HOW
CREDIT-MONEY SHAPES
THE
ECONOMY

COLUMBIA UNIVERSITY SEMINAR SERIES

The University Seminars at Columbia University welcomes this study of *How Credit-Money Shapes the Economy: The United States in a Global System* by Robert Guttmann to the Columbia University Seminars Series. The study has benefited from Seminar discussions and reflects the advantages of scholarly exchange provided by the Seminar movement.

Aaron W. Warner
Director, University Seminars
Columbia University

HOW
CREDIT-MONEY
SHAPES
THE
ECONOMY

The United States
in a Global System

Robert Guttmann

M.E. Sharpe
Armonk, New York
London, England

Library of Congress Cataloging-in-Publication Data

Guttmann, Robert, 1951–
How credit-money shapes the economy: the United States in
a global system / Robert Guttmann.
p.   cm.
Includes bibliographical references and index.
ISBN 1-56324-100-5 (cloth)—ISBN 1-56324-101-3 (pbk)
1. Monetary policy—United States
2. Money—Social aspects—United States.
3. Gold standard—History.
4. Credit—United States.
5. Banks and banking—United States.
6. International finance.
I. Title.
HG501.G87   1994
332.4'973—dc20   93-45466
CIP

Printed in the United States of America

The paper used in this publication meets the minimum requirements of
American National Standard for Information Sciences—
Permanence of Paper for Printed Library Materials,
ANSI Z 39.48-1984.

BM (c)   10   9   8   7   6   5   4   3   2   1
BM (p)   10   9   8   7   6   5   4   3   2

*Dedicated to Gina Philogene
and our son Sascha*

Contents

PART IV
The Monetary Regime in Transition

PART V
The International Dimension of Money

Tables and Figures

Figures

Preface

This is a book about money. If you expect to find advice in these pages about the safest or quickest routes to wealth, however, you will be disappointed. All I can say about those how-to-get-rich books, especially the best-sellers among them, is that their authors have found a quick way to riches themselves. Their sales confirm that a great many people want to be told how to "make money." I am more interested in the "why" than in the "how to." Why are we so obsessed with getting rich? What is it about money that makes it so attractive?

Apart from the most basic human emotions of love and fear, there is probably no more powerful motivating force in our lives than money. Its attraction stems from an ironic combination of exclusivity and omnipresence. Money is the only means through which we may lawfully gain access to goods, services, and assets. This monopoly position as the one socially accepted representative of income gives its owners command in the marketplace, power, and social status. We all need a minimum of it and want a maximum of it. There is enough money around for many of us to be well off but never enough for all of us to live comfortably. In that setting of relative deprivation, we are all forced to pursue its acquisition in competition with each other. To the extent that we expend our income, we are continuously forced to repeat the pursuit.

Given that we spend most of our days earning income and spending it, we tend to take the role of money as "the only thing that counts" for granted. We learn early on that having money is prerequisite to satisfying most of our needs and desires. Soon we internalize its representation and stop questioning its existence. At that point we easily forget that money is not a natural but a human construct, something we created and refined to regulate a wide range of interactions among ourselves. We use it to price goods and services, to pay for them, to acquire assets that produce even more income, and to settle debts. All of these activities are essential to the proper functioning of our economic system.

Most economists understand these functions of money only in a purely descriptive manner. They approach the object as if it were a good, with its own unique demand and supply conditions. That view of money sets it apart from the rest of the economy, an exogenous variable which exists somehow separated from the "real" economy of production and exchange. Yet money is more than just another good. It is above all a social institution which integrates diverse economic activities—production, exchange, credit—into interconnected circuits. At the same time, money is the force most responsible for breaking those circuits apart and preventing their successful completion. Whether its hoarding prevents markets from being cleared or its sudden abundance invites overextension, its potential for disruption is quite impressive.

How well (or poorly) our economy functions depends, therefore, to a significant degree on the modalities that guide the creation, distribution, and circulation of money. These are neither arbitrary nor exogenous to the rest of the economy. On the contrary, they are determined by key agents in our economy who exercise their relative control over the monetary process for specific purposes. Ever since the fourth millennium B.C., when the rulers of Egypt, Sumer, and China managed to replace agrarian forms of money produced by farmers with metal coins from mines which they themselves owned, control over the issue of money has always been a foundation of state power. The ability to determine and regulate the socially accepted medium of exchange gives governments not only a powerful tool to shape the economic space of their nation but also a great responsibility, on which their legitimacy depends. Yet the monetary authorities of the state have never had full control over the money supply. Private agents have always been able to issue their own forms of money—farmers in prehistoric times, goldsmiths in antiquity and the Middle Ages, and banks with the emergence of capitalism. Forced to accept such private alternatives, governments have consistently tried to regulate their issue. As I shall try to show here in the case of the United States, the rules and practices defining the coexistence of different public and private money forms have always had a powerful impact on a nation's economy.

Probably the most important evolution in this regard occurred during the Great Depression of the 1930s, when the United States and other industrial nations abandoned the gold standard ("commodity-money") in favor of a payments system based on central bank notes and private bank checks. The introduction of such inconvertible paper money, which is created in acts of credit extension ("credit-money"), gave their domestic economies an elastic currency. Its issue responded much more flexibly to the needs of the public than did gold or silver. This innovation revolutionized the ways in which the advanced capitalist economies worked. It did so by providing the institutional underpinnings in support of monopolistic pricing strategies, regulation of wages by collective bargaining, and deficit spending by the public sector, as well as lender-of-last-resort interventions of the monetary authorities. These changes, none of which would have been sustainable in the absence of credit-money, helped to stabilize the level of economic activity and greatly contributed to the amazing economic expansion of the first two postwar decades.

The boom ended in the late 1960s and gave way to more than a decade of gradually intensifying stagflation, a combination of rising prices and slowing growth which helped to bring down three U.S. presidents in a row. This unique confluence of two cyclically opposite phenomena, inflation and unemployment, stemmed from structural imbalances which, during the era of the gold standard, would in all likelihood have triggered a depression. But the presence of an elastic currency—that is, credit-money issued in acts of lending—gave the economy a shock absorber that moderated the crisis.

Still, the stagflation of the 1970s also exposed the social costs of private bank money. Since most of our money supply consists of checking accounts in commercial banks, its creation is heavily influenced by the profit motive of bankers and their clients. Those tend to vacillate in procyclical fashion between aggressive pursuit of profit opportunities and periods of pessimism characterized by caution and retrenchment. As stagflation deepened during the late 1970s, ever-rising borrowing needs of many debtors collided with their declining creditworthiness. Accelerating inflation and artificially low interest rates kept the actual burden of that debt tolerable. In this situation it was only a question of time before banks and other lenders would have to conclude that their returns from traditional lending activity no longer matched risks. When they finally revolted, in 1979, the U.S. economy suffered a classic debt-deflation adjustment not seen since the 1930s.

This time, however, the economy was prevented from falling off the cliff by the active use of fiscal and monetary stabilizers, most notably record budget deficits and gradual extension of our various lender-of-last-resort mechanisms. Belt-tightening in the early 1980s was accompanied by policy changes under President Reagan, and both encouraged a resumption of debt financing at an even more hectic pace than before. Lenders participated eagerly in this debt explosion, after their returns had been boosted by disinflation and the deregulation of interest rates. The extraordinarily rapid growth of private and public debt kept the U.S. economy growing at a moderate pace for nearly eight years.

The expansion could not last. When debt grows faster than income and interest rates are higher than growth rates, borrowers will eventually be squeezed by an intolerably heavy debt-servicing burden. That situation arose in 1989 and blossomed into a full-blown recession by mid-1990. The essentially finance-driven downturn of 1990–92 marked the end of an era. The U.S. economy is now forced to undergo long-term restructuring. That process involves not only the reorganization of industry but also a fundamental transformation of our credit system. The banking sector, suffering steady erosion of its key markets and large bad-debt losses, needs a new regulatory structure to revive. The relation between industry and finance, the two dominant forms of capital, is in urgent need of a new balance.

We experience the realities of this long-term restructuring on a daily basis, whether in the form of deindustrialization, structural unemployment, asset deflation, shifting fiscal priorities of our government, or pressure from intensifying foreign competition. Less obvious, but equally decisive for the outcome of this painful process, is what happens to our financial institutions and markets. Those are in a state of tremendous flux. The remaking of our financial system, which we are currently witnessing, puts into question the very existence of credit-money. The prospects of the U.S. economy depend not least on how well we manage to contain the social costs of private bank money—the tendency toward credit overextension, the propensity for high interest rates, and the growing dominance of short-term financial capital. All this arises at a time when the emergence of a new money form, "electronic" money, is fundamentally altering the ways in which our credit system operates. Our capital markets and payments system are in the midst of a technological revolution which complicates the tasks of regulators.

The challenge of monetary reform extends beyond the boundaries of the United States to the international arena. During the entire postwar period the dollar has been the principal form of world money, which has made it easier for the United States to finance large balance-of-payments deficits. But over the last decade, we as a nation have become heavily indebted to the rest of the world. Unfortunately, there is a contradiction between being the issuer of the key currency and at the same time also the world's largest debtor nation. The former status depends on maintaining a stable currency, whereas the latter encourages lower exchange rates. Great Britain, which preceded us as issuer of world money, could not escape this contradiction during the late 1920s and early 1930s. Nor will the United States in the 1990s.

As the dollar's world-money status gradually erodes, the question of succession arises. Who or what will replace the dollar? Three scenarios are possible. One is continuation of the route begun in the mid-1980s when the leading industrial nations decided to cooperate in managing the emerging multicurrency system. But efforts in this direction have recently faltered, raising the specter of a much less sanguine future. It is quite possible, even likely, that in the absence of renewed cooperation the world economy will gradually disintegrate into three competing blocs (the Americas, Europe, and the Pacific Rim), in which the leaders (the United States, Germany, and Japan) maintain hegemonic control over their regions by imposing their respective currencies (dollar, mark or ECU, and yen) as the medium of exchange on their respective zones of influence. A third possibility, by far the most difficult and yet the only one providing a satisfactory solution for the kind of international monetary system required by the emerging pattern of global integration, is to replace all key currencies with a supranational form of credit-money. Toward the end of the book (chapters 15 and 16) I sketch how such a global money form could work.

Since the issue of money's regulation is by and large removed from the public and confined to experts, yet affects everyone, I have tried to write this book for the widest audience possible without compromising on the side of simplification.

The issues raised here may be complex, but they should not remain the domain of insiders. They are too important to be left to the experts. I have therefore tried to make the issue of credit-money comprehensible even to those without a great deal of prior knowledge of economics. Of course, the book also addresses my colleagues in an attempt to move forward the often sterile debate on money among economists.

Acknowledgments

Many people have shaped my thinking on the subject of money and helped me formulate my ideas in this book. I would like to thank in particular Robert Boyer, Suzanne de Brunhoff, Robert Delorme, Alain Lipietz, Marty Kenner, Pascal Petit, Bruce Steinberg, and my colleagues at both Hofstra University and the Université de Paris–Nord for the patience and guidance they have given me. Without their contribution over the years I would not have been able to write this book. I have also greatly benefited from participation in the Columbia University Seminar on monetary and financial reform organized by Professor Albert Hart. Having access to some of the greatest thinkers in the field, such as Al himself, Hyman Minsky, Stephen Rousseas, Robert Mundell, and many others, has had a profound effect on my thinking and, by extension, on the book. I would like to thank Columbia University Seminars and Professor Aaron Warner for allowing this work to be published in their series and for the generous support they have provided me. Finally, I would like to express my deeply felt gratitude to Richard Bartel of M. E. Sharpe, Inc., whose support and insights have been invaluable.

Part I

The Theory of Money

1

The Economy
in Transition

1.1. The Bitter Taste of Victory

The collapse of Communist rule in the former Soviet empire during 1989–91 is probably the most dramatic indication that we live in a period of great historic change. Four decades of confrontation between two superpowers, the United States and the Soviet Union, have suddenly come to an end. From our perspective, as the victors of the cold war, the disintegration of the Soviet command economy looks like the final triumph of capitalism over communism. These self-congratulatory sentiments are quite understandable. After all, it is their system which is falling apart, not ours.

Central planning and government monopoly, although initially capable of redirecting resources toward rapid industrialization, lacked the technological dynamism and adjustment capacity of a system based on markets and free enterprise. Moreover, these pillars of Stalinism were prone to inefficiency and misallocation of resources. The lack of competition limited the range of available products and invited shoddy quality. The imposition of output targets from above prompted producing units to fudge their figures, hoard inventories, and focus on aggregate production quantities to the exclusion of other goals. Artificial price controls encouraged a combination of waste and shortages. These distortions ate up scarce resources while forcing brutal rationing on a discontented population. The absence of markets not only stifled entrepreneurial initiative but also deprived decision-makers of a crucial signaling device. In the end this repressive system could not maintain its social contract of providing its citizens with a great deal of economic security in exchange for forsaking political and commercial freedom.

While the failure of central planning illustrates the superiority of our own system, the liberalization now under way in hitherto mostly government-run economies also shows tellingly how brutal the logic of the market mechanism can be: a high degree of economic insecurity, the terrible divisiveness and social costs of mass unemployment, a more unequal distribution of income and wealth, the clash between private profit and social benefits. The crisis in Eastern Europe, the Soviet Union, and many one-party states of the developing world is certainly for the most part a reflection of the degree to which these economies have been mismanaged over decades. But its rapid deepening is also at least partly caused by the switch to market regulation. Poland, the former East Germany, Ukraine, and Russia are clear cases in point. Political turmoil in these countries forced policy-makers to introduce a market economy practically overnight, with traumatic results for large segments of the population. Although most economists regard this as a transitional problem which will be alleviated once the necessary restructuring has run its course, the drama unfolding there should make us think some more about the social costs and benefits of a market-based economy.

The transformation of a defunct economic system is an experiment with few precedents in history, and much will be learned from it. The lessons from this revolutionary process will have a profound impact on political discourse and economic policy throughout the world. It may well be that the principal concern of reformers here and there—how to construct a "mixed" economy which combines the virtues of the marketplace with the coordinating capacities of representative government carrying out a broadly shared social contract—will finally move to the forefront of public debate now that the recipes of the dogmatic Left appear to have become obsolete.

In the meantime, the monumental events of 1989–91 raise more immediate questions for the United States. These have already begun to catch up with us, cutting our euphoria short and leaving us in a state of growing anxiety. The cold war shaped the political organizations and economic structures of our country as profoundly as it shaped those of the former Soviet Union. What, for example, will happen to our military-industrial complex or bipartisan foreign policy consensus now that this period is finally coming to an end? How do we redefine national security in an era of reduced superpower tensions? Can we convert our bloated defense industry for civilian uses, or do we have to write off its excess capacity? Finally, how can we best use the "peace dividend" from reduced military spending to meet future challenges?

Correct answers to these questions require an understanding of the present as history. We no longer live in a world dominated by the political and military confrontation of two superpowers. The geopolitical era of the cold war has given way to a new epoch in which the strength of nations will be defined primarily by their industrial competitiveness, mastery of technology, financial position, and entrepreunerial talents. Moreover, in this emerging *geoeconomic* era the United States faces powerful challengers, most notably Japan and a reunited Germany. In the developing world several countries with large populations and important natural resources, such as Mexico, Brazil, Nigeria, South Africa, India, or China, have the potential of becoming important producers in key industries. The principal question then becomes whether we as a nation are prepared for this intense global competition and, if not, what to do about it.

It is fair to say that the United States enters the new geoeconomic era with several handicaps. Our economy, though still by far the largest, is no longer in the position of absolute dominance that it held since the end of World War II. In a growing number of industries the Japanese and Europeans have caught up with, if not already surpassed, us. The accelerating decline of competitiveness during the 1980s shows up in many ways, most dramatically in the loss of market shares by U.S. corporations both at home and abroad, huge trade deficits, and the rapid accumulation of debt owed to foreigners. Within a span of few years the United States has turned from being the world's leading creditor nation, a position occupied for nearly seventy years, into its largest debtor. It does not take much knowledge of economics, politics, or history to understand at least intuitively that it makes quite a difference whether a country is a creditor or debtor vis-à-vis the rest of the world. For one, our dependence on foreign capital restricts our economic policy options and puts at risk the future generations of Americans who will have to service that debt.

There are many reasons for this erosion in our position. Those causes are often rooted at home. U.S. productivity growth, a key determinant of competitiveness, has slowed to a crawl over the past two decades. Recent improvements in this regard by our manufacturing sector have come about largely as a result of radical streamlining and cost-cutting. Such a defensive posture of squeezing and retrenchment does not necessarily lay the foundations for sustainable increases in productivity over the long run. When it comes to those, we are not doing well at all in relation to other industrial nations. We invest much less, proportionally speaking, than does either Germany or Japan. Therefore, our income growth and saving rate are low by comparison. We also lag behind in research and development, while still directing a much larger portion of our research and development spending toward the military. The U.S. economy has consequently lost its once seemingly unassailable technological leadership in a relatively short period of time. This particular aspect is especially troubling in a period of very rapid technical progress, during which many growth industries of the future are passing through the early stages of their life cycle. Our dismal education system deprives young citizens of crucial skills just when job assignments are becoming increasingly knowledge-intensive. Other structural weaknesses include the nation's crumbling infrastructure (e.g., roads, railroads, airports, water and sewer systems), a history of adversarial labor-management relations, the short-term planning and investment horizon of our chief executives, and the high cost of capital for firms that are trying to raise funds.

These problems are structural in nature—that is they emanate from the amalgam of institutional characteristics, policy compromises, and cultural attitudes that gives every national economy its distinct societal features from deep within.

As such, they often take a long time to develop before becoming a focus of national attention. The process of our declining competitiveness, for example, began more than two decades ago. But it only reached a critical stage in the mid-1980s, when other countries finally caught up with our productivity levels. Of course, governments have at their disposal short-term expedients that postpone the moment of truth. We shall see below how consecutive U.S. administrations have tried to mask the underlying deterioration of our world market position and to delay painful adjustments for as long as possible.

It may be difficult for many Americans to accept the new realities of a polycentric world economy which we no longer dominate. There is an age-old political tradition of isolationism in this country which in uncertain times tends to breed protectionism, xenophobia, and an insular outlook toward the rest of the world. Politicians are often tempted to stir and exploit these sentiments for their own agenda. This undercurrent in American politics, already showing troubling signs of revival, is quite dangerous. Instead of turning inward, the United States must maintain a leadership role in favor of free trade and multilateral solutions to global problems. Otherwise, industrial nations may regroup and divide into distinct power blocs. Europe's efforts at greater integration, the growing influence of Japan in the Pacific Basin, and the U.S. pursuit of free-trade agreements with Canada and Mexico all point in this direction. History, especially that of Europe during the nineteenth and early twentieth centuries, shows how easily the formation of hegemonic spheres of influences leads to conflict and how difficult it is to manage a triangular web of adversarial relations.

Americans cannot isolate themselves from the rest of the world without risking lower living standards and suffering a loss of influence in international affairs. As large as our domestic economy is, it is by no means self-sufficient. We need to import crucial products, such as oil, steel, machine tools, semiconductors, and consumer electronics. Shortages of skilled workers require the United States to tap foreign labor supplies. Our traditional reliance on the "brain drain" from the rest of the world is thus likely to continue. Many firms have production capacities that far exceed what they can sell at home. They must compete in the global marketplace. The pressure to export will, if anything, only increase in the near future. Enormous U.S. budget and trade deficits over the past decade have forced us to import capital from abroad, and our foreign debt in excess of $600 billion is best serviced out of export earnings.[1]

1.2. Globalization of Economic Activity

These developments are only surface reflections of a much deeper historical process now under way—the globalization of economic activity. This trend is the single most important aspect of the transition referred to earlier. Our economic system has an inherent tendency to expand its activities beyond national frontiers. From its very inception in the sixteenth and seventeenth centuries, when

European powers colonized resource-rich regions and organized a slave trade across the globe, capitalism has always contained a strongly international dimension. U.S. policy-makers realized the importance of this aspect after World War II. They used America's position of absolute dominance in the world to introduce a new international monetary system (Bretton Woods Conference, 1944), liberalize trade (General Agreement on Tariffs and Trade, 1947), and finance the rebuilding of Western Europe (Marshall Plan, 1948). These reforms paved the way for a rapid expansion of world trade and overseas investments, both of which played a crucial role in the worldwide economic boom of the 1950s and 1960s.

But the globalization we face today is not merely a quantitative extension of those trends. It is a qualitative leap forward. During the last decade a variety of forces have coalesced to foster a much higher degree of global integration. The world is rapidly becoming a single economy. This new entity is more than just the sum of its parts, the nation-states.

• All countries have become dependent on trade for their prosperity, whether to import goods and services produced more cheaply elsewhere or to pursue export-led growth strategies. Even the United States, until recently a relatively closed economy, has turned into a much more open economy, in which exports and imports absorb nearly a quarter of its gross national product (GNP). Trade has many benefits. It allows producers to sell more, gives consumers greater choice at lower prices, encourages competition, and facilitates specialization. Countries must export in order to pay for their imports or service their foreign debts.

• Large corporations, turning multinational in the postwar period, have now reached the next stage in their development. They are rapidly becoming global corporations that operate integrated production networks stretching over several countries and compete with each other across the globe. The most dramatic expression of this trend has been the amazing wave of cross-country mergers and joint ventures during the last few years, often spurred by the need to share the otherwise prohibitive costs of product development and to gain access to new market opportunities. These giants are no longer bound to any particular nation-state. Their ability to avoid regulations and taxes considered too burdensome poses a major challenge to governments. Threats of relocation to cheap-labor areas give them an upper hand against nationally organized unions. More than a third of world trade consists today of intracompany transactions between subsidiaries, making traditional means of correcting trade imbalances between countries much less effective.

• Electronics has turned the world into a "global village." Spaces and people in every corner of the world have become connected through computer networks, fax machines, fiber-optics cables, and satellite dishes. Information abounds and is now shared everywhere. The emergence of global communication technologies has vastly increased the tradability of once local services (e.g., television, education, accounting) and has made it possible to move huge sums of money across the globe with the push of a button. In their wake, financial markets have become globally linked. The "information age" also transforms skill requirements and job specifications while creating new forms of poverty for those who are deprived of access to the data. Long-run effects of this technological revolution on politics and culture will be profound as well.

• Large migrations of people across national borders are likely in the future. Even though the world has always experienced major waves of migration, human capital has traditionally been much less mobile than physical or financial capital. This too is changing fast. Population movements are no longer confined to economic crisis or war, the traditional reasons for relocation. Uneven development, the increasingly precarious state of food supplies in many parts of the world, and a major demographic imbalance (i.e., explosive population growth in developing countries, coupled with stagnant and aging populations in the industrial world) will prompt many to seek their fortunes elsewhere. Global communication reduces language and cultural barriers, making it easier for people to move. Managerial careers will increasingly require foreign work experience or education abroad. Cross-cultural interaction can and should be a truly enriching experience for all involved. Immigrant communities contribute everywhere to the wealth of nations. Despite these facts, we see a frightening intensification of anti-immigrant sentiment and racist incidents in the United States and Europe. The pathological need for scapegoats, against whom to direct one's feelings of economic insecurity and social despair, has once again created an opening for reckless demagogues with political ambitions.

• Since the early 1970s the business cycles of industrial nations have become a great deal more synchronized. When the economies of the United States, Western Europe, and Japan all slow down at the same time, any downturn becomes that much stronger. The deep recessions of 1974–75 and 1979–82 bear dramatic witness to this danger. The synchronization of cyclical fluctuations has had many causes, the most important of which was the emergence of floating exchange rates following the disintegration of Bretton Woods in 1971–73. As we shall see (in chapter 7), that deregulation of currency prices encouraged destabilizing movements of capital and procyclical economic policies emanating from the United States, which triggered recessionary adjustments on a global scale. The oil-price hikes of 1973 and 1979, the most obvious trigger events, must in this context be understood as direct consequences of a flawed international monetary system, rather than be reduced to "external shocks," as most mainstream economists are prone to do. Since 1982 the industrial nations have become locked into an even more tightly interdependent growth pattern, with surplus countries recycling their excess savings to the United States so as to maintain large U.S. budget and trade deficits as the principal stimulant of global recovery (see chapter 8). Policy-makers have begun to realize that this situation requires international policy coordination, but first steps in this direction have stalled.

• The globalization process now under way has gained added impetus from the plethora of truly international problems that affect the future survivability of the entire planet. These include the debt crisis of developing countries, the shortage of savings to meet long-term investment needs across the globe, the degradation of our environment (e.g., acid rain, the depletion of the ozone layer, the greenhouse effect, toxic-waste disposal), threats to the world's food supply, the arms race, the AIDS epidemic, and explosive population growth. No one can really escape these crises. Even though their most virulent manifestations may be found in faraway places, they all impact more or less directly on the well-being of Americans. We must also recognize that their universal nature demands multilateral solutions.

The globally integrated economy has unique features—world money, exchange rates, movements of capital forms with different degrees of mobility, trade regimes, foreign debts of sovereign nations, the absence of fully developed state institutions at the international level. This entity also behaves in ways that differ from those of national economies, creating its own logic of uneven development, resource transfers, and power relations. In that sense it is more than just the sum of its parts. Neither politicians nor economists have yet fully come to grips with this essential difference, leaving both at this point ill prepared for the policy challenges of the geoeconomic era. The standard projection of microeconomic behavior by individual agents onto the larger economy through simple aggregation (see section 1.3 below for more detail) is particularly misleading here. John Maynard Keynes, the famous British economist, has shown the fallacy of composition embodied in this methodology of linear extension. That which may be regarded as perfectly rational behavior for individuals can produce disastrous results for the economy as a whole, as is the case when firms try to cut wages and employment in response to declining sales. The same holds when moving from the level of national economies to the level of the global economy. We therefore need what Keynes did for macroeconomics, a new "megaeconomic" theory of the emerging international economy.[2]

1.3. The Limits of Neoclassical Orthodoxy

The main task of social scientists is to explain a changing world. In this regard economists ought to be very busy these days. We live, after all, in a period of profound transformation which affects all of the constituent elements of our economic system. Whether we focus on the world of work, technology, the structure of key industries, economic policy, or international relations, each has experienced significant changes in recent years. These, as we shall demonstrate in this book, have significantly altered the modus operandi of our economy.

Yet most economists face this dynamic era with a good deal of myopia. The high degree of specialization, forced upon them during their early years in graduate school, makes it very difficult for anyone in the profession to "see the whole picture." Economic analysis has also increasingly been turned into a marketable product. Whether publishing (often narrowly focused and mostly mathematical) articles in academic journals to assure tenure at the nation's colleges, running forecasting models through the computer for interested parties, writing investment letters, or giving policy advice for government agencies, the output of economists is nowadays shaped by the needs of buyers. This commercialization is detrimental to the experimental spirit of scientific investigation. A form of censorship, it limits the scope of investigation and predetermines what can be said. General theoreticians, the only ones with freedom to think in broad terms about the evolution of our economy and as such indispensable to progress in the field, have become a dying breed.

Unfortunately, the problem goes even deeper. Mainstream dogma itself lacks the tools to figure out the dramatic changes we are currently witnessing in the world economy. The vast majority of American economists adhere to the so-called *neoclassical* school. This tradition has produced some important insights into the adjustment capacity of markets and the behavior of individual agents, but it has not developed a coherent picture of the economy as a whole in forward motion. Seeking to prove *equilibrium*, an ideal state of balance, its protagonists make simplifying assumptions that abstract from fundamental characteristics of our economic system.

The neoclassical orthodoxy, to which most economists still adhere, replaced the classical theory of accumulation with the analysis of market equilibrium in a stationary state.[3] Behind the increasingly sophisticated mathematical formulations of this model lies a relatively simple structure of basic properties.

• At the core of the neoclassical world we find the *homo oeconomicus*, whose "rational" behavior it is to maximize benefits (utility, profit) within a given budget constraint. That fictional character, whether consumer or producer, acts as if in possession of perfect knowledge and foresight when making decisions. Those occur at the margin, by comparing additional ("marginal") costs and benefits, according to specific rules of optimizing behavior: in the case of consumers, a budget allocation in which the last dollars spent on different goods yield the same marginal utility; in the case of producers, the output level at which marginal cost and revenue are equal.

• Neoclassicists analyze the market as a direct extension of these microeconomic optimization rules. They simply add up the optimizing quantities of individual consumers and producers at different price levels. This exercise yields a market's demand and supply curves. The intersection of these two curves in turn determines the market-clearing equilibrium price.

• The theory then moves from the partial-equilibrium analysis of specific markets to the "general equilibrium" model of Leon Walras. There, output quantities and prices of all commodities are determined by a process of haggling in the market, so that no participant can improve his/her position by changing the amount of any commodity he/she produces or consumes. That process assumes an auctioneer soliciting bids from buyers and sellers to find the equilibrium set of prices and outputs before production and exchange actually take place.[4]

• Embodied in the Walrasian scheme is a notion of resource inputs as "factors of production" (labor, machines, land), whose hire prices for their services yield their suppliers income in the form of wages, interest, and rent. Depending on technical conditions, various combinations of inputs can be used to produce a given commodity, and substitution between different factors goes on in response to changes in their relative prices until an optimal mix is found. Based on this theory, neoclassical economists have constructed physical "production functions" to determine the best input combination at given factor prices for specific output levels.

• The combination of factor substitutability, perfect foresight, and freely flexible prices in resource markets also provides the underpinnings of neoclassical steady-state growth models.[5]

• On the macroeconomic level those same assumptions are used to show the economy automatically tending toward full-employment equilibrium between aggregate demand and supply.

That multilevel analysis of equilibrium conditions is a beautiful logical construction. It also offers some useful insights concerning individual reactions and market adjustments to changing conditions. Beyond that it has very little to say about the reality of our capitalist economy. Rather than trying to explain how our economic system truly functions, neoclassical economists are more driven by ideological justifications of its virtues. Their equilibrium model "shows" how the blind pursuit of self-interest by individual agents, bound together and constrained by the marketplace, also leads to socially optimal outcomes for the rest of society and a stable economy. Such an exercise rests on highly unrealistic assumptions and excludes systemic forces of destabilization from proper consideration.

Let us briefly illustrate that last point. Take, for example, the standard notion that individual agents have perfect knowledge and foresight or at least act as if they were in possession of these superhuman qualities. That assumption conveniently ignores the existence of uncertainty which in reality prevents market participants from defining optimal outcomes a priori and forces them to aim for merely satisfactory objectives ("satisficing") instead. The problem is not resolved by turning uncertainty, an intangible quality, into its opposite, quantifiable risk that can be measured on the basis of probability distributions.[6]

The concepts of certainty and risk, so essential to the neoclassical theories of optimizing behavior and rational expectations, rest on a unique notion of time. The standard equilibrium model uses "logical" time, a purely quantitative variable $(t-n, \ldots \ldots \ldots, t-1, t, t+1, \ldots \ldots \ldots, t+n)$ which operates in both directions and is therefore assumed to be reversible. This implies, among other things, that mistakes can be undone simply by starting all over again and that market adjustments occur quasi-instantaneously. The real world offers no such conveniences. There time unfolds as a historic process of irreversible actions and decisions in continuous forward motion. Mistakes cannot be avoided, adjustments take time, and their actual duration has a bearing on the outcome.

The time aspect is crucial to economic activity. Producers face a variety of temporal constraints, such as turnover time and depreciation of capital, the pay-off period during which investments are at risk, debt maturities and other contractual commitments, as well as worker productivity. All these affect profitability and need careful management. The equilibrium model, with its effectively timeless notion of "logical" time, has no sense of those. Even worse, the processes it describes take place in a temporal vacuum and therefore lack any historic context.

Apart from its ahistoric nature, neoclassical theory also ignores what makes our economy a social system. Its equilibrium model moves straight from individual behavior to the economy as a whole by means of simple aggregation. Lost in this linear extension from "microeconomics" to "macroeconomics" are the human interactions and social relations that arise in the course of economic activity. Those shape fundamental characteristics of our economy, such as its class structure, the creation and absorption of its surplus, the formation of capital, and its tendency toward cyclical instability. Abstraction from the social is not just a problem of methodology. Neoclassicists consciously abandoned the classical notion of *value*, rooted in production and measurable in terms of labor time, in favor of "utility." The latter is a subjective value concept, based entirely on individual preferences.[7] With this substitution, the problem of economics came to be redefined from growth and distribution of wealth to one of allocating given resources so as to obtain maximum satisfaction. Such a shift in focus reflected the emergence of utilitarian individualism as the dominant ideology in Great Britain and the United States during the second half of the nineteenth century.

A good example of its consciously nonsocial analysis is the neoclassical treatment of markets in terms of demand and supply curves representing hypothetical price-quantity combinations and intersecting at an equilibrium price. This is a simplistic representation of what in reality is a complex and often highly differentiated institution. Markets organize exchange, a crucial aspect of human interaction. They usually contain a large number of players whose interests conflict but who depend on each other. Market participants observe each other in order to form expectations and make decisions. This social context of shared experiences and communicated signals may encourage behavior that does not appear to be rational from the neoclassical perspective of isolated individuals trying to maximize their strictly private benefits in the face of impersonal constraints. Each market is unique in terms of who its buyers and sellers are, the distribution of power among them, the type of product traded, the nature of its contractual commitments, and its rules of socialized behavior (e.g., forms of competition, modes of adjustment to imbalances). This high degree of institutional differentiation, itself reflecting the complex nature of social interaction in exchange activities, gets lost when all markets are reduced to mere demand and supply curves.

Neoclassical equilibrium theory is a logically consistent model of great beauty. It also has the added advantage of legitimating the pillars of utilitarian individualism—"free" markets, private enterprise, profit maximization—as in the best interests of society. But its underlying assumptions, those of logical time, optimizing individuals, and automatically self-correcting markets, have very little bearing on reality. They do not explain how our economy actually works.

The reality of capitalism is a good deal more problematic and contradictory than the idyllic world of neoclassical equilibrium theory implies. True, the system is very dynamic. Even its critics acknowledge that.[8] But its very capacity for change is also a source of social tension and economic instability. The system creates winners and losers, and its inherently unequal distribution of opportunities is often beyond the control of individual agents. The system also moves through time in distinct sequences of boom and bust. Yet in the neoclassical world of perfect foresight, flexible prices, and quasi-instantaneous market adjustments, there is no room for proper consideration of such cyclical behavior. Inherently destabilizing forces are reduced to disturbances emanating from outside the model, and the key focus is then on showing how market participants respond to such external shocks in a rational manner so as to restore equilibrium. This comparative-static approach, besides tailoring its behavioral assumptions to a preconceived outcome, views the economy as merely moving from one equilibrium position to another.

Both income inequality and cyclical instability engender political pressures for government to become involved in the management of the economy. The standard equilibrium model, however, has a very limited view of economic policy. Conservative neoclassicists in particular, such as the followers of the "rational expectations" school, monetarists, or supply-siders, resist any activist role for government in dealing with the long-range problems of the U.S. economy. Their belief in the self-balancing virtues of "free" markets is so unflinching, even in the face of evidence to the contrary, that it takes on the characteristics of religious conviction. They want government intervention to be kept to an absolute minimum and to be based on fixed policy rules, especially balanced budgets and steady money-supply growth. Discretionary policies, such as the countercyclical "fine-tuning" of aggregate demand prescribed by Keynesians or market regulation for social policy purposes, are condemned as disrupting the equilibrating forces of the economy.

These apostles of laissez-faire capitalism now dominate both the economics profession and the political discourse in our country. The disintegration of centrally planned command economies and worldwide movement toward deregulation have given their "free market" arguments added weight. Yet today's problems of widening income gaps, speculative excesses, uneven development, and environmental degradation go beyond the neoclassical concept of limited "market failures" and have their roots in the very operation of our economic system. There is no question that advanced capitalist economies are highly adaptable and resilient structures which provide large segments of their population with the benefit of enrichment. But they also engender major social costs, such as pollution and inequity. Nor are they stable. They move through cyclical fluctuations and long waves. The latter give rise to periods of large-scale restructuring that can only come to a successful resolution if specific new policies are put into place. We are currently in the midst of such a period.

Eight years of uninterrupted growth during the Reagan-Bush era gave us—at least for a while—the illusion of renewed vigor and lasting prosperity. But the principal driving forces of this long recovery period, a rapidly growing pyramid of debts and major rechanneling of capital flows, left us exposed to new tremors of instability that began to appear in the early 1990s. Moreover, the relatively stable growth pattern after 1982 masked the extent to which our economy has been transformed since then by massive industrial reorganization, accelerating technological change, new financial instruments, the shift from manual work to mental work, and increased global interdependence. Those changes are long-run processes rather than purely cyclical phenomena. Finally, we shall see that governments, even those led by conservative politicians full of "free-market" rhetoric, have not so much disengaged from the economy as dismantled old policies that had become counterproductive. Their reforms do not yet amount to a coherent policy regime. A great deal remains to be done, especially on the international level. The new geoeconomic era requires an unprecedented degree of cooperation among nations to assure both stability and prosperity.

The challenge we now face is to figure out the kinds of policy reforms still needed to give the ongoing process of structural change greater coherence. This task cannot rely on standard equilibrium theory, whose comparative-static perspective is deprived of historic sense and social context. We need a different approach to the amazing and often puzzling complexities of our economy. That alternative focuses on the analysis of capitalism's long-run tendencies and sources of instability. Earlier attempts to do precisely that, most notably by Karl Marx in the second half of the nineteenth century and by John Maynard Keynes during the 1930s, give us a valuable starting point in this endeavor. Their questions and insights concerning the evolutionary dynamics of our economy, today largely crowded out by the linear logic and ahistoric nature of equilibrium models, deserve revival. Of course, the institutional characteristics and development level of contemporary capitalism are quite different from those observed more than a century ago or during the Great Depression. Nonetheless, these two economists discovered essential features and tendencies of our system that are still relevant today.

Marx? Keynes? Are these two economists not associated with failure? Both Marx and Keynes shaped the policies of an epoch, and neither today seems to have been vindicated by the judgment of history. Marxism, leading to Lenin's prescription for a one-party state and to Stalin's ruthless implementation of collectivization, ultimately proved to be unworkable. The Soviet-style command economy is certainly not a convincing alternative to capitalism. And Keynesianism, the theoretical foundation of New Deal liberalism, died a painful death in the stagflation and tax revolts of the late 1970s. Note the reference to the "-isms" here. Marxism and Keynesianism were reinterpretations of original thought, designed to provide apparatchiks or Washington bureaucrats with tools for policymaking. As policy prescriptions they were simplified extracts, the butchering work of many followers and critics. True, both lent themselves to such application, and what either one of them had said turned out to be problematic when their word became the deed of others. But it is important not to "throw out the baby with the bathwater." Anyone who reads the works of these two writers should find much of interest and relevance between the lines. Each tried to grapple with fundamental questions about the nature of our economic system that still demand answers.

It is no coincidence that Marx and Keynes were in essence monetary economists. Seeking to show how our system as a whole reproduces itself over time in forward motion, both identified money as the central unifying element. Building on these heterodox traditions, I share that position. My attempt here to shed some light on the ongoing transformation of our economic system focuses to a major extent on the meaning of money.

1.4. The Central Role of Money

If we want to understand the structural changes that are transforming our economy, we need to go beyond neoclassical theory. Although its focus on efficient allocation of scarce resources among alternative uses is not necessarily wrong or irrelevant, it is certainly too narrow. It does not cover other fundamental aspects of our economic system, most importantly the creation and distribution of income. Those were at the center of economic analysis during the heyday of classical political economy more than a century ago, and they need to be brought back to life.

Any realistic analysis of our economy has to clarify the central role of money in this system. It is no coincidence that Marx and Keynes, arguably the two most important critics of standard equilibrium theory, based their own heterodox alternatives on presenting money as the unifying force that integrates otherwise separate and disparate activities into a coherent whole capable of reproducing itself in expanding fashion. Irrespective of their fascinating differences in approach, both economists understood the standard treatment of money to be the Achilles' heel at which to aim their attacks against orthodox economists.

Neoclassical theory describes an essentially money-less world. Individual optimization rules, for example, depend solely on relative price ratios. Exchange takes the form of barter between goods. Production is depicted as a merely physical process of combining resource inputs in an optimal mix. Credit appears, if at all, as a passive residual which equalizes saving and investment at a certain market-clearing interest rate and thereby assures macroeconomic equilibrium. In this world of barterlike exchange and physical production functions money is artificially separated from the rest of the economy to allow for definition of (essentially nonmonetary) equilibrium conditions. Once money is placed at the center of economic activity, where it belongs, those conditions disappear. A monetary economy such as ours renders invalid any notion of equilibrium other than that of a purely coincidental and fleeting moment of market balance between demand and supply.[9]

How, then, do neoclassical economists cope with the challenge posed by the existence of money? Obviously, they have to define money in such a way that equilibrium conditions remain intact. Standard theory manages to do just that by reducing money to the status of one good among many (see, for example, the Walrasian general equilibrium model). As such, it is defined in terms of distinct supply and demand functions, each with specific properties. On the supply side, money is considered an exogenously fixed stock under the direct control of the central bank, which acts as the monetary authority of the state. And in terms of demand, money represents an asset which gives its holders liquidity. Standard monetary theory assumes that households and firms hold cash balances primarily for transaction purposes as a constant proportion of income. Less stable reasons for money demand, such as the precautionary or speculative motives, can be modeled as an optimizing choice between this liquid asset and interest-earning financial assets (e.g., bonds). In these so-called portfolio-choice models, money demand is shown to depend on interest rates and, while not stable, to be at least predictable.[10]

This particular characterization of money as exogenous stock (supply) and liquid asset (demand) defines a distinct "monetary" sphere which complements, and thereby also keeps intact, the nonmonetary equilibrium conditions in the "real" sphere of exchange and production. The two separate spheres are then linked in the so-called quantity theory of money. Assuming balanced growth of output Q and stable velocity of money V (the reciprocal of money demand), this theory reinterprets the accounting identity $M \times V = P \times Q$ into a monocausal relation between money supply M and price level P. In other words, changes in the money supply are assumed to affect (in the long run) only nominal prices, not underlying equilibrium conditions in the "real" output sphere. From this follows a very simple prescription for monetary policy: the central bank should aim for a stable long-term expansion of the money supply in line with the natural growth capacity of output. If labor-supply growth and productivity gains allow the economy to expand each year on average by, say, 3 percent without reigniting inflation, then the money supply should also increase by 3 percent to keep prices stable.[11]

Reduced to a mere good and as such separated from the rest of the economy, money is a rather marginal phenomenon in standard equilibrium theory. Most neoclassicists justify its existence in terms of its practicality and, in doing so, stress above all its functions. By acting as medium of exchange and standard of prices, money removes barter's drawbacks of "double coincidence" and multiple pricing of each good. A third function, that of store of value, is often mentioned to explain the origins of saving and to stress money's attraction as the most liquid of assets. This functional view presents money as a purely technical instrument which facilitates both exchange and the accumulation of wealth. Apart from these advantages, money has no discernible impact on economic activity in the neoclassical world. Orthodox economists like to invoke the images of money as a "veil" or as "manna from heaven" when describing either its neutrality or its exogeneity vis-à-vis the rest of the economy.

This treatment of money as a residual variable may be necessary for the construction of logically consistent equilibrium models. But such an approach makes little sense when analyzing the actual workings of advanced capitalist economies. We live, after all, in a cash-flow economy. There money acts as representative of income and thus gives its individual holders command in the marketplace. Its acquisition, the most important measure of success and source of power in our society, shapes the decisions and actions of all economic agents. But money is more than the irresistible object of private desires. It is also a powerfully homogenizing force, making otherwise heterogenous products commensurable and subjecting private activities to social validation in the marketplace. Finally, money forces individual market participants into a complex network of social relations, with everyone's income depending on the actions of others.

Money enjoys godlike status in our society. Its omnipresence is pervasive and generally taken for granted. Even though we chase it obsessively, we hardly ever question how it actually works. From the point of view of an individual consumer or investor, money appears as a given, its operation automatic, its force like natural law. Yet money is a social institution, and as such it is subject to regulation by the state in order to maintain its smooth circulation and general acceptability. As we shall see, the precise modalities of this institutional regulation have a decisive impact on the inner workings of our economy and are by no means a historic given. They change over time due to innovation or in response to financial instability. And these changes usually alter the prevailing growth pattern of our economy.

The next two chapters clarify the central role of money in our cash-flow economy. Theoretical conclusions drawn from this analysis can then be put into a historic context. Chapter 4 provides a brief outline of how money and its regulation evolved in the United States, focusing in particular on the gradual transition from the gold standard to a system based on credit-money. Chapters 5 to 7 illustrate the far-reaching implications of this change in the form of money, especially its contribution to both the postwar boom and the subsequent stagflation crisis of the 1970s. In chapter 8 we analyze "Reaganomics," a conservative counterrevolution in response to this crisis. That reform program, while profoundly shaping a broader process of restructuring in our economy, led to new imbalances that need to be addressed. How these pertain to U.S. banking is the subject of chapters 9 to 11. In chapter 12 we analyze the growing importance of short-term speculation and how this trend has transformed financial markets across the globe. Finally, we take up the issue of monetary reform (in chapters 13 to 17), in particular the kinds of policies and regulations required to give the globally integrated economy a stabilizing institutional framework. At the center is a proposal for a new international monetary order.

2

Economic Activities as Monetary Circuits

We are in the midst of a transition period in which our economy is undergoing major restructuring. As the world community enters a new epoch, a geoeconomic era, it faces a much more integrated and multipolar system. Standard economic theory has little to say about this globalization process, and the reasons for this omission lie in the very methodology of its equilibrium model. We need to consider a different approach to economic analysis, drawing from various heterodox traditions. Such an alternative, besides providing a historic context for the structural changes under way, should enable us to analyze our capitalist system as a *monetary production economy* in forward motion. That exercise requires a more extensive understanding of money's role than is generally found in the neoclassical Quantity Theory of Money.

2.1. Defining Money as a Social Institution

Throughout history the operations and forms of money have changed, depending on the type of economic system and its stage of development. Money is a social institution subject to historic evolution. Its modus operandi varies according to period and place. This is true even today. Money has very different meanings and appearances for the aborigines of Papua–New Guinea than it has for brokers on Wall Street. More generally, money can only be properly analyzed in the broader societal context within which it operates. In Communist economies, for example, money functioned in ways that were quite different from its existence in advanced capitalist economies. Mikhail Gorbachev's successors there have become painfully aware of this difference, as they struggle with the thorny issue of currency convertibility.

If we investigate the role of money in capitalism, we have to begin by placing it in the context of the marketplace. The structural features of any market, including its demand and supply curves, are invisible to the naked eye. What we can see instead are customers, prices, and payments. All these are expressed in terms of money. It is therefore fair to say that money makes markets. Those, after all, are spaces of monetary exchange. As such, markets consist of payments from buyers to sellers of a particular product at a predetermined price. These transactions occur on the basis of legally enforceable contracts between two parties engaged in exchange.

Noteworthy here is a qualitative difference between expenditures and receipts. These are two sides of the same transaction. But they are also two separate acts by one and the same economic agent. Every agent, whether producer or consumer, has to first earn money-income in acts of selling before being able to spend money-income in acts of buying. Spending money is comparatively easy, because it depends only on oneself. Receiving money is a wholly different matter. That event depends entirely on others, those who are willing and able to buy the product offered by the seller. It is consequently a much less certain event, beyond the full control of even those sellers who do their best to induce potential customers into purchasing their products.

Everyone can feel that essential difference between buying and selling in an intensely personal manner. It is what makes you get up early in the morning and hustle. Money is easily spent, whereas earning it takes real effort. No matter how much you chase it, money always remains ephemeral. The moment you have it, you will want to spend it. If you do respond in that fashion to temptations or needs, then you will have to regain the income you spent in order to restore your depleted purchasing power. So you must find someone else to whom to sell goods or services in your possession. We all face this unsettling reality of a *monetary constraint*: the constant pressure of having to sell, which may or may not happen, in order to be able to buy.[1]

Income expended in the act of purchase may be lost to the buyer, but it continues to exist. It has simply been transferred to the seller, who in turn will spend it in yet another market, and so forth. Exchange transactions basically circulate income, and buyers must eventually redirect that income back to themselves by acting as sellers. In that *circular flow* all of us are both buyers and sellers at different times, and anyone who wants to buy needs someone else to sell to. Thus we all depend on each other. Workers, for example, can only be consumers to the extent that they manage to sell their labor services to businesses for a wage. Businesses, on the other hand, will only hire those workers if they can sell their output to consumers. The system as a whole reproduces itself, therefore, through a continuous sequence of payments between interdependent market participants who constantly alter their respective roles as buyers and sellers.

So far we have discussed the marketplace only in terms of concrete events— decisions, transactions, and payments. These events reproduce the system. At the same time they also provide information about the system to anyone who cares to know. Markets consist of events as well as observations. What happens in our economic system is observed, and what is observed in turn shapes what happens. Observations provide the raw material for expectations upon which to base decisions about concrete actions. From this we can draw several important conclusions.

• Any observer in the marketplace only sees what can actually be seen. It is therefore futile to assume, as the neoclassicists do, that individuals form "rational" expectations which do not correspond to their own experience. Nor can we argue that the economy follows automatic rules, detached from the subjective and inherently volatile assessments of its participants.[2]

• The importance of observation, even though mostly neglected in standard economic analysis, has not escaped market participants. Today the processing of "information" about markets has become a big business, whether in the form of advertising, consumer reports, trade magazines, consultants, investment letters, or software programs for data processing. Many people are obviously willing to pay others for doing the observing. In other words, the knowledge to observe has itself become a commodity. This also puts economists in a position of marketability, and their conclusions reverberate on the behavior of those they analyze.

• Finally, market participants look mostly for monetary variables, such as prices and transactions. In that sense money acts as a common point of reference, much like a language, for the processing of information. This role of money as signaling device facilitates socialization of behavior in the marketplace. When, for example, individuals see others buying up a "hot" product and driving up its price in the process, they may well be tempted to buy it themselves. This seemingly paradoxical reaction, growing demand in response to higher prices, is particularly evident in the case of speculation or with luxury consumer goods that carry a strong "snob" appeal.

Observers of markets will also note that our economic system is both highly mobile and inert at the same time. On the one hand, it is composed of industrial structures which by their very nature evolve only gradually and remain relatively fixed in the short run. That sluggishness is precisely what makes a given structure attractive to those who operate within it. Firms, for example, know the structural features of their industry and can expect them to continue for some time to come. Their investment decisions and marketing strategies are thus made less uncertain. On the other hand, our economic system also possesses a high degree of mobility. Market participants, whether individuals or firms, can disengage from previous payments commitments when better investment opportunities arise. The ease with which funds can be moved compensates for the inert nature of underlying structures and forces them to adjust to changing conditions. The reconciliation between mobile payments flows and slow structural changes occurs through legally enforceable money contracts that impose a socially necessary degree of patience on market participants.[3]

2.2. Going Beyond a Functional Approach to Money

Let us briefly summarize how standard theory discusses money. For most orthodox economists, money is just another good that provides its holders with utility in the form of liquidity. As such, individual agents have a certain demand for cash balances with which to conduct their transactions. Its supply is supposed to be a stock fixed by the state's monetary authorities. This definition as a good turns money into an exogenous variable which affects only the absolute price level and otherwise has no long-run impact on underlying equilibrium conditions in the "real" sphere of production and exchange (see section 1.4). From this perspective it is easy to justify the existence of money solely in terms of its practicality as a facilitator of exchange. In support of this argument, neoclassicists usually refer to one or the other "function" of money.

Now let us briefly compare that functional approach to money with the reality of its existence. Our introductory comments (in section 2.1) already indicated that money is more than just another good. It is, above all, a social institution subject to both historic change and, as we shall see, complex institutional regulation. Circulating as income through sequences of market transactions, money behaves more like an endogenous flow variable than an exogenous stock variable. Since its circulation affects economic outcomes, money is anything but neutral vis-à-vis volumes of production or terms of exchange. We shall analyze these attributes of money more closely in section 2.4 below. Suffice it to say here that they contrast sharply with the views of standard monetary theory.

The central position of money emerges only when we take a closer look at what lies behind its so-called functions. So let us discuss these in some detail:

1) Money as Price Standard. What enables money to become a unit of account so that goods and services can each be priced in terms of dollars and cents? Obviously, irrespective of their different physical properties and uses, all commodities must have something in common that allows them to be measured by one and the same standard. According to classical political economists, such as Adam Smith, David Ricardo, and Karl Marx, each commodity is the product of human effort. As such it embodies a certain quantity of *value*, depending on how much labor-time is expended on its production under average conditions and with a given state of technological know-how.[4] That value quantity remains invisible to the naked eye, except for its social representation by money. It is precisely as measure of value that money makes otherwise heterogeneous commodities commensurable in terms of money-prices.

2) Money as Medium of Exchange. This unique ability to represent value is also what gives money purchasing power. A given sum of money commands an equivalent quantity of commodity value in the marketplace. From the point of view of individual agents, money thus comes to symbolize income that can be spent on desired products. These expenditures form a coherent whole of circulating commodities and parallel transfers of income flowing in the opposite direction. Money is the glue that keeps this circular flow together. It does so by forcing individual market participants into interdependent sequences of exchange transactions in which they alternate as sellers earning income and buyers spending income (see section 2.1 above).

When buyers and sellers interact, they do so with opposing interests. Sellers want to sell at the highest possible price; buyers want to buy at the lowest possible price. Market transactions underlying flows of money are thus characterized by both interdependence and conflict, a tension that must be resolved each time by contractual agreement for these transactions to take place. This dual nature of market relations reflects the ambivalent nature of money. As a socially accepted medium of exchange it binds agents and is thus an integrative force. As representative of private income, on the other hand, it sets those agents apart and thus acts as a separating force. Much of its institutional regulation by the state as well as private agents focuses on balancing this contradictory aspect of money.

Let us return once again to the circular flow mentioned in the paragraph before last. That circulation of commodities and income is by no means automatic. Once commodities are produced, they embody value. But their value has not yet materialized in its general form, as money-income, the only useful form for the producers. At this point the commodities are merely a potential source of income. Only when they are sold does their value become realized as cash. In the absence of such sales no new income is earned, and old income invested in the production of these unsold commodities is lost. The sale validates the commodity in terms of social demand: someone is willing to spend money on it. This social sanction of validation expresses the link between money and value in dramatic fashion.

3) Money as Store of Value. This function adds yet another dimension to money's linkage with value. Provided it does not get devalued by accelerating inflation, money preserves purchasing power over time. It does not have to be spent right away and therefore can be saved until later. That ability to store value enables money to bridge time gaps between interdependent market transactions which, as we shall see in the next section, occur as a matter of course in production and other types of investments. Moreover, if the spending of one's income can be delayed, why not lend that otherwise unspent income in the meantime to others who intend to spend in excess of their current income? Surplus-saving units and deficit-spending units interact with each other as lenders and borrowers in credit transactions.

It is precisely as measure, representative, and store of value that money gains its special position at the center of our economy. One of the virtues of classical political economy has been to explore that relation between money and value in order to understand how money accumulates as *capital* (see section 2.3 below).

The classical tradition reached its climax in the 1860s with Marx, who analyzed wage-labor as a commodity to derive the origins of profit from the "surplus-value" produced by workers and appropriated by capitalists. This so-called labor theory of value, which Marx derived from Ricardo, challenged the capitalist system head on with its emphasis on exploitation and class conflict. At the same time, the classical economists had also failed to formulate a coherent theory of distribution and prices, as evidenced by the problems Marx had with the "transformation" of values into prices. Neoclassical equilibrium theory, which has remained dominant, emerged during the 1870s to deflect the political challenge posed by Marx and to address these unresolved questions.[5]

As already mentioned earlier (in section 1.3), the founders of this alternative abandoned the classical concept of value. In its place they put "utility" as the characteristic of commodities that makes individuals want to buy them. This redefinition of value in purely subjective terms shifted the analysis from the dynamics of capital accumulation to market equilibrium between demand and supply in a stationary state. The new value concept formed the basis for a theory of relative prices of commodities which assumes that rational consumers allocate their income among different commodities so as to maximize their utility. This shift in focus from production to exchange moved the class origin of income, a key question in classical political economy, into the background. The main concern was now with the conditions for rational decision-making by individuals in the marketplace, thereby framing standards of judgments in terms of utilitarian individualism. But by removing the classical value concept, the neoclassicists also ended up severing the link between money and the activities of exchange and production. What they were left with was a very truncated notion of money as just another good and thus separated from the rest of the economy.

2.3. The Circuits of Exchange, Production, and Credit

The central position of money in our cash-flow economy is illustrated most dramatically when we consider that all economic activities take the form of distinct monetary circuits. Whether comprising exchange, production, or credit-financing, these circuits produce together a cyclical, thus inherently unstable, growth pattern (see chapter 3). In other words, they exhibit fundamentally different behavioral characteristics from those depicted in neoclassical (nonmonetary) equilibrium models.[6]

1) Monetary Exchange. Let us begin with exchange. In the absence of money this activity takes the form of barter; that is, the direct exchange of goods between two people. Here the acts of buying and selling are synonymous, and everyone is both buyer and seller at the same time. Such barter trades require exactly matching reciprocity of needs between the two sides in the transaction. Each party must have what the other wants and at the same time want what the other has. Moreover, each good has to be priced in terms of all other goods for which it can be traded.

The insertion of money into exchange allows the acts of buying and selling to be separated both in time and space. You can now sell your product to anyone who desires it and then take the income earned from this sale to someone else who has what you want. No longer does exchange depend on exactly matching needs, and all goods have just one (money) price. Neoclassical economists recognize these advantages of monetary exchange over barter in terms of lower transaction costs, but they have failed to consider more problematic differences between these two types of exchange.

Although it overcomes barter's double coincidence of wants, money's separation of purchase and sale imposes its own restriction in the form of a monetary constraint (see section 2.1 above). Market participants have to sell something for money before they can make purchases. Their products must satisfy some social demand to yield income. Monetary exchange thus subjects otherwise private production activities to "social (ex-post) validation" in the marketplace. Yet such validation is by no means assured. Money's temporal and spatial separation of buying and selling, allowing income to be spent anywhere and at any point of time, also means that no product offered for sale is a priori assured of a buyer. Say's Law of automatic equality between demand and supply, the core of neoclassical equilibrium theory, does not hold in a monetary economy.[7]

When market imbalances between supply and demand do occur, they may not be self-correcting. This is especially the case when prices no longer decline in response to excess supplies. That loss of price flexibility is widespread in advanced capitalist economies. In contrast to the neoclassical view of price formation as a market-clearing auction (see Walras, 1874), products enter monetary exchange with a predetermined money-price. That price must be high enough to cover production-related unit costs and include an adequate profit margin on top. Sellers thus have a vested interest in maintaining sufficiently high prices for their products. This has encouraged various price-support arrangements (e.g., multi-year wage contracts, fixed-price supply contracts, price coordination in oligopolistic industries, subsidy programs by the government) that have made prices more sticky. In this environment of downwardly rigid prices any buildup of unsold inventories may prompt producers to cut back output and employment before considering price cuts. Even if excess supplies are sold off at lower prices, their costs cannot be reduced a posteriori, and profits will suffer a decline. In either case producers are likely to decrease their purchases, thereby causing falling sales and excess supplies elsewhere. Market disequilibria thus tend to spread, possibly to the point of a generalized downturn in the economy.

Monetary exchange involves swapping a commodity for an equivalent amount of money. Both sides of the transaction depend on each other. The buyer needs a seller to acquire the desired product, and the seller has to have a buyer for income. But the relation between buyer and seller is also one of opposing interests. The seller wants to charge the highest possible price, and the buyer wants to pay the lowest price necessary. While ostensibly regulated by contractual agreement, this conflict over price is resolved on the basis of relative market power.

2) Monetary Production Circuits. Whereas monetary exchange transfers income from buyer to seller, it is production which creates that income in the first place. This activity begins with producers who purchase resource inputs, mostly in the form of labor services, raw materials, plant, and equipment. Those inputs are then combined in the actual production process which transforms them into marketable output for sale. Since this process involves the expenditure of human labor activities, it creates value (see the preceding section). That value added in production is the source of new income. A portion of it is realized as additional profit, if and when the output is sold for an adequate price.

Neoclassical production functions focus solely on the (nonmonetary) middle part of that circuit, the transformation of input into output. They abstract from the monetary transactions required at the beginning and end of the production process (input purchases, output sales). This omission leads standard theory to ignore an essential feature of our capitalist economy; namely, the accumulation of money as capital by engaging it in production as a process of self-expanding value.[8] What motivates producers is not the creation of output per se but its profitable sale. Producers spend money now in order to earn more money later. Production process and exchange transactions form a sequential unity held together by money. Any separation of these activities, as in standard equilibrium theory, is therefore artificial and distorts their actual significance.

It is also worth noting here that the depiction of capital and labor as merely physical inputs in neoclassical production functions abstracts from their complex interaction in this accumulation process. The labor–management relation is not confined to wage determination in the labor market but extends to production itself. Competition with other firms forces managers to obtain as much output from their work force as possible. This objective shapes their organization of production in terms of choice of technology, control over the flow of work, job categorization, and length of working day. Although Marx emphasized its potential for conflict and crisis, the labor–management relationship in production is also one of interdependence. Successful firms are those in which both sides cooperate closely to make production more efficient and in which large productivity gains form the basis for rapid wage growth.

Our discussion of monetary exchange above pointed to the possibility of crisis when anticipated sales fail to materialize. The dynamics of the production circuit turns this phenomenon into a recurrent necessity. The search for higher profits in the face of competition induces producers to strive for productivity gains, better technology, and greater market share. Whenever these measures increase supply capacity beyond demand, firms build up unsold inventories (see chapter 3 for more on this overproduction tendency). In the face of such excess supplies, producers tend to reduce production volumes, lay off workers, and cancel investment projects. Such retrenchment, if widespread enough, leads to recession.

In addition to excess supplies, the production process is also destabilized by inherently volatile investment behavior. Producers face a particularly difficult monetary constraint, since any investment requires spending of money now in order to make more money later. Their cost outlays necessarily precede revenue inflows. Because they cannot know in advance, at the time of their spending decision, what future market conditions (and revenue inflows) will be, they face uncertainty. Under these conditions their willingness to invest depends on expectations about the future. Those are subject to sudden shifts, especially when a particular expectational bias is widely shared. The greater the homogeneity of expectations, the more violent may be the reaction to unanticipated events that clearly contradict the prevailing bias (see the theory of "reflexivity" developed by Soros, 1987).[9] In addition, when making investment decisions, firms typically estimate a project's expected rate of return and then compare it to the minimum rate of return required ("hurdle rate"), which is set by the prevailing interest rate. Investment spending thus tends to fluctuate not only with shifting expectations but also in response to changing interest rates.[10]

The problem of uncertainty arises because producers all face time as a historic process of decisions and events in continuous forward motion. This historic time is irreversible. Mistakes, once made, cannot be simply undone by returning to the status quo ante and starting all over again, as so conveniently assumed in the neoclassical concept of "logical" time (see section 1.3 above). Operating instead in historic time, producers confront a variety of temporal constraints: the labor time per unit of output (productivity) as the determinant of competitiveness; the effects of capital turnover time on profitability; the devaluation of fixed capital goods over time (depreciation and technological obsolescence); the pay-off period as an inverse function of the "hurdle rate;" the diffusion of innovation in relation to the life cycle of products. These time constraints all have a direct impact on corporate profits and therefore require careful management.[11]

3) Credit Circuits. As store of value, money preserves purchasing power over time. Income may therefore be saved for later expenditures. Such savings can then be loaned out to someone else for a finite period. This gives rise to a third type of circuit/activity in our cash-flow economy, credit financing. Except for "trade credit" based on mere deferral of payment (accounts receivables/payables), most credit transactions transfer loanable funds from creditor to debtor. When the loan matures, the debtor has to repay principal and pay interest on top. Money functions here as means of payment to settle outstanding debt obligations.[12]

Credit benefits both sides of the transaction. It provides lenders with a profitable outlet for funds they do not want to spend at the moment. By allowing others temporary use of their own income, they gain a legally enforceable claim on the borrowers' future income in the form of interest. Borrowers in turn receive access to someone else's income and can therefore spend beyond their own means. When used to finance production activities, credit bridges the gaps between cost outflows and revenue inflows and shortens capital turnover. To the extent that credit expands the volume of investment, it helps to generate additional profit income. When financing consumer durables (e.g., homes, cars), credit permits large-ticket purchases which, in the absence of adequate savings, would otherwise have occurred only much later or not at all. In general, credit financing accelerates economic activity by increasing aggregate spending levels.

According to neoclassical theory, credit has a stabilizing influence. It mobilizes otherwise unutilized funds, which as savings would leak out of circulation, to finance current spending. Credit is treated here as a passive residual, an automatic transfer mechanism which equates saving and investment (at a market-clearing rate of interest) and thereby maintains macroeconomic equilibrium. This view has been effectively refuted in Keynes (1936). In his model, interest rates are determined by the interplay between money-supply and money-demand, and the causality runs from investments (via income) to savings rather than the other way around. Moreover, we shall see later (in chapter 3) that credit financing follows a procyclical pattern and thereby reinforces the business-cycle fluctuations of our economy.

As is the case with the other monetary circuits (exchange, production), credit embodies a social relation of interdependence and conflict. Creditors share both gains and losses with their debtors. When those default on their loans, creditors lose their original investment. Their willingness to lend depends therefore on their confidence in the ability of borrowers to service debt out of future income. In other words, their loans amount to a "private (ex-ante) validation" of the borrowers' anticipated income gains. When lenders perceive greater risk, they will want to tighten their credit terms (i.e. higher interest, shorter maturity, demanding collateral) and may even refuse to offer new credit or refinancing facilities.

Lenders and borrowers typically have conflicting interests with regard to the interest rate, length, size, and collateral of a loan. These inherent conflicts can be bridged by several institutional arrangements. First, financial institutions can act as intermediaries in the credit circuit. Such institutions (e.g., commercial banks, thrifts, mutual funds) issue their own instruments tailored to the preferences of lenders for liquidity, safety, and small denominations. Given these attractive characteristics, lenders are willing to accept lower interest rates on those claims than on direct loans to ultimate borrowers. The funds collected thereby are then loaned out in return for different claims that correspond to the needs of the issuing borrowers in terms of, say, larger denomination or longer maturity. This intermediation service earns a profit when interest earned exceeds interest paid. Financial institutions therefore try to maintain a positive yield spread between assets and liabilities.

A second institutional arrangement that facilitates credit financing has been the emergence of financial markets. Any credit transaction is in effect a money contract which gives the lender a financial claim against the borrower's future income. That claim, as the physical expression of the contract, specifies all relevant credit terms (denomination, interest, collateral, etc.) and is legally enforceable. A large variety of these claims have become securities that can be traded in financial markets. This enables creditors to liquidate their claims before maturity, whenever they want their money back. Being thus more liquid than loan contracts, the holders of such securities demand a comparatively lower return. By issuing securities directly to the financial markets, borrowers have a source of funds which is cheaper than bank loans. Certain financial institutions (e.g., investment banks) help to organize these markets by acting as brokers, dealers, and underwriters of securities.

Financial claims can be distinguished on the basis of maturity (money-market instruments versus bonds and equity shares) and liquidity (illiquid loans versus tradable securities). The longer their maturity, the more volatile the market-values of securities ("price risk") and the more uncertain the prospects of the borrowers' ability to service their debt ("default risk"). Higher risks, including that of illiquidity, have to be compensated for by higher returns. The credit-system is therefore based on a hierarchical structure of interest rates which reflects perceived risk differentials between various financial instruments.[13] That structure alters over time due to reevaluation of relative risks in light of changing expectations and corresponding adjustments in credit supplies (e.g., flight into "quality" by nervous creditors). Within that rate structure, certain key interest rates form the basis for other rates (e.g., the Treasury bill rate as the "default-free" rate; the prime rate for all bank loans).

Orthodox economists, such as Gurley and Shaw (1960), treat financial institutions as just another industry whose function it is to sell such financial services as risk reduction, liquidity, and maturity transformation in the process of intermediation between ultimate lenders and borrowers. Heterodox theorists tend to reject this "industry" view as too narrow. Marx (1967, vol. 3, chs. 19 and 21), for example, argued that financial institutions occupy a strategic position in capitalist economies, unlike any industry, by mobilizing and distributing money as capital for different investment uses.

2.4. Credit-Money and the Strategic Role of Banks

As mentioned in chapter 1, neoclassical theory separates money from all economic activities. Its followers treat exchange as if it were barter, only focus on physical inputs in the production process, and analyze credit merely as a passive residual. In this framework the existence of money can be shown to have no lasting impact on the relative prices and individual choices that together bring about equilibrium in the "real" economy. In other words, money is exogenous to the equilibrium model and neutral vis-à-vis its conditions. The logical construction of this argument requires money to be presented as a good which exists separately from all other goods. If we want to claim the exogeneity and neutrality of money, we must therefore assume that it is commodity-money.

Such a conception of money may be fine for the construction of logically consistent equilibrium models. But it has little to do with reality. We do not live in a barter economy, and our prevalent form of money is certainly not a commodity that comes out of a regular production process. Today we operate in a regime of *credit-money*, a form of money whose behavioral characteristics escape the majority of economists still fixated on defining money as just another good. Let us therefore briefly spell out in this section what credit-money is and how it differs from the standard theory of money.

1) Money Is Not a Good. An economy that uses as money a commodity (e.g., precious metals), which producers can produce for themselves, cannot be distinguished from a barter economy. If money had ever been just another good, we would have had barter and not monetary exchange. In reality, throughout modern civilization we have never truly had commodity-money. Instead, we always used tokens as money, mostly paper currency and bank notes. Even gold and silver coins, which we usually refer to as commodity-money, were actually tokens and as such, strictly speaking, credit-money.[14]

While money has not been a commodity since prehistoric times, we did until fairly recently operate in a regime of commodity-money. Under that institutional arrangement the total domestic supply of various tokens circulating as money was supposedly backed by a nation's stock of precious metals, and gold functioned as an international means of payment for settling debts between nations. That so-called gold standard had serious shortcomings. Whenever the issue of tokens exceeded available gold reserves, as happened inevitably during boom phases, overextended banks would at the first signs of trouble become subject to panic runs that forced the inflated money supply back to its "metallic" base in often violent depressions. Moreover, gold flows between nations would easily destabilize their respective economies, forcing the deficit country into deflationary adjustment and exacerbating inflationary pressures in the surplus country. These problems led eventually, during the Great Depression, to the abandonment of the gold standard and its replacement by credit-money proper (see chapter 4).

2) Money Must Originate Outside the Marketplace. Were money to originate within the marketplace for goods and services, buyers could pay for their purchases simply by issuing their own money. In this case money does not function as an effective means of payment capable of settling debts. In this context it is important to bear in mind that tokens representing credit-money are per se nothing but a promise of future payment. If sellers accept such tokens, they in effect give their buyers a line of credit. By continuously issuing new tokens, buyers could permanently postpone final payment. Such a privilege, an expression of what economists call *seigniorage*, violates the fundamental rule of a monetary economy, because it prevents proper settlement of debts.[15]

Since money must not grant seigniorage benefits to economic agents who make payments, no buyer of goods and services can be allowed to issue it. This is why money creation has been confined to banks that do not operate in the marketplace. Of course, these institutions do buy goods (e.g., buildings, computers) and services (e.g., labor) on a regular basis. But these purchases are entirely financed out of their profits. In other words, their buying is strictly separate from their specialization in money-dealing activities through which the banks issue credit-money in the form of transaction deposits with check-writing privileges.

3) Monetary Payments Are Triangular Transactions. When a buyer wants to pay for his purchase, he simply gives the seller a check with the amount due written on it. That check represents a promise to pay by a third agent. It orders the bank, on which the check is drawn, to pay the seller the sum in question. Any monetary payment is thus necessarily a triangular transaction between buyer, seller, and bank. Payments by check turn the buyer into a debtor of the bank and the seller into a creditor of the bank. These debts are settled as soon as the bank deducts the amount due from the buyer's account and credits it to the seller's account.

When a seller receives a check from a buyer for payment, he may not have an account with the same bank. How then can the bank of the payer credit that money to the payee? The answer is that it cannot, at least not directly. Instead, the payee presents the check to his own bank for credit to his account. His bank then becomes a creditor of the other bank on which the check was drawn. Here we run into an already familiar complication. A bank may be able to issue a promise to pay on behalf of its depositor, but it cannot do the same to settle its own debt. In that regard a bank is no different from the buyer of a good. Neither can effectively meet payment obligations by issuing promises to pay. In other words, a bank cannot just write a check drawn on itself and give it to another bank as a means of payment. The problem is resolved in similar fashion as in the case of payments between agents in the marketplace, through interjection of a third party. That party is the central bank, which runs a check-clearing mechanism as part of the national payments system.

The banks keep deposit accounts with the central bank which represent their so-called reserves. When a bank receives a check, it sends it to the central bank for credit to its reserve account. The same amount is debited from the reserve account of the other bank on which the check was drawn. In this way debts between banks are settled by reserve transfers, with the central bank acting as bookkeeper debiting and crediting the appropriate accounts. Each payment by check thus actually involves two triangular transactions. The first one occurs when a buyer orders his bank to pay a seller, followed by a second transaction in which the central bank moves the same amount in reserves from the buyer's bank to the seller's bank.

4) Money Creation Is Tied to Bank Lending. When a payee deposits a check, his bank will gain an equivalent amount in reserves. That bank has to set aside a certain portion of that reserve addition to meet the reserve requirements imposed by the central bank. The rest represents excess reserves. Since those do not earn interest, banks will under normal conditions try to turn their excess reserves into income-earning assets by lending them out. It is precisely this step that creates new money. Reserves in the banking system are thus the "raw material" for the issue of private bank money.

When a bank lends out its excess reserves, it gives the borrower a book of empty checks. These tokens become real money the moment the borrower uses them to pay for purchases. Anyone who borrows from a bank will inevitably do so, since it is irrational not to spend a loan which requires payment of interest. The moment the loan is spent, the bank loses its excess reserves. But, as shown above in our discussion of the check-clearing mechanism, another bank receives the borrower's check and thereby gains those reserves. After deducting a portion to meet reserve requirements, that second bank can lend out the rest and initiate another round of money creation. The same process may repeat itself with a third bank, a fourth bank, and so forth until the original excess reserves of the first bank have been transformed step by step into required reserves. In this way the banking system as a whole can create a multiple of the original excess reserves in new money. The size of that multiplier depends on the reserve requirement imposed by the central bank, the extent to which banks lend out their excess reserves, and the public's preference for cash over deposits.

5) The Central Bank Does Not Control the Money Supply. So far we have depicted the central bank as merely a passive bookkeeper crediting and debiting the reserve accounts of banks, with the additional power of setting reserve requirements on bank deposits. But its role in our monetary economy goes far beyond that. For one, it issues its own credit-money in the form of paper currency. When you look at any dollar bill, for example, you will see the sign "Federal Reserve Note" imprinted on it. In addition, the central bank operates the nation's payments system so as to maintain the automatic convertibility of all tokens circulating as credit-money, including exchange of domestic currency with foreign monies for cross-border payments. This convertibility guarantee is precisely what enables private bank money to become a socially accepted medium of exchange. Thirdly, it acts as the fiscal agent of the state and in this role trades large amounts of securities to maintain an orderly market for government debt. Finally, the central bank is the only agent in the economy able to write checks drawn on itself. In this way it can extend credit at will.

These unique powers allow the central bank to exercise a significant influence in our monetary economy by manipulating the amount of reserves in the banking system. If it wants to add reserves, for example, it can lend funds through its discount window to overextended banks that are facing reserve deficiencies. Those discount loans are one of the principal lender-of-last-resort channels in our economy. The central bank can also buy government securities and pay for these by crediting the bank that receives its check with an equivalent amount in reserves. These so-called open-market purchases facilitate deficit spending by the government, because they create liquidity injections to finance a portion of the public debt. When the central bank pumps additional reserves into the banking system, it supplies more "raw material" for private bank money. In this case banks can extend more credit and thereby accelerate their money creation. Conversely, the central bank can remove reserves by restricting its lending to banks or by selling government securities. Ceteris paribus, this will slow down the money-creation process by banks.

The central bank issues its own paper currency and can manipulate the amount of total reserves in the banking system. By setting reserve requirements, it can also determine what portion of total reserves constitutes excess reserves available to banks for money creation. Yet these powers do not amount to direct control over the money supply, as most standard economists would have us believe. The central bank controls only the excess reserves that enable banks to create new money. It does not control the willingness of banks to lend out these excess reserves. In times of great uncertainty banks may want to keep more reserves than the required minimum as a liquidity cushion. In euphoric times, on the other hand, banks may borrow additional funds in order to meet strong credit demand. Some of these funding sources, such as the Euromarket, are beyond the reach of any monetary authority. Banks can thus drive the money-creation process beyond available excess reserves, if they want to. Finally, the central bank does not control the public's demand for bank loans. When economic activity is depressed, most agents will not want to borrow. In that situation, pumping additional reserves into the banking system will not have much of a stimulative effect.

6) Banks Are More than Just Intermediaries. Because money creation derives ostensibly from banks that collect deposits and lend them at interest, it reinforces the idea held by most economists that banks act as mere intermediaries between depositors and investors. Another way of expressing this widely held belief is that banks collect savings and finance investments. From there it is only a small step to conclude that an adequate amount of saving needs to be formed before any investment can actually be undertaken—the standard equilibrium condition of ex ante saving equaling ex ante investment at a market-clearing interest rate.

This notion is an illusion. Banks cannot really lend out deposits, because these may be withdrawn at any time on demand. When banks make loans, they consequently do not simply transfer liquidity from depositor to borrower. Instead, the loan must represent new liquidity in addition to the liquidity embodied in the demand deposit. It is precisely for this reason that credit extension by banks automatically involves the issuance of new money. This ability to add liquidity gives banks a much more important role in our economy than their reduction to the status of intermediaries in standard economics would imply.

In order to understand the strategic position of banks in advanced capitalist societies, we must abandon the neoclassical emphasis on individual choices by isolated agents and focus instead on the relationships among socioeconomic groups. In our economic system the interaction between industrial enterprises and banking institutions is of special importance. Even though these two groups may forge very close ties (see our discussion of Hilferding's "finance capital" in section 2.5), banks and firms cannot be aggregated into a single sector—a mistake commonly found in macroeconomic models. The two are distinctly different agents, each engaged in a unique activity.

Firms mobilize the production of goods and services. This activity allocates available resources among different uses, creates income, and provides our society with a *surplus*. It is precisely that surplus which enables the economy to grow. In the absence of a surplus, the entire output would be spent on current consumption. Nothing would be left for investing in productive capacity. Banks, on the other hand, do not engage in production. They specialize in financing and thereby supply firms with the means of payment to carry out their production plans. In return for this assistance they obtain a share of the firm's income gain. In other words, the surplus of the economy is divided between profits to industry and interest to the banking sector. That division is subject to negotiations between firms and banks in the money market and depends on their relative social power.

7) Money Flows in the Form of a Circuit. The standard notion of money as an exogenous stock variable misrepresents its actual existence. In our monetary production economy money carries precisely opposite characteristics, that of an endogenous flow variable. We have already shown (in section 2.3) that all of our economic activities take the form of monetary circuits. The theory of the "dynamic circuit," popular among certain post-Keynesians in France, Italy, and Canada, goes one step further and describes the intertwining of bank credit and industrial production itself in terms of a distinct circuit. This theory is not entirely new. It extends earlier analyses of money's creation and circulation, most notably those undertaken by Wicksell (1898), Schumpeter (1912), and Keynes (1930a).[16]

The dynamic circuit begins with firms determining their output targets for the current period and the inputs going into the production process. This decision requires two sets of negotiations. In the labor market, firms and wage-earners negotiate the level of money wages. Since firms have to spend money now in order to make more money later, they often face expenditures in excess of income and need to take on debt. In the money market they negotiate with banks the amount of credit granted and the rate of interest charged. These two price determinations are obviously interdependent, because the level of money wages affects the credit needs of firms and banks may be more reluctant to lend if firms agree to pay excessively high wages.

Since firms buy inventories from each other, these purchases cancel each other out when considering firms as a whole. Their only external payments at this point are wages to workers. These must then decide what to do with their money wages, how much to spend on consumer goods and how much to save. Concerning savings, wage-earners have a choice. They can keep their savings liquid in bank deposits. Alternatively, they can buy corporate securities (e.g., bonds, equity shares), which in the absence of a government deficit are the only ones issued in the capital markets.[17]

As long as workers spend their money wages on consumption goods or invest their savings in corporate securities, firms receive their original wage payments back and can use those funds to repay their bank loans. Such repayment destroys the money created initially when the banks made their loans to the firms, and the circuit is closed. But if wage-earners place some of their savings in bank deposits, then firms will receive less money back than they originally expended. Such leakage prevents them from repaying all of their bank loans. Since in that situation not all of the money is destroyed, some of it—the portion of wages deposited in banks—will survive into the next period. This failure to close the circuit does not matter as long as banks use the excess reserves gained from these deposits to grant firms in the next period the same amount of credit as was granted in the previous period. When that happens, the money supply will increase over time. Implicit here is an assumption that wage-earners have a need for liquidity (savings deposited in banks) in response to uncertainty and therefore do not spend all of their income at once. In the neoclassical equilibrium model, where no uncertainty exists, there is no need for such bank deposits. If that were truly the case, credit-money would tend to disappear and the velocity of its circulation would become infinite.

What emerges clearly from the "dynamic circuit" approach is the endogeneity and non-neutrality of money in our economy. Money is endogenous, because its supply arises in the wake of credit extension and therefore as a direct result of spending decisions by firms or other agents.[18] Money is non-neutral, because firms need finance in order to carry out their production plans. The extent to which new money is issued determines how much industry can spend on wages and the means of production. The decisions by banks, its issuers, as to the amounts lent and interest rates charged thus affect the real economy profoundly in both the short run and the long run.

8) Interest Rates Do Affect Investment Behavior. The monetary circuit described above distinguishes between two types of finance. Bank loans supply firms with "initial" finance of a temporary nature to help them pay their wages and inventory purchases of intermediate goods. This source of short-term liquidity therefore covers only the current cost of output and is not specifically connected with investment in plant and equipment. The latter activity requires long-term finance, which firms obtain by issuing debt and equity securities. Circuit theorists refer to these corporate securities as "final" finance, reflecting their assumption that firms purchase their capital goods only at the end of a given production period for use in the next period. Firms issue those securities not least in order to attract the savings of workers which, if deposited in banks instead, would be lost to them and thus prevent them from repaying their bank loans in full.

Circuit theorists differentiate between bank loans and corporate securities to argue that interest rates do not affect the investment behavior of industrial firms. In their model there is principally no limit as to how much interest firms can pay savers on their securities, since these interest payments flow right back to them. This, of course, does not apply to interest paid on their loans, which represents a transfer of income from firms to banks. Since purchases of capital goods are financed only by securities (and not bank loans), the level of interest rates is shown to have no impact on corporate investment activity. This, by the way, enables circuit theorists to conclude also that there is no "crowding out" effect from large government deficits and that monetary policy efforts to keep interest rates down do not stimulate investment.[19]

The claim that interest rates have no impact on industrial investment behavior rests on problematic assumptions. For one, it is somewhat arbitrary to say that firms only purchase capital goods at the end of a production period. If they need to replace worn-out plant and equipment or expand capacity, they may have to buy capital goods before they can meet current production targets. Secondly, only larger firms have access to the capital markets. The majority of firms in our economy must still rely on bank loans as the exclusive source of finance for all of their inputs. Most importantly, circuit theorists suffer from a fallacy of composition when they argue that interest on corporate securities is paid at no cost by firms to savers. Those interest payments may flow back to industry as a whole, if and when savers spend their investment income on goods and services. But this does not hold for single firms. No firm can know a priori to what extent it will earn back its payments to bondholders and shareholders. Yet it is on the level of individual firms that investment decisions are made. Consequently, from the point of view of a firm, payments to holders of its securities are costs. And these costs do impact on both its ability and its willingness to invest in capital goods.[20]

The level of long-term interest rates affects corporate investment behavior in a variety of ways. For one, interest and dividend payments are costs that are deducted from corporate income. They reduce "retained earnings"; that is, the proportion of profit available to the firm for reinvestment. In addition, the interest rate plays a crucial role in the investment decision of a firm by determining the minimum rate of return required for investment projects to qualify as profitable. In other words, firms will undertake only those projects whose expected rates of return exceed that required minimum rate. There are two reasons why the interest rate functions as such a hurdle rate in the investment decisions of firms. One is the "cost of capital." If firms have to pay, say, 10 percent per year to obtain external finance, then it makes little sense for them to invest those funds in anything that yields less than 10 percent in return. If they did, they would have a net loss.[21] The other reason is that of "opportunity cost." If financial assets (e.g., bank deposits, government bonds) pay 10 percent in interest, why should a firm invest in its own line of business at a profit rate below that? Finally, interest rates move inversely with security prices. The prospect of rising interest rates will discourage savers from holding securities whose value is expected to decline. This situation makes it more difficult for firms to issue new bonds or stocks, thereby undermining their capacity to finance new investment. For all these reasons, rising or already high interest rates are an impediment to industrial investment activity.

2.5. The Bifurcation of Money-Capital: Industrial Capital versus Financial Capital

Our cash-flow economy grows when money is invested in production circuits. There it accumulates in the form of *industrial capital*. Alternatively, investors can lend their money and in the process acquire claims on the borrower's future income. In such credit circuits money accumulates as *financial capital*. Each alternative provides the investor with its own type of return: profits from industrial investments; interest, dividends, and capital gains from financial investments. Both provide outlets for the accumulation of money-capital, but they do so in distinctly different activities. Industrial capital creates marketable goods and services. In the process it mobilizes the *production economy*, which is made up of the intersectoral matrix of industries, social consumption norms, labor markets, and technological change. Financial capital, on the other hand, originates from credit-financing. There it gives rise to the *portfolio economy*, which comprises the instruments, markets, and institutions of the credit system.

Even though financial data are quite incomplete, it is clear from flow-of-funds accounts and other statistical sources that in contemporary America financial capital is larger and growing more rapidly than is industrial capital. Although the collapse of stock and bond prices in 1987 may have altered the balance somewhat, it did not fundamentally reverse the trend. At the end of 1990 the U.S. production economy used $16.2 trillion worth of tangible assets (plant, equipment, inventories) to create a gross domestic product of just over $5.5 trillion per year. At the same time the U.S. portfolio economy had accumulated $27.5 trillion worth of financial assets (e.g., stocks, bonds, bank accounts), which supported a total debt outstanding of more than $8.4 trillion. Unlike industrial capital, many financial assets are turned over several times a year, so that their trading volume is much larger than the purchases of goods and services.[22] The growing dominance of financial capital is also reflected in the fact that throughout the 1980s U.S. debt expanded twice as rapidly as did our production volume (see Figure 2.1).

Most economists focus primarily on the production economy and pay little attention to the portfolio economy. That bias results from an underlying conviction, commonly shared in the profession, that there is nothing peculiar to the

Figure 2.1 **The Growing Dominance of Financial Capital**

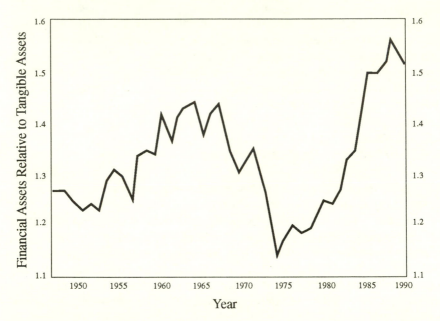

Year

Source: Keith Carlson (1991). "The U.S. Balance Sheet: What Is It and What Does It Tell Us?" Federal Reserve Bank of St. Louis, *Review,* 73(5), p. 13.

Note: Financial assets relative to tangible assets (both in 1982 dollars). That ratio's decline in the mid-1970s was due to inverse effect of inflation on financial assets (devaluation) versus tangible assets (revaluation).

portfolio economy. Microeconomists apply the same choice-optimization principles to financial portfolio decisions that they use when modeling decisions by firms and consumers. Financial institutions are viewed as just another service industry, on a par with manufacturing sectors, such as cars or machine tools. Macroeconomists, confining credit to the status of a passive residual with which to equilibrate savings and investments, spend most of their time trying to explain variations in the gross national product from which financial transactions are excluded.

The orthodox bias in favor of the production economy downplays the important role of the credit system in our economy. Even worse, it ignores many important differences between financial capital and industrial capital in terms of time constraints, liquidity, riskiness, cash-balance requirements, income form, and price formation.

• Financial capital forms a two-step circuit (purchase of financial asset - its sale or repayment of principal), whereas industrial capital has to go through a three-step transformation (inputs - output - sales) before returning to its owner.

• Financial assets tend to be quite liquid. That means it is usually quite easy and does not take much time to turn them into money without suffering a loss. By comparison, industrial capital is much less liquid, since plant and equipment cannot normally be resold at a reasonable price and are liquidated only very gradually in the production process.

• Financial capital is for the most part based on contracts with predetermined cash flows (e.g., interest, repayment of principal). It is therefore less exposed to unforeseen disruption and more predictable in its timing than is industrial capital, whose outcome and duration cannot be easily anticipated with accuracy.

• The two forms of capital each have their own specific connections to money. Industrial firms demand money for transaction purposes, as insurance against unforeseen mishaps during periods of heightened uncertainty ("precautionary" motive), and for cash advances to start planned investment projects (see the "finance" motive of Keynes, 1937). Financial capital comprises two additional sources of money demand: the holding of cash to benefit from anticipated price movements of financial assets (the "speculative" motive), and debtors who need money to honor their debt obligations.

• Industrial capital yields investors a profit. The precise nature of this income form has been one of the more hotly debated subjects in economics.[23] Financial capital, in contrast, yields interest. In neoclassical equilibrium models, interest is the rate of return, which equates savings and investments, and is equal to the profit rate. Heterodox economists reject this standard notion of a "natural" interest rate and emphasize instead the difference between interest and profit rates. In any case, interest is a deduction from the borrower's income, to which the lender is entitled in return for supplying loanable funds.[24] We shall discuss dividends and capital gains, two additional forms of income associated with financial capital, in the next section.

• Output prices in industry are determined by the (past and current) cost outlays required to operate the production process. Large corporations with a degree of market control price their output nowadays by first calculating a given period's total operating costs per unit of output and then adding a mark-up, their profit margin, on top of these unit costs. The size of this mark-up depends both on the market power of firms and the cyclical variations of demand. In contrast, securities traded in financial markets are valued on the basis of expected future returns. Their valuation involves discounting prospective yields at a risk-adjusted rate of interest to determine their present value as the market price. Based on this so-called *capitalization of income* procedure, security prices and interest rates move in opposite directions. In addition, security prices also vary with changing expectations about future returns and with reassessments of risks. Given the inherently volatile nature of all these valuation factors, security prices fluctuate much more than do the cost-based output prices of industry.

2.6. Finance Capital and Fictitious Capital

The price volatility in financial markets attracts a great deal of speculation, in which investors set up trading positions to benefit from correctly anticipated changes in security prices. Neoclassical economists consider speculation to be like arbitrage by individuals in response to temporary price deviations from some presumed equilibrium level. In this framework, speculators are a stabilizing force, returning the price to where it belongs. In reality, however, speculation may be a highly destabilizing force.[25] Speculators do not operate in isolation but follow short-term shifts in market psychology and, in the process, take each other as reference points. Once their activity begins to dominate a market, then a widely shared expectational bias of speculators often becomes a self-fulfilling prophecy. For example, anticipated price increases may trigger such a wave of speculative buying that this prediction cannot but come true. Such self-validation only feeds further speculation. However, to the extent that the price movements thereby exacerbated are increasingly out of line with underlying economic realities, they become unsustainable. The speculative bubble bursts when the often sudden reversal of the expectational bias triggers panic selling. Speculative waves thus tend to follow a pronounced boom-bust cycle, as was so clearly evident during recent years in the stock and foreign exchange markets.

Such propensity for speculation in financial markets underlines the fact that the relationship between industry and finance contains two seemingly contradictory aspects; namely, integration and separation. On the one hand, industry and finance are obviously interdependent. Industrial firms require access to loanable funds in order to cover the cash-flow gaps in their investment activities. By providing these funds, the creditors can claim a share of the borrowing firms' future profit income. Here the two sides share both gains and losses. On the other hand, industrial capital and financial capital represent two separate investment alternatives, each with its own attributes (see section 2.5 above). This dimension of separation is especially clear in the case of financial speculation, a form of investment with a certain degree of "relative autonomy" from the vicissitudes and constraints of industrial capital.

The duality of interdependence and separation dominates the relationship between production and portfolio economies. Concerning the first aspect in this relation, there is a clear historic trend toward the growing integration of finance and industry. Technology-based concentration of industrial capital (e.g., mass-production technologies), monopolistic market structures, and the centralization of financial capital all go hand in hand. The emergence of giant banks parallels that of huge corporations. Both need and reinforce each other. Growing size alone makes industrial firms more dependent (and able to rely) on external funds to finance their production activities. That in turn leads to growing investments by financial institutions in industry, both through loans and through equity positions.

By investing their own funds in industry, banks and other financial institutions tie their income to the profits of those firms they support. This is true whatever form their investment takes, whether it be loans, equity positions, or underwriting (issuing and marketing) new securities. When firms supported thereby face a decline in profits, the banks cannot simply withdraw their funds and put them somewhere else. To do so would endanger their own investments in industry by undermining the financial position of already troubled firms even more. They are therefore often compelled to stay with their financially weak corporate customers, providing refinancing facilities and agreeing to restructure outstanding debt whenever necessary. It is this close link to the fortunes of industry that induces financial institutions to control the management and operations of enterprises in an effort to protect their own assets. That trend toward greater integration led Hilferding (1985, ch. 14) to conclude in 1910 that industrial capital and interest-bearing money-capital in the hands of banks would merge into a whole new form of capital, *finance capital*. Since then, this form of capital has evolved especially in those countries (e.g., Germany, Japan) in which commercial banks have been permitted to own equity shares of industrial firms.[26]

Yet banks and other financial institutions also have strong incentives to avoid this direct dependence on industry. After all, profits are notoriously volatile, and those institutions do not like to have to "throw good money after bad money." In addition, many institutions tend to face highly liquid liabilities (e.g., bank deposits, mutual fund shares) and run therefore large risks, if they hold too many illiquid loan assets. Thus they seek more liquid and mobile alternatives that at the same time shield them from the vicissitudes of industry. In particular, financial institutions have developed various "money-dealing" activities which are not directly tied to corporate profits and which can thus expand in relative separation from industry (e.g., money transfers, foreign exchange transactions, trading of financial instruments). Whereas the integration of finance and industry through interest-bearing credit gives rise to "finance capital" (see note 26), the money-dealing activities of financial institutions engender their own distinct form of capital. Marx (1967, vol. 3, chs. 25, 29, and 33) has analyzed those activities as the basis for so-called *fictitious capital*. This concept refers to all those financial assets whose values are based on the capitalization of a future income stream (see the last paragraph of section 2.5 above) and which as such have no counterpart in actual industrial capital. Based on this definition, Marx identified several types of "fictitious" capital, all of which have become pillars of our modern portfolio economy:

• Equity shares traded in the stock market do not represent the actual industrial capital accumulated by firms but are only ownership titles to that capital. While the valuation of a share depends to some degree on the expected profitability of the issuer's investment in plant and equipment, it can also be influenced by market manipulation and speculation (see chapter 12 for more).

Shareholders earn dividends which, like interest on bonds and bank loans, are paid out of the income gains of firms.

• Another form of fictitious capital discussed by Marx is credit to the state, financed either through government securities or bank loans. Because these funds are not used in private production activities, they do not represent industrial capital. Correspondingly, the servicing of this public debt is not a direct deduction from gross profits but depends on future tax revenues. State debt, especially the $4 trillion worth of U.S. Treasury securities, gives financial institutions an extremely liquid and nearly risk-free asset in which to invest.

• Finally, writing during the heyday of the gold standard, Marx also stressed the fictitious nature of all forms of money whose circulation was not backed by equivalent gold reserves. These include state-issued inconvertible currency and all private credit-money through which banks can create a multiple of their deposit reserves in new credit. Since the Great Depression our payment system has been entirely based on such credit-money (see chapters 4 and 5).[27]

Even though largely ignored in the literature, the notion of fictitious capital is of crucial importance in giving us a better understanding of finance. Its key characteristic, the formation of credit circuits and security values that are relatively divorced from the accumulation of industrial capital, enables individual financial institutions to expand without being directly tied to industry, as in the case of finance capital. It is the form of capital that best satisfies their preference for a mobile asset structure and yields income within the shortest period of time (e.g., service fees, capital gains).

In recent years various forces have fueled the extraordinary growth of fictitious capital in the U.S. economy. Persistently high interest rates since 1979/80 made financial investments in many instances more attractive than industrial investments, causing a major shift in investment preferences. Banking deregulation intensified competitive pressures among financial institutions and spurred innovation. Many new instruments, such as junk bonds, mortgage-backed securities, financial futures, swaps, repurchasing agreements, and deposit brokerage, involved complex sequences of interrelated fund transfers and claim issues (see chapter 11). Such multiple layering of credit circuits relied heavily on financial institutions lending funds to each other. Thereby creating business among themselves, those institutions could earn more income (and at the same time spread risks) without being tied to illiquid loan assets. Add to this the explosive growth since 1981 of financial futures contracts, which give holders the right to buy or sell financial assets (e.g., stocks, currencies) at a certain future date and predetermined price. These instruments have come to be widely used for short-term trading strategies in government securities, corporate equity, and currencies. Their dramatic growth soon turned bond, stock, and foreign-exchange markets into a casino-like domain of speculators seeking to benefit from price volatility.[28]

Marx, Keynes, and other heterodox economists had good reason to focus attention on the complex interaction between finance and industry. In advanced capitalist economies this relation assumes a most strategic position. For one, it shapes investment priorities and time horizons of investors. The credit system also tends to reinforce business-cycle fluctuations, and its tension between "enterprise" and "speculation" has a profound impact on the long-run performance of capitalist economies. It is in this context that we must understand the explosive growth of fictitious capital over the last decade as a major force in the structural transformation of our economy (see chapters 11 and 12 for more).

The Cyclical Growth Pattern
of Capital Accumulation

Our economy grows because individual agents invest money in income-creating projects. Motivated by the desire for profit that accrues to investors whenever new income revenues exceed original cost outlays, these investments add value and expand production capacity. In this way money accumulates as capital. That process of *capital accumulation*, which the classical economists analyzed so beautifully as one of "self-expanding value," gives the capitalist system its powerful dynamism. Competition forces producers to invest constantly in the development of new products and better production technologies. Otherwise they run the risk of falling behind in the race for profits and market share. On the sidelines are all kinds of financial investors who want to capture a share of those profits and who in the process make bets on the relative strengths and weaknesses of producers. Their choices reinforce the perceived qualitative differences in competitiveness. Firms, and in today's globalized economy even entire nations, must therefore shape up or decline. That pressure is sweetened by the prospect of enjoying the fruits of their effort. Investment and reorganization may eventually pay off.

But investors, whether industrial producers or financial assetholders, face a particularly stringent monetary constraint. They must spend now in order to earn more later. And they need to have their spending activities and choices validated ex post by others before they can earn any income. Neither the extent nor the timing of those future inflows can be predicted accurately. In this climate of uncertainty, investment activity fluctuates a great deal in response to changes in earnings performance and expectations. When investors cut back, their spending reductions filter through the circular flow and thereby feed on themselves. Eventually this shrinkage process will have destroyed enough of the excess build-up on the supply side to have run its course.

Capital accumulation is therefore an inherently cyclical process, reinforced by the social psychology of "markets" as places of human interaction (see section 2.1). Markets adjust precisely in sequences of overextension and retrenchment. They do not automatically tend toward equilibrium or remain there. In this chapter we distinguish between two different kinds of cycles, relatively short-term "business cycles" and the much more gradual "long waves." The former can be counteracted by appropriate countercyclical policies of macroeconomic stabilization. The latter, on the other hand, engender major ("structural") crises during their downswing phases which require large-scale restructuring and major policy reforms.

3.1. Business-Cycle Dynamics

In contrast to neoclassical equilibrium models, capitalist economies do not move along a steady-state path of "balanced" growth. Instead, their growth pattern typically exhibits alternate phases of crisis and prosperity. Implying that these ups and downs cancel each other out and can therefore be compressed into a linear path simply ignores the dynamic motions of instability in our economy. It is the market mechanism itself that drives our cash-flow economy through regularly recurrent sequences of destabilization, rupture, and readjustment. These result in business cycles which last on average from four to seven years. Even though they all have their own distinct features, those cycles share certain characteristics.[1]

Let us begin with recovery. That first phase of a business cycle begins when cost-cutting measures during the preceding slump finally bear fruit. As profits show signs of improvement, expectations about future demand conditions and prospective yields turn more optimistic. Competitive pressures, coupled with the fear of falling behind other rivals, induce industrial firms to expand production in response to improved profit opportunities. Lenders share the optimistic expectations and eagerly seek to expand their loan assets in response to reviving credit demand. Following a period of weak lending activity, financial institutions have accumulated large supplies of loanable funds which they are willing to make cheaply available. At this point, firms invest primarily to enlarge their employment and inventory stocks in line with growing production volumes. Their outlays create more income for workers and inventory suppliers, who in turn increase their own spending. These positive multiplier effects feed gradually through the industrial matrix and labor markets to result in a broadening recovery.

After a while, as firms become increasingly confident and begin to approach their capacity limit, they begin larger-scale investment projects in new plant and equipment. This additional business spending accelerates economic activity, and the recovery gives way to a boom. But it is precisely this speed-up which causes its own demise by overshooting. The very process of increased investment activity eventually puts downward pressure on profits, as firms exhaust their most profitable investment opportunities.[2]

Such profit erosion occurs not least because of rising cost pressures. The surge of spending on plant and equipment in the boom phase typically causes order backlogs and higher prices in the capital goods sectors, which make investment projects more expensive than originally envisaged. Supply bottlenecks in raw-materials industries and labor shortages add to cost pressures. Speculative euphoria, with a growing number of investors seeking short-term capital gains from rising prices, reinforces the speed-up of inflation. Boom-related increases in credit demand begin to push interest rates upward.

Those increases in production costs are accompanied by slowing revenue growth for firms. The latter results from industry's inherent tendency toward overproduction, a problem rooted in the contradictory double nature of the wage. On the one hand, wages constitute a business cost to be kept at a minimum. On the other hand, they are the largest source of social demand for industry's products (consumption). The wage is thus a simultaneous determinant of both costs and revenues of industry, but in opposite directions. Each firm wants the wages of its own work force to be as low as possible (as a cost factor) and the wages of all other workers to be as high as possible (as a source of revenue). Yet wages are determined in the labor market as a private cost. Competition among firms induces capacity-expanding investments, while forcing them to keep their labor costs under control. The result is that industry's production capacity tends to outgrow the consumption ability of its workers, eventually leading to a situation of unsold excess supplies.[3]

Industry's overproduction is fed by a simultaneous process of credit overextension. During the upswing, creditors aggressively compete with each other to pursue profitable lending opportunities. This makes it much easier for firms to finance rapid capacity expansion. The resulting boom conditions cause overconfident creditors to make loans which under less euphoric circumstances would have been rejected as too risky. Certain debtors receive more funds than warranted by their long-term performance trends. In addition, accelerating inflation encourages speculative activity. Lenders direct more and more funds into short-term investments that promise rapid gains from continuous price increases (e.g., stocks, real estate, gold).

Near the peak of the cycle, even while the boom-induced euphoria persists, industrial firms suddenly find their balance sheets eroding. Because of the boom-induced surge in investment spending, both their cash outflows and debt levels will have risen. With new production facilities often coming on stream just when demand is peaking, the then-emerging problem of excess capacity rapidly grows worse. This situation of overproduction ruptures the expansion process. Decelerating revenue growth usually coincides with large increases in fixed costs of firms from their investment boom, most importantly debt servicing and depreciation. This combination results in sharp profit declines.

In this situation a growing number of firms will find it increasingly difficult to service debt. With loan defaults spreading, expectations suddenly turn sour. In the face of growing risks and pessimism lenders become more cautions. They demand higher interest rates and shorter maturities to compensate for risk. More conservative standards in loan applications shut out debtors with weak balance sheets. This tightening of credit terms typically comes at a time when the refinancing needs of many heavily indebted borrowers are rising. The preceding process of credit overextension now explodes into the open in the form of bankruptcies, loan defaults, and creditor panics. Speculative bubbles, built on expectations of continuously accelerating inflation, burst as expected price increases suddenly fail to materialize. These incidences of financial crisis spread pessimism, paralyze lending activity, and force spending cutbacks.[4]

The ensuing recession serves as a cleaning-out mechanism which eventually removes underlying market imbalances. For example, speculative excesses sparked by the inflationary boom are eliminated. Bankruptcies or plant closures reduce surplus capacity. Surviving firms win a larger market share, either by takeover or by elimination of their weaker competitors. Labor costs are lowered by layoffs, with the fear of unemployment also restraining wages and disciplining the work force. Debt-servicing burdens decline, as interest rates fall and firms actively seek to reduce their debt levels. The downturn reaches bottom when firms have cut supplies below demand and have, in the process, reduced costs faster than their decline in revenues. Thus it is the very process of retrenchment that sets the stage for a new recovery.

The conclusion of this discussion is simple: the market mechanism itself creates recurrent instability! The profit motive, competitive pressures, and optimistic expectations all drive firms to expand their production volume beyond the growth of effective demand. In standard theory such a situation of overproduction is swiftly corrected by corresponding price declines in affected markets. Not so in the real world! Prices may not be reduced sufficiently, especially in oligopolistic markets and given the downward rigidity of fixed costs. Furthermore, competition-induced price and cost cutting in the face of excess supplies, far from correcting the situation, may actually exacerbate losses. Because costs are simultaneously revenues for others, efforts to reduce them are likely to spread losses through interconnected markets.

The mutually reinforcing and intertwined nature of business and credit cycles can also be seen clearly in the changing relationship between profit and interest (see Table 3.1).

• At the end of a downturn, interest rates are low and profit margins are finally beginning to recover (e.g., 1971, 1975, 1983). This situation encourages debt-financed investment and consumption spending to grow more rapidly.

• During the recovery triggered thereby the relationship gradually reverses. The combination of strong credit demand and gradually accelerating inflation induces rising interest rates. At the same time, profit margins begin to decline in

Table 3.1

The Profit-Interest Relationship in the Growth Cycle (percent)

Year	Corporate profits (per unit of output)	Corporate bond yields (Aaa)	Prime rate
1966	5.6	5.13	5.63
1967	5.2	5.51	5.61
1968	5.3	6.18	6.30
1969	4.8	7.03	7.96
1970	3.9	8.04	7.91
1971	4.4	7.39	5.72
1972	4.7	7.21	5.25
1973	4.9	7.44	8.03
1974	4.2	8.57	10.81
1975	5.6	8.83	7.86
1976	6.4	8.43	6.84
1977	7.1	8.02	6.83
1978	7.4	8.73	9.06
1979	6.9	9.63	12.67
1980	6.1	11.94	15.27
1981	6.7	14.17	18.87
1982	5.6	13.79	14.86
1983	7.6	12.04	10.79
1984	9.4	12.71	12.04
1985	9.4	11.37	9.93
1986	8.3	9.02	8.33
1987	9.6	9.38	8.21
1988	10.2	9.71	9.32
1989	9.6	9.26	10.87
1990	8.3	9.32	10.01
1991	7.6	8.77	8.46

Source: Council of Economic Advisers, *Economic Report of the President,* 1992, Washington, DC, Tables B–11, B–69.

Notes: Current-dollar before-tax profits of nonfinancial corporate business (with inventory valuation and capital consumption adjustments) as percentage of output. Output is measured by gross domestic product of nonfinancial corporate business in 1987 dollars. Corporate bond yields and prime rate are yearly averages.

the wake of increased investment activity, as industry exhausts its most profitable investment opportunities and experiences large increases in fixed costs.

• The growing divergence between falling profit margins and rising interest rates causes cutbacks in spending and borrowing that trigger a downturn (e.g., 1969, 1974, 1979).

• Weak credit demand and the cooling of inflationary pressures during the recession result in lower interest rates. At the same time, cost-cutting and capacity reductions in industry gradually begin to improve profitability. This reversal in the profit–interest relationship sets the stage once again for debt-driven recovery.

3.2. Long Waves: The Structural Dimension of Capital Accumulation

Business and credit cycles are not the only type of instability we face. The long-term trend around which these short-term cycles fluctuate is itself subject to change. Periods of rapid expansion, characterized by strong upturns and weak recessions, alternate with periods of stagnation. The latter tend to culminate in deep crises (see the depressions of the U.S. economy in 1837–43, 1873–79, 1892–97, 1929–39, and, to a lesser extent, 1979–82). Kondratieff (1926) identified this pattern as a recurrent long wave with an average duration of 40 to 60 years. Only a few economists, most notably Schumpeter (1912, 1939), Garvy (1943), or Batra (1987), have paid attention to those long waves.[5]

Based on time-series data of key variables (e.g., prices, income distribution, industrial production, productivity, world trade), these economists have identified four long waves of capitalist development: 1793–1848, 1849–1897, 1898–1938, and the one beginning in the wake of World War II. That last wave peaked in 1968 and was followed by a decade of intensifying stagflation which culminated in a serious global downturn between 1979 and 1982. Primarily concerned with empirical verification of a pattern, those studies had a narrow theoretical focus. Each emphasized one specific factor as the primary cause of long waves, such as technological developments affecting long-lived capital goods (Kondratieff), cluster-like bursts of innovative activity by entrepreneurs (Schumpeter), or excessive wealth concentration (Batra). In reality, however, long-wave dynamics are shaped by a complex variety of cyclical, structural, and institutional forces.

Long waves exhibit the same dynamics of destabilization and readjustment as business cycles, except that here the cyclical factors are more stretched out. Primary forces of instability, such as the balance-sheet erosion of increasingly indebted and illiquid firms (see Minsky, 1964), are not sufficiently "cleaned out" during the short and shallow recessions that typify the expansion phase. Their cumulative build-up over several business cycles eventually creates serious crisis conditions. Of course, the same process also works in reverse during downswing phases of long waves. Years of stagnation, punctuated by sharp downturns, create conditions for an eventual return to sustained expansion: pent-up consumer demand for large-ticket items, large capital replacement needs following a long period of depressed investment activity, improved financial conditions due to debt reduction and increased savings, and cheapening of goods and services by deflationary pressures.

Long waves are also shaped by structural factors; that is, long-term forces affecting the structure of our economic system. Of great importance in this context are technological progress, financial innovation, and capitalism's globalization tendency. During expansion phases each of these forces contributes to the acceleration of growth. For example, breakthroughs in technology give rise to new industries, typically with very rapid growth in the early stages of their life cycle. Technological change also improves corporate profitability by cheapening fixed capital goods and increasing productivity. Financial innovations boost credit supplies, which in turn facilitate larger volumes of investment and consumption. Finally, expansion phases are usually fueled by rapid growth of world trade and international capital flows. But these structural forces eventually exhaust themselves. The inevitable maturing of industries and technologies deprives the economy of stimulative impetus. Financial innovations often lead to speculative excess and thereby destabilize the credit system. Finally, expansion phases have typically ended in major disruptions of global economic relations, triggered by international monetary crises (e.g., 1931, 1971) and protectionism.

In order to understand the institutional dimension of long-wave dynamics, we have to recall the discussion of our cash-flow economy in chapter 2. Its various monetary circuits force individual agents to interact with each other. These social relationships, whether as competitors, as sellers and buyers in exchange, as workers and managers in the production process, or as creditors and debtors, embody aspects of both interdependence and conflict. The latter tends to intensify in downswing phases of long waves. As losses spread, more and more agents try to protect their own income by transferring losses to others. Stronger firms squeeze weaker suppliers or competitors. Employers lay off workers and push for give-backs. Lenders tighten credit conditions. Open conflicts of interest are therefore part and parcel of the market's adjustment process during crisis periods.

That propensity of our economic system for instability and conflict can be counteracted by specific institutional arrangements. These may originate from the private sector (e.g., insurance and other "forward money" contracts, collective bargaining agreements, price coordination strategies) or as government initiatives (e.g., welfare programs, subsidies). When working well, they promote faster growth by reducing uncertainty, regulating conflict, promoting confidence, and directly supporting economic activity. But their continued effectiveness is by no means assured. For one, they often have negative side effects that may intensify over time. Furthermore, they may become obsolete or even counterproductive in the face of structural changes in the economy. Serious erosion of existing institutional arrangements in the face of mounting imbalances typically plays a major role in the transition of long waves from expansion to stagnation. Conversely, a resumption of expansion requires major policy changes. Institutional reform is therefore one dimension of crisis-induced reorganization.

3.3. Strategic (Im)balances of the Monetary Production Economy

The equilibrium framework of neoclassical theory leaves little room to consider business cycles and long waves as endogenous phenomena. Yet both patterns of fluctuation recur with a reasonable degree of regularity. How, then, can we account for those forces as part of our system?

Any economic system must be able to organize income-creating activities on a continuous basis. Otherwise, its productive capacity cannot be maintained, let alone expand. Labor power needs constant restoration by allowing workers to consume goods and services. Physical capital goods depreciate and eventually have to be replaced. Inventories are used up in production and require restocking. Debts must be paid off in time to keep the credit system functioning smoothly. So the entire system of economic activities has to reproduce itself in forward motion. If that reproduction works well, enough surplus is produced for total income to grow relative to the preceding period. If not, then both the volume of economic activities and income levels shrink.

Heterodox economists have always focused their attention on analyzing how a capitalist economy reproduces itself. Frequently they did so by dividing the economy into two sectors, Department I producing capital goods and Department II producing consumer goods. The first sector absorbs the industrial profits that firms in both sectors reinvest in plant and equipment. The second sector absorbs the wages and salaries paid to workers employed in capital-goods and consumer-goods industries. (Sometimes a Department III is added for the luxury goods consumed by capitalists and other wealthy classes.) Depending on the income distribution between profits and wages, we can then specify proportionate relations between the two departments to identify the conditions for simple (static), expanded, or contracted reproduction.[6]

There is, however, another way to look at reproduction. Our economic system is best described as a monetary production economy whose activities all take the form of monetary circuits (see section 2.3). These circuits form intertwined circular flows of money centered on production (see Figure 3.1). Businesses have a certain sum of money-capital (M) for purchases of inputs (I) to create output (Q), which they then sell for a profit (M') in product markets. Successful completion of that circuit supplies them with new money-capital for the next production cycle. Workers sell their labor power as an input (I) for wages (M) that are spent on a portion of the business output. The consumer goods (C) they acquire help them to restore their labor power as a marketable commodity (L) ready to be hired again. Both circuits divert funds as savings and for debt-servicing charges to financial institutions (FIs), which in turn provide businesses and workers with loans. All of those circuits are interdependent. Failure by businesses to sell their output for a profit leads to fewer hirings of workers, and flows to financial institutions will slow from both circuits. Failure in one circuit thus disrupts the other circuits.

These circular flows reproduce themselves through sequences of metamorphosis in the forms of capital: money-capital - productive capital (inputs) - commodity capital (output) - money-capital. And they reproduce each other in their dependence on mutual validation. Successful reproduction of the entire

Figure 3.1 **The Circular Flows of the Monetary Production Economy**

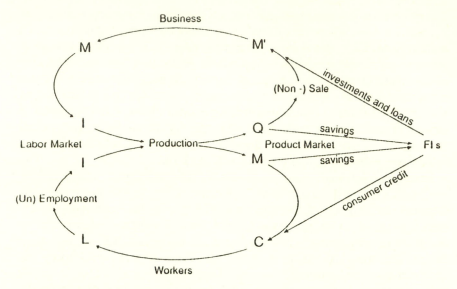

Abbreviations: M (or M) for Money: I for inputs, Q for Output, C for consumption, L for Labor, FIs for Financial Institutions.

monetary production economy depends on certain balances between key variables that occupy a strategic position within its intertwined circuits.

1) Market (Dis)equilibrium. There must be rough equivalence between supply and demand in any given market. The underlying forces, which bring the two sides of the market into balance, are the focus of neoclassical theory. But the standard adjustment mechanism, price fluctuations in response to disequilibria, may not always operate effectively or may take too long for successful completion. Today many prices are quite sticky on the downward side, refusing to decline sufficiently in the face of excess supplies. Instead, firms may well be inclined to cut output and employment, a response which tends to reduce demand in related markets.

2) Sectoral (Im)balances. The amalgam of resource and product markets making up the economy forms a matrix of interdependent industries. There must be a certain consistency within that industrial matrix for a stable growth pattern to exist. The traditional reproduction schemata of Marx, Kalecki, and others have stressed the proportionality between capital-goods sectors and consumer-goods sectors in this context. More generally, there are always certain key industries that have a huge multiplier effect on the rest of the economy—for example, real estate during the postwar boom or computers over the past decade.

3) Resource Waste. Investment is the engine that drives the economy forward. It adds value, it creates income, it produces the social surplus that can be reinvested. But not all investment projects are equally productive in this regard. Resources can be wasted on relatively unproductive uses. Conservatives stress the inefficiency of state-run enterprises that operate as protected monopolies outside normal market constraints. Liberals attack military spending. Our military-industrial complex may create jobs and support corporate profits, but armaments themselves are neither consumption goods nor investment goods. Speculative position-taking in financial markets also absorbs funds that could be spent more meaningfully elsewhere. The strength of a nation's economy depends not least on channeling most of its resources into productive activities and on minimizing waste.

4) Labor Unit Costs. Industrial performance depends fundamentally on the relationship between money wages and labor productivity. Firms need high wages to sell their output. This holds true even for producers in Department I. Their customers will only buy capital goods if they themselves manage a sufficiently large volume of sales. But wages are also a major cost factor for businesses. What managers care about is not so much the wage level per se but the cost per unit of output. If wages go up by x percent and productivity increases at the same rate, then the labor unit cost remains stable. A successful economy is inevitably one in which both variables grow rapidly. If wages rise faster than labor productivity, businesses face pressures on the cost side to raise prices or face a squeeze in their profit margins. If, on the other hand, productivity growth outpaces wage increases, industries may face overproduction.[7]

5) The Profit-Investment Link. How do firms assure the kind of productivity growth that affords all of us better living standards? Productivity, measured as output per worker, depends on many factors. Some of these are quite intangible, such as the ability of managers to coordinate diverse production processes or the motivation of workers. Among the most important determinants of productivity is how much firms spend on their means of production. Investment affects not only total production capacity but also the quality of inputs. Well-trained workers and modern technology obviously perform better than do unskilled laborers and obsolete machines. The level of investment spending depends fundamentally on profits. These provide firms with the funds to invest and shape how managers evaluate future prospects. Corporate profitability determines both ability and willingness of firms to invest, but the volume of investment spending has a major impact on how much income firms will earn in the next production cycle. Hence there exists a mutually interdependent relationship between profits and investment that shapes industrial performance.[8]

6) Interest Rates and Profit Rates. That dynamic interaction between profits and investment is fundamentally affected by a third variable, the current level of interest rates. From the point of view of individual enterprises, interest represents an actual cost outlay paid to creditors as well as an alternative form of income;

that is, an opportunity cost. For both reasons, firms treat the relevant interest rate as their "cost of capital," which defines the minimum rate of return they require for investment projects to qualify as worthwhile (see section 2.4). Managers make investment decisions by comparing that required rate of return with the rate of return they expect to earn from the project considered. Expectations are based on current returns. Interest rates, especially in relation to profit rates, thus have a powerful impact on industrial investment spending.

7) *Financial Assets and Gross National Product.* The credit system mobilizes otherwise unused funds or creates new liquidity for spending purposes. In that sense it contributes to faster growth. Additional income gains, which the credit system helps to generate, can be used by borrowers to pay off their debts. That process eliminates financial assets, including the destruction of money. Under normal conditions, financial assets will therefore grow roughly in line with gross national product. When they grow faster, it is because deficit-spending units use too much debt or because speculation crowds out enterprise. Either situation has troublesome implications for the health of our economy.

3.4. The Theory of "Regulation"

It is precisely through business cycles and long waves that our monetary production economy corrects imbalances in those strategic relations. In this context we must understand recession as a cleaning-out mechanism. When the economy turns down, firms cut output and thereby eliminate market gluts. They will also be hard pressed to limit wage growth and strive for greater gains in productivity. Cost-cutting will eventually improve profit rates, while lack of credit demand and easing by the central bank help to push interest rates lower. The write-down of bad debts brings financial assets back in line with gross national product. These cyclical adjustments set the stage for recovery.

It is quite easy to show how the wage–productivity balance, the relationship between profit and interest rates, and other pairings discussed above behave in the course of the business cycle. The same cannot be said for long waves. These are a much more complicated phenomenon, shaped by structural forces and institutional features in addition to the usual cyclical variables. *Regulation Theory*, first developed in France during the late 1970s, has tried to study capitalism's long-wave dynamics by focusing on the interaction between these cyclical, structural, and institutional factors.[9] What makes this theory such an original contribution, apart from unifying different heterodox traditions in economics, is its focus on the real-life forces that have shaped the historic evolution of the capitalist system.

The key question in Regulation Theory is how our inherently unstable and conflict-prone economy manages to maintain the order required for its reproduction. The approach first identifies the principal organizing forces of capital accumulation, the engine of growth. These are money, competition, wage labor, the state, and the international division of labor. Each of these organizing forces is subject to change, reflecting necessary adjustments in response to underlying tensions. In order to understand how the various organizing forces are mobilized and made to interact with each other, we need to understand precisely the nature of these adjustments. Regulation Theory accomplishes this task by analyzing the evolution of each organizing force in terms of institutional forms. Those can be characterized as regulatory substructures which shape social relations in ways that give economic activities a certain coherence.

Corresponding to the principal organizing forces of capital accumulation, we can identify five main institutional forms:

• The monetary regime comprises money creation, credit extension, and their respective management by the state's monetary authorities. It regulates creditor–debtor relations and determines the distribution of money-capital among different investment uses. The features of any given monetary regime shape the balance between finance capital and fictitious capital within our credit system and their respective relationship to industrial capital. As we shall see throughout this book, that triangular organization of capital explains much of the prevailing growth pattern in our economy.

• Competition, the dominant social relationship between producers operating in the same market, is also subject to regulation. The prevailing institutional forms of competition (e.g., price coordination, advertising, product differentiation) influence the behavior of different producers in a given sector and play a major role in the formation of prices. These forms of competition depend, in turn, on corporate organization and the structure of industries (e.g., their degree of concentration).

• The sociotechnical system covers all aspects of the capital–labor relationship, including the means to control the work process, the social and technical division of labor (e.g. skill formation, internal job hierarchies, labor–market segmentation), and wage determinants (e.g., direct wage, fringe benefits, social insurance programs), as well as the living standards and consumption norms of wage-earners.

• Another institutional form of great importance in our economy is state intervention. Operating outside the confines of the market mechanism, the government is in a unique position to intervene on behalf of the economic system as a whole. The very existence of markets has always depended on government for enforcement of contracts, protection of private property, maintenance of social order, and representation of national interests in international relations. Nowadays the government typically also conducts stabilization policies, actively promotes science and technology, and runs a public sector to provide collective goods, social services, and infrastructure investments.

• Global trade and capital flows, which play a crucial role in the macroeconomic performance of individual countries, depend on such institutional factors as multilateral trade agreements and the international monetary system. Together these form an international policy regime with which to regulate economic relations between competing nation-states toward a required minimum of cooperation.

These different institutional forms combine to determine the conditions that allow the economic system to reproduce itself in a stable manner and on an expanding scale. In other words, they regulate our economy by coordinating its decentralized decisions and integrating its separate activities into a unified structure capable of forward motion. Replacing the static analysis of market equilibrium, the concept of regulation is used to show how various economic agents manage to achieve a certain degree of compatibility between their activities and of balance in their social relations.[10] Different *modes of regulation* can be distinguished, depending on the prevailing set of monetary rules, corporate organization and competition, wage labor nexus, public policies, and international arrangements.

The long-run evolution of our economy can then be conceptualized in terms of historically specific *accumulation regimes*, each with its own distinct institutional forms and modes of regulation. During the expansion phase of a long wave, these are capable of establishing and maintaining a relatively stable growth pattern. The shift toward the stagnation phase typically occurs when prevailing regulatory mechanisms are no longer able to cope with changing conditions in the structure of our economy. Economic imbalances and social tensions are allowed to build up to the point of structural crisis, at which point they destroy the cohesion of the existing accumulation regime in a series of ruptures. But this disintegration is simultaneously an impetus for massive reorganization efforts. Eventually these may go far enough to create a new accumulation regime, with different social characteristics, regulatory mechanisms, and policy institutions. The precise outcome of this process is by no means predetermined and depends on strategic choices by managers, unions, and government officials to give the restructuring the coherence required for sustainable expansion.

3.5. The Accumulation Regimes in the Evolution of Capitalism

Regulation Theory identifies three different accumulation regimes in the history of capitalism. The first one was the *old regulation*, culminating in the emergence of modern industry (i.e., factory production) during the early decades of the nineteenth century. In that particular regime, agriculture dominated as the leading sector. Bad harvests had a major destabilizing effect on the economy through price increases for agricultural goods and declining purchases of manufactured goods by peasants. Price formation was controlled by guilds. State intervention confined itself to general functions (contract enforcement, legal protection of property, and national security) and protection of infant industries from foreign competition ("mercantilism"). Money creation was limited by available gold reserves.

Economic stagnation and major upheavals in the middle of the nineteenth century (e.g., Europe's 1848 revolution, the United States' Civil War between 1861 and 65) led to a new regime of *competitive regulation*. Large productivity increases in agriculture reduced the labor required to till the land, thus creating the supply of workers required for rapid industrialization. The Industrial Revolution destroyed the autonomy of independent artisans, giving the emerging industries an ample supply of highly skilled workers. Central to this revolution was the application of energy to the production of goods. This tied people to factories, which in turn were located near energy resources, such as coal or iron ore (e.g., Germany's Ruhr Valley, the Midwest in the United States). Urbanization was further encouraged by expanding trade in factory goods, which required "physical" markets in strategic places, such as crossroads or harbors. The dominance of manufacturing then gave rise to the modern business cycle (i.e., mildly inflationary booms, deflationary downturns), with industrial overproduction replacing agricultural underproduction as the principal barrier to growth. This was the Golden Age of "free markets," as most prices responded flexibly to demand. The role of the state was still limited, with the exception of crucial assistance to certain key industries (e.g., railroads). Financial capital grew rapidly in response to credit-enhancing innovations. Great Britain's dominance, its emphasis on "free trade," colonization of resource-rich countries by industrial powers, and a relatively stable gold standard all encouraged the rapid growth of world trade.

Around the turn of the century this accumulation regime gradually began to transform into one of *monopolistic regulation*, a crisis-prone process that reached its climax in the Great Depression of the 1930s. The merger boom in the late 1890s and early 1900s gave rise to large corporations and much more concentrated industrial structures. The development of electricity and its application to motors led to assembly-line production ("Fordism"). In the United States this new technology of mass production started in 1913 and expanded rapidly during World War I. That was followed by the introduction of modern management practices as well as large-scale retailing outlets during the 1920s. The (often violent) destruction of craft unions during the postwar depression of 1920–21 allowed a massive reorganization of the labor force in key industries ("Taylorism"). The combination of large productivity growth and lower wages, while initially enlarging profits and spurring investment activity, led ultimately to a structural overproduction crisis in the late 1920s. This disequilibrium was the underlying cause for extremely serious financial instability, which exploded into the open with the collapse of the stock market in October 1929.

The resulting depression of the 1930s forced significant policy reforms and industrial restructuring, which gave the emerging regime of monopolistic regulation its required degree of coherence. The spread of industrial unions, especially after the National Labor Relations Act of 1935, combined with the oligopolistic price-coordination strategies of industrial firms and created a downwardly rigid price structure. Consumer-good industries (e.g., cars, housing) became the leading sectors, combining mass-production technologies and social norms of "consumerism." State intervention expanded rapidly to manage aggregate demand (e.g., social wage, military-industrial complex) and to stabilize credit financing. The United States replaced Great Britain as the world leader and used its hegemony to establish a new international economic order. Its components included trade liberalization (i.e., the 1947 General Agreement on Tariffs and Trade, or GATT), a gold-backed dollar standard (Bretton Woods 1944), decolonization, and large-scale capital transfers to U.S. allies (e.g., Marshall Plan 1948). These measures, encouraged not least by the cold war with the Soviet Union, led to the emergence of multinational corporations and transnational banks as the global extension of monopolistic regulation.

This postwar accumulation regime enjoyed a long boom, as its different institutional forms managed to maintain the strategic balances in our economy. Union contracts and full employment encouraged rapid wage growth. At the same time, the spread of mass-production technology made productivity gains easier to come by. Consumerism, symbolized by home ownership and America's love affair with the automobile, allowed for much better integration between Departments I and II. Deficit spending by the government counteracted overproduction by stimulating aggregate demand. Central bank accommodation kept interest rates low, while large U.S. firms managed to protect their profits by investing aggressively abroad. The international policy regime set up at the end of World War II boosted world trade and capital transfers, giving the boom a truly global dimension.

After two decades of extraordinarily rapid growth those strategic balances began to break down one by one. The monopolistic accumulation regime entered a structural crisis in the late 1960s, which manifested itself in the form of intensifying stagflation (see chapters 6 and 7). Today we are in the midst of a transition to yet another accumulation regime, which may most accurately be termed as one of *global regulation*. Certain features of this new regime, the fourth in the history of capitalism, have already taken root. But these do not yet form a coherent whole, therefore requiring additional policy changes and institutional adjustments.

• The "electronic revolution," especially the development of computer-aided manufacturing and design, is radically changing production processes in many industries. The spread of information technology has made knowledge-dependent services (e.g., data processing, financial services, education, health care) the new growth sectors. Recent technological advances provide the basis for important new industries in the future, such as superconductivity, artificial intelligence, robotics, and biogenetics.

• Markets are being transformed from physical "places" to communication networks, allowing capital to move more easily on a global scale.

• The focus of state intervention has shifted from Keynesian demand-management to providing incentives on the supply side, with special emphasis on subsidies for private capital formation, lower tax rates, and deregulation.

• Most importantly, the globalization of economic activities is advancing rapidly toward a whole new level of integration (see also section 1.2). The leading firms now compete worldwide, including a growing number of joint ventures and cross-ownership ties among firms of different countries. Advances in technology and corporate organization have allowed production and finance to become more globally integrated than ever. Manufacturing is increasingly shifting to newly industrialized countries (e.g., Mexico, Brazil, Malaysia, Taiwan, South Korea). Increased reliance on export-led growth strategies has made domestic economies much more open and has intensified international competition. The global mobility of capital poses a major threat to national sovereignty and undermines domestic policy-making. International trade agreements and monetary relations have to be adjusted to reflect the polycentricity of several power centers competing for leadership (United States, Japan, Europe). Amid a dangerous combination of global debt crisis, persistent trade imbalances, volatile exchange rates, and massive short-term capital flows, those economic superpowers will have to contain deepening conflicts among themselves and to find creative solutions based on increased multilateral coordination.

In the remainder of the book we shall focus in particular on the regulation of money creation and credit financing as one of the key regulatory substructures shaping the growth pattern of any given accumulation regime. Once we have analyzed the long-term tendencies in the historic evolution of this institutional form, we can shed more light on one crucial aspect of the ongoing transition toward a new (global) accumulation regime, the dramatic changes in the credit system during the 1980s that combined financial innovation, deregulation, and globalization.

Part II

The Historic Evolution of Money Management

The Transition from Commodity-Money to Credit-Money

In the last two chapters we analyzed essential characteristics of our capitalist market economy: the mobilization of economic activities in the form of inter-dependent monetary circuits; the investment of money as capital for accumulation purposes; the coexistence of "industrial" and "financial" forms of money-capital; and the unstable (business-cycle and long-wave) dynamics of their expansion. This analysis makes it clear that money plays a crucial role in our economy.

We can now proceed to see how money creation, credit financing, and production activities interrelate as an organizing force in the accumulation process to shape a given growth pattern. The precise configuration of this triangular relation depends on a variety of institutions and policies regulating money and credit. Together these form a distinct substructure of the prevailing accumulation regime, the so-called monetary regime.[1] We start this chapter by first defining at greater length what such a monetary regime consists of and how it is supposed to work. Then we analyze its historic evolution in the United States, with special emphasis on the gradual crowding out of the gold standard by credit-money.

4.1. Defining the Concept of Monetary Regimes

The monetary regime, a crucial institutional form of any given accumulation regime (see section 3.4), includes several distinct and interrelated dimensions.

1) The Money-Creation Process. Given the strategic role of money (as income and capital) in our economy, the modalities of its creation are bound to have a major impact. If certain private agents were able to create their own money and impose it as a socially accepted medium of exchange, they would obviously gain an unfair advantage over all other market participants who lacked this power. They could simply issue new money to increase their purchasing power or pay off their debts. Hence money creation has to be placed outside the markets for goods and services; that is, in the banking system. Moreover, the different needs for cash balances (i.e., transaction, precautionary, speculative, and finance motives of money demand) must be met by adequate liquidity injections to assure the smooth operation of economic activities. It is for this reason that the money-creation process has become subject to government regulation. This so-called monetary policy comprises integration of the different money-forms into a coherent payments system and management of the latter by the monetary authorities of the state.

2) International Monetary Arrangements. Both trade and the inherent globalization tendency of capital give rise to monetary transactions between nations. Those require exchange of different currencies. Hence monetary regimes typically have their international dimension, secured by multilateral agreement among leading industrial powers, to accommodate this need for foreign exchange. Such an international monetary system needs to define acceptable forms of world-money, regulate exchange rates, and determine how countries can meet their payment obligations.

3) Financial Regulations. Financial institutions and markets are subject to a variety of government regulations that are designed to affect their behavior. These regulations, termed here "financial policy," enable the government to shape the nation's credit system and its allocation of resources. A crucial aspect of financial policy is the stabilization of the relation between creditors and debtors.

4) Crisis Management. Nowadays the monetary authorities of the state have several mechanisms at their disposal to counteract instability in the credit system, mostly by acting as a *lender of last resort.* Such interventions contain and resolve financial crises before their spread paralyzes the banking system and threatens to turn a normal cyclical downturn into a depression.

In this chapter we shall see how and why the monetary regime evolved from a financial system based on a metallic standard to one centered around the much more flexible credit-money. This change in the money-form began in the middle of the nineteenth century but only reached its climax in the Great Depression when the simultaneous collapse of domestic banks and the gold standard (in 1931) forced U.S. policy-makers to undertake major monetary reforms. The gradual transition toward a regime based on credit-money deserves closer scrutiny. Besides confirming the importance of institutional change in the historic evolution of our economy, it tells us much about the socio-economic foundations of money and finance. Let us therefore take a brief look at the development of U.S. monetary regimes from the 1790s to the 1930s.

4.2. The Bimetallic Standard and State Banking, 1792–1862

In the aftermath of the Revolutionary War and its hyperinflation, the U.S. Congress passed the Coinage Act of 1792, which linked the dollar to gold and silver.[2] This represented our first effort to introduce a metallic monetary standard. In such a regime of commodity-money a country's currency was both defined in terms of precious metals (gold, silver) and freely convertible with them. That link had two important characteristics. First, the convertibility requirement meant that the amount of government-minted coins and bank-issued paper money was limited by the available specie reserves backing them. Second, the metallic standard created fixed exchange relations between the currencies of the various countries by defining each monetary unit (e.g., dollar, pound, franc, yen) in terms of specific amounts of gold. This international arrangement also included the unrestricted right to import and export the precious metal at the officially fixed rate of exchange, so that it could function effectively as world-money. Together, these two features subjected the issue of money to automatic discipline exerted by the moneyholders' right to demand redemption in precious metals.

The bimetallic standard of 1792 soon ran into trouble. The price of silver began to fall relative to gold. This encouraged people to trade in silver for gold at the U.S. Mint at the official ratio of 15:1 and then to exchange this gold in the world market at the market-price ratio of 15.5:1. Gold therefore began to disappear from domestic circulation, putting the United States on a de facto silver standard. This was a dramatic illustration of Gresham's Law, according to which "good" (officially undervalued) money is driven out by "bad" (overvalued) money.[3] To stem the gold outflows, the dollar was devalued (in the Coinage Act of 1834) to 23.22 grains of gold. Since the new mint ratio of 16:1 exceeded the then-prevailing world-market ratio of 15.73:1, gold was consciously overvalued to reverse the flow of metals. This moved the United States to a gold standard, with silver gradually reduced to a subsidiary status for coins of less than one dollar (see the Coinage Act of 1853).

The establishment of bimetallism in the United States coincided with the emergence of the first private banks in the 1780s. These institutions soon found that they could greatly expand their lending activity by linking their loans to the simultaneous issue of new money. A variety of innovations combined to make this linkage possible:

• First, trade credit, which consisted of deferred payments in transactions between businesses, gave rise to so-called bills of exchange, representing the claims of sellers. Once these bills were allowed to cancel each other out, they themselves became means of payment in lieu of cash. Undertaking this clearing-house function, banks began to buy these bills in exchange for their own bank notes. In this way their own credit replaced the trade credit.

• Second, once those bank notes became sufficiently standardized, their holders could directly exchange them for goods and services, provided the recipient knew that those notes would be redeemed by the issuing bank. Thus increasingly used as a medium of exchange, these bank notes became an early form of bank-issued currency. The same process of standardization and growing circulation as a socially accepted medium of exchange also occurred with receipts issued by banks in return for deposits.

• Third, banks observed that their deposits were not withdrawn all at once. Thus they only needed to keep a fraction of those on reserve to meet withdrawals and could use the rest to finance additional credit. This became known as "fractional reserve banking." In that process, banks issued new notes and loaned them out, because these were now accepted as a medium of exchange.

The rapid growth of banks in the early 1800s was very controversial, reflecting deep economic conflicts and corresponding political divisions in the country. Industrial and commercial interests in the East favored a strong banking system. Because banks supplied credit and issued money (in the form of notes that were freely convertible into specie), they were seen to stimulate capital formation and to promote trade. But the plantation owners of the South, backed by the farmers in the frontier areas of the West, opposed banks, which they saw as aiding industry and commerce in the East at their expense. They also attacked banks for lowering the quality of the nation's money by displacing metallic coins with bank notes and deposit receipts.

This conflict between agrarian and industrial interests, embodying the crucial contradiction of the first accumulation regime ("old" regulation), also manifested itself over the question of whether banks should be controlled on the federal level or by the states. In 1791 the federal government set up the Bank of the United States, America's first attempt at central banking. But this institution embodied a contradiction which led to its eventual demise. On the one hand, it operated just like any other commercial bank, making business loans, taking deposits, and issuing bank notes. On the other hand, it also functioned as a central bank, empowered to control the amount of bank notes that state banks could issue, to transfer funds across the country, and to act as the fiscal agent of the U.S. government.[4]

State banks, besides strenuously objecting to the bank's practice of draining their reserves (see note 4), argued that the Bank's dual role as their competitor and their regulator put them at an unfair disadvantage. They won the backing of southern landowners and the West's rural population. Both of these groups feared that the Bank would use its powers to divert their local funds to the East Coast cities for industrial investment. This coalition of state banks, agricultural interests, and anti-federalist politicians blocked the renewal of the Bank in 1811. But massive inflation following the War of 1812 led Congress to authorize another central bank in 1816, the Second Bank of the United States. Continuing opposition, fed by sharp economic downturns during "tight money" periods (1818, 1820), prompted Andrew Jackson, a populist president and advocate of states' rights, to veto a renewal of the Second Bank's twenty-year charter in

1832. From 1836 onward the United States was thus left without a central bank until the Federal Reserve Act of 1913.[5]

These attempts at federal control over state banks reflected the concern of commercial and industrial interests for a sound currency and for safe banks, which would facilitate trade and finance industrial investment. In light of the repeated failure to establish nationwide control over the banking system, it was not surprising that eastern state governments encouraged their own banks to cooperate in ways that also benefited their regional economies. For example, Boston banks agreed to redeem the otherwise discounted notes of New England country banks at par, provided those banks kept large enough specie reserves with them to cover any redemption. During the 1820s this so-called Suffolk System gave booming New England the soundest currency and banks in the entire country, with notes circulating freely and its country banks avoiding excessive issue of notes for fear of large-scale redemption by the Boston banks. In 1829 New York set up a Safety Fund which protected bank creditors (noteholders, depositors) as "lender of last resort" and was financed by pro-rata contributions of its banks. It effectively halted panic runs and thereby stabilized the local economy, allowing New York to become a major trading center, until a wave of bank failures exhausted the fund in the early 1840s.

The defeat of the Second Bank also sparked a major expansion of state banks in the South and West. Agricultural interests strongly favored a policy of "easy money." Plantation owners benefited from inflation, either as land speculators or as sellers of inelastic commodities with a strong potential for especially high price increases during boom periods. Relying on slaves and labor-intensive production methods, they did not worry about inflation's effects on costs. Farmers in the frontier areas of the West wanted cheap credit to buy land and to build an infrastructure for their new communities. Being chronic debtors, they also favored inflation as an easy way to reduce their debt-servicing burden. In both regions banks, seeking to build a political coalition with the ruling local interests against the federal government, complied as much as possible.

In 1837, a year after the end of the Second Bank, Michigan allowed any group that met preestablished legal requirements to operate a bank without obtaining special legislative approval. This system of *free banking* was designed to eliminate both rampant corruption in the granting of bank charters and monopolistic protection of politically favored banks from competition. Its widespread popular appeal led eighteen other states to adopt free banking. Between 1834 and 1840 the number of state banks nearly doubled. Their rapid spread fed major speculative waves in the agricultural areas of the country, such as the land boom in 1835–36 and the cotton boom in 1839.

But the ease of chartering and lack of proper supervision by state governments encouraged unscrupulous practices. For example, many free banks were established in remote locations, which made it difficult for noteholders to redeem their notes for gold. "Wildcat banking" was the result. A variety of deficiencies combined to make state banks very vulnerable to failure. For one, most of them were severely undercapitalized, thus often giving them insufficient protection against losses. Moreover, many banks made high-risk loans without adequate security, often to their own shareholders or bank officers. Speculative lending, especially in land-development schemes or real estate finance, was rampant during inflationary periods. Many states imposed either no or very small reserve requirements, thus allowing their banks to issue a large quantity of bank notes without regard for specie reserves. Such overextended banks faced collapse whenever a large number of their depositors or noteholders demanded payment in gold or silver coins. The practice of discounting the circulating notes of banks with inadequate reserves by varying amounts operated as a powerful market signal of default risk. Rapid increases in those discounts prompted frequent runs by worried depositors and noteholders. This structural vulnerability of state banks was especially manifest during the depression of the early 1840s, when many overextended banks collapsed amid widespread debt repudiation.[6]

The expansion of state banking after 1834 also led to serious problems with the money supply. For one, the lack of uniformity with regard to the notes issued by state banks created much confusion. In 1860, for example, the United States had 1,600 state banks operating under the diverse laws of some thirty states, and each bank issued a variety of notes.[7] In addition, state banks tended to issue their notes in a pro-cyclical manner, thus causing sharp fluctuations in the money supply (see Table 4.1). Rapid growth during periods of economic recovery prompted banks to resume aggressive credit extension, which they financed by issuing new bank notes. This was followed by speculative euphoria amid accelerating inflation, which enticed banks into excessive lending and issuing of notes relative to their specie reserves (e.g., the land boom of 1835–36; the cotton boom of 1839; the Mexican War of 1846–47; the California gold rush of the early 1850s). In subsequent deflationary downturns (e.g., the panic of 1837; the debt-repudiation depression of 1840–43; the panic of 1857), a large number of these overextended banks either failed or had to curtail their activities to stay solvent, thereby reducing the money supply.[8]

The pronounced cyclical instability of this era reflected a structural contradiction in the monetary regime between limited specie reserves and the tendency of state banks to issue excessive amounts of paper-money (freely redeemable notes) in the face of strong credit demand. The gold standard thus acted as a "metallic barrier" to expansion, which made itself regularly felt at the cyclical peak through violent banking crises and sharp deflationary downturns. That problem was exacerbated in the agrarian South and the frontier West. There the absence of government regulation encouraged the rapid spread of banks and often unsound lending practices, while most of the country's specie reserves were concentrated in the East. This uneven reserve distribution was somewhat alleviated by the massive gold discoveries in California after 1849 that, besides expanding the credit base of the entire country, shifted trade to the West. Still, the conflict

Table 4.1

Money-Supply Volatility During the "Free Banking" Era

Period	Change in money supply (in percent)
1834–37	+ 61
1837–43	− 58
1843–48	+102
1848–49	− 11
1849–54	+109
1854–55	− 12
1855–57	+ 18
1857–58	− 23
1858–61	+ 35

Source: John J. Knox (1903), *A History of Banking in the United States.*

between agrarian and industrial interests continued to sharpen, exploding finally in the Civil War of 1861–65.

4.3. The Greenback Era, 1862–1879

The Civil War marked a major turning point in the evolution of our monetary regime. For one, it led to the temporary suspension of the gold standard. The war-related surge in government expenditures soon confronted the federal government with a major fiscal crisis, because the Treasury was unwilling to raise taxes for fear of thereby undermining public morale. At first, in the fall of 1861, the Treasury embarked on a massive borrowing program.[9] But lack of investor interest foiled this plan. The government was once again forced to rely on commercial banks for short-term help in return for ending its independent payment system (see note 6). The banks, having more than adequate gold reserves at this point, agreed to give the Treasury's regional offices ("subtreasuries") $5 million in gold every ten days for a six-month period in exchange for government bonds. Once these were sold to the public, the proceeds would go to the Treasury, which in turn would return the gold to the banks.

But in late 1861 this "circuit" broke amid a run on gold when the Treasury announced deficits that were much larger than had been expected. On December 30, 1861, banks suspended specie payments. Two months later, after a very tumultuous debate in Congress, President Lincoln signed the First Legal Tender Act, which provided for the issuance of $150 million worth of so-called U.S. notes in denominations of $5 or more. This new money-form, which became known as "Greenbacks," could be exchanged at any time for an equivalent amount in specified government bonds. At the same time, the United States decided to let the dollar float against other currencies, thus introducing for the first time flexible exchange rates for a key currency. Between 1862 and 1864 the United States issued a total of $450 million of these Greenbacks.

Apart from thereby replacing the gold standard with inconvertible fiat currency, the Treasury also pushed for a major banking reform to supersede the inherently deficient state banks. The National Banking Act of 1863 put into place a new banking system, which was to remain unchanged until the creation of the Federal Reserve in 1913. The act introduced the so-called national banks, which were federally chartered and supervised by a new monetary authority, the Treasury's Office of the Comptroller of Currency. Those banks had to meet much hgher minimum capital requirements, keep reserve requirements (ranging between 15 percent and 25 percent) against deposits or bank notes, and face restrictions on the type and amount of loans made (e.g., no single loan in excess of 10 percent of the bank's capital). These safety provisions, designed to avoid the structural weaknesses of state banks, are still in place today. Congress also took a giant step toward developing a uniform and safe national currency by allowing the new banks to issue national bank notes, which each bank had to accept at par value. These notes were printed by the Treasury to insure standardization and thus make counterfeiting more difficult (see note 7). Because the national banks were also required to hold government bonds as security against any bank notes they issued, they were induced to purchase and hold Treasury securities. This made it much easier for the government to finance its war effort.

The introduction of inconvertible paper money—Greenbacks as well as national bank notes—permitted a dramatic expansion of the money-supply from $682 million in mid-1862 to $1,634 million at the end of the war in mid-1865, a 150 percent increase in three years. Because both forms of paper money were backed by government bonds, their issue was directly tied to additional government borrowing.[10] This helped to close a deep budgetary gap. Government spending during the war exceeded $3.3 billion, compared to only $753 million in revenues. This combination of a rapidly growing money supply and large budget deficits facilitated a sharp acceleration of inflation, as a result of which the price level nearly doubled between the end of 1861 and mid-1865.

Such inflation is typical for periods of war, but it was exacerbated during the Civil War by the tension between new and old money-forms. Fearing higher prices from any major injection of new money, people bought gold in anticipation of accelerating inflation. This speculation worked like a self-fulfilling prophecy, driving up the money-price of gold. In addition, manufacturers needed gold, either for payment of imports and tariffs or for settlement with those suppliers who refused to accept the depreciating paper notes as a means of payment. To compensate for the increased cost of gold purchases, manufacturers would try to raise their own prices and thereby spread the inflationary acceleration. At one point, in June 1864, speculation became so virulent that Congress suspended in the Gold Act all gold contracts for future delivery and all gold transactions outside a broker's office. After two weeks of chaos, in which business transactions were disrupted and the price of gold shot up, Congress revoked this restriction.

The government's deficit spending and its automatic "monetization" (through issuance of additional Greenbacks and bank notes) translated into direct demand for industrial products. Much of the more than $3.3 billion spent by the U.S. government for its war effort went directly to industry in the form of high-priced supply contracts. Evidence taken by congressional investigating committees indicates that the average profit on material supplied to the army (e.g., guns, munitions, uniforms, blankets, food, railroad transportation) exceeded 50 percent. Generous bribes to government officials assured not only excessively priced contracts but also legislative opposition to public pressure for more government-operated facilities. With government contracts so large and profitable, private producers withheld their facilities from civilian production—until they succeeded in driving up the price of civilian goods. This circuit of money issue, government borrowing, and high-priced procurement contracts thus enabled industry to use inflation as a money-skimming program. Not surprisingly, contractors and other manufacturers consistently backed the issue of Greenbacks, because most of that new money would fall into their own hands.[11]

This war-induced and self-financed demand gave industrial accumulation a major boost. In many industries (e.g., iron ore, lumber, wheat and other grains, rubber, wool, shoes, machine tools) output doubled or even tripled in the 1861–65 period. The war also gave rise to new industries that had just begun to emerge before its outbreak. For example, only in 1859 had the first successful oil well been drilled in Pennsylvania. But by the end of 1864, 1,100 oil companies had been formed, which managed to attract the very large sum of $90 million in new capital. Similarly spectacular was the increase in iron furnaces, steel plants, and railroads. This explosive industrial growth allowed many individuals to amass huge fortunes and build up industrial empires. During the 1860s net national wealth doubled, from $16.1 billion in 1860 to $32.3 billion in 1870.[12]

The regime of inconvertible paper money continued after the war ended. The inflated cost-price structure made it difficult to return to the gold standard, for lack of agreement over an appropriate gold–dollar exchange rate and because of widepread fears of causing too sharp a deflation. In the late 1860s and early 1870s the political debates over the appropriate money-forms sharpened considerably. Agrarian interests in the South and frontier farmers in the West, as perennial debtors traditionally in favor of "easy money" and cheap credit, merged with some industrialists (e.g., steel, railroads) and certain factions of organized labor to back the continuation of the Greenbacks. That position was also supported by the silver-mining companies that, in the wake of large domestic discoveries of silver, had an interest in continued inflation. This heterogenous coalition successfully blocked several legislative attempts between 1868 and 1874 to phase out the Greenbacks.[13]

4.4. The Return to a Gold Standard, 1879–1914

The continuation of Greenbacks, coupled with the increased circulation of national bank notes, helped to fuel a strong recovery after a brief postwar depression in 1865. But the boom in the early 1870s soon led to industrial overexpansion as capacity increases outpaced consumption. The result was the first major overproduction crisis of the new industrial accumulation regime—the one we referred to in section 3.5 as "competitive" regulation—starting with the panic of 1873. The end of postwar prosperity and the 1875 elections strengthened the eastern industrialists and bankers, who favored "sound money" and therefore a return to a metallic standard.

In 1873 Congress ended the free and unlimited coinage of silver coins, an action which the "cheap money" proponents called the "Crime of '73." This was followed by the Gold Resumption Act of 1875, which specified the return to a gold-based dollar. When the prolonged deflation finally restored the parity between Greenbacks and gold, Congress passed the Monetary Acts of 1878 and 1879 to restore gold convertibility. The quantity of Greenbacks in circulation was frozen at then-prevailing levels, and the United States returned de jure to a bimetallic monetary standard at prewar mint-ratios. To appease silver-mining interests and to make use of new silver supplies, the Treasury received legislative approval (in 1878 and 1890) to resume purchases and coining of silver as "backing" for silver certificates circulating as paper money.

But this renaissance of silver was short-lived, because the subsidiary status of the metal was not changed. The Treasury still could not use silver to meet its obligation. De facto the United States was therefore on a gold standard. This was especially true after 1896, when major discoveries of gold (e.g., Alaska, Colorado, South Africa) and improvements in mining technology led to large increases in gold supplies. The electoral defeat of William Jennings Bryan in the same year, following a bitter presidential campaign in which the monetary system was the main issue of contention, was a decisive setback for silver supporters. The Gold Standard Act of 1900 put the United States finally on an official, gold-based standard. Figure 4.1 shows the complex changes in the composition of the U.S. money-supply during this dramatic period of monetary experimentation. Three subperiods are discernible: the Greenback Era, 1862–1879; Bimetallism, 1879–1896; and the Gold Standard, 1896–1914.

The struggle over money-forms was accompanied by the postwar evolution toward a dual structure of domestic banking. The framers of the 1863 bank reform had hoped that state banks would switch to national charters. Despite tougher safety regulations and stricter government supervision, these were considered more attractive because of the right to issue national bank notes. To reinforce such switching, in 1865 Congress imposed a prohibitive 10 percent annual tax on state bank notes that made their issue unprofitable. This caused a sharp decline in the number of state banks during the 1860s.

Figure 4.1 **Money Forms in the United States, 1860–1915**

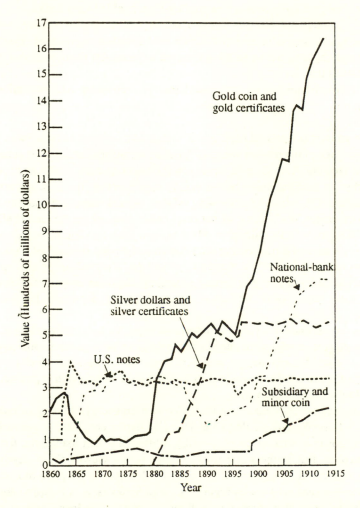

Source: Board of Governors of the Federal Reserve System: reprinted from Robert Boyer and Benjamin Coriat (1984), "Les Greenbacks Revisites: Innovations dans les Institutions et l'Analyse Monetaires Americaines (1862–1913)," CEPREMAP mimeo no. 8420. Paris, p. 4.

Yet state banking still managed to survive. The Civil War had triggered rapid industrialization and had established nationally integrated markets. Propelled by the growing size of businesses and improved communications and transportation, the volume of transactions increased both regionally and on a national scale. To facilitate these transactions, state banks began to offer their customers a new type of bank deposit—the "demand deposit"—which was payable on demand and against which checks could be written. Soon these checking accounts gained widespread acceptance as a more convenient payment mechanism than paper currency. The popularity of this new money-form enabled state banks once again to grow in number and size (see Table 4.2). Another reason for their revival was the attraction of generally less restrictive state banking regulations. Both dual banking and checking accounts have endured as structural features of our monetary regime to this day.

The national banking system established in 1863 also had several major deficiencies:

• The amount of national bank notes, which any bank could issue, was based on a percentage of the market value of Treasury securities owned by that bank as collateral (see our discussion in section 4.3). Although such coverage protected noteholders, it made money creation solely dependent on the U.S. government bond market. For example, following higher interest rates and consequently lower bond prices, the volume of national bank notes fell in the late 1880s and early 1890s, from $350 million to $160 million (see also Figure 4.1).[14] Given rigid enforcement of those reserve requirements, the issue of national bank notes could not respond flexibly to economic expansion, seasonal needs arising from the agricultural cycle, or emergency situations. In other words, that form of private bank money was "inelastic" to the liquidity needs of the domestic economy.

• The correspondent network of interbank deposits, through which thousands of banks cleared checks with each other, proved to be a cumbersome payment system. It caused major delays and high costs in intraregional fund transfers. Because of these inefficiencies out-of-town checks were often redeemed at a discount rather than at par value.

• That same correspondent network also encouraged pyramiding of reserves, which made banks quite vulnerable. Big-city banks competed vigorously for reserve deposits of smaller country banks, which they then loaned out for additional income. But at the same time country banks viewed these deposits as reserves that could be exchanged for cash on demand. When they did, such as during harvest seasons or in emergencies, large banks faced a liquidity squeeze. Those banks were then forced to call back outstanding loans and to curtail lending, which in turn led cash-strapped debtors to liquidate their financial assets. That sell-off, combined with the inherently inelastic currency, caused collapsing security markets and bank runs as everybody scrambled to gain a share of the diminishing supply of cash.

When the post–Civil War expansion in domestic industry finally gave way to a period of prolonged stagnation (1873–96), these shortcomings of the national banking system came to the fore in dramatic fashion. The combination of industrial excess capacity and vulnerable banks caused three panics. Each financial

Table 4.2

Dual Banking in the United States, 1860–1914

Year	National Banks	State Banks
1860	—	1,529
1865	1,294	349
1870	1,612	325
1875	2,076	586
1880	2,076	650
1890	3,484	2,250
1900	3,731	5,007
1910	7,138	14,348
1914	7,518	17,498

Source: Board of Governors of the Federal Reserve System, *Banking Studies*, Washington, DC, 1941.

crisis, usually a mutually reinforcing sequence of money-market pressure, bank runs, and collapsing security prices, triggered a serious depression (1873–78, 1884–85, and 1893–97). The 1873 crisis began when European investors withdrew funds from the United States to cover their exposed cash positions after the collapse of massive real estate speculation in Germany and Austria. The temporary prosperity following the return to the gold standard in 1878–79 ended in 1884, when rising interest rates and falling bond values triggered a money famine. The 1893 panic came after both the aforementioned decline in the supply of national bank notes between 1888 and 1892 and the resurgence of silver (culminating in the Sherman Silver Act of 1890) had eroded confidence in the ability of the United States to maintain a gold standard.

In all of these financial crises during the stagnation period of 1873–96, the situation was made worse by the systemic "inelasticity" of currency. With the issue of bank notes tied to the U.S. government bond market, there was simply no way to respond to rising interest rates and financial distress with an "easy money" policy. In the absence of effective lender-of-last-resort intervention, any financial panic tended to spread rapidly by triggering multiple bank runs. The only mechanism that encouraged banks to cooperate in the face of incipient crisis was set up during the panic of 1873. Under that system banks accepted payment on cleared checks in so-called clearinghouse certificates (obligations of the clearinghouse as a whole) rather than demanding currency or bank notes. This reduced the incentive of any bank to try to bid deposits away from its competitors. But the mechanism worked only with an agreement to pool reserves so that the accepting banks, which now no longer received cash in clearings, would be able to honor their own payment obligations. In the later crises such pooling was no longer forthcoming, thus making the repetition of this crisis management impossible. Furthermore, the mechanism worked only within the locally confined area of the respective clearinghouses, but not for the flow of payments between cities.[15]

The vulnerability of the U.S. banking system seemed to recede after 1896. Several factors contributed to the rapid increase in the U.S. money supply (see Figure 4.1). Gold reserves increased sharply in the wake of new discoveries and improved mining techniques. Ever since 1879 the Treasury had issued gold certificates to pay for its purchases of the precious metal. When that new currency was deposited in the banks, it increased bank reserves and thus allowed further credit expansion under the system of "fractional reserve" banking. In addition, the spectacular growth in the number of banks (see Table 4.2) allowed much larger circulation of both national bank notes and demand deposits, the other principal forms of money.

The rapid growth in the money supply after 1896 helped U.S. industry to resume a period of sustained expansion which was to last until the end of World War I. This was an era of mergers and corporate prosperity. Ambitious and ruthless entrepreneurs (the "robber barons") built major industrial empires by taking over other firms through the formation of holding companies and the issuance of trust certificates. Many of today's dominant firms in the banking, insurance, railroad, steel, meatpacking, and petroleum industries were formed during that first merger boom in U.S. history. In 1907, however, another financial crisis occurred. Although that episode had only limited impact on industry, as is typical during expansion phases of long waves, it hit New York banks and the stock market particularly hard. Governmental officials and city bankers were now convinced that some sort of centralized control over the nation's monetary system was needed.

4.5. The Introduction of Central Banking in the United States

Adopting the principal recommendations of the 1910 report on U.S. banking by the Aldrich Commission, Congress enacted the Federal Reserve Act of 1913.[16] That act was meant to rectify the most serious shortcomings of the national banking system, which had become so acutely apparent during the 1907 crisis. Its key provision was the establishment of a central bank, the Federal Reserve System (Fed). Congress empowered this new monetary authority to issue currency, to run the nation's payment system, to act as lender of last resort in emergency cases, and to supervise large banks. Because of the long-standing opposition to centralized control of banks by the federal government (see section 4.2), Congress gave the Fed a relatively decentralized structure, which consisted of twelve regional Federal Reserve Banks coordinated by a seven-member Board of Governors in Washington, DC. Each regional bank was responsible for the economic needs of its particular geographic area. In practice, however, changing economic circumstances caused the Fed to become increasingly centralized (see below), so that today most of the authority rests with the Federal Reserve Board of Governors in the nation's capital.

The autonomy of the Fed from the other branches of government was assured by a variety of measures. The governors of the Federal Reserve are appointed (by the president subject to Senate approval) to fourteen-year terms, and the chairman's four-year tenure does not coincide with the presidential term. These provisions make it difficult for any president to stack the board with his appointees. Moreover, the Fed is one of the few government institutions that operates outside Congress's budget-appropriation process. Instead, the central bank was given a corporate structure in which the member banks (all national banks and 10 percent of the state banks that joined voluntarily) bought stock in their regional Federal Reserve bank and helped to elect its board of directors. This de jure ownership of the Fed by its member banks also meant that the central bank was run by bankers and that it represented their interests.

The principal function of the new monetary authority was to manage the domestic money supply in accordance with the needs of the economy. To provide for such an "elastic" currency, the Fed was authorized to issue a new form of paper money, the so-called Federal Reserve notes. Member banks could obtain these notes from their regional Federal Reserve bank whenever they needed extra currency. These notes soon became the principal form of paper currency in circulation, a position of dominance they have kept until today. Accustomed to the gold standard and having just gone through massive peacetime inflation (with average prices increasing by nearly 50 percent between 1897 and 1914), many Americans feared that the Fed's money-issuing powers would only exacerbate inflationary pressures. To calm those concerns, the regional Federal Reserve banks were required to keep a gold reserve against their liabilities (40 percent against their notes, 35 percent against their deposits). But the board could set aside those requirements whenever needed. In effect, the Fed never allowed its management of money to be influenced by these requirements, and Congress reduced them repeatedly and finally removed them in 1968.

The Fed also imposed reserve requirements on the deposit liabilities of its member banks. These bank reserves were primarily kept as deposits at the regional Federal Reserve banks, where they were used to clear checks (at par) by simple transfer of an equivalent amount of reserve deposits from the bank on which the check was drawn, to the bank in which the check was deposited. Such interbank transfers of reserves established an efficient payment system for clearing and collecting checks throughout the country.[17] By altering the reserve requirements of member banks within specified limits, the Fed could regulate money creation (in the form of new demand deposits) and credit extension of member banks. Increased reserve requirements restricted the issuance of private bank money, and vice versa.

In addition, the Fed could act as a "lender of last resort" to reduce the likelihood of damaging banking crises. For one, the central bank was given the power to supervise its member banks and thereby to assure prudent banking practices. And in moments of acute crisis the Fed was to offer failing member banks emergency credit, so-called discount loans. Usually lent only for fifteen days (but with possible rollover extension) at rates set by the Fed, these loans would help the threatened bank with cash infusions until the crisis subsided. The loan took the form of an addition to the borrowing bank's reserve position at the Fed and was available only to banks with reserve deficiencies. Still, if the Fed wanted to increase bank reserves (and thereby the nation's money supply) without issuing more of its own notes, it could lower the discount rate and thereby encourage more qualifying banks to borrow from its discount window.

4.6. World War I and the United States' Emerging Global Dominance

The start of World War I in 1914 forced most countries to eliminate convertibility and the free exporting of gold. With the gold standard temporarily suspended, Federal Reserve notes and demand deposits became the two primary sources of new money to finance America's war expenditure. The war gave our domestic economy, the only one among the major powers to escape serious damage, a powerful boost. Under the guidance and with the financial assistance of the federal government (i.e., the War Industries Board), U.S. industry became the main producer of armaments and other essential products for the Allied forces. Its output nearly doubled between 1914 and 1918. The war-related export boom opened many foreign markets to American businesses and within a few years turned the United States from the world's largest net debtor to the dominant net creditor.

Initially Great Britain and France financed their purchases of U.S. products by reselling us more than $2 billion of their American investments. But that was not enough. Hence American banks lent Great Britain, France, and other friendly nations in Europe some $2.6 billion between 1914 and 1917. Those loans represented more than twice (!) the U.S. government's own debt at the time. The Allies relied heavily on J. P. Morgan and Company, one of our nation's most prominent banking institutions, to manage their debt issues and to act as their American purchasing agent. U.S. banks thus suddenly gained a leadership position in global banking, only two decades after their first sovereign loans to Caribbean countries and China. This dramatic step in the internationalization of banking was further facilitated by the Federal Reserve Act of 1913 which allowed nationally chartered banks to establish foreign branches. After the United States entered the war in April 1917, the private loans to our Allies were replaced by official loans of the U.S. government, which totaled $9.6 billion over the next two years.

Reflecting its much-strengthened international position, the United States was the first country after the war to return to a full-fledged "gold coin" standard (in 1919) without any change in the dollar's prewar gold content. With the gold-dollar relationship left unchanged despite massive wartime inflation, deflationary pressures were exacerbated. The result was a steep postwar depression in 1920–21. During that downturn, industrial managers successfully attacked the unions, reduced the war-related build-up in excess capacity, and further boosted their competitiveness via lower prices.

In the early 1920s Wall Street used its new global influence to initiate stabilization loans for the collapsing economies of Central and Eastern Europe, culminating in the huge $1.4 billion credit for Germany in 1924. These initiatives reflected a new "internationalist" vision of American bankers, centered on liberalized trade rules, U.S. aid for European reconstruction, and American leadership in the global economy. But isolationist sentiments, a powerful tradition in American politics, undermined this strategy. First Congress blocked the United States' entry into the League of Nations, thereby destroying this attempt at international cooperation. Then, in the wake of the depression of 1920–21, Congress gave in to pressures from domestic industries and raised tariffs. The ensuing reduction of our imports made it much more difficult for the Allies to service their $10 billion debt to the United States, forcing them to extract huge reparations from defeated Germany as a source of foreign-exchange reserves. Finally, Congress rejected the bankers' plea to facilitate recovery in Europe through debt cancellation, since such a step would have meant a significant loss of U.S. government revenues.[18]

4.7. From Speculative Excess to the Great Depression

While the United States returned to a metallic standard soon after the end of World War I, other countries postponed the return to gold-backed money. Great Britain took that step in 1925, and it sparked the general strike of 1926 in response to industry's wage-cutting efforts. France returned to gold in 1928. Typically, these and other European economies adopted a more limited "gold bullion" standard, under which gold coinage was abolished and other types of money were not necessarily redeemable in gold. In addition, central banks bought and sold gold in unlimited quantities at a fixed price. Those provisions reduced the metal's role as a domestic medium of exchange and strengthened central banks by concentrating domestic gold supplies in their hands. A similar relaxation occurred on the international level with the introduction of the so-called gold exchange standard. Under this system, gold still served as a monetary reserve and as a means of international payment to settle balances between central banks. However, monetary units were defined not in gold but in the currency of the particular country that was on either a gold coin or gold bullion standard. This made it easier for national currencies to be used as an international medium of exchange.[19]

The adoption of a more relaxed version of the gold standard during the 1920s did not establish an effectively functioning international monetary system. War debts and reparations burdened international trade and finance relations. The relative strengths of the different industrial powers had been permanently altered during the war. But the readoption of prewar exchange rates failed to reflect these changes accurately. The British pound was overvalued, especially relative to the then-emerging industrial and financial dominance of the United States. With the pound still the world's key currency, the absence of realistic adjustments in exchange rates further distorted trade and capital flows.[20]

Soon the monetary authorities of the two leading countries had to coordinate policy in order to maintain the integrity of the international monetary system in the face of deepening imbalances. After Great Britain's return to the gold standard and the defeat of its unions in the general strike, the Bank of England tried to aid British industry through a "cheap money" policy. But with the pound already overvalued, such an inflationary low-interest policy threatened major gold losses for London. To prevent this, other countries, especially the United States, had to keep their interest rates in line with those in Great Britain. Throughout 1926 and 1927 the Fed therefore followed a policy of lowering discount rates to stay in step with rate cuts by the Bank of England. The Fed agreed to this policy course for two reasons. For one, it needed to avoid a flight from the pound, for such a crisis of confidence would seriously weaken, if not destroy, the fragile gold exchange standard. Nor did the Fed want to invite massive capital inflows, for fear that the resulting revaluation of the dollar would undermine the ability of American industry to hold on to newly captured export markets. But its "cheap money" policy also encouraged speculation after 1926.

A second factor contributing to the speculation-driven expansion of financial capital during the late 1920s was the success of U.S. industry in diversifying its sources of funds. Following the rapid spread of electricity, public utilities increasingly managed to finance a power-plant construction boom by issuing long-term debt securities. This became the engine for a major expansion of the corporate bond market during the 1920s. In addition, once the stock market started its upward trend in 1925, firms could afford to lower dividend payouts without triggering a decline in the price of their equity. They were thus able to increase internal financing of investment outlays through retained earnings. Larger reinvestment of profits also boosted expectations of future gains, which in turn made stocks more attractive to investors. With the bull market thus starting to feed on itself by late 1926, it became easier for large companies to issue new shares as another means of financing large-scale investment projects.

Being able to retain more of their earnings and issue more securities, companies became less dependent on bank loans, which until then had been their principal source of funds. The loss of traditional corporate customers and the consequently shrinking asset base caught banks unprepared. Many of them were further weakened by intensifying competition over funds, especially time deposits, which increased from $12.2 billion in 1921 to nearly $20 billion in 1929 (compared to the slower expansion of demand deposits, from $18 billion to $22.7 billion). This type of savings deposit, with which banks tried to tap the increased pool of savings during a period of prosperity, was more stable than demand deposits and had the added advantage of lower reserve requirements. But stiff competition led banks to offer relatively high interest rates on their time deposits. These costly funds had to be invested in higher-yielding assets in order to maintain the profit margins of banks. Real estate loans, for example, grew from $2.1 billion in 1921 to $5 billion in 1929, while bank investments in stocks and bonds rose from $8.4 billion to $13.4 billion in the same period. Those assets carried higher returns, precisely because they were riskier and/or had longer maturities. The switch from business loans to longer-term and higher-yielding assets also made banks less liquid. These conditions of vulnerability caused a major shake-out, with 5,209 banks failing during the 1920s.[21]

The combination of competitive pressures and weakened banks encouraged a major merger wave, as large city banks sought to expand their deposit base by absorbing smaller and often vulnerable banks. The McFadden Act of 1927 subjected national banks to the branching restrictions of the state in which they were headquartered and prohibited them from branching across state lines. On the one hand, this prohibition of nationwide banking protected many small banks from inroads by larger competitors into their local markets. This was especially true in those fourteen midwestern states (e.g., Minnesota, Illinois, Texas) in which unit banking (one branch per bank) predominated. But in states with statewide branching (mostly in the Far West and the East Coast) or with limited county-based branching (in states east of the Mississippi River), large banks acquired many of their smaller competitors and operated them as branches, thus coming to dominate their home cities.

Squeezed between costly funds (time deposits) and a decline of their traditional assets (business loans), surviving banks were eagerly looking for new and profitable investment opportunities. Naturally, their attention soon began to focus on the booming stock market. Since commercial banks were not allowed to own equity shares of industrial corporations, a prohibition dating from the National Bank Acts of 1863 and 1864, they had to enter the stock market indirectly.[22] They did this in three different ways.

• First, banks began to make active use of a provision in the Federal Reserve Act which allowed them to offer trust services. By either buying trust companies or opening their own trust departments, they could thus trade in stocks on behalf of their wealthy customers.

• Second, commercial banks dramatically expanded their investment banking subsidiaries, which had come into their own during the first merger boom around the turn of the century. Profits from underwriting new equity issues were large in this period, as euphoric investors were willing to pay high premium prices on any type of security. By 1929 investment affiliates of commercial banks had taken a 41 percent share of the underwriting business, compared to only a 10 percent share in 1921. This gave banks considerable control over the supply of shares.

• Finally, the banks also found a way to manipulate the speculative demand for stocks by increasing broker loans (from $800 million in 1921 to $2.6 billion in 1929). Brokers in turn lent most of these funds to customers who bought stock on credit. With margin (downpayment) requirements as low as 10 percent, investors could move a great deal of stock with very little capital of their own. This leveraging also meant that even relatively small price increases translated into proportionately high returns, allowing many margin buyers to pyramid their paper profits into additional investments.[23]

Despite the outright prohibition on equity ownership, banks were thus able to feed the stock market boom and to benefit from its capital gains. The combination of trust accounts, stock underwriting, and broker loans allowed banks to affect both sides of the market. Their active funding of margin credit fed speculative demand for stocks. This, in turn, helped their trust departments to boost trading volumes and commissions. The bull market also made it easier for their investment-bank subsidiaries to expand underwriting activities and to resell new issues at a larger profit. New shares, which did not fetch a sufficiently profitable market price, were often placed into trust accounts. This practice not only transferred price risks to their clients but also acted to support a higher price level by restricting the supply of new stocks.

But the stock market boom had to exhaust itself. A major reason for the profit increases during the 1924–28 period, which started the bull market rolling in the first place, were relatively low wage costs. This was made possible by the (often violent) destruction of unions during the depression in the early 1920s which weakened the workers' bargaining power and lowered their wage levels. With consumption thereby limited, the industrial expansion of the 1920s eventually had to end in overproduction. When profits finally began to stagnate in 1928, price-earnings ratios in the stock market rapidly became unsupportable. In addition, brokers began to be concerned about overextended customers and raised their margin requirements (up to 22 percent). It was in this situation of growing vulnerability that the Fed decided to tighten monetary policy in order to counteract excessive speculation. Its discount rate was raised from 3.5 percent in February 1928 to 6 percent in August 1929. The combination of these dampening factors finally triggered a collapse of the stock market in late October 1929.

Much has been said about this crash as the trigger for the worst depression in our history.[24] What concerns us here are the structural deficiencies of the then-prevailing monetary regime that intensified the stock market panic and its spillover to the rest of the economy. For one, margin credit proved to be a house of cards once the speculative bubble burst. The rapid decline in stock prices prompted "margin calls," in which brokers demanded additional cash (within one day) from their customers to make up for the decline in the value of the collateral backing their margin credits. When many customers failed to meet these calls, the brokers sold the equities held as collateral. Massive selling into a falling market only reinforced the price decline, triggering even more margin calls. Banks were hit hard, as brokers defaulted on their loans, margin buyers scrambled for cash, underwriting activity collapsed, and trust accounts shrank. Large losses wiped out the relatively small capital base of many banks. Occasional runs on banks by worried depositors only added to the vulnerability of the banking system. Some 800 banks failed in 1930 alone. By wiping out billions of dollars in wealth in two days, the stock market crash certainly undermined confidence and depressed consumer buying. Massive layoffs ensued, which only reinforced the decline in demand.

By late 1930 the economy had recovered somewhat, mostly as a result of sharply lower interest rates (to a record low of 2 percent for the discount rate). But this improvement could not be sustained. First, a trade war ensued when the United States imposed a 40 percent tariff on most imports (in the Smoot-Hawley Act of 1930). Other countries retaliated immediately. This wave of protectionism only exacerbated the debt-servicing problems of many European countries, since the collapse of international trade further restricted their already inadequate foreign exchange earnings. In April 1931 the Kredit-Anstalt Bank of Austria collapsed. Great Britain, at that time facing its first current-account deficit since its return to the gold standard, was no longer in a position to act effectively as international lender of last resort. The result was a rapidly spreading financial panic, which first led Germany to freeze foreign accounts and then forced Great Britain (in late September) to abandon gold-pound convertibility. From there the panic spread across the Atlantic, hitting first those U.S. banks with foreign holdings that suddenly had been blocked and then causing another major plunge on Wall Street.

U.S. government officials made matters worse. In October 1931, just when the financial crisis began to hit at home, the Fed raised the discount rate from 1.5 percent to 3.5 percent in an effort to stem gold losses. When the rate of bank collapses accelerated sharply, the central bank failed miserably to intervene as lender of last resort. Its crucial mistake was to follow the "real bills" doctrine, which led it to accept only the short-term business loans of member banks as collateral for its discount loans. Since the corporate shift to other sources of funds in the 1920s and the sharp downturn after 1929 had drastically reduced these bank assets, many banks did not qualify for enough discount loans to prevent their collapse. The spread of bank failures soon became self-feeding, due to panic runs by worried depositors. Between 1930 and 1933 more than 9,000 banks (40 percent of the total) failed, with depositors losing $1.3 billion in the process. This led, in turn, to a sharp reduction of liquidity and to a decline in credit, squeezing industry and reinforcing its overproduction crisis.[25] Finally, during the election campaign of 1932, Herbert Hoover answered Franklin Roosevelt's call for a balanced budget by tightening fiscal policy, thus further reducing aggregate demand.

4.8. Roosevelt's Reforms of the Monetary Regime, 1933–1944

The collapse of the interwar monetary regime in 1931 and Roosevelt's election victory in 1932 opened the way for fundamental institutional reforms designed to revive the moribund credit system. One crucial change was the official abandonment of the gold standard. The Emergency Banking Act (of March 1933) took the United States off the gold coin standard and gave the government control over the export and hoarding of the precious metal. That act also expanded the Reconstruction Finance Corporation (RFC), a government-sponsored lending institution set up a year earlier by Hoover to beef up bank capital and to disburse funds to holders of blocked accounts. By the end of 1935 the RFC had supplied more than $3.7 billion to commercial banks, which amounted to more than half of the reported bank capital during that year. This strategic injection of funds enabled many closed banks to reopen, thereby boosting the credit system and stimulating consumption and employment. The Gold Reserve Act (of January 1934) established a highly modified gold bullion standard, whereby gold was available from the Treasury for settlement of international transactions. The gold price was fixed at $35 per ounce, which represented a significant devaluation of the dollar from 13.61 grains of gold (the ratio established in 1834) to 23.22 grains. But within the domestic economy all monetary uses of gold were suspended, giving way to a monetary standard that leaned heavily toward inconvertible paper currency. This two-step abolition of the gold standard in 1933–34 was primarily designed to give the central bank more flexibility in controlling the money supply.

In addition, the intervention capacity of U.S. monetary authorities was significantly strengthened by several measures.

• First, the Glass-Steagall Banking Act (of June 1933) gave the Fed greater flexibility to alter reserve requirements as a tool of monetary policy.

• Second, that same act also established the Federal Deposit Insurance Corporation (FDIC). Besides examining those state banks outside the Federal Reserve System, the FDIC was to prevent panic runs on banks by insuring bank deposits and assisting in the orderly removal of failing banks (through merger with a healthy institution or asset liquidation).

• Third, the Banking Act of 1935 broadened the range of bank assets that would qualify as collateral for discount loans, thus allowing the Fed to use this lender-of-last-resort mechanism more vigorously than during the Great Depression.

• Fourth, that same law also set up the Federal Open Market Committee (FOMC) to coordinate and direct the Fed's trading of government securities in the open market, a practice begun in the early 1920s in its function as the government's "fiscal agent."[26] When the Fed buys government securities, its payment adds an equivalent sum to bank reserves no matter whether it bought these securities from banks directly or from the nonbank public. This enables the banks to issue more money (demand deposits) and to extend new credit. The opposite occurs with open-market sales, which reduce bank reserves, money issue, and credit supplies. These open-market operations allowed better management of the money-supply and gave the Fed a powerful mechanism with which to inject additional liquidity into the banking system during periods of financial crisis.

Besides abolishing the gold standard and boosting monetary policy tools, the Roosevelt administration also embarked on a major overhaul of financial regulations to revive and strengthen our credit system. The Glass-Steagall Act of 1933 prohibited banks from paying any interest on demand deposits and subjected the interest rates paid on savings and time deposits to ceilings set by the Fed (Regulation Q). Coupled with the states' usury ceilings on consumer credit, these deposit-rate ceilings were instituted to reduce price competition between banks, which in the 1920s had forced them into riskier investments. Those ceilings gave the Fed a powerful tool with which to control interest rates and to assure a cheap supply of funds for banks. Moreover, Glass-Steagall also separated commercial and investment banking, forcing banks to divest themselves of their investment affiliates. This division of banking into two distinct types was designed to eliminate potential conflicts of interest, market manipulation, and abusive practices. These problems were rampant in the 1920s when banks related to corporations both as creditors and as underwriters. The stock market crash also convinced regulators that investment banking was too risky an activity for commercial banks. Finally, in an effort to control speculation in the stock market, the Fed was empowered to impose minimum down-payment requirements for margin credit purchases of stocks.[27]

The reforms of 1933–35 transformed three dimensions of the monetary regime. Elastic management of the money supply by the state's monetary authorities was strengthened by the de facto abandonment of the gold standard and the broadening of the Fed's monetary policy tools (reserve requirements, discount window, open market operations). Learning from history, the federal government was given much more extensive powers to act as lender of last resort during financial crises, whether through the highly effective FDIC (and a similar agency for thrifts, the Federal Savings and Loans Insurance Corporation, or FSLIC), through the expanded use of discount loans, or through open-market purchases of the Fed. Financial regulations of commercial banks, investment banks, and security markets were introduced to make these institutions safer and to prohibit unsound practices.

The fourth dimension of the monetary regime, the international monetary system, could only be reformed after World War II had established a new global hierarchy of power relations. That war left the United States in a position of absolute dominance among capitalist nations, and this time around the U.S.

government finally accepted the internationalist agenda first proposed by American bankers a quarter of a century earlier. At the Bretton Woods Conference in 1944 the leading industrial powers agreed to a new gold exchange standard. This system established the U.S. dollar as the principal form of world money. The dollar was backed by (and thus as good as) gold. The United States guaranteed full convertibility between foreign dollar holdings and its gold reserves at the 1934 price of $35 per ounce. This price relation formed the basis for defining fixed exchange-rates between all member currencies. The International Monetary Fund (IMF) was set up to oversee exchange-rate changes and to help member countries deal with balance-of-payments crises through short-term loans in exchange for supervised policy adjustments. A second multilateral lending agency, the International Bank for Reconstruction and Development (IBRD, the "World Bank"), was introduced to give developing countries (LDCs) cheap loans for infrastructure investments.[28]

The Postwar Monetary Regime
and Its Inflationary Bias

Roosevelt's reforms established a new monetary regime based on credit-money. We have already discussed the modalities of this money-form in section 2.4. Here we analyze the broader implications of credit-money, especially its interaction with the other institutional forms of monopolistic regulation.

5.1. The Advantages of Elastic Money

Most economists believe that we used commodity-money before the Great Depression forced its abolition. This widespread belief is erroneous. Other than agrarian forms of money during the earliest phases of human civilization, we have never really had commodity-money. All of our forms of money since then, including gold coins, have been tokens rather than commodities. What we did have, however, were monetary regimes rooted in commodity-money—the various metallic standards discussed in the last chapter (see also chapter 14 for more). This distinction is important. Using commodities as money gives rise to a barter economy and allows producers to create their own medium of exchange. Yet even during periods of a metallic standard we had a monetary economy, and the creation of money tokens has always been restricted to the banking system.

The monetary regimes preceding the Great Depression were all, with the exception of the Greenback Era of 1862–79 and World War I, based on some sort of metallic standard (see chapter 4). Over time this institutional form of money developed several shortcomings which led to its eventual collapse in the 1930s. For one, by limiting credit supply and money issue to previously accumulated specie reserves, it constituted a "metallic barrier" to continuous and stable capacity expansion. Of course, under the aforementioned system of "fractional reserve banking," banks could issue socially accepted money tokens (e.g., bank notes, demand deposits) beyond available specie reserves to finance strong credit demand during recoveries. But that process was only temporary. Whenever industrial overproduction began to set off debt-servicing problems, overextended banks would collapse in violent financial crises. In the subsequent downturn, both credit activity and the money supply would shrink back to the metallic reserve base (see Table 4.1). Apart from its procyclical operation, the gold standard also prevented effective crisis management. Monetary authorities, themselves restricted by the nation's gold reserves, often found themselves unable to inject additional liquidity into the banking system when needed.

On the international level, the gold standard provided for automatic correction of trade imbalances between countries. Deficit countries experienced a net outflow of gold and, with the domestic money supply thus reduced, price deflation. The exact opposite tended to occur in surplus countries, where specie inflows triggered rising inflation. The resulting shifts in relative price ratios (the "terms of trade") would then alter trade patterns toward a better equilibrium. While thus balancing trade, the gold standard ended up destabilizing entire national economies through deflationary or inflationary shocks.

Moreover, the smooth operation of this international adjustment mechanism via specie flows depended on two conditions. Market prices, including above all wages, had to respond rapidly to changes in the money supply. And trade volumes had to react sensitively to changes in relative prices. While still prevailing in the accumulation regime of competitive regulation during the second half of the nineteenth century, both prerequisites were gradually undermined in the transition to monopolistic regulation. The emergence of oligopolistic market structures around the turn of the century engendered increasing downward rigidity of prices. And as national economies industrialized, they became more dependent on both vital imports and export-led growth. This made their trade volumes less responsive to changes in their terms of trade. Another problem with the gold standard on the international level was the negligible elasticity of gold production. Its supply was relatively fixed and hardly reacted to price changes. There simply was not enough additional gold available worldwide to satisfy the growing needs for international liquidity in the wake of expanding world trade.

With all these shortcomings the eventual demise of the gold standard was inevitable, a process that reached its final climax in the global banking collapse of 1931. Its replacement, which we shall term the *postwar monetary regime*, contained two forms of credit-money. One is state-issued currency (Treasury coins, Federal Reserve notes), which is put into public circulation via the banking system. The other, by far the largest component of our money supply, is the demand deposits issued by commercial banks in the wake of credit extension and out of excess reserves.[1]

Standard monetary theory assumes that money is an exogenously fixed stock (see section 1.4). This characterization is doubly wrong. To begin with, credit-money is an endogenous variable. It is issued in response to credit-financed demand for money and to meet liquidity needs of individual agents in excess of their existing cash positions.[2] Moreover, even though credit-money may be measured at any given point of time as a stock, it also has the characteristics of a flow. Credit-money can only be issued outside the marketplace for goods and services if it is to assure proper settlement of debts (see section 2.4). New tokens thus have to be first transferred from their issuers to users before they can enter the marketplace as a medium of exchange. This transfer occurs through credit circuits, even in the case of state-issued currency (coins, central bank notes).[3] Once the tokens have become money, they circulate as spendable income in monetary circuits until their destruction upon repayment of the originating bank loan.

It is precisely as an endogenous flow variable that credit-money manages to overcome the defects of the gold standard. Its issue is no longer constrained by inelastic specie reserves. Instead, we have an elastic money supply which responds directly to the liquidity needs of economic agents. Whenever those need more funds beyond their own cash reserves, they can borrow from banks. Such acts of bank lending in turn create new money. As we shall see below, this elasticity of the money supply has given our economic system much greater flexibility and stability.

5.2. State Management of Credit-Money: Monetary Policy

The various tokens representing money are, on their own, worthless paper devoid of any intrinsic value. They only function as money because of their backing by the state as legal tender. The state has to maintain the purchasing power of these tokens or risk losing public confidence. This is the job of central banks, such as our Federal Reserve. The Fed issues its own currency. It also regulates private bank money by operating an integrated payments system which assures the proper circulation of money.

The public keeps deposits in commercial banks, and those banks in turn keep deposits with the Fed which count as their reserves. These reserve accounts form the core of the payments system. By allowing banks to keep their reserves either in currency or deposits at the Fed, the central bank maintains automatic convertibility between different money forms (coins, notes, demand deposits), so that these can be exchanged with each other at par and on demand. This convertibility guarantee extends to the international circulation of U.S. dollars as world-money, as manifest in the backing of international dollars by U.S. gold reserves under Bretton Woods or the Fed's foreign-exchange operations. In addition, the bank reserves kept with the Fed are also used to clear checks. The bank on which the check is drawn loses an equivalent amount in reserves; the bank in which the check was deposited gains that amount in reserves (see section 2.4).

Reflecting the modern version of "fractional reserve banking," a certain portion of check deposits at a particular commercial bank has to be set aside as required reserves. That bank can treat the rest as excess reserves, which can be loaned out. Under normal circumstances banks will try to turn their *nonearning* excess reserves into *income-yielding* loan assets in order to earn a profit. It is precisely this use of excess reserves for credit extension that enables private banks to create new money (in the form of demand deposits) by giving their borrowers a checking account. But no single bank can create more money than its excess reserves, because these are lost once the borrowers spend the new checks. Of course, because that check payment transfers an equivalent amount of reserves to other banks, the banking system as a whole can create a multiple of the original excess reserves in new money (see note 1). The size of that multiplier is inversely related to leakages of funds out of the banking system, such as reserve requirements, cash withdrawals, banks not loaning out their excess reserves, and switching funds between deposits with different reserve requirements. It should be noted that both technological change—for instance, electronic fund transfers—and new money forms (e.g., Eurodollars in the 1960s, Negotiable Order of Withdrawal [NOW] accounts in the 1970s) have played a major role in shaping the evolution of our payments system.

The central bank controls the ability of commercial banks to create money by manipulating their excess reserves within its payments system. This is the purpose of what we economists term *monetary policy*. Toward this objective the Fed uses three different policy tools:

• The central bank buys and sells Treasury securities in so-called open-market operations, which originated in the 1920s from its role as the "fiscal agent" of the U.S. government. These operations have a direct effect on total bank reserves. When the Fed buys government securities, it pays for these purchases by adding an equivalent amount to bank reserves. The reverse, a reduction in bank reserves, occurs in Fed sales of securities. These effects are the same no matter with whom the Fed trades.

• The Fed's discount window provides mostly reserve-deficient banks with borrowed funds that are booked as additional reserves. The Fed can influence the demand for those discount loans and thereby alter total bank reserves by changing either the discount rate or eligibility criteria.

• Finally, the Fed has the power to decide what percentage of different deposits the banks have to set aside as reserves. These reserve requirements determine which proportion of total bank reserves are excess and can be used for the creation of new money via credit extension. Moreover, changes in those reserve requirements alter the size of the aforementioned money-creation multiplier in the banking system.

These policy tools enable the central bank to control the "monetary base," the sum of currency and total bank reserves. The Fed uses this control to counteract business-cycle fluctuations. Whenever an overheating economy threatens higher inflation, the Fed tends to slow growth by tightening its policy. Economic downturns, on the other hand, induce the Fed to allow more rapid growth of bank reserves and to push for lower interest rates as means of stimulation. But this countercyclical monetary policy should not be confused with direct central bank control over the money supply, as wrongly implied by the standard assumption of an exogenously fixed money stock.

The Fed only controls the monetary base and, as such, the banks' ability to create new money out of available excess reserves. Yet it controls neither the banks' willingness to lend out these excess reserves nor the public's demand for bank loans, the other two determinants in the creation of private bank money.[4] At times, especially during downturn periods, banks may prefer to keep more excess reserves as a safety cushion rather than lending them out to possibly shaky borrowers. Moreover, credit demand may be low due to depressed activity. Under such conditions monetary stimulation tends to be quite ineffective. A similar problem, albeit in the opposite direction, may occur during boom periods. To the extent that banks manage to meet high loan demand by attracting funds other than regulated deposit liabilities, they can bypass the Fed's tightening efforts. The ability of the central bank to intervene against the dynamics of the business cycle is therefore limited at best. It cannot eliminate cyclical fluctuations of our economy, but it may reduce their amplitude.

More generally, the problem here is that the issue of credit-money is determined by the private profit motive of the issuing banks and their borrowing clients. In their risk-return calculations banks face a direct trade-off between safety and profitability. Safety-oriented strategies, such as holding larger reserves, increasing their capital base, or investing in low-risk assets, all come at the expense of profits. Conversely, more profitable investment strategies are inherently riskier.

Bank executives tend to manage this trade-off in distinctly procyclical fashion. During recovery periods banks share the optimistic expectations of the public and, in the face of competitive pressures, eagerly seek to expand their assets in response to strong credit demand. The search for higher returns encourages investments that under less euphoric circumstances would have been rejected as too risky. Industry's overproduction tendency is thereby exacerbated by overextension of credit (see section 3.1). That situation, characterized by emerging signs of excess capacity, declining profits, and the burst of speculative bubbles, prompts expectations to turn sour. Mounting losses and risks then force banks into a sudden emphasis on safety, with most of them insisting on tougher credit terms and/or cutting back their loan supplies. Bank lending therefore engenders its own credit-cycle dynamic. Because money creation is directly tied to bank lending, the supply of private bank money tends to fluctuate in procyclical fashion as well.[5]

5.3. State Management of Credit-Money: Financial Policy

The limited capacity of monetary policy to control procyclical money creation by private banks has prompted the monetary authorities to develop complementary measures—best termed *financial policy*—with which to stabilize the credit cycle. Usually introduced in response to major banking crises (see our discussion of the National Banking Acts of 1863–64 and the Glass-Steagall Act of 1933 in chapter 4), these measures typically have taken the form of regulations designed to influence the behavior of financial institutions and markets.

Financial policy in the post-Depression United States used three different types of regulations. The first category comprised all those measures that impact directly on the terms and allocation of credit, most notably selective credit controls and central bank manipulation of key interest rates. A second group of regulations aimed at the structure and competitive practices of financial institutions to promote "safer" banking. Third, in the wake of repeated panic runs on banks (see chapter 4), monetary authorities gained special powers to contain acute financial crises by intervening as "lender of last resort." The regulatory agencies supervise and examine financial institutions on a regular basis in order to assure compliance with regulations and early identification of problems. Let us now analyze these three areas of financial policy in greater detail.

1) Credit Allocation and Interest Rates. In times of strong inflationary pressures the central bank has repeatedly reinforced its monetary policy by restricting lending in specified areas of the credit system. Among many examples of such selective credit controls are minimum downpayment requirements and maximum repayment periods for consumer installment credit during World War II (Fed Regulation W) and the Korean War (Regulation X), increased margin requirements for credit-financed stock purchases in 1968 and 1971, and limiting the growth of consumer credit in 1980 (under the Credit Control Act of 1969).

The Fed has also tried to counteract the credit cycle by influencing key interest rates:

• Its power to set discount rates may not have much actual impact, because banks do not take on many discount loans unless they are forced to. But changes in the discount rate have an important "announcement" effect, providing the financial markets with a clear signal of the central bank's intended policy course.

• Through its open-market operations the Fed has also been able to influence yields on government securities. These act as the default-free rates and thereby set a floor for all riskier private debt instruments of similar maturity.

• Aggressive use of open-market operations or Treasury debt management to change relative supplies of short- and long-term securities may in addition manipulate the yield curve, or what is called the "maturity structure" of interest rates.

• Deposit rate ceilings (Regulation Q) proved to be an especially powerful tool. Given the strategic importance of savings deposits, these ceilings influenced the entire interest-rate structure. They assured banks of relatively cheap deposit funds, which in turn kept their loan rates down.

• In exceptional circumstances the monetary authorities also pressured banks to alter their key lending rate, the prime rate, in the desired direction.[6]

• Finally, in recent years, especially during 1972–79 and from 1984 to the present, the Fed has often used the Federal funds rate as its principal policy variable, defining rate targets compatible with its long-run objectives for money growth. With Federal funds involving primarily very short-term (overnight) loans from banks with excess reserves to banks with reserve deficiencies, their rate is a very sensitive indicator of money-market conditions. When a relatively tight reserve position of banks causes upward pressure on the Federal funds rate, the Fed adds bank reserves through open-market purchases to keep the rate within its target range. The opposite, draining the banking system of reserves, happens when large excess reserves threaten to depress the rate below its target floor. Such a policy of "pegging" the Federal funds rate may temporarily stabilize otherwise highly volatile short-run interest rates, but only by giving up control over bank reserves.

At times the Fed's manipulation of interest rates reinforced its overall monetary policy objectives. For example, during World War II it "pegged" the government securities market at very low yields. Under this policy, in effect until the accord between the Treasury and the Federal Reserve in 1951, the central bank purchased any securities not bought by the private sector at prices that maintained yields at fixed levels (ranging from 0.375 percent for very short-term Treasury bills to 2.5 percent for long-term bonds). These security purchases added to bank reserves. With aforementioned credit controls restricting consumer loans, banks either had to lend these reserves to firms with legal priorities for activities related to war production or buy additional government securities. This "peg" proved to be a vtal link in organizing the war economy as an essentially self-financing accumulation circuit. Industry, apart from being given priority status over other private borrowers, was helped by guaranteed demand in the form of large government contracts and by subsidies that reduced the costs of capacity expansion. The resulting budget deficits were then financed at low yields and through automatic "monetization" of the public debt.

Another example of reinforcing monetary policy by manipulation of interest rates occurred in 1961, when the Fed abandoned the "bills-only" policy it had first adopted eight years earlier. Instead, the central bank began to buy long-term Treasury bonds and at the same time sell short-term Treasury bills. This so-called operation twist aimed at flattening the yield curve to deal with the twin problems of sluggish growth (requiring lower long-term rates) and balance-of-payments problems (calling for higher short-term rates).

But simultaneous management of interest rates and monetary aggregates has clar limits. In periods of rapidly rising prices central bank efforts to keep interest rates low eventually become untenable, because they tend to accelerate money supply growth and to feed inflationary expectations. In this situation the central bank cannot effectively tighten unless it abandons its "low-interest" policy. This was the case during the early stages of the Korean War, when a sudden burst of inflation forced the end of the peg in the Fed-Treasury Accord of 1951. A similar policy reversal occurred during the double-digit inflation of the late 1970s, when the Fed's peg of the Federal funds rate within an artificially low target range encouraged excessively rapid growth in bank reserves and the money supply. In October 1979 this procyclical policy was suspended amid a major financial crisis (see chapter 7).

2) Regulating the Behavior of Financial Institutions. Monetary authorities have tried to promote bank safety by imposing a variety of balance sheet restrictions on the investment strategies of banks. Here are some of the most important examples:

• Bank capital, which serves as a safety cushion against losses, is subject to minimum requirements (as a proportion of assets).

• Various procedures, such as loan classifications, debt rescheduling, setting aside of loss reserves, and write-offs, determine how banks deal with losses from defaulting loans.

• Banks are not allowed to commit more than 10 percent of their capital to any individual loan. This lending restriction is designed to assure that banks maintain sufficiently diversified loan portfolios and are not overexposed vis-à-vis any particular borrower.

• In addition, banks cannot lend to their shareholders or bank officials, a practice with a high potential for fraud and conflicts of interest.

• Banks were also prohibited from engaging in certain high-risk activities and investments, in particular underwriting of corporate securities and equity ownership.

• Regulation Q ceilings on deposit rates, in effect from 1933 to 1980, prevented all-out price competition between banks. In the absence of such ceilings banks are inclined to push up their deposit rates and then maintain their profit margins by investing those costly funds in high-yield but risky assets.

• Finally, the Fed's reserve requirements, apart from controlling credit-linked money creation, enforce a minimum degree of liquidity in case of sudden cash withdrawals.

These safety regulations were complemented by additional balance-sheet restrictions that regulated the structure of our banking system. Such structure regulations impact directly on the competitive behavior and investment strategies of financial institutions. They also influence the allocation of credit, thus affecting the distribution of resources in our economy. For example, the limitations on bank branching mentioned first in section 4.7 (i.e., the McFadden Act of 1927) restricted the geographic expansion capacity of large banks and thereby shielded small banks from excessive competition. Until the deregulation of the 1980s,

U.S. banking had therefore been dominated by a large number of small- to medium-sized institutions (see Table 5.1). Many of those enjoyed regulatory protection to operate as a local monopoly or oligopoly in their local communities.

Other regulations of banking structure included the Bank Holding Company Acts of 1956 and 1970. These empowered the Federal Reserve to regulate the activities of bank holding companies that became the most popular form of corporate organization for U.S. banks in the postwar period. The Bank Merger Act of 1966 introduced special restrictions and regulatory procedures for bank mergers and acquisitions. Commercial banks were also kept apart from other financial institutions (e.g., investment banks, thrifts, mutual funds) by regulatory barriers that specified the types of assets and liabilities permitted for each type of institution. In addition, nonbank institutions, such as thrifts, credit unions, investment banks, mutual funds, or pension funds, each had their own framework of laws and regulators to guide their respective activities.

3) Crisis Management. Given the propensity of banks for credit overextension and undercapitalization, neither contracyclical monetary policy nor financial safety regulations were sufficient to rule out the possibility of bank failures. History has shown consistently that those situations, if left alone, may spread into very damaging financial crises. The postwar monetary regime therefore included various lender-of-last-resort mechanisms with which to reduce the number of bank failures and contain financial crises.

• In response to the disastrous chain bankruptcies in the banking system during the Great Depression, the Banking Act of 1935 made it easier for the Fed to supply troubled banks with discount loans in emergency situations (see section 4.8).

• The deposit insurance of the FDIC, first introduced in 1933, proved to be extremely effective in eliminating panic runs by worried depositors which in earlier times had so often marked the onset of depression. The FDIC also organized the orderly removal of insolvent banks. In most instances this has involved merging the failed bank into a healthier institution, with various forms of financial assistance provided by the FDIC as an incentive. In exceptionally severe cases the FDIC may take over the failed bank to pay off depositors and liquidate its assets. A similar organization, FSLIC, was set up for thrifts.

• Finally, the Fed can conduct massive open-market purchases of government securities on short notice to counter sudden credit squeezes through additional liquidity injections, as was the case during the crisis in the commercial paper market following the collapse of Penn Central in 1970, the global debt crisis in 1982, and the stock market crash in October 1987.

5.4. Credit-Money in the Regime of Monopolistic Regulation

As already indicated, the standard notion of the money supply as an exogenously fixed stock places great emphasis on its direct control by the central bank. In this

Table 5.1

Size Distribution of U.S. Banks (end–1981)

Asset size (million dollars)	Number of banks	Percent of banks	Percent of total assets
Less than 5	470	3	<1
5–25	6,233	44	5
25–50	3,660	25	8
50–100	2,186	15	9
100–500	1,474	10	16
500–1000	188	1	8
1000 or more	204	2	54

Source: Federal Deposit Insurance Corporation *Bank Operating Statistics, 1981,* Washington, DC.

extension of the neoclassical paradigm the market economy is seen as tending automatically toward full-employment equilibrium, provided the central bank allows the money supply to grow at a rate consistent with the economy's long-term expansion capacity (see section 1.4). From this monetarist perspective it becomes easy to blame financial instability and the economic crises it triggers on mistaken policies by the monetary authorities.[7] In contrast, our alternative theory of credit-money as an endogenous flow variable stresses the limited control capacity of the central bank in an inherently unstable economy. Of course, monetary policy has a major impact on the precise course of the cyclical growth pattern. But it cannot eliminate those cycles. Therefore, rather than focusing on the control function of the central bank, as is the case in standard monetary theory, our alternative emphasizes its *support* function instead.

To analyze how the central bank supports economic activity in a regime of elastic credit-money, we need to go back to our discussion of the credit circuit in section 2.3. There it was emphasized that lenders and borrowers share in the gains as well as the losses from this activity. In other words, they face the monetary constraint together. This is why industrial overproduction is usually accompanied by financial instability in the form of spreading loan defaults and bank failures. In the face of such risks, lenders will only extend credit if they are reasonably certain of the borrower's ability to earn future income and to service the debt. Their credit extension thus amounts to a "private prevalidation" of production activities. The Fed's primary objective is to accommodate credit-financed activities by linking bank lending to the issue of new money. This *monetization* of debt does not in itself guarantee the future profit realization of borrowers and their banks. But it certainly facilitates that outcome, because it provides an automatic liquidity injection to back credit-financed spending. Such accommodation by the central bank has been accurately characterized as a "social pseudo-validation" of private production activities (De Brunhoff, 1978, p. 47).

The emphasis on the central bank's support function allows us to analyze how contracyclical state management of credit-money tied in with other components of the postwar accumulation regime. We shall focus here specifically on three major transformations in our economy during the interwar period, each of which required credit-money as an institutional prerequisite. First and foremost was the transition from "competitive" to "monopolistic" pricing in industry. The second change centered around the expanded role of government spending in the economy, especially the active use of fiscal policy to manage aggregate demand. Finally, the global economy was fundamentally restructured after World War II under U.S. leadership. Each of these structural changes contributed to faster growth by regulating otherwise conflict-prone social relations—those between competing firms, between capital and labor, and among nations—on the basis of mutually beneficial consensus and cooperation.

1) "Monopolistic" Regulation of Prices and Wages

The accumulation regime that dominated the United States from the Civil War to the Great Depression linked the underlying value of a commodity, defined by the average labor time expended in its production (see section 2.1), and its money price in fairly direct fashion. Productivity gains, which lowered the value per unit of output by economizing labor time, usually led to correspondingly reduced money prices.

What enforced this direct linkage? For one, that regime was characterized by active price competition. Producers with a technological edge or better organizational efficiency enjoyed a unit-cost advantage and could afford to attack their competitors by charging lower prices. The other firms in the industry had to adopt the improved production methods or lose market share. Price wars, accompanied by managerial efforts to reduce wages, tended to become especially virulent when producers faced excess supplies. Such industrial overproduction, recurring regularly at the cyclical peak, typically coincided with widespread failures of overextended banks through which inelastic commodity-money imposed itself as a barrier to growth. With the money supply falling back to its metallic base, the inflated price structure collapsed. In that regime of competitive price regulation and commodity-money, the monetary constraint operated in unmitigated fashion, with output prices and asset values forced down sharply during regular depression-type crises: 1873–78, 1884, 1893–96, 1907, 1920–21, and 1929–37. These declines represented a *deflationary* mode of market adjustment to the preceding reduction in the value per unit of output by improved productivity.

As pointed out earlier (see section 3.5), price competition gave way gradually to monopolistic regulation. Starting with the merger movement in the 1890s and 1900s, key industries became more concentrated. The trend toward oligopolistic market structures, which accelerated during the interwar period, encouraged greater price coordination and a corresponding shift to product-based forms of competition, introducing, for example, product differentiation and advertising to promote brand identification. Oligopolies were increasingly capable of "administering" their prices. Mark-up pricing, with output prices based on unit-costs at normal rates of capacity utilization plus the industry's average profit margin, became standard practice.[8]

This evolution toward administered (mark-up) prices was accompanied by an equally important change in wage determination. The expanding size of corporations coincided with a major reorganization of the production process. Especially after the destruction of both craft and political unions following World War I, managers replaced highly skilled workers and batch production with unskilled workers and mass production techniques. Crucial in this context were Ford's introduction of the assembly line in 1913 and Taylor's "scientific management," which combined time-motion studies, work-flow integration, and performance-based pay.[9] These developments encouraged the spread of industrial unions and their eventual integration into the New Deal under the Wagner Act of 1935. In a major strike wave (1936–37), led by the United Auto Workers (UAW), blue-collar workers forced management to implement the legislation, especially its provisions for union recognition and collective bargaining. In 1948, in the wake of yet another wave of industrial unrest, the UAW and General Motors (GM) agreed on a three-year contract which tied increases in real wages to the rate of productivity growth. This wage formula soon became standard in U.S. industry.

Such monopolistic regulation of prices (i.e., administered pricing) and wages (i.e., collective-bargaining agreements) in the postwar period enabled competing firms to avoid self-defeating price wars that tended to reduce profits for all. Competition continued to generalize improved production techniques, but without pushing prices down. The most efficient firm still exerted strong pressure on its competitors to improve performance or fall behind. At given prices, lower unit costs translated into a higher profit margin, making it easier for the market leader to raise capital and develop new products.

Productivity gains thus no longer led to falling prices, as had been the case earlier. Following the standard collective-bargaining formula established by the GM–UAW agreement in 1948, they were instead used to compensate for regular wage increases. This allowed aggregate demand to expand more in line with supply capacity, thereby leading to a significant moderation of economic instability. In other words, the contradictory double nature of the wage as private cost and largest source of aggregate demand (see section 3.1) came to be managed in more stable fashion by maintaining a balance between productivity gains and wage increases.[10]

Even though collective bargaining led to downwardly rigid money wages, the multiyear pay agreements made it easier for managers to plan their labor costs and to prepare for strikes. Those were now mostly confined to specified periods of contract renegotiation and thus became quite predictable. The regular wage increases provided for in collective-bargaining agreements did not have to cause higher labor unit costs as long as they were accompanied by proportionate gains in productivity. At the same time the higher wages boosted demand, making it easier for firms to limit overproduction and to avoid ultimately self-defeating price wars. With sales strong, companies were in a better position to coordinate their pricing strategies and to realize their desired mark-ups. In oligopolistic industries, especially those with large barriers to entry, the leading firms often set prices high enough to allow their less efficient competitors adequate profit margins for survival ("umbrella pricing"). Whenever wages rose faster than productivity, firms could try to pass the resulting increase in unit costs onto higher output prices and thereby maintain their profit margins. This response proved especially effective in markets with relatively inelastic demand, such as health care or real estate.

Monopolistic price regulation thus enhanced the stability of our economic system. But it did so only at the expense of an *inflationary bias* which manifested itself as a continuing devaluation of money. A proper understanding of this phenomenon requires us to specify first what exactly is meant by the value of money. In a regime of commodity-money this question poses no problem. Precious metals have intrinsic value, depending on the production costs and market conditions for gold (or silver). But in the postwar monetary regime this internal value basis for money disappears. Modern credit-money, itself just a piece of paper, has no intrinsic value. Instead, its value is defined externally by its social purchasing power; that is, by the amount of physical output a given monetary unit, such as one dollar, commands in the marketplace. In other words, credit-money is valued on the basis of how much average labor time, the common value denominator of physical output, it represents at any given moment (see section 2.3).

In the earlier regime of competitive regulation, declines in the value of commodities would lead to correspondingly lower money prices, mediated by price wars during regular overproduction crises. In the postwar regime of monopolistic regulation, however, this once-close linkage between value and price has been significantly loosened. Productivity gains, which reduce the labor-time necessary to produce a given sum of physical output, no longer trigger recurrent price deflation. They support wage increases instead (see Table 5.2). But when nominal prices fail to decline in correspondence with productivity-induced reductions in value per unit of output, a given monetary unit buys a smaller quantity of value and thus ends up having lost (external) value. It should be noted that the external value of money can fall even at relatively stable prices.[11]

In the postwar regime deflation thus gave way to an *inflationary* mode of market adjustment. No longer were output prices forced lower during economic downturns, and any cyclical decline of asset values remained by and large modest. Productivity gains formed the basis for regular wage increases rather than price wars. Though rooted in the accumulation conditions of industrial capital

Table 5.2

The Inflationary Bias of the Post-War Regime—the Boom of 1948–1968

Year	Private non-farm			Manufacturing	
	Output per man-hour (percent of change)	Compensation per man-hour (percent of change)	Implicit price deflator (percent of change)	After-tax profit margins (per dollar sold)	Money (M1) supply (percent of change
1948	3.0	9.0	6.8	7.0	−1.2
1949	4.0	2.9	0.8	5.8	−0.3
1950	6.3	5.5	1.1	7.1	4.5
1951	2.0	8.7	6.5	4.9	5.6
1952	0.9	5.5	2.6	4.3	3.8
1953	2.9	5.6	1.8	4.3	1.1
1954	2.3	3.2	1.7	4.5	2.7
1955	4.4	3.5	1.3	5.4	2.2
1956	−0.6	5.8	3.4	5.3	1.2
1957	2.2	5.7	3.7	4.8	−0.7
1958	2.5	3.8	1.7	4.2	3.8
1959	3.4	4.3	1.8	4.8	1.6
1960	1.2	4.1	1.4	4.4	0.6
1961	3.0	3.2	0.9	4.3	3.1
1962	4.6	4.0	0.9	4.5	1.5
1963	3.1	3.6	1.2	4.7	3.7
1964	3.7	4.7	1.3	5.2	4.6
1965	2.9	3.7	1.4	5.6	4.6
1966	3.5	6.1	2.2	5.6	2.4
1967	1.6	5.7	3.3	5.0	6.6
1968	2.9	7.3	3.5	5.1	7.8
1969	−0.1	7.0	4.5	4.8	3.5
1970	0.7	7.3	5.0	4.0	6.0

Source: Council of Economic Advisers, *Economic Report of the President*, 1974, Washington, DC, (selected tables).

(i.e., oligopolistic price formation, wage-productivity balance), this inflationary bias depended on credit-money as an institutional prerequisite. Its elastic creation, in response to credit demand, helped to loosen the monetary constraint by providing individual agents with extra liquidity whenever it was needed to cover cash-flow gaps. In other words, this new form of money supported the entire structure of "administered" prices by endogenously financing cash-flow commitments arising from such monopolistic price regulation. The result was a better balance between supply and demand, with deflationary pressures countered through automatic injection of loanable funds.

2) Keynesian Demand Management

The second major transformation of the interwar period was the active use of fiscal policy to counteract business cycles. The impetus for this change came from Roosevelt's New Deal reforms in response to the Great Depression and their theoretical justification by Keynes (1936). The "Keynesian Revolution," given an institutional basis in both Great Britain and the United States by their respective Employment Acts of 1946, called for active management of aggregate demand via government spending. Budget deficits, adding net injections of spending, stimulate the economy while budget surpluses (or reduced deficits) have the opposite effect.

Ever since the New Deal, the U.S. budget has contained automatic fiscal stabilizers designed to operate in countercyclical fashion. Any slowdown would cause more than proportionate reductions in tax revenues (through the graduated income tax system) and larger government spending on income-maintenance programs (e.g., unemployment compensation, welfare benefits), so that budget deficits increased in times of recession. During recoveries these fiscal stabilizers would operate in the opposite direction. In addition, the government could always reinforce its stabilizers through discretionary policy action in the annual budget process. Ever since the late 1950s the U.S. government has run regular budget deficits (see Table 5.3). This feature of the postwar regime also depended on elastic credit-money. The Federal Reserve has supported the government's deficit spending by acquiring Treasury securities. Such open-market purchases tied federal budget deficits to automatic money creation and thus monetized a portion of the national debt.

Postwar fiscal policy, reflecting a much-expanded role of government in the economy, was not confined to countercyclical management of aggregate demand. The progressive rate structure of our income taxes and various antipoverty programs aimed at redistributing income from the rich to the poor, whose higher marginal propensity to consume would spur additional consumer spending. Industrial investment was encouraged by tax incentives, such as accelerated depreciation allowances and investment tax credits, as well as subsidies that often took the form of lucrative contracts (e.g., the military-industrial complex). Government provided industry with an infrastructure by constructing roads, airports, mass-transit systems, industrial parks, waste disposal plants, water supplies, and so forth. Most important, however, was a complex web of policies to manage the social reproduction of wage labor as a productive resource. Income maintenance programs offered a safety net for people pushed outside the labor market (e.g., Social Security benefits for retirees, disability insurance, unemployment compensation). Increased access to education and job-training programs facilitated the skill formation of workers, which in turn helped to sustain productivity growth. Other social services included government support for public-health programs, for low-income housing, and for community-development projects.

Table 5.3

Deficit Spending and Monetization of the Public Debt

Year	Government expenditures	Transfer payments (in billions of dollars)	Budget surplus/deficit	Federal Reserve holdings of T-securities (as percent of total outstanding)
1949	59.1	12.4	−3.2	7.3
1950	60.8	15.1	7.9	8.1
1951	79.0	12.5	5.8	9.1
1952	93.7	13.0	−3.8	9.2
1953	101.2	14.0	−6.9	9.4
1954	96.7	16.0	−7.0	9.0
1955	97.6	17.3	2.7	8.8
1956	104.1	18.5	4.9	9.0
1957	114.9	21.4	0.7	8.8
1958	127.2	25.7	−12.5	9.3
1959	131.0	26.6	−2.1	9.1
1960	136..1	28.5	3.7	9.4
1961	149.0	32.4	−4.3	9.7
1962	159.9	33.3	−2.9	10.1
1963	166.9	35.3	1.8	10.9
1964	175.4	36.7	−1.4	11.6
1965	186.9	39.9	2.2	12.7
1966	212.3	44.1	1.1	13.5
1967	242.9	51.8	−13.9	14.2
1968	270.3	59.6	−6.8	14.8
1969	287.9	65.8	8.8	15.5
1970	312.7	79.1	−10.1	16.0
1971	340.2	93.2	−18.1	16.5
1972	370.9	103.0	−2.8	15.6

Source: Council of Economic Advisers, *Economic Report of the President*, 1974, Washington, DC (selected tables); Board of Governors of the Federal Reserve System, *Federal Reserve Bulletin* (selected issues for Fed holdings of Treasury securities).

Notes: Data for government spending, transfer payments, and budget surplus/deficit comprise all levels of government. Transfer payments exclude interest payments on public debt to private bondholders and are gross of personal contributions for social insurance.

3) The International Policy Regime of Bretton Woods

A third socioeconomic transformation occurred on the international level. The United States used its new status as the absolutely dominant superpower at the end of World War II to initiate a major reorganization of international economic relations. This included a concerted push for the liberalization of trade and capital flows, culminating in GATT in 1947. That and subsequent multilateral agreements, including the Kennedy Round of the 1960s and the Tokyo Round of the 1970s, provided for phased-in reductions in trade barriers and regulated protectionist conflicts between nations. Both the emergence of newly independent nations following the massive wave of decolonization in Asia and Africa and the regional treaties for economic cooperation between neighboring countries (the European Community, and the Association of South East Asian Nations, or ASEAN) served to reinforce the global opening of markets.

Also crucial to the successful postwar reorganization of the world economy was the international monetary system put into place at the Bretton Woods Conference in 1944 (see section 4.8). That system had several beneficial results:

• It facilitated international transactions by restoring full convertibility between key currencies at stable exchange rates, a process completed by the late 1950s.

• The International Monetary Fund, controlled by the United States through its veto power, enforced adjustment programs in countries with balance-of-payment problems that kept their markets open.

• Cheap loans by the World Bank enabled many newly independent nations to undertake needed investments in their social infrastructure.

• Bretton Woods' new "gold exchange" standard provided for more elastic supply of international liquidity. Its imposition of the (gold-backed) dollar as world money meant that the United States had to run large balance-of-payment deficits in order to generate much-needed dollar outflows to the rest of the world (see Table 5.4). Given chronic U.S. trade surpluses, the only way this could be achieved was through massive capital exports. U.S. military commitments abroad in the wake of security treaties (e.g., the North Atlantic Treaty Organization, or NATO; Australia-New Zealand-United States [ANZUS] Pact; the Organization of American States, or OAS), direct overseas investments of U.S. firms, and official aid programs (e.g., the Marshall Plan in 1948) were all channels for capital exports with which to transfer U.S. dollars overseas. These transfers served both sides. The United States was allowed to make profitable use of its global hegemony, while our allies received much-needed foreign-exchange reserves to pay for imports.

5.5. The Postwar Monetary Regime as a "Debt Economy"

The Fed's support function can thus be defined in terms of helping other institutional transformations, most notably the monopolistic regulation of prices and wages, deficit spending by the government, and a rapid expansion of world trade and capital flows. Each of these changes accelerated growth, provided they were backed by accommodative state management of elastic credit-money. Administered prices and collective-bargaining agreements promoted stability in the production economy. Industry managed to counteract its overproduction tendency

Table 5.4

The Balance of Payments of the United States, 1946–1961
(in millions of dollars)

Year	Merchandise trade surplus	Overseas military expenditures	Government grants and capital outflow (–)	Private direct and portfolio investments (–)	Overall balance of payments surplus (+) or deficit (–)
1947	+10,036	+455	−6,415	−987	+4,567
1948	+5,630	+799	−5,361	−936	+1,005
1949	+5,270	+621	−5,854	−553	+175
1950	+1,009	+576	−3,935	−1,265	−3,580
1951	+2,921	+1,270	−3,496	−1,048	−305
1952	+2,481	+2,054	−2,809	−1,160	−1,046
1953	+1,291	+2,615	−2,542	−383	−2,152
1954	+2,445	+2,642	−2,061	−1,622	−1,550
1955	+2,753	+2,901	−2,627	−1,255	−1,145
1956	+4,575	+2,949	−2,841	−3,071	−935
1957	+6,099	+3,216	−3,233	−3,577	+520
1958	+3,312	+3,435	−3,131	−2,936	−3,529
1959	+972	+3,107	−3,040	−2,375	−3,743
1960	+4,736	+3,048	−3,405	−3,882	−3,925
1961	+5,401	+2,947	−4,051	−3,953	−2,461

Source: Council of Economic Advisers, *Economic Report of the President*, 1963, Washington, DC, Table C–78.

by combining productivity gains from mass-production technologies, downwardly rigid mark-up pricing, and regular wage increases. This combination required adequate credit supplies, both to industry for financing of large-scale investment projects and long-term contracts with unions or suppliers and to consumers for purchases of large-ticket items. Government deficits, backed by Federal Reserve purchases of Treasury securities, further boosted aggregate demand. Finally, global expansion benefited from the creation of international (dollar-based) liquidity through consciously orchestrated capital exports from the United States.

The resulting stabilization and acceleration of economic activity during the postwar boom (1948–68) was therefore due not least to better integration of production, credit financing, and money creation. Corporate investment activity, itself encouraged by stronger demand and more stable prices, was further increased by a larger supply of credit funds at relatively low interest rates. The same held true for spending by government units and consumers. Cheap and ample credit supplies depended in turn on central bank accommodation that allowed the banking system to monetize a sufficient proportion of the new debt. The result was the emergence in the postwar period of a *debt economy*, characterized by credit-financed spending in excess of current income and by demand-driven acceleration of growth.

Two crucial developments, both helped by the transition from commodity-money to credit-money, played a very important role in this debt economy. One was the rapid spread after World War II of *forward-money contracts*. Those took a great variety of forms, such as financial contracts in credit relations, collective-bargaining agreements with unions, long-term supply contracts (including the provision of trade credit), pension plans, insurance policies for risk protection, or government-sponsored income maintenance programs, such as Social Security and unemployment compensation. These different forward-money contracts had two crucial advantages. They predetermined otherwise uncertain cash flows in advance and regulated potentially conflict-prone relations on the basis of mutual agreement. Adequate injection of additional liquidity in response to credit demand assured the funding of these various contractual cash-flow commitments.

The other development was a significant shift within the credit system from direct transfer of funds between lenders and borrowers to financial intermediation. During the 1920s half of all loanable funds in the United States were still absorbed by direct financing. But since the mid-1960s the share of intermediation-based financing has generally exceeded 90 percent. That switch was very much rooted in the transition to credit-money, whose issue and circulation in an integrated "check-clearing" system requires continuous depositing and lending of funds in the banking system. Financial intermediation lowers borrowing costs because of the economies of scale achieved by financial institutions in large transfers of funds. Even more important, it helps to overcome the conflict of interest between creditors and debtors over maturity, denomination, risk, and liquidity (see sections 2.3–2.5). The switch from direct financing to intermediation was a key factor behind the rapid postwar expansion of different financial institutions (see Table 5.5).

The growing importance of intermediation and the rapid expansion of financial institutions reflected a major increase in credit-financing of economic activities. In the postwar debt economy the continuous supply of credit and issue of (credit-) money merged with new, debt-based norms of production and exchange, so current expenditures could be driven beyond current income. Such debt-financed additions of demand occurred in every sector of the economy, whether industrial firms, consumers, government units, or financial institutions.

1) Industry

Producers acquire external funds to increase their investment outlays beyond the level permitted by sole reliance on internally generated profits. For example, companies receive trade credit, in essence a deferral of payment ("accounts payable"), from their suppliers. They may also finance their inventory purchases by taking out short-term bank loans or by issuing commercial paper. The expan-

Table 5.5

Size and Growth of U.S. Financial Institutions, 1950–1989

Intermediary	December 1950		December 1989		Growth (Percent per year)
	Assets (in billions of dollars)	Percent of total	Assets (in billions of dollars)	Percent of total	
Commercial banks	150	52	3,231	32	8.0
Life insurance companies	63	22	1,268	13	7.9
Savings & loan associations	17	6	1,233	12	11.2
Private pension funds	7	2	1,163	11	13.6
State & local government pension funds	5	2	727	7	13.3
Mutual funds	3	1	555	6	13.9
Finance companies	9	3	519	5	10.6
Casualty insurance companies	12	4	491	5	9.7
Money-market funds	0	0	428	4	n.a.
Mutual savings banks	22	8	283	3	6.5
Credit unions	1		200	2	14.2
Total	289	100	10,098	100	9.1
GNP	286		5,340		7.4

Sources: Board of Governors of the Federal Reserve System, *Flow of Funds Accounts, Assets & Liabilities Outstanding,* 1981, Washington, D.C. (for 1950 data); *Flow of Funds Accounts Financial Assets and Liabilities, Year-End 1966– 1989,* 1990, Washington, D.C. (for 1989 data).

sion of plant and equipment can be funded by long-term debt instruments (corporate bonds) or through issue of new equity. The latter instrument has indefinite maturity and is actively traded on the exchange where the stock is listed. The return on equity to shareholders takes the form of dividends and capital gains from increases in the stock price. Both are tied to the company's earnings and are thus, in contrast to debt-servicing obligations, neither fixed nor legally enforceable. The expansion of its capital base through issue of new equity also gives a firm an additional safety cushion out of which losses can be written off. Its risk of insolvency is thereby reduced.

Yet despite the obvious usefulness of equity, the financial structure of U.S. industry is clearly biased toward corporate debt. Until the tax reform of 1986 firms could fully deduct their interest payments from their taxable profit income, while dividend payments to shareholders did not receive any preferential tax treatment.[12] In general, the cost of debt to the firm tends to be lower than that of equity, because creditors are better protected and face lower risk than do shareholders. By increasing their debt–equity ratios, companies may lower their average cost of financing and improve the profitability of their investment projects. The increased use of debt will also lead to a proportionately smaller capital base, so that for any given nominal sum of profits there will be a larger rate of return on equity. Finally, because increases in equity through new issues of common stock dilute earnings as well as control for existing shareholders, they are often resisted.

While debt thus carries important advantages, its excessive use may well have potentially destabilizing consequences. To begin with, debt-servicing obligations are by and large fixed costs that have to be paid out at any level of sales revenues. The larger they become, the greater the possibility of default and bankruptcy. Any further increase in the company's leverage beyond a certain debt–equity ratio will thus cause both creditors and shareholders to raise their required rates of return as compensation for this increase in risk. Such risk premiums add to the firm's cost of capital, thereby undermining its profitability and investment activity. The larger a firm's fixed costs, whether reflecting depreciation charges from past investments in plant and equipment or debt-servicing charges, the greater also the variation in profits from any given change in sales revenues. Highly automated and/or leveraged firms thus face a greater risk of large losses from any decline in sales. This tendency toward an increasingly rigid cost structure intensifies the need to stabilize corporate earnings and cash flows at high levels of sales.[13]

One such effort at cash-flow stabilization was a major change in the way in which corporations have come to deal with the devaluation of their plant and equipment. These fixed capital assets decline in value over time, because they are subject to natural wear and tear as well as to technological obsolescence. They thus have a finite period of usefulness during which the initial investment outlay can be recovered and additional profits be earned. In the era of competitive regulation this constraint made itself felt as a sudden and violent devaluation of capital during overproduction crises that forced firms into plant closures, asset liquidations at depressed prices, and write-downs of (excess) capacity. Nowadays, with companies administering their prices, such losses are moderated by treating the decline in the value of fixed capital as a nonoutlay cost ("depreciation") and by incorporating it as such into the pricing structure. This cost does not involve an actual cash outlay, because the plant and equipment have already been paid for at the time of their purchase. Together with net profits, it thus becomes part of the corporate cash flow. As such, it is a source of funds that can be set aside to finance the orderly replacement of fixed capital. Representing a less violent alternative to the forced destruction of capital during earlier depressions, depreciation enables a firm to tie the devaluation of its plant and equipment over time more closely to their validation as income-producing assets.[14]

Depreciation has the added advantage that its time schedules can be manipulated to the advantage of firms. Provided that prevailing market demand is strong enough to stand higher prices and that the pricing strategies of competitors permit it, companies can speed up depreciation. In this endeavor of cash-flow manipulation, our industries have been regulated by governmental accounting standards. Given the difficulty of measuring actual depreciation and the need for standard write-off procedures to make financial statements comparable, in the 1920s the U.S. government began to specify depreciation rules irrespective of the actual timing of sales revenues. Repeatedly, in 1954, 1962, 1972, and 1981, it allowed faster depreciation schedules to encourage industrial investments. With depreciation charges deductible from corporate income tax, their acceleration created larger tax deductions early in the life cycle of fixed capital assets. Booked as a nonoutlay cost, they also reduced taxable income while increasing cash flow. Both tax benefits shortened the payback period for new investments. Today such accelerated depreciation has also become an increasingly important means with which to counteract the trend toward more rapid technological obsolescence.

Depreciation has traditionally been measured in terms of historic costs rather than current replacement costs. When inflation accelerated in the 1970s, this practice led to a growing undervaluation of depreciation. Reported earnings were consequently overstated, giving rise to "paper" profits that masked the actual profit decline considerably (see Figure 5.1).[15]

These nominal accounting profits illustrate how the regime of elastic credit-money relaxes the aforementioned monetary constraint (see section 2.3). Yet in this case the relaxation is inherently limited. For one, companies have to pay real taxes and dividends on those fictitious gains. During a period of steadily rising inflation this excess tax liability from historic-cost accounting soared from \$3.2 billion in 1960 to \$19.1 billion in 1977. Moreover, these accounting profits last only until plant and equipment have to be replaced at much higher costs than those used in the calculation of depreciation charges.

The transformation of fixed capital's devaluation into a source of funds via depreciation accounting is one of the central features of monopolistic regulation (see section 3.5). That treatment of fixed capital's declining value as a nonoutlay cost, factored into the output prices charged by the users of that capital, is itself a by-product of "administered" prices and clearly expresses the inflationary bias in our postwar economy. Moreover, these depreciation charges are also tied to credit-financed excess spending and thus constitute part of our modern debt economy. This is so because depreciation charges represent expenditures without engendering at the same time any equivalent amount of income. Incorporated into the prices paid for goods and services, depreciation is obviously a current expenditure item. But it has no counterpart in the value added that forms the

Figure 5.1 **Inflation-Based Paper Profits**

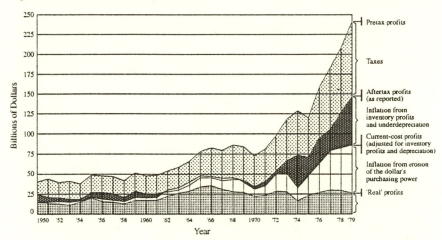

Source: Business Week (1982), The Reindustrialization of America (McGraw-Hill: New York), p. 45. Reprinted from 1982 issue of *Business Week* by special permission, copyright © 1982 by McGraw-Hill.

basis for current income. Instead, it only represents a decline in previously produced value, which is charged and paid for as a current expenditure. Depreciation becomes part of corporate cash flow, precisely because it involves spending in excess of income-generating value added. The only way in which such a gap between current income and expenditure can be bridged is by means of continuous credit expansion and money issue.

Corporate indebtedness and reliance on indirectly credit-financed depreciation rose steadily in the postwar United States (see Table 5.6). The share of private business debt in the GNP grew from 29.4 percent in 1946 to 52.2 percent in 1979. And corporate depreciation allowances of $197.7 billion in 1981 amounted to 213 percent of undistributed profits and 184 percent of personal savings.

2) Consumer Spending

The "debt economy" allowed households to finance consumer spending in excess of their current income. Various forms of consumer debt played a major role in the formation of new social consumption norms, which drove the postwar boom. For example, mortgages, supplied by thrifts and commercial banks, financed the rapid spread of homeownership after World War II. This was a crucial propellant for faster growth, for the housing sector occupied a strategic position in our industrial matrix. Construction, a labor-intensive industry, created many well-paid jobs. And home purchases have traditionally had significant

Table 5.6

Corporate Debt and Depreciation Allowances in U.S. Industry
(in billions of dollars)

Year	Total liabilities	Current liabilities	Undistrib- uted profits	External credit market funds	Depreciation allowances (total)	Depreciation allowances (as percent of output)
1966	380.8	209.7	25.0	24.6	34.1	7.9
1970	537.4	298.4	12.6	38.9	49.4	8.8
1974	730.2	388.9	45.3	54.6	76.8	9.4
1978	1,027.4	523.2	78.7	71.0	131.1	10.2
1982	1,490.2	849.2	30.6	50.7	227.6	12.6
1983	1,623.8	929.6	30.5	81.0	240.2	12.4
1984	1,862.8	1,072.1	46.4	92.5	246.2	11.4
1985	2,051.5	1,163.7	21.7	52.4	256.1	11.2
1986	2,312.8	1,244.2	–2.1	126.7	269.3	11.3
1987	2,542.3	1,303.2	41.3	63.0	279.3	11.0
1988	2,816.8	1,419.7	73.6	63.0	295.2	11.6
1989	3,082.5	1,529.7	48.5	42.1	313.9	10.8

Sources: Board of Governors of the Federal Reserve System, *Flow of Funds Accounts, Financial Assets and Liabilities, Year-End 1966–1989,* 1990, Washington, D.C., Tables 9 and 10 (for total and current corporate liabilities); Council of Economic Advisers, *Economic Report of the President,* 1992, Washington, D.C., Tables B–10 and B–90 (for other variables).

Notes: Quarterly data at seasonally adjusted annual rates for non-farm non-financial corporations. External credit market funds comprise securities, mortgages, loans and short-term paper. Depreciation allowances measured at replacement cost.

multiplier effects on other sectors, such as domestic appliances, road construction, or housing materials. Carrying a large and long-term mortgage disciplined many workers who could not afford to lose their jobs and fall behind in their repayments. At the same time, homeowners acquired an asset which turned out to be an excellent hedge against inflation. Its large capital gains created what economists have called a "wealth effect" in support of increased consumption.

Similarly stimulating effects were engendered by car loans of banks, finance companies, and the automobile companies themselves. The automobile industry, besides embodying the most advanced application of mass-production technology, represented a major source of demand for other industries like steel, petroleum, and rubber. The role of the car in our society cannot be overestimated, whether as a status symbol or in terms of shaping our social space as an amalgam of sprawling suburbs, shopping malls, highways, and gridlocked urban centers.

Besides home mortgages and car loans, consumer debt has recently developed a third component, the widespread use of credit cards. These amount to a revolving line of credit which can be used in market transactions. Such deferral of payment frequently tempts consumers into spontaneous buying, which boosts retail sales.

Several government initiatives have supported consumer debt. For one, interest payments could be deducted from income tax, thus reducing the after-tax cost of debt. State governments set maximum interest rates ("usury ceilings") for different types of consumer debt. Recognizing the unequal power relation between the lending institution and the borrowing consumer, Congress enacted several laws to protect the latter. The Truth-in-Lending Act of 1968 (Regulation Z) and the Home Mortgage Disclosure Act of 1975 (Regulation C) required lenders to disclose relevant credit terms and regulated the processing of disputes. The Equal Credit Opportunity Act of 1974 (and Regulation B) made it easier for certain groups (women, minorities), which tended to suffer widespread discrimination by lenders, to obtain credit. The Community Reinvestment Act of 1977 (Regulation BB) aimed to prevent "redlining" of specific communities by lenders refusing to invest their funds in designated areas. Thrifts were given tax breaks for investing heavily in qualifying assets and at the same time were prohibited from making certain loans. This regulatory framework created a special institution whose main purpose was to attract household savings and channel those funds into mortgage lending. Government-sponsored institutions—the Federal National Mortgage Association, the Government National Mortgage Association, and the Federal Home Loan Mortgage Corporation—aided the supply of mortgages by offering insurance, guarantees, or interest subsidies. Finally, the government offered student loans at concessionary terms to increase access to otherwise very expensive college educations.

Consumer debt accelerated growth by helping to finance excess spending of households on a widespread scale. Debt-financing of large-ticket purchases (homes, cars, education) helped to create "mass markets" for key consumer products and to stimulate large segments of the economy. Consumers, starting the postwar period with much pent-up demand and in a relatively strong financial position, finally could go on a spending spree. Accelerating inflation, starting in the late 1960s, contributed to further indebtedness. The frequency of negative "real" interest rates in the 1970s prompted households to take on additional debt while running down their savings (see Table 5.7). This strategy enabled many Americans to compensate for declining real wages and to beat future price hikes through accelerated purchasing.

3) Deficit Spending by the Government

This component of our domestic debt economy has already been discussed (see section 5.4). Several additional points are worth keeping in mind here.

Table 5.7

Consumer Debt Among U.S. Households (yearly averages in billions of dollars)

Year	Residential mortgages	Consumer credit	Interest paid by persons	Personal saving (as percent of disposable income)
1946–50	41.24	14.66	2.14	6.4
1951–55	80.94	30.58	4.12	6.9
1956–60	136.62	48.00	6.74	6.2
1961–65	216.56	72.74	9.82	5.7
1966–70	304.43	111.22	15.32	7.0
1971–75	493.94	181.62	21.70	8.4
1976–80	879.98	299.63	37.76	7.1
1981–85	1,400.48	456.92	67.54	7.7
1986–90	2,504.12	727.56	97.20	4.8

Source: Council of Economic Advisers, *Economic Report of the President*, 1974, Washington, DC, Tables C–8 and C–63 (for 1946–60 data); 1992, Tables B–24 and B–71 (for 1961–90 data).

• For one, budget deficits often replace private debt with public debt. Many government-financed activities, such as medical insurance, social security, manpower training, or infrastructure investments, would otherwise have had to be undertaken by the private sector. Extra-high profit margins on lucrative government contracts allow corporations to finance their expansion into civilian markets (e.g., aerospace firms). Targeted tax breaks for industry, such as accelerated depreciation allowances or investment tax credits, subsidize investment spending at the expense of lower government revenues. All of these government activities have acted as means of "socializing" private-sector costs and risks by allowing beneficiaries to transfer a portion of their expenditures to the general public.

• Secondly, as long as budget deficits expand in line with overall economic growth and fund productive investments that enhance the nation's income-creation capacity, they benefit our economy without causing any problems in servicing or refinancing the growing national debt.

• Finally, the increased circulation of Treasury securities in the wake of annual budget deficits gave creditors—banks, corporations, households, foreign dollar-holders—an extremely liquid and essentially default-free instrument to hold. This has made our credit system safer and more efficient (see Table 5.8).

4) Credit Between Financial Institutions

Banks supply each other with funds through the correspondent system, the interbank segment of the Euromarket, and the Federal funds market. They also pro-

Table 5.8

Budget Deficits and Public Debt Monetization (yearly averages in billions of dollars)

Year	Budget deficits (–) and surpluses (+)	Gross federal debt	Federal Reserve holdings of U.S. government securities
1948–52	+2.8	255.2	22.3
1953–57	–0.7	271.2	25.0
1958–62	–5.1	290.6	28.0
1963–67	–4.9	323.5	41.0
1968–72	–14.2	391.9	62.5
1973–77	–40.3	565.5	87.9
1978–82	–76.0	929.0	121.7
1983–87	–195.3	1,843.6	181.6
1988–92	–217.7	3,270.5	241.4

Sources: Council of Economic Advisers, *Economic Report of the President*, 1992, Table B–74, Washington, DC (for budget deficits/surpluses and gross federal debt); Board of Governors of the Federal Reserve System, *Federal Reserve Bulletin*, selected issues (for Fed holdings of Treasury securities).

Note: Federal holdings of Treasury securities only until 1991.

vide frequent credit to thrifts, finance companies, and brokers while borrowing actively from money-market funds. These credit transfers enhance the ability of various financial institutions to increase their own lending activity.

Starting in the mid-1960s, accelerating inflation led to rising loan demand while making the no-yield demand deposits or low-yield savings deposits of banks and thrifts increasingly unattractive (see chapter 6 for more details). That financing gap encouraged a new banking strategy called "liability management." By introducing and/or expanding a series of new debt instruments, such as Federal funds, negotiable certificates of deposit, Euroloans, bankers' acceptances, or repurchasing agreements, the banks gained access to a larger supply of funds. Increased reliance on these "borrowed" liabilities enabled banks to reduce their holdings of low-yield assets, such as excess reserves or Treasury securities, as a liquidity cushion and to expand their loan assets without proportionate increases in equity or deposit liabilities. Funds were also increasingly transferred from the low-yield deposits of banks to less-regulated institutions, like Eurobanks and money market funds, in order to escape such government restrictions as Regulation Q rate ceilings. The banks then borrowed these funds back at higher interest rates. The rise of borrowed liabilities in the late 1960s and 1970s (see Table 5.9)

Table 5.9

Borrowing by U.S. Commercial Banks (negotiable certificates of deposits and borrowed liabilities)

Year	In billions of dollars	As a percent of total bank liabilities and capital
1950	3	2
1955	3	1
1960	6	2
1965	29	7
1970	80	14
1978	270	21
1984	612	28
1989	964	31

Source: Board of Governors of the Federal Reserve System, *Federal Reserve Bulletin, Washington, D.C. (selected issues).*

thus facilitated continued credit extension by the banking sector even during phases of more rapid inflation and more restrictive monetary policies.

5) External Deficits

The domestic debt economy and its funding of continuous excess spending by U.S. corporations, consumers, government, and financial institutions was supported on an international scale by the Bretton Woods system. A growing gap between foreign dollar-holdings and U.S. gold reserves after 1955 meant that the international circulation of U.S. dollars as world money was no longer supported by adequate gold backing. The system could then only survive if foreigners were willing to hold dollars as reserve without demanding their redemption in gold. Such global acceptance of the de facto inconvertible dollar reserves allowed the United States to finance its balance-of-payment deficits by issuing its own money as a buyer in the world market. Foreigners, who were the recipients of those dollar outflows, were then in effect giving the United States a continuous line of credit. Of course, they accepted this arrangement only because these dollar reserves enabled them to meet their own international payment obligations.

This so-called *seigniorage* benefit freed the United States from any external constraint.[16] With its own currency having a monopoly status as world money, it was the only country whose capacity to run external deficits was not restricted by its available foreign-exchange reserves. We could therefore run much more stimulative policies and escape recessionary policy adjustments much longer than would otherwise have been possible. This was especially true during the era of the Vietnam War. The postwar expansion of our domestic debt economy was thus given a crucial international extension, with dollar-holders abroad financing much of our excess spending in the United States.

Part III
The End of the New Deal

6

Stagflation and Financial Instability

6.1. From Boom to Stagnation

In the preceding chapter we analyzed how the postwar monetary regime contributed to an unprecedented economic boom during the 1950s and 1960s. Its institutional provision of continuous credit extension and automatic "monetization" of debt helped to finance various channels for spending in excess of current income. The most important sources of excess spending were depreciation charges on industrial capital, consumer purchases of large-ticket items, regular budget deficits, and America's seigniorage benefit. The resulting stimulation on the demand side combined with monopolistic price regulation on the supply side to support real wage growth in line with productivity gains. This combination relaxed the monetary constraint in the production economy, as illustrated by the ability of firms to avoid deflationary price adjustments and to turn the devaluation of their plant and equipment into a source of cash flow.

The stable growth pattern of the postwar boom was very much contingent on increasing debt and regular liquidity injections via endogenous money creation. This debt economy had its roots in the Great Depression, a deflationary crisis which prompted massive debt reduction and monetary reforms toward elastic currency. During World War II, a period of rapid income growth and forced savings, both U.S. consumers and industrial firms further strengthened their balance sheets. Once the war ended, they were therefore in a good position to take on significantly more debt. At the same time, U.S. budget deficits fell from their exceptionally high levels of the war period, thus creating space for more rapid credit extension to the private sector. While the level of total debt in the United States rose in line with the gross national product during the postwar boom, its composition shifted quite dramatically from public debt to private debt. This remarkable long-run stability in the ratio of total debt to GNP illustrates the essentially self-financing nature of the "debt economy," with debtors creating sufficient income gains to meet their debt-servicing commitments. Such balance between debt growth and income gains lasted well into the 1970s.

However, just as earlier expansion phases of long waves inevitably exhausted themselves after two or three decades of rapid growth, so also did the postwar boom eventually come to a close. Profit rates in U.S. industry peaked in 1966 and began a steady decline thereafter. This trend (see Table 6.1) resulted partly from the gradual maturation of many previous "growth" industries, such as automobiles, household appliances, chemicals, and steel, which had initially driven the postwar boom. The accompanying saturation of their markets intensified with the successful reconstruction of the war-damaged economies in Western Europe and East Asia. By the late 1960s other industrial nations, most notably West Germany and Japan, began to challenge the dominance of U.S. industry. Falling rates of return on industrial capital depressed corporate investment activity. This in turn caused capital stock to age more rapidly and the pace of technological change to slow, thereby further eroding profitability. That downward profit-investment spiral slowed the long-term growth capacity of the U.S. economy.[1]

During the 1960s and 1970s the United States devoted about 15 percent of GNP to gross domestic private investment, which was three-fourths of the average among other industrial nations. This ratio seemed to have changed very little during those two decades. But such apparent stability masks a significant deterioration of investment activity during the 1970s. Due to more rapid aging of plant and equipment in U.S. industry, an average three-fifths of that investment was required to replace worn-out capital stock. Hence our net investment share averaged only 6 percent during the 1970s. Half of that went into housing and inventories. So only some 3 percent of GNP was devoted to increasing the stock of plant and equipment, less than half the average share of our major competitors. And that net share exhibited a disturbingly downward tendency, falling by 40 percent from 4.2 percent of GNP in the late 1960s to only 2.6 percent of GNP in the late 1970s.

The spreading stagnation of the 1970s coincided with a trend of accelerating inflation. After years of near stability, prices began to rise more rapidly in the late 1960s. That first inflationary surge was clearly of the classic "demand-pull" variety that which typically characterizes a booming economy (see Table 6.2). An unusually strong and durable recovery (1961–68), only briefly interrupted by the "growth recession" of 1966, had pushed the U.S. economy close to full employment. The key driving force behind this unprecedented expansion was a strongly stimulative fiscal policy. Facing recession (1960–61), President Kennedy introduced large tax cuts and public-works programs. A few years later, in response to the civil rights movement, President Johnson expanded social spending to combat poverty, the so-called Great Society programs, such as Medicaid in 1965. Then his administration had to let military spending grow rapidly in the wake of escalating warfare in

Table 6.1

The Profit-Investment Dynamic of Stagnation

Year	Profit rate	Real investment spending (annual percent change)	Real growth rate of business output
1965	9.9	17.1	6.1
1966	9.7	13.9	5.5
1967	8.8	−2.1	2.3
1968	8.1	3.4	4.5
1969	6.9	5.8	3.0
1970	5.5	−1.5	−0.4
1971	6.1	0.2	3.3
1972	6.7	6.5	6.0
1973	7.7	14.7	6.3
1974	8.2	−0.2	−1.3
1975	7.8	−1.1	−1.7
1976	8.5	3.6	5.7
1977	8.8	10.8	5.3
1978	9.1	13.3	5.8
1979	8.8	8.7	2.3
1980	7.4	−2.4	−1.0
1981	6.7	3.9	1.8
1982	4.8	−4.6	−2.0
1983	5.0	−3.2	4.2

Source: Council of Economic Advisers, *Economic Report of the President,* 1992, Washington, DC, Tables B–10, B–2, and B–9.

Notes: Ratio of after-tax profits (with inventory valuation and capital consumption allowances) to gross domestic product of nonfinancial corporate businesses. Nonresidential fixed investment in plant and equipment in 1987 dollars. Gross domestic product of nonfarm businesses.

Vietnam. Faced with intensifying domestic opposition to the war, Johnson delayed the inevitable tax increase until 1968. This policy combination caused an overheating of the economy.[2]

With the U.S. economy cooling off during the recession of 1969–70, the nature of inflation changed. Slower growth and an accelerating shift in resources from manufacturing to services contributed to stagnant productivity levels throughout the 1970s. At the same time nominal wages began to rise more rapidly, as inflationary expectations took hold in the work force and unions won automatic cost-of-living adjustments in their contracts. This breakdown in the balance between productivity gains and wage growth resulted in rising unit labor costs. Whenever market conditions permitted it, firms passed those cost increases onto higher output prices to prevent their profit margins from shrinking too much. Additional cost pressures arose from explosive price increases for raw materials, most notably food and energy, in global commodities markets during 1972–73 and 1978–79.

Table 6.2

The Demand-Pull Inflation of the Late 1960s

Year	Federal budget surplus (+) or deficit (−) (in billions of dollars)	Unemployment (percent)	Capacity utilization (percent)	Inflation (percent)
1964	−5.9	5.0	85.6	1.8
1965	−1.4	4.4	89.5	2.5
1966	−3.7	3.7	91.1	3.5
1967	−8.6	3.7	87.2	3.1
1968	−25.2	3.5	87.2	4.6
1969	+3.2	3.4	86.8	5.0

Source: Council of Economic Advisers, *Economic Report of the President*, 1992, Washington, DC, Tables B–74, B–37, B–49, and B–3.

Notes: Unemployment rate, all workers (including resident Armed Forces). Capacity utilization is manufacturing output as percent of capacity. Inflation is measured by implicit price deflator of gross domestic product.

6.2. Standard Inflation Theories

The traditional view of ("demand-pull") inflation as a phenomenon of wars and economic booms obviously did not apply to the 1970s. For one, U.S. military spending fell as a share of GNP during that period, following the pullout from Vietnam and the détente with the Soviet Union in the early 1970s. Even more significantly, the long-term secular growth trend clearly slowed down after 1968. This unprecedented combination of rising prices and spreading economic stagnation, commonly referred to as *stagflation*, gave rise to several new inflation theories.

1) "Cost-Push" Theory of Inflation. This approach has its roots in Keynes (1930).[3] Modern cost-push theorists, such as Bowen (1960) or Okun (1975), attribute inflation to nonmonetary influences on the supply side which raise costs and hence prices. They have focused in particular on union wage pressure and administered mark-up pricing as the principal forces of inflation. Other frequently mentioned cost-push factors are resource immobilities contributing to price and wage rigidities, job-information deficiencies, "ratchet" effects resulting from the downward inflexibility of specific prices in response to shifts in the composition of demand, and, more recently, random nonmonetary price shocks, like crop failures, commodity shortages, or oil-price hikes by the Organization of Petroleum Exporting Countries (OPEC).

That approach downplays monetary factors which affect demand. And it relegates expansive monetary and fiscal policy to a passive role of accommodating cost increases in order to maintain high levels of production and employment. From this, it follows that cost- or supply-induced inflation cannot be fought successfully with demand-management weapons, such as restrictive monetary policy. With prices downwardly sticky, a policy of slow money-supply growth is not able to compensate for particular price increases by reductions in other prices and instead triggers declines in output and employment.

2) "Conflict" Theory of Inflation. Quite closely related to the Keynesian theory of cost-push inflation, this approach was developed by left-leaning economists in the United States and Great Britain, most notably Glyn and Sutcliffe (1972), Rowthorn (1977), and Rosenberg and Weisskopf (1981). Following the neo-Ricardian emphasis on distributional conflict, these authors point to the competitive struggle for relative income shares between different groups, especially workers and their employers, as the key impetus for inflation. That struggle tends to intensify during periods of stagnation, when the economic pie does not grow sufficiently to satisfy the claims of all groups at the same time.

3) The "Accelerationist" Hypothesis. Monetarism, a modern version of the age-old Quantity Theory of Money, analyzes inflation as the result of excessively rapid growth in the money supply. From this, it follows that inflation can only be reduced and kept in check if the central bank exercises tight control over the money supply to assure its stable expansion in line with the economy's natural growth capacity (see section 1.4). monetarists thus tend to reject the Keynesian prescription for contracyclical monetary policy.[4] This rejection was based on a critique of the so-called Phillips Curve, which measures a trade-off between unemployment and inflation (see Phillips, 1958).

Introducing adaptive expectations into the Phillips Curve, some monetarists, such as Phelps (1976) and Laidler (1976), have argued that economic agents form expectations about future price behavior on the basis of past experience and learn from error by adjusting their forecasts and behavior in response to unanticipated inflation. Changes in monetary growth can then be shown to have merely transitory effects on excess demand and associated real variables by causing temporary divergences between actual and expected rates of inflation. Eventually, however, expectations will be fulfilled due to error-learning adaptation, so that excess demand will be zero. Thus in the long run monetary growth will influence only the rate of inflation; it cannot affect real variables in steady-state equilibrium. In other words, the long-run Phillips Curve is a vertical line at the economy's "natural" (equilibrium) rate of unemployment. From this, it follows that policy efforts to reduce unemployment below its "natural" level will inevitably lead to ever-accelerating inflation. Here only monetary growth matters as a determinant of inflation, and cost-push factors are ignored.

4) The "Rational Expectations" Approach. Some neoclassical economists have criticized the concept of adaptive expectations in the "accelerationist" hypothesis of monetarists as an inadequate description of how price anticipations are formed. Rational individuals, these critics argued, do not look just at past price changes; they utilize all relevant information about current developments to improve the accuracy of their price forecasts. Consequently, forecasting errors can only arise from random, and thus unforeseen, shocks to the economy, because rational agents will quickly try to learn from any initial mistakes due to incomplete information and will apply any new knowledge to their forecasting procedures.

This theory of "rational expectations," as formulated by Sargent and Wallace (1976) or Poole (1976), has fairly radical implications. To begin with, the only source of departure from steady-state equilibrium accepted here are expectational errors which themselves are short lived and random in nature. Policy-induced changes in the money supply tend to be rapidly absorbed by rational price expectations. Because such changes fail to cause surprises, they have no impact on real variables. Anticipated policy changes only affect the price level. Any trade-offs are purely coincidental and cannot be exploited by systematic policy rules, even in the short run. Hence this approach denies any role for contracylical stabilization policy other than as an influence on the rate of inflation.

Even though they move away from the standard notion of "demand-pull" inflation, the new inflation theories do not give us adequate explanations for stagflation.

• Keynesian "cost-push" theories have the advantage of analyzing inflation as a nonmonetary phenomenon caused by structural changes in the economy, such as downward price rigidity due to monopoly power or the breakdown of the wage-productivity balance. But their emphasis on the wage-price spiral and other cost-push factors boils down to mere tautology, with rising (output) prices viewed as the result of higher (input) prices. Left unexplained here are the origins of cost-price pressures on industry. These are by and large reduced to "exogenous shocks."

• Neo-Ricardian "conflict" theories focus on struggles over income shares but often do not adequately clarify the interrelation between distribution and growth. The size of the pie to be divided up is usually taken as a given. Thus we are not told what made the pie grow more slowly in the first place.

• monetarists completely ignore the structural dimensions of inflation, defining it instead as a purely monetary phenomenon caused by erroneous central bank policy. Their claim of a direct relation between money growth and inflation assumes that goods and services somehow enter the marketplace without price. But in reality producers price their output before exchange takes place. Their price decisions depend on production conditions (unit costs) and market structures (power relations, types of adjustment response to current imbalances). Money supply growth enters the picture ex post, as one of the factors that determine whether or not the prices charged generate sufficient revenues.

• Expectations surely play an important role in determining how well markets function and what the level of economic activity will be. But it is difficult to see how the now-dominant notion of rational expectations can work in practice. If markets are in balance, the presumed state of normality, then everyone must believe that products are correctly priced. Why should anyone in this situation want to look for new information? Thus there seems to be an inherent contradiction between equilibrium and informationally efficient markets. The advocates of "rational" expectations also suffer from a fallacy of composition. What seems rational in the case of an individual is often not so when looked at from a broader social perspective. Operating in the market together, economic agents do not form expectations in isolation. Instead, they are prompted by uncertainty to take each other as a reference point. Correct processing of information in the face of market imbalances may thus give rise to widely shared expectational biases which feed destabilizing overshooting behavior (e.g., speculative manias, panic selling). Moreover, these biases often shift dramatically when they are proved to be mistaken. Such volatile expectations contribute to instability and reinforce the cyclical fluctuations of our economy. In this environment contracyclical policy continues to be a valid undertaking, especially if it manages to stabilize otherwise procyclical expectations.

More generally, the phenomenon of stagflation can only be understood properly if we abandon the neoclassical framework of full-employment equilibrium. Otherwise, we are forced to regard the combination of slowing growth and rising prices as solely the product of mistaken government policies. This is precisely what standard theorists end up arguing. Yet there are deeper reasons why the U.S. economy was rarely near full-employment equilibrium and did not move along a balanced (steady-state) growth path during the 1970s. Actual growth fluctuates around a long-term trend line which is itself subject to change (see our discussion of "long waves" in section 3.2). After 1968 that trend line turned downward.

A second justification for moving beyond the traditional equilibrium framework in any analysis of stagflation is its erroneous assumption of flexible prices capable of quasi-instantaneous adjustments. In reality we can observe often considerable price-adjustment lags in crucial markets. These cannot be explained solely by expectational errors, as neoclassical economists like to believe. Price setters just do not take that long to react to forecasting mistakes. Instead, these delays must be seen as the result of contractual and institutional rigidities which prevent rapid adjustments. With prices responding slowly, restrictive policy tends to trigger protracted output and employment effects. Conservative policy rules, such as letting the money supply grow at 3 percent per year or keeping the budget balanced, may thus reduce inflation only at the expense of inducing recession. This is exactly what happened in 1969–70, 1973–75, and 1979–

82. Each time the downturn took longer before inflation subsided enough to lay the foundations for renewed recovery.

6.3. Stagflation as a New Form of Structural Crisis

None of the aforementioned cost-push or expectation-based theories of inflation related the process of rising prices to deepening stagnation. Although the U.S. economy had experienced simultaneous increases in inflation and unemployment earlier (e.g., 1914–15, 1945–46), those incidences were short lived and mostly due to war-related dislocations. In contrast, the stagflation of the 1970s was much more persistent and, as it endured for more than a decade, grew progressively worse from cycle to cycle (see Table 6.3). What we have here is an historically unique phenomenon. Stagflation has to be understood as a structural feature endemic to the monopolistic accumulation regime during the downswing phase of a long wave.

Such a notion of stagflation as a new form of structural crisis must be able to analyze inflation and stagnation as interrelated, mutually feeding, and therefore necessarily simultaneous processes. The nodal points connecting these two phenomena lie in the production economy where accumulation conditions affecting both growth and price formation are determined. For example, the introduction of highly mechanized production technologies (e.g., assembly lines, robots, computer-aided automation) and the growing use of debt raised industry's share of fixed costs in the postwar period. As a result any decline in output was less likely to be followed by an equiproportional reduction in total production costs. The growing dominance of fixed costs thus caused costs per unit of output to rise whenever production volumes declined, and it is precisely those unit costs that form the basis for administered cost-plus pricing by oligopolistic firms. Stagnation thus fed inflation. But the interrelation operated also in reverse. Intensifying inflation created greater uncertainty about future costs and revenues, thus undermining investment activity and shortening the planning horizon of firms.

Besides stressing the mutually reinforcing linkage between stagnation and rising prices, we must avoid the mistake of the aforementioned approaches that characterized inflation either as the result of nonmonetary (e.g., cost-push) factors or as a purely monetary phenomenon. It comprises both dimensions. Earlier (see section 1.3) we criticized the neoclassical separation between "real" variables (e.g., output, employment) and "monetary" variables (i.e., money supply, nominal prices) as artificial. Obviously, individual decisions and market behavior are profoundly shaped by such nonmonetary factors as technology, contracts, laws, social convention, and policy institutions. Yet at the same time all economic activities are essentially monetary in nature, taking the form of interdependent cash flows between market participants and over time. Any realistic analysis of stagflation must therefore address both the nonmonetary and the monetary dimensions of our cash-flow economy.

Table 6.3

The Stagflation Dynamics of the 1970s

Year	Inflation	Unemployment	Productivity (percent)	Real GDP growth
1966	2.9	3.8	2.1	6.0
1967	3.1	3.8	2.1	2.6
1968	4.2	3.6	2.9	4.1
1969	5.5	3.5	0.0	2.7
1970	5.7	4.9	0.9	0.0
1971	4.4	5.9	3.5	3.1
1972	3.2	5.6	2.7	4.8
1973	6.2	4.9	2.5	5.2
1974	11.0	5.6	–2.0	–0.6
1975	9.1	8.5	2.3	–0.8
1976·	5.8	7.7	2.7	4.9
1977	6.5	7.1	1.4	4.5
1978	7.6	6.1	0.7	4.8
1979	11.3	5.8	–1.4	2.5
1980	13.5	7.1	–0.9	–0.5
1981	10.3	7.6	0.9	1.8
1982	6.2	9.7	0.1	–2.2
1983	3.2	9.6	2.4	3.9

Source: Council of Economic Advisers, *Economc Report of the President*, 1992, Washington, DC, Tables B–59, B–37, B–45, and B–2.

Notes: Inflation based on seasonally adjusted year-to-year consumer price index. Unemployment rate of all civilian workers. Productivity measured as output per hour of all persons employed in the nonfarm business sector. Gross domestic product in 1987 dollars, percentage change from preceding period.

Although the monetarist argument of a direct and unidirectional link between money supply and nominal prices is clearly too simplistic, inflation is certainly related to money. After all, it involves a devaluation of money. In the preceding chapter (see section 5.4) we discussed how the interplay between monopolistic price regulation and elastic credit-money created an inflationary bias in the post-war accumulation regime. That bias expressed the ability of firms to avoid deflationary price wars and to use productivity gains as the basis for regular pay increases. It was precisely this institutional relaxation of the monetary constraint embodied in the inflationary bias that moderated the form of structural crisis from depression to stagflation once the economy moved into the downswing phase of a long wave during the late 1960s.

In order to analyze this fundamental change in the form of crisis we need to understand that the prevailing growth pattern of our cash-flow economy depends on the interrelation between exchange transactions, production activities, credit financing, and creation/circulation of money (see section 2.3). Based on this understanding it becomes possible to analyze how these different monetary circuits may feed inflationary pressures to the point of undermining their own stable expansion.

1) Transfer Gains in Monetary Exchange. In the regime of monopolistic regulation many firms became price-setters rather than price-takers. Highly concentrated market structures facilitated price coordination among firms, and a continuously growing debt economy supported high enough spending levels to make their administrated (mark-up) prices stick in the marketplace. Crucial to this relaxation of the monetary constraint was the institution of elastic credit-money, which allowed debt-financed excess spending to be monetized (see section 5.5). With the linkage of values and prices thus significantly loosened, producers gained greater control over their output prices.

The usual measure of inflation as a rise of the general price level obscures the fact that individual prices do not move in tandem. They do not change at the same rate, either in absolute terms or relative to the prevailing value of the commodity purchased. Instead, in any period their respective changes fluctuate unevenly around a moving average which represents the value of money at the time. For example, some producers may be in a market position to charge extra-high prices, which exceed the level reflecting the given social (average) value of money, without suffering a proportionate decline in sales volume. This is especially likely in the case of firms with a considerable degree of monopoly power (as in oligopolistic industries) and/or highly inelastic demand for their products.

When charging such extra-high prices, sellers gain a sum of money income that is larger than the value embodied in the quantity of output given up in their sales. Conversely, the buyers spend more money than the value gained in their purchases. In other words, sales at prices above those representing the average value of money give rise to *unequal exchange*. In those market situations sellers receive additional income at the expense of losses for their buying customers (or, more generally, those selling at below-average prices). Of course, these buyers can try to recover some of their losses by raising their own sales-prices. But such compensation occurs only later, if at all. In the meantime their losses will have restricted their spending capacity. Transfer gains from "unequal exchange" disappear if and when buyers succeed in passing their cost increases onto their own revenue prices. Initially extra-high prices will then have been generalized into a new average price-level, reducing (ceteris paribus) the value of money in the process.

The temporary nature of transfer gains explains the self-feeding character of the inflationary process. Price-setters will always be tempted to resume their gains through a new round of price increases. In addition, the redistributive effects of inflation contribute directly to stagnation. Agents whose prices tend to rise less rapidly than the average experience continuous income erosion. During the 1970s this was especially true for a majority of workers, all those on relatively fixed incomes (e.g., retirees, welfare recipients), savers, and creditors. Eventually even the initial beneficiaries of accelerating inflation may end up suffering. Their high profitability will at first attract new capital and induce them to expand their production capacity. But at the same time their extra-high price increases will force buyers to cut back purchases and find cheaper substitutes, thereby restricting demand for their products. After 1979 such inflation-induced overproduction especially afflicted oil- and coal-based energy, metals and minerals, agricultural products, and commercial real estate. It is not surprising that all of these sectors were somehow tied to land. That unique resource, characterized by a relatively fixed supply and thus an attractive object of speculation in inflationary periods, made all land-based activities inflation winners during the 1970s.

2) Nominal Accumulation Gains in Production. Firms must spend money now in order to make more money later. Production activities are therefore characterized by the temporal separation of cost outlays and revenue inflows. When the value of money declines over time due to inflation, firms end up measuring their current investment outlays and operating costs at a higher money-value (and thus as a proportionately smaller quantity of money) than later sales revenues. This creates paper profits. During the 1970s, a period of accelerating inflation, paper profits actually masked falling profitability in U.S. industry. Additional accounting profits accrued to firms from conscious undervaluation of depreciation and inventory charges measured in their balance sheets on the basis of historic cost rather than current dollars (see section 5.5).

As is the case with transfer gains in monetary exchange, nominal accumulation gains in production last only for a limited time. Eventually absorbed by the inevitable replacement of obsolete plant and equipment or restocking of inventories at higher cost, they too can only be continued through renewed price increases. Furthermore, the growing reliance of industrial firms on fictitious paper profits had insidious side effects which contributed to slowing growth.

• Shareholders gradually lost confidence in the validity of financial statements as those deviated more and more from reality. This had negative consequences for the stock market, with share prices performing dismally during much of the 1970s. From its peak in 1968 the inflation-adjusted value of shares, as measured most broadly by the Standard & Poor's 500 index, fell by more than 50 percent until 1980.

• Corporate managers themselves lacked accurate data with which to evaluate investment projects and operating performance. That problem compounded the difficulty of making correct investment decisions in an inflationary environment when future cost- and revenue-prices become that much more uncertain.

• At the same time, managers earned a great deal more as a result of those paper profits, because much of their pay was directly tied to reported earnings. Management remuneration thus came to be increasingly divorced from performance.

• It should also be noted that corporations had to pay real tax and dividend dollars on their accounting-based paper profits.[5]

3) Destabilization of Credit Financing. Accelerating inflation made U.S. industry more dependent on external funds. Just to stay even during periods of rising prices, companies had to expand their sales, assets, and profits at the average rate of inflation. But because profits were smaller (in dollar volume) than sales or total assets, an expansion of all these items at the same rate meant that the volume of the former grew by lower dollar amounts than the volume of the latter. This funding gap, translating into correspondingly larger needs for external funds, rose even further in the wake of declining profitability.

Stagflation, besides making firms more dependent on external funding, also reinforced industry's aforementioned preference for debt over equity (see section 5.5). With the stock market entering a sustained period of decline after 1968, issue of new equity shares became increasingly difficult and costly. At the same time, the prospect of repaying the debt later with devalued dollars further encouraged borrowing. This was especially true whenever interest rates lagged behind the inflation rate, something that happened frequently during the 1970s.

As firms became more leveraged, they ended up in a more vulnerable position (see Figures 7.2.c and 7.2.d in the next chapter). Rising debt-servicing commitments added to fixed costs. The increasingly rigid cost structure meant higher break-even points and greater fluctuations of profits for any given change in sales, thus greater risks. Firms reach a critical level of overextension when their debt-servicing costs rise faster than their income gains and have to be covered by additional borrowing.[6]

While on the one hand engendering more credit demand by debtors, accelerating inflation created on the other hand worsening credit risks and losses for the suppliers of those funds. Inflation is characterized by two simultaneous but opposite price movements: rising output prices (of goods and services) and falling asset prices (of financial instruments).[7] The paper profits in production activities mentioned above were thus accompanied by inflation-induced capital losses in the credit system. Additional income transfers from creditors to debtors occurred whenever interest rates lagged behind accelerating inflation. Those losses came on top of larger risks from increasingly volatile interest rates ("price risk") and declining creditworthiness of many highly leveraged debtors ("default risk").

As those losses and risks grew with rising inflation, creditors would eventually try to protect themselves by tightening their credit terms. This response occurred repeatedly during the 1970s, usually near the cyclical peak (1969, 1974, 1979, 1981), when both inflation and credit demand tended to accelerate rapidly. In that environment worried creditors suddenly demanded higher nominal interest rates, removed funds from low-yielding assets (disintermediation), and shortened the time horizon ("maturity") of their loans.

This recurrent tightening contributed to the spectacular rise in the cost of capital for businesses during the 1970s, which exceeded that of their labor costs per unit of output. Capital costs include interest rates on bank loans, the cost of raising money in securities markets, as well as price levels for plant and equipment. Together with unit labor costs they determine the "core" inflation rate. Moreover, the cost of capital functions as the so-called hurdle rate, the minimum rate of return required for investment projects. Squeezed between rising hurdle rates and falling profit rates, U.S. industry cut back its capacity-enhancing net investments during the 1970s (see also section 6.1 above).[8]

4) The Declining Quality of Money. Gradual devaluation of money by persistent inflation undermines each of its functions.

• Rising prices erode money's ability to serve as store of value, undermining the incentives for saving. Consumers spend a larger share of their income more rapidly to beat future price hikes, a shift in behavior which tends to feed accelerating inflation. And whatever small portion of income households still save is moved out of zero-interest transaction deposits or low-yield savings accounts to avoid inflation-induced losses in the value of their holdings.

• At the same time, money's function as a means of debt settlement suffers. Inflation reduces the effective debt burden of borrowers. This in turn induces greater credit demand. To avoid transfer losses, creditors will be forced to charge more for their loans.

• The growing uncertainty about future prices, indicating a less effective role for money as the standard for prices, increases investment risks and makes long-term planning more difficult. Forward-money contracts require indexing to protect the value of their cash-flow commitments, but that practice only reinforces the spread of inflation.

• Finally, in situations of acute hyperinflation even money's most basic function, that of a medium of exchange, suffers. Workers demand shorter pay periods and prefer to do their shopping early. Hoarding of goods spreads. This feeds panic buying and causes acute shortages. Market participants spend a growing amount of time trying to keep up with rapid price changes. Once-easy transactions become more cumbersome, as the entire complex structure of payment deferrals (e.g., trade credit, check-clearing) breaks down. Sellers demand immediate cash and then scurry to transform their money-income into tangible assets. Finally, barter begins to crowd out monetary exchange as the public loses all confidence in the increasingly worthless currency.

The inflation-induced erosion of money's functions during the 1970s destabilized economic activity. The simultaneous decline of savings and increase in credit demand in response to accelerating inflation created strong pressures in the credit markets for higher interest rates, especially near cyclical peaks. It was also typically then that massive disintermediation of funds out of deposits subject to the rate ceilings of the Federal Reserve squeezed banks and thrifts. Unstable prices harmed long-term investment activity while they encouraged speculative activity seeking to exploit expected price movements for short-term gains. At times, as in 1973 and 1979, speculation grew into a flight out of money itself. This translated into sharply rising prices for certain speculative objects (e.g., oil, gold, other metals, diamonds, artwork, real estate) and massive sell-offs of high-inflation currencies in the foreign exchange markets. Both reactions accelerated inflation further. The hidden effects of inflation on taxes (bracket creep, tax liabilities on paper profits from historic cost accounting) encouraged the rapid growth of an "underground economy" made up of off-the-book barter and cash transactions without a paper trail.

Eventually, when inflation is out of control, the erosion of money's functions can unleash such powerful forces of destabilization that the monetary authorities are forced into drastic action. This happened in the United States, especially in 1969–70, 1973–75 and 1979–81, when the central bank imposed much more restrictive policies to slow down inflation and counteract rampant speculation. Although standard economists, especially monetarists, define such tightening in purely quantitative terms of slower money-supply growth, the actually dominant objective of the central bank is to restore the quality of money in the face of its abandonment. We should not forget that in each instance of tightening the Federal Reserve responded to rapidly spreading speculative flights out of the dollar. In situations of hyperinflation the collapse of money's functions can become so acute that the monetary authorities have to introduce new currency units amid a broad austerity program, as happened during the 1980s in Israel, Argentina, and Brazil.

Spreading stagnation and accelerating inflation are thus two sides of the same coin, that of a deepening structural crisis which typifies the downswing phase of a long wave. The interplay between worsening profit prospects and declining net investments slows the growth capacity of the economy. Individual agents try to counter this slowdown through an inflationary process of transfer gains and paper profits. But the aggregate effects of this process serve only to reinforce the stagnation of industrial capital while they undermine the prevailing circuits of financial capital.

This type of crisis is much more gradual and moderate than earlier depressions. The latter typically involved a brutal shrinkage process based on large-scale destruction of physical capital, mass unemployment, and widespread defaults and bankruptcies, as well as collapsing financial institutions. Individual agents, facing the monetary constraint then with unmitigated force, responded to conditions of overproduction with price wars and a mad scramble for scarce liquidity. Stagflation, in contrast, avoids such deflationary adjustment ("debt-deflation spiral") because of the institutional relaxation of the monetary constraint. Monopolistic regulation of prices and wages has encouraged a downwardly rigid price structure. Fiscal stabilizers counteract any decline in economic activity through automatic increases in budget deficits. Lender-of-last-resort mechanisms support financial asset values through additional liquidity injections during incidences of acute instability in the credit system. As long as the central bank accommodates increased lending and the banking system continues its asset expansion, borrowers can maintain spending levels despite stagnating income by taking on more debt.

6.4. The Debt-Inflation Spiral and Credit Crunches

This institutional relaxation of the monetary constraint allows producers to reduce the effects of their profit squeeze and defer final settlement of their mounting payment obligations by taking on more debt. But rising debt-servicing charges in the wake of growing indebtedness add in turn to fixed costs. Their increase intensifies inflationary pressures. As prices rise rapidly in response to higher unit costs, the debt burden becomes less onerous. Debtors are now in a position to repay their loans with devalued dollars. At the core of stagflation is therefore a *debt-inflation spiral*. In this spiral, inflation serves as the mechanism that spreads private losses and risks in the wake of overproduction as well as credit overextension to everyone using the national currency. Such socialization of losses and risks moderates the otherwise violent destruction of industrial capital and the devalorization of financial assets through the devaluation of money itself.

This debt-inflation spiral had its inherent limits, giving rise to a growing tension between rising credit demand by increasingly leveraged borrowers and mounting losses for lenders in the wake of accelerating inflation. Eventually creditors would respond by tightening their credit terms. This step usually began with a speculative euphoria after recovery had given way to a highly inflationary boom, as happened in 1968, 1973, and 1978. Then creditors abandoned long-term financing and increasingly switched their funds to activities with good potential for short-term capital gains from rapid price increases (e.g., energy and other raw materials, "hard" currencies of low-inflation countries, real estate). Such speculation was typically the first sign of a spreading creditors' revolt, not just against risks and losses from long-term credit financing but also in response to the declining quality of money.

Those speculative movements into short-term investments often triggered a credit crunch soon thereafter.

• For one, the tightening of credit terms for long-term funds thereby engendered acutely restricted the ability of already heavily indebted borrowers to maintain their current spending levels. In this context it is worth noting that industrial firms typically undertake their major expansion projects and begin to face eroding profit margins precisely then, in the late stages of recovery just before the cyclical peak.

• Many debtors would at that point switch to short-term borrowing so as not to lock themselves into expensive long-term funds. But such growing reliance on short-term debt created its own tensions. The financial position of debtors would only grow more precarious in the face of shorter repayment schedules and maturity mismatch between long-term assets and short-term liabilities. Moreover, that switch pushed up short-term rates faster than and finally above long-term rates, thereby reversing the normal maturity structure of interest rates (a positively sloped "yield curve"). This switch to a negatively sloped yield curve has been a standard feature of every "credit crunch" in the United States since 1966.

• This reversal of the yield curve tended to squeeze the profits of financial institutions with short-term liabilities and long-term assets (e.g., thrifts, banks), as their cost of new funds began to exceed revenues from their investments. Central bank ceilings, which prohibited banks and (after 1966) thrifts from raising their deposit rates beyond an artificially low maximum, helped to prevent such a negative yield spread, but only at the expense of triggering massive disintermediation of funds out of those low-yield instruments. Coming on top of capital losses from devaluing assets with below-market coupon rates and growing default risks, either type of squeeze forced banks to curtail lending activity and instead raise their liquid cash assets.

• In the wake of these multiplying cutbacks, credit-financed speculation tended to collapse as expected increases in prices and sales failed to materialize in the wake of declining demand. Resulting losses only reinforced the credit crunch.[9]

That credit-crunch dynamic gave the stagflation crisis of the 1970s a decidedly cyclical character. Whenever inflation heated up too much and credit demand reached unsustainable levels, financial instability would trigger a lending squeeze and subsequent recession. Those downturns (i.e., 1966, 1969–70, 1973–75, 1979–82) would force inflation, interest rates, and debt levels of many debtors lower, while allowing financial institutions to rebuild liquidity. Eventually these market adjustments set the stage for renewed recovery, which would last for a few years until its inevitable demise in the next credit crunch.

Starting with the short slowdown ("growth recession") in 1966, each subsequent recovery phase ended in the United States with progressively higher inflation rates and more excessive debt levels. Consequently, each cyclical turning point engendered worse credit crunches and deeper recessions. Underlying that supracyclical intensification of stagflation was a gradual deterioration of accumulation conditions in industry. Capacity utilization rates peaked each time at lower levels (see Table 6.4). On the one hand, this build-up of excess capacity acted as a disincentive for capacity-enhancing net investment. On the other hand, the resulting deficiency in modernization contributed to the rapid aging of plant and equipment.[10] This increasing obsolescence of its capital stock hurt the pro-

Table 6.4

Capacity Utilization Rates in U.S. Industry (output as percent of capacity)

Year	Total industry	Manufacturing
1966	—	91.1
1967	86.4	87.2
1968	86.8	87.2
1969	86.9	86.8
1970	80.8	79.7
1971	79.2	78.2
1972	84.3	83.7
1973	88.4	88.1
1974	84.2	83.8
1975	74.6	73.2
1976	79.3	78.5
1977	83.3	82.8
1978	85.5	85.1
1979	86.2	85.4
1980	82.1	80.2
1981	80.9	78.8
1982	75.0	72.8
1983	75.8	74.9
1984	81.1	80.4
1985	80.3	79.5
1986	79.2	79.0
1987	81.4	80.4
1988	84.0	83.9
1989	84.2	83.9
1990	83.0	82.3
1991	79.4	78.2

Source: Council of Economic Advisers, *Economic Report of the President*, 1992, Washington, DC, Table B–49.

ductivity and competitiveness of U.S. industry, making it in turn much more difficult to run production at high levels.

The long-term erosion of industry's productive apparatus was the primary reason for its rising unit costs and falling profit rates. Against this background the growing use of debt financing inevitably led to weaker balance sheets, as debt-servicing charges took increasingly large bites out of corporate income. The gradual intensification of stagflation was thus at least partly fed by the deepening financial fragility of U.S. industry. A steadily expanding number of producers required more and more external funds to make up for their cash-flow gaps even as they were becoming less able to afford those funds. Eventually lenders would respond to this declining creditworthiness of their largest borrowers by tightening their credit terms or altogether refusing to supply new funds. Such belated efforts to impose discipline tended to come with sudden force, usually in response to signs of acute distress in credit markets. As stagflation deepened for more than a decade, those incidences of financial instability grew in force, until they reached a dramatic climax in the Great Recession of 1979–82.

The Disintegration of the Postwar Monetary Regime

In our preceding discussion of stagflation we referred to this phenomenon as a form of structural crisis (see section 6.3). That type of crisis has to be distinguished from recessions, which represent relatively short-lived adjustment processes in the normal course of business cycles. A structural crisis has much deeper roots. It typically occurs only during the downswing phases of long waves, when the tendencies of our economic system toward overproduction and credit overextension have become sufficiently dominant. In such a situation the required balances for stable expansion break down, and hitherto effective modes of regulation no longer assure a modicum of stability. Structural crisis, whether in the form of stagflation or depression, therefore denotes a long-term process of institutional erosion and policy failure. The tensions set off in its wake cause the existing accumulation regime to disintegrate in a series of interdependent ruptures. These in turn trigger forces of reorganization which may eventually lead to a new and more viable regime.

We can observe precisely such a combination of paralysis, disintegration, and restructuring during the 1970s. What concerns us in this chapter is how stagflation, with its debt-inflation spiral and credit crunches, destroyed the pillars of the postwar monetary regime one by one.

7.1. The Collapse of Bretton Woods

The international monetary system put into place at the end of World War II was the first component of the postwar monetary regime to break down. On the surface, such a collapse appears to be a sudden chain of events. But that is only the final outcome of underlying and gradually deepening disequilibria which at some point explode into the open as acute moments of crisis. In the case of Bretton Woods, this process began when one of its key institutional features, the convertibility of international dollars into gold on demand at a fixed rate of exchange, could no longer be guaranteed by the United States.

Worldwide production of gold, a metal with notoriously inelastic supply, failed to keep up with the rapid growth of international trade. For example, between 1929 and 1966 the annual global production volume of gold slightly more than doubled, from 18.3 million ounces to 40.3 million ounces. But during the same period the volume of world trade quintupled. Thus gold's role diminished steadily. Its share in total world money fell from 68.6 percent in 1951 to 62.7 percent in 1961 and 41.3 percent in 1970, while the combined share of international dollars and members' reserves at the IMF grew in inverse proportion.

In addition, the limited gold supplies underwent major redistribution. Due to redemptions and speculation, U.S. gold reserves declined from $22.7 billion in 1951 (equal to 68.3 percent of the non-Communist world's total gold reserves) to $17 billion (43.7 percent) in 1961 and $11.8 billion (29.9 percent) in 1970. During the same period total currency reserves of the capitalist world (except the United States), which were all supposedly convertible with U.S. gold reserves, rose from $13.8 billion in 1951 to $21.3 billion in 1961 and $49.7 billion in 1970.[1] By the late 1950s U.S. gold reserves no longer sufficed to back all dollars in international circulation.

The return to currency convertibility during 1958 made the economies of Western Europe less dependent on dollars and suddenly turned the dollar shortage of the 1950s into a glut. This prompted European central banks to cash in their excess dollars for gold at a massive rate. Between 1958 and 1960 U.S. gold reserves fell by an alarming $5.1 billion because of such conversions (compared to only $1.7 billion before 1958). At the same time the formation of the European Economic Community, under the Treaty of Rome in 1957, sparked a massive wave of direct investments by U.S. multinationals in the new Common Market. This capital outflow only added to the excess supply of international dollars.

When Charles De Gaulle, a strongly nationalistic and anti-American politician, returned to power in France during 1958, he adopted the proposal of Jacques Rueff to "solve" the problem of the dollar glut through a doubling or tripling of the gold price. The Eisenhower administration rejected this idea, and in the process American antipathy to gold as an instrument of pressure by other nations on the United States sharpened considerably. President Kennedy then made the U.S. balance-of-payments problem a key issue in his election campaign. His statements fed expectations abroad of an imminent dollar devaluation. This triggered a speculative run into gold during October 1960, which pushed its price on the open (and unofficial) market in London from the official level of $35 per ounce to $40.

The United States, under the leadership of Robert Roosa at the U.S. Treasury, introduced several counteracting measures to deal with this first crisis of the Bretton Woods system:

• The leading industrial powers set up a gold pool to feed gold to the private market and thereby keep its free-market price near the official price.

• The U.S. Treasury also agreed to issue bonds denominated in other currencies ("Roosa bonds"), which allowed foreign governments to reduce their dollar holdings.

• The Federal Reserve set up currency "swap lines" with other central banks and in the process used foreign currencies for dollar purchases to relieve the dollar glut.

• In 1961 the Federal Reserve launched its aforementioned operation twist. That maneuver aimed at higher short-term rates to slow capital outflows, while it pushed long-term rates down to stimulate a sluggish domestic economy (see section 5.3).

• Finally, in 1964, the United States introduced capital controls to slow dollar outflows.[2]

But these initiatives were no substitute for what was really needed, a more fundamental adjustment mechanism to deal with the persistent dollar glut. In 1959 Robert Triffin had defined the fundamental dilemma of the Bretton Woods system in a compelling and prophetic testimony before the Joint Economic Committee of the Congress. The rapid growth of trade and investment, he argued, could only be sustained with more rapid reserve creation than hitherto possible. In the present system this could only come about by means of much larger U.S. payments deficits. But such increases in our external deficits would eventually create growing doubts abroad about the quality of the dollar. Those could easily trigger large conversion demands, which in the end would destroy the gold-dollar link, akin to what happened with the pound in 1931. Should the United States want to avoid this situation by returning to a surplus, it would reduce global liquidity and thereby inhibit the expansion of world trade. As the only way out of this dilemma Triffin proposed the creation of an international reserve unit, much like Keynes's original Bancor Plan for the Bretton Woods Conference in 1944, as a new liquidity device capable of replacing gold and dollars.[3]

Underlying the "Triffin dilemma" is the inherent inadequacy of national currencies as a form of world money. The international economy consists of exchange transactions and money transfers, in which the various national economies confront each other as buyers and sellers. Payment obligations between countries from their participation in international exchange are for this reason direct debts of buyers to sellers (via their respective central banks). Just as individual buyers or private banks within domestic circulation cannot properly settle their debts by simply issuing their own money, so can no country effectively pay for its excess purchases abroad by issuing and then transferring its own currency to foreign sellers. This is why the country whose currency serves as an internationally accepted medium of exchange has the unique advantage of being able to finance its own imports and capital exports by what amounts to continuous credit supplied by foreigners.[4]

This so-called seigniorage benefit accruing to the issuer of world money (see section 5.5, including note 16) came into full play once dollars in international circulation had become de facto inconvertible by the late 1950s. To the extent that foreigners agreed to hold their excess dollars without reconversion into gold, the United States in effect did not have to pay for its external deficits with other countries. Under those conditions the system in place could only survive as long as foreigners continued to have confidence in the dollar. But, given Bretton Woods' particular institutional arrangements, that confidence was bound to erode eventually.

A national currency typically emerges as world money, because its issuer is the dominant power in the world economy at that time (e.g., Great Britain before World War I, the United States after 1945). But that dominance usually does not last. Because the industries of the hegemonic power set the international standards of technology, product development, and organizational efficiency, the competitive pressure they exert on others is often stronger than their own drive for continuous innovation to maintain market leadership. In addition, lower wage rates, more modern capital stock (reflecting more recent investments), and various protectionist measures typically facilitate the "catching up" process of other countries, such as West Germany and Japan during the 1960s. Incapable of adjusting currency prices in response to those changes in international competitiveness, the Bretton Woods' system of fixed exchange rates actually ended up reinforcing this "catching up" process. The failure after 1961 to devalue the dollar relative to the mark and yen kept German and Japanese exports artificially cheap and made imports into those countries more expensive.

In the absence of appropriate exchange-rate adjustments, the United States could have defended the overvalued dollar by imposing a dose of fiscal or monetary restraint to lower the excessive U.S. balance-of-payments deficits. But our policy-makers, freed from any acute external constraint by America's seigniorage benefit, failed to take this kind of action. Following President Kennedy's large tax cuts, the Johnson administration introduced new social programs in the mid-1960s and then rapidly expanded the United States' military involvement in Vietnam.[5] Add to these fiscal stimuli the reflationary effects from the rapid build-up of excess dollars abroad whose reflux increased the supply of funds to the U.S. banking system (see note 4). This policy combination further weakened the dollar by feeding import demand and inflation in the United States.

By 1968 the dollar's twin sources of vulnerability, its inconvertibility vis-à-vis gold and overvaluation relative to other currencies, had become serious enough to undermine confidence in the key currency. U.S. inflation suddenly began to accelerate above the rates experienced elsewhere (from 1.9 percent in 1965 to 4.7 percent in 1968) without providing foreign dollar-holders adequate compensation through sufficiently higher interest rates. At the same time, a flood of imports had sharply reduced the U.S. trade surplus (from $4.9 billion in 1965 to only $600 million in 1968). When speculative sell-offs started to put acute downward pressure on the dollar, the United States had to act.

• In January 1968 mandatory controls were imposed on direct foreign investments by American firms.
• In March 1968, amid panic purchases of gold, the exhausted "gold pool" was replaced by a two-tier system which allowed a private gold market with fluctuating free-market prices to coexist with official gold transfers at the fixed price of $35 per ounce.
• During the same month the 25 percent gold coverage requirement for the U.S. money supply was eliminated. This freed the remaining gold supplies for conversion demands by foreign dollar-holders.

In March 1968 the leading industrial nations also agreed to introduce so-called Special Drawing Rights (SDRs), which were issued by the IMF and backed by the fund's gold reserves. Surplus countries committed themselves to accepting $9.5 billion worth of newly issued SDRs between 1970 and 1972 in exchange for an equivalent amount of their own currencies, which could then be distributed to debtor countries. In this way the SDRs acted as a reserve asset with which to settle official payments obligations among central banks arising from trade and investment imbalances between member countries. But the introduction of this new liquidity device, a decade after Triffin's proposal, came at a time when the world was already awash in liquidity and needed instead an adjustment mechanism to deal with the overvalued dollar.[6]

Later in 1968 the Johnson administration finally agreed to a tax increase, followed by tighter monetary policy. This policy switch helped to strengthen the dollar, but only at the expense of triggering a recession during 1969–70. With unemployment rising, the newly elected Nixon administration adopted strongly reflationary fiscal and monetary policies during 1970. But renewed acceleration of inflation and deteriorating U.S. trade figures in the wake of this policy switch soon began to once again exert downward pressure on the dollar.

By now a new factor had entered the equation. With U.S. balance-of-payments deficits pumping a growing amount of excess dollars into international circulation, it was only a question of time before banks outside the United States began to accept dollar-denominated deposits and loans. Starting in the late 1950s, this so-called *Eurodollar* market emerged as a global private banking network beyond the reach of national governments. Transnational banks and their corporate customers used this parallel credit system not least to circumvent domestic regulations.[7] During 1968–69, in response to rising interest rates and a severe credit shortage at home, U.S. banks borrowed heavily from the Eurodollar market through their foreign subsidiaries. This reduced foreign dollar holdings and thereby alleviated the dollar glut temporarily. But when U.S. credit conditions eased, the repayments of these loans combined with additional dollar outflows in response to higher interest rates abroad. As a result, short-term U.S. capital flows shifted dramatically from a positive (inflow) $5.8 billion average for 1968–69 to a negative $6.5 billion in 1970.

Such massive capital outflows set the stage for a major dollar crisis in 1971. Dollars accumulating in the Euromarket could be easily switched in and out of currencies and countries. That unregulated and globally integrated banking system thus became a perfect conduit for currency speculation. Pressure on the dollar continued to mount throughout 1970 and early 1971 in response to rising interest rates in Europe as well as steadily worsening U.S. inflation and balance-of-payments figures. The Nixon administration faced this situation with a policy of "benign neglect," thereby forcing foreign central banks to absorb most of the dollar sales by private holders and speculators.[8] Their dollar purchases, having the same effect as open-market purchases, expanded domestic bank reserves and money creation. In this way U.S. inflation was effectively "exported" to the rest of the world. Efforts by foreign central banks to counteract this involuntary monetary expansion proved futile, since the interest rates increased thereby only attracted further dollar outflows and sales.

This gradually building dollar crisis reached an explosive peak in August 1971 amid news of the first U.S. trade deficit since 1893 and publication of a report by the highly respected Reuss subcommittee of the Congressional Joint Economic Committee, which recommended a devaluation of the dollar. Faced with conversion demands by France and a British request to reactivate the Fed's swap lines, the Nixon administration finally severed the dollar's link with gold on August 15. The closure of the U.S. gold window was part of a broader program which included wage and price controls as well as an import surcharge. This so-called New Economic Policy completed a gradual turn toward a more nationalistic U.S. course begun earlier with the policy of benign neglect. The strategy was designed to turn the dollar problem into a bargaining chip with which to pressure Europe and Japan into trade concessions. Moreover, Nixon's convertibility suspension transformed the inevitable dollar devaluation from a sign of weakness into a show of American power and shifted the blame for domestic unemployment to the Japanese and Europeans. Finally, the move also reduced gold's role in the international monetary system and thus reasserted the monopoly status of the dollar as world money.

The declaration of inconvertibility addressed the first dollar problem but left open the question of what to do about its overvaluation. Continued instability in the foreign-exchange markets made coordinated exchange-rate adjustment among the leading industrial nations a matter of great urgency. Even though Nixon's import surcharge had soured relations between the United States, Japan, and Western Europe, in December 1971 their governments managed to agree on a comprehensive overhaul of currency prices. That so-called *Smithsonian Agree-*

ment combined simultaneous currency revaluations, ranging from 7.5 percent for the Italian lira to 17 percent for the yen, with a devaluation of the dollar against gold by 8 percent. It also tried to make the system of fixed exchange rates somewhat more flexible by widening the "band" for permissible currency price fluctuations from plus or minus 1 percent from the set level to plus or minus 2.25 percent.

But the new exchange rates failed to calm the foreign-exchange markets. As uncertainty over the future capacity of the dollar to maintain its monopoly status as world money deepened, transnational banks and multinational corporations decided to diversify their currency portfolios. Much of this diversification took place in the Euromarket, where the market share of other key currencies (e.g., mark, yen, Swiss franc) began to grow rapidly. Banks and corporations soon found that they could avoid exchange losses and earn large capital gains by altering the currency composition of their assets and liabilities. This institutionalization of currency speculation in the early 1970s fed an extraordinary growth of currency trading. The daily volume of the global foreign-exchange market rose, according to estimates by Giddy (1979), from \$25 billion in 1970 to more than \$50 billion in early 1973 and to \$100 billion by the end of that year.[9]

In this environment it became impossible to defend fixed exchange rates, once market sentiment had shifted against a particular country and its currency. In June 1972 Great Britain responded to a speculative run out of the pound by letting its currency float downward. Near the end of 1972 the dollar came under pressure, mostly in response to a large increase in the U.S. trade deficit (from \$2.9 billion in 1971 to \$6.4 billion in 1972). Then, during the crisis-ridden first quarter of 1973, about \$10 billion in private capital flows left the United States for the Euromarket, where they were changed into other currencies. These outflows first forced the Swiss to let the franc float and then triggered a second dollar devaluation (by 10 percent) in February. Barely two weeks later a new wave of dollar selling hit Europe, forcing the closure of the currency markets after European central banks had spent \$4 billion in a single day (March 1) to defend the dollar. When the markets reopened in mid-March, Germany and other member nations of the European Economic Community had agreed to a joint float against the dollar.

7.2. Flexible Exchange Rates as a Source of Global Instability

Such a system of floating (i.e., market-determined) exchange rates had long been urged by many economists, especially monetarists.[10] Their advocacy of price deregulation in foreign-exchange markets stressed two benefits, greater stability and an increased degree of autonomy for domestic policy-makers. In their opinion, trade imbalances between countries would disappear rather quickly, once currency prices could adjust immediately to any underlying disequilibria. This improved market response should also remove much of the incentive for speculation, thereby reducing short-term capital flows. Moreover, central banks would no longer have to maintain artificially fixed exchange rates by intervening in the foreign-exchange markets and adjusting the money supply. Freed from such constraints, monetary authorities could then pursue domestic policy objectives more effectively.

However, the actual experience with flexible exchange rates after 1973 did not bear out these arguments. For one, market-determined currency prices failed to balance international trade. In addition, as payments imbalances between countries intensified, capital flows between countries grew dramatically in volume. A large proportion of these capital flows consisted of speculative "hot money" flows in and out of currencies, which made exchange rates increasingly volatile. Consequently, central banks continued to intervene very actively in currency markets and force often dramatic adjustments in the domestic money supply in order to reverse damaging movements in exchange rates. In other words, most predictions by the advocates of freely fluctuating exchange rates turned out to have been wrong.

This dismal predictive record is not surprising, considering that many of their assumptions were erroneous:

• monetarists saw flexible exchange rates as determined by rapid adjustments in trade flows. Therefore, they argued, a depreciation would quickly reduce imports and boost exports, so that any such decline in the currency price was ultimately self-limiting. But this argument underestimated the degree to which global interdependence and intracompany trade between different subsidiaries of multinational corporations had reduced the price elasticity in foreign trade.

• This inelasticity meant that exchange-rate movements affected prices of exports and imports much more quickly than trade volumes. Given this difference in response time, currency depreciation often had the perverse *(J-curve)* effect of initially increasing trade deficits. With price changes outpacing volume adjustments, a lower currency would at first raise the import bill of the depreciating country while at the same time lowering its exports earnings.[11]

• The J-curve effect, by raising the trade deficit at first, brought additional supplies of the depreciating currency into the market. With import prices rising more rapidly, domestic inflation typically heated up as well. Both factors tended to reinforce downward pressure on an already declining exchange rate. The reverse occurred with appreciating currencies. These factors help to explain the unmistakable tendency of exchange-rate movements to overshoot supposed equilibrium levels of "purchasing power parity" in both directions. During the last two decades, currency prices have moved in distinct multiyear cycles with increasingly large amplitudes (see Figure 7.1).

• Since the early 1970s many countries have engaged in competitive devaluations as a new form of monetary protectionism (see section 7.3). These "currency wars," first among the industrial nations and since the onset of the global debt crisis in 1982 extending to the majority of developing countries, have reduced the effectiveness of each individual currency devaluation and have necessitated correspondingly larger downward movements in exchange rates.

• The monetarist advocacy of deregulated currency prices assumed that national economies remained separated from each other by barriers to resource mobility and could therefore be shielded from international disturbances. This insular view implied the absence of globally integrated capital markets, as if the Euromarket did not exist. In reality, however, huge sums nowadays move into and out of countries and currencies within seconds, at the push of a button. Short-term capital flows across the globe, motivated by exchange-rate expectations or seeking to exploit interest-rate differentials, have come to dominate the world economy.[12] No single country can defend itself against a concerted speculative attack on its currency. Starting with the failure of Britain's Labour government in 1967 to prevent a pound devaluation, we have seen many instances of speculators forcing governments into dramatic policy reversals. It is also worth noting that such "hot money" flows thrive on and in turn exacerbate exchange-rate instability.

7.3. Dollar Devaluation and Global Stagflation

These negative repercussions of flexible exchange rates occurred in the context of a steadily weakening dollar during the 1970s (see Figure 7.1). The initial dollar devaluations in 1971 and 1973 marked a long overdue adjustment to the catching up of Europe and Japan in the 1960s. With the collapse of fixed exchange rates in March 1973, the United States was free to seek an additional edge for its producers in an increasingly competitive environment by letting the dollar float downward. This strategy, actively pursued during the second quarter of 1973, in late 1974, and from mid-1976 to the fall of 1978, was an extension of the nationalistic policy course adopted in 1971 (see section 7.1). By making imports more expensive and exports cheaper, a lower dollar could be expected to improve the competitive position of U.S. industry both at home and abroad.

Normally, countries with large balance-of-payments deficits have to combine currency devaluation with restrictive policies aimed at reducing domestic demand. In other words, they must cut trade and budget deficits in order to calm speculative pressure on their currency or to comply with IMF conditions. Not so the United States! As the sole beneficiary of seigniorage it could escape such an external constraint, provided that foreigners continued to accept its currency as an international medium of exchange. Its currency devaluation, rather than being part of a larger austerity package, was actually tied to the exactly opposite policy course. In 1971–73 both U.S. budget deficits and money supply expanded rapidly (see Table 7.1). These stimulative policies triggered lower U.S. interest rates and higher trade deficits, which in turn created downward pressure on the dollar.[13]

Figure 7.1 **Exchange Rate (Mark/Dollar) and Purchasing Power Parity**

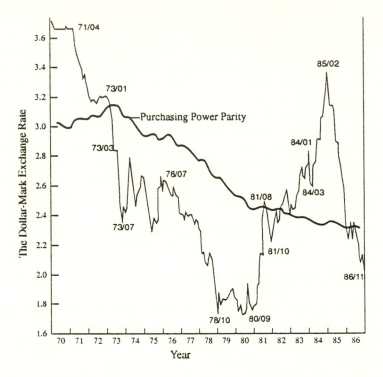

Source: Stephan Schulmeister (1987), "An Essay on Exchange Rate Dynamics," Discussion Paper no. 8(87), Wissenschaftszentrum Berlin—Research Unit Labor Market and Employment, p.7. Reprinted with permission of the author.

This depreciation strategy was coupled with active U.S. steps against alternative forms of world money in order to protect the international status of the dollar.

• After closing its gold window in 1971, the United States tried to undermine gold's continued importance as a reserve asset and for official settlements between countries. Its policy of "demonetizing" gold, pursued between 1973 and 1976, comprised regular sales of U.S. gold reserves, abolition of the official gold price, and elimination of both the IMF's "gold tranche" (i.e., the portion of a member's quota that was contributed in gold) and the "gold coverage" of the IMF-issued SDRs.

• After 1972 the United States also used its veto power to block new issues of SDRs, a limited form of world money to begin with (see note 6).

• At this point other currencies, such as the mark and yen, were not in a position to challenge the dollar. Chronic trade surpluses of Germany and Japan

Table 7.1

U.S. Policy Reflation and Dollar Devaluation 1971–1973

Year	Money supply growth (in percent)	Federal budget deficits (in billions of dollars)	International value of the dollar (3/73 = 100)	Increase in global reserves (in billions of dollars)
1970	6.5	–2.8	121.1	92.6
1971	13.5	–23.0	117.8	130.6
1972	13.0	–23.4	109.1	158.7
1973	6.9	–14.9	99.1	180.9

Source: Council of Economic Advisers, *Economic Report of the President*, 1992, Washington, DC, Table B–65, B–74, B–107; 1974, Table C–92 (global reserves);

Notes: Money supply M2. Multilateral trade-weighted value (nominal) of the U.S. dollar, March 1973 = 100. International reserves comprised of monetary authorities holdings of gold (valued at 38 dollars per ounce), Special Drawing Rights and Reserve Positions in the International Monetary Fund, and convertible foreign exchange.

limited the supply of these currencies to the rest of the world, and both countries resisted the growing use of their monies in international transactions. Fearing that such a movement to world-money status would cause their currencies to appreciate, they did not want to hurt their export industries.

The dollar devaluation, while helping to improve U.S. trade performance by 1973, also fueled inflationary pressures both at home (via higher import prices) and abroad (via larger U.S. capital outflows). Rising U.S. balance-of-payments deficits in 1972 pumped a great deal of extra liquidity into the global economy. This led to a rapid expansion of world trade, with especially strong demand for raw materials. At the same time the suppliers of these commodities, paid across the globe in dollars, suffered eroding profit margins because of the decline in the value of that currency. Helped by strong demand and mounting speculation in commodities, they responded with massive price hikes. This process culminated in a quadrupling of oil prices (from $3 to $12 per barrel) in October 1973, following supply disruptions from the "Yom Kippur" war between Israel and its Arab neighbors.[14]

Most mainstream economists have characterized the oil price explosion in 1973 (and again in 1979) as an "external" shock. This view ignores, or at least downplays, the direct effect of dollar depreciation on commodity prices as the underlying structural trigger for that market disruption. Instead, standard theory stresses the existence of an international cartel among thirteen oil-producing nations, OPEC, and its exploitation of temporary disruptions in oil supplies (i.e., the Arab-Israeli War in 1973, the Iranian Revolution in 1979). While surely reinforcing the price hike, those factors could not have arisen so forcefully without prior destabilization of global commodity markets by the depreciation-driven acceleration of inflation. It is no coincidence that precisely the same sequence of policy reflation in the United States' dollar decline and more rapid inflation set off another explosive increase in oil prices during 1979.

Because of oil's strategic role as a basic energy input in most industries, OPEC's price hike in late 1973 had a huge impact on the entire world economy. Much like a large tax increase, that move left everyone using oil suddenly with much less income to spend on other products. Moreover, most oil-importing nations adopted more restrictive macroeconomic policies to combat sharply accelerating inflation and deteriorating trade balances in the wake of OPEC's price hike. These effects caused a synchronized global recession which only began to bottom out in early 1975.

The international monetary system survived this downturn remarkably well. Flexible exchange rates, even though themselves a reinforcing element in the destabilization of the world economy during the early 1970s, also facilitated market adjustments. To the extent that OPEC's price hikes increased the differences in inflation rates among industrial nations, relative currency prices could now change more easily to reflect that divergence. Of course, at times the often sudden shifts of exchange rates in this process created huge losses among currency speculators. Between June and October 1974 two transnational banks, Germany's Bankhaus Herstatt and the Franklin National Bank of New York, collapsed from losses suffered in speculative currency trades. Their failures sent shock waves through the Euromarket, with only blue-chip banks able to obtain funds there during late 1974 and early 1975. Foreign-exchange trading slowed dramatically during that period. But this crisis was successfully contained, with the central banks of the leading industrial nations agreeing in the *Basle Concordat* to extend their lender-of-last-resort support and bank supervision to the Euromarket.[15]

Following the steep decline of economic activity and disinflation during the first half of 1975, the United States resumed more stimulative monetary and fiscal policies. Once again that policy reflation was accompanied by continued dollar devaluation (with its trade-weighted index declining from 105.6 in 1976 to 88.1 in 1979). Rising U.S. balance-of-payments deficits spread domestic monetary expansion abroad, as increases thereby engendered in dollar outflows added to international monetary reserves. With the United States and Western Europe actively discouraging long-term investments by OPEC in their own economies, a large portion of these surplus funds ended up in short-term Eurodollar deposits. The industrial nations, under domestic pressure to cut foreign assistance, then urged their banks to lend these surplus OPEC funds to developing countries with large external deficits. This so-called recycling of "petro-dollars" allowed world trade to expand rapidly in the late 1970s.

During that recovery, U.S. trade performance worsened significantly, moving from a surplus of $9.5 billion in 1975 to a deficit of $33.9 billion in 1978. That deterioration was due in part to continued erosion in competitiveness of U.S. industry, with import penetration of U.S. markets actually rising despite a falling dollar. In addition, the continuous dollar decline prevented the United States from reaching the upward leg of the J-curve, because volume adjustments in trade constantly lagged behind devaluation-induced changes in prices. This worsening trade balance fed the dollar overhang abroad. Coupled with rising domestic inflation fueled by more expensive imports, it therefore added to the downward pressure on the currency.

In the first half of 1977 the Carter administration urged Germany and Japan to allow more imports from the United States and to stop central bank interventions which prevented appreciation of their currencies ("dirty float"). When this failed, U.S. Treasury Secretary W. Michael Blumenthal began to "talk down" the dollar. His June 24 speech, introducing what the Europeans called a policy of "malign neglect," poured gasoline on simmering embers in nervous foreign-exchange markets. Speculative sentiments against the dollar intensified rapidly, and the currency weakened considerably. In the absence of any counteracting response from the Federal Reserve, the central banks of Western Europe and Japan were forced to support the dollar in order to protect their export-dependent industries. In 1977 they spent about $35 billion, which added to their already excessive dollar reserves and forced a rapid expansion of their domestic money supplies.[16]

After more than $70 billion had flowed out of the United States in just sixteen months, the Carter administration finally abandoned its policy of malign neglect. On November 1, 1978, the industrial nations announced a dollar rescue package. Its centerpiece was a $30 billion war chest of foreign-currency reserves, acquired by currency swaps and U.S. bonds denominated in other currencies ("Carter bonds"), which the Federal Reserve would use to buy dollars thrown into the market by speculators. As part of the package the Fed also raised its discount rate by a full point. For the first time since the introduction of Bretton Woods in 1944, U.S. domestic economic policy had become subject to external constraint.

The rescue package did not calm the foreign-exchange markets for long. By then the expectational bias against the dollar had grown so strong that the support program was simply "too little, too late" to stop the bandwagon effect among speculators. The prospect of exchange-rate gains from portfolio shifts into appreciating currencies proved irresistible. Moreover, the rise in U.S. interest rates associated with the dollar-defense program was not enough to compensate for rapidly rising inflation. "Real" (inflation-adjusted) returns on dollar-denominated assets were much lower than comparable rates in other currencies. Consequently, speculators soon resumed their dumping of dollars. Besides snapping up marks and yen, they also bought large amounts of gold and silver, the last refuge of scared investors.

In early 1979 the global economy experienced its second "oil shock" in six years. The same combination of accelerating inflation, dollar weakness, and supply disruption (in the aftermath of the Iranian Revolution) at a time of high demand allowed oil producers to once again drive the price of oil sharply higher (from $13 at the end of 1978 to $22 by October 1979). That shock spilled rapidly over into the currency markets, not least because OPEC members decided to diversify out of the dollar.[17]

At that point it became clear that the weakness of the dollar had finally begun to threaten its status as world money:

• OPEC announced its intention to be paid in a basket of currencies rather than dollars.

• The formation of the European Monetary System (EMS) in the same year promised to lessen Europe's dependence on dollars and to boost the global position of the mark.

• The IMF began discussing plans for a "Substitution Account" which would have reduced the global dollar overhang and significantly expanded the role of SDRs.

• Most dramatically, the phenomenal rise in the price of gold (from $200 per ounce at the end of 1978 to $450 in October 1979) amid panic buying once again proved gold's continued importance as the most attractive store of value during periods of uncontrolled inflation or depression. The U.S. strategy of "demonetizing" gold had ended in spectacular failure.

Against this background of acute crisis, the world's leading central bankers gathered in Belgrade (Yugoslavia) for the annual meeting of the IMF. There Paul Volcker, the new chair of the Federal Reserve, came under heavy pressure to do something about the combination of exploding U.S. inflation and a collapsing dollar. In the midst of these deliberations Volcker suddenly departed. A few days later, on October 6, he announced his dramatic response—the abandonment of accommodation. Henceforth, the Federal Reserve would aim to restrict money creation in the banking system by restricting the growth of bank reserves rather than try to keep short-term interest rates low. This shift in operating targets caused U.S. interest rates to double within three months. In March 1980 the Fed reinforced its new policy of restraint through selective controls on consumer credit. That double squeeze plunged first the U.S. economy and then the rest of the world into the deepest slump since the Great Depression.

7.4. The Limits of Accommodating Monetary Policy

Volcker's dramatic policy reversal has been widely characterized as the conversion of the U.S. central bank to Monetarism. That variant of standard theory rejects the Keynesian prescription of discretionary central bank actions for short-term stabilization purposes and instead favors a long-term policy of stable money growth (see section 1.4). For this purpose the monetarists have all along wanted the central bank to focus on monetary aggregates and to keep the annual expansion of the money supply within a certain supposedly non-inflationary range. This is precisely what Volcker appeared to have done when he adopted the growth of bank reserves as the Fed's new operating target in October 1979.

Until then, and for most of the postwar period, the Federal Reserve had shown a distinctly Keynesian bias. After the accord with the Treasury in 1951 (see section 5.3) had removed its obligation to "peg" Treasury bond yields at artificially low levels, the central bank was free to develop a discretionary policy course. During the 1950s and early 1960s the Fed focused primarily on stabilizing money-market conditions. In practice this meant a policy of accommodating shifts in the public's demand for money (and bank credit) by corresponding changes in money-supply growth, in order to keep interest rates stable. Besides using open-market operations toward this objective, the Fed had several means at its disposal to influence interest rates. These included changes in the discount rate, pegging the Federal funds rate below a fixed target, imposing deposit rate ceilings on bank deposits (Regulation Q), and pressuring commercial banks to change the prime rate ("moral suasion"). Between 1951 and 1965, when inflationary pressures were by and large absent, the Fed could successfully accommodate rapid credit expansion while it assured low interest rates.[18]

With inflation taking root in the United States during the mid-1960s and continuing to accelerate thereafter, the Keynesian dominance began to wane. Following the influential article by Friedman (1968), a growing number of economists began to stress the connection between a rapidly growing money supply and higher prices. At the same time, policy-makers saw their efforts at policy stimulation repeatedly threatened by the often sudden surges of inflation during the late stages of recovery, as in 1968, 1972–73, and 1978–79. With price stability gradually replacing full employment as the primary policy issue during the 1970s, monetarists were in a strong position to push their agenda of balanced budgets and steady monetary expansion.

The acceleration of inflation during the 1970s thus enabled the monetarists to gain steadily in influence.[19]

• Their first big policy success came with the collapse of Bretton Woods and its replacement by a system of flexible exchange rates and inconvertible currencies as world money in 1971–73. Ironically, it was precisely that deregulation of currency prices which, as a trigger for competitive devaluations, fed inflationary pressures across the globe (see section 7.3).

• At the same time, monetarists pressured the Federal Reserve to focus more on bank reserves and monetary aggregates and less on credit conditions. In early 1972, amid rapidly rising inflation, the Fed finally complied by choosing "reserves available for private nonbank deposits" (RPDs) as its new operating target. This policy experiment was abandoned in early 1976, because the RPDs proved to be a highly elusive target and did not relate in stable fashion to monetary aggregates.

• In late 1972 the Fed for the first time began to set specific numerical growth ranges for the key money-supply measures M1 and M2, a practice continued to date.[20] In March 1975, amid growing concerns about persistent inflation despite a deepening recession, Congress asked the Fed to specify and disclose annual growth targets for monetary and credit aggregates on a quarterly basis (House Concurrent Resolution #133).

• In October 1979 the monetarists gained their last and most decisive victory in the United States, when the Fed abandoned its post-1976 policy of keeping short-term interest rates below inflation in favor of tight restrictions on money growth.

Even though the growing influence of Monetarism during the 1970s is indisputable, it is nonetheless inaccurate to characterize the dramatic shift in monetary policy during 1979–80 solely in voluntaristic terms of an ideological conversion within the Federal Reserve. The declining influence of Keynesianism, and with it the corresponding reemergence of the Quantity Theory of Money, merely reflected the eroding effectiveness of essentially accommodating monetary policy in an environment of deepening stagflation. In other words, that policy reversal must be placed in a structural context, as a spectacular expression of institutional limitations on the type of contracyclical monetary policy favored by the orthodox Keynesians.

The stagflation conditions, which emerged in the 1960s, limited the effectiveness of central bank accommodation. Beginning in 1965–66, each business cycle saw the Federal Reserve reverse its "easy money" policy near the cyclical peak.

• In December 1965 the Fed raised the discount rate (from 4 percent to 4.5 percent) to slow down an overheating economy. This was followed by restricting the growth of bank reserves in April and May of 1966 (see note 20 on the "proviso" clause). When these measures failed to slow down the extremely rapid pace of bank lending, the Fed squeezed the commercial banks in June by raising the discount rate to 5 percent, limiting bank access to the discount window, and lowering the rate ceilings on small time deposits.

• In response to rapidly rising inflation during 1968, the Fed raised the discount rate in December 1968 and again in April 1969. This was followed by tight restrictions on bank reserves through open-market sales and higher reserve requirements. At the same time the Fed kept deposit rate ceilings below market rates, thus triggering disintermediation of funds out of deposits and forcing banks to rely on more expensive sources of funds. That squeeze was reinforced in July 1969, when the Fed made Eurodollar loans and repurchase agreements, two hitherto unregulated sources of bank funds, subject to reserve requirements.

• Throughout 1973 the Fed tightened gradually, to keep once again rapidly rising inflation in check. But OPEC's price hike in October 1973 prompted a temporary easing of monetary policy in response to a supply-induced recession. In early 1974, however, heavy loan demand and rapid expansion of monetary aggregates resumed, while inflation continued unabated. Monetary policy tightened again, pushing interest rates to historic highs. By September 1974 the economy had entered the second stage of the recession, which in early 1975 led to a remarkably steep decline in economic activity.

Such tightening by the central bank near the cyclical peak occurred each time against a background of mounting imbalances in the credit system. On the one hand, the late stages of recovery were typically a period of very strong credit demand, fueled by booming investment activity in industry and the cheapening of credit due to accelerating inflation (i.e., negative "real" interest rates, the prospect of repaying loans at maturity with devalued dollars). The final surge of borrowing activity usually came when industrial firms suddenly experienced larger funding gaps because of declining profitability and rising cost pressures (see Figure 7.2). At the same time, lenders faced not only higher default risks from excessively leveraged borrowers but also the prospect of growing losses from the inflation-induced decline in the value of their financial assets. They responded to this deteriorating investment climate by withdrawing funds from low-yield and/or high-risk assets, by shortening the maturities of their loans, and by pursuing speculative short-term gains. These responses only served to undermine the already precarious position of many debtors. The result of this clash between growing borrowing needs and tightening supplies of loanable funds was a full-blown "credit crunch" which inevitably triggered recessionary readjustment (see also section 6.4).

Let us now return to the last and most virulent credit crunch in 1979. After the Federal Reserve ended its experiment with RPDs in 1976, it once again chose the Federal funds rate on short-term loans by banks with excess reserves to reserve-deficient banks as its key operating target. In an effort to support the post-1975 recovery, this rate was kept within a fairly low range. Whenever the rate approached its upper limit, the Fed simply added bank reserves through open-market purchases. This particular practice of accommodation revealed a key dilemma for the central bank: its inability to control interest rates and monetary aggregates at the same time. If the Fed wanted to keep short-term rates low relative to inflation, then it had to allow for procyclical money creation.

From 1976 to 1979 this policy of "pegging" the Federal funds rate at artificially low levels exacerbated both inflationary pressures and related imbalances in the financial markets. Strong credit demand, itself a by-product of recovery, was automatically "monetized" through injections of additional bank reserves.

Figure 7.2a **Cyclical Dynamics of Credit Crunches, 1966–1982: Investment Contracts and Orders**

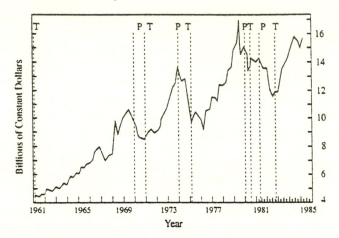

Source: Based on data from U.S. Department of Commerce, Bureau of Economic Analysis, *Business Conditions Digest.*

Notes: Contracts and orders for plant and equipment. Seasonally adjusted quarterly averages of monthly data. In constant (1972) dollars. P and T indicate business-cycle peaks and troughs, as defined by the National Bureau of Economic Research..

Figure 7.2b **Cyclical Dynamics of Credit Crunches, 1966–1982: Profit Rate**

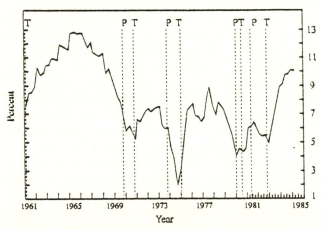

Source: Based on data from U.S. Department of Commerce, Bureau of Economic Analysis, *Survey of Current Business.*

Notes: Profits of nonfinancial corporations as a percentage of domestic income. Profits are after taxes with inventory valuation and capital consumption adjustments. Seasonally adjusted quarterly flows at annual rates.

Figure 7.2c **Cyclical Dynamics of Credit Crunches, 1966–1982: Financing Gap**

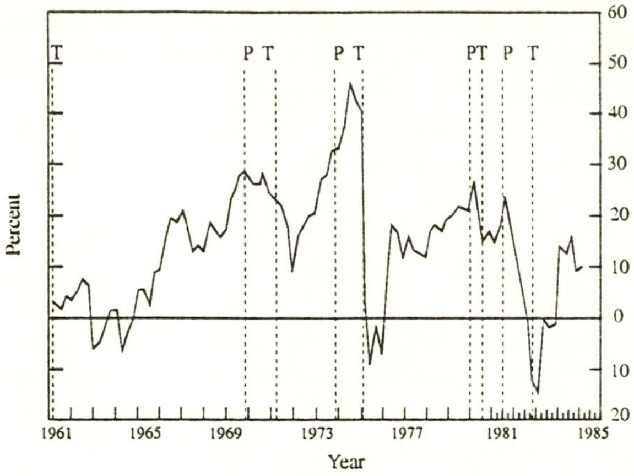

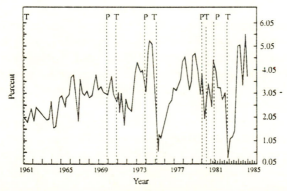

Source: Based on data from Board of Governors of the Federal Reserve System, *Flow of Funds Accounts.*

Notes: Financing gap (equals capital expenditures minus internal funds) of nonfinancial corporations as a percentage of capital expenditures. Seasonally adjusted quarterly flows at annual rates.

Figure 7.2d **Cyclical Dynamics of Credit Crunches, 1966–1982:**
Nonfinancial Corporate Debt

Source: Copyright © Martin Wolfson (1982), *Financial Crises: Understanding the Postwar U.S. Experience*, pp. 142, 143, 145, 152. Reprinted with special permission of the author.

Notes: Credit market borrowing of nonfinancial corporations, calculated from seasonally adjusted quarterly data, as percentage of gross national product. Based on data from Board of Governors of the Federal Reserve System, *Flow of Funds Accounts* (for debt of nonfinancial corporations) and U.S. Department of Commerce, Bureau of Economic Analysis, *Survey of Current Business*, National Income and Product Accounts (GNP).

The resulting acceleration of money creation acted as an institutional underpinning for gradually rising inflation, not least because it facilitated the realization of higher prices. Keeping interest rates constantly below inflation rates, that "easy money" policy soon set off a self-reinforcing debt-inflation spiral of growing demand for cheap credit and rapid money creation. Low U.S. interest rates also fed the decline of the dollar and increases in U.S. balance-of-payment deficits, which further aggravated inflationary pressures both at home and abroad (see section 7.3).

This spiral of debt financing and its monetization, with the falling dollar as its global transmission mechanism, triggered increasingly serious stress conditions in the credit system during 1978–1979 (see Table 7.2). The combination of negative "real" interest rates and spreading inflationary expectations engendered a borrowing binge of already heavily leveraged debtors and made creditors increasingly nervous. Disintermediation, shortened investment horizons, and speculation all began to spread as expressions of jittery financial markets. When this *creditors' revolt* finally took the form of a flight out of money itself, with the dollar collapse and gold price explosion as its most dramatic manifestations, the Fed could no longer sustain accommodation of credit demand. At that point the policy of keeping interest rates below inflation had so exacerbated underlying imbalances that it had to be abandoned.

In this context the aforementioned policy switch by the Fed in October 1979 takes on a rather different meaning from simply marking a conversion to Monetarism. Even though targeting the quantity of money, the new policy must be understood as a desperate attempt by the Fed to restore the seriously eroded quality of money. The primary motivation of the central bank was to let U.S. interest rates rise dramatically in order to halt the decline of the dollar and to break the debt-inflation spiral. As emphasized in the fascinating account of recent Federal Reserve actions by Greider (1988), Volcker used the growing influence of Monetarism as a convenient legitimation to justify abandonment of the increasingly counterproductive focus on low interest rates in the midst of a dangerous crisis of confidence.

Stagflation thus rendered Keynesian policy prescriptions for contracyclical monetary policy focused on money-market conditions and short-term interest rates increasingly impotent. Such a policy course contributed to credit overextension amid accelerating inflation, followed by retrenchment of nervous lenders. Faced with a combination of excessive leveraging by debtors' and creditors' revolts at the cyclical peak, the Fed had to abandon its "easy money" policy (as in 1965, 1968, 1973–74, and 1979). The adoption of a more restrictive, anti-inflationary policy course, while aiming to restore the eroded quality of money, also helped to deepen the credit crunch and to push the economy into recession. Once that downturn had forced inflation, interest rates, and corporate debt levels sufficiently lower, the Fed could resume its accommodating policy and thereby encourage recovery (as in 1966, 1970, 1975–76, or 1980).

Table 7.2

The Credit Crunch of 1978–1979

Year	Consumer price index (in percent)	Treasury bills rate (in percent)	Savings deposits (in billions of dollars)	Dollar index
1977	6.7	5.27	492.0	103.4
1978	9.0	7.22	481.8	92.4
1979	13.3	10.04	423.7	88.1
1980	12.5	11.51	400.1	87.4

Source: Council of Economic Advisers, *Economic Report of the President*, 1992, Washington, DC, Tables B–60, B–69, B–66, B–107.

Notes: Consumer price index measured from year-end to year-end rather than average per year to show rising trend more clearly. The Treasury bills rate applies to new 3-month issues. The currency index measured as multilateral trade-weighted value (nominal) of the U.S. dollar, March 1973 = 100.

Recurrent central bank switches between restraint and accommodation indicate a process of endogenous limitation imposed by the business cycle on monetary policy. These procyclical policy shifts were required to contain the particular form of financial instability characterizing the different phases of the credit cycle. Credit overextension and speculation at the top of the cycle ("upward limit") necessitated tightening. Spreading defaults and losses at the bottom of the cycle ("downward limit") induced easing. Thus captured in a "stop-go" pattern, monetary policy contributed to the progressive deepening of cyclical fluctuations after 1965.

7.5. Financial Innovation and Regulatory Erosion

In addition to these cyclical "stop-go" policy switches, the postwar monetary regime was further weakened by accelerating financial innovation. Beginning in the early 1960s, commercial banks and other credit institutions introduced new instruments designed to circumvent existing regulations and avoid the sudden cut-off of funds in the wake of central bank restraint. In addition, financial institutions exploited regulatory loopholes to expand their operations beyond the control of domestic monetary authorities. Unlike other forms of product development in industry, financial innovations can be rapidly introduced and do not normally require large initial capital outlays.

The first wave of innovation took place during the 1960s, when rising inflation made zero-yield checking accounts and low-yield savings deposits less attractive (see Table 7.3). While thus suffering an erosion of their traditional deposit base, the banks faced continuously large loan demand. To bridge this gap between sources and uses of funds, commercial banks began to rely increasingly on a variety of borrowed liabilities.

• In 1961 Citibank introduced so-called negotiable certificates of deposit (CDs). Their large denominations (usually $1 million) and relatively high yields, coupled with the ability to resell them before maturity, made these CDs attractive to corporations.

• Following the legal clarification of their status (in the Bank Holding Company Acts of 1956 and 1970) the number of bank holding companies (BHCs) spread rapidly, from only 50 in 1957 to 3,500 in 1981. BHCs had several advantages over banks, including their ability to sell commercial paper (i.e., short-term notes with an active resale market) and then to deposit the borrowed funds in their bank subsidiaries.[21]

• In the Federal funds market, banks traded large amounts of liquid funds (i.e., excess reserve balances held at the Federal Reserve) with one another for periods as short as one day.

• So-called repurchase agreements (RPs, repos) involved a bank selling short-term securities, mostly Treasury bills, with the stipulation that, after a period of time, it would buy those back at a predetermined price. Such repos were thus in effect collateralized short-term loans.

• Finally, domestic banks often borrowed funds from their foreign subsidiaries in the Eurodollar market. In the absence of any regulatory costs these Euroloans carried lower rates than comparable domestic sources of funds.

Growing use of borrowed liabilities had a profound impact on banking strategy during the 1960s. Historically, banks had managed their need for liquidity to accommodate deposit withdrawals by holding a sizable portion of assets which could be easily converted into cash (e.g., reserves, Treasury bills). Such "asset management" had forced banks to take their liability structure as fixed and to tailor their asset holdings to the deposit variability characteristics of their liabilities. But borrowed liabilities freed banks from having to rely on low-yielding assets for liquidity. Whenever they needed additional funds for liquidity, they could simply borrow those funds in the money market. Sudden or unexpected deposit outflows could be offset by purchase of new funds. This enabled banks to target their asset growth as given and then to adjust their liabilities as needed. The new strategy allowed banks to grow more rapidly and to invest a larger portion of their funds in higher-yielding assets, such as bank loans or long-term municipal bonds.

The shift from asset management to liability management in the 1960s marked a major turning point in the postwar evolution of our debt economy. Banks soon found that, as long as expected marginal returns on new loans

Table 7.3

Deposit and Borrowed Liabilities of U.S. Commercial Banks
(in billions of dollars)

Year	Demand deposits	Small time and savings deposits	Negotiable CDs	Federal funds and security RPs	Commercial paper	Miscellaneous liabilities
1966	150.4	127.7	33.4	1.7	3.6	8.0
1967	162.5	145.8	39.3	1.7	4.4	9.1
1968	175.8	159.7	46.0	2.6	4.5	13.0
1969	180.5	165.8	30.5	8.7	9.8	21.4
1970	189.9	179.9	54.0	4.7	9.5	26.4
1971	202.9	208.5	66.6	8.7	9.9	33.7
1972	222.6	233.0	84.5	10.8	9.6	49.7
1973	235.4	245.6	122.5	27.1	13.9	58.4
1974	235.2	263.7	161.9	28.5	27.0	59.8
1975	242.8	303.5	152.0	29.9	27.6	75.8
1976	256.1	358.0	136.7	43.8	30.6	80.8
1977	280.6	386.1	162.7	54.4	35.0	93.4
1978	306.0	399.3	211.2	76.9	41.1	115.9
1979	332.4	428.8	225.0	94.3	54.5	123.8
1980	342.0	473.6	272.2	114.8	68.2	139.4
1981	350.6	513.7	323.8	129.6	86.9	199.9
1982	369.8	611.4	329.5	138.8	99.6	194.2
1983	385.7	742.2	281.2	153.6	108.3	216.6
1984	414.9	816.8	319.5	155.2	118.1	232.7
1985	468.8	897.2	331.2	186.4	111.0	255.7
1986	562.9	968.7	334.4	205.6	101.9	289.3
1987	543.1	996.1	376.6	215.8	108.9	338.8
1988	560.0	1,069.2	418.6	236.6	106.0	380.9
1989	556.2	1,165.8	450.7	274.4	106.1	484.7

Source: Board of Governors of the Federal Reserve System, *Flow of Funds Accounts, Financial Assets and Liabilities, Year-End 1966–1989*, September 1990, Washington, DC, pp. 17–18.

exceeded the expected marginal cost of funds, they could increase income by acquiring additional funds through liability management. More and more they used borrowed liabilities to meet increases in loan demand. Customers no longer had to be denied loans because of a lack of funds. But the rapid expansion of their lending activity made possible by such liability management ultimately left U.S. banks in a more vulnerable position. For one, the ratio of bank capital to risk assets fell precipitously through the 1960s. Moreover, the maturity mismatch from funding loans with short-term liabilities exposed banks to added risk during periods of volatile interest-rate movements. Especially in times of credit crunch, when the yield curve typically turned negative, the costs of their variable-rate liabilities could easily rise above their fixed-rate loans and thus cause operating losses.

Liability management had an impact on the effectiveness of monetary policy. This practice allowed banks to lend irrespective of available excess reserves, thereby moving the money-creation process beyond the reach of the central bank.[22] However, this was not the only factor that reduced central bank control over private bank money. The Federal Reserve also had to contend with the proliferation of new "near money" deposits beyond its regulatory reach. These deposits were not subject to reserve requirements and avoided interest-rate ceilings, so they were attractive to both issuers and depositors.

• In the late 1960s, when inflation rose for the first time above domestic rate-ceilings on savings deposits, the leading U.S. banks encouraged their largest corporate customers to deposit excess funds at market yields in Eurodollar deposits. Then they simply borrowed these funds back from their Euromarket branches. This circuit conveniently bypassed Regulation Q, even after the imposition of reserve requirements on Eurodollar loans in July 1969 (see section 7.4).

• During the 1970s, with (zero-interest) demand deposits made increasingly unattractive by rising inflation, banks and other depository institutions (thrifts, credit unions) introduced several alternative transaction accounts which paid interest. Key among those were share drafts offered by credit unions, negotiable orders of withdrawal (NOWs), and the use of automatic transfer systems between customer savings accounts and checking accounts in commercial banks (Automatic Transfer of Savings, or ATS). By offering depositors check-writing privileges, these accounts could effectively be used as a medium of exchange.

• Starting in 1978, depository institutions began to face intense competition from money-market mutual funds (MMMFs). These offered depositors higher yields and limited check-writing privileges (allowing checks above $500). Since deposits there were invested in money-market instruments, a large portion of these funds returned to banks in exchange for negotiable CDs, bankers' acceptances, repos, or commercial paper issued by BHCs. The net effect of this circuit was therefore not so much disintermediation of funds out of the banking system but a significant rise in their cost to depository institutions.

The combination of borrowed liabilities and "near money" deposits allowed private banks to lend irrespective of available excess reserves and thereby weakened central bank influence over the money-creation process. At the same time, the Federal Reserve also suffered from a gradually intensifying "membership crisis." Between 1947 and 1978 the proportion of commercial banks that were members of the Federal Reserve System dropped from 48.8 percent to 38.5 percent, and the fraction of all deposits held by member banks decreased from 85 percent to 72.3 percent. Between 1967 and 1977 alone, 551 banks left the system. The trend became especially worrisome in the mid-1970s, when a growing number of larger national banks decided to switch to a state charter. The move allowed them to relinquish membership in the Federal Reserve System and enjoy the less onerous reserve requirements of state banking commissions. Each withdrawal lessened the Fed's control over bank reserves.[23]

7.6. Financial Instability and the Lender of Last Resort

During the postwar boom the number of bank failures averaged fewer than 10 per year and involved mostly small banks that were suffering from mismanagement or fraud. They were easily taken care of by the FDIC, which arranged for their takeover by a healthier bank. Otherwise, no serious financial crisis requiring active central bank intervention occurred between 1945 and 1965.

That picture of tranquillity changed with the onset of stagflation. As this structural crisis deepened from the late 1960s onwards, it triggered increasingly serious incidences of financial instability in the domestic banking system. These were themselves a clear indication of deteriorating conditions in the U.S. economy. Over the long run, they reflected the growing financial fragility of debtors who had taken on a great deal of debt and could no longer generate the same kind of income gains as during the boom years. What aggravated the problem even more was the tendency of corporations and households to cover widening funding gaps in the face of stagnant income through increased borrowing.

Apart from this structural dimension of financial fragility, the incidences of acute crisis in the credit system during the 1960s and 1970s were a decidedly cyclical phenomenon. They all occurred in the aftermath of credit crunches, as a by-product of recessionary adjustment to overproduction in industry and to credit overextension (see section 3.1). These conditions typically originated earlier, in the boom phase of recovery near the cyclical peak, when speculative euphoria and rising inflation fueled excessive leveraging.

The gradual erosion of the postwar monetary regime contributed directly to the progressive deepening of financial crisis. With banks increasingly able to borrow funds and bypass interest-rate ceilings (see section 7.5), the Federal Reserve could no longer restrain bank lending as effectively. Wojnilower (1980) and Wolfson (1986, part II) have convincingly documented how banks used borrowed liabilities, "near money" deposits, and lines of credit to accelerate their lending activity even after the central bank had already decided to tighten their reserves. This phenomenon grew more pronounced from one cyclical peak to the next. The Fed's inability to rein in the banks helped to prolong the process of credit overextension, and with each cycle the end result of this policy failure, acute financial instability, became more severe.

For nearly four decades, from the late 1930s to the mid-1960s, the U.S. monetary authorities had not had to intervene as lender of last resort, except for occasional FDIC assistance to failing banks. But starting with the "growth recession" in 1966, each downturn required progressively more extensive crisis management by the Federal Reserve.

• Worried by rising inflation, the Fed had introduced a series of tightening moves after December 1965 to slow down the rapid pace of bank lending. These measures, which included raising the discount rate, limiting access to its discount window, higher reserve requirements for large time deposits, and keeping Regulation Q ceilings on time deposits and negotiable CDs below market rates, eventually squeezed depository institutions. First, thrifts suffered massive disintermediation. Then commercial banks, cut off from their normal sources of funds, began to sell off municipal bonds to generate needed funds. With financial markets increasingly unsettled as a result, in August 1966 the Fed decided to reverse its policy course and pump more reserves into the banking system. Banks, which agreed to cut back on their business loans and stop liquidating their municipal bonds, were given easier access to the discount window.[24]

• From December 1968 onward monetary policy once again turned restrictive, to cool inflationary pressures and excessive bank lending. In July 1969 the Fed even made outstanding drafts due to Eurodollar transactions, net borrowings of banks from their own foreign branches, and funds obtained from repurchase agreements subject to reserve requirements. Then, in June 1970, the bankruptcy of Penn Central triggered a flight to quality in the commercial paper market. Because most corporate borrowers maintained backup lines of credit from the banks in case holders of commercial paper refused to roll them over, this crisis threatened to create a potentially enormous demand for bank funds. The Fed responded by opening up the discount window for banks in need and by suspending rate ceilings on large-denomination CDs.

• The two-stage recession of 1973–75, the deepest downturn since the 1930s and itself a period of repeated tightening efforts by the Fed in response to stubbornly high inflation, created several episodes of distress in the credit markets. In early 1974 a combination of rising interest rates, tighter credit supplies, rising construction costs aggravated by materials shortages, and a depressed housing market created serious liquidity pressures for so-called Real Estate Investment Trusts (REITs).[25] Some banks purchased bad mortgage loans from affiliated REITs to prevent their failure and ended up insolvent themselves. The second major shock occurred in May 1974, when Franklin National, the twentieth largest U.S. bank, with deposits of $3.7 billion, announced major losses. The Federal Reserve kept the bank afloat by extending $1.7 billion in discount loans and by guaranteeing a daily average of $300 million in Fed funds, until the FDIC could arrange for another bank to purchase Franklin's assets and assume its liabilities in October. This crisis marked an important extension of the lender of last resort toward the international operations of a domestic bank, for the Fed also protected Franklin's Eurodollar liabilities and assumed its foreign-exchange commitments.

• Volcker's abrupt change of operating targets in October 1979 triggered a period of great turbulence in the financial markets. In January 1980 the government extended a $1.7 billion loan guarantee to Chrysler in order to prevent bankruptcy. During the first three months of 1980 many firms sharply increased their loan commitments at commercial banks to assure themselves of funds in a highly volatile environment. Those commitments increased by 45.9 percent in the first three months of 1980. With inflation and borrowing rising rapidly, in March 1980 the Fed for the first time invoked its powers under the Credit Control Act of 1969 to restrict credit.[26] These tough new credit controls had immediate ripple effects, bursting several speculative bubbles at the same time. In late March 1980 the Hunt brothers, who had driven up the price of silver through the highly leveraged accumulation of silver futures contracts, could not meet margin calls after the price of the metal had begun to fall sharply. Many banks and brokers, which had lent the Hunts huge sums, suddenly found themselves in jeopardy. The crisis ended when Bache, the broker most exposed to this crisis, managed to sell off most of Hunt's silver contracts and a consortium of thirteen banks lent the Hunts $1.1 billion. In April 1980 the FDIC and a consortium of banks arranged for a $500 million loan to bail out the First Pennsylvania Bank. The bank collapsed after financing heavy investments in long-term bonds with short-term borrowed liabilities whose costs suddenly rose.

7.7. The Great Recession of 1979–1982 as an Historic Turn

By 1979, after a decade of intensifying stagflation, the postwar monetary regime was in shambles. This new form of structural crisis, indicating the downswing phase of a long wave, had turned the initially growth-promoting "debt economy" into a highly destabilizing debt-inflation spiral. One by one, each institutional pillar of the postwar monetary regime experienced signs of serious stress as this spiral triggered recurrent credit crunches (i.e., 1966, 1969–70, 1973–75, 1979–80).

• First, the gold-dollar standard known as Bretton Woods collapsed in 1971. The subsequent U.S. strategy of simultaneous policy reflation and currency depreciation backfired twice, first in 1973 and then in 1979, amid acute speculative pressure on the dollar and explosive price hikes in global commodity prices. All this ill-fated strategy did was to export domestic inflation and to synchronize the business cycle across the globe.
• The innovative efforts of banks and other depository institutions gradually eroded financial regulations and made monetary policy less effective. Borrowed liabilities and "near money" deposits in particular complicated the job of the Fed.
• Credit crunches, a form of stagflation-induced financial instability, forced the Federal Reserve to repeatedly abandon accommodation and impose anti-inflationary restraint instead (e.g., 1966, 1969, 1973–74, 1979–80). In effect, the central bank ended up locked into a procyclical policy.

• As the financial fragility of debtors worsened over time and as credit crunches grew more intense with each cycle, the U.S. monetary authorities had to intervene with growing frequency as lender of last resort to contain incidences of financial crisis.

Stagflation, and with it the progressive disintegration of the postwar monetary regime, reached its climax in 1979. During that year oil prices exploded once again, the dollar plummeted to an all-time low, and the fever of speculation spread across global currency and commodity markets. For the first time in the postwar era the very status of the dollar as world money was in question. The reflation-devaluation strategy adopted by the United States eight years earlier had obviously failed. In addition, sharply rising inflation also acted as a hidden tax because of "bracket creep" and undervaluation of depreciation costs from historic-cost accounting. By 1979, amid double-digit inflation, this effect had created a fiscal drag on domestic growth in the United States. Conditions were ripe for a major downturn in the economy. All that was needed was a spark.

That came in October 1979. Under mounting pressure, the Fed finally acted to halt the run out of the dollar. Unlike earlier credit crunches, during which monetary policy had tightened gradually, this time restraint came with sudden force. From one day to the next the U.S. central bank switched to a new operating target (nonborrowed bank reserves) and then, six months later, reinforced its squeeze through hitherto-unused powers (the Credit Control Act of 1969). These dramatic moves marked the official end of Keynesian monetary policy. The Fed's decision to let interest rates rise to whatever level market forces required, which was intended to counter inflationary pressures and strengthen the dollar, also triggered a major decline in economic activity.

The ensuing recession, much like the downturn of 1973–75, was a two-step process (see Table 7.4). The doubling of interest rates between October 1979 and March 1980, followed by credit controls that same month, had a sharply restraining effect. During the second quarter of 1980 real GNP fell at an annualized rate of more than 9 percent. In the wake of lower credit demand, interest rates dropped significantly from their record levels. This allowed the economy to recover during the second half of 1980, and by the first quarter of 1981 real GNP expanded at an annual rate of 8.7 percent. But inflationary pressures reappeared rapidly, with the GNP deflator rising above 10 percent by late 1980. In response the Fed tightened once again, sharply restricting the growth of nonborrowed bank reserves and raising the discount rate three times between September and December. In July 1981 the U.S. economy started to turn down again, and depressed conditions prevailed until the end of 1982.

From the point of view of long-wave dynamics (see section 3.2), the mini-depression of the early 1980s was a decisive turning point. It marked the culmination of a gradually deepening structural crisis which had begun in the late 1960s. Recall from our earlier discussion that downswing phases usually end

Table 7.4

The Mini-Depression of 1979–1982

Year	Consumer price index	Unemployment (in percent)	Industrial production	Real GDP	Prime rate
1978	7.6	6.0	5.6	4.8	9.06
1979	11.3	5.8	3.7	2.5	12.67
1980	13.5	7.0	−1.9	−0.5	15.27
1981	10.3	7.5	1.9	1.8	18.87
1982	6.2	9.5	−4.4	−2.2	14.86
1983	3.2	9.5	3.7	3.9	10.79

Source: Council of Economic Advisers, *Economic Report of the President*, 1992, Washington, DC, Tables B–60, B–37, B–47, B–2, and B–69.

Notes: Consumer price index, industrial production, and real GDP all measured as percent change per year. Unemployment (of all workers) and prime rate (charged on bank loans) measured as percentage. Consumer price index is year-to-year.

in depression-like conditions. Only then do we see the kind of fundamental adjustment responses that can lay the foundations for an eventual return to long-term expansion. The Great Recession of 1979–82 was no different in this regard. It broke the debt-inflation spiral of the 1970s. Facing a sudden burst of deflationary pressures, both creditors and debtors had to strengthen their balance sheets in order to survive. Finally, in the face of such acute crisis policy-makers abandoned long-established policies in their search for new solutions. A revolution in economic theory, bringing first Monetarism and then supply-side theory to the fore, provided justification for major institutional reforms in both fiscal and monetary policy.

8

The Legacy of Reaganomics

The Great Recession of 1979–82 came at the end of a gradual deterioration process in our economy, the dramatic culmination of a long wave in its downswing phase. Like previous manifestations of acute structural crisis, it marked a turning point. In its wake the economy had to undergo restructuring on a scale far beyond mere recessionary adjustments in the normal course of business cycles. Existing policies, no longer able to counteract rapidly worsening conditions in the economy, lost their legitimacy. New economic theories and politicians able to turn those ideas into a vision of change emerged. Frightened and frustrated voters were willing to give both a try. And so the way was paved for reform. In 1980 this scenario catapulted Ronald Reagan into the White House.

Whether they supported or opposed his policies, most Americans agree that Reagan's presidency was one of great historic significance. Very few presidents before him had managed to alter the political landscape of our nation as profoundly as he did. His policies marked a radical break with the dominant (New Deal) tradition of the past five decades. The first president since Eisenhower to serve two full terms, Reagan had enough time to implement his reform program and to see it bear fruit. In crucial areas of economic policy (e.g., taxes, budget deficits, trade, exchange rates) his administration had to change course in the face of unforeseen problems, and it did so without losing face. In the end Reagan retired with his extraordinary popularity largely intact, a truly amazing feat after such a long string of failed presidencies following Kennedy's assassination in 1963.

His political achievements notwithstanding, Reagan's policies failed in the end to revive the U.S. economy. They helped to bring about short-term prosperity, but only at the expense of deepening long-term erosion. His successor, former Vice President George Bush, won in 1988 by presenting himself as the guardian of the Reagan Revolution. Elected as a caretaker president, he also acted like one throughout his term. Having spent most of his political career in the arena of foreign policy, Bush was not particularly drawn to domestic policy issues. In that area there were only a few initiatives under his presidency, and even those were usually mishandled (e.g., the budget accord of 1990, the banking reform plan of 1991). When the failures of the Reagan Revolution finally began to show their long-term effects on the U.S. economy, Bush had no response and lost his bid for a second term. With the Reagan-Bush era now behind us, it is a good time to assess its legacy. This is a particularly meaningful exercise, for the impact of Reagan's policies will be felt for a long time to come.

8.1. Defining Reagan's Conservative Counterrevolution

Ronald Reagan's landslide victory over Jimmy Carter in 1980 gave him a strong mandate to turn the major themes of his successful campaign into reality. His mission was that of a reformer coming to power at a time of acute crisis and widespread dissatisfaction with the status quo. His program was one of change, nothing less than a complete overhaul and reversal of long-standing policies. His message was simple and popular, getting "government off our backs" and "making America strong again." These slogans were not just empty promises. Instead, they symbolized a dramatic reversal of existing policy traditions.

His program, commonly referred to as *Reaganomics*, comprised tax cuts, a reorientation of fiscal priorities from social to military spending, an anti-inflationary monetary policy, deregulation of industry, and a "free market" approach to trade and exchange rates. Liberals may not want to admit this, but these policies corresponded to the public mood of the time and had solid roots in the problems then afflicting the U.S. economy. With inflation in the double digits and unemployment rising, many Americans wanted change in 1980. Their disaffection reflected the breakdown of the liberal consensus that had dominated our body politic ever since Roosevelt's New Deal in the 1930s. More than a decade of stagflation, a new form of crisis combining rising prices and slowing growth, had eroded its Keynesian policy prescriptions to the point that those increasingly came to be seen as part of the problem.[1] In this context Reagan managed to present a conservative alternative in each area of policy erosion.

1) Tax Policy. Throughout the 1970s accelerating inflation had acted as a hidden tax. Households receiving higher money wages, which in any case barely compensated for rising consumer prices, were pushed into higher tax brackets ("bracket creep"). Corporations also found their effective tax burden increased. In periods of rising prices their practice of "historic-cost" accounting understated the depreciation of their fixed capital and thus created fictitious accounting profits subject to taxation (see section 5.4). Lower taxes, besides accommodating widespread anti-tax sentiments, would thus remove an inflation-induced "fiscal drag" on the economy.

During the 1980 election campaign Reagan supported the position of so-called supply-siders, who blamed the slow growth of the U.S. economy during the 1970s on our progressive income tax system and its excessively high marginal tax rates in the upper-income brackets (peaking at 70 percent). Those rates made it less worthwhile to pursue income gains and thus discouraged work effort, saving, investment, and entrepreneurial risk-taking. Supply-siders favored a substantial reduction of tax rates to restore incentives for these growth-promoting activities. Some even predicted that this step would create such rapid income growth that after a while tax revenues would actually increase despite lower rates—the infamous "Laffer Curve."

Reagan lost no time in putting supply-side prescriptions into effect. His first budget proposal, passed by Congress as one package in the Economic Recovery Tax Act (ERTA) of 1981, included the largest tax cut in U.S. history. An across-the-board cut of personal income taxes by 25 percent gave upper-income households the largest breaks, leaving the richest one-third of taxpayers with two-thirds of the tax savings. The income tax system came to be fully indexed for inflation, with personal exemptions, standard deductions, and tax brackets annually adjusted upward. ERTA also greatly expanded access to Individual Retirement Accounts (IRAs) in order to induce more personal saving. These IRAs allowed tax deferral on investment income until actual withdrawal of these funds and gave individuals up to $2,000 in annual contributions as a tax deduction. Corporations received large tax breaks, especially a 25 percent tax credit on research and development expenses and dramatically accelerated depreciation allowances.[2]

As it turned out, ERTA 1981 actually weakened the income tax system. It provided new channels for already rampant tax evasion (e.g., use of "limited" partnerships as tax shelters), and it encouraged inefficient resource allocation by treating different industries and types of investment unequally. Congress tried to correct some of these problems in the Tax Reform Act of 1986. In exchange for limiting or eliminating many tax deductions, credits, and exceptions to expand the tax base, the measure lowered tax rates even more. The fourteen-bracket range of 11 percent to 50 percent for personal income gave way to just two brackets, 15 percent and 28 percent, with a temporary 5 percent surcharge for some upper-income taxpayers. The corporate tax rate fell from 46 percent to 34 percent. Higher standard deductions, besides "simplifying" tax returns for many who no longer qualified for itemized deductions, combined with a doubling of personal exemptions to provide major tax relief for the working poor.[3] Though neutral in terms of overall revenues, this 1986 reform shifted about 15 percent of the total tax burden from individuals to corporations.

2) A Shift in Spending Priorities. In 1980 the majority of Americans backed Reagan's proposed reorientation from social to military spending. Declining "real" (inflation-adjusted) wages and higher tax burdens during much of the 1970s made middle-income households much less willing to support welfare and other antipoverty programs. Reagan's overdrawn characterization of these programs as wasteful and counterproductive thus fell on fertile ground. At the same time, many Americans supported higher military spending. Soviet expansion, especially the invasion of Afghanistan in late 1979, had left them skeptical of the policy of détente started a decade earlier by Nixon. This, together with the revolutions in Iran and Nicaragua during the same year, created the political climate for reversing the post-Vietnam decline in military spending.

As can be seen in Table 8.1, Reagan managed to shift spending priorities from social to military programs. In 1981 he convinced Congress to approve fairly deep cuts in many antipoverty programs, above all food stamps, child nutrition, low-income housing assistance, student grants, and later also Medicaid. Strong popular support for entitlement programs benefiting the middle class (e.g., Social Security) prevented similar reductions there. Farm-support programs continued to rise rapidly throughout the early 1980s to cope with a deep depression in rural America. At the same time, the Reagan administration undertook a huge rearmament effort to develop new missiles and aircraft, to expand the Navy, to set up a mobile "rapid deployment" force, and to launch a space-based antimissile defense system.

Reagan's military advisers thought that an arms race with the economically weakened Soviet Union would eventually force the "evil empire" into major concessions. This is exactly what began to happen in 1985, when a new generation of reformers under the innovative leadership of Mikhail Gorbachev came to power in the Kremlin. But there was another strategic purpose behind the shift in fiscal priorities from social to military spending. The former benefits primarily individual consumers, whereas the latter, ever since World War II, has become a peculiarly American form of industrial policy. The rearmament program was thus also a means of government support for some of our largest corporations.

Apart from creating jobs for millions and offering many poor Americans a convenient vehicle for a successful career, the Pentagon annually spends huge sums of money for purchases of goods and services from private industry. These outlays feed a unique institutional structure, the *military-industrial complex*, comprising large military contractors, thousands of smaller subcontractors, key Congressional representatives of districts depending on military spending for jobs, the Pentagon bureaucracy, and the national-security apparatus in the White House.

This military-industrial complex is largely exempt from market rules and operates instead more like a centrally planned economy. On the demand side, the government acts as the sole buyer. Its purchases are shaped by classified Pentagon claims of "gaps" in our arsenal, by intense competition between the different military services, and by coalition-building in Congress to spread contracts across different regions. Producers usually specialize in a particular weapons category, sometimes to the point of becoming its sole supplier (as in the case of General Dynamics producing all of our tanks). This monopoly structure assures contractors of follow-up orders, makes it easier to build up expertise, and allows high fixed costs to be spread over a larger production volume. But it also means that the Pentagon has to award most of its contracts without competitive bidding.[4]

Table 8.1

Changes in the Composition of the U.S. Budget, 1981–1989
(as percent of total)

Year	Military	Social programs	Health	Income security	Social security	Net interest	Personal income tax	Corporate income tax
1981	23.3	6.5	9.7	14.7	20.6	10.1	47.7	10.2
1982	24.8	4.7	9.9	14.4	20.9	11.4	48.2	8.0
1983	26.0	4.2	10.0	15.2	21.1	11.1	48.1	6.2
1984	26.7	4.1	10.3	13.2	20.9	13.0	44.8	8.5
1985	26.7	3.9	10.5	13.5	19.9	13.7	45.6	8.4
1986	27.6	3.8	10.7	12.1	20.1	13.7	45.4	8.2
1987	28.1	3.5	11.5	12.3	20.7	13.8	46.0	9.8
1988	27.2	3.5	11.6	12.2	20.6	14.3	44.1	10.4
1989	26.5	3.6	11.7	11.9	20.3	14.8	45.0	10.4

Source: Council of Economic Advisers, *Economic Report of the President,* 1992, Washington, DC, Table B–75.

Notes: All expenditure items as percentages of total federal spending; all revenue sources as percentages of federal taxes. Social programs include community and regional development, education, training, employment, and social services.

These contracts use a formula which reimburses suppliers for production-related costs and guarantees a "fair return" on top. Such "cost-plus" pricing is standard practice in oligopolistic industries that are dominated by a few large corporations. However, in contrast to the rest of private industry, military contractors are not subject to market regulation. In other words, normal market constraints on output prices in the form of competition with other suppliers or elastic (price-sensitive) demand do not apply in the case of military contractors. These are, after all, monopolies in their specialized product categories. And they also enjoy highly inelastic demand, facing a monopsonistic buyer (the Pentagon) with an open purse (your tax dollars) and few, if any, substitutes (French missiles for our nuclear arsenal?).

In the absence of these normal market constraints, the "cost-plus" pricing formula used by the Pentagon becomes an invitation for inefficiency. Guaranteed a "fair return" as a fixed percentage of costs, contractors can earn more profit simply by incurring higher costs. For example, a 15 percent return on costs of $10 generates twice the profit ($1.50) than does the same return on $5 (75 cents). Military contractors thus have a powerful incentive to inflate costs by paying (often outrageously) high prices for components, by slowing product development, and by favoring high-cost production methods. They know that Pentagon enforcement tends to be lax and that Congress is unwilling to cancel projects before completion even in the face of delays and huge cost overruns.[5]

Studies of the Pentagon's procurement practices during the arms build-up of the 1980s have revealed some interesting facts:

• Weapons contracts, making up about one-third of the Pentagon's annual ($300 billion) budget, were heavily concentrated among the largest contractors. In 1984 the top fifteen firms received 41 percent of all weapons contracts.

• In 1981 the Pentagon expanded financial "incentives" for military contractors while it reduced outside scrutiny of their profits. Several studies by Congress and the Pentagon since then have proved these steps to be a failure. The improved incentives did not induce increased investment in plant and equipment. Relaxed supervision encouraged weapons-producing firms to pay their subcontractors too much (costing taxpayers more than $1.3 billion in 1984). Besides being reimbursed for certain items not included in normal cost accounting (e.g., the "cost of money"), those contractors also received about $10 billion a year in progress payments before actually incurring reimbursable expenses.[6]

• After 1981 the Pentagon used a revised pricing formula that allowed higher profit. Negotiated profit rates on weapons contracts rose from 10.7 percent in 1979 to 13.1 percent in 1983. A survey of 1983 results for 1,000 corporations by *Forbes* magazine showed that the ten largest military contractors earned a 25.6 percent return on shareholder equity. This rate of return was higher than that in any other industry and compared to a 15.1 percent average for the entire survey. That fact illustrates the importance of the military-industrial complex as a safety net in support of corporate profitability— especially when profit-rates suffer from long-term decline, as has been the case for U.S. industry since 1966.

• Military contractors used a special accounting method, the so-called completed-contract method, to book huge losses for tax purposes and to thereby gain tax deductions which they could apply against past and future income.[7] Until restriction of this accounting method by the tax reform of 1986, most military contractors did not have to pay any taxes even though they earned billions in profits from weapons contracts and civilian output.

• Until recently the Pentagon spent more than $40 billion per year on research and development. Even though gradually being scaled back in the aftermath of the Soviet Union's demise, Pentagon-sponsored research and development spending remains significant. These outlays underwrite and socialize the large risks associated with new technology. In this context Reagan's Strategic Defense Initiative (SDI), for example, is primarily a subsidy program for such high-tech sectors as artificial intelligence, satellite communications, computer software, lasers, and metals. But spillover effects of military research and development for nonmilitary applications are increasingly limited, and in an era of intense global competition it may be more effective to channel government support directly into civilian technologies.

3) Monetary Policy. This area of macroeconomic stabilization policy concerns management of money creation and credit conditions by the state's monetary authorities. For much of the postwar period the Federal Reserve, the U.S. central bank, followed a Keynesian policy course which favored fixed exchange rates and low interest rates. But accelerating inflation made these positions increasingly difficult to sustain during the 1970s and boosted the influence of monetarists (see section 7.4). Those conservative critics pushed for flexible exchange rates determined by market forces and urged a central bank policy of slow and steady increases in the money supply as the only means of assuring long-run price stability.[8] Monetarism experienced a first success with the transition from government-regulated ("fixed") to market-determined ("flexible") exchange rates in 1973. But their true breakthrough came in October 1979, when the Federal Reserve, under the initiative of its newly appointed chair, Paul Volcker, abandoned the essentially Keynesian policy of "pegging" interest rates below inflation and instead began to target monetary aggregates within a narrow growth range. In the same year Monetarism also took hold in Great Britain following Margaret Thatcher's election.

These successes notwithstanding, the monetarists have since suffered considerable erosion. Though still dominant in academe, on Wall Street, and in the government bureaucracy, their theory has been overtaken by new realities:

• Volcker's historic policy switch in 1979 did manage to tame inflationary pressures, but only at the expense of a deep recession. At the bottom of this downturn, in the summer of 1982, a series of spectacular financial failures (Drysdale, Penn Square, and Mexico) prompted the Federal Reserve to abandon its "tight money" policy. From then on, for seven years, the central bank successfully walked a tightrope between accommodating strong credit demand to sustain recovery and responding to early signs of rising inflation by temporary tightening, as in 1984, 1987, and 1988–89.

• Interest-rate deregulation in the early 1980s encouraged many new types of banking deposits with monetary attributes and carrying market rates (e.g., consumer CDs, money-market funds). Some of these are included in the various measures for the money supply; others are not. Frequent shifts of funds between different deposit accounts in response to changes in the level and maturity structure of interest rates have disturbed the traditional relation between bank reserves and the larger money-supply aggregates. This has made it much more difficult for the central bank to enforce a monetarist "quantity rule" of steady money-supply growth via effective control of bank reserves.

• Another sacred assumption of the monetarists, that of constant money velocity reflecting a stable relation between money supply and the gross national product, has also proved to be unreliable. Although recoveries normally cause the velocity of money to rise, that variable exhibited a remarkably sustained decline during 1983–85, years of strong growth. This surprising development had several causes, including net outflows due to exploding trade deficits and a massive shift of resources into financial transactions not counted in the GNP. Whatever the reasons, it made a "tight money" policy obsolete.

• Finally, the monetarist experiment in flexible exchange rates ended in September 1985 amid growing trade imbalances and speculation-driven volatility in foreign-exchange markets. In one of its most spectacular yet relatively little-discussed policy reversals, the Reagan administration abandoned its "free-market" approach to currency prices in favor of coordinated exchange-rate management by the central banks of leading industrial nations.

Compounding these declining fortunes, Monetarism also faced a challenge from a second conservative alternative within the Reagan administration. Supply-siders in the Treasury (e.g., Norman Ture, Manuel Johnson) and in Congress (e.g., Jack Kemp) wanted a "price rule" which would tie the money supply to a commodity, preferably gold, at a fixed rate of exchange. In the absence of such backing by gold, they rejected the monetarists' "quantity rule" as an unnecessary barrier to more rapid growth.[9] However, a commission set up in 1981 to study the role of gold in international monetary arrangements failed to recommend a return to the gold standard. Reagan then appointed several supply-siders to the Federal Reserve Board of Governors. Their opposition to Volcker's "tight money" course in 1987 surely played a role in his decision to resign. The central bank's principal policy-making body, the FOMC, is now fairly evenly split between supply-siders and monetarists. The latter group is led by Alan Greenspan, Volcker's successor, and includes several presidents of the Federal Reserve Banks who occupy five of the twelve seats on the FOMC.

4) Deregulation. This aspect of "Reaganomics" aimed at a complete overhaul of the government's regulatory apparatus vis-à-vis private industry. The Reagan administration wanted to relax or abolish many existing regulations in order to reduce business costs and to give corporate managers a greater degree of freedom in their actions. The motives for such a policy course ranged from its ideological "free-market" conviction to concern about the declining competitiveness of U.S. industry. In practice, deregulation included a variety of different policy initiatives.

• For one, the Reagan administration expanded Carter's efforts to relax "price and quantity" regulations in the transportation, energy, telecommunications, and finance sectors. By the late 1970s these regulations had begun to have a negative impact on industry performance, as rate-setting agencies kept prices lagging behind costs. New technologies also made the structure of many regulated industries obsolete. When the government deregulated those sectors, it removed its protective umbrella over their structure and thereby triggered major restructuring. Given their strategic position as producers of basic material inputs, the reorganization of those sectors had significant spillover effects on the rest of the economy.

• The Reagan administration also launched a frontal attack on so-called social policy regulations of harmful business practices across the entire spectrum of industry, including antipollution rules, consumer-protection provisions, workplace safety standards, and antidiscrimination rules. With Congress unwilling to repeal or relax relevant legislation, the White House simply used its executive powers to gut the enforcement agencies (e.g., the Environmental Protection Agency [EPA], the Occupational Safety and Health Administration [OSHA], the Equal Employment Opportunity Commission [EEOC]). It appointed proven foes to head those agencies, cut their operating budgets, and blocked their rule-making capacity.

• Finally, the Reagan administration decided early on not to enforce antitrust laws. This hands-off attitude toward mergers and monopoly behavior paved the way for the largest merger wave in U.S. history. Between 1983 and 1988 "deal mania" on Wall Street dramatically transformed the structure of most industries toward a much higher degree of concentration.[10] In the absence of policies that helped to reorganize troubled sectors in an orderly fashion, takeovers and divestitures became the principal means for restructuring industries. The massive scale of this process had its roots in the deep recession of the early 1980s that left many firms with weaker balance sheets, undervalued equity, and excess capacity. Add to this more intense global competition and often prohibitive costs of product development. That merger wave, a key driving force behind the bull market (pushing the Dow Jones from a low of around 750 in 1982 to 2,722 in 1987), also involved dramatic changes in the organization of the stock market. These included the growing dominance of large institutional investors (pension funds, insurance companies, mutual funds), the transformation of investment banks from advisors to active deal-makers, and the emergence of low-grade, high-yield "junk bonds" to finance hostile takeover bids by so-called raiders.

5) International Economic Policy. Reagan began his term committed to free trade, flexible exchange rates, and providing assistance to strategic allies (e.g., Israel, Egypt, Pakistan, El Salvador). But these priorities did not translate into an integrated approach which addressed the challenges of a rapidly changing global economy. Hence Reagan's policy-makers were not in a position to anticipate certain developments and to cope with them in an other than ad hoc manner.

For example, the debt crisis of developing economies caught Treasury Secretary Donald Regan completely off guard, even though signs of that problem abounded before Mexico's default in August 1982 (e.g., Turkey, Zaire, Jamaica). Only after an intense internal debate did Volcker receive White House approval to arrange for a new international lender-of-last-resort mechanism which combined assistance by the IMF and debt reschedulings with austerity programs. When James Baker took over at the Treasury following Reagan's reelection, he extended this case-by-case approach by urging that new funds be provided to fifteen selected countries in exchange for structural reforms aimed at reducing the role of government in their economies.

In the face of exploding U.S. trade deficits, the Reagan administration also found itself exposed to mounting protectionist pressures at home and to trade conflicts with some of our closest allies. It responded with import restrictions against Japanese cars, Caribbean sugar, and steel from the Common Market. Other steps, such as a return to bilateralism (see trade and cooperation agreements with Israel and Canada), pressure for "voluntary" export restrictions by surplus countries, its hard-line stance in the Uruguay Round concerning agricultural products and services, and provisions for unilateral retaliation under the "Super 301" provision of the Omnibus Trade and Competitiveness Act of 1988, all indicate Reagan's gradual abandonment of his initial "free-trade" position.

Nor could the Reagan administration maintain its laissez-faire approach to currency prices in the face of growing trade imbalances and exchange-rate volatility. Just a year after celebrating the strong dollar as a symbol of America's resurgence during the 1984 campaign, it adopted a policy of multilateral coordination among the central banks of the leading industrial nations to drive the dollar down in an orderly manner.

Finally, we must also make brief mention of Reagan's emphasis on military aid for repressive regimes and "freedom fighters." This was not a new policy. Beginning with the "gunboat diplomacy" in the Caribbean around the turn of the century and dramatically expanded into the role of "global policeman" after World War II, the United States has had a long tradition of intervening in the internal affairs of supposedly sovereign nations. The pace of intervention quickened with the global extension of the cold war following the decolonization of Africa and Asia in the 1950s and 1960s, culminating in defeat in the jungles of Southeast Asia in 1975. Reagan wanted Americans to overcome their "Vietnam syndrome" and to resume a more aggressive stance against the "evil empire." In that sense his policy of fueling proxy wars across the globe marked a dramatic change from the relatively inactive and introspective post-Vietnam years. Except for Lebanon, he managed a string of successes. And toward the end of his second term the Soviet Union began its retreat from the rest of the globe.

But against this picture of apparent success we must weigh huge costs which remain generally hidden to most Americans. Throughout the 1980s, the developing countries, already facing depression conditions from the global debt crisis, spent more on the military than on housing, health, and education combined. That not only constitutes a profound misallocation of very scarce resources but also strengthens the least democratic segments of their torn societies—religious fundamentalists, the landowning oligarchy, the armed forces.

Many conflicts, in which our national security apparatus saw only the seeds for a possible Communist takeover, have in essence been domestic class conflicts created by conditions of unbearable inequality and repression. The engagement of both superpowers often fueled these conflicts to the point of turning them into large-scale regional wars involving a number of nations (e.g., Southeast Asia, the Middle East, Southern Africa, Central America). The Iran-Contra scandal of 1986–87 illustrated what happens when the logic of our national security apparatus comes to dominate our foreign policy. In the coming geoeconomic era the dual challenge of economic development and political reform will require different kinds of U.S. assistance.

8.2. Twin Deficits and Global Recovery

Reagan presided over the longest peacetime recovery in our history. During that period the U.S. economy proved remarkably resilient in the face of all kinds of shocks, such as the huge fluctuations of the dollar and the stock market crash. Eight years of continued expansion pushed both inflation and unemployment far below the levels that prevailed when Reagan took office. The deep downturn of 1981–82, easily attributed to earlier "mistakes" by the unpopular Carter administration, caused dramatic disinflation. Since then a combination of weaker unions, intense global competition, and occasional tightening by the Federal Reserve has kept inflation below 5 percent, even when the U.S. economy approached full-employment levels in the late 1980s.

The tax cuts and rearmament program of ERTA 1981 (see section 8.1 above) represented a heavy dose of fiscal stimulation, which began to pull the economy out of recession in mid-1982. At the same time the Federal Reserve abandoned its "tight money" policy in favor of a more accommodating course. The resulting decline in nominal interest rates triggered a stock market revival, which in turn reinforced investor and consumer confidence. The stage was set for recovery. Low rates of capacity utilization and high unemployment left much space for rapid expansion, and the U.S. economy grew at a 5–6 percent pace per year in 1983–84.

The recovery was in large part driven by stubbornly high budget deficits, which represent a net addition to aggregate demand. Those deficits, which reached a record $225 billion in 1985 before declining gradually until 1990, had several causes. One was the double-step recession of 1979–82 that activated automatic fiscal stabilizers of declining tax revenues and growing entitlement outlays for the unemployed and the poor. In their wake the budget deficit nearly doubled in just three years, from $40 billion in 1979 to $79 billion in 1981. Another cause was the loss of extra tax revenues from bracket creep and historic-cost accounting in the aftermath of both disinflation and indexing of our income tax system. But the most important factor was surely the combination of large tax cuts and increased military spending enacted in 1981. These discretionary policy changes added at least a $100 billion per year to our so-called structural (full-employment) deficit.

Budget deficits can be financed internally, either out of domestic savings or through additions to the money supply. But neither of these methods sufficed.

Contrary to the predictions of supply-siders, lower marginal tax rates failed to boost domestic saving. The private saving rate of U.S. households and businesses actually declined, from an average 9.7 percent of net national product in the 1970s to just 6.1 percent in 1987.[11] In addition, although the rate of money creation accelerated significantly after the Federal Reserve abandoned its monetarist experiment in mid-1982, it did not suffice to compensate for the decline in saving and to fund the extraordinarily rapid pace of debt additions during this recovery. Not only did our public debt double between 1981 and 1986, but private debt of households, corporations, and financial institutions also grew very rapidly during those years.

In the absence of adequate internal funding, the United States came to rely increasingly on foreign savings to make up for the shortfall. Foreigners were willing to supply us their excess surplus for a variety of reasons. The U.S. economy recovered earlier than did the economies of other industrial nations, and this meant that investment opportunities were better here than elsewhere. Stable political conditions in the United States under the leadership of a popular president committed to probusiness policies helped as well. In addition, U.S. interest rates compared favorably to those of other countries, especially when adjusted for inflation. This made U.S. securities relatively more attractive than, say, those of Japan or West Germany.

To the extent that these capital imports were in foreign denominations, they had to be converted into dollars. Thus they represented a net addition to the demand for dollars in foreign-exchange markets. With the Reagan administration adopting a laissez-faire policy toward exchange rates, that extra demand helped to drive up the value of the dollar. Between 1981 and 1985 the dollar rose by 60 percent against other key currencies, such as the mark, yen, or pound. That revaluation made imports into the United States correspondingly cheaper and, at the same time, made U.S. exports that much more expensive. Exacerbating a long-term and structural decline in the international competitiveness of U.S. industry, such a dramatic change in our terms of trade exploded our merchandise trade deficit with the rest of the world from $28 billion in 1981 to a record $175 billion in 1987.

Initially this situation had several important advantages. The expensive dollar greatly intensified competitive pressures for domestic producers in trade-dependent sectors, which forced them to restructure, to cut costs, to improve product quality, and to price their products aggressively. Cheap imports kept domestic inflation down and raised the living standards of many Americans despite relatively stagnant wage growth. Moreover, the trade deficit represented a drag on economic growth, slowing the rate of expansion by late 1984 from the torrid 5–6 percent pace to a more sustainable 2–3 percent per year. Conversely, our negative trade balance allowed our domestic recovery to spill over to the rest of the world. Other countries, mostly the industrial nations of Western Europe and Japan, the newly industrializing countries of the Pacific Basin (e.g., South Korea,

Hong Kong, Taiwan, Singapore), and some of the larger developing economies with big debt-servicing problems (e.g., Mexico, Brazil), could now recover by pushing their products aggressively into the huge U.S. market. In that sense Americans became the "consumers of last resort" for the rest of the world, the U.S. economy acted as the locomotive for worldwide recovery, and Reaganomics must be understood as a new form of "global Keynesianism."

In 1985, however, the long-term dangers of these twin (budget and trade) deficits began to emerge.

• That year it became clear that the two deficits reinforced each other. The slowdown in growth due to the trade deficit led to an unexpectedly rapid increase of the budget deficit (from $185 billion to $225 billion), after it had begun to decline in the previous year. The illusion that "we can simply grow our way out of the deficit" could no longer be maintained. A gradually building budgetary stalemate between Republicans and Democrats turned into an open political crisis when Congress failed to come up with a deficit-reducing budget for the next fiscal year.

• The market shares lost by our trade-dependent sectors at home and abroad plunged entire regions of our nation into near-depression (e.g., the farm belt, the industrial heartland around the Great Lakes, Texas). Protectionist pressures grew rapidly amid mass bankruptcy of farmers and the loss of many high-paying manufacturing jobs. Unions, weakened by declining membership and under relentless management pressure to grant concessions, supported businesses' lobbying for import restrictions. And there was much worried talk about uneven growth turning the United States into a "bicoastal" or "service" economy.

• In early 1985 the spectacular rise of the dollar came to an end when the exploding U.S. trade deficit finally emerged as the dominant factor in foreign-exchange markets. Remembering earlier out-of-hand dollar devaluations (e.g., 1973, 1979) and fearing the herd-like behavior of speculators when they share the same expectational bias, many economists soon began to worry that too rapid a decline of the dollar would make foreign investors less willing to supply us their funds. Should this occur, U.S. interest rates would inevitably shoot up and endanger the global recovery. Against this background, the news of the United States having become a net debtor for the first time in seventy years created a good deal of nervousness in domestic political circles.

The time was ripe for a significant change in U.S. economic policy to bring both deficits down. Reagan's landslide victory in 1984 gave him a strong political mandate to act. And the replacement of Donald Regan by James Baker at the Treasury opened the way for a much more pragmatic policy course. In September 1985 Baker invited officials from other leading industrial nations to New York and concluded the so-called *Plaza Agreement* for coordinated market intervention by their respective central banks to assure an orderly decline of the dollar.[12] This measure aimed at a gradual reduction of U.S. trade deficits. And in December 1985 a panicky Congress passed the Balanced Budget and Emergency Deficit Control Act, better known as *Gramm-Rudman-Hollings,* with Reagan's approval. That law set annual targets to reduce the budget deficit in equal install-ments over a five-year period. Should Congress fail to pass a budget by pre-scribed deadlines within $10 billion of that deficit target, then automatic and equiproportional spending cuts across the board would have to make up the difference ("sequestration"). These cuts were to be shared evenly between mili-tary and social programs, exempting nine welfare and entitlement programs al-ready squeezed earlier.

For a while, until 1990, these deficit-reduction measures lowered the twin deficits without aborting the recovery. The budget deficit fell from its record $225 billion in 1985 to below $170 billion four years later. A 50 percent devalu-ation of the dollar between 1985 and 1988 gave our export industries a much-needed boost, helping to reduce our trade deficit from its 1987 peak of $175 billion to around $110 billion in 1989. Although these adjustments surely helped, the United States continued to absorb a major portion of the world's excess savings at a time when other countries needed large infusions of capital to rebuild their economies.

8.3. The Darker Side of Reaganomics

The successes of the Reagan administration were significant. Seven years of uninterrupted expansion reduced unemployment (to 5 percent) while inflation remained moderate (hovering around 4 percent). The West won the cold war, raising the prospect of lasting improvements in superpower relations and disar-mament. For a while these improvements fed an often self-congratulatory eupho-ria among a large number of Americans who believed the Republican message of "peace and prosperity." But such optimism proved premature. It ignored a vari-ety of shortcomings which festered during the Reagan years and came to the fore during Bush's first term. Those will require major efforts to correct.

1) Growing Income Inequality. During the Reagan years the gap between poor and rich widened considerably (see Table 8.2). Reagan's fiscal policies contributed to this growing inequity of personal income distribution. His 1981 tax cuts, only partially reversed by the tax reform in 1986, mostly benefited upper-income households. On the other hand, his reductions in antipoverty programs and in federal assistance to local governments aggravated the pre-carious situation of many poor families already devastated by the deindustri-alization and decaying infrastructure of our inner cities. The cumulative effects of these spending cuts in terms of hunger, homelessness, inadequate health care, and decline of affordable public education are difficult to de-scribe. The long-term costs of dealing with these effects far outweigh the initial fiscal savings. We as a nation waste many productive resources by

Table 8.2

Shifts in Personal Income Distribution

Quintile	1969	1979	1987
Lowest	5.6	5.3	4.6
Second	12.4	11.6	10.8
Third	17.7	17.5	16.9
Fourth	23.7	24.1	24.1
Highest	40.6	41.6	43.7
Top Five	15.6	15.7	16.9

Source: U.S. Bureau of the Census, *Current Population Reports*, Washington, DC (selected issues).

Note: Percentage of before-tax income received by each one-fifth of families.

allowing millions of Americans to be locked into often-hopeless poverty. The social tensions that arise from segregating society by class and race can explode suddenly with amazing force, as witnessed in the widespread riots of May 1992.

The widening income gap also had its roots in structural changes that limited wage growth. Stubbornly high unemployment following the deep recession of 1981–82 and intensifying global competition made it much harder for American workers to push for higher wages. The labor movement weakened considerably. Many once-powerful unions became stuck in mature sectors with declining employment and failed to attract new members in significant numbers. They also had to put up with a hostile White House, whose actions (e.g., the firing of striking air-traffic controllers in 1981, the de facto destruction of the National Labor Relations Board [NLRB], the attack on employee protection laws) emboldened managers to take a much tougher line vis-à-vis their work force. Changes in top management following mergers often brought about dramatic downsizing of the work force. Finally, the shift within our industrial matrix from manufacturing to services accelerated during the 1980s. This meant elimination of many high-paying industrial jobs and massive creation of lower-paying service jobs. Despite these limits on wage growth, many Americans managed to maintain high consumption levels by working more hours (including an increase in the number of two-earner families), borrowing more or saving less, and buying cheaper imports.

This polarization of our personal income distribution during the 1980s shifted the composition of aggregate demand (and output mix) from basic social goods and services to luxury goods. Cuts in social programs aggravated the decline in the purchasing power of poor people and reduced the supply of government-assisted necessities (e.g., food stamps, low-income housing, medical insurance, public education). At the same time, upper-income Americans used their gains in after-tax income to a large degree in conspicuous consumption. Many of the expensive status symbols of the 1980s were imported (e.g., luxury cars, diamonds, fur coats, designer clothes, cocaine), thereby adding to our trade deficit.

In our contemporary society acute deprivation and mindless excess coexist tensely, with potentially frightening consequences for economic stability and social peace. Poverty is not just a moral issue stressing the fabric of our society. It also has severe economic consequences. People deprived of opportunity represent a loss of valuable resources to all of us, because they cannot contribute fully to the creation of the nation's wealth. In addition, the misery and despair in impoverished communities creates major social costs which society has to bear, one way or another. The expenditure of money on imprisoning the criminals, sheltering the homeless, feeding the hungry, and treating the sick could have been avoided if we as a nation had invested more in those human resources early on. Being poor is not a personal choice. It is the result of institutionalized discrimination and local disinvestment, compounded by the social pathologies of a dramatically unequal society.

2) Finding a Regulatory Balance. Despite significant effects in terms of lower prices, efficiency gains, and accelerated pace of industrial restructuring, Reagan's deregulation measures had their share of negative side effects. These have already begun to shift the public mood toward some degree of reregulation.

• The removal of "price and quantity" restrictions at first led to more intense price competition in strategic sectors of our economy. But lower prices often forced cost-cutting measures, which hurt the quality of output. Moreover, self-feeding merger waves in those deregulated sectors ultimately led to such an increase in concentration that initial price reductions have gradually been reversed. These problems are especially acute among the airlines, in broadcasting, and in consumer banking. The thrifts are a classic case study of all that can go wrong in the aftermath of deregulation. Industries still operating as natural monopolies (e.g., electricity, local telephone, cable television) have been allowed to charge much higher prices.

• Reagan's relaxation of "social policy" regulations greatly relieved the regulatory burden on industry. But businesses have also abused their newly won freedoms, with many negative results. These include environmental degradation, more work-place accidents, erosion of consumer safety standards and employee protection, and the government's unwillingness to act as impartial arbitrator in discrimination cases and labor-management conflicts.

• The deal mania of the 1980s has left many firms with extremely heavy debt burdens and under great pressure to generate cash through asset sales and radical cost-cutting measures. Firms subject to takeovers and reorganization have tended to suffer a great deal of turmoil, leaving their work force demoralized and their managers obsessed with short-term results. Too many companies spend valuable cash resources buying existing (paper) assets rather than investing in more modern equipment, employee skills, and product development—the long-run sources of commercial success. Finally, there is a real question as to how the dramatic increase in concentration will affect the future performance of industries.

3) Misdirected Investment Priorities. Despite Reagan's tax incentives and regulatory relief, corporate investment levels remained quite low. Here it is necessary to distinguish between mere replacement of worn-out assets and investing beyond that, especially in light of the rapidly aging capital stock in many U.S. industries. Investment thus needs to be measured net of depreciation. During the 1980s this net investment share ranged between 5 percent and 6 percent of net national product, compared to an average of nearly 8 percent between 1950 and 1980. If we also exclude from this figure consumer durables (e.g., housing, cars) which do not boost productivity, the share of net private business investment has fallen from its postwar average of 3.3 percent to a mere 2.4 percent after 1983. That anemic investment performance has slowed the annual growth rate of our manufacturing capital stock from an average of 3.7 percent in the 1950–82 period to less than 1 percent since 1983.[13] Such a sluggish pace of industrial capital formation threatens America's economic progress and may lead to further declines in the world market share of U.S. industry.

Apart from inadequate levels of investment, we have also witnessed harmful shifts in the composition of investment during the last decade.

• Given that interest rates determine the degree to which future dollars are discounted to present value, the high real interest rates of the 1980s reinforced a bias in favor of investments with rapid payoff potential. This has meant a preference for short-lived equipment, most notably computer technology. But such equipment adds less to capacity and productivity gains than do other types of capital goods (e.g., heavy machinery, new plant) which incorporate the latest technological advances in a more integrated manner. The bias toward short planning horizons also constrained long-term investments in intangible capital, such as product development, skill formation, accumulation of knowledge, and marketing and distribution networks, as well as the willingness of managers to take initial losses until sufficiently large market shares are secured. But these activities are often precisely the ones that eventually contribute the most to corporate profitability and industrial growth.

• In the 1980s our industry increasingly lost its once-unassailable technological leadership. This came as no surprise. Today we have fallen behind other industrial nations in scientific education and in the technical knowledge of top managers. U.S. expenditures on research and development (as a share of GNP) are substantially lower than are those of Japan and Germany. And in recent years more than half of our national research and development effort has been devoted to the military, whose spillover effects for civilian applications are at best limited and laggard. In contrast, other industrial nations spend most of their research and development funds directly on civilian technology.

• The Pentagon still absorbs a quarter of our federal budget, much of it to meet obsolete commitments concluded nearly half a century ago to protect allies which have turned into our toughest competitors. Although military spending is clearly an effective federal job-creation program and a huge channel of public subsidy to the private sector, it is an inefficient use of resources. It encourages costly production processes and results in "dead-end" products that are not usable for either consumption or investment.

• At the same time, U.S. spending on civilian public works has declined from 2.3 percent of total output in 1965 to just 1 percent per year since 1985. In this area the United States now ranks 55th (!) in the world. As a result our infrastructure, especially transportation (roads and bridges, railroad tracks, airports), water supply, and waste disposal, is old and deteriorating rapidly. Since this infrastructure supports our nation's productive capacity, its erosion imposes great costs on industry.

• Nor do we as a nation invest enough in long-term projects with large social returns that directly benefit industry, such as basic research, skill formation and education, and environmental protection. Often considered too risky or lacking the prospect of short-term profits, these activities tend to be undersupplied by the private sector unless they are adequately subsidized by the government. Yet Reagan reduced budget expenditures in those areas as well as for other socially beneficial activities, including mass transit, low-income housing, and health care.

• Most problematic of all, during the Reagan era we saw a dramatic shift in corporate investment priorities, from industrial assets to financial assets. U.S. corporations spent much of their cash flow on financial instruments to benefit from their relatively high returns, to exploit the volatility of interest and exchange rates for speculative gains, or to acquire other firms in the stock market. This "portfolio economy" of financial transactions is today nearly four times the size of our "production economy" comprising output. The dramatic expansion of financial assets during the 1980s may well have come at the expense of more productive spending on industrial plant and equipment.

4) The Erosion of Government. If Reagan's hidden agenda was to weaken the intervention capacity of the government, as suggested by his first budget director, David Stockman (1986), he was very successful. Huge budget deficits made it much more difficult for his successors to launch new federal programs, no matter how great the need. Years of neglect left costly legacies, such as the thrift bailout or the clean-up of nuclear weapons plants.[14] Regulatory agencies (e.g., EPA, OSHA, EEOC) suffered a great deal under the leadership of ideological zealots and in the wake of budget cuts. They will need a long time and decisive leadership to recuperate. The self-destruction of the federal government affected many other departments. Major scandals during the second half of the Reagan-

Bush era (the National Aeronautics and Space Administration, National Security Council, Pentagon, Energy, Housing and Urban Development, Food and Drug Administration) illustrated the decline of many important government programs because of incompetence, mismanagement, greed, and corruption.

These signs of institutional decline had their roots not least in Reagan's ideology of laissez-faire capitalism, which denied government a positive role in addressing the country's problems and stressed personal advancement over social concerns. The revival of utilitarian individualism in the Reagan era justified a "get-rich-quick" mentality among many Americans. That focus on material self-interest undermined our sense of civic responsibility and ethical behavior. The widespread indifference, even hostility, toward the rest of society embodied in this individualistic attitude had very negative effects on the quality of public discourse. Self-serving politicians, for whom incumbency had come to dominate all other motives, and a disengaged electorate colluded to leave deepening problems unattended for far too long. It was only when the recession of 1990–92 created a climate of fear and pain across the country that inaction became a political liability. Bill Clinton read the shifting mood well, promised a rejuvenated government, called on individual citizens to do their share for the social good, and won the presidential election. The Reagan era may have ended with Bush's spectacular electoral defeat, but its legacy continues to cast long shadows.

8.4. An Unbalanced Growth Pattern

President Clinton's success will depend much on whether his policies revive the U.S. economy. The long recovery of 1982–90 notwithstanding, Reaganomics created a dangerously unbalanced growth pattern. For eight years we as a nation consumed 4 percent per year more than we produced, leaving us with an exploding foreign debt that approached $600 billion. Even if we manage to lower budget and trade deficits from their current levels, we will remain dependent on foreign savings for years to come. Yet it will be more difficult to attract those imports of capital in the 1990s than it was during the past decade. The world faces a growing shortfall of savings relative to the massive investment needs of Eastern Europe and developing nations. Global disarmament may release funds that are currently tied up in unproductive activities, but even then international competition for scarce capital will heat up.

America's dependence on foreign savings was already recognized as a potentially serious problem when the United States first became a debtor nation in 1985. But the deficit-reduction strategy put in place then (see section 8.2) failed to reduce America's twin deficits sufficiently and in time to avoid the squeeze from slowing capital inflows. Even with a steep dollar devaluation boosting our exports, the trade deficit declined only slowly, for America's appetite for imports continued unabated. And progress on reducing the federal budget deficit was limited by an unwillingness, shared by politicians and the public, to digest the bitter doses of fiscal austerity.

In 1987 Congress revised the deficit targets under Gramm-Rudman and stretched the process out by two years (to balance the budget by 1993), delaying most of the pain until after the 1988 election. Moreover, much of the deficit reduction until then had been fictitious. Congress counted the Social Security surplus, a sum that exceeded $50 billion, toward the budget deficit. But this trust fund is a separate "off budget" item, and its surplus is scheduled to rise rapidly between now and 2010 to pay for the retirement of the "baby-boom" generation. On the other hand, only a small portion of the thrift bailout, which may ultimately cost up to $500 billion, with interest, was actually counted in the budget. The rest was "off budget" even though it has been borne by taxpayers. Congress and the White House also used various accounting gimmicks to make the budget deficit appear smaller than it really was.[15]

Had the budget deficit truly been cut in accordance with Gramm-Rudman's actual targets, the required spending cuts and negative multiplier effects would have reduced the GNP by about 1.7 percent each year. Such a heavy dose of fiscal restraint during the late stages of recovery might well have triggered recession unless compensated by new sources of stimulation. In the second half of the 1980s we still had the benefit of three such sources. But each of those had its limits.

• The collapse of oil prices in 1985–86 (from $30 per barrel to $9) acted like a tax cut for energy users, leaving them with more cash to spend elsewhere. But energy producers and their creditors were immediately hurt. Oil prices have climbed back since then to about $20 per barrel due to strong global demand, elimination of many marginal producers, and new production quotas by OPEC.

• These lower prices for oil, the most dramatic expression of deflationary pressures in commodity markets, convinced bondholders and other financial investors to abandon their hitherto stubborn inflationary expectations. This in turn enabled the Federal Reserve to reverse its tightening of late 1984. Falling interest rates during 1985–86 helped to maintain a high level of (largely credit-financed) demand and fueled the bull market on Wall Street. However, U.S. interest rates could not decline too far without endangering capital inflows. In order to attract foreign savings, we had to offer higher yields than Europe and Japan.

• By making exports cheaper and imports more expensive, a lower dollar eventually managed to improve our trade balance. This took a while, because price adjustments in response to such currency depreciation operated more rapidly than did the changes in trade volumes thereby engendered. Therefore the dollar depreciation of 1985–86 initially had the perverse (J-curve) effect of increasing the trade deficit by raising import costs and reducing export earnings.[16] This only served to reinforce the speculation-driven decline of our currency which in turn aggravated the trade imbalance further. When private foreign investors finally began to lose confidence in response to this sliding J-curve and began to cut back their dollar-denominated investments, the Group of Seven (G–7) (i.e., the United States, Japan, Germany, Britain, France, Canada, Italy) countries concluded the so-called *Louvre Agreement* in February 1987 to keep exchange rates between their currencies within secret, relatively broad, and adjustable target ranges. This currency-stabilization strategy succeeded only because of massive dollar purchases by foreign central banks (amounting to $125 billion in 1987 alone) and higher U.S. interest rates. In the aftermath of the stock market crash of October 1987, the Federal Reserve used that moment of exploding recession fears to push both exchange and interest rates aggressively lower. Those moves turned the corner. Soon thereafter the U.S. trade balance began its long-expected improvement (from the record monthly deficit of $15.6 billion for August 1987 to just $8.2 billion in June 1989 and less than $5 billion during much of 1991–92). Export-led growth kept the domestic recovery alive for more than two years following the crash.

The simultaneous reduction of our twin deficits was a delicate undertaking in the best of circumstances. It resembled driving along an icy road and having to push brakes and accelerator at the same time. One wrong move and the car was bound to start sliding. Should fiscal austerity outweigh improved trade performance, domestic growth would slow down. The reverse case—of trade-deficit reduction outpacing budget-deficit reduction—risked a slowdown abroad, as foreign companies lost sales in their largest export market. Any downturn abroad would hurt U.S. exports. In either case it was imperative for other industrial nations, especially Germany and Japan, to stimulate their domestic economies and thus pick up some of the global slack likely to be caused by lower U.S. twin deficits. As it turned out, neither country helped in time. And the United States failed to put its own fiscal house in order while our economy was still strong enough to absorb a heavy dose of austerity without too much trouble.

In late 1989 foreign-capital inflows into the U.S. economy began to slow down significantly. European investors shifted their focus to investment opportunities closer to home in preparation for a single European Community (EC) market by 1992. Great Britain's recession caused major losses for investors there. With the Berlin Wall gone, Germany turned inward and soon came to depend on foreign capital itself. Japanese investors, who had already started to disengage from the United States in 1987 in favor of an increased presence in the Pacific Rim region, became increasingly preoccupied with financial crisis conditions at home caused by excessive speculation in land and on the Tokyo stock exchange. At that point, in late 1989, the postcrash influx of capital in search of cheap U.S. takeover targets had run its course. As our economy approached "full" employment (5 percent unemployment, 85 percent capacity utilization), prices started to rise more rapidly here. The prospect of higher inflation and continued dollar devaluation made foreign investors wary of U.S. investments.

The combination of slowing capital inflows, revived inflationary pressures, and pressure on the dollar forced the Fed to let U.S. interest rates rise. This policy turned the gradually building financial fragility into an acute credit crunch, and by July 1990 the U.S. economy had entered a finance-induced recession.

8.5. Mounting Financial Imbalances

The growth pattern evolving under Reaganomics fed a worrisome build-up of imbalances and tensions in our credit system. Those reflected significant changes in the relation between money creation, debt financing, and industrial accumulation in the aftermath of financial deregulation.

1) High Interest Rates as an Investment Barrier. Throughout the 1980s U.S. interest rates remained very high, fluctuating between 4 and 6 percent in "real" (inflation-adjusted) terms (see Table 8.3). The first shift toward higher rates occurred in October 1979, when the Federal Reserve shifted from a low-interest policy to restraint of money-supply growth. In 1980 Congress decided to phase out interest-rate ceilings on bank deposits and loans. This deregulation of interest rates made it much easier for lenders to increase the price of their loans. Bond-holders, in particular, insisted on high rates because of stubborn inflationary expectations and the perception of greater credit risk. Their high-price strategy benefited from extraordinarily strong credit demand after 1982. Finally, U.S. interest rates had to remain above those in other industrial nations in order to attract foreign-capital inflows. This constrained the ability of the Federal Reserve to push interest rates below a certain threshold. Even during the recession of the early 1990s, when short-term rates fell steeply in the wake of declining credit demand, long-term rates remained stubbornly elevated.

The high interest rates raised the minimum rate of return required on investment projects ("hurdle rate") and thus were one factor in the aforementioned decline of the net business investment share during the 1980s (see section 8.3). They also altered the composition of corporate investments, to the detriment of our industry's long-term strength. For one, the negative effect of high interest rates on the present value of future cash-flows created a bias in favor of projects with faster payoff periods, such as computers. Yet those short-lived capital goods usually contribute less to capacity or productivity than do longer-term projects in plant, skill formation, or product development. In addition, high interest rates also made yields on many financial instruments more attractive than the returns on industrial investments. The resulting shift in corporate investment priorities turned chief executives more and more into "paper entrepreneurs" who preferred to buy up existing assets in the stock market or trade securities for speculative gain.[17]

Table 8.3

Key Inflation-adjusted Interest Rates (percent per annum)

Year	Treasury bill rates (6-month)		Corporate bond yields (Aaa)		Prime rate charged by banks		New-home mortgage yields	
	Nominal	Real	Nominal	Real	Nominal	Real	Nominal	Real
1978	7.57	−0.33	8.73	0.83	9.06	1.16	9.56	1.96
1979	10.02	1.42	9.63	−1.57	12.67	1.47	10.78	−0.52
1980	11.37	1.87	11.94	−1.46	15.27	1.87	12.66	−0.84
1981	13.78	3.78	14.17	4.97	18.87	9.67	14.70	4.40
1982	11.08	4.88	13.79	9.69	14.86	10.76	15.14	8.94
1983	8.75	4.65	12.04	10.44	10.79	9.19	12.57	9.37
1984	9.80	5.40	12.71	10.61	12.04	9.94	12.38	5.07
1985	7.66	3.96	11.37	10.37	9.93	8.93	11.55	7.95
1986	6.03	3.43	9.02	10.42	8.33	9.73	10.17	8.20
1987	6.05	2.85	9.38	7.28	8.21	6.11	9.31	5.71
1988	6.92	3.02	9.71	7.21	9.32	6.82	9.19	5.09
1989	8.04	3.74	9.26	4.06	10.87	5.67	10.13	5.33
1990	7.47	3.27	9.32	4.42	10.01	5.11	10.05	4.65
1991	5.49	1.89	8.77	6.67	8.46	6.36	9.32	5.12

Source: Council of Economic Advisers, *Economic Report of the President*, 1992, Washington, DC, Tables B–69 (all nominal yields), B–3 (GDP price deflator), B–64 (producer price index), B–60 (consumer price index).

Notes: Real rates are calculated as Treasury bill rates minus percent change of GDP implicit price deflator, corporate bond yields and prime rates minus percent change in producer price index (total finished goods, year to year), home mortgage rates minus percent change in consumer price index (all items, year to year).

2) The Debt Explosion. As long as it creates sufficient income gains, debt stimulates economic activity by giving borrowers additional income to spend before they have earned it. But whenever the debt-servicing burden grows faster than income, debtors face eroding balance sheets and become more vulnerable. This situation is bound to arise eventually. Widely shared optimism during upturns encourages credit overextension, which in turn propels industrial investment to the point of overproduction. The ensuing recession corrects this imbalance, forcing liquidation of debt and capacity reductions. The tendency of taking on too much debt also has a long-term dimension. Throughout the postwar period U.S. consumers and businesses have gradually increased their use of debt, as their memory of depression faded and earlier decisions to borrow more proved successful.[18]

That trend accelerated during the stagflation crisis of the 1970s, when debt began to grow more rapidly in order to compensate for slowing income growth.

The relatively high spending levels sustained by this increased use of debt made it easier to raise prices. As long as the Federal Reserve pursued a policy of low interest rates, inflation held the effective debt burden down. Debtors could repay their debt in devalued dollars. But this process had its limit in the inevitable response of lenders to negative "real" interest rates, devalued principal, and declining creditworthiness of overextended debtors. Faced with such a combination of losses and risks, creditors would eventually insist on tougher credit terms or would simply stop lending. The result was a series of credit crunches followed by recessionary downturns, as occurred during 1969–70, 1973–75, and 1979–82 (see section 6.4 for more detail).

The deep downturn of the early 1980s broke this cycle by triggering massive debt deflation in many sectors and by forcing the central bank to deregulate interest rates. With lenders able to charge higher interest rates, the supply of credit funds has not been subject to the kind of crunch-induced rationing so common during the turbulent 1970s. That recession forced many in the private sector to liquidate debt, enabling them to start the recovery in much better financial shape. These adjustments created the conditions for a new phase of rapidly growing debt levels. The post-1982 recovery was driven by an extraordinary borrowing binge in all sectors of the U.S. economy. With total debt rising more rapidly than total income, many borrowers eventually became quite vulnerable to significant financial distress in case of declining income (see Table 8.4). This caused a great deal of pain when the U.S. economy finally went through a recessionary adjustment in 1990–92.

3) Financial Instability. Incidences of financial crisis used to be confined to cyclical downturns. This changed in the 1980s, when banks and thrifts failed at a record postwar rate. These insolvencies reflect excessively aggressive expansion into new markets in the aftermath of deregulation and major losses from previous credit overextension in certain sectors, such as sovereign loans to developing countries, energy, farming, and real estate. In the process, existing lender-of-last-resort mechanisms were pushed to the limit and required gradual extension. Many high-risk financing arrangements using new and thus untested instruments, such as junk bonds, came under duress during the recent downturn. Financial instability can pose a major threat to the health of our economy, and there is clearly a growing propensity for it.

4) The Dramatic Consequences of Financial Deregulation. The removal or relaxation of many financial regulations in the early 1980s led to major changes in our credit system. These included the transition toward variable-rate bank deposits and loans, proliferation of new money forms, and an unprecedented wave of financial innovation. The spread of new technologies and instruments profoundly transformed our credit circuits and security markets. Gradual loosening of regulatory barriers allowed previously separated institutions to merge, attack each other's traditional markets, and offer a greater variety of products. The trend toward globally integrated financial markets and institutions acceler-

Table 8.4

Increase in U.S. Debt

Credit market debt outstanding (year-end), by borrowing sector
(in billions of dollars)

Year	U.S. government securities	State and local government	House-holds	Nonfinancial business	Financial institutions	GDP
1979	893.2	274.9	1,310.4	1,311.3	265.8	2,488.6
1980	1,016.1	286.6	1,430.2	1,438.1	286.4	2,708.0
1981	1,149.1	303.7	1,549.2	1,596.6	341.8	3,030.6
1982	1,375.0	331.4	1,626.3	1,718.5	370.4	3,149.6
1983	1,629.4	355.0	1,791.9	1,883.7	403.2	3,405.0
1984	1,902.8	383.0	2,018.8	2,180.8	479.0	3,777.2
1985	2,227.0	473.9	2,296.0	2,434.2	580.5	4,038.7
1986	2,620.0	510.1	2,596.1	2,724.8	719.5	4,268.6
1987	2,933.9	558.9	2,879.1	2,945.6	858.2	4,539.9
1988	3,211.1	604.5	3,191.5	3,182.2	986.1	4,900.4
1989	3,512.4	634.1	3,501.5	3,399.9	1,073.0	5,244.0
1990	3,982.5	649.1	3,847.2	3,492.2	1,109.3	5,513.8
1991 (Q2)	4,147.9	652.8	3,911.3	3,503.6	1,082.2	5,652.6

Sources: Board of Governors of the Federal Reserve System, *Flow of Funds Accounts, Financial Assets and Liabilities, Year-End 1966–1989*, September 1990, p. 2 (for 1979–89); *Federal Reserve Bulletin*, January 1992, Table 1.59 (for 1990–91); Council of Economic Advisers, *Economic Report of the President*, Washington, DC, Table B–8 (for GNP).

ated, with significant consequences for credit allocation and power relations between creditors and debtors.

In some respects this process went too far. Greatly intensified competition between financial institutions encouraged excessive risk-taking. The costly thrift crisis illustrates this point most dramatically, even though it is only one of many examples. New financial instruments, such as reverse repurchase agreements by government securities dealers, deposit brokerage, junk-bonds, mortgage-backed securities, and stock-index futures, caused major losses, which prompted our monetary authorities to limit their use. Deregulation of exchange rates (in 1973) and interest rates (in 1980) made these crucial prices of money much less stable. Their growing volatility increased both the attractiveness of short-term financial speculation and the uncertainty associated with long-term industrial investment. The uneven and piecemeal nature of deregulation also created problematic changes in the structure of the financial services industry, which still have not been addressed properly.

So far our policy-makers have responded to these problems in an ad hoc fashion. That will no longer do. Instead, they will have to develop an integrated regulatory framework for financial institutions and markets capable of their stabilization. Such a task involves finding a workable balance between market-driven restructuring of our credit system and effective measures to counteract the inherent instability of this process. In earlier periods of transition such comprehensive regulatory reform usually occurred only in the aftermath of acute crisis, such as the Civil War in the 1860s or the Great Depression of the 1930s (see chapter 4).

5) The Complications of Monetary Policy. With fiscal policy locked into a gradual reduction of our large structural budget deficit, the burden of macroeconomic stabilization fell more heavily on the central bank. After 1982 the Federal Reserve proved remarkably effective in steering the economy between inflationary overheating and recession. Its frequent policy adjustments during the post-1982 recovery were helped by the new variable-rate regime, which allowed the effects of interest-rate changes to spread much more rapidly through the credit system. This improved the central bank's capacity to counteract the cyclical fluctuations of economic growth, making relatively moderate policy shifts sufficient.

At the same time the U.S. central bank was forced to operate in a much more complex environment, which has made monetary policy more difficult to execute. For one, financial innovation following deregulation made the interrelations between bank reserves, monetary aggregates, and the gross national product significantly less stable. Any policy course aiming to limit the growth of the money supply by targeting bank reserves, as recommended by the monetarists, therefore became less accurate. Moreover, the Federal Reserve had to keep domestic interest rates high enough to attract needed capital inflows from abroad and to prevent a dollar crisis. On the other hand, our central bank could not allow those rates to rise too much without risking recession. This dilemma was aggravated by current international monetary arrangements, especially the new system of "managed floating" introduced under the Louvre Agreement in 1987. That accord among the leading (G–7) countries made it very difficult, and during episodes of acute instability in foreign-exchange markets even impossible, to control interest rates and exchange rates at the same time.

6) The United States as Net Debtor. Our twin deficits have made the United States dependent on continuous borrowing from abroad. Today, in 1993, we owe the rest of the world close to $600 billion. For seventy years the United States dominated the global economy as the principal creditor to the rest of the world, but in less than a decade it has become the world's largest debtor. While this new status surely symbolizes the decline of our economic might, most Americans are not too sure about its effects, except for rather vague premonitions about the future erosion of our living standard. Since we operate now in uncharted territory, it is not easy to predict what that external debt will eventually mean for the U.S. economy. However, certain implications can already be identified.

• There is a real (moral as well as economic) problem when the richest country in the world absorbs a large chunk of the world's scarce savings to satisfy its own excess consumption.[19] Many LDCs face severe socio-economic conditions and are starved for investment capital, a situation exacerbated by massive capital flight of their ruling oligarchies into dollar-based assets. Eventually the LDCs will need more of the world's excess funds to rebuild their devastated economies and resume imports of industrial products. Such reopening of lost export markets would also benefit the United States and other industrial nations.

• In order to attract continuous inflows of funds from abroad, the United States had to maintain a positive differential between its interest rates and those of its principal lenders. From early 1987 onward the Federal Reserve found that it could no longer lower U.S. interest rates unless they also declined in Western Europe and Japan. Such a dependency situation required coordination of simultaneous interest cuts among the G–7 countries. Those occurred three times in the late 1980s but have become more difficult to implement in the early 1990s with the erosion of the Louvre mechanism. The absence of international policy coordination since 1990 has not mattered much until now. As long as the recession forced private credit demands lower, it was easier to finance our public-sector borrowing requirement even though fiscal stabilizers pushed the U.S. budget deficit to $300 billion in 1992. That year the Fed was actually in a position to drive short-term interest rates to their lowest level in nearly three decades. But the downward rigidity of long-term rates during the most recent recession should serve as a warning signal that America's continued dependence on foreign capital inflows might well restrict the growth capacity of the U.S. economy in years to come. That constraint is a major reason why the recovery that began in late 1992 has been much slower than previous ones.

• When public debt is financed internally, the only effect is a redistribution of income within the country from (on average middle-income) taxpayers to (usually upper-income) bondholders. But external debt reduces a country's available resources, because its servicing costs constitute a net outflow to the rest of the world. With up to a third of our annual income gains flowing abroad each year, Americans will have to produce that much more from now on just to maintain the current (meager) pace of improvement in living standards. It might be that foreign investors reinvest their gains here, but that too depends on making our economy more competitive.

• Besides depressing our future living standards, foreign debt-servicing charges count as a debit item that adds to our current account deficit. In the second quarter of 1989 the balance of trade in the services and investment sector of the U.S. economy posted its first deficit in decades. Servicing charges for our external debt and income to foreign owners of American assets have finally begun to exceed repatriated income from our foreign assets. Unless compensated by improvements elsewhere in our trade balance, we run the risk of continuously worsening current account deficits.

7) The Dollar as World Money. For all those who worry about our capacity to repay the debt to foreigners, let it be understood that the United States is unlike any other debtor in the world. After all, the dollar remains the world's key currency. Between one-half and two-thirds of international trade and capital flows are still denominated in dollars. The world-money status of its currency makes the United States a unique debtor nation, capable of settling its foreign debt obligations in its own money.[20] Of course, that so-called seigniorage benefit lasts only as long as foreigners remain confident in the dollar and accept it as an international medium of exchange. Under these conditions, repayment of our foreign debt is for all practical purposes automatic. To the extent that foreigners are willing to hold dollar-denominated assets, U.S. debt can be simply rolled over. Our only actual outlays in this case are the debt-servicing charges we pay on our foreign liabilities.

When a currency acts as world money, the country of its issue must actually run a deficit in its balance-of-payments accounts of capital flows and trade with the rest of the world. Such a deficit generates the net outflows that transfer the currency from its domestic origin into international circulation. A country becomes issuer of world money because of its hegemonic dominance of the world economy, so it will normally run trade surpluses. In that case it must be a net exporter of capital (e.g., official foreign aid, direct investment of multinational corporations, or bank loans) to create the required balance-of-payments deficits. But when its global hegemony erodes, the issuer of world money experiences a reversal in its balance of payments. It begins to run chronic trade deficits and eventually becomes a net importer of capital. This is precisely what happened to Great Britain during the interwar period and to the United States over the last two decades.

Such a situation is inherently unstable. There is a fundamental contradiction between being the principal issuer of world money and simultaneously also the world's largest debtor. The need for a strong and stable currency eventually clashes with mounting devaluation pressures. This crisis can be avoided as long as existing international monetary arrangements tie foreign investors to the dollar. For lack of alternative investment opportunities these investors simply do not have much choice, other than to invest a significant portion of their excess funds in dollar-denominated assets. And they also know that any panicky unloading of these dollar assets would create havoc in the international monetary system and disrupt the world economy, thus hurting their own investment portfolios. But the large U.S. trade deficits are bound to weaken the dollar over time, since they represent excess supplies of that currency and affect market expectations. Such dollar devaluation is bound to erode investor confidence, which threatens the world-money status of our currency in the long run.

How this contradiction will unfold in the next few years depends not least on how well the G–7 countries manage to contain inevitable pressures. So far they have performed rather badly on that score. The mechanism for international policy coordination set up under the Plaza and Louvre agreements soon fell apart. The central banks found that they could no longer control interest rates and exchange rates at the same time unless there was greater convergence among the G–7 economies and appropriate changes in their respective fiscal policies. And there was simply not sufficient political will to move in that direction. On the contrary, by 1990 each of the three principal powers had turned inward, away from international cooperation. The United States, while finally replacing the discredited Gramm-Rudman approach with a bipartisan budget agreement of multiyear spending caps and revenue enhancements, decided that it needed to fight recession at home with lower interest and exchange rates. Germany, on the other hand, mishandled its reunification and then responded to the inflationary shock it thereby created with a policy of very high interest rates which was bound to create great difficulties within the European Community and further erode the Louvre mechanism. Japan has been consumed by the collapse of its stock market and land prices, a bursting of speculative bubbles which wiped out a great deal of capital and threw the domestic economy into its worst postwar recession.

The domestic problems of Germany and Japan, the world's two dominant creditor nations, have given the dollar's threatened international status a temporary reprieve. The United States, under a new leadership committed to long-term reindustrialization and deficit reduction, might use that window of opportunity to strengthen its economic base and external position. Even then it is doubtful that existing international monetary arrangements can last much longer. At issue is not only how the three key currencies can coexist but also how to contain exchange-rate instability, speculative capital flows, and divergences in the macroeconomic policy mix of different countries. In the absence of a more stable international monetary order, the multilateral trade regime set up under GATT threatens to disintegrate into a triad of adversarial blocs engaged in a proliferation of trade conflicts. The atrophy of the Louvre Agreement, the stalemate concerning the Uruguay Round, and Europe's failure to implement the Maastricht Treaty on Economic and Monetary Union all clearly point in that direction. As these crises run their course, political leaders and their economic advisors may finally come to realize that the world needs a radical overhaul of the international monetary system—a subject to which we shall return in the last part of this book.

Part IV
The Monetary Regime in Transition

9

The Dilemmas of Monetary Policy

The mounting signs of financial instability discussed at the end of the preceding chapter (see section 8.5) are part and parcel of the transition toward a new global accumulation regime. They are both the manifestation of a collapsed monetary regime and the driving force behind deeper structural changes which are transforming our economy. As such, they deserve the close attention of policy-makers who are struggling with the challenges of a new era.

The changes in our credit system, a mixture of destabilization and restructuring, need to be analyzed carefully, not least in order to define the direction of monetary reform. We are, after all, in the middle of a gradual transformation toward a new monetary regime. That process has involved a series of initiatives by the U.S. government over the last dozen or so years. In the following four chapters we shall try to identify the underlying thread of these seemingly disparate measures, starting with a discussion of monetary policy changes during the 1980s.

9.1. The Banking Act of 1980

The historic demise of the postwar monetary regime can be traced back to the dramatic switch by the Federal Reserve from a Keynesian low-interest policy to a monetarist focus on slow and steady money-supply growth in October 1979. As already discussed (see section 7.7), that policy change aimed at breaking the "debt-inflation" spiral underlying the stagflation crisis of the 1970s. It did so, but only by triggering the worst downturn since the 1930s. Insofar as this Great Recession of 1979–82 marked the beginning of a major restructuring process in our economy, its historic significance reaches far beyond that of a purely cyclical event. In this chapter we shall analyze how the monetary policy of the Federal Reserve has evolved since then.

Six months after Volcker's fateful policy switch, in March 1980, Congress passed the Depository Institutions Deregulation and Monetary Control Act

(DIDMCA). This was the most significant banking legislation since Roosevelt's monetary reforms of 1933–35 and a major first step toward constructing a new monetary regime. As its name indicates, the act had two different purposes. On the one hand, it removed harmful or ineffective regulatory restraints on the banking industry. On the other hand, it sought to strengthen the Fed's influence over the money-creation process by private banks. These apparently contradictory goals of deregulation and increased central bank control corresponded to actual conditions of institutional erosion, prompting Congress to pursue both objectives simultaneously.

I will first summarize DIDMCA's key provisions pertaining to deregulation of the banking sector. Various "near money" deposits (e.g., NOW accounts, ATS accounts, share drafts, and accounts accessible through remote service units), which had emerged on a regionally limited basis during the 1970s, now became available on a nationwide basis. These interest-bearing checking accounts could also be offered by thrifts (savings and loans associations, mutual savings banks) and credit unions, thereby extending money-creation powers for the first time to these depository institutions. The law also phased out Regulation Q ceilings on deposit rates and overrode various state usury ceilings on loan rates.[1] These price controls had played a crucial role in the recurrent credit crunches of the preceding decade by triggering disintermediation and cutbacks in lending whenever market rates rose above set ceilings. Thrifts, battered by their particularly pronounced maturity mismatch between short-term deposit liabilities and long-term (mostly fixed-rate) mortgage assets, were allowed to enlarge their proportion of nonmortgage loans and to lend over a bigger geographic area. Finally, DIDMCA also simplified truth-in-lending regulations and required different regulatory agencies to lower the compliance burden associated with their regulations.

Concurrent with these deregulation measures, DIDMCA strengthened central bank control over the money-creation process of private banks. The act established identical reserve requirement standards for all depository institutions, thereby extending the Fed's most powerful monetary policy tool from 5,500 member banks to more than 40,000 depository institutions (including 9,000 nonmember banks, 5,500 thrifts, and 20,500 credit unions). Reserve requirements were themselves greatly simplified, replacing a highly graduated system with fewer brackets.[2] All depository institutions subject to reserve requirements gained access to the discount window and payments services of the Federal Reserve. The law also provided for explicit pricing of these services which until then had been offered for free. Deposit insurance increased from $40,000 to $100,000 per bank deposit.

These provisions expanded the control net of the Federal Reserve in two significant ways. For one, various "near money" deposits, which previously had existed outside its regulatory umbrella, became subject to reserve requirements. In addition, the basic monetary policy tools of the central bank now applied to all commercial banks, savings and loans associations, mutual savings banks, and credit unions rather than just to member banks. That extension meant that both our dual banking system and regulatory differences between different types of financial institutions lost much of their significance. All depository institutions could now issue new money, and in return they all had to accept the same degree of Federal Reserve control over their money-creation process.

Congress also redefined the procedures for implementing selective credit controls in DIDMCA. Two weeks before the law was passed President Carter had for the first time used the emergency powers of the Credit Control Act of 1969 and authorized the central bank to restrict credit in the face of exploding inflation pressures. The Fed responded by imposing special deposit requirements on consumer credit, money-market mutual funds, and borrowed liabilities of banks (see section 7.7). The dramatic impact of this tough credit-restraint program created an immediate political backlash against the central bank. Congress then included a provision in DIDMCA which authorized the Federal Reserve Board to impose any reserve requirements it deems necessary in a national emergency situation. But such action can only be undertaken after consultation with appropriate House and Senate committees, requires a prompt explanatory report to Congress, and is limited to 180 days unless five of the seven board members vote for an extension. At the same time, the Credit Control Act of 1969 was allowed to expire in June 1982. With this legislative substitution, lawmakers narrowed the discretionary powers of the Federal Reserve to control credit extension when the economy overheats. Of course, the Fed should be made accountable when it uses such a potent and exceptional weapon. But there is also much to be said in favor of selective credit controls as an effective tool to curtail potentially damaging financing activities and influence the direction of credit allocation.[3]

Apart from restricting its emergency powers over credit controls, DIDMCA presented additional complications for the central bank. Even though the law expanded the Fed's control net over the banking system, it introduced new difficulties for the effective conduct of monetary policy. These arose in particular from the various provisions of deregulation. The legalization of "near money" deposits made accurate targeting of monetary aggregates more difficult. The elimination of rate ceilings on bank deposits and loans had a profound impact on interest rates, which made it harder to stabilize them. Finally, explicit pricing of previously free payments services confronted the central bank with the prospect of intensifying competition from the private sector and threatened its traditional control over the nation's payments system. Each of these complications deserves to be looked at in some detail.

9.2. The Deregulation of Private Bank Money

The banking act of 1980 legalized a variety of interest-bearing transaction deposits on a nationwide basis (e.g., NOW accounts, ATS accounts, credit-union share drafts) and made them part of the money supply. It also opened the way for an entire generation of new deposit types by phasing out Regulation Q over a six-year period. In 1982 bank regulators, grouped together by DIDMCA in the Depository Institutions Deregulation Committee (DIDC), decided to speed up the timetable of that phase-out. What prompted their decision was the phenomenal success of unregulated deposits which nonbank institutions had introduced a few years earlier. Money-market mutual funds (MMMFs) and cash management accounts (CMAs) in particular diverted billions from depository institutions whose regulated deposits carried much lower yields.[4]

During 1982–83 the DIDC authorized a host of new bank deposit instruments capable of competing with the MMMFs and the CMAs. These included removal of interest ceilings on deposits with maturities of 3.5 years or more, a new three-month account with an interest rate tied to Treasury bills and a $7,500 minimum deposit, permission for Citibank's "personal-asset management account," which competed directly with the CMAs, and so-called SuperNOW accounts. The Depository Institutions Act (DIA) of 1982, enacted principally to expand the deregulation of thrifts (see section 10.3), also created a new "money-market deposit account" (MMDA) with no rate ceilings, no reserve requirements, and only limited checking privileges (three checks per month). Both SuperNOW and MMDA accounts proved to be very successful, attracting more than $300 billion within the first three months of their introduction. When the last remnants of Regulation Q finally disappeared in 1986, depository institutions introduced small-denomination certificates of deposit yielding current market rates. Those "consumer CDs" largely replaced traditional passbook savings accounts and time deposits, which had been subject to rate ceilings.

These new deposit instruments have allowed banks and thrifts to compete more effectively for funds. But since most carry current market yields, they cost more than the old zero-interest demand deposits and fixed-rate savings deposits. In response to this increase in the cost of funds, many depository institutions have aggressively gone after upper-scale customers and encouraged consolidation of accounts. Rich clients were offered more services in return for higher minimum deposits, separate teller lines, personal account officers, and fee waivers on safe-deposit boxes or other amenities. In addition, banks introduced fees for many previously free services and stiff penalties for below-minimum balances. Banks defend such *relationship pricing* on the grounds that they have lost the interest-cost subsidy provided by Regulation Q. But this practice, coupled with widespread branch closures in poor neighborhoods during the 1980s, has hurt the majority of (low-income) Americans. In large cities, especially, millions of people have been deprived of access to banking services and are forced to use often seedy "check-clearing" establishments, which may charge up to 10 percent to cash a check. The emergence of class-tiered banking has caused enough popular discontent to get the attention of Congress. Some banks have responded to this pressure by providing no-frills "lifeline" accounts for low-income customers.[5]

The deregulation of deposits has made the cost side of depository institutions much more susceptible to interest-rate fluctuations. With most of their short-term deposit liabilities now carrying variable rates, interest payments by banks and thrifts increase immediately whenever market rates rise. Their revenue side, on the other hand, responds much more sluggishly to higher rates. This is especially true to the extent that they carry longer-term assets with fixed interest rates. In that case, higher rates have to paid on most deposits but can only be charged on new loans. To counteract such a profit squeeze, depository institutions have increasingly offered floating-rate rather than fixed-rate loans. In this way they could match the greater variability of their costs on the revenue side.

• Business loans used to be the mainstay of commercial banking. But for more than two decades now, corporations have increasingly come to rely on commercial paper as a more attractive source of short-term funding. This trend continued during the 1980s, and the share of business loans fell from 38 percent of total bank credit in 1980 to 31 percent in 1988. Banks responded by diversifying into new areas of lending, in which they could charge variable rates.

• Their first major diversification took place during the 1970s, when the largest U.S. banks became heavily involved in the recycling of "petrodollars" through the Euromarket. These loans to developing countries carried variable rates, which typically were readjusted twice a year.

• In 1981 the Federal Home Loan Bank Board, the thrifts' main regulator, allowed adjustable-rate mortgages (ARMs). These ARMs, which now account for about 70 percent of new home loans, have their interest rates adjusted annually, with a cap that limits the rate increase in any one year. With loans to industrial corporations lagging due to the growing popularity of commercial paper and junk-bonds, banks aggressively expanded real estate lending from 25 percent of their loan total in 1982 to 37 percent in 1989.

• The Tax Reform Act of 1986 restricted the tax deductibility of interest expenses on most consumer loans. In its wake home equity loans, which remained fully deductible, gained in popularity. Between end–1985 and mid-1988 their volume quadrupled to about $70 billion. The interest rates on these loans are typically pegged to the prime rate and can change anytime.

• Fluctuating rates have also spread in the category of personal loans and credit cards. According to Federal Reserve estimates in June 1988, 10 percent of the $628.75 billion in consumer installment debt then outstanding carried floating rates.

Today nearly half of the bank loans provide for some kind of regular price adjustment to reflect current market yields. To the extent that this share is likely to rise further, we are in effect gradually moving toward a *variable-rate regime* of bank deposits and loans. Depository institutions are thus in a better position to protect their profit margins. Whenever their deposit rates rise, banks and thrifts simply adjust their loan rates upward. This practice of *spread banking* is facilitated by a large degree of price coordination. Although depository institutions often compete intensely for deposits by offering higher yields, they tend to price their loans in unison. Leading banks usually change the prime rate—the rate charged to their best (corporate) customers and the basis for other loan rates—at the same time. The banks' margins on business loans have been razor thin, but they have priced mortgages, consumer loans, and credit card lines far above their cost of funds.

The proliferation of unregulated deposit instruments has also complicated monetary policy in significant ways. For one, traditional money-supply measures became obsolete when new transaction deposits with check-writing privileges (e.g., NOW accounts, MMMFs) appeared in the late 1970s. This prompted the Fed to undertake a major revision of monetary aggregates in February 1980: M1A, the old M1 consisting of currency and domestically owned demand deposits in commercial banks; M1B comprising NOW and ATS accounts in addition; an amended M2, which included not only savings accounts and bank-issued RPs but also the money-market mutual funds; a revision of M3 to take account of all other RPs and large time deposits; and an entirely new measure named L (for liquidity), which included U.S.-owned Eurodollars, commercial paper, bankers' acceptances, and some Treasury obligations. In January 1982 the Fed dropped M1A as no longer relevant. Its new M1 measure, the former M1B, was amended in December 1982 to include MMDAs, while SuperNOW accounts were counted toward M2 after January 1983.

These repeated redefinitions of monetary aggregates did not resolve the problem posed by the quickening pace of financial innovation. Throughout 1981 and 1982 the new money measures behaved in erratic fashion. In the face of such unpredictability the Fed downgraded M1 and abandoned monetary targeting in October 1982. By that point the central bank governors had come to realize that they could not target the money supply precisely, no matter how they measured it. Deregulation of private bank money had made the monetary aggregates more volatile.[6]

Most of the new deposit types mentioned above (e.g., MMMFs, MMDAs, SuperNOW) have effectively abolished the traditional separation between checking and savings accounts. They combine both transaction and investment features. It thus becomes hard to predict whether money kept in those various accounts is used for spending or saving purposes. Yet that distinction is crucial. Money about to be expended in transactions has a much more direct effect on economic activity after a relatively short time lag than does money hoarded in otherwise liquid accounts to earn interest. It will be a while before policy-makers know with a reasonable degree of accuracy the spending propensities of funds deposited in new types of checking accounts. In the meantime, long-standing patterns between bank reserves, money, and the economy, which the Federal Reserve used to rely on as a guide for its monetary policy, have clearly broken down. Nor does it help the effectiveness of monetary targeting that some deposits used predominantly for investment purposes (e.g., SuperNOW, MMMFs) are included in the narrow money-supply measures M1 or M2, while other deposit types, which are essentially transaction balances or easily converted into those, are not. The latter category comprises negotiable CDs and the growing number of credit lines secured by real estate or other investments which are accessible by check.

With so many liquid instruments at their disposal, businesses and consumers have become much more inclined to move funds constantly in and out of different deposits. Debit cards, transfers by telephone, and multideposit "sweep" accounts (e.g., CMAs) have all made it much easier to shift funds at a moment's notice. Sometimes, as in 1981, these movements are prompted by the desire to earn better yields. At other times—during 1982, for instance—people are nervous and prefer to build up liquidity in lower-yielding funds. Movements of funds between deposits also depend on the pricing strategies of banks. Bankers offer their customers different yields on various deposit types depending on where they think interest rates are headed. Expectations of rising interest rates, for example, usually lead banks to offer comparatively better yields on longer-term CDs in order to lock in depositors' money. As a result, funds flow out of the more liquid deposits counted in M1 or M2. The reverse happens when interest rates are expected to go down.

Constant switching of funds between different deposit types shows up as unpredictable swings in monetary aggregates which seem entirely divorced from any corresponding changes in economic activity. In other words, money-supply measures no longer conform to GNP growth. Instead, they reflect investment strategies of depository institutions and their customers. The narrow measure M1, comprising currency and checking accounts, has shrunk in size relative to the economy because under normal conditions many depositors prefer to hold their cash in higher-yielding alternatives. As new deposit types paying market rates have absorbed a growing share of M2 and M3, these broader money aggregates have become less responsive to overall movements in interest rates. Yet they both react quite sensitively to relative changes in yield differentials; that is, to movements in the structure of interest rates. "Transaction" and "investment" components of multideposit sweep accounts also have different reserve requirements, so that any shifting of funds within these accounts has an immediate impact on the money multiplier that links bank reserves and money aggregates.

Financial deregulation has thus opened a whole new chapter in the historic evolution of credit-money. We now face an array of deposit instruments with monetary attributes. Not only has this development dramatically altered the behavior of various monetary aggregates, it also poses a major challenge to monetary theory. monetarists, who have always argued in favor of deregulation and privatization of credit-money, now find these very steps to have invalidated their most cherished assumptions.

• To begin, the proliferation of different deposit types has made it difficult to define an accurate transaction measure of the money stock.

• Private bank money, the dominant form of credit-money, is neither stable nor under the direct control of the central bank. It is essentially an endogenous variable subject to the profit motive of depository institutions and their customers. Dependent on volatile expectations and cyclical credit extension, monetary aggregates behave in inherently unstable fashion.[7] If anything, this instability has deepened with deregulation. Today deposit-holders constantly move funds among a large number of accounts, and these transfers often reflect portfolio adjustments rather than market transactions.

• Worst of all, the velocity of money behaved very strangely during much of the 1980s. That variable is the ratio of GNP and M1 and, as such, is the reciprocal of the transaction demand for money. When velocity is unstable, the relationship between the money supply and economic activity is no longer predictable. In this case targeting of monetary aggregates loses its rationale as an effective stabilization policy.

The velocity of money rose consistently at an annual rate of between 3 and 4 percent for most of the postwar period, but it fell by 2 to 6 percent per year between 1981 and 1986 (see Figure 9.1). Such a decline in velocity could be expected for the kind of deflationary downturn we had in 1981–82. But it is highly unusual for it to occur during a recovery period. Why, then, did the circulation of money continue to slow after 1982? One reason could have been that M1 included interest-bearing deposits after 1980. These are held more for investment purposes and turn over less frequently than transaction accounts. That period also saw an explosion in the volume of financial transactions which are not counted in GNP. Finally, Americans began to spend a great deal more on imports which cut into GNP, thereby shrinking the numerator in the velocity equation. Whatever caused it, the decline in money's velocity during the first half of the 1980s allowed the Fed to tolerate much faster money-creation without reigniting inflation.

The monetarists are not the only victims of deregulation. Portfolio-choice models, a mainstay of the Neoclassical/Keynesian synthesis (see chapter 1, note 10), have lost much of whatever explanatory power they used to have. Their distinction between money and other financial assets (e.g., bonds) makes little sense today, when many deposits combine both transaction and investment features. Their emphasis on the transaction motive of money demand, which they share with the monetarists, no longer corresponds to the reality of the last decade, during which the less stable precautionary, speculative, and finance motives of money demand have frequently dominated. It is for this reason that we need to revive Keynes's theory of money demand, including his highly original analysis of sectoral differences in the circulation of deposits found in the *Treatise* (1930).

Figure 9.1 **The Velocity of Money**

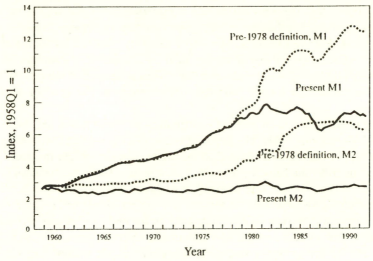

Year

Source: Council of Economic Advisers, *Economic Report of the President*, 1992, Washington, DC, Chart 7–1.

Note: 1958Q1=1.0. Pre–1978 M2 is a proxy which excludes all large time deposits.

Monetarists do recognize that the central bank operates in a new environment. What is needed, they argue, is for the central bank to improve its control over the money supply. They have made several suggestions in this direction. For example, Federal Reserve economists have developed new money-calculation techniques to distinguish between the transaction and investment components of money.[8] In February 1984 the Fed also heeded the monetarists' call for a switch from "lagged" to "contemporaneous" reserve accounting. Under the new system required reserves, which banks have to set aside, are computed on the basis of deposits over the current reporting period rather than the preceding two weeks. This change in procedure gave the Fed better short-term control over the money supply but also caused significant compliance costs for reporting institutions and greater volatility in the money markets.[9]

Apart from suggesting procedural changes, monetarists have also pushed the Fed to change its operating targets. In July 1981 Treasury Under Secretary for Monetary Affairs Beryl Sprinkel argued that the central bank should focus on the broader monetary base (cash plus total reserves), rather than just nonborrowed reserves, and should at the same time correlate the discount rate for borrowed reserves more closely with other money-market rates. In his opinion, these steps would reduce "erratic" money-supply growth and thereby also stabilize interest rates. In June 1987 another monetarist at the U.S. Treasury, Assistant Secretary for Economic Policy Michael Darby, urged the Fed to return to M1A as its principal target. That measure excludes interest-bearing checking accounts

(NOW, MMDAs) and should therefore reflect spending activity more accurately. Darby noted that the behavior of M1A in relation to GNP was more stable throughout the 1980s than any of the other monetary aggregates. What he forgot to consider was the likelihood of reverse causality: that the level of economic activity affects the amount of money held by the public. Nowadays M1A is dominated by business accounts, and this makes it likely that the growth of the M1A aggregate has merely reflected, not determined, the pace of economic activity.

The most important monetarist contribution in recent years has come from Ronald McKinnon (1984). The Stanford economist argued that the global mobility of capital has made traditional Monetarism obsolete. When investors move huge sums from one currency to another on a regular basis, the standard notions that the demand for any one currency is stable and that the central bank need only watch its own domestic money supply are no longer valid. Once Bretton Woods gave way to floating exchange rates in the early 1970s (see section 7.2), the dollar lost its status as the only acceptable reserve currency. With both the mark and the yen gradually emerging as alternatives, the money supplies of the United States, Germany, and Japan became inextricably linked. The domestic monetary policy of one country may now be easily offset by the actions of other countries. For this reason central bankers of the leading industrial nations should coordinate their money-supply targets to keep the growth of the *global* money supply stable.

McKinnon's empirical work has shown that movements in the world money supply, defined here as the combined money supplies of the ten largest economies, predicted both the two global bouts with inflation in the 1970s and the worldwide recession of 1981–82 better than did changes in purely domestic money supplies. In his opinion this is not a statistical accident but proof of a causal relationship. The key to this connection is a synchronizing transmission mechanism via exchange rates. When, for instance, U.S. money-supply growth slowed after 1979, domestic interest rates rose and the dollar strengthened. Because Germany and Japan both depend heavily on raw material imports that are priced in dollars, the depreciation of their currencies quickly threatened to increase inflationary pressures at home. Both countries then tried to contain this spillover effect by tightening their money supplies and driving up their interest rates. The result was a deepening of the global contraction. In other words, monetary policies nowadays have a tendency to move in lockstep, with the Fed setting the basic direction. The problem is that most industrial nations are heavily dependent on trade and therefore pursue exchange-rate objectives, while the United States, as the provider of the major reserve currency, does not. This situation began to change with the Louvre Agreement in 1987 (see section 8.4). But such exchange-rate coordination among the G–7 is, in McKinnon's opinion, only a first step. Unless monetary policies are harmonized, the misalignment of exchange rates will remain.

Although monetarists continue to push for a policy of stable money-supply growth, the Fed has actually long since abandoned pursuit of this elusive objective. In the summer of 1982 Volcker, faced with dramatic disinflation and a series of spectacular financial collapses (e.g., Penn Square, Drysdale, Mexico), decided to allow faster money growth. Although the Fed resumed monetary targets in 1983, it has missed those often and no longer responds to short-term deviations of the money supply. Instead, since the early Reagan years the Fed has supported credit demand by injecting additional reserves into the banking system through open-market purchases whenever needed. The extent of this accommodation has been regulated by pegging the Federal funds rate within a target range. The Fed has managed this peg more flexibly than it did during the 1970s by adjusting the targets more often. For these adjustments the Fed uses several leading indicators of inflationary expectations, most notably the yield curve, commodity prices, the exchange rate, and also, since early 1988, labor-market data.

9.3. The Contradictory Effects of Interest Deregulation

Given the renewed importance of interest rates in the formulation of U.S. monetary policy, we must analyze significant changes in their behavior following their deregulation in 1979–80. Between 1966 and 1981 low rate ceilings on bank deposits and loans triggered recurrent credit crunches. Whenever unregulated interest rates rose above those ceilings, banks faced massive disintermediation and had to cut back their lending activity. In the absence of rate ceilings we no longer have this automatic shut-down mechanism with which to cool down accelerating inflation. Nowadays financial institutions and borrowers can obtain new funds as long as they are willing and able to pay whatever interest rates their lenders require. Quantitative rationing of credit, with its sudden crunch dynamic, has given way to a more moderate restraint on credit via the price mechanism. That restoration of market-based adjustment counteracts cyclical episodes of credit overextension more gradually.

The removal of interest-rate ceilings thus had the fundamentally beneficial effect of stabilizing the business cycle and extending the longevity of the recovery. But, as often happens with efforts to strengthen the market mechanism, this deregulation also had its share of negative repercussions.

• For one, the restoration of price competition has made the banking system more prone to risk. When depository institutions bid up rates to attract depositors, they are under pressure to invest these costlier funds in correspondingly higher-yielding assets. But in their frantic search for more profitable investment outlets, financial institutions have often forgotten the inescapable trade-off between risk and return: investments with higher yields also tend to carry greater risks.[10]

• In the absence of price controls the credit system regulates itself through market forces of demand and supply. Unfortunately, neither borrowers nor their lenders are normally inclined to exercise prudent self-restraint. Successful validation of previous financing decisions often prompts both sides to accept higher leveraging in their joint chase for greater profits. The longer the recovery lasts, the less conservative financial standards tend to become. Unless constrained by rising interest rates, borrowers are therefore likely to accumulate more debt over time than used to be the case when sudden credit crunches forced debt levels down in regular intervals.

• Finally, variable-rate loans have allowed lenders to transfer much of their price risk to borrowers, a dramatic change in credit relations which the oligopolistic practice of spread banking has only served to reinforce. Higher interest rates no longer have an impact just on the margin, when borrowers take out new loans; they raise the debt-servicing burden of all outstanding loans carrying adjustable rates. This has meant that any dose of restraint, whether initiated by private lenders or the central bank, now affects a much larger group of debtors and spreads more rapidly through the credit system than it did under the old fixed-rate regime. Tightening by the Fed may thus require less time to take effect. However, should the Fed ever be forced to keep interest rates high for a while, say in response to capital flight out of the dollar, then borrowers with a large variable-rate debt would suddenly face significant increases in their debt-servicing charges. From now on any sustained rise in interest rates may therefore trigger massive debt-servicing problems and loan defaults.

The deregulation of interest rates may have lengthened (debt-financed) recoveries, but it has also made subsequent credit crunches potentially more difficult to overcome. We saw this dynamic at work during the past decade. The post-1982 recovery lasted far beyond the average duration of postwar upswings not least because debt financing of excess spending went on for so long. Deflationary pressures and excess capacity in key sectors helped by keeping the overall inflation rate low. It was only when the U.S. economy started to approach the full-employment barrier in 1989 that inflation began to edge up. At that point the Fed pushed the brake, a reaction that was also prompted by a slowdown in capital inflows from abroad.

But the tightening of the central bank, initially designed as a "soft landing" scenario, turned into a low-altitude crash. After seven years of rapid increases in debt, the credit system had reached such a point of vulnerability that a relatively modest dose of restraint by the Fed sufficed to force credit demand and bank lending into sharp retrenchment. Facing the first financial squeeze in the new variable-rate regime, the Fed also underestimated how much more rapidly any tightening nowadays spreads through the credit system. In the summer of 1990, even before the Gulf crisis pushed oil prices temporarily much higher (from $18 dollars a barrel to $40), the decelerating U.S. economy finally slipped into recession. None of the normal triggers, such as sharply rising inflation, panic runs out of the dollar, or bulging business inventories, played a significant role this time. Instead, the downturn was entirely finance-driven, the result of a new kind of credit crunch which lasted for nearly three years.

Let us now turn to a structural rather than purely cyclical feature of interest deregulation. Although U.S. interest rates declined gradually between August 1982 and February 1987, they fell much less than the inflation rate. This led "real" (inflation-adjusted) interest rates to remain constantly above 4 percent— the highest level since the Civil War (see Table 9.1). Such a dramatic turn from extremely low "real" rates during the 1970s had several causes. In part it surely reflected market conditions of very strong credit demand from all sectors of the economy clashing with stagnant domestic savings. Creditors may also have demanded higher risk premiums in response to considerable uncertainty during a period of dramatic structural change in our economy. Ever since the United States became dependent on foreign savings in 1983, our interest rates have had to remain above those of our key competitors (e.g., Japan, Germany) in order to attract capital from abroad. Another important impetus for higher real rates came from the Fed's policy switch in October 1979 and DIDMCA 1980. These measures ended the Keynesian prodebtor bias of the postwar monetary regime in favor of low interest rates (see section 5.5). In the absence of rate ceilings it is much easier for creditors to demand higher yields, especially when credit demand is strong. Finally, borrowers are now more likely to refinance their debts at lower rates whenever such a "window of opportunity" presents itself. Their rush into the credit markets has made interest rates more sticky on the downward side.[11]

The high real interest rates have had profound effects on U.S. industry. For one, they have made financial assets quite attractive. During the 1980s U.S. corporations invested huge sums of money in all kinds of high-yielding financial instruments. The boom in the stock and bond markets from 1982 to 1987 also generated significant capital gains. This accumulation of financial assets provided firms with a great deal of short-term income and counteracted similarly steep increases in their liabilities. At the same time, high real interest rates undermine industrial investment activity (see chapters 2 and 3). Despite generous tax breaks in 1981 and a recovery that was stronger than expected, the share of industrial investment in U.S. national product remained significantly below its postwar average (see Figure 9.2).

In addition to investing less, the composition of industrial investment has changed for the worse. In the face of high interest rates most firms do not want to put their capital "at risk" for long. They will therefore prefer projects with relatively short payback periods (e.g., computer equipment, differentiation of already existing products). Yet it is precisely investments with typically longer gestation periods, such as construction of new plant, research and development projects, or worker training, which lay the foundation for the competitive

Table 9.1

High Real Interest Rates and Their Causes (annual averages; percent per annum)

Year	Treasury note yields (10-year) Nominal	Real	Debt growth	Savings rate	Risk premium
1960–64	4.03	2.42	5.06	16.48	0.97
1965–69	5.32	1.70	6.14	17.96	0.99
1970–74	6.82	0.66	8.16	16.87	1.89
1975–79	8.14	0.35	10.76 ˙	17.41	1.93
1980	11.46	1.96	8.80	17.20	2.21
1981	13.91	3.91	9.40	18.39	2.13
1982	13.00	6.80	8.80	16.16	3.11
1983	11.10	7.00	11.00	14.74	2.45
1984	12.44	8.04	13.90	16.79	1.75
1985	10.62	6.92	13.90	15.13	2.10
1986	7.86	5.26	12.60	13.47	2.71
1987	8.39	5.19	9.40	13.65	2.19
1988	8.85	4.95	8.90	14.38	1.98
1989	8.49	4.19	7.60	14.19	1.69
1990	8.55	4.35	6.30	12.91	1.81
1991 (3 Q)	7.86	4.26	4.55	12.23	1.94

Source: Council of Economic Advisers, *Economic Report of the President*, 1992, Washington, DC, Tables B–69 (Treasury notes yields; risk premium), B–3 (implicit GDP price deflator), B–65 (debt growth), B–26 and B–8 (savings rate).

Notes: Real rate on ten-year Treasury notes calculated by deducting implicit GDP price deflator. Debt consists of outstanding credit market debt of the U.S. government, state and local governments, and private nonfinancial sectors. Savings rate is ratio of total gross savings and gross domestic product in current dollars. Risk premium is yield difference between Baa-rated corporate bonds and ten-year Treasury notes.

strength of a company. The disappointing investment levels in U.S. industry, coupled with the short planning horizons of its corporate managers, further jeopardize America's technological edge and competitive advantage in an increasingly polycentric and integrated world economy.

9.4. The Coming Reign of "Electronic Money"

The emergence of a new monetary regime always brings with it major changes in the form of money—whether we are talking about the emergence of demand deposits in the 1880s or the abolition of the gold standard in the 1930s. The current transition is no exception. DIDMCA 1980 played a crucial role in this

Figure 9.2 **Investment Shares of Output**

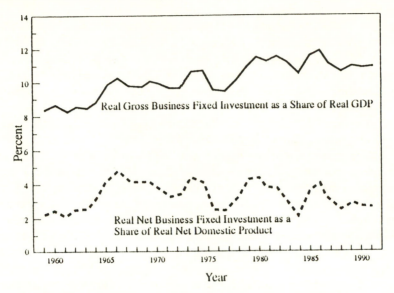

Source: Council of Economic Advisers, *Economic Report of the President*, 1992, Washington, DC, Chart 7–2.

Note: Investment and domestic product are measured in 1987 prices.

regard. Besides deregulating private bank money (see sections 9.1 and 9.2), it also forced major changes in the nation's payments system. The Fed could now offer payments services to all depository institutions, not just to member banks, but it had to price those services instead of providing them for free. The significance of these provisions cannot be understood properly unless we put them into the broader context of *electronic money*.

In the late 1970s banks began to automate their operations. Crucial in this regard was the introduction of automated teller machines (ATMs) operated by magnetic cards ("debit cards"). Replacing human bank tellers, these machines dispense cash and perform other transactions twenty-four hours a day. Initially ATMs spread slowly, because they were expensive and met consumer resistance. But after a few years more consumers began to appreciate their convenience, and technological improvements created much better machines. ATMs are capital-intensive and therefore constitute mostly fixed costs, so they generate major economies of scale when they operate at high volume. Throughout the last decade banks have therefore looked for ways to increase the use of ATMs.

Customers can now access account information and move funds between different deposits through ATMs. Banks across state lines have also entered into sharing agreements with each other to standardize the information encoded on their respective debit cards so that these can activate each others' teller machines. These multistate ATM networks enable participating banks to bypass the prohibition against interstate banking under the McFadden Act of 1927 (see chapter 11). The central switches in those ATM networks make it possible for banks to hook up to electronic cash registers in retail stores around the country. In such "point-of-sale" transactions customers can use debit cards to deduct purchases directly from their bank accounts. Finally, shared tellers have also facilitated the development of "home banking" by computer, via cable television, or by telephone.[12]

ATM networks, point-of-sale transactions, and home banking have all spread less rapidly than originally expected. Several factors have so far hampered their growth, including limited availability of hardware (e.g., personal computers, modems), their high user cost (up to $15 a month on top of checking-account fees), and loss of float due to instant debiting of bill payments. More generally, consumer acceptance of new financial technology usually takes a long time, because payment habits are deeply ingrained and change only very gradually. As is typical for new products, the technological evolution of electronic banking has been quite chaotic during its first decade. System components and machines have often lacked the kind of standardization and compatibility required for large-volume operations. Yet without volume the massive capital outlays and high fixed costs associated with electronic banking create formidable barriers to entry for banks. As the product matures, these problems can be expected to diminish. By the year 2000 electronic retail banking will most likely have greatly reduced the use of cash, checks, traveler's cheques, and credit cards in transactions.

The automation of consumer banking is only one aspect in the movement toward electronic money. Facing a decline in commercial lending, banks have tried to keep corporate customers by offering them payments-processing services in return for fee income. Initially companies used these services primarily to exploit time differences in the crediting and debiting of checks by the Fed, the so-called float. Banks helped corporate treasurers to get the maximum float time on checks they issue through "remote disbursements," in which company accounts were kept at branches or correspondent banks sufficiently out of the check-collection mainstream to slow payments. Check deposits, on the other hand, were directed toward centrally located branches to speed up collections. Banks could assist these "lead and lag" manipulations of corporate cash flows because they received their own float from the Fed in the check-collection process.

The passage of DIDMCA in 1980 had a major impact on these money-dealing activities of banks. The law ordered the Fed to reduce its float or to charge banks for it. Caused by the central bank practice of crediting checks before debiting them, the float in effect represented an interest-free loan by the Fed to any bank on which a check was drawn.[13] This cost the U.S. government about $700 million per year in lost income and complicated the task of controlling the money supply by inadvertently adding to bank reserves. Between 1981 and 1983 the Fed managed to reduce its float by more than half through a variety of operational improvements, and in October 1983 it began to impose charges for the remaining float. These measures increased the processing costs per check to $1. Suddenly this traditional form of money had become very expensive. By comparison, electronic funds transfers (EFTs) cost only about 25 cents.[14]

That cost differential accelerated the use of EFTs, which are processed through automated clearinghouses (ACHs). By 1983 banks had set up more than 3,000 of these processing centers. Apart from lower cost, EFTs have the added advantages of speed and predictability. Today many corporations value these qualities more than the benefits of gaining a few days of float. By allowing earlier notification, EFTs also made it easier for banks to grant their corporate clients automatic overdraft privileges. As industrial enterprises began to increase their holdings of financial assets during the 1980s, banks extended their services beyond the processing of payments to cash management. They provided clients with information about investment opportunities, managed their portfolios, and presented cash-flow statements. All these services benefited greatly from computerization.

When DIDMCA extended the payments services of the Fed to all depository institutions, it also spread the diffusion of EFTs by radically transforming the so-called correspondent banking network. Suddenly nonmember banks and other institutions gained direct access to the Fed for payments services which they used to buy from member banks.[15] Large money-center banks had to reorganize their correspondent services. If they ran automated clearinghouses, they could easily make supplementary use of these computer and communications systems to offer respondents processing of EFTs, computer software for home banking, and specialized-accounts systems, as well as training and consulting programs.

Besides encouraging the spread of computerized payments services, the banking act of 1980 reopened the age-old battle over who should control the nation's payments system. Before 1914 check clearing and settlement had been entirely the domain of the private sector. Under that system checks were not always honored for their full amount and made their way back to the paying bank by a slow and circuitous network of other banks. The check-clearing mechanism set up under the Federal Reserve Act of 1913 overcame these disadvantages. Our peculiar dual banking structure, in which some banks were members of the Federal Reserve System while others were not, led to a mixed payments system. The Fed processed checks and other fund transfers for member banks, which in turn used their access to the central bank to offer those services to nonmember banks in the aforementioned correspondent banking network.

DIDMCA of 1980 altered that arrangement by granting all depository institutions access to the Fed's payments services while requiring that those be paid for. With this provision Congress basically decided that the Fed had to compete directly with the payments-processing services offered by commercial banks and that the market should determine the precise mix. At question here is not only the comparative efficiency of these two components but also the Fed's ability to manage the conflict of interest inherent in its double role as competitor and regulator of banks. Since it writes the rules for our payments system, it can easily give itself significant advantages over private banks.

The Fed does not want to give up control over the nation's payments system. The check-clearing mechanism is, after all, the primary locus of its interventions to influence the money-creation process by private banks (see section 2.4). It is for this reason that the Fed has since 1980 made active use of its ability to regulate the payments system to its own advantage. In August 1981 it complied with DIDMCA and introduced prices for its hitherto free payments services.[16] In the wake of this first price list the Fed saw its quarterly volume of processed checks decline from 4.1 billion in the second quarter of 1981 to barely 3 billion in the first quarter of 1982, a loss in market share from 44 percent to 35 percent. Lower volume caused a revenue shortfall and higher unit costs, which raised the prospect of further price increases. The Fed wanted to avoid this situation by regaining lost market share. In September 1982 it extended the deadline after which it would debit the accounts of paying banks for checks presented only during the next day, from 10 A.M. to midday. This switch to "noon presentment" gave out-of-town banks more time to deliver their checks for same-day credit, thus making its service more attractive. In addition, the later deadline helped to reduce the Fed's float by increasing the number of checks subject to same-day debiting.

The Fed also made its electronic funds transfers more attractive (see note 14). Since those require very capital-intensive technology, they generate large economies of scale. The Fed's volume allows it to process EFTs at lower unit costs than its private competitors. This advantage has already led to a major shake-out among bank-operated ACHs, whose number may decline from 3,000 in 1983 to possibly only 300 in the mid-1990s.

A third payments service offered by the Fed, in addition to check-clearing and electronic funds transfers, is a system of wire transfers through which participants can transmit funds and securities both quickly and efficiently. The only remaining private competitor of Fedwire is the Clearing House Interbank Payments System (CHIPS), a computerized network owned by eleven New York banks and used for transferring international dollar payments. The transaction volume of these systems has reached truly staggering amounts. Between 1960 and 1985 the ratio of banks' wire payments relative to their reserves with the Fed grew by a factor of thirty. In 1983 Fedwire averaged $330 billion a day, and CHIPS about $200 billion. By 1992, the daily amount moving through the Fedwire averaged $900 billion, while CHIPS could clear $1,000 billion on a normal day. Most of these transfers involve settlements for financial transactions, illustrating the spectacular expansion of financial capital during the 1980s.

In both Fedwire and CHIPS, payments are made instantaneously by wire throughout the working day. But settlement, the actual transfer of funds from the

Federal Reserve account of one bank to that of another, occurs only at the end of the day. This practice encourages so-called daylight overdrafts, which arise when a bank sends more funds over Fedwire than it receives. In other words, banks routinely make payments for corporate customers without funds to cover them. Such overdrafts are in effect unsecured loans from the Fed to banks and their customers, thus amounting to a taxpayer subsidy. In 1985 these daily overdrafts averaged $120 billion a day. In light of these sums the Fed began to worry about what might happen if a bank found itself unable to honor its wire-transfer commitments at the end of a day. That could threaten other banks which had committed money on the assumption that they would receive payment. The potential ripple effect could create gridlock and chaos in our financial system. Because the Fed guarantees these payments, in such a situation it could be forced to inject huge sums of money into the system on short notice.[17]

In February 1986 fear of such a disruption prompted the Fed to restrict daylight overdrafts among financial institutions. Under its new guidelines, bank directors had to rate the financial condition of their institution in one of four categories and then set a limit on total overdrafts. That cap, expressed as a multiple of the bank's capital, varied with the creditworthiness of the institution and was subject to Fed review. Banks that refused to cooperate or that were found to have unsatisfactory ratings would lose their overdraft privilege altogether. On top of this "consolidated" cap the Fed required private wire transfers to impose both aggregate and bilateral caps on their customers. These regulations engendered significant compliance costs, which banks could reduce by cutting the number of wire systems they used. In practice this meant that Fedwire, the largest system, gained a great deal of additional business at the expense of three privately operated wire-transfer systems, Bankwire and two regional services. These had to close down in May 1986.

Those caps prompted banks to charge their customers higher fees for wire transfers and to give certain customers priority status. The overdraft limits have also caused delays of up to two hours in the payments system, for banks that bump against the cap have to wait until their balance is replenished. Operational inefficiencies in the computer operations of many banks have aggravated those delays, making it difficult for the Fed to reduce overdrafts further by gradually tightening caps. Instead of relying on further restriction, Congress could instead remove the continuing interest ban on corporate demand deposits which DIDMCA had phased out earlier for consumer deposits. This prohibition has prompted cash managers to transfer their bank balances every night to New York and other money-centers for overnight investment in government securities and commercial paper. The funds are wired back the next morning for disposal as needed. In effect, most corporate cash balances are thus turned over every day. Removing the interest ban on corporate deposits would dramatically lower the volume of wire transfers.[18]

The technological revolution of financial capital extends beyond banking services and funds transfers. Securities markets all over the world are currently busy computerizing their price quotation, settlement, and delivery systems. These efforts will surely improve market efficiency and capacity. But they also promise to change the ways in which these markets are organized and how they function (see chapter 12). At this point I only want to discuss one aspect of this trend, which directly involves the Fed's payments services. Bookkeeping entries in our computerized payments system have replaced engraved pieces of paper as the primary form of government securities. Since 1976 Treasury securities owned or held by member banks have only existed in the Fed's computer memory bank. In January 1986 the Fed introduced book-entry accounts for states and municipalities to provide for better safekeeping and third-party verification of securities pledged as collateral in repurchasing agreements with dealers. The Fed undertook this step after a series of costly failures by government securities dealers who engaged in various fraudulent practices (see chapter 11). Such book-entry securities are a logical extension of the Fed's check-clearing and wire transfer services. They reduce transaction costs. They also allow commercial banks to become involved in financial market transactions by acting as depositories for dealers.

The computerization of banking and financial markets, in all its multifaceted manifestations, is a truly profound phenomenon. It promises to transform the way we spend money, move capital, shift assets, deploy resources. For centuries financial capital, itself inclined toward cyclical motions and therefore quite unstable, had at least a relatively stable technological evolution focused on coins, paper, and ledger accounts. But now this volatile form of capital suddenly finds itself at the threshold of a completely new socio-technological organization which promises to transform its modus operandi with accelerating speed. In the process we are moving toward a new form of money—electronic money—whose international circulation capacity propels our ongoing transition to a global accumulation regime forward. Economists and policy-makers have not yet caught up with the enormous implications of this structural change in our economy. They are just beginning to see the first signs that there might be more to this process than just another industry going through a period of restructuring.

• Money is intimately tied to information, as agents observe markets to deploy their liquid capital across an ever-growing range of alternatives. The diffusion of new computer and telecommunications technologies among financial institutions has begun to expand beyond payments processing to data processing. Today economic agents can access market information at an unprecedented scale and can execute their investment decisions with much greater speed than ever before. The question of access is a complex one. It requires funds, inclusion by those controlling market entry, and specialized knowledge all at once. We will have a new cause of poverty, one which afflicts those who lack access to information. But the new technology is also powerfully decentralizing (e.g., debit cards, personal computers), ready to be used by millions.

• Until recently banks used to manage financial portfolios and process payments for corporations, other financial institutions, and very wealthy individuals. Now, however, these services can be supplied to a much larger group of households at low cost. A growing number of Americans are in the process of becoming increasingly sophisticated investors who manage complex financial portfolios. Torn between more liquidity and higher returns, they constantly move funds around or instruct others to do so on their behalf. This has serious repercussions for monetary policy. Long gone are the days when the transaction motive dominated and the key prices of money, exchange rates or interest rates, were essentially stable. Nowadays the Fed must take account of speculative, precautionary, and finance motives playing themselves out in increasingly volatile financial markets that are linked across the globe. It has to learn how a large number of agents might react to its actions or to other developments. Finally, it has to tailor its own decisions to the likely portfolio adjustments.

• The movement toward electronic money has opened tremendous economies of scope for banks and other financial institutions. It has become much easier for them to introduce new products and to link existing ones. Especially important has been the innovation of integrated "sweep" accounts (e.g., cash management accounts, mutual fund families, multideposit bank accounts) which allow customers to move funds easily within a diversified portfolio. The economies of scope apply in particular to new products which bypass regulatory restrictions, such as ATM networks or Eurodollars. Those allow banks and their clients to operate more freely.

• The spread of computer technology in securities markets is bound to transform the way in which these markets function. Examples of that evolution abound, such as the move toward book-entry securities, the importance of computer-driven "program trading" in the stock market, and efforts to replace traders with computers in the financial futures markets. One important effect of computerizing the financial markets has been to accommodate a much larger trading volume, with capital-intensive technology itself facilitating volume-enhancing innovation to exploit economies of scale and scope. Increased volume and improved efficiency have engendered greater market volatility, which in turn has fed more speculation and created a need for risk-hedging techniques. Finally, the ability to move funds at the push of a button through computer networks that span the planet has greatly accelerated the global integration of financial markets—a powerful new transmission mechanism toward more synchronized price movements and business cycles.

9.5. The International Dimension of U.S. Monetary Policy

The trend toward globally integrated financial markets has made purely national monetary policy objectives obsolete. Today any central bank has to focus on exchange rates and international capital movements as well. Its actions can be magnified or offset by other central banks. For more than thirty years the United States was relatively protected from this interdependence, because the international status of the dollar freed our economy from any external constraint. But now this seigniorage benefit is coming to an end, and the Federal Reserve must adjust to new realities. It too is forced today to consider the emerging global policy dimension in its decisions.

During the 1980s the Fed managed to guide the domestic economy onto a sustainable path of moderate growth and to keep it there without reigniting a surge of inflationary pressures. In this endeavor the central bank had to walk a tightrope between accommodating strong credit demand and responding to first signs of higher inflation with doses of restraint. It did so through consecutive sequences of loosening and tightening within comparatively short time periods.

In this mode of "fine-tuning," different sectors and regions could undergo recessionary adjustments at different times (e.g., energy and agriculture in 1985–86, financial services after late 1987) without aborting the recovery for the rest of the economy. Although those sectoral downturns had their underlying roots in the long-wave dynamics of industrial restructuring toward a new accumulation regime (see chapter 3), Federal Reserve actions had a great deal to do with containing their potential for spreading. Most important, the central bank responded to various crisis situations by pumping a great deal of liquidity into the banking system and then tightening very gradually after the financial markets had calmed: loosening after the collapse of Continental Illinois in mid-1984; driving the dollar down in 1985 to ease deflationary pressures on America's trade-dependent sectors; containing the fallout from the stock market crash of October 1987 by aggressively pushing interest and exchange rates down.

This careful balancing act of the Fed was welcome news. It did not matter much at that point that its middle-of-the-road course was very much the result of a sometimes fragile compromise between monetarists and supply-siders at the Fed's policy-setting Open Market Committee. With U.S. fiscal policy locked for nearly a decade into record budget deficits and political stalemate, the role of countercyclical stabilization fell predominantly on monetary policy. Moreover, its timely actions made it possible for the Fed to regain the confidence of financial investors, which it had lost in the late 1970s. Of course, the use of multiple intermediate targets and the lack of clearly identifiable policy rules might have made financial markets more nervous at times. But by and large both domestic and foreign holders of dollar-denominated assets seemed reasonably assured that the Fed would, if anything, err on the side of caution and not let inflation get out of hand again.

While U.S. monetary policy steered the domestic economy toward a sustained upswing after 1982, during that period its effectiveness also became increasingly dependent on other actors. The Fed is no longer master of its domain; it is hostage to international financial conditions. We have already indicated earlier, when discussing McKinnon's theory of the "world money supply" (see section

9.2), that in today's world of global capital mobility and alternative key currencies, domestic monetary policy is no longer insulated. The policy actions of the
United States, which is still the major supplier of international liquidity, have
especially powerful effects on the rest of the world. Take, for example, the
global debt crisis whose intensity at any given point in time depends to a large
degree on U.S. interest rates. So do compensatory actions by other industrial
nations to shield their own economies from exchange-rate misalignments perpet-
uated by our twin deficits. But, as a large recipient of foreign capital, the United
States can no longer insulate itself from the global repercussions of its own
actions as it did in the past, when it was still the world's dominant creditor
nation. The Fed's ability to manage domestic growth is now much more affected
by shifting sentiments of foreign suppliers of capital about the United States'
relative prospects.

Over the last decade the United States has seen its net international investment position shift by about $800 billion due to massive capital imports, includ-
ing a near quadrupling of foreign direct investment. Until 1990 it managed to
receive a large chunk of the world's savings on relatively favorable terms. Japan
and Germany generated huge surpluses, much of it in dollars ready for recycling.
Many LDCs became mired in the global debt crisis after 1982 and lost their
ability to attract funds from industrial nations. As a matter of fact, they have
since then been net exporters of capital, a perverse and damaging situation
forced upon those troubled countries by a combination of heavy debt-servicing
charges and capital flight. Most of that money, especially from Latin America,
was denominated in dollars and remained within the U.S. banking system (even
if reinvested in the Eurodollar market). In the 1980s the United States thus
became the prime recipient of foreign cash reserves. During the first four years
of the post-1982 recovery, especially, foreign investors were drawn to high U.S.
interest rates, a rapidly growing economy, a soaring dollar, and a booming stock
market. This allowed United States to fund exploding budget and trade deficits
quite easily.

The first time this situation changed was during 1987. With the dollar at that
point devaluing rapidly and with private foreign investors becoming skittish
about accumulating more dollar-denominated assets, the G–7 nations decided in
February 1987 to stabilize the U.S. currency through coordinated central bank
intervention in foreign-exchange markets. This so-called Louvre Agreement (see
section 8.4) did not in itself shift market sentiments against the dollar. What it
did do, however, was to lock the G–7 into a particular set of support actions. The
central banks of the surplus nations, above all Germany's Bundesbank and the
Bank of Japan, agreed to fill the void created by private investors. In 1987 alone
they used nearly $125 billion of their reserves to buy dollar-denominated assets,
mostly Treasury securities. The U.S. central bank, in turn, pushed domestic
interest rates higher to stop the slide of its currency. Under this international
monetary arrangement it became clear that the Federal Reserve could no longer

control interest and exchange rates at the same time. It was precisely this rise in U.S. interest rates, with its negative impact on security prices, that ultimately helped to trigger the stock market crash of October 1987. Only after that crash, when market expectations shifted massively toward recession, was the Fed temporarily in a position to push both exchange and interest rates lower.

Since then the external constraint faced by U.S. policy-makers has, if anything, intensified. Although a cheaper dollar and domestic recession helped to lower our trade deficits to less than half of their 1987-peak, we may soon see those rise again as U.S. recovery begins to clash with sluggish conditions almost everywhere else. Moreover, the U.S. budget deficit has risen sharply over the last four years, especially if we include the surging costs of the thrift bailout. Even though the widely abused Gramm-Rudman rules gave way to a tighter multiyear budget agreement in 1990, the annual budget deficit has since doubled to $300 billion. At the same time, the fiscal position of state and local governments deteriorated markedly during the last recession, with combined deficits in that sector reaching $100 billion in 1992. Even though American corporations and consumers have ended their borrowing binge, domestic savings have not recovered much since their postwar low in 1987. In sum, the U.S. economy still faces a significant financing shortfall, which necessitates continuous capital imports.

But the supply of foreign savings to the United States began to dry up in late 1989 after a last surge of postcrash investment opportunities had finally run its course. During the first quarter of 1990 foreign investors sold a net $4.2 billion in U.S. bonds and stocks. This was the first time since the third quarter of 1983 that foreigners pulled money out of U.S. securities markets. That sudden reversal of capital flows, a major trigger factor for the recession shortly thereafter, had a number of causes. With interest rates rising abroad but falling in the United States, the rate differential between the industrial nations disappeared. U.S. securities also became less attractive due to dollar weakness and a recession-induced decline in corporate profits.

Sentiments of foreign investors may well shift even more against the United States in coming years. The abolition of trade and investment barriers by the twelve-nation EC has already created a new magnet for foreign investors. Add to this the recent opening and coming reconstruction of Eastern European economies. Germany must use much of its surplus for the huge financing needs of its reunification. Japan too seems more self-absorbed, preoccupied by volatile financial conditions and restructuring at home. Its long-term capital flows reversed from an outflow of $140 billion in 1987 to an inflow of almost $40 billion in 1991. Some newly industrialized countries—for instance, China, Thailand, and Malaysia—have emerged as new lures for international investment capital. Mexico, in the middle of a major restructuring program and soon part of a North American free-trade zone, may soon join that list. To sum up, the United States faces a growing number of countries with which it will have to compete for capital at a time when worldwide savings are in a downward trend.

This shift in global investment preferences has made the Fed's balancing act more difficult. The dollar has faced steady depreciation since the adoption of target zones for the key currency prices in early 1987, punctuated by occasional unward movements of rather limited duration. U.S. policy-makers have not resisted this currency trend, because a cheaper dollar has helped make American products more competitive. But at the same time they cannot tolerate exchange-rate declines becoming so rapid that they might trigger potentially massive portfolio shifts out of the dollar. The Fed can no longer count on help from its G–7 partners. The Louvre Agreement has evaporated gradually, and central banks of other industrial nations are nowadays less inclined to support the dollar. Long-term U.S. interest rates have consequently not been allowed to decline much despite recession. They had to remain high enough, in real terms and relative to those in other countries trying to attract foreign savings, to contain capital flight out of the dollar during a period of rising U.S. public-sector borrowing requirements.

Since early 1991 the Fed has tried to stimulate our economy, pushing short-term U.S. interest rates to the lowest levels since the early 1960s. But with our currency weak, our twin deficits stubbornly high, our long-term interest rates downwardly rigid, and our attractiveness to foreigners declining, its "easy money" policy has been difficult to implement effectively. When investor confidence is shattered, credit demand is low no matter how much interest rates decline. Despite the spectacular drop of short-term interest rates during 1991–92, lending activity has remained essentially flat, which in turn has left money-supply aggregates growing very slowly. This time the stimulative effect of U.S. monetary policy therefore took much longer to materialize.

The primary impact of monetary easing by the Fed during the recession of the early 1990s has been to relax the conditions of financial fragility reached after two decades of growing indebtedness across the entire U.S. economy. The credit crunch, which took hold after the slowdown of foreign capital inflows in late 1989, required major reliquefication and debt-restructuring efforts within the domestic credit system. The sharp and sudden decline in bank lending at the onset of the crunch allowed the Fed to drive short-term interest rates down while long-term rates remained high. That combination caused the steepest yield curve in decades. The great beneficiaries of such widening differentials in the term structure of interest rates were American commercial banks and thrifts. Carrying short-term liabilities and long-term assets on their books, they saw their profit margins widen significantly. The improved profitability of their current funding operations allowed especially the weaker institutions to write off losses on old debt. The crisis conditions afflicting the U.S. banking sector thus eased considerably before they required yet another huge taxpayer bailout. At the same time the exceptionally low money-market rates, not least a reflection of deepening debt-deflation pressures in many sectors of the U.S. economy, gradually began to drag down long-term bond yields. This easing in capital markets sparked large-scale refinancing of old debt at lower yields, which reduced debt-servicing burdens. By late 1992 financial-market conditions had recovered enough to allow for a gradual resumption of growth.

For the nascent recovery to become self-sustaining and create sufficient numbers of new jobs, long-term rates in dollar-denominated capital markets will have to come down farther. That requires continuous reductions of U.S. budget deficits in coming years, best achievable by a multi-year agreement involving a combination of targeted tax increases, military spending cuts, and domestic spending caps. Such an austerity program, much like the approach proposed by President Clinton shortly after he took office in 1993, must spread budget economies and revenue enhancements broadly if they are to be politically feasible and economically successful. As the U.S. budget deficit begins to weigh less heavily in capital markets, long-term rates on dollar-denominated claims will have more room to move downward. This reduction in the "cost of capital" is a key prerequisite for any sustained recovery in domestic industrial investment activity.

Financial Fragility and the Lender of Last Resort

Business cycles engender financial instability as part of the recessionary adjustment to overproduction. This cyclical phenomenon must be distinguished from financial fragility, a gradual build-up of structural imbalances in the credit system which is part of the long-wave dynamic of the economy (see sections 3.1 and 3.2). During an expansion phase both borrowers and lenders will become more risk-prone and will accept higher debt levels when they see earlier investment decisions successfully validated. The usually short and shallow recessions during that phase are too weak to force much of a retrenchment in this debt-driven expansion. Gradually rising indebtedness is one major reason why the boom eventually ends (see Minsky, 1964).

Once the long wave turns down, the credit system typically experiences continued deterioration. Since finance capital is tied to industrial capital (see section 2.3), it will naturally experience losses when profit-rates suffer a sustained decline. The combination of slowing income gains and rising debt-servicing charges makes heavily leveraged borrowers vulnerable to loan defaults. Bad-debt losses in turn threaten the solvency of many lenders. These trends usually become more pronounced as the downswing phase persists. It is then, after such financial fragility has built up for a decade or more, that recessionary adjustments to overproduction have typically disintegrated into depressions in the past. See, for example, the deepening financial crises between 1873 and 1896 or the growing number of bank failures during the 1920s that led to the catastrophic collapse of the entire credit system between 1929 and 1933 (see chapter 4).

The latest downswing phase has been no exception to this pattern. In 1966 profit-rates reached their postwar peak and began a long-term decline. U.S. industry came to rely on more debt financing to cover a rapidly growing financing gap. That jump in corporate borrowing needs coincided with the shift to "liability management" by banks whose use of borrowed liabilities allowed them to fund a much larger lending volume (see section 7.5). Financial ratios of both industrial corporations and commercial banks deteriorated dramatically during the second half of the 1960s. This set the stage for progressively worse credit crunches in 1966, 1969–70, 1973–75, and 1979–82.

The growing intensity of credit crunches and recessions after 1966 indicated gradually worsening accumulation conditions. Such supracyclical deterioration is quite typical for the downswing phase of a long wave. Previously that process had always led to full-blown depression, as during the 1890s and 1930s. This time, however, the structural crisis took the more moderate form of stagflation. This was due to several institutional safeguards that had been built into our postwar accumulation regime following Roosevelt's New Deal. Endogenous credit-money allowed continuous monetization of debt and counteracted liquidity squeezes in the banking system. The monopolistic regulation of prices and wages created a better balance between aggregate supply and demand. And policy stabilizers, primarily deficit spending and lender-of-last-resort interventions by the government, managed to stop recessions before they could turn into depressions. Initially these safeguards moderated the latest downswing phase by turning previously deflationary pressures into rising inflation.

The crisis-related acceleration of inflation during the 1970s amounted to a complex process of socializing otherwise private losses and risks to everyone using the domestic currency (see sections 6.3 and 6.4). But the transfer gains from unequal exchange and the accumulation of paper profits involved in this socialization process required additional debt financing for support. At the same time, rising inflation hurt savers and lenders the most. America's two-pronged strategy of currency devaluation and policy reflation gave this debt-inflation spiral an international dimension, spreading inflationary pressures abroad and forcing foreigners to hold excess dollars of declining value. When the spiral finally began to threaten the world-money status of the dollar, the Fed had to abandon its accommodating stance in October 1979.

That historic shift in monetary policy had a devastating impact on all of the sectors which had benefited from accelerating inflation. In a position to charge extra-high prices, those sectors had managed to accumulate especially rapid income gains from unequal exchange and accounting profits during the 1970s. Their above-average profitability attracted a great deal of capital to finance accelerated capacity expansion. At the same time, demand could not keep pace with these supply increases, because the extra-large price hikes prompted buyers to cut back on purchases and to seek cheaper alternatives. The inevitable overproduction came to the fore when the Fed finally decided to break the debt-inflation spiral in 1979.

In the aftermath of this policy shift, inflation-gaining sectors and their lenders suffered major losses and retrenchment, the first debt-deflation adjustments in the postwar period. Unlike earlier incidences of isolated financial instability in the late 1960s and 1970s, these sectoral debt crises were serious enough to threaten many banks and to require sustained assistance by the federal government. In the summer of 1982 America's largest money-center banks faced a serious threat to their solvency when several developing countries defaulted. Management of this global debt crisis necessitated a new international lender-of-last-resort mechanism (section 10.1). Then hundreds of small farm banks failed when land speculation collapsed. This crisis was followed by a deflationary shock in the oil industry, which knocked out some of the largest regional banks in the Southwest. After the stock market collapse of October 1987 banks also began to suffer substantial loan losses in two previously booming segments of the domestic economy, real estate and Wall Street (section 10.2). Thrifts, depository institutions that are inherently weaker than banks, suffered even greater damage when those speculative bubbles finally burst (section 10.3). With record numbers of banks and thrifts threatened by insolvency, the government's role as lender of last resort has come under renewed scrutiny (section 10.4).

10.1. The Global Debt Crisis

When the Fed's tightening in 1979 broke the debt-inflation spiral of the preceding decade, it hit certain sectors with special force. Those sectors had been in a particularly advantageous position during the 1970s, when they benefited more than others from accelerating inflation. It is no coincidence that all of them were tied in one way or another to land. This fixed-supply resource is prone to especially rapid price increases during inflationary periods. Activities tied to land thus became an irresistible object of speculative fever in the 1970s. Developing countries with comparative advantages in the production of natural resources grew rapidly, as global commodity inflation improved their terms of trade. Similar inflation gains boosted domestic agriculture and oil production (see section 10.2). When these bubbles burst in the wake of the Fed's switch to an anti-inflation policy, all three land-based sectors suddenly found it difficult to service their debt obligations. Widespread defaults amid brutal deflation pressures hurt their overextended lenders as well, causing large bad-debt losses.

Let us begin this chapter with the global debt crisis of developing nations. In August 1982 Mexico declared itself unable to honor its debt-servicing obligations, followed shortly thereafter by defaults of Brazil and Argentina. Since then the majority of countries in Latin America, Africa, Eastern Europe, and Asia have found themselves in a similar predicament. As of today, LDCs owe more than $1.3 trillion, of which about $450 billion are uncollectable.

The crisis had its origins in a borrowing binge by the LDCs which increased their foreign debts from $100 billion to $640 billion between 1973 and 1982. That process began with massive debt financing of large external deficits caused by the first oil shock in 1973.[1] Then many LDCs launched ambitious industrialization programs. Centered on large-scale infrastructure investments, these programs aimed at diversifying their hitherto rather narrow industrial base for import substitution and export expansion purposes. Billions were also absorbed quite unproductively by a corrupt bureaucracy, to cover losses of inefficient firms either run by the state or operated privately as licensed monopolies, in armament purchases to keep an overblown military happy, on consumer goods imports, and in capital flight.

Commercial banks, especially the large transnational banks that operated in the Euromarket, gladly financed this borrowing binge of LDCs. After 1973 a large portion of OPEC's surplus ended up in short-term Eurodollar deposits, because oil producers could only spend a fraction of the massive wealth transfer on imports and had at best very limited access to long-term investments in industrial nations. Flush with funds and under great pressure to reinvest those profitably, Eurobanks aggressively pursued lending to LDCs. Their governments actively encouraged this *petrodollar recycling*, because it enabled them to cut domestically unpopular foreign aid at a time of rising budget deficits.[2] Those government officials also knew very well that much of the LDC debt would be spent on imports and would thus help to create jobs at home.

From the point of view of the commercial banks, most LDCs looked like an excellent credit risk at the time. Many developing economies specialized in the export of raw materials whose rapidly rising world market prices led the inflationary acceleration during the 1970s. These countries were inflation gainers. In possession of highly valued resource assets, they appeared to have strong earnings potential. In the process both sides obviously overestimated future inflation trends. Had they foreseen the commodity deflation of the 1980s, they would have acted more prudently. Benefiting from favorable terms of trade and easy access to large credits, many LDCs had boom-like growth rates for much of the 1970s. This rosy picture reinforced the erroneous belief of bankers that sovereign nations could not default. Ultimately it was pure greed that drove our banks into such overextension. For them, lending to LDCs through the Euromarket had several irresistible advantages. Unlike domestic loans, these Euroloans carried adjustable rates, thus transferring the price risk to borrowers. Nor were they subject to any regulatory limitations, so that Eurobanks could lend as much as they wanted to individual countries. Finally, they generated a great deal of extra fee income for the lead banks organizing the loan syndication on behalf of LDCs.

The petrodollar recycling process worked quite well for about six years. But then, in 1979, the Islamic Revolution in Iran triggered another worldwide hike in oil prices. Amid surging global inflation, speculation against the dollar became rampant. Six months later U.S. monetary policy switched dramatically toward restraint. Shortly thereafter the world economy entered its worst downturn since the Great Depression of the 1930s. This sequence of events hit the LDCs with a double whammy. Their borrowing needs and interest payments exploded, while their debt-servicing capacity eroded precipitously at the same time (see Table 10.1).

Table 10.1

Selected Data for Non-OPEC Developing Countries

Year	Growth rate (percent)	Gross external debt (in billions dollars)	Debt service as percent of exports	Change in commodity prices (percent)	Gross oil imports	Current account
					(billion dollars)	
1973	6.7	110	n.a.	53.2	4	−6
1974	5.6	135	15.9	28.0	15	−24
1975	4.2	165	17.9	−18.2	14	−32
1976	6.6	200	16.8	13.2	16	−19
1977	5.4	250	17.4	20.7	19	−14
1978	5.6	310	21.9	−4.7	20	−26
1979	5.0	365	21.9	16.5	31	−41
1980	4.7	430	20.0	9.7	50	−64
1981	2.5	505	22.9	−14.8	53	−74
1982	1.2	550	28.0	−12.1	47	−60

Source: Paul Volcker, "How Serious Is U.S. Bank Exposure?" in Robert Guttmann, *Reforming Money and Finance: Institutions and Markets in Flux* (Armonk, NY: M.E. Sharpe, 1989), pp. 181–82.

Note: All data for 1982 are based on estimates.

The events of 1979, largely beyond the control of LDCs, had a devastating impact on their financial position (see Figure 10.1).

• Facing sharply widening trade and budget deficits in the wake of the second oil shock, the non-OPEC developing countries suddenly needed to borrow a great deal more. The combined LDC debt grew from $340 billion at the end of 1978 to $640 billion four years later, of which nearly two-thirds were owed to the banks.

• Short-term debt increased even more rapidly, from $60 billion to $160 billion. Such a trend toward shorter maturities is typical for the last phase of a credit overextension process, when lenders begin to sour on granting riskier long-term debt and borrowers are increasingly forced to refinance old debt. That very trend, of course, puts great pressure on overextended debtors. In 1982 Mexico, Argentina, South Korea, Chile, the Philippines, and several smaller countries faced refinancing or repayment of close to half of their debt within one year.

• The Federal Reserve's decision in October 1979 to break the debt-inflation spiral with a heavy dose of restraint greatly increased the debt-servicing burden of LDCs. After all, 75 percent of their private bank loans—that is, about half of their total foreign debt—carried adjustable rates which were closely linked to the

Figure 10.1 The Debt-Servicing Squeeze of Non-oil LDCs

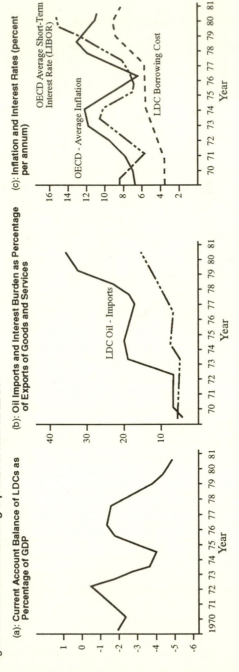

Source: Morgan Guaranty Trust Company, *World Financial Markets,* December 1980.

Note: Horizontal axes indicate end of year.

U.S. prime rate. Higher rates, growing debt, and shorter maturities combined to triple interest payments of non-oil LDCs between 1978 and 1982.

• Capital flight by the ruling oligarchies in many developing countries took off after 1979. The local elites, whose practically exclusive political control over the economic resources of their countries gave them direct access to the inflows of foreign loan capital, preferred to invest a large chunk of the borrowed dollars under their control in safer places abroad. According to various estimates, some $70 billion left the debtor countries between 1980 and 1982 as flight capital for asset investments in the United States and Europe. In Mexico, Venezuela, Argentina, and Nigeria the exodus of money drained away over half of the funds borrowed abroad during those years.[3]

• To make matters worse, by 1981 the gradually intensifying global downturn had reached such intensity that it triggered rather severe deflationary pressures in global raw material markets. Commodity prices declined by more than 25 percent in 1981–82. The combination of lower prices and shrinking trade volumes cut into the export earnings of commodity-producing LDCs. By 1982 the ratio of debt-servicing costs to export income for the poorer oil-importing countries had risen to an average of 28 percent from 14 percent in 1973, far in excess of the 20 percent level that bankers normally considered the worry threshold for any one country. In key debtor nations, such as Mexico, Argentina, Brazil, and Chile, that ratio rose during 1982–83 to more than 50 percent—to well over 100 percent, if short-term obligations are included.

In the face of these deteriorating conditions, many LDCs rapidly found themselves on the brink of default. Signs of the impending LDC debt crisis already began to emerge in 1981 and early 1982 when some two dozen countries (including Turkey, Bolivia, Peru, Costa Rica, Jamaica, Nicaragua, Togo, Malawi, Sudan, and Zaire) could no longer keep up with their interest payments and had to reschedule their loans. Several other countries, including East Germany, Romania, and Nigeria, faced serious financial difficulties. Then came the near-defaults of Poland in the aftermath of martial law, and of Argentina following the Falklands War. By mid-1982 those storm clouds had caused enough concern among banks in the United States and Europe that they began to pull back on loans to poor countries.[4]

The crisis took a decisive turn for the worse in August 20, 1982, when Mexico declared itself unable to meet its payment obligations. This de facto default of the largest LDC debtor—which then owed a total of $80 billion, of which $58 billion had been borrowed from commercial banks—sent shock waves through the international credit markets. Loans to other countries dried up, and within a few weeks both Brazil and Argentina, with commercial bank debt totaling $52 billion and $27 billion, respectively, also failed to keep up with their debt-servicing charges. That situation posed an immediate threat to the solvency of the entire international banking system. At that point the nine largest U.S.

banks, for example, had lent nearly 120 percent of their entire capital base to those three countries alone and 222 percent to all non-OPEC developing economies as a whole. Had those defaults of the three largest LDC debtors been allowed to happen, our money-center banks could have faced imminent insolvency. Such an event, akin to a heart attack, might very well have set off a paralyzing chain reaction and pushed the world economy into depression.

This scenario had to be prevented. But no international lender-of-last-resort mechanism existed at the time to cope with the rapidly spreading defaults and credit cutbacks in the largely unregulated Euromarkets. Thus central bankers had to come up with a new solution, and they could not afford to lose much time. Under the leadership of Federal Reserve Chairman Paul Volcker, who managed to overcome the initial laissez-faire attitude among key U.S. Treasury officials, a three-step mechanism was set up to manage that crisis on a case-by-case basis.[5]

• First, central bankers of industrial nations would arrange short-term "bridge" loans for troubled debtor nations, in order to prevent their actual default. These immediate cash infusions came from two sources in particular. One was the U.S. Treasury's Exchange Stabilization Fund, set up originally under the Gold Reserve Act of 1934 to help the United States stabilize the value of the dollar through buying and selling currencies. In the summer of 1982 the fund had nearly $11 billion in assets, of which $600 million were lent to Mexico and $1.23 billion to Brazil. The other source was the Swiss-based Bank for International Settlements (BIS), which was set up in 1930 to help European nations collect German war reparations and has since evolved into a central banks' bank. With assets exceeding $40 billion, the BIS arranged bridge loans of $1.8 billion for Mexico, $1.5 billion for Brazil, and $500 million each for Argentina, Hungary, and Yugoslavia between August 1982 and February 1983. These short-term loans helped to keep borrowers afloat until longer-term arrangements could be worked out.

• Second, LDCs with debt-servicing problems then had to negotiate an agreement with the IMF for additional funds in exchange for accepting specific macroeconomic performance targets and austerity measures. The sums given to them in those deals were quite small relative to their funding needs and were mostly used for repayment of bridge loans. The key advantage, from the point of view of LDCs, was that these IMF agreements usually paved the way for negotiations with the commercial banks for repayment delays and new funds. Previous debt reschedulings, such as the one negotiated with Peru in 1978, had taught banks that they could not force sovereign nations into policy changes. Only the IMF had the power to impose belt-tightening measures on its member countries. Hence the banks insisted that troubled debtors accept the tough medicine prescribed by the IMF before they would consider additional assistance.

• Finally, with the IMF agreement acting as a "green light," advisory committees representing the private creditors would negotiate deals with the debtor countries to stretch out repayment schedules. If necessary, the banks offered new funds with which to pay the interest on the old debt. Similar debt reschedulings were negotiated directly between governments for official loans in default.

That three-step bailout mechanism mobilized the creditors (i.e., the central banks of industrial nations, the IMF, commercial banks) into a sort of informal cartel. Together they insisted on dealing with cash-strapped LDCs one by one. This case-by-case approach succeeded in preventing the much-feared formation of a debtors' cartel, which would have given the LDCs a great deal more leverage by simply threatening a moratorium or other concerted actions. Alone the debtor countries were in a much weaker bargaining position. Their only alternative was to repudiate their debt. In that case they would have lost access to foreign loans for years to come, as happened to many Latin American countries during the 1930s or to Peru after 1985.

Having institutionally secured their power advantage, the creditors then proceeded with a strategy of crisis management which defined the problem as one of short-term illiquidity among cash-strapped LDCs. From this perspective all that seemed to be required was to tide over the debtor nations until global recovery helped them to overcome their temporary cash squeeze. Creditors could simply stretch out the maturity of loans coming due and, if necessary, offer additional funds to help the debtors keep up with their interest payments. In return debtors had to promise specific policy actions which would reduce their need for new credits by lowering trade and budget deficits.

This strategy also allowed banks to manipulate accounting rules governing loan losses to their advantage. Normally, if a debtor falls behind in paying interest due by ninety days or more, the affected loan becomes "nonperforming" and must be rated according to probability of default (special mention, substandard, doubtful, loss). In this case the bank can no longer include interest on that problem loan as income and may have to subtract up to six months of already booked interest. Loans that are classified as doubtful have to be covered by setting aside additional "loan-loss reserves" which are deducted from earnings and counted as part of bank capital. Loans that are considered a loss have to be written off as a charge against those loss reserves, thus reducing the capital of the bank by an equivalent amount.[6] With regulators (i.e., the Fed, the FDIC) usually examining only a small portion of any bank's loan portfolio, banks can often apply these rules at their own discretion. Since the various steps of loan-loss accounting cause lower income or capital erosion, banks have a vested interest in avoiding or delaying them as long as possible.

The temptation to delay the day of reckoning was especially pronounced in the case of large loans to LDCs that originated in the largely self-regulated Euromarket. The crisis management designed in 1982 accommodated U.S. banks in this regard. They could, for example, continue to record interest income on loans that were actually nonperforming, as long as they considered those "well secured" and "in the process of collection." Their willingness to give LDCs new funds for payment of interest on old loans was precisely aimed at assuring that status. Moreover, restructured loans only had to be considered as nonperforming, if they carried "below market" rates of interest. In the first round of reschedulings during 1982–83 the banks charged LDCs a "risk premium" of up to 2 percent above the rate they charge each other (the London Inter-Bank Offer Rate, or LIBOR), high enough to avoid classifying those renegotiated credits as nonperforming. Debt reschedulings also generated large syndication fees for large banks, which they often booked all at once as income at the beginning of the loan agreement. Finally, banks had to write down only those loans deemed "likely to be impaired at the date of the financial statement" and whose "losses can be reasonably estimated." This deliberatedly vague rule gave banks a great deal of discretion in deciding when to declare a loan loss.

Under the IMF-led bailout mechanism the banks agreed to delay repayment of old loans indefinitely and to supply their debtors with additional funds, so that those could continue servicing their old loans. In this way banks could keep LDC loans on their books at face value and count interest payments on those loans as current income. Thus they ended up showing increased earnings, an additional $35 billion or so each year for U.S. banks, even though the quality of their loan portfolios deteriorated steadily.

Although the management of the global debt crisis protected the international banking community, it forced most of the initial adjustment burden onto the debtor countries. With foreign debts averaging about 60 percent of their gross national product, Latin American countries and other LDCs in a similar position (e.g., Nigeria, the Philippines) have had to set aside about 5 percent of their GNP each year for interest payments. In the absence of new loans, such a resource transfer could only be financed out of a similarly large trade surplus. That, in turn, was only possible if the LDCs saved 5 percent of GNP more than they invested. Such large increases in trade surpluses and savings required drastic cuts in consumption and budget deficits. After 1982 many LDCs undertook precisely those policy adjustments and managed to achieve impressive trade surpluses. However, those were not enough, and more austerity eventually became politically impossible. Creditors thus still had to arrange new loans which paid for about half of the foreign interest bills. One problem with such a Ponzi scheme, in which new loans are used to pay the interest on old debt, is that it continuously increases the indebtedness of already troubled borrowers. To the extent that their debts and interest payments have grown faster than their national income or export earnings, LDCs have become caught in a "debt trap" (see Table 10.2)

While their debts and servicing charges increased steadily after 1982, many LDCs also faced deepening slumps, which impaired their ability to grow out of this debt trap. The adjustment programs of the IMF typically imposed painful austerity policies that were aimed at reducing the budget and trade deficits of the LDCs. Such steps as currency devaluations, cuts in social programs, phase-outs

Table 10.2

The Debt Trap for LDCs

	Total debt (in billions of dollars)		Total foreign debt (as percent of exports)		
	1982	1986	1982	1986	1987
Argentina	45.4	51.7	405	536	554
Brazil	85.3	110.3	339	425	471
Chile	18.0	21.5	333	402	370
Colombia	10.6	14.1	191	198	235
Ecuador	7.5	9.1	239	333	464
Mexico	87.6	100.3	299	413	366
Nigeria	14.3	23.4	84	300	310
Peru	12.2	16.2	269	497	551
Philippines	29.5	28.3	269	308	309
Venezuela	37.2	34.1	84	322	278

Source: Morgan Guaranty Trust Company, *World Financial Markets*, June–July 1987, p. 4.

of price subsidies, mass layoffs, and wage freezes hit their citizens hard. In the wake of these belt-tightening measures, growth in many LDCs decelerated while inflation rates rose sharply (see Table 10.3). Growing internal and external debt-servicing burdens forced governments to slash much-needed spending on education, health care, and infrastructure investments. The push for trade surpluses led to drastic import reductions, which retarded the modernization of their industries, and distorted development (e.g., rising malnutrition in food-exporting LDCs). Sharply lower living standards caused social tensions and political unrest to intensify in many LDCs during the 1980s.[7]

The crisis management set up in 1982 was inherently flawed. It added to the debt burden of LDCs, while it undermined their income-generating capacity. As the crisis deepened, banks became increasingly unwilling to "throw good money after bad money." Smaller regional banks, especially, cut back their sovereign debt exposure. Unable to secure adequate supplies of new funds, troubled LDCs lacked the capital to grow out of this crisis. With interest payments and flight capital exceeding new loans and direct foreign investment after 1982, LDCs actually became new exporters of capital. Their trade surpluses were not enough to compensate for this perverse capital transfer. Finally, the very logic of IMF-enforced adjustment programs was self-defeating. Having to cut imports and push exports at the same time, the LDCs ended up throwing supplies into already glutted world markets. During much of the 1980s commodity prices continued to decline, despite recovery in the industrial nations. Thus the commodity-producing

Table 10.3

The Burden of Adjustment in Latin America (annual average percent)

	Real GDP growth		Gross fixed investment (as percent of GDP)		Fiscal balances (as percent of GDP)		Inflation	
	1970–1982	1982–1989	1970–1982	1983–1989	1982–1984	1985–1990	1985–1989	1990
Argentina	0.9	-0.4	20.2	13.7	-12.0	-9.5	474	1,344
Brazil	5.7	3.1	24.5	20.1	-21.3	-41.5	465	1,585
Chile	2.4	2.8	15.1	14.8	-4.1	0.2	20	27
Colombia	5.1	3.4	19.0	19.8	-6.7	-2.3	24	32
Mexico	6.3	0.4	20.9	19.1	-8.6	-11.9	74	30
Peru	3.4	-1.0	17.6	20.1	-8.4	-6.7	443	7,649
Venezuela	3.4	0.5	27.6	19.4	-0.5	-4.8	33	37

Source: Morgan Guaranty Trust Company, *World Financial Markets*, July–August 1992, Tables 1, 2, 8, 10.

Notes: Fiscal balances include interest payments. Inflation based on consumer price index.

LDCs had to export ever-larger volumes just to earn the same amount of money, a classic debt-deflation spiral. If LDCs faced a temporary illiquidity problem in 1982, they faced insolvency a few years later.

Given those shortcomings of its crisis management, the creditors' cartel soon faced pressure to make adjustments. In November 1983 Congress passed legislation which brought foreign lending by U.S. banks under regulatory control and called for more stringent accounting treatment of troubled LDC debt.[8] During 1984 the banks realized that the crisis was more serious than they had originally thought. Under pressure from LDCs and policy-makers, they accepted lower interest rates on new loans and multiyear debt reschedulings. In October 1985 the U.S. Treasury announced a new approach to the global debt crisis. This so-called *Baker Plan* proposed that fifteen major debtor countries commit themselves to reforming their economies, with special emphasis on balancing budgets, privatizing state-run companies, and removing limits on imports as well as on foreign ownership, to make their industries more competitive. In return, those countries would receive $29 billion in new (long-term) funds from the World Bank and commercial banks. That plan, even though it was introduced to preserve the case-by-case approach to the LDC debt crisis, reflected at least a recognition that the problem required a longer-term solution.

In late 1986 the new U.S. initiative led to a loan package for Mexico which offered significantly more lenient terms than previous reschedulings.[9] Despite this innovative agreement and efforts by several countries (e.g., Mexico, Argentina, Chile, Uruguay, Morocco, Nigeria, the Philippines) to restructure their their economies, the Baker Plan never really got off the ground. The structural reforms implemented in those LDCs proved to be destabilizing and fostered political opposition at home before they had a chance to boost economic growth. Commercial banks refused to commit more money to LDCs. Even the IMF and the World Bank reduced their assistance in 1986–87.

When interest rates began to rise in early 1987, the global debt crisis intensified once again. Following the collapse of its anti-inflation program, Brazil decided to challenge the creditors' cartel in February 1987. It suspended its interest payments on $67 billion owed to commercial banks and called for multilateral negotiations between governments to come up with a more balanced approach to crisis management. The Reagan administration rejected its appeal. Our money-center banks, which had managed to increase their capital by 60 percent since 1982, were no longer threatened with insolvency and could afford to hold firm. They restricted Brazil's access to short-term trade finance and ignored its proposals for substantial debt reduction. Eventually, in May 1988, the two sides compromised on terms that closely resembled the 1986 deal with Mexico (see note 9).

Even though Brazil ultimately had to give in, its suspension of interest payments threatened banks with a major hit in their income. Facing the prospect of having to declare its Brazilian loans nonperforming, in May 1987 Citibank decided to set aside $3 billion in reserves. By forcing weaker U.S. banks to follow suit, Citibank managed to strengthen its own competitive position. Within two months U.S. banks had added $16.7 billion in reserves and had taken a $10 billion loss for the second quarter of 1987. By the end of the year their reserve additions came to $33 billion. The banks had finally decided that they had to write down a portion of their LDC claims.[10]

That decision to bolster reserves gave banks a larger cushion with which to cover the inevitable losses incurred when they rid themselves of unwanted LDC debts. Now they could intensify their efforts to sell off or swap a large chunk of their LDC loans. In 1983 banks had already started to sell some of their LDC loans at a discount to the debtor countries or to investors who hoped for capital gains. These loan sales provided a market valuation of debts owed by different countries, with discounts increasing in direct relation to perceived default risks. Soon thereafter banks began to use this secondary market for loan swaps at prevailing discounts to diversify their portfolios in light of more stringent disclosure and accounting rules (see note 8). After the Baker Plan of 1985, debt-equity swaps became popular. These turn a dollar-denominated external debt into an equity investment denominated in local currency within the LDC. In 1988 Brazil and Mexico offered debt-for-bond swaps in which banks tendered their loans in return for a smaller amount of tradable "exit bonds" carrying below-market yields.[11]

In March 1989 the newly elected Bush administration announced a major shift in LDC debt-crisis management. The so-called *Brady Plan* emphasized debt reduction as the primary objective and debt-for-bond swaps as its principal tool. Bank claims would be written down and replaced by "exit bonds." These were to be backed by U.S. Treasury securities which the debtor countries would purchase. Such coverage would insure their value and enable them to carry low fixed rates, thereby making these new bonds attractive to both issuers and holders.

The first swap, negotiated with Mexico in February 1990, lowered that country's annual debt-servicing charges by $1.5 billion—a reduction of about 12 percent.[12] This relief, even though rather modest, gave President Carlos Salinas the breathing room he needed in order to initiate a major restructuring of Mexico's economy, which led to the creation of a free-trade zone with Canada and the United States (the North American Free Trade Agreement, or NAFTA), in August 1992. A second deal, concluded in late 1990 with Venezuela, had less fortunate consequences. Venezuela's debt reduction was too small to allow relaxation of a tough austerity program, and soon Latin America's oldest democracy found itself facing major social unrest. Subsequent loan-for-bond swaps with Argentina (in April 1992) and Brazil (in July 1992) offered debtors more significant relief and creditors greater flexibility. Both gave banks the option of either forgiving 35 percent of their loans in exchange for floating-rate bonds or receiving the face value of their loans in below-market, fixed-rate bonds.

The Brady Plan signaled a new phase in the global debt crisis. The debtor countries were finally given some reduction in their debt principals and interest payments. In return, they have begun the difficult process of economic restructuring, a decisive break from their postcolonial reliance on protectionism, state ownership, and price subsidies. Banks had enough time during the initial crisis management, from 1982 to 1989, to build up their capital. They are no longer threatened with insolvency. Now they can use various refinancing methods (e.g., loan sales, debt-equity swaps, debt-for-bond swaps) to reduce their LDC loan exposure while they limit their losses. The swaps, especially the last two, involving Argentina and Brazil, have actually been quite lucrative. The new bonds earn more interest. They also carry a higher market value than the loans they replaced. Banks can sell their bonds and book the difference as income. Or they may hold on to these securities and revalue the asset side of their balance sheets accordingly. Finally, the deals freed some of the bank reserves set aside for LDC debt to shore up loan-loss provisions against other bad loans, especially commercial real estate.

Banks have used the Brady Plan primarily to socialize their risks and losses. As they gradually disengage from LDC loans, others have to fill the void. Governments of industrial nations and international lending institutions (the IMF, the World Bank) have had to increase their share of funding and at the same time guarantee the exit bonds that are held by banks. These official lenders will continue to supply the lion's share of new funds, to provide backing for debt reduction schemes, and to socialize some of the bank losses.

The evolution of crisis management since 1982 has dramatically transformed the role of the IMF. The fund was set up in 1944 to manage the international monetary system and help member countries cope with temporary balance-of-payments problems. During the 1980s, however, it became the international lender of last resort for more than fifty developing countries that were caught in a structural debt crisis. That change expanded the scope of its interventions, and its lending capacity grew from $65 billion in 1982 to $180 billion in 1991. Much of that increase has gone into several new emergency funds which offer long-term loans at concessionary terms. The once-clear institutional distinction between the IMF and the World Bank is now quite blurred.[13]

10.2. Sectoral Debt Deflation in the United States

1) The Farm Crisis. From the late 1950s to the late 1970s American farmers had enjoyed strong growth. During that period the productivity of land tripled on a per-acre basis due to the introduction of modern farm machinery, hybrid seeds, pesticides, and irrigation equipment at a time of generally favorable world markets and farm policies. As income from farm assets surged, land prices soared twelvefold between 1950 and 1979.[14] In the 1970s, when real interest rates averaged only 1 percent, many farmers borrowed heavily for purchases of land, which appreciated at an annual compound rate of more than 25 percent. Such capital gains only increased their borrowing power, since the land served as collateral for loans. By 1979 the total U.S. farm debt exceeded $200 billion.

Then the Fed suddenly switched to an anti-inflationary policy and pushed interest rates sharply higher. Between 1980 and 1984 interest expense of farmers rose by 90 percent from the 1975–79 average to $21 billion per year, while their income fell by 15 percent to $19 billion per year. The agricultural sector could no longer service its debt without resorting to additional borrowing. But new loans became harder to obtain, as expectations of future land-price appreciation waned and lenders turned cautious. The speculative bubble had finally burst.

Between 1981 and 1987 land prices fell by 55 percent nationwide. Since land served as collateral for farm loans, such deflation exacerbated the financial squeeze of domestic agriculture. At the same time U.S. farmers, who relied on export sales for up to 40 percent of their total output, lost their once-unassailable edge in world markets. Hurt by a high-flying dollar, they also faced increased protectionism by the EC and Japan, an aggressive push of farm exports by debt-ridden LDCs (e.g., Mexico, Argentina, Brazil) as well as other developing countries whose "green revolutions" had succeeded (e.g. India, China), and diversification of suppliers by the Soviet Union after Carter's grain embargo in 1979. Record harvests at home and abroad glutted world markets and kept farm prices low.

In the face of this acute crisis, farmers used their traditional clout in Congress to obtain more help from the government. In fiscal 1987 the various federal assistance programs, exceeding $35 billion that year, constituted nearly three-fourths of farmers' income.[15] But that money was not spent well. By linking the amount of its payments to the size of output, the government encouraged farmers to produce more than market conditions warranted. For the same reason federal subsidies went primarily to the largest farmers, who had relatively light debt loads and few, if any, cash-flow problems. Only a minor portion, about 17 percent of total aid, benefited the small- and medium-sized family farms in financial trouble. These owed two-thirds of the farm debt but controlled merely one-third of the assets. In light of these huge costs and misallocation, the government has recently begun to cut its farm assistance and to negotiate a phased-in deregulation of global agriculture under the Uruguay Round of trade agreements.

With government aid programs doing little to help the most burdened producers, one-third of all farmers faced bankruptcy in the mid-1980s. About 20 percent of the $200 billion in agricultural loans were in jeopardy of having to be written off. As a result many of the nation's 5,000 farm banks, mostly small institutions with at least a quarter of their loans in agriculture, found themselves in trouble as well. Between late 1981 and late 1986 the number of farm banks on the FDIC's problem-bank list rose from 45 to 615. In the second quarter of 1985 only 60 farm banks had more problem loans than capital, a sign of severe weakness and potential failure, but by the third quarter of 1987 that figure had risen to 209. During that period 129 farm banks failed.[16] Responding to the steep increases in loan defaults and bank failures, the FDIC relaxed its regulation for farm banks in March 1986. It allowed "well-managed" farm banks to operate temporarily below minimum capital requirements, which then stood at 6 percent of total assets. It also introduced more liberal accounting, reporting, and disclosure requirements for renegotiated problem loans so as not to penalize banks when they restructured debts.

In mid-1985 commercial banks held about $50 billion in farm loans; the Farm Credit System (FCS) accounted for another $76 billion. Ever since its beginning in 1917, the FCS has been the primary lender to farmers. It is a nationwide network of borrower-owned cooperative banks.[17] It funds its farm loans by issuing its own securities. These have "agency" status, trading as if they were backed by the U.S. government and offering exemptions from state and local taxes. Because the FCS is owned and controlled by farmers who are also borrowers, there is a conflict of interest that puts pressure on the system to keep out professional managers and underprice loans. Its units are basically run as nonprofit organizations.

During the late 1970s and early 1980s, years of rapid growth, the system had borrowed money for long periods at the higher rates then prevailing. Trying to maintain some positive yield spread after rates began to decline in 1982, the system ended up charging uncompetitive rates on its loans. This prompted healthy borrowers to shift to commercial banks. As they left the FCS, they withdrew the stock that customers are required to buy in the system, further draining it of low-cost funds. As a result of this exodus, the system's loan assets dwindled from a peak of $80 billion in 1983 to just below $50 billion in late 1987. When the farm debt crisis exploded in 1985 and 1986, it hit the already weakened FCS with special force. During those two years, 20 percent of its loans became nonperforming, and the system lost $4.6 billion. This huge loss wiped out half of its capital. The collapse of its regional banks in Omaha and Spokane during 1985 triggered a series of measures to keep the system afloat.[18]

In December 1985 Congress proposed a loss-sharing arrangement whereby the stronger units of the system would move some of their capital to weaker units in danger of collapse. In return, the FCS would be given a line of credit from the Treasury. But healthier units of the FCS blocked this loss-sharing arrangement in court. This was followed in September 1986 by regulatory relief in the form of lower capital-adequacy rules, reserve requirements, and interest rates. The system banks agreed to show forbearance and to restructure loans whenever the reduction in repayment of principal or in interest charges would cause a smaller loss to the lender than foreclosure. Congress allowed the FCS to refinance outstanding bonds at lower interest rates. The costs of that refinancing operation and of bad-debt losses could be stretched out over twenty years to give the system a healthier financial picture. One year later the FCS, under pressure from Congress to slash costs, proposed a sweeping consolidation of its far-flung network through a series of mergers. Finally, Congress passed the Agricultural Credit Act to bail out the system with a $4 billion bond issue and an interest subsidy that cost an estimated $1.2 billion. The Federal Agriculture Mortgage Corporation was set up with a $1.5 billion credit line from the Treasury to guarantee securitized packages of farm loans for resale. Finally, the act also required both FCS and the Farmers Home Administration, another major farm lender run by the U.S. Department of Agriculture, to adopt more liberal rules on loan restructuring and forgiveness.

2) Crisis in the Oil and Gas Industry. Much like our nation's farmers, the domestic oil and gas industry also suffered a major debt crisis in the wake of global commodity deflation. During the boom years U.S. banks had increased their share of energy loans from 10.6 percent of total bank credit in 1979 to 17.6 percent in 1982. But a relatively modest 7 percent decline of oil prices starting in late 1980 caused a 40 percent decline in domestic drilling activity during 1981.

The first casualty of this downturn was the Penn Square Bank of Oklahoma City which had lent hundreds of millions of dollars to regional oil drillers in the energy-rich Southwest through negotiable CDs and brokered deposits that pulled in funds from all over the country. Between 1980 and 1982 its loan portfolio had tripled. Lending decisions were based on highly optimistic assumptions about future energy prices and drilling output. Many of its loans were to local wildcatters who were directors or major shareholders of the bank. In one instance it had lent more than twice its capital to the subsidiaries of one such bank insider. Its loans lacked proper documentation and collateral. Ironically, Penn Square's lending practices had been questioned by the bank examiners of the Comptroller of Currency in April 1980. But in October 1981 the bank, having covered up many of its souring loans by granting overdrafts, won a reprieve from that regulator. This decision made the loan officers of Penn Square even more reckless. In July 1982 the bank collapsed.

Penn Square was not a large bank. The fourth-largest bank in Oklahoma, it had capital of $33 million and about $500 million in assets. Yet its insolvency became the most expensive bank failure in U.S. history, testimony to the growing interdependence of banks. Penn Square had amassed $250 million in uninsured deposits from credit unions, savings and loan associations, commercial banks, and other financial institutions. The bank was in such bad shape that it had to be liquidated by the FDIC, so those uninsured depositors lost about $50 million. That led in turn to a rather massive "flight to quality" out of negotiable CDs and into Treasury bills. Moreover, by the time of its failure Penn Square had sold more than $2 billion in loan participations to larger banks.[19] With most of these loans uncollectible, participating banks lost more than $1.2 billion. These losses left two large banks mortally wounded. SeattleFirst, which had bought about $400 million in loans from Penn Square, required a $1.5 billion safety net from fourteen banks and a $700 million discount loan from the Fed in

June 1983. Ultimately it was saved from certain bankruptcy only by an FDIC-assisted merger with the Bank of America. Continental Illinois had booked more than $1 billion in loan participations from Penn Square. It never recovered from its $350 million loss, and in May 1984 the nation's sixth-largest bank required a $4.5 billion federal bailout.

The sectoral downturn of the energy sector took a dramatic turn for the worse in late 1985 and early 1986. Global oil overproduction of up to 3 million barrels a day finally triggered a price war within OPEC, started by the Saudis in an effort to discipline other cartel members who routinely violated their production quotas. In six months oil prices collapsed from about $29 per barrel to less than $10, before finally settling in a $15–$18 range. Such sudden and brutal deflation after three years of depressed conditions had a devastating impact on the domestic oil industry and its lenders in Texas, Oklahoma, and Louisiana. The situation was especially bad in Texas, where the bust extended to real estate and agriculture, two other sectors whose boom in the late 1970s had been heavily debt-financed.

In the aftermath of the oil-price slide the region's banks suffered sharply rising loan losses, depressed earnings, and deposit withdrawals. Regulators still remembered the Penn Square debacle and the collapse of First National Bank of Midland (Texas), whose liquidation had cost the FDIC $346 million. With 92 percent of the $61 billion in energy loans concentrated in just 59 banks with assets in excess of $1 billion, the potential for costly failures was great. The regulatory agencies did not want to be surprised again, so they began to prepare for a full-blown regional banking crisis in the first half of 1986. The Fed extended to energy banks the regulatory and accounting relief measures announced earlier for ailing farm banks. Those could now continue lending, even after their capital-to-assets ratio had dropped below the required minimum of 6 percent, and they were given easier accounting treatment to invite more concessionary debt reschedulings. The FDIC declared itself ready to help keep failing institutions alive, an important break with its established practice of assisting only already failed banks. Congress relaxed the Garn–St. Germain Depository Institutions Act of 1982 to facilitate acquisitions of troubled banks across state lines. Now out-of-state banks could take over failing (not just already failed) banks with assets of $250 million or more (instead of $500 million or more). Finally, in September 1986 the Texas legislature passed a law allowing out-of-state take-overs of its banks.

Those initiatives came just in time to cope with a major wave of energy bank failures. In July 1986 the First National Bank of Oklahoma City, with $1.6 billion in assets, could not repay a $296 million emergency discount loan from the Fed. The FDIC arranged for its purchase by First Interstate Bancorp of Los Angeles. In August 1986 the FDIC pumped $130 million into BancOklahoma Corp in return for a 55 percent stake in the bank holding company. Chemical Bank of New York bought Texas Commerce Bancshares, the state's preeminent energy lender, for $1.19 billion in December 1986, and less than 48 hours later

RepublicBank purchased its crosstown rival InterFirst Corp of Dallas. In July 1987 BancTexas Group of Dallas was bailed out with $150 million in FDIC funds and $50 million from the Hallwood Group. In January 1988 First Interstate Bancorp of Los Angeles acquired Allied Bancshares of Houston without federal assistance for $296 million. In April 1988 First City Bancorp of Houston received a $500 million capital injection from an investment group led by former Chicago banker Robert Abboud. The FDIC covered up to $970 million in losses on loan write-offs. Then the biggest Texas bank, the recently merged First RepublicBank, with $27 billion in assets, collapsed in July 1988. The FDIC took over the bank. NCNB of North Carolina later acquired a 20 percent share for $210 million, with the possibility of raising its stake over a five-year span. NCNB also secured a $4 billion assistance package from the FDIC, which erased First Republic's negative equity and covered all of its bad-loan losses. Finally, the FDIC assisted the takeover of the insolvent Dallas-based MCorp by Banc One Corp in July 1989 by promising to cover up to $2 billion in sour loans.

3) The Real Estate Boom and Bust. Although the debt crises of LDCs, farmers, and energy firms have all subsided somewhat since 1987, commercial banks have encountered new problems. During the second half of the 1980s they engaged in yet another wave of land-based speculation, financing a boom in housing and construction driven by rapid appreciation of real estate values. Between 1986 and early 1990 the banks increased their real estate lending by 50 percent to $765 billion. The loans fueled massive overbuilding, especially of office space. In 1989 office vacancies soared and housing prices started to decline, especially in the Northeast and later also in California. Since then many banks based in those regions have faced a surge in defaults and foreclosures resulting in significant loan-losses.

4) The Leveraged Buyout Debacle. In addition, over the past few years banks have come to regret their rush into funding leveraged buyouts during the deal mania of the late 1980s. Once the recession hit, many of these restructured companies found it difficult to meet burdensome debt obligations. Some of the largest buyouts have since gone bankrupt (e.g., Campeau, Macy's), and many others faced cash-flow problems that required refinancing and debt reschedulings.

10.3. The Thrift Disaster

Among the sectoral debt crises of the 1980s, none was more spectacular than the collapse of hundreds of thrifts. In early 1989 the Bush administration and Congress agreed to a federal bailout of the thrift industry which may cost U.S. taxpayers $350 billion or more over the next thirty years. This was followed by revelations of massive fraud and a series of scandals involving well-known politicians (e.g., the "Keating Five," Jim Wright, Tony Coelho, Neil Bush). Even though most Americans only began to focus on the thrift problem in the late

1980s, the crisis had built beneath the surface of public attention for nearly a decade. Moreover, even though embezzlement and corruption were important ingredients in the collapse of many thrifts, the root causes of the mess went much deeper.

Thrift institutions, whether savings and loan associations (S&Ls) or mutual savings banks (MSBs), traditionally specialized in attracting savings deposits and using these funds for mortgage lending. In other words, they offered liquid deposit liabilities to savers while obtaining less-liquid, longer-maturity assets. Under normal conditions (an upward-sloped yield curve) the thrifts could charge higher rates on their loans than they had to pay on their deposits. But their maturity mismatch had its dangers, and these came to the fore with growing force once the postwar era of price stability ended in the mid-1960s.

Whenever accelerating inflation in the late 1960s and 1970s pushed up interest rates, earnings of thrifts declined. Because their deposits were mostly short-term, any increase in interest rates quickly affected their liability side. However, the same was not true for their asset side. Low-rate mortgages were repaid only slowly, so the thrifts could not quickly alter their loan portfolios in favor of higher-rate mortgages. Hence their costs tended to increase more rapidly than their revenues in periods of rising interest rates. This earnings squeeze became especially pronounced each time the term structure of interest rates inversed during a credit crunch, thereby causing an abnormal, negatively sloped yield curve. With short-term rates rising above long-term rates, the thrifts would actually experience a negative yield spread and suffer operating losses.

That inherent vulnerability was not lessened by the decision of Congress in 1966, during the first postwar credit crunch, to extend Regulation Q ceilings to thrifts. Even though their deposit rates were set 0.25 percent above those of commercial banks, the thrifts too faced disintermediation by depositors who sought higher yields elsewhere whenever market rates rose above the ceiling. The loss of funds forced thrifts to stop making loans, which is why each credit crunch between 1966 and 1979 hit the real estate industry especially hard. Sometimes they even had to sell assets in order to obtain the cash they needed for withdrawals. Because mortgages were long-term and carried low fixed rates, their market value declined strongly when interest rates rose. Forced asset sales thus tended to create large losses for the thrifts.

In the 1970s these problems prompted regulatory authorities to help thrifts retain or obtain funds at minimum cost and increase their asset flexibility and returns.[20] DIDMCA 1980 (see section 9.1) abolished the rate ceilings on deposits and mortgages, allowed S&Ls to offer NOW accounts, boosted the net worth of federal thrifts by letting them issue mutual capital certificates, let S&Ls lend in a wider geographic area, and expanded their product range to include consumer loans, credit cards, and trust services. The Garn–St. Germain DIA of 1982 helped thrifts to diversify even more. S&Ls could offer demand deposits for loan customers and expand into futures transactions, commercial lending, leasing services, municipal bond purchases, and additional consumer lending. The act also let out-of-state banks and thrifts acquire failing S&Ls and gave regulators permission to inject more capital into weak thrifts by buying their "net worth certificates."

It has become commonplace to blame those deregulation measures of the early 1980s for the subsequent thrift disaster. There is some truth in this criticism, but it tends to ignore that Congress passed both the DIDMCA of 1980 and the DIA of 1982 at a time of acute crisis in the thrift industry. Stuck with $70 billion in mortgages yielding less than 7.5 percent, the nation's 5,000 thrifts suffered negative yield spreads and massive disintermediation when interest rates surged to more than twice that level in late 1979. Throughout the postwar period the FSLIC, the main insurer of S&L deposits, with $6.5 billion in funds, had faced on average just one thrift failure per year. But in 1980 and 1981 it had to assist 34 mergers, at a cost of $2.23 billion. In 1981 alone the thrift industry suffered a $6 billion loss and net withdrawals of deposits in excess of $39 billion. Additional losses of $3.3 billion during the first half of 1982 brought 400 thrifts to the brink of collapse. It was against this background that Congress decided it needed to assist the battered industry. Its vehicle, the DIA of 1982, provided weaker S&Ls with additional capital so that they could survive the cyclical downturn. And it expanded both liabilities and assets of thrifts so that those institutions would never again face maturity imbalances. As we shall see, both strategies caused major problems later on.

The DIA's capital infusion was a purely cosmetic financial transaction. The FDIC, which insured mutual savings banks, and the FSLIC, which insured savings and loan associations, had the authority to issue promissory notes that covered up to 70 percent of an institution's losses. Any thrift thus assisted would in turn issue an equivalent amount in so-called net worth certificates, which were held by the regulators and counted as capital. In essence, the government committed itself to cover private losses while allowing the debt incurred in the process to be turned into capital.[21]

This ingenious method of socializing losses was only one in a series of accounting gimmicks that were designed to hide losses and keep insolvent thrifts open. Under conventional accounting rules the FSLIC simply did not have enough reserves to cover all potential losses when assisting mergers involving failing thrifts, its preferred bailout method. It was thus forced to let many thrifts operate with negative net worth and defer losses through so-called regulatory accounting principles (RAP).

• In September 1981 the Federal Home Loan Bank Board (FHLBB), the principal thrift regulator, had facilitated acquisitions of sick thrifts. Instead of forcing the acquiring institution to write down the low-yield loans held by the failed S&L to market value, as required under normal accounting rules, the FHLBB allowed these write-down losses to be treated as "good will" and thus to be amortized over forty years. But interest and repayments of principal from the acquired mortgages could be reported over the life of these loans, usually ten to twelve years. This so-called purchase method of accounting created significant paper profits for the first few years after a merger.[22]

• In February 1982 purchase accounting was extended to sales of old low-yield mortgages at market value by all thrifts as well as to mergers between two or more failed thrifts, thus combining them into a new and apparently profitable institution. The FSLIC helped those "basket mergers" by issuing promissory notes to keep the net worth of the new institutions at 1 percent of liabilities for five years.

• At first those creative accounting methods seemed to have done the trick. In 1984 the thrift industry reported $2.1 billion in profits, half of which were paper profits created by those special RAP rules for thrift losses. But then a second wave of thrift failures hit in late 1984 which sent FSLIC reserves plummeting by $1.34 billion. In the face of these huge costs the agency adopted a new bailout method in April 1985. Under the so-called management consignment program (MCP) the FSLIC replaced the management of a failed institution, then set it up as a new thrift and provided it with capital in the form of net worth certificates. If no buyer was found within ninety days, the new thrift would gradually liquidate the bad assets. Losses from these liquidations would be covered by FSLIC issue of additional certificates. But lack of buyers turned the MCP into a long-term program of warehousing insolvent thrifts, each of which kept losing millions every month. In just two years the MCP's sixty thrifts lost $4.6 billion, in addition to losses of $1.28 billion reported earlier, before their takeover by the FSLIC.

The use of more liberal RAP rules assumed that sick thrifts would become viable again once the recession was over and interest rates dropped. But most of them never recovered. By keeping insolvent thrifts open rather than removing them from the market, the regulators allowed operating losses to accumulate over time. Many of those institutions engaged in high-risk strategies, facilitated by deregulation, in the hope of rapidly earning their way out of bankruptcy. In addition, they tried to attract brokered deposits from across the nation by offering higher rates. This practice undermined the health of other thrifts, because it raised their cost of funds. The various accounting gimmicks also masked the full extent of thrift losses and thus prevented regulators from enforcing needed reorganization measures in time to prevent eventual failure. In 1985 and 1986 many thrifts, which had relied heavily on net worth certificates and other RAP relief, collapsed. Contingent liabilities of the FSLIC suddenly became actual losses.

At the end of 1986 the FSLIC had only $500 million in usable cash left, but it had accumulated a deficit of $6.3 billion from its contingent liabilities. Now the insurer had to be bailed out. The Competitive Equality Banking Act (CEBA) of 1987 offered $10.8 billion in bonds over three years for the recapitalization of the FSLIC. Interest payments on these bonds would be financed out of special insurance assessments. In addition, the act also required thrifts to phase out their regulatory accounting practices over five years. This measure was wholly inadequate to deal with the problem. It did not provide the FSLIC with sufficient funds to cover its losses, let alone close down or merge insolvent institutions. And the rise in premiums prompted many healthier thrifts to leave the insurance system by converting into banks, thus weakening the FSLIC.

The second strategy of the DIA of 1982, that of extensive thrift deregulation, also backfired. The law unwittingly created a tailor-made vehicle for speculators and criminals who were intent on using the public's money for their own personal gain. For one, the act made it much easier to acquire failing thrifts across state lines. Because thrifts had a minimal capital requirement of 3 percent of assets and could count debt certificates as well as intangibles (e.g., good will) toward net worth, they were cheap to buy. Their low capital base also allowed for highly leveraged transactions which, if successful, gave thrift owners attractive rates of return.[23] Under the management of unscrupulous investors, once small and sleepy thrifts turned rapidly into much larger institutions. The extraordinary growth of many "go-go" thrifts was due to aggressive pursuit of brokered deposits by offering above-average rates. These relatively expensive funds were then invested in risky instruments and trading strategies with potentially high yields—real estate development, land speculation, mortgage-backed securities, repurchase agreements, junk-bonds, financial futures, and even the acquisition of failing thrifts to get more government assistance and book additional paper profits.

Making matters worse, government regulators lacked both will and resources to prevent the spread of unsound funding and lending practices among thrifts. The FHLBB in particular was what we may call a "captured" agency. Its directors maintained close ties to large thrifts and frequently consulted their managers. The U.S. League of Savings Institutions, the powerful trade group of the thrifts, had a de facto veto over the FHLBB's regulatory decisions. Thus the private interests of regulated institutions tended to crowd out the public interest. Thrift examiners, besides being reduced in numbers by budget cuts at the regulatory agencies, lacked the training to investigate accounting manipulations and evaluated complex investments. When the thrift regulators allowed widespread use of accounting gimmicks to cook the books, they sent a strong message that abuse would be tolerated. Many thrift owners tried to influence regulatory decisions in their favor by hiring big-name lobbyists or making contributions to lawmakers. All of this created a climate of rampant corruption, collusion, and negligence. Fraud reached epidemic proportions and contributed to many thrift failures.[24] Insider misconduct was especially common. Thrift officers made personal loans to shareholders and managers of thrifts or funded real estate projects in which thrift owners had a hidden interest.

It was inevitable that the flawed policy toward thrifts should eventually produce such disastrous results. The moment of truth arrived in 1987, when U.S. interest rates moved up sharply and security prices collapsed. These unfavorable developments in financial markets caused some of the largest and most aggressive "go-go" thrifts to suffer huge losses on their high-risk investments and to become insolvent. Other thrifts, which had been kept artificially alive, could no longer hide their staggering operating losses and asset devaluations behind accounting gimmicks. Thrift failures were especially concentrated in states with the most lenient regulation of state-chartered thrifts and the largest excess supplies of commercial real estate—Florida, Texas, and California. During 1987 and 1988 the FSLIC's deficit grew from $6.3 billion to $16 billion, the thrift industry recorded a loss of $19.9 billion, and the estimated cost of rescuing or closing about 500 insolvent thrifts rose from $20 billion to $75 billion. This deterioration rapidly consumed the $10.8 billion capital infusion into FSLIC under the CEBA of 1987.

A much larger bailout had become necessary, possibly involving taxpayer money for the first time. But during 1988 neither a Congress distracted by the election campaign nor a lame-duck president could come up with any long-term solution to the problem. With losses of insolvent thrifts soaring to $1 billion a month, the FHLBB decided it could not wait any longer. The agency's partisan chairman, Danny Wall, tried to keep a lid on the thrift crisis so as to shield George Bush from criticism during his election campaign. He also wanted to avoid dumping thousands of office buildings and shopping malls, which were in default, on an already weak market. Finally, tax benefits that were attractive to outside investors were about to expire by the end of the year. For all these reasons, in late 1988 the FLRBB rushed into 205 guarantee-assisted mergers, so-called resolutions, which removed sick thrifts from its insolvent list. Most of them were acquired by banks, home builders, industrial corporations (e.g., Ford), corporate raiders (e.g., Bass Group, Perelman), and investment groups that specialized in the acquisition of failing S&Ls, such as the WestFed Holding Company, run by former Treasury Secretary William Simon and former Fed Vice Chair Preston Martin.

These buyers made great deals. They had to put up little of their own money, usually receiving between $8 and $10 in assets for each dollar they spent. They also obtained FHLBB guarantees against any future losses. These guarantees usually in the form of promissory notes of the FSLIC backed by a special pocket-charter device in case the de facto bankrupt regulator ever defaulted, enabled the new owners to mark up bad loans to original book value and to eliminate reserves for losses. In this way they could start to report large gains even though those loans were still nonperforming. In addition, the acquirers also received tax breaks on operating losses. The FHLBB kept the terms of these deals secret, arguing that publicity would weaken its bargaining position vis-à-vis other potential buyers of insolvent thrifts. When Congress finally started to investigate those deals in early 1989, lawmakers were horrified to see that the FHLBB still bore the full risk of continuing losses on the "resolved" loans and to learn how little capital the buyers had to put up on their own.

Soon after taking office, President Bush proposed a bailout plan for the thrift industry which was passed into law in August 1989. This so-called Financial Institutions Reform, Recovery and Enforcement Act (FIRREA) of 1989 was the most important measure of banking regulation since the Great Depression. It set up the Resolution Trust Corporation (RTC), an "off-budget" agency managed by the FDIC, which was authorized to borrow $30 billion over two years to help cover the cost of liquidating about 600 insolvent S&Ls. For that same purpose the Treasury would raise an additional $20 billion "on budget." Together with interest payments and the costs of covering losses until the thrift assets could be sold off, the total bailout expense was estimated at $166 billion over ten years. In addition, the law replaced the FHLBB and FSLIC with a new regulatory structure, allowed banks to buy healthy thrifts, phased in higher minimum capital requirements for thrifts based on risk, prohibited thrifts from using brokered deposits and junk bonds while requiring 70 percent of their loans to go toward housing-related investments, and raised penalties for lending fraud. Eventually these provisions will remove up to two-thirds of the nation's 2,900 thrifts.[25]

The RTC had a difficult time getting off the ground, and it liquidated only 40 of the 600 thrifts it had seized during the first six months of its existence. There were several reasons for this slow start. The labyrinthine bureaucracy set up under FIRREA of 1989 led to turf battles, diffused responsibilities, and cumbersome decision-making. Trying to avoid the abuses of the past, Congress also saddled the cleanup effort with crippling constraints. It ruled out enticements used earlier to attract bidders for sick thrifts, such as tax breaks and exemptions from onerous regulations. In order to avoid depressing property prices by "dumping" assets of seized thrifts, the RTC could not sell real estate below market value. But with thrifts seized by the RTC suffering $5 million in daily operating losses and $9-million-a-day plunges in the value of their investments, delays were expensive. Currently the eventual costs of the thrift bailout, including future interest payments, are estimated to exceed a staggering $350 billion.

Looking back on this thrift disaster, the U.S. government could have covered the losses at troubled thrifts in 1985 by writing a check to depositors for $20 billion and closing those S&Ls down. Instead, it allowed insolvent institutions to stay open and gamble with federally insured deposits on risky ventures. It thereby created a time bomb which has now exploded. The debris from this explosion has created lasting and widespread damage—pushing the budget deficit to new record levels, crowding out much-needed federal spending on our infrastructure and social services, triggering tax increases, forcing depository institutions to cut back lending in order to comply with tougher capital requirements, and depressing the real estate industry for years to come.

10.4. Credit Crunch, Moral Hazard, and Deposit Insurance Reform

The Great Depression convinced economists and policy-makers that financial crises, if left unchecked, could paralyze the economy and that they therefore had to be contained. Since then the U.S. government has actively intervened as lender of last resort to overcome such crises. When financial markets face major disturbances, the Federal Reserve can pump additional reserves into the system through open-market purchases and can then direct banks to make funds available to adversely affected institutions. The central bank can also use its discount window to help depository institutions which face illiquidity due to deposit withdrawals. Deposit insurance aims to forestall panic runs on banks or thrifts. When a bank has incurred losses exceeding its capital and thus becomes insolvent, the FDIC steps in and organizes its orderly removal. The agency can liquidate the bank and pay off insured depositors. Alternatively, it can take over the bad assets of the failed bank and sell the rest to another institution—the preferred method, which is used in 80 percent of bank failures. The proceeds from selling off the bad assets, usually at a discount, are then distributed to creditors and shareholders.

This type of policy stabilizer was largely inactive during the expansion phase between 1945 and 1966, when the credit system was free of any major disturbances. In the first phase of the postwar downswing, between 1966 and 1979, the existing mechanisms contained financial instability quite well. Isolated incidences of bank failure were easily taken care of by FDIC-assisted mergers. And whenever a credit crunch put too much pressure on financial institutions and markets, the Fed would ease up and supply the banking system with additional reserves.

During the 1980s financial instability intensified, as entire sectors experienced debt-deflation adjustments to speculation-driven overextension of credit that was followed in each case by collapsing prices and spreading defaults. Together they left our domestic banking sector in a much weakened state. Each hit a particular segment of the banking sector. The LDC debt crisis had the greatest impact on the large money-center banks, some of whom suffered additional losses when the merger wave collapsed in the late 1980s. The farm crisis primarily hurt small community banks in rural America. The energy crisis stopped the rapid expansion of superregionals in the Southwest. And the real estate downturn after 1989 has affected thrifts and superregionals in the Northeast the most.

Those deflationary adjustments required significant extensions of crisis management. The LDC debt crisis, for example, led to the creation of an entirely new international lender of last resort. This meant transforming the IMF and beefing up its capital. Other agencies, most notably the FCS and the FSLIC, also needed recapitalization. In the face of a rapidly growing number of failures, the existing ban on interstate banking had to be circumvented to allow acquisition of insolvent banks and thrifts by out-of-state institutions (DIA of 1982; CEBA of 1987). Repeatedly the Fed used its discount window for what in effect became long-term loans to failing banks, most notably $8 billion to Continental Illinois, $600 million to First City, $3 billion to First Republic, and $1.75 billion to MCorp. Ever since the rescue of Continental Illinois in 1984 the FDIC followed a "too-big-to-fail" policy of insuring all deposits of large money-center banks, even those with denominations larger than $100,000.[26] The ConIll takeover by the FDIC was also the first time a bank was nationalized. In order to hold down bailout costs the FDIC even attempted to help sick institutions before they actually failed, starting with its "open-bank" assistance to the Bank of Oklahoma in October 1986. Similarly, the Fed pushed bank holding companies into helping their ailing subsidiaries or into merging strong and weak units.

As bank and thrift failures mounted throughout the 1980s, both the FDIC and the FSLIC tried to preserve their own scarce resources by keeping severely undercapitalized and even insolvent institutions open. Troubled energy banks, farm banks, and thrifts could continue to operate even though their capital had fallen below the required minimum. Moreover, that capital included net worth certificates, a debt instrument, as well as good will, a paper gain. Most importantly, banks and thrifts could use more lenient RAPs to avoid marking down devalued assets, to keep booking income from nonperforming loans, to make concessions in debt restructurings without taking a hit in income, and to report artificial gains in mergers of failed institutions. Such accounting gimmicks relax the monetary constraint by deferring economic losses or, even better, by turning them into accounting profits.[27]

Even though these lender-of-last-resort extensions during the 1980s prevented the kind of banking collapse last seen in the 1930s, they were not without problems.

• Protected by the government's deposit insurance and bailout guarantee, banks and thrifts are in the enviable position of not having to pay for their mistakes. They can pocket profits for themselves and transfer their losses to the rest of society. In other words, they are not subject to the same kind of market discipline as other private firms. Hence they may be inclined to take larger risks than would be prudent. When regulators extended their safety net, they only made this moral hazard problem worse.

• The policy of deferring losses and keeping bankrupt institutions open, which had been designed to reduce the costs of government assistance, actually ended up doing exactly the opposite. The longer insolvent banks and S&Ls continued to operate, the greater were the risks they took in the false hope of returning to solvency. In order to stay liquid, these troubled institutions tried to attract brokered deposits by offering higher interest rates. Not only did their losses grow over time because of excessive risk-taking, but their practice of bidding up the cost of deposit funds also weakened healthier institutions.

• Government protection of banks transfers private losses to, and thus imposes costs on, others. Depending on the mode of loss socialization, these costs may accrue to debtors (e.g., LDCs), to healthier competitors having to pay extra insurance premiums, to investors misled by the accounting distortion of financial statements, to taxpayers (e.g., the S&L bailout), or to anyone using money if the Fed's reserve injections prove to be inflationary.

It is by no means surprising that deregulation tended to aggravate these problems. Higher cost of funds and intensifying competition propelled many depository institutions into pursuing inherently riskier investment opportunities, with which they had little past experience. At the same time the Reagan administration made the decisive mistake of confusing deregulation with lax supervision. If anything, deregulated institutions need to be supervised more closely, lest they take too many chances with their new-found freedoms. But Reagan's attack on the regulatory apparatus of the federal government weakened the capacity of various regulators, especially the Comptroller of Currency, the FDIC, the Securities and Exchange Commission (SEC), and the FHLBB, to carry out their supervision effectively. While bank failures surged, the number of enforcement actions by bank supervisors (e.g., cease-and-desist orders, penalties) fell from 814 in 1986 to 411 in 1989. These agencies lacked the staff, both in numbers and quality, to examine the increasingly complex investment strategies and linkages in the banking sector.[28] In that environment it was to be expected that banks and thrifts became more vulnerable to failure. Extensions of lender-of-last-resort mechanisms to deal with a much larger number of insolvencies only raised the ultimate cost of government assistance.

The dangerous combination of deregulation, lax supervision, and bailout guarantee came to full fruition when domestic growth slowed to a trickle in 1989. Deprived of income gains and no longer able to deduct most interest expenses, borrowers began to feel debt burdens much more heavily. The banks, already under pressure from many problem loans during the uneven recovery, began to take very heavy hits from asset deflation (especially high-risk securities and real estate). The crisis began gradually, overshadowed at the time by the thrift debacle, but accelerated rapidly once the economy fell into outright recession during 1990.

Our banks had managed to recover somewhat from large bad-debt losses in 1986–87, when they had to write off a large number of LDC, farm, and energy loans. Record earnings of $23 billion in 1988 and $14.3 billion in the first half of 1989 enabled them to build up their capital base to $206 billion in 1989, the highest level in fifteen years. However, these improvements proved to be ephemeral. When the Fed tightened in late 1988 and much of 1989 in response to full-employment conditions which moved inflation higher (from 4 percent to 5.5 percent over the same period), interest rates rose. This put renewed pressure on bank earnings. More importantly, the rate hike pushed many heavily indebted

consumers and corporations to the brink of default. The retrenchment was especially pronounced in the real estate sector, which was hit hard by overcapacity,
loss of tax benefits (in the wake of the 1986 tax reform), RTC liquidations of
thrift assets, and regional recessions in the Mid-Atlantic and New England states.

During 1990 the financial position of commercial banks deteriorated rapidly.
Their profits fell from $6.3 billion in the first quarter to $2.6 billion in the fourth
quarter of that year. Nonperforming loans rose from an average 2.24 percent of
assets in 1989 to 3.03 percent by the end of 1990, a postwar high. Between July
1989 and July 1990 restructured loans grew an amazing 433 percent at the
nation's leading 100 commercial banks. Net write-offs of bad loans, which had
averaged an already significant $15 billion per year during the mid-1980s, rose
to almost $25 billion in 1989 and 1990 among FDIC-insured banks. Even though
their loan-loss reserves rose, those additions did not keep pace with the jump in
their potential loan losses. In 1990 reserves covered only 58.5 percent of nonperforming loans, compared to 82.1 percent in 1989.

This gap virtually guaranteed future earning hits among banks that were
forced to increase their reserves significantly (e.g., Citibank's $885 million loss
during the third quarter of 1991). The prospect made investors sour on bank
stocks and bonds, and banks found it more difficult to raise capital that way. In
1990 bank issues of new equity and debt securities were less than half of what
they had been during the preceding year. At the same time, regulators demanded
that depository institutions boost their capital. In July 1988 twelve leading industrial nations concluded the so-called Basel Agreement to impose uniform capital
requirements for their banks. By the end of 1992 banks operating in those countries were supposed to have capital equivalent to 8 percent of assets, weighted by
risk.[29] The old requirement for U.S. banks was 6 percent irrespective of risk.
FIRREA of 1989 imposed the same increase for thrift capital.

Although a larger capital base increases the cushion against losses, the new
rule turned out to have been the right policy at the wrong time. With investors
dumping their stocks and with earnings depressed, depository institutions could
not increase their capital-asset rations except by cutting back their lending and
by selling off their best assets. At the same time, consumers and corporations
decided to reduce their loan demand. Consumer loans peaked in early 1990 and
started to shrink thereafter. Commercial loan growth slowed from 6.68 percent in
1989 to just 1.9 percent in 1990, with loan balances actually beginning to decline
in the fourth quarter of that year. They fell from a peak of $330 billion in August
1990 to $302 billion a year later, as the U.S. economy slipped into a full-blown
recession.

That credit crunch, a mutually reinforcing chain reaction of cutbacks by excessively leveraged borrowers and loss-plagued lenders, differed from crunches
in the 1970s. Those had been essentially short-lived adjustments to cool off
accelerating inflation. The most recent squeeze, by contrast, was a longer-term
correction of excessive leveraging. As such, it more closely resembled the tradi-

tional debt-deflation processes that were common before World War II. Those kinds of finance-driven downturns are hard to get out of, as our policy-makers have found out. The Fed began easing in late 1990. But its efforts to push interest rates lower and to increase bank reserves failed to revive credit activity. Worried lenders did not loosen their standards, and pessimistic borrowers still hesitated to take on new debt. Only after the Fed abandoned its gradualist approach in December 1991 and lowered the discount rate by a full percentage point, to its lowest level in nearly thirty years, did we see the first signs of a turnaround—better yield spreads for banks, a rush of refinancings that saved debtors large amounts of interest expense, improving stock and bond markets, and a pick-up in retail and home sales. Banks used that more favorable climate to accelerate their sales of bonds and stocks, thereby finally managing to improve their dangerously eroded capital position during the first half of 1992.

With bad-debt losses the worst since the Great Depression, one out of ten U.S. banks was in serious trouble at the beginning of the recession in 1990. Even though the number of "problem" banks on the FDIC's list declined slightly that year, from 1,109 to 1,046, their average size increased dramatically. Assets of these troubled institutions totaled $408.8 billion at the end of 1990, or 12.1 percent of the industry aggregate, compared to $235.5 billion (7.1 percent) a year earlier. By the end of 1991 the list contained 1,069 banks with assets of $611.1 billion.

Throughout the 1980s the number of bank failures had risen steadily from an annual average of fewer than 10 in 1980–81 to more than 200 each year in 1988 and 1989 (see Table 10.4). These had gradually eaten up the FDIC's resources, especially the costly wave of bank failures that hit Texas after the oil-price collapse of 1986. And now, with recession spreading across the economy, the FDIC had to face the prospect of insolvencies whose potential costs could far exceed its dwindling resources. The possibility of yet another taxpayer bailout so soon after the thrift debacle began to raise questions about the viability of our deposit insurance system.

During 1990 the FDIC lost $4 billion in the course of its bailout operations, and that loss consumed all of the increase in deposit insurance premiums, from 12 cents per $100 of deposits to 19.5 cents imposed in August 1990. Anticipated losses of at least $5 billion in 1991 threatened to reduce its reserves to a mere $4 billion (compared to $18 billion in 1987). Only about two-thirds of that sum represented actual cash; the rest consisted of illiquid assets from failed institutions. At that point it was clear that the FDIC faced imminent insolvency. With Congress and the Bush administration still reeling from the thrift debacle, the politicians were intent on avoiding yet another expensive taxpayer bailout.

In February 1991 the U.S. Treasury proposed a comprehensive bank reform (see section 11.3 below), which would have limited insurance to $100,000 per institution rather than for each individual account, and would have eliminated coverage for pension fund deposits as well as brokered deposits. The administra-

Table 10.4

Bank Failures and Depletion of the Deposit Insurance Fund in the 1980s

Year	Number of problem banks	Number of failed banks	Total assets of failed banks (in billions of dollars)	Size of deposit insurance fund (in billions of dollars)	Ratio of deposit insurance fund to total deposits
1985	1,140	116	2.8	17.95	.91
1986	1,484	138	7.0	18.25	.84
1987	1,575	184	6.9	18.30	.83
1988	1,406	200	35.7	14.06	.60
1989	1,109	206	29.2	13.21	.54

Source: Federal Deposit Insurance Corporation, *Annual Report*, 1989, pp. 27, 113, 114.

tion also wanted to link deposit insurance premiums and expansion of banks' activities to capital rations. But the opportunity for a broader overhaul of deposit insurance died when Congress rejected the Treasury proposal.

Washington then focused its attention on a narrower law to replenish the FDIC's depleted Bank Insurance Fund.[30] In December 1991 President Bush signed a bill, the Federal Deposit Insurance Corporation Improvement Act (FDICIA), which allowed the bank insurance fund to borrow about $70 billion from the Treasury. The banks are supposed to pay back those loans with interest over a period of fifteen years. The FDIC was authorized to borrow an additional $45 billion for working-capital needs which would be repaid (with interest) from the proceeds of selling the assets of failed banks. This recapitalization implied further increases in deposit insurance premiums to assure repayment by the banks of any FDIC loans. In late 1990 Congress had authorized the FDIC to raise premiums beyond the statutory limit. Those were subsequently increased to 23 cents per $100 of domestic deposits, and in the wake of its new line of credit from the Treasury the FDIC announced a further increase to an average 28 cents, effective January 1993. Proposing a risk-based premium schedule for the first time, the insurer staggered the new rates from 25 cents for the strongest banks to 31 cents for the weakest ones. Each one-cent rise in those premiums cost the banking industry about $250 million a year. Such a steep rise in insurance premiums, which already absorb on average about 15 percent of their pretax earnings, could therefore have a significant impact on the profitability of banks and make it even harder to boost their capital base. A small number of very weak banks might even be pushed into bankruptcy by higher premiums, especially after implementation of the FDIC's new risk-based rate schedule. On the other hand, if banks are not able to pay back large FDIC loans, then the rescue operation would in effect become a taxpayer bailout.

The FDICIA of 1991 also phased in a series of procedural changes which toughened federal banking regulations to reduce the number of future bank failures. Most importantly, it introduced an early-intervention regime which would force banks to undertake "prompt corrective action," such as caps on growth, dividend reductions or suspensions, stock sales, and management changes, whenever capital declined below a specified threshold. Toward this objective regulators would set five capital levels for banks and thrifts (ranging from well capitalized to critically undercapitalized), introduce new noncapital measures of bank safety (e.g., underwriting standards, minimum earnings levels), and perform annual on-site bank examinations. They were also authorized to limit real estate lending by banks and to tighten auditing requirements.

Congress complemented the "stick" of tougher regulation with a few small "carrots" for well-run banks. Only the best-capitalized banks would be able to offer insured brokered deposits or receive deposit-insurance protection for accounts established under employee pension plans. Starting in 1993, conservatively run banks would be charged lower insurance premiums than those engaging in risky practices. But these rewards were minor compared to the expansion of banking-related activities under President Bush's original proposal, which Congress rejected (see chapter 11).

At the same time the legislators curbed the regulators' ability to prop up sick banks, in the hope of thereby lowering bailout costs. Regulators will no longer have to wait until a bank has actually failed before intervening. Under the new law they will be able to close a bank when its capital-asset ratio falls below 2 percent. The FDIC will have to abandon its "too-big-to-fail" doctrine after 1994. It has already relaxed this policy. In nearly half of the bank failures during the first quarter of 1992 uninsured depositors suffered a loss, averaging 20 cents on the dollar, when a bank closed. Finally, the Fed will have to limit its long-term lending to troubled banks. In the past such extended discount-window borrowing had often failed to avoid bank failure and only increased the eventual bailout costs for the FDIC.

Recently the FDIC has clearly slowed the pace of bank closings, for it spent only $4.3 billion during the first six months of fiscal year 1992 (October 1, 1991, to March 31, 1992), which was considerably less than half of the $14.5 billion estimate for the whole year. Some of that slowdown was certainly due to the improved capital position and earnings picture of banks following the Fed's dramatic easing. But political considerations might also have played a role here, especially during an election year. Early in the campaign the respective chairs of the House and Senate Banking Committees accused the Bush administration of leaning on regulators to overlook bank problems as a way to ease the credit crunch. Key congressional leaders favored a different strategy to contain the political fall-out from the banking crisis. They pushed the White House to discuss "open bank assistance" proposals for regulatory relief and government investments in weaker banks and thrifts to keep them open. However, these proposals did not go very far, since past experience with forbearance suggested strongly that efforts to nurse sick banks back to health often ended up boosting the cost of bank or thrift failures.

The FDIC recapitalization, even though tied to rolling back some of the costlier lender-of-last-resort extensions of the last decade, is at best a stopgap measure. It does not address the fundamental weaknesses of deposit insurance. As currently constituted, the bailout guarantee encourages banks to take excessive risks and leaves taxpayers with potentially huge liabilities. The entire system breaks down, if and when the benefits of protection for depositors are taxed away. If we combine the thrift bailout and the possibility of similarly large costs to deal with bank failures over the next decade, American taxpayers may well end up paying more to foot the bill than the average value of their insured funds in the depository institutions. The question of how to reform the system is therefore still with us. In recent years there have been three alternative reform proposals worth mentioning.

• Some economists (see Todd, 1991) have proposed abolishing deposit insurance altogether. They argue that default-free instruments, such as U.S. saving bonds or Treasury bills, could take the place of insured deposits. Bills could be paid with travelers' cheques, postal money orders, or credit cards. We could also revive the now-defunct U.S. Postal Savings System as a government-operated alternative to the banking system. These suggestions leave entirely open what future role, if any, the banks would play in our economy. Moreover, the proponents of insurance removal forget that "market discipline" in banking usually meant panics in the past.

• Robert Litan (1987) proposed investing insured deposits only in Treasury securities. It is not clear why such "narrow" banks need any insurance protection at all, if their assets are free of any default risk. We already have practically fail-safe mutual funds which channel investor money into government bonds. Moreover, Litan's proposal strips insured institutions of the primary function of banking, that of financial intermediation. In his plan this activity would be carried out by uninsured banks that make loans. But failures among those institutions could still set off serious financial panics.

• The most interesting reform suggestion has come from Jane D'Arista (1991). She wants to replace the present deposit insurance system with a financial guarantee program that would cover interest-free transactions accounts held in federally regulated depository institutions up to a certain limit. That change, she argues, would restore the system's original purpose of protecting individual savers against loss. In recent years deposit insurance has taken on a rather different objective, that of bailing out failing institutions. Such a shift in focus led directly to adoption of the FDIC's "too-big-to-fail" policy in 1984. The result has been increasingly costly government intervention which now has bankrupted the system. By shifting coverage from institutions to individual savers and cash balances of businesses, taxpayer liability could be contained more effectively. The banking system as a whole would be kept safe even though individual institutions might be allowed to go under. The regulators would simply withdraw permission to advertise insurance from any bank that failed to meet certain safety standards. Such an announcement would most likely cause depositors to move their funds to safer institutions and sink the suddenly uninsured bank. The prospect of near-certain failure should induce banks to be more careful than they tend to be under the current system of blanket protection. D'Arista would complement this disciplining force with stronger safety regulations and an automatic trigger mechanism for corrective action once an institution approached a certain threshold of weakness. Her proposal covers all transaction balances, even those deposited in nonbank institutions, such as pension plans.

No matter what kind of reform we ultimately adopt, some form of deposit insurance is of fundamental importance to the stability of our economy. After all, banks invest other people's money and therefore have a special fiduciary responsibility. In the past, making them subject to "market discipline" always meant exposing them to panics, which in turn could easily paralyze economic activity. At the same time, it is important to stress that the term deposit insurance, as currently constituted, is a misnomer. The size of the Bank Insurance Fund of the FDIC bears no relation to the risks it is supposed to cover. The premiums paid by the insured banks bear no relation to the risks these institutions impose on the fund. Nor do they affect behavior. They are in reality a tax on the banking industry in return for taxpayer backing of its liabilities. In addition, we must not forget that reforming the deposit insurance system is not the key issue. More important is to keep banks from failing in the first place. And this issue touches on the broader question of what banks should or should not do—in other words, on the need to define an appropriate structure for a safe and profitable banking industry.

11

Regulatory Overhaul and the Restructuring of U.S. Banks

The costly bank failures of the 1980s, which nearly bankrupted our deposit insurance fund, were neither a passing cyclical phenomenon nor simply isolated instances of bad management decisions. They reflected deeper structural problems which have evolved to the point of threatening the very existence of our banking system. Should this crisis remain unresolved, its consequences for the U.S. economy could be quite detrimental. We need healthy and stable banks to promote economic growth. Banks collect savings and channel them back into the circular spending flow, thereby funding growth-promoting activities. In the process they create new money in support of the circulation of goods and services. The strategic position of banks is analogous to that of a human heart which pumps blood through the body to keep it going. Just as humans do not function well with a sick heart, so does the economy suffer when banks are weak.

American banks have been hit over the last two decades by a variety of adverse developments. Their traditional functions, taking deposits and making loans, have been subjected to increasing competition from less-regulated institutions. In the face of such market erosion on both sides of their balance-sheet ledger, the banks have had to find new profit opportunities. Their search for market alternatives, itself responsible for an unprecedented wave of *financial innovation*, was fundamentally shaped by two sources of pressure.

- Funds became significantly more expensive for banks to attract once interest-rate ceilings on bank deposits were phased out in the early 1980s. Carrying costlier liabilities, the banks had to look for higher-yielding assets which could help them maintain a positive yield spread. But financial instruments are always subject to the risk-return logic of valuation; they carry higher returns because of greater riskiness. At that point, however, banks were no longer in a position to manage this trade-off between safety and profitability in a prudent manner. Ever since the rescue of Franklin National in 1974, when the Fed for the first time opened its discount window to long-term assistance to the tune of $1.7 billion, the U.S. government had in fact protected banks against the consequences of failure. The increase in deposit insurance from $40,000 to $100,000 under DIDMCA of 1980 and the FDIC's adoption of a "too-big-to-fail" policy after its takeover of Continental Illinois in 1984 only reinforced this protection. With the lender-of-last-resort mechanisms thus transformed into an automatic bailout guarantee, the normal market discipline against excessive risk-taking no longer applied to banks. This made the pursuit of high-yield, high-risk assets irresistible for them. Thrifts succumbed to the same moral hazard, with even more devastating results.

• As the banks faced intensifying competition from less-regulated financial institutions and attempted to branch out into new products, they found themselves severely constrained by existing structure regulations. A relic from the New Deal, these had separated traditional commercial banking activity from other financial institutions and functions. During the past decade the banks have tried, with varying degrees of success, to circumvent existing restrictions. Financial innovation, as Edward Kane (1981) argued convincingly, has always had the avoidance of regulations as one of its main objectives. These evasion efforts have left the current regulatory framework much weakened. But to the extent that they are still in force, these outmoded regulations have prevented full-scale reorganization of the banking sector. In the meantime banks atrophy, an untenable situation that needs to be corrected.

In 1991 the Bush administration tried to address that problem with a proposal for a wholesale overhaul of banking regulations, but it failed miserably in key congressional committees. All that the lawmakers passed was a much narrower piece of legislation, the FDICIA, which recapitalized the bank insurance fund and rolled back some of the recent lender-of-last-resort extensions (see section 10.4 for details). So the challenge of comprehensive bank reform is still with us. How that issue is eventually resolved will reshape the financial system well into the next century. Because the banking system plays a central role in determining the level and distribution of investments, its restructuring is bound to have a major impact on the long-term performance of our economy. The same argument can be made for the U.S. government's ability to stabilize economic fluctuations, because both fiscal and monetary policy tools rely heavily on banks.

The merits and drawbacks of various reform plans can be judged only if we have a clear idea of how financial institutions can best contribute to the expansion of our "real" economy. It may well be that banks, as currently constituted, are in the process of becoming obsolete. Increasingly their traditional functions can be carried out more effectively by other institutions (section 11.1). The two-pronged response of banks to this challenge has created its own problems. In many instances forays into new areas have proved to be risky and a source of losses. Efforts to evade existing legal restrictions have undermined the current regulatory framework (section 11.2). In the face of this precarious situation, the U.S. Treasury proposed a radical overhaul of increasingly outdated banking laws, but after an intense debate Congress rejected that plan (section 11.3). Since then we have seen a major consolidation in the banking sector, most notably several mergers among the United States' largest money-center banks. But these measures are defensive in nature and are no substitute for more basic reform based on a new legal framework of regulations that better fit current conditions in our financial system (section 11.4).

11.1. The Slow Death of Traditional Commercial Banking

In recent years U.S. banks have had to write off large chunks of nonperforming loans to developing countries, farmers, oil drillers, real estate developers, and takeover artists. As a result of these mounting bad-debt losses, more than 900 banks, with assets of $162 billion, failed between 1987 and 1991. The FDIC had to pay out $56 billion to close these insolvent institutions. Fortunately, initial agency estimates of $30 billion in additional losses for its Bank Insurance Fund during 1992 and 1993 proved to be too pessimistic. Starting in mid-1992, when the yield curve steepened considerably in response to sharply declining short-term rates, the profit margins of financial intermediation widened enough to keep many weaker banks afloat. The worst of the crisis seems to be behind us—for now. But the structure of the banking system remains quite fragile. If the trend of the past decade continues, a distinct possibility unless there is a strong and sustained rebound, future bailout expenses of the FDIC may eventually consume its entire $70 billion recapitalization loan from the Treasury. This worst-case scenario would leave the fund in need of additional capital infusions.

Apart from possibly having to foot the bill for yet another multibillion rescue operation, the public has already paid for this banking crisis in more indirect ways. In retrospect it is quite clear that the weakness of the banking sector played a crucial role in throwing the domestic economy into a long and difficult downturn. When commercial banks and thrifts had to liquidate assets and tighten lending terms in the face of growing bad-debt losses, they created a credit crunch that choked off growth (see sections 9.5 and 10.4). That squeeze has lasted longer than necessary, because banks have relaxed their credit conditions much less than warranted. They have maintained loan rates far above their borrowing costs, which have fallen to new lows since the Fed decided in late 1991 to push short-term interest rates dramatically lower. Nowadays bankers charge many borrowers very high rates, using the exceptionally large yield spread as a source of profit with which to counteract bad-debt losses. Finally, banks have aggressively pushed up their user charges and fees for all kinds of once-free services, not least to finance higher insurance premiums.

Underlying these developments has been a dramatic erosion of the position that commercial banks occupy in the credit system. Their once-secure dominance of financial capital is evaporating rapidly. Between 1974 and 1989 their share of assets held by all financial institutions declined from 37 percent to 27 percent, a stunning reduction. During the same period they suffered an even worse loss of market share in their core business, short-term corporate loans, from 79 percent to only 55 percent. Our commercial banks have also faced serious erosion vis-à-vis their foreign counterparts. In 1960, at the peak of American hegemony, we had six of the world's ten largest banks, and nineteen among the top fifty. Today no U.S. bank is among the top ten, and only two are left among the fifty largest. Foreign banks have also established a strong presence in the U.S. market, and nowadays they make a quarter of all our commercial and industrial loans. This relative decline has left our banking sector with massive overcapacity, the principal reason why more than 1,000 banks have failed during the last six years. The shake-out is likely to continue for quite some time, because this overcapacity has become systemic. Our commercial banks have lost market share to other financial institutions, because their once-special role in the economy is no longer unique.

Until not so long ago America's credit system was essentially built around three pillars. Commercial banks specialized in taking liquid deposits and in making short-term loans to businesses. Insurance companies, which enjoyed illiquid liabilities and actuarially predictable outflows, could afford to provide businesses with long-term loans. And investment banks organized financial markets as underwriters, brokers, and dealers of marketable securities. Other institutions filled market niches, such as thrifts funding mortgages or finance companies making personal loans, but industrial firms relied almost exclusively on commercial banks, insurance companies, or investment banks for capital. Each of these three had its own unique intermediation function, and regulatory walls between them secured a rather rational division of labor.

Within that post-Depression structure of our financial capital, commercial banks played a special, if not dominant, role. They possessed several characteristics which made them the financial intermediaries par excellence. On the liability side, they offered small household savers a safe repository for their savings and large business depositors access to the nation's payments system. On the asset side, bankers maintained close personal relations with their corporate clients and consequently knew the financial conditions of those firms very well. This gave them an information edge over direct lenders. Their knowledge advantage enabled bankers to value (loan) assets, which markets found inherently difficult to assess, more accurately than anyone else. Many creditors therefore entrusted their funds to banks instead of lending out their excess cash directly.

As intermediaries, commercial banks were able to bridge several decisive gaps between ultimate lenders and borrowers. Household savers would often deposit only small amounts, wanted liquidity, and were for the most part averse to risk. Corporate debtors typically had precisely opposite characteristics.

They typically borrowed large amounts all at once, wanted to keep those as long as possible, and represented more risk than the average saver was willing to bear directly. Banks traditionally resolved that conflict of interest by interjecting their own credit into the relationship, issuing their own claims to ultimate lenders and using those funds to buy yet another set of claims from ultimate borrowers. In that process they could pool many small deposits into one loan package and satisfy the need of corporate borrowers for large-denomination credit. Moreover, they offered depositors liquidity while they accommodated the demand for longer maturities among their debtors from industry. Of course, banks benefited in the process from positive yield spreads between their deposit rates and their loan rates. A large portion of their deposits consisted of zero-interest transaction accounts which they alone could offer as issuers of private bank money. These so-called demand deposits were a cheap source of funds which could be loaned out at a profit. Enjoying such a monopoly over money creation, commercial banks were subject to special regulations associated with the government's constitutional responsibility over the money supply, such as reserve require- ments. For the same reason they also had certain privileges, most notably access to the Fed's discount window, to the nation's payments system, and to deposit insurance.

This combination of regulatory restraint and privileged treatment worked well as long as banks were truly the only money-creating intermediaries taking depos- its and making commercial loans. During the past two decades, however, banks have faced challenges from several directions and have lost this monopoly posi- tion. Ever since the 1960s other financial institutions have come to the fore. These are not truly intermediaries but instead act on behalf of other money- holders. Pension funds, for example, represent workers as a collective of invest- ors subject to "forced savings" which are paid back in a prescribed manner upon retirement. Mutual funds are pools of funds which sell the public shares in their own portfolios. Unlike commercial banks, these two institutions do not create new assets. All they do is to choose among already existing assets created by others on behalf of the individual investors they represent. This activity earns them fee income. Hence their profits do not depend on a positive yield spread between their cost of funds and the returns earned from reinvesting those, as is the case with commercial banks and other intermediaries. Depending on fees rather than yield spreads shields their income from interest-rate fluctua- tions and the vicissitudes of financial markets. Moreover, these institutions provide their customers with very few services and are therefore significantly more cost efficient than are service-oriented banks. Their share has expanded dramatically over the last quarter of a century at the expense of banks and other intermediaries.

The emergence of no-frills investment pools, such as pension funds and mu- tual funds, has coincided with a dramatic shift away from loans to securities. The rapid growth of these so-called institutional investors has itself contributed to the trend, because they invest primarily in corporate securities and therefore have provided capital markets with a large source of funds. The technological revolution in communications and data processing has made it possible for nonbank institutions, including mutual funds and pension funds, to develop their own information-gathering capacities. This leaves them in a position to make their own valuation and creditworthiness assessments on behalf of clients cheaply. They can access computerized information networks to get the latest data about the economy and financial market conditions. And they can get ample information directly from corporations whose securities they may want to buy. Most corporations are quite willing to tell investors, market analysts, fund managers, and financial data services about themselves as a price they have to pay for issuing securities. Much of their data is packaged in easily comparable fashion under rules specified by the SEC and the Financial Accounting Standard Board (FASB).

Securities are issued as standardized bundles of claims which can be resold in the marketplace and are therefore more liquid than loans. They are subject to a constant market test, and a whole army of market analysts is busy valuing the different securities based on assessing risks and expected returns. Of course, their judgments are built on inherently speculative expectations and subject to exaggerated adjustments when investor sentiment shifts (see section 12.2). Bank lending tends to be more stable in that regard.1 But the relative instability of financial markets impairs the ability of firms to issue securities only at times of acute crisis (e.g., the temporary paralysis of the commercial-paper market in the wake of Penn Central's failure in 1970; junk-bond market jitters following the collapse of Drexel in 1990), because the price risk is normally borne by the investment banks or by investors. Corporate treasurers prefer securities over loans, not least because they would rather deal with underwriters who are competing for bids or with investors who are able to resell their investments than with loan officers of commercial banks. The latter relationship is intrusive and one of direct dependence. Securities are also more attractive from the point of view of costs and returns. Having eliminated the yield spread required by banks as the price of their intermediation, corporate issuers of securities can offer investors better yields than bank deposits while paying less than the rates on bank loans.

The first major movement away from lending and toward securities came during the 1960s when top-notch corporations discovered the usefulness of commercial paper as a cheaper alternative to short-term bank loans.[2] Today the volume of commercial paper outstanding in the United States almost equals the commercial and industrial loan assets of banks. Corporate bonds grew rapidly in the 1970s, with issues outstanding rising from $202 billion in 1970 to $504 billion in 1980. During the next decade high-yield, high-risk bonds became popular. They carried low ratings and could therefore be issued by a potentially much larger number of firms. These so-called junk bonds were frequently used to finance hostile takeover bids of corporate raiders, a practice that fueled an unprecedented merger boom.

As corporations switched from loans to securities for funding, commercial banks faced an erosion of their core business. They had to respond, and their diverse reactions have had a huge impact on the way the financial system has interacted with the real economy.

• In the early 1960s, when commercial paper first took off, banks began to search for new funding sources. The immediate impetus for this desire to diversify was a gradually accelerating erosion of their corporate deposit base. Many of these deposits were held to cover corporate loans and disappeared when the underlying credit relation between bank and corporate client stopped. In 1961 Citibank found an answer when it introduced negotiable certificates of deposit in large denominations which could be sold before maturity in a secondary market. These CDs proved to be especially popular among nonfinancial businesses, giving banks a useful tool to keep some of their corporate customers from leaving them altogether.

• Negotiable CDs had the additional advantage of allowing banks access to large sums of borrowed money on short notice. Throughout the 1960s they developed additional channels for short-term funds. Banks found that they could pursue all these so-called borrowed liabilities (e.g., bankers' acceptances, repurchase agreements, Federal funds) aggressively whenever needed and no longer had to wait passively for depositors to carry their money to the local branch. This easy access to funds prompted banks to switch their portfolio management strategy. Until then they had restricted their loan assets to the size and composition of their deposit liabilities ("asset management"), keeping large amounts of cash reserves and liquid securities to meet sudden surges of deposit withdrawals. However, once the banks were able to issue their own money-market instruments, they could target faster growth of loan assets and finance any funding shortfall ("liability management"). Reliance on these borrowed liabilities helped banks to expand their loan assets more rapidly, but it also added to their volatility. These instruments typically carried shorter maturities than did the loans they helped to finance, so the interest banks had to pay could change more rapidly than the interest they received on the loans. Especially during the 1970s, when the term structure of interest inverted repeatedly (negative yield curves), such maturity mismatches between borrowed liabilities and loan assets often squeezed bank income.

• Starting in the mid-1960s, when international dollars began to accumulate rapidly in surplus countries, American banks expanded their overseas operations by doing business abroad in dollars. Such global extension of dollar deposits and loans, the so-called Eurodollar market, enabled them to follow their largest corporate customers overseas. At that point these multinational corporations could only issue securities in national financial markets and hence appreciated a transnational banking network which was ready to do business with them on a global scale. Our banks liked the Euromarket for its absence of regulatory restrictions, which saved costs and allowed them to do things they could not do at home. For instance, they could expand into investment banking, so they soon launched a market for Eurobonds, a major first step toward globally integrated financial markets. Eurodollar deposits from their foreign subsidiaries also became a key borrowed liability for our money-center banks.

• Despite these responses, the banks could not stem the continuous erosion of their core business, commercial, and industrial loans. They had gained much greater access to funds, yet they could no longer lend out these added funds quite as easily to their preferred customers. At the same time the cost of their funds had gradually begun to rise, as they came to rely more heavily on borrowed liabilities and less on noninterest demand deposits. For both reasons American banks began to search for new lending opportunities which promised higher returns to maintain a positive yield spread. They expanded their lending operations to smaller firms, consumers, and homebuyers. In the early 1970s they poured money into real estate investment trusts. And money-center banks, organizing the recycling of petrodollars after OPEC's price hike in 1973, flooded developing countries with Eurodollar loans.

• Starting in 1978 money-market mutual funds, which offered investors higher yields and limited rights to write checks against their shares, suddenly emerged as a major threat to commercial banks. Providing very few services, using telephone and computer networks instead of branch offices, and running their highly automated operations at large volume, the funds could keep their customer charges to a minimum. Banks could not compete with the funds and faced massive disintermediation whenever unregulated market rates surged in response to accelerating inflation. In the early 1980s (DIDMCA 1980; DIA 1982) Congress helped the banks to compete on a level playing field with money-market funds when it phased out interest-rate ceilings (see section 9.1). This deregulation undermined the health of depository institutions in the long run. Banks and thrifts, now in a position to bid aggressively for funds, ended up paying returns that were much higher than warranted by the insignificant riskiness of insured deposits. Under pressure to reinvest these costly funds profitably in higher-yielding assets, they extended credit on terms that ultimately proved much too generous relative to default and price risks. If those high-risk loans worked out, the banks and thrifts would pocket the gains. If they failed, the insurers (and ultimately the taxpayers) would pick up the tab.

To the extent that the combination of deregulated deposit rates and extended deposit insurance created an environment for overgenerous bank credit, it helped to feed speculation throughout much of the 1980s. Deregulated thrifts, many of them growing 1,000 percent or more per year by attracting brokered deposits at very high yields, rushed into high-risk real estate development deals. Banks tried to compensate for declining commercial loan demand and higher deposit rates by pursuing new lending opportunities that looked promising at the time. They lent heavily to developing countries, farmers, domestic energy producers, real estate developers, and leveraged buyouts. In each case the banks ended up overextending credit and facing huge losses when those speculative bubbles burst one after another (see chapter 10).

Even though most commercial banks have managed to survive the surge in bad-debt losses during the latest downturn, they still face major competitive threats from less-regulated institutions. It is doubtful whether they can stop the market inroads made by pension funds, mutual funds, investment banks, and other institutions that benefit from the "marketization" of our financial system. Commercial bankers have simply lost their traditional information advantage, which previously had convinced so many households, industrial firms, and non-bank institutions to leave their excess cash with them for investment. The revolution in computer and communications technologies has enabled others to access and process data at low cost. Neither lenders nor borrowers need banks anymore. Both sides may find it increasingly more appealing to deal directly with each other.[3]

11.2. Financial Innovation and Regulatory Evasion

As commercial banks faced an erosion of their traditional intermediation role and growing bad-debt losses, they understood that attracting costlier funds and lending those out to riskier borrowers was not sufficient. They had to find other ways to survive in a new environment. Encouraged by an administration sympathetic to a relaxation of regulation, bankers began to pursue a two-pronged strategy in the early 1980s. One was to accelerate the development of new financial instruments and services with which to generate profits. The other was to attack existing regulatory restrictions, with the expressed objective of weakening them or escaping their reach. Both activities have made the banking crisis as well as its eventual resolution more complicated. Forays into new areas are not without risk. Some have already caused significant losses and have prompted regulators to respond. And the ability of banks to bypass existing restrictions has weakened the entire regulatory framework. The end result has been to make comprehensive bank reform both more urgent and, at the same time, more difficult (see section 11.3).

Let us first discuss some of the more important innovations that emanated from the banking sector during the last decade, as well as their repercussions.

1) Deposit Brokerage. Interest deregulation in the early 1980s prompted securities firms (e.g., Merrill Lynch, Dean Witter, Shearson) and small specialists to broker to the highest bidders large deposits held by either institutional investors or rich individuals. This turned out to be a very lucrative business, with brokers charging up to 1 percent in commissions. Banks and thrifts were willing to pay, because that service allowed them to attract funds from across the country and to save themselves the costs of servicing small local deposits. Institutional depositors, in turn, received the highest possible rates without any search costs.

These advantages notwithstanding, deposit brokerage caused significant problems for the banking system as a whole. The practice enabled bank and thrift managers to lay their hands on huge amounts of deposits simply by offering to pay above-market rates. Troubled institutions could thereby cover financing problems while expanding their questionable lending practices. With brokers dividing large sums into smaller parcels to assure full deposit-insurance coverage, depositors did not have to worry about whether their funds went to well-managed and responsible institutions. Many brokers only looked for the highest rates, regardless of an institution's reliability or financial strength. As a result deposit brokerage greatly intensified the moral-hazard problem of deposit insurance (see section 10.4). With many banks and thrifts using brokered deposits in a last-ditch effort to stay afloat, their subsequent failures ended up costing the FDIC and the FSLIC much more than would otherwise have been the case.[4] In addition, by bidding up deposit rates the troubled institutions forced up the cost of funds for others.

In March 1984 regulators decided that the increase in the cost of bank failures from excessive use of deposit brokerage required action. The FDIC and the FHLBB tried to limit deposit insurance to the first $100,000 any broker brought to a depository institution. After that insurance cap was thrown out in court, in July 1984 the FDIC required banks to report the total amounts of brokered deposits and deposits placed by other financial institutions on a monthly basis whenever those exceeded either a bank's capital or 5 percent of its deposits. In October 1984 the FHLBB limited brokered deposits to 5 percent of total deposits for any thrift whose capital had fallen below 3 percent of deposits. A month later both agencies urged criminal investigations of tie-in arrangements at failed institutions which had received brokered deposits in exchange for making loans to certain high-risk borrowers. In December 1984 the FDIC required banks to report all of their brokered deposits. In July 1985 both the FDIC and the FHLBB required brokers to disclose the holders of any deposit they placed. The 1991 law recapitalizing the FDIC also limited the use of brokered deposits to well-capitalized depository institutions (see section 10.4).

2) Repurchasing Agreements. Soon the exploding federal budget deficits of the early 1980s could no longer be handled by the thirty-six primary government securities dealers which at the time had authorization to trade directly with the Federal Reserve. Even though their own daily trading volume rose from $13 billion in 1979 to $42.5 billion in 1983, the post-1979 environment of high interest rates forced those dealers to reduce the amount of government securities held in inventory. Demand from their traditional customers, mostly financial institutions and corporations with excess cash to park, did not increase enough to accommodate that need for increased turnover. This void soon led hundreds of smaller dealers to enter the Treasuries market, the world's largest securities market.[5] Unlike stock-market dealers, Treasury bond dealers did not have to meet minimum-capital rules or impose margin requirements on customers who wanted to trade on borrowed funds. Hence these "secondary" dealers entering the market were usually thinly capitalized and engaged in highly leveraged transactions.

At the same time the government securities market came to depend heavily on a complex financing technique called a "repurchase agreement" (repo, or RP). In such a transaction one party (often a bank or a thrift) sold securities to another party (the dealer) and agreed to repurchase them at a higher price, usually a few days later. Repos, whose daily volume reached $150 billion in 1984, were in essence short-term collateralized loans in which the price difference represented the lender's return on the deal. Both sides benefited from these transactions. The depository institutions could turn their considerable holdings of Treasury securities into credit to earn additional income, and dealers obtained cash in the deal which they then used to buy additional securities and to repeat the process.

The dealer made his profit when the value of the securities in his portfolio rose or when the securities paid a yield that was greater than the cost of the repo. By pyramiding security purchases through repos into a complex web of speculative positions, dealers could control a large amount of securities with a much smaller cash investment of their own. It was quite typical that dealer capital was only 1 to 2 percent of total security holdings. That kind of leveraging allowed potentially high returns, but it carried also great risks of loss, especially considering that interest rates (and bond prices) had become a great deal more unstable since 1979.

The combination of price volatility and extreme leveraging caused several spectacular failures of secondary dealers. In May 1982 Drysdale collapsed after having used a complex credit-pyramiding technique based on reverse repos to build a huge $2 billion portfolio with only $20 million of its own capital. Its failure led Chase Manhattan to lose $160 million and required a $1.4 billion injection by the Fed to calm a jittery market. The failure of Lombard-Wall in August 1982 caused $107.8 million in losses. In April 1984 Marsh & McLennan, the nation's largest insurance broker, took a $165 million hit on "unauthorized" government-securities trades. During the following month two small dealers, Lion Capital and RTD Securities Inc., failed due to trading losses which stemmed from rising interest rates and from demands for collateral by nervous customers. The most damaging failure was that of E.S.M. Government Securities Inc. in March 1985, which caused its clients to lose an estimated $315 million. Nearly half of that loss occurred in reverse repo transactions with Home State, a thrift controlled by the largest shareholder of E.S.M. Its insolvency, in turn, triggered a panic run on seventy other privately insured Ohio thrifts, half of which were eventually reopened after qualifying for federal insurance. Finally, the $240 million loss from the failure of Bevill, Bressler & Schulman (BBS) in April 1985 wiped out a dozen thrifts.

Many of these costly failures involved abusive or fraudulent practices which worsened losses. Drysdale, for example, had routinely used an arbitrage strategy called "match book." This enabled it to exploit an industry practice of not including accrued interest paid by the government in repos but of counting that interest when those same securities were sold outright.[6] Drysdale simply pocketed that difference as working capital while it bought bonds on which semiannual interest had just been paid and whose purchase price would therefore have included a relatively small amount of accrued interest. E.S.M. colluded with several hidden shareholders to obtain an excessive amount of securities in reverse repos. Many of the failed dealers used the same securities for several repo transactions or traded securities which had yet to be issued. Regulatory oversight was lax, to say the least, as proved by the ability of E.S.M. or BBS to continue their fraudulent practices despite repeated investigations by the SEC and the Justice Department.

Drysdale's collapse in 1982 led to only minor regulatory adjustments, such as expanded Fed surveillance of government securities dealers and an end to match-book arbitrage. Only after the failures of E.S.M. and BBS in the spring of 1985 did government officials become convinced that self-regulation of the market was not enough. Something had to be done to restore investor confidence. Within six months all federal bank and thrift regulators had endorsed a set of guidelines for institutions under their supervision which included credit checks on unregulated securities dealers, methods of securing legal control of collateral, and limits on the size of repo transactions. In January 1986 the Federal Reserve introduced book-entry accounts for repo transactions that involved states and municipalities. In early 1986 the SEC also required financial institutions and other publicly held concerns to disclose their liabilities from repos if those amounted to more than 10 percent of their total assets or loss risk from those transactions that exceeded 10 percent of capital. Similar disclosure rules were adopted by the Government Accounting Standards Board for state and local governments. In October 1986 Congress passed a law to tighten federal oversight of dealers, including the more than one hundred previously unsupervised secondary dealers. The lawmakers authorized the Treasury to issue net capital, bookkeeping, and financial reporting rules and to regulate the transfer and control of securities used in repos. These rules would then be enforced by the SEC and relevant banking regulators. Since that law was passed no dealer has collapsed. The Salomon scandal of 1991, in which the primary dealer was caught violating existing regulations in an attempt to manipulate auctions to its own advantage, may well trigger a broader overhaul of the market for Treasuries.

3) Mortgage-Backed Securities. The U.S. government, as part of its postwar policy to encourage homeownership, sponsored several institutions which insured, guaranteed, and organized a secondary market for mortgages. In the 1970s the Federal National Mortgage Association (Fannie Mae), the Government National Mortgage Association (Ginnie Mae), and the Federal Home Loan Mortgage Corporation (Freddie Mac) began to buy pools of mortgages from thrifts or banks and to repackage them into securities. Investors, mostly insurance companies and pension funds, found mortgage-backed securities very attractive because of their high yields and collateral levels. By 1979 they financed 15.6 percent of all new one-family mortgages.

Having secured a critical mass, this instrument took off in the early 1980s. At that point banks and thrifts realized that those securities enabled them to borrow against the value of mortgages already in their portfolio. Rather than having to sell off old low-yield mortgages during a credit crunch, these institutions could now obtain relatively low-cost funds whenever their own savings inflows proved inadequate. The traditional (fixed-rate, thirty-year) mortgage is essentially a steady stream of monthly payments. Mortgage-backed securities are created by pooling a group of similar mortgages and then selling a slice of that stable cash flow to investors. By late 1986 two-thirds of all new mortgages and nearly 31 percent of the $1.7 trillion in total home loans outstanding were securitized. During 1986 alone issues of new mortgage-backed securities grew from $110 billion to $300 billion, and trading volume in that market reached $2.5 trillion. This was more than all of the trades on the world's stock exchanges and five times the level of 1981.[7]

Yet mortgage-backed securities carry unique risks. One such risk is prepayment. Because mortgages can be prepaid at any time, these securities in effect have a call option. When interest rates fall sufficiently, homeowners rush to prepay their high-interest mortgages. Such refinancing simply evaporates high-yielding mortgage pools and the securities they back. This in turn limits what investors would pay for mortgage-backed securities. Falling interest rates, good news for other securities markets, thus may bring heavy losses to the market for mortgage-backed securities, as happened in the latter half of 1986.[8] Then there is extension risk. Rising interest rates slow the number of prepayments, and bondholders will have to wait longer for their money. This makes their bonds less valuable. The value of mortgage-backed securities depends heavily on guessing how quickly borrowers will prepay their loans, so the price behavior of these bonds is inherently very volatile. Moreover, the overall volume of new security issues fluctuates a great deal. In 1987, for example, only about 30 percent of new residential mortgages were securitized, as opposed to nearly 70 percent in 1986. During 1987 most new loans and refinancings were adjustable-rate mortgages, which lenders prefer to hold on to because of the protection they provide against fluctuations in interest rates. Finally, loan securitization has made mortgage rates more volatile, since lenders now peg them directly to the prevailing market rates on mortgage-backed securities.

The complexity and price volatility of mortgage-backed securities caused several market players to suffer heavy losses.

• In February 1985 Bank of America took a $95 million loss when twenty-two thrifts forced the bank to repurchase mortgage-backed securities which were based on fraudulently inflated values. In response, Fannie Mae and Freddie Mac acted to tighten appraisals of home mortgages.

• In August 1985 Equity Programs Investment Corporation (EPIC), a real estate syndication subsidiary of Community Savings & Loan Association based in Bethesda, Maryland, could not make payments due on mortgages and mortgage-backed securities valued at $1.4 billion. EPIC bought homes, turned those into highly leveraged partnerships sold as tax shelters, and packaged the mortgages of these partnerships into securities.[9] That Ponzi scheme fell apart when rental income from its homes fell below mortgage payments. Investors ultimately bailed out EPIC rather than suffer potentially huge losses. Community S&L, which had been heavily involved in the operations of its subsidiary, was taken over by the Maryland Deposit Insurance Fund. Its insolvency triggered a run on other state-insured thrifts in Maryland, much like the one in Ohio that had been triggered by the failure of E.S.M. six months earlier. TMIC, the private insurer with the largest liability from having backed EPIC paper, had to be liquidated.

• During 1986 First Boston Inc., a leading underwriter of mortgage-backed securities, lost $100 million before taxes from trading risky new mortgage products, so-called interest-only (IO) and principal-only (PO) securities stripped from underlying mortgage-backed securities. And in February 1988 First Boston announced that it had lost another $50 million from mismarking certain mortgage-backed securities.

• In April 1987 Merrill Lynch's traders mispriced a large issue of IO/PO securities. Investors snapped up the underpriced IOs, leaving Merrill with a huge $900 million inventory in POs. Such an unhedged position can be disastrous due to the extreme price volatility of POs, and Merrill suffered a $377 million loss when rising interest rates sharply devalued its POs.

• The interest hike during that month also hit large bondholders with significant capital losses of between 6 percent and 9 percent. One victim was Financial Corporation of America (FCA), the nation's largest thrift. FCA had pledged about $12 billion of its mortgage-backed securities as collateral for reverse repos with government-securities dealers. When the value of these securities fell, it had to put up nearly $900 million in additional collateral.

4) Off-Balance-Sheet Commitments. Facing a steady erosion of their traditional lending business, commercial banks began to look for other ways to make money during the 1980s. This search spawned a myriad of new financial transactions and instruments which generate fee income. Nowadays money-center banks often earn between 30 percent and 50 percent of their income from fees rather than from interest. Moreover, many of these innovations are kept off their balance sheets. In this way the banks do not have to set aside capital to cover the risk. Thus they can conduct a large volume of fee-earning business without having to tie up capital.

Let us briefly analyze the most important off-balance-sheet transactions and instruments developed by banks in the 1980s.[10]

• Repurchase agreements, discussed earlier in connection with government-securities dealers, are one such item kept off the balance sheets. Regulators have not yet decided whether such repos should be classified as loans or as sales. How this issue is resolved is important not only for accounting purposes but also with regard to the availability of securities as collateral in case of defaults.

• Some derivatives of mortgage-backed securities (e.g., Collateralized Mortgage Obligations, Real Estate Mortgage Investment Conduits) are currently exempt from disclosure.

• All standardized loan contracts with a predictable cash flow can be repackaged into securities and sold to investors. Starting in 1986, securities backed by credit-card receivables, auto loans, and computer leases took off. Their market now exceeds $100 billion. Unlike mortgage-backed securities, those asset-backed securities do not have a prepayment risk. Such securitizing of loans not only liquefies an otherwise illiquid asset but also transfers credit and interest-rate risks from banks to investors. Even though those loan securitizations usually have a reserve fund and a supporting letter of credit to protect bondholders from default losses, they do raise serious questions. One worry is that banks may become weaker by selling off their best, most marketable loans. Moreover, bankers may not be as careful in evaluating the credit risk of their borrowers if they know they will sell off these loans quickly. And in this informal market most investors lack information to monitor credit risk.

• In the early 1980s banks began selling loans to pension funds, corporations, insurance companies, and thrifts on a massive scale. Such loan sales spread risk and free up capital for new business while still allowing banks to collect fee income for originating and servicing the loans. Banks have also sold off nonperforming loans at a discount to reduce their loan-loss reserves and make at least some money on those, as in the case of LDC debt or when failing institutions restructure.[11] Of course, the practice of loan-selling is not without problems. As the Penn Square failure clearly showed (see section 10.2), the ability to transfer risk to others through loan sales could make banks more careless in their lending decisions. Loan buyers in turn might end up taking risks they do not understand and cannot afford to carry. Finally, regulators are more likely to lose track of who owes what to whom. This makes their task of supervision and examination more difficult.

• Banks have also developed a host of off-balance-sheet (OBS) liabilities that generate fee income in the form of guarantees. In the case of standby letters of credit, for example, they guarantee payments by a purchaser of goods. In the early 1980s banks and insurance companies did a booming business selling private guarantees to back mortgages, municipal bonds, and a host of new instruments. In this way borrowers could essentially rent someone else's credit rating for a fee to reduce their financing costs. Such private guarantees rose from $162 billion in 1980 to $437 billion at the end of 1984 (see *Business Week,* 1985b, p. 86) but slowed after the defaults of the Washington Public Power Supply System and EPIC. In so-called note issuance facilities (NIFs), which soared to $50 billion within a year or two of their inception in 1983, banks promise to buy commercial paper that a borrower cannot sell in the Euromarkets at an agreed price. Volatile interest rates and the proliferation of floating-rate debt in the early 1980s led borrowers to protect themselves against interest-rate risk by taking on debt whose rates are guaranteed not to go beyond a set limit. Banks charge fees for these rate caps and hedge their own risks through a variety of techniques that include futures, swaps, and options. Borrowers can in turn sell their caps to others. Prime customers for someone else's rate caps are thrifts, which want to match their liabilities more closely to capped floating-rate mortgage assets, or lower-rated companies that are unable to sell their own capped debt.

• Finally, banks help to bring together borrowers who want to swap financial instruments. Such swaps, which originated in 1982, have become one of the most popular forms of international financing. They protect corporations and financial institutions against increasingly volatile exchange and interest rates. Besides hedging risks, swaps are also used to reduce borrowing costs. In currency swaps two parties might trade one currency for another, pay each other interest on the borrowed funds, and then exchange the principal amounts at maturity. Interest-rate swaps, in which borrowers trade floating-rate debt for fixed-rate debt, take advantage or rate differences among markets and among borrowers. Depending on interest-rate expectations, firms use these swaps to switch between different types of debt.[12] Investment and commercial banks arrange these swaps for hefty fees. Acting as middlemen, they receive and disperse the interest payments on a pass-through basis. In mid-1987 the debts underlying currency and interest-rate swaps amounted to an estimated $600 billion.

The exact size of these various off-balance-sheet items is difficult to measure, for they do not appear in financial statements. Various studies, such as those by the FDIC in 1985 and by the BIS in 1986, estimated that at that point the off-balance-sheet liabilities of large money-center banks already exceeded their balance-sheet or "book" liabilities including deposits. A more recent study by the General Accounting Office shows off-balance-sheet activities exceeding total bank assets by 1987 (see Table 11.1). The explosive growth of repos, loan securitizations, loan sales, financial guarantees, and swaps soon caught the attention of regulators. They worried that the risks associated with the various off-balance-sheet commitments were neither laid out in a bank's basic financial statement nor covered by its capital. Each of these inventions carries specific credit, interest-rate, or market risks. In guarantees and swaps, for example, banks agree to step in and complete a deal between two parties should one default. In this case they are liable for lost interest, whereas in loan securitizations and loan

Table 11.1

The Growth of Off-Balance-Sheet (OBS) Activities by U.S. Banks

Reported activities (in billions of dollars)	1984	1985	1986	1987
Loan commitments	494	531	572	586
Commitments to buy futures/forward contracts	40	57	99	129
Commitments to sell futures/forward contracts	28	40	80	124
Commitments to buy when-issued securities	4	4	10	10
Obligations to buy under-option contracts	3	11	28	35
Obligations to sell under-option contracts	2	5	12	18
Foreign-exchange commitments	584	735	893	1,419
Standby letters of credit	146	175	170	167
Commercial letters of credit	30	28	28	33
Participations in acceptances bought	2	1	1	1
Securities borrowed	3	4	5	7
Other significant commitments	25	59	71	81
Annual totals	1,364	1,840	2,342	3,140
OBS activities as a percentage of total assets, 1985–1987 (all banks)	—	67.4	79.6	107.8

Source: U.S. General Accounting Office, *Banking: Off-Balance-Sheet Activities*, March 1988, Washington, DC, Tables I.1 and I.3.

Note: Annual figures are for end of year.

sales they may also have to pay off principal to investors. Transfer of risks to investors tends to make banks less careful. Moreover, the extremely rapid growth of off-balance-sheet items has not given banks enough time to adopt standard operating procedures on a systemwide basis.[13]

In 1985, following several meetings to discuss financial innovation and bank risk, the regulatory agencies decided on a multistep strategy. The FASB began a study to determine the accounting treatment of different off-balance-sheet commitments, should their disclosure eventually become mandatory. At the same time the SEC embarked on a major rule-making effort to cover those new financial transactions, with particular emphasis on repos, loan securitizations, and swaps. The second step was to encourage standardization of these transactions. During 1986 Fannie Mae and Freddie Mac began work on creating a national market exchange for mortgage-backed securities. And in March 1987 the International Swap Dealers Association designed a standard contract for interest-rate and currency swaps. Finally, regulators undertook several measures to cope with the risks involved in off-balance-sheet transactions. In 1986 the Federal Financial Institutions Examination Council, comprising the Fed, the FDIC, and the

Comptroller of Currency, proposed that loan securitizations and sales be backed by reserve funds. In November 1988 the council also required banks to count the income from interest-rate swaps over the life of a contract rather than immediately. In December 1987 the FASB proposed that companies disclose credit risk of off-balance-sheet instruments they use in the footnotes of their financial statements. The Basel Agreement in 1988 included off-balance-sheet commitments in its new risk-based system of capital-adequacy rules. Toward this end the FASB and the SEC are expected soon to announce final accounting and disclosure rules for these items, so that the Fed can make sure that they are adequately backed by bank capital.

New financial products, such as the ones discussed in this section, have made a significant difference to the bottom line of individual banks. But considering the banking system as a whole, these innovations have had at best a marginal impact. They are no substitutes to its core activities of taking deposits and making loans. At best they complement that traditional intermediation function. Banks have therefore relied on a second, more basic response to the invasion of their market by less-regulated competitors. They have challenged existing regulatory restrictions which have confined their activities. The banking acts of 1980 (DIDMCA) and 1982 (DIA) provided for only partial deregulation of banking. Left intact were two key regulations that affect the structure of our financial-services industry, the ban on nationwide banking and the separation of commercial and investment banking. Larger banks argue that these restrictions have kept them locked out of lucrative markets and have put them at a competitive disadvantage against more integrated European and Japanese banks. We shall now look at how banks have tried to circumvent these regulations in recent years.

The McFadden Act of 1927 prohibited interstate banking and left it up to the states to regulate bank branching within their own borders. These geographic branching restrictions have allowed a very large number of small community banks to operate as local monopolies, shielded from direct competition with larger regional banks or money-center banks. This resulted in a highly decentralized U.S. banking system. So far Congress has refused to repeal the McFadden Act and to permit interstate banking. Its resistance reflects a long populist tradition against excessive concentration of economic power in the hands of banks (see section 4.2). The small banks, relying on strong local support, have argued that allowing large out-of-town banks into their hitherto protected markets would hurt not only them but also their communities. The newcomers would divert deposit funds to metropolitan areas while starving local producers and home-owners of much-needed loans. The considerable lobbying power of small banks has blocked bills in Congress and has forced large banks to emphasize other deregulation issues.[14]

Yet despite inaction by Congress, the movement toward interstate and ultimately nationwide banking has accelerated greatly over the past decade. Even though restrictions against interstate branching remain in force, banks have found several ways to offer services outside their own home state.

• Congress amended the BHC Act of 1956 in 1970 so that one-bank holding companies could conduct such banking-related activities as consumer finance, leasing, commercial finance, and mortgage banking outside the state in which they were based. By early 1982 more than 5,500 such offices were in operation. In addition, at that time BHCs had 202 "loan-production offices" for commercial business and 143 Edge Act banks offering international-transaction services outside their home state.[15]

• The BHC Act of 1956 defined a bank as an institution which takes in demand deposits and makes commercial loans at the same time. As long as an institution refrained from offering either transaction deposits or loans to businesses, it did not qualify as a bank and was therefore exempted from geographic branching restrictions. In February 1981 Delaware used this loophole to allow so-called limited-service banks (LSBs). Other states soon followed suit. Many banks then bought small community banks and turned them into LSBs by selling off their business loan portfolios. LSBs typically offered a wide range of consumer banking services, including federally insured deposits, various types of loans, and credit cards. Besides providing a vehicle for interstate banking, LSBs also proved attractive to nonbank institutions (e.g., investment banks, mutual funds, insurance companies) and even industrial corporations (e.g., Sears, Gulf & Western) as a means to enter the commercial banking business. By July 1987, when Congress imposed a moratorium on new LSBs and restricted the asset growth of already existing ones to 7 percent per year in the CEBA, there were 166 LSBs in operation and 300 applications to form such institutions pending with regulators.

• In 1980 the Comptroller of Currency determined that agreements among banks of different states to allow their customers to use each other's ATMs did not violate the McFadden Act. Most of the first ATM networks set up in the aftermath of this decision were in large metropolitan areas, many of which stretched across state lines (e.g., New York, Philadelphia, Washington, Boston, Chicago). In late 1981 banks went a step further and set up multistate ATM networks to compete directly with new cash-dispensing networks operated by MasterCard and Visa across the nation. By late 1983 there were more than 175 regional ATM networks and 6 competing national networks, together covering more than 3,000 banks and approximately 16,000 ATMs.

• The so-called Douglas Amendment to the BHC Act of 1956 allowed states to authorize acquisitions of banks in their jurisdiction by out-of-state banks.[16] In 1975 this led Maine to allow its banks to be acquired by out-of-state institutions, provided the acquirer's home state allowed Maine banks to do the same thing there. In 1982 Massachusetts allowed bank tie-ins with institutions from neighboring states, provided those responded in kind. In 1983 Connecticut and Rhode

Island followed suit, and the first regional compact was born. New York banks, explicitly shut out of New England, challenged this arrangement. But in June 1985 the Supreme Court upheld the regional compact, paving the way for other multistate agreements during 1985–86 in the Southeast, the West, the Midwest, and the densely populated Mid-Atlantic region. Each of these interstate zones excluded the banking giants of California and New York. In this way regional banks could consolidate and obtain the size needed to eventually compete with the large money-center banks.

• Two laws, DIA of 1982 and FIRREA of 1989, allowed failing thrifts to be acquired by out-of-state banks, provided they were run as a strictly separate entity. Thrifts became attractive takeover targets when deregulation in 1980 and 1982 made them much more similar to commercial banks, and several New York banks used this route to establish a foothold in key markets (e.g., Florida, Ohio, Maryland).[17] The 1982 law also permitted a commercial bank in one state to acquire a failed bank with assets of more than $500 million in another state. This provision allowed BankAmerica in April 1983 to buy Seafirst Corp., enabled New York's money-center banks to enter the lucrative Sun Belt region, and was used by the FDIC to cope with several bank failures in Texas following the collapse of oil prices in 1985–86. CEBA of 1987 further relaxed the conditions for out-of-state takeovers (see section 10.2).

This piecemeal evolution of interstate banking has shaped a merger-driven process of restructuring in the domestic banking sector. A crucial engine in the ongoing consolidation has been a new tier of large banks with assets that range from $20 billion to $50 billion, the so-called superregionals. These emerged during the mid-1980s as the most aggressive and profitable segment of the industry by exploiting certain strategic advantages: domination of the respective multistate markets by regulatory design, location in booming regional economies, significant economies of scale from postmerger centralization, emphasis on efficient retail banking operations with a large deposit base, and close relations with small- and medium-sized firms.[18] Many superregionals earned consistently higher returns on assets and equity than did the larger money-center banks. This in turn made them very popular on Wall Street, especially during the boom years of 1985–87. Their comparatively high market value allowed them to raise money more cheaply in the capital markets, made it easier to acquire other banks by swapping stocks, and protected them from takeovers by bigger banks. In recent years some superregionals have experienced setbacks, especially New England banks that were hurt by a regional recession and the real-estate slump.

Money-center banks, on the other hand, faced hard times throughout the 1980s. The long-term erosion of their traditional core business, commercial lending to large corporations, accelerated. Foreign banks managed to establish a large presence in the American market, while our largest banks cut back many of their operations abroad. Because French, German, and Japanese banks have closer ties to their governments, they are not required to set aside as much capital as their U.S. counterparts.[19] Higher regulatory costs (e.g., deposit insurance premiums, reserve requirements, capital requirements) have also hurt the money center banks in their increasingly fierce head-on competition with investment banks.[20] Those institutions offer a cost-efficient alternative to bank loans by helping their corporate clients to issue securities.

In the face of intensifying competition larger banks have lobbied hard in favor of repealing the Glass-Steagall Act of 1933, which separated commercial and investment banking. For much of the 1980s the securities industry looked very attractive. According to a study by the Federal Reserve Bank of New York, investment banking earned an average after-tax return on equity of 26 percent between 1980 and 1984 while the comparable rate for commercial banking amounted only to 12.2 percent.[21] After 1982 Wall Street experienced explosive growth when the combination of durable recovery and falling interest rates sparked a powerful boom in the stock and bond markets. This bull market spurred new issues and more trading of securities, thereby allowing brokers, dealers, and underwriters to operate a much higher volume. Feeding this boom was an unprecedented wave of mergers, and investment banks played a crucial role in this deal mania (see chapter 12). Add to this the growing trend of turning loans into tradable securities ("loan securitization"), and it becomes clear why commercial banks found investment banking irresistible.

The prohibition in Glass-Steagal against underwriting corporate securities (e.g., bonds, stocks) has not prevented money-center banks from engaging in other market-making activities, such as trading securities for their customers through trust departments, helping to issue U.S. government securities, and trading currencies. During the 1980s money-center banks searched for new ways to enter the rapidly expanding world of securities trading and deal origination.[22] To the extent that the banks succeeded in this effort, they could earn lucrative fees and trading profits while avoiding the credit risk that more loans would have brought to their balance sheets. Noninterest revenue, a rough proxy for investment banking activity, has increased steadily for the leading U.S. banks, from one-quarter of total revenue earned in 1981 to more than one-third now. Their forays into investment banking relied heavily on the introduction and propagation of new financial instruments which fell outside the domain of Glass-Steagall. Examples include arranging private placements of corporate securities, advisory services (e.g., merger advice, helping firms to design takeover defenses, identifying possible acquisition targets), arranging foreign financing for their domestic clients, and trading financial futures for corporations eager to hedge their borrowing costs. In general, commercial banks have achieved their greatest success when offering new types of instruments which limit a client's exposure to the increasingly large swings in interest and exchange rates (e.g., interest-rate swaps, currency swaps, caps, collars). They control more than 50 percent of this business.

In addition to regulation-evading innovation, money-center banks have challenged Glass-Steagall in a more direct fashion. In the process they have been helped by regulators and/or courts ruling in their favor. A good example was the decision in November 1981 by BankAmerica to purchase Charles Schwab & Company, the nation's largest discount brokerage house, which was later approved by the Federal Reserve and the Supreme Court.[23] In 1982 the Comptroller of Currency allowed Citibank to operate investment funds for its IRA customers, thus paving the way for banks to offer mutual funds. Between 1984 and 1987 many state-chartered banks gained broader powers to engage in securities underwriting, to offer insurance, and to develop or own real estate.[24] That, in turn, led national banks to argue with their federal regulators for comparable treatment. In January 1989 the Federal Reserve allowed banks to underwrite corporate bonds, commercial paper, mortgage-backed securities, and municipal revenue bonds through a separate subsidiary. It limited the subsidiary's revenues from these activities to 10 percent, with the rest coming from less-risky underwriting of federal debt. In September 1990 the Fed used the same restrictions when it gave Morgan permission to underwrite corporate equity. This regulatory extension eliminated the last remaining barrier between commercial and investment banking. The 10 percent revenue cap, however, is too low to attract any but the largest money-center banks into the securities business.

11.3. Bank Reform: A Difficult Balancing Act

Existing bank regulations, most of which were introduced more than half a century ago, clearly no longer correspond to the emerging structure of the financial-services industry. In the age of the computer, geographic restrictions on bank branches or the artificial separation of commercial and investment banking functions no longer make much sense. But the ad hoc adjustments of regulatory agencies to changing realities offer no good solution. Such piecemeal deregulation by loopholes and circumvention has only added to uncertainty and created unequal competitive conditions between different banks, depending on who regulates them. As the banking crisis deepened with the onset of recession in 1990, it became clear that something more drastic and far-reaching was needed. The prospect of having to bail out the FDIC, something Congress would have to pass into law, gave the Bush administration a welcome opportunity to break a decade-long legislative stalemate and to propose a complete overhaul of existing bank regulations. In February 1991 the Treasury offered its long-awaited plan for comprehensive bank reform.

The Treasury plan had several major objectives. One was to give big banks vastly broader powers by repealing the McFadden Act of 1927, the Glass-Steagall Act of 1933, and the BHC Act of 1956. National banks would be permitted to open branches in other states, provided there were no intrastate restrictions. Full nationwide banking would be authorized for bank holding companies in three years. Well-capitalized banks could set up securities, mutual-fund, and insurance affiliates, provided those were separately capitalized. In return, nonbank financial companies would be permitted to own well-capitalized banks. The plan also wanted to strengthen bank capital, the (now much eroded) cushion against bad-debt losses. Toward this objective it allowed commercial ownership of new financial holding companies for the first time since the 1930s, in the hope of attracting massive capital infusions from industry. The Treasury proposal also offered bankers inducements for better capitalization. Well-capitalized institutions would be subject to less regulation, while undercapitalized institutions would face much more stringent restrictions. Premiums for deposit insurance would be based on capital levels. That last provision was part of a broader overhaul of deposit insurance. That aspect of reform also included limiting deposit insurance (to $100,000 per institution for checking and saving accounts and an additional $100,000 per institution for retirement accounts) and eliminating insurance for brokered deposits. Bank supervision would be tightened, including annual on-site examinations and early regulatory intervention to correct deficiencies at problem banks before they fail. Finally, the Treasury proposal called for streamlining the existing regulatory apparatus of overlapping and competing agencies. Each banking organization would have only one regulator. The Fed would regulate all state banks, while national banks and thrifts would become the domain of a new federal banking agency under the direction of the Treasury Department. The FDIC would lose its regulatory powers and would be confined to deposit insurance.

This far-reaching and radical proposal faced rough going in Congress, where it fell under the jurisdiction of many different committees and soon became subject to intense lobbying pressures. Small banks, grouped together in the influential Independent Bankers Association (IBA), mobilized against nationwide banking. Insurance companies, which are also highly influential in Congress, resisted the intrusion of banks into their own hitherto protected markets. Bankers of all stripes opposed the limitations on deposit insurance. In the end even the securities firms, which had initially agreed to support the repeal of Glass-Steagall in return for being allowed to own banks themselves, soured on the idea of comprehensive bank reform. These powerful special-interest groups could put a great deal of pressure on lawmakers with their large political action committees and lobbyists, but there was very little pressure for action from the general public, which by and large cared little about banking legislation.

Except for strong support in the House Banking Committee, the Treasury proposal encountered stiff opposition in a number of Congressional committees. Donald Riegle (D–Mich.), chair of the Senate Banking Committee, proposed an alternative which prohibited commercial ownership of banks and the expansion of banks into the insurance business. The Treasury proposal suffered another setback when the bipartisan leadership of the House Banking Committee (Reps. Henry Gonzales of Texas and Chalmers Wylie of Ohio) decided in May 1991 to focus instead on a narrower bill to recapitalize the FDIC as its top legislative priority. Then came a summer in which financial scandals (Salomon; Bank of Commerce and Credit International [BCCI]), a wave of big-bank mergers, and new warnings of costly bank failures further weakened the proreform forces on Capitol Hill. These developments strengthened the hand of the powerful chair of the House Energy and Commerce Committee, John Dingell (D–Mich.), who vehemently opposed letting banks enter the securities business. His committee passed repeal of Glass-Steagall but attached such onerous "fire-wall" and accounting restrictions that the large money-center banks and the Bush administration lobbied hard against a Dingell-Gonzales compromise that included these restrictions. In November 1991 the House defeated this bill by 324 to 89. That lopsided vote dissuaded the Senate from taking up its own version, proposed by Senator Riegle, and the whole overhaul effort collapsed. President Bush, who had never lobbied hard for the Treasury proposal, saw one of his top domestic priorities unravel. In the end, Congress managed only to pass a much narrower FDIC recapitalization law (see section 10.4) before it adjourned in December.

The failure of the Treasury proposal had roots that went deeper than divisive lobbying and congressional gridlock. Lawmakers feared the unpredictable repercussions of such far-reaching reform. They were especially afraid of further weakening an already fragile banking system. Moreover, many features of the plan revived long-standing controversies regarding the structure and operations of our financial-services industry. Comprehensive bank reform will only be possible if these issues are addressed in a way that allows for a broader consensus.

1) The Push for Nationwide Banking. Banks have already found several ways to establish interstate or even national operations (see the preceding section), but the continued existence of geographic branching restrictions has prevented them from full nationwide integration. These restrictions have been one of the principal reasons for pushing America's largest banks far down on the list of the world's banking giants. Without a nationwide network of full-banking branches they could never achieve the size of their European and Japanese counterparts. Size alone is no guarantee of market power, but it allows for a critical mass which helps expansion into other markets. Moreover, continuing limitations on interstate banking have made our banks more susceptible to failure. They lack geographic diversification and depend on what happens to the regional economies in which they are located. Whenever a region faces a downturn (e.g., Texas in the mid-1980s; New England in the early 1990s), its banks will suffer too. They are also more vulnerable, because these restrictions have forced them to have a comparatively narrow base of stable consumer deposits. As long as the McFadden Act remains in force, no U.S. bank can accurately reflect the strength of the American economy as a whole.

Despite these obvious disadvantages, opposition to changing the status quo is strong. Numerous small banks, which have long relied on these branching restrictions for protection against direct competition with larger city banks, maintain close relations with their congressional representatives (especially in the House). They have consistently argued that allowing money-center banks into their markets would deprive their local industry of access to credit and would remove funds from their communities. These arguments feed into an old populist tradition of widespread suspicion about excessive economic concentration and fears of domination by outside forces. Yet it is also clear that the prohibition against interstate or nationwide banking has been a key reason for the massive overcapacity that currently plagues our banking industry. We simply have too many banks operating below optimal efficiency. The introduction of nationwide banking would certainly eliminate many small banks and help reduce the number of branch offices. This trend is inevitable anyway, because technology has given people across the country a new place to store their cash. Money-market funds offer most of the benefits of a bank account (liquidity, check-writing privileges, market yields) with no up-front cost. But our banking industry as a whole might survive the coming shake-out in much better shape if its better-run representatives were given permission to integrate and diversify their operations on a nationwide basis.

2) The Integration of Commercial and Investment Banking. The separation of these two banking functions has certainly hampered U.S. banks in their battles for global market share against more integrated European and Japanese institutions. The same holds true for other existing product-line restrictions which have kept our banks out of the insurance business and out of direct loans to real estate. Unable to participate directly in the underwriting and selling of securities, our commercial banks have been hurt by the trend toward the "marketization" of credit and have been forced to compensate for the loss of corporate customers with riskier loans. As a result of these restrictions they are less profitable. And as long as they cannot be directly involved in securities underwriting, insurance, and real estate at home, they will lack the skills to compete effectively in these areas overseas.

But there are some good reasons for caution when considering the abolition of existing product-line restrictions. Should commercial banks, already suffering heavy losses from nonperforming loans, be allowed to expand into inherently volatile markets and cyclical activities? Highly integrated financial-services giants would inevitably exercise even more power over access to financing and the distribution of resources in our economy. Regulators also have to worry about problems which may arise when banks relate to corporate clients both as creditors and investors. Congress separated commercial and investment banking precisely in order to avoid the conflicts of interest and abusive market-manipulation practices that had contributed to the stock market crash of 1929.[25] Tight "fire walls" between separately capitalized bank affiliates could help to contain these problems. But the more stringent the separation of these subsidiaries, the less integrated the holding company and the less effective its ability to offer customers a complete package of financial services.[26]

Moreover, it is doubtful whether commercial banks can perform well as underwriters, dealers, or brokers without experience in securities markets. These activities involve fictitious capital, a form of capital which is quite different from the traditional financial capital of making loans (see section 2.6). Investment bankers focus on market risk, trying to determine precisely the timing and pricing of any deals they bring to market for their clients. Their preoccupation with quick trading profits and deal origination fosters a freewheeling and risk-taking style of operation. Because speed of action is essential to their success, they have a great deal of autonomy in their decisions. Commercial bankers, on the other hand, focus on credit risk and are thus conservative in their investment outlook. They take their time in analyzing a customer's creditworthiness and follow a strict hierarchy of reporting and decision-making, from account officer all the way up to senior management level, which consumes additional time. Their fixed salaries tend to be much lower than the performance-based bonuses of investment bankers.

This cultural clash is difficult to reconcile. Most banks have been racked by internal tensions and turf battles between their commercial lending and investment banking subsidiaries.[27] They have yet to figure out how to design the kinds of compensation packages, promotion tracks, operating procedures, and reporting requirements needed to attract and retain talented investment bankers without making their traditional account officers too resentful. It may take years to turn their moneylenders' culture into a fee-earners' culture.

3) Possible Fusion of Commerce and Banking. For decades now these two economic activities have been kept strictly separate in the United States. Close links between bankers and industrial managers prevail in Germany, where banks own controlling interests in many large manufacturing firms, as well as in Japan, where banks and industrial groups form integrated combines called *keiretsu.* There are good reasons to consider such fusion of banking and commerce into "finance" capital (see section 2.6) for our economy, also. It would provide our undercapitalized banking system with a much needed infusion of capital. And it would make it much easier for bank holding companies to diversify out of deposit-taking and loan-making at a time when technological change threatens to make these traditional intermediation activities of banks obsolete. Once data-processing equipment and communications facilities emerged to bring up-to-date information on prospective borrowers to worldwide capital markets, banks lost their advantage of knowing more than anyone else about the financial conditions of borrowers (see section 11.1). With their value added thus much lower, many managers of bank holding companies will find it attractive to expand their activities into new fields. Enabling them to branch out into more profitable areas, instead of forcing them by regulation to fight for a share of a declining market, as is now the case, would make the inevitable shrinkage of our banking industry that much easier to accomplish.

But Americans have traditionally been opposed to the kind of concentration of economic power that any fusion between banking and commerce might entail. Another reason for resisting any change in the status quo is the fear that a commercial company might try to exploit the privileged position of its bank subsidiary for its own purposes. The ability to take deposits and create money means that commercial banks bear a unique fiduciary responsibility and enjoy special government protection. Some nonbank financial institutions and industrial enterprises could use the bailout mechanisms and access to the interbank payments system to socialize their losses. These problems could be avoided by regulations which would keep bank subsidiaries strictly separate from the rest of the company. On the other hand, if those restrictions are too onerous, not many commercial and industrial companies may be willing to acquire banks.[28]

4) The Creation of Core Banks. The Treasury proposal envisaged as the typical financial institution of the future a large holding company in which the bank affiliate would be kept strictly separate from other subsidiaries in terms of product differentiation, capitalization, accounting, and restrictions on intracompany dealings. This is a less stringent version of the "narrow" banking proposal first put forward by Robert Litan (1987) and pushed in Congress by Rep. Charles Schumer (D–New York). Such core bank subsidiaries, insulated by fire walls from the rest of the otherwise fully integrated financial-services companies, would enjoy the privileges of money creation and deposit insurance in exchange for a higher degree of government supervision. Under such a structure savers have a choice, a trade-off between returns and risks. They can either leave their money with the core banks, which offer insured deposits and invest only in low-risk assets (e.g., government securities), or seek better returns from uninsured "wholesale" bank affiliates, which engage in riskier activities. Schumer's core-bank proposal, which the House Banking Committee narrowly defeated in June 1991, would also have limited the interest that banks could pay on deposits and restricted the maximum size of their loans.[29]

The proponents of core banking argue that these conservatively managed units would hardly ever fail and would thus reduce the government's bailout costs. Its opponents worry that the proposal might open the back door for increased government regulation of credit allocation. There are other problems associated with the idea.

• Its restrictions would prevent banks from competing effectively with other financial institutions.

• Forced by regulation to pay low yields, core banks would not be able to keep their depositors from moving funds into substantially higher-yielding investments whose risks appear low. Banks could thus face the same kind of massive disintermediation they experienced in the late 1970s, when nonbank competitors offered money-market investments.

• Although the inevitable shrinkage of insured deposits would reduce the government's exposure to bailout costs, it would also leave the FDIC with many fewer deposits to assess and would thereby endanger its recapitalization effort.

• Core banks might also have fewer funds available for lending, especially when they face large outflows of funds and also because of larger overhead costs from having to maintain two banking entities instead of one.

• Tighter loan limits would not necessarily reduce the riskiness of insured banks, for there is no convincing evidence that small loans inherently perform better than do large loans. Litan's proposal to confine the assets of "narrow" banks to default-free government securities would deal with that problem. But the increasingly popular government bond funds already do precisely that, with much lower operating costs than banks.

• Finally, it is by no means clear whether the government could afford to let the larger uninsured wholesale banks fail. The FDIC might face increased pressure to maintain its "too-big-to-fail" policy while facing lower premium income with fewer deposits to assess.

5) The Restoration of Market Discipline. The Treasury plan tried to introduce a modicum of market discipline into banking. It did so by proposing limits on deposit insurance (see above), curtailment of the "too-big-to-fail" policy, and a discriminatory approach by regulators in favor of stronger banks. All of these provisions should encourage depositors to demand higher returns from weaker banks or to move funds to stronger banks. Implied here is a triage mechanism that would separate the healthy institutions from the badly managed ones. But this intention may well backfire. Given that bank assets (loans) are difficult for outsiders to evaluate properly, depositors have a hard time assessing the health of a bank in an efficient manner. Instead of making their decisions coolly and rationally, they are prone to panic when their bank faces a loss of confidence. Sudden mass withdrawals of uninsured deposits can even sink otherwise solvent banks. Banks may protect themselves against such "runs" by keeping a large amount of liquid assets of shorter maturity. But this response would hurt their profits, because such assets yield less. In the process they would reduce the availability of commercial and consumer loans, which have longer maturities and are less liquid. Nervous depositors might even move funds out of the banking system altogether into relatively safe alternatives, such as money-market funds or government bond funds. Be that as it may, the Treasury's deposit insurance proposals would most likely force many of the weaker institutions into insolvency. Although this strategy has the advantage of reducing the overcapacity of our domestic banking sector in a fairly rapid manner, the proposed methods for such downsizing may make the banking system as a whole even more unstable than it already is. The government does not seem well prepared for the increased costs of an approach that might result in a significantly larger number of bank failures.

11.4. Financial Capital and Economic Development

The failure of the Treasury proposal leaves the issue of banking reform unresolved. That task is not likely to go away anytime soon, because the current situation is untenable. The combination of price deregulation and continued product-line restrictions has squeezed banks. They have to pay more for deposits, but they cannot invest these costlier funds profitably other than by lending them out to risky borrowers. Facing an invasion of their traditional turf by foreign banks and less regulated nonbank institutions, they cannot respond in kind. Existing restrictions hamper their ability to enter new areas of the financial-services industry. As currently structured, our commercial banks face massive excess capacity. Consequently, we see many more bank failures and mergers now than we did in the past. Selective repeal of restrictions by regulatory fiat creates limited openings for individual banks, but it is no answer to the challenges faced by the system as a whole.

In the absence of a comprehensive reform, banks have tried to deal with the pressures of systemic crisis on their own. Most important, they have begun to consolidate. Over the past decade some 2,000 banks have disappeared, close to 15 percent of the total. This trend will accelerate in coming years. In October 1991 the FDIC predicted a decline of up to 4,000 banks over the next five to six years from the current 12,000, and the Fed projected that the number of banks would fall to between 6,000 and 7,000 by the year 2010. Apart from failures, this shake-out has been driven mainly by mergers. Starting with the acquisitions of Crocker by Wells Fargo in 1986 and of Irving Trust by the Bank of New York in 1988, the merger wave has spread to the nation's largest commercial banks. Such megamergers exploded in 1991 (e.g., Chemical and Manufacturers Hanover, NCNB and C&S/Sovran, Bank of America and Security Pacific, Bank of Boston and Shawmut). Unlike earlier acquisitions of failed institutions by out-of-state banks, these recent mergers occurred between banks that compete in the same regional market. Such consolidation allows significant cost reductions by eliminating duplication, and most of these megamergers have in fact been followed by massive branch closures and layoffs. Other prospective benefits from mergers for the banks involved are building on complementary market strengths and beefing up capital. For all these reasons regulators have actively encouraged the current wave of megamergers.

Whereas the recent merger wave among banks has not been found in violation of existing antitrust restrictions, there is clear evidence that the resulting increase in local or regional market concentration has hurt customers. Evidence (see Lipin and Charliers, 1992) suggests that many small businesses have had a far more difficult time receiving credit since their traditional local bank lender was bought by a larger out-of-state bank. In markets that are dominated by just a few banks, deposit rates tend to be lower and loan rates tend to be higher than in less concentrated markets. User fees and other service charges tend to be higher, the smaller the number of banks in any given market.[30] That correlation between price behavior and market structure can be found across the entire spectrum of the banking sector for all kinds of mergers, no matter whether those involve small community banks, superregionals, or the money-center banks of New York and California. The decline in price competition following a merger-induced increase in concentration is particularly pronounced in banking for two reasons. Bank prices are highly visible, and their coordination is easily administered. In addition, consumers are quite immobile. They still rely on banks more than on nonbank alternatives, they tend to stick with the same bank, and they rarely compare the profusion of financial products. The decline in price competition, which this combination of mergers and consumer immobility has allowed, was especially manifest during 1991–92 when banks enjoyed unprecedented yield spreads between deposit and loan rates to boost their earnings.[31]

Mergers will reduce excess capacity, but they are essentially defensive in nature and will not suffice to cope with the broader crisis conditions that afflict our domestic banking system. There has to be a new regulatory framework for the rapidly changing world of financial services. Banks are caught in an intermediate stage of structural transformation, one in which their traditional functions are no longer their exclusive domain and their future role is still ill defined. Whatever the eventual outcome of the inevitable regulatory reform, between now and then the debate has to focus on one question above all: how can our banks best contribute to the overall performance of the U.S. economy?

Politicians and bank regulators have two basic options. Either they can reestablish a tight regulatory framework, setting commercial banks clearly apart from other types of financial institutions, or they can deregulate, along the lines of the Treasury proposal to promote a more integrated financial-services structure. Each alternative has its merits and disadvantages.

Why should our policy-makers opt for reregulation? That would, after all, mean going against the trend of recent decades toward deregulation. At least two broad reasons justify such an historic reversal.

• For one, the traditional functions of commercial banking remain essential. Households still want a safe place in which to put their savings. The majority of businesses are too small to issue securities and continue to rely on bank loans as their only source of external funding. It is no surprise that community banks that specialize in commercial loans to businesses ranging from sole proprietors to medium-sized corporations have continued to do well, especially those banks with a diversified loan portfolio and a stable base of consumer deposits. Perhaps the most important reason for keeping commercial banks separate from nonbank institutions is that they create money. That exclusive power makes their interme-

diation activity uniquely important for our economy and requires special regulatory restraints by the government, which has a constitutional responsibility to
manage the money supply.

• Reregulation may also be justified on the grounds that recent deregulation
moves have played a major role in exacerbating systemic problems. Lawmakers
still remember the debacle of the thrifts, which rushed straight into disaster upon
deregulation in the early 1980s (see section 10.3). A quite convincing case could
be made that partial deregulation of commercial banks has contributed in large
measure to major problems in that sector. Certainly the abolition of interest-rate
ceilings on deposits a decade ago has forced bankers to pursue much riskier
investment strategies in order to afford the cost increase on the liabilities side.[32]

For all of these reasons, we may want to consider some form of reregulation
to preserve traditional commercial banking. There is, after all, historic prece-
dence for such a policy reversal. When the wave of innovation and deregulation
in the 1920s triggered speculative excesses with disastrous results, we did not
hesitate to impose a tight regulatory structure on financial institutions and markets during the early 1930s. That reform (see section 4.8) gave us four decades
of financial stability and steady growth.

Once we have decided in favor of reregulation, we must ask what kind of
regulations will best serve the real economy. We need stable banks that promote
economic development. The "core banking" proposal may cause too much turbulence from massive movements of funds between regulated and unregulated
bank subsidiaries. Parent companies may be tempted to channel funds surreptitiously from the insured core bank to other affiliates in trouble, and regulators
may not be able to resist bailing out the uninsured "wholesale" banks. There is
much to be said, however, in favor of limiting the maximum interest that banks
pay on insured deposits, because this would keep the cost of bank credit down
and would contain ruinous price competition of the kind last seen via brokered
deposits. Such price regulation on the deposit side would be more flexible than
the rigid limitation under Regulation Q, which triggered major disintermediation
during the 1970s whenever inflationary spurts drove market rates above set
ceilings. The deposit-rate maximum could be tied to the Treasury bills rate or to
some other floating formula that reflects current market conditions for default-
free instruments. The banks should pay slightly less than going market rates in
exchange for federal deposit insurance. Regulators should probably permit interstate banking, and Congress is now debating several proposals to permit nationwide bank branching. At the same time, lawmakers should retain existing
product-line restrictions that keep commercial banks by and large confined to
deposit-taking and loan-making activities.

The U.S. government might also want to set up an agency, much like the RFC
of the 1930s and 1940s, which would provide capital infusions for undercapitalized banks and make its assistance contingent on certain restructuring mea-

sures by the recipient bank. Such recapitalization is bound to be cheaper than our current practice of bailing out insolvent banks after they fail. Finally, Congress could design appropriate tax incentives to direct bank credit into desirable directions. Depositors might receive (at least a partial) tax exemption for interest earned on bank deposits. Such tax-based savings incentives already exist in many other industrial nations. Banks themselves should enjoy tax breaks for investments that clearly serve economic development.

Any new regulatory framework for banking will have to take account of the globally integrated nature of contemporary financial capital. Policy-makers have already begun to adjust to this reality. In 1975, following the collapses of Herstatt and Franklin National, the central bankers of the leading industrial nations met under the auspices of the BIS and concluded the so-called Basel Concordat to define their intervention responsibilities when Euromarket subsidiaries of transnational banks fail. Out of this secret agreement emerged the BIS-sponsored Committee on Banking Regulations and Supervisory Practices (Cooke Committee), which serves as a sort of global intelligence network for central bankers. In 1982 the committee members agreed on a framework for consolidated supervision of banking operations in the Euromarket.[33] Central banks have also increased their cooperation to reduce price volatility in foreign-exchange markets (see section 8.4) and to manage the LDC debt crisis (see section 10.1).

The global integration of financial institutions and markets will ultimately require an international regulatory framework. Otherwise, banks will not operate on a level playing field, and high-risk activities will move to the least-regulated areas. In recent years we have witnessed increased activity toward creating such a framework.

• In 1988 twelve industrial nations concluded the Basel Agreement to impose uniform capital guidelines on their respective banks. This agreement forced banks operating in those countries to raise their capital-asset ratios to 8 percent. The capital guidelines are weighted by risk, and the Fed recently announced a preliminary system of risk weights for different asset categories. Its rather crude categorization of risk could use further refinement.

• More recently, the United States also concluded bilateral agreements with Japan and the European Economic Community for reciprocal access by their financial institutions to each other's domestic credit system.

• Further initiatives can be expected soon to harmonize national rules for increasingly interconnected stock and bond markets.[34]

• Pressure for tighter regulation of the Euromarket has grown since the summer of 1991 when the BCCI affair revealed just how inadequate purely national regulation of transnational banking activities has been. The BIS responded to this unprecedented scandal by intensifying its efforts to create more uniform global banking rules. In July 1992 its twelve member nations agreed to tighten minimum standards for the supervision of international banking groups and their cross-border operations. If regulators from a "host country," in which a foreign bank seeks to set up operations, find the supervisory system of the bank's home country inadequate, they can impose their own restrictions on that bank. Complementing this international agreement, the Federal Reserve will gain additional powers to collect financial and ownership information about foreign banks that operate in the United States and to supersede state authority over those institutions. The European Community also plans to require the home countries to pay any deposit insurance losses by their banks, even those incurred in foreign branches, to stress the costs of inadequate supervision. The next major step toward the construction of a global regulatory regime will be to place monitoring powers over transnational banking operations into the hands of a single international agency, such as the BIS.

The second option for regulators, and a radically different one from the reregulation of commercial banks to keep them separated from the rest of the financial-services sector, is to go along with the basic outlines of the Treasury proposal and to phase out existing geographic branching, product-line, and ownership restrictions. The strongest argument in favor of such full-scale deregulation is that it would help to improve the international competitiveness of American banks. Right now they cannot compete on a level playing field with the more integrated European and Japanese banks. At a time when financial capital is becoming fully globalized, our banks are forced by regulation into a smaller deposit base and a much more limited range of activities than their foreign counterparts. Thus they lose out in the battle for global market shares.

Proponents of this kind of comprehensive reform can also point to the experience with "universal" banking in Germany and Japan, where banks have maintained close relations with industrial corporations for more than a century. Although the precise modalities differ, the basic features of this fusion between financial capital and industrial capital are similar in those countries. They include cross ownership, interlocking directorates, joint strategic planning, and steady supplies of long-term funds. In Germany the three national banks play a crucial role in determining both structure and market behavior of key industries because of their presence on the powerful supervisory boards of competing firms. Japan's dominant banks are part of larger multifirm combinations, the keiretsu, which integrate key industrial enterprises, their suppliers, customers, and lenders into a tightly knit network of coordination and interaction. Both economies have obviously benefited from having a few powerful full-service banks that are actively involved in the management and investment decisions of industrial corporations. Their success raises the question of whether the United States should reorganize its own economy in a similar fashion.

Obviously, the kind of financial system and the various facets of its relationship with domestic industry will have a huge impact on how a nation's economy performs in the long run. The fundamental advantage of such close ties between finance and industry in either Germany or Japan is that these produce informed and patient capital. Being allowed to own the equity of industrial firms, banks there have a vested interest in the long-term success of their corporate clients. As shareholders they benefit directly if and when their customers succeed. Their capital gains from stock ownership often exceed loan profits, which in turn allows them to charge less for loans. Owner-banks are also inclined to help their clients through hard times. Their support enables corporations to take on much more debt without incurring a greater risk of default. As a matter of fact, comparatively few German or Japanese firms go bankrupt even though they are highly leveraged. Greater use of debt, a cheaper source of capital than equity, means lower cost of capital and a decisive competitive advantage over their American counterparts. Finally, German or Japanese managers can afford to take a longer-term perspective in their investment decisions and product development, knowing that their source of capital is reliable and patient. Their corporate managers and bankers share information on a regular basis, which improves the quality of investment decisions.

In the fifty years preceding the Great Depression the United States had a banking system not unlike that of present-day Germany and Japan. During that period U.S. banks could underwrite and distribute securities. They played a major role in the restructuring of troubled industries, they actively promoted corporate mergers, and (before the Clayton Act of 1914) they were closely linked to railroad companies as well as manufacturing firms through a complex web of interlocking directorates. Our leading banks, such as J.P. Morgan, were thus in a powerful position to shape the course of industrialization in the United States. But passage of the Glass-Steagall Act in 1933, which prohibited banks from engaging in the securities business, changed all that. Since then, banks have essentially been providers of short-term loans to corporations.

This reduced role vis-à-vis industry has dramatically altered the outlook of our banks. Relationships with their corporate customers have become adversarial, where once they were cooperative. Being collateralized lenders without equity investment, American banks often feel they have little to lose from pulling the plug on delinquent borrowers. All that really matters to them is that the underlying collateral is worth at least as much as the outstanding loan balance when those assets have to be liquidated in the case of default. From that perspective it is not difficult to see that our bankers lend to assets rather than to corporations. They would rather fund tangible structures than intangible technologies. Worst of all, they prefer dealing with borrowers that have already succeeded to supporting those that might succeed in the future. As short-term lenders, they lack a stake in the long-term success of their borrowers. These harmful biases reinforce the short-term and risk-averse investment horizons of our industrial managers.

In the absence of close cooperation between banks and their corporate clients, American industry has traditionally had to rely much more on the stock market for funding. In bank-dominated capitalist systems, such as those of Germany or Japan, the stock market matters much less. As a result, corporations in those countries operate with higher leverage ratios and lower dividend payout ratios than those in the United States. Hostile takeover bids are comparatively rare. Replacement of poor management or change of ill-conceived business strategies is done by banks (in Germany) or industrial groups (in Japan) through a process of boardroom discussions and interfirm consultations. In the United States this disciplinary function is vested with the stock market. Disgruntled investors sell the stock of a firm, pushing down its stock price until the firm either changes strategy or faces a takeover bid. This is why corporate restructurings in the United States typically involve more savage cuts in employment and investment than do those in Germany or Japan.

America's heavy reliance on the stock market has had some benefits for domestic industry. Our corporate managers have greater autonomy in their decision-making than do their more tightly controlled German or Japanese counterparts, and this increased flexibility may foster better entrepreneurship. Many more small companies have gone public here than there, and we have much more highly developed venture capital to fund start-ups. But securities markets, in particular the stock market, are a much more volatile source of funds than are those derived from a long-term liaison with a commercial banker or from the interfirm dealings of an industrial group like Japan's keiretsu. The drawbacks of our marketization-based form of financial capital, in terms of encouraging speculation and short time horizons, have emerged with special clarity in the aftermath of the takeover boom of the 1980s (see chapter 12). As our industries face increasingly intense competitive threats from different directions, we may want to rethink our current regulatory structure and to replace it with a new system of financial capital that better serves the needs of the real economy. This issue, which centers on the ambiguous relationship between financial capital and industrial capital in a system with a strong bias toward "marketization," is taken up in the next chapter.

Deal Mania and Fictitious Capital

*Speculators may do no harm as bubbles on a steady stream of enterprise.
But the position is serious when enterprise becomes the bubble
on a whirlpool of speculation. When the capital development of a country
becomes a by-product of the activities of a casino, the job is likely to be ill-done.*
—John Maynard Keynes, 1936, p. 159

Never have Keynes's words been more relevant than during the past decade, when speculation came to dominate enterprise. In the early 1980s deregulation triggered a revolution in our hitherto highly structured and regulated credit system. Financial institutions introduced a vast array of instruments and created whole new markets around them. That combination of deregulation and innovation benefited almost anyone who held excess cash, from small savers finally earning the going market rate of interest to the giant pension funds hedging risks in the futures markets. But that very revolution also helped to turn our nation into a "casino society" of investors who engaged in high-stakes financial maneuvering as a shortcut to wealth. During the Reagan era a get-rich-quick mentality took hold in our country and soon pervaded the securities markets. With the onset of recovery in late 1982, the volume of financial transactions in the United States soared to unbelievable levels, and securities trading became the fastest-growing activity in our economy.

It is surely no coincidence that the United States possesses the world's largest economy as well as its most developed capital markets. The two went hand in hand. However, the advent of the casino society has thrown this symbiotic relationship out of whack. Trading of stocks, bonds, and other kinds of securities in financial markets, amounting nowadays to several tens of trillions of dollars per year, represents mere shuffling of paper assets. This is not a productive activity and is therefore excluded from our GNP, except for brokerage commissions and service fees generated in those trades. Moreover, it is by no means clear that our economy needs these huge financial transaction volumes to produce the current level of GNP. On the contrary, a strong case can be made that the spread of financial maneuvering has diverted resources from productive enterprise. After all, even though securities trading has grown explosively, industrial investment activity has remained relatively stagnant and productivity growth has continued to lag.

Why have investment priorities shifted from enterprise to speculation? The answer to this question requires us to focus on so-called fictitious capital and its role in long-wave dynamics. We briefly introduced this peculiar form of capital at the end of chapter 2, but now we have to analyze its historic significance in the context of the current transition (section 12.1). Among the numerous layers of fictitious capital that exist today in our economy, equity shares deserve special attention. Their volatile price behavior makes them a particularly attractive object of financial speculation (section 12.2). The stock market boom of 1982–87, like earlier ones (e.g., 1896–1907, 1923–29, 1962–68), coincided with a merger wave and so became the primary vehicle for industrial restructuring (section 12.3). At the same time, the computerization of securities trading and the spread of financial futures transformed the modus operandi of the stock market (section 12.4). Eventually the speculative bubble burst in a one-day panic on October 19, 1987. Unlike the crash of October 1929, this latest stock market collapse did not cause the economy to tumble right away. Its repercussions were more gradual and subtle, illustrating the relative autonomy of fictitious capital vis-à-vis the rest of the economy (section 12.5).

12.1. The Dominance of Fictitious Capital

An economy only grows to the extent that it creates more output during any given production cycle than is needed to satisfy current consumption needs. That excess output, the surplus, can then be directed toward long-term investments in education and equipment which increase a nation's productive capacity. It is industry that produces and reinvests this surplus. Keynes's emphasis on "enterprise," like Marx's discussion of "productive capital" and "surplus-value," captures the importance of industry as the engine of growth in our economy.

Because industrial investments require cost outlays before revenue inflows can be earned, firms often have to borrow funds. By attracting otherwise idle income ("savings"), the credit system supplies borrowers with additional funds to cover their cash-flow gaps. It actually does not matter here whether the loans go to industrial firms for purchase of inputs needed in the production process or to households for purchase of consumer goods. In the latter case firms benefit too, albeit more indirectly, by being able to sell a larger quantity of output than would have been the case without consumer loans.

Neoclassical theory recognizes this support function of credit. It views the credit system as a mechanism which channels savings—a leakage from the circular spending flow—into investments—an injection—so as to equate the two and thereby to maintain macroeconomic equilibrium. Financial institutions, which organize these fund transfers, are seen simply as mediating between ultimate lenders and ultimate borrowers. In that process of intermediation they produce and sell financial services, such as risk reduction or maturity transformation. From this point of view, financial intermediaries appear as a service sector on a par with manufacturing industries, such as steel or automobiles, except that their product is less tangible. Commercial banks are the most representative among various financial-services institutions. Even though the liquidity of their liabilities accords them a special role in orthodox monetary theory as creators of money, that role too is seen solely in terms of financial intermediation.[1]

The money-creation process of commercial banks is much more than a mere act of financial intermediation, however (see section 2.4). It represents a source of capital formation, in this case financial capital. This form of capital is quite different from industrial capital. Most important, it represents an alternative investment channel whose basic features are often more attractive than are those found in industry (see section 2.5). Unlike industrial capital, investments in financial capital are not productive per se unless they direct more funds into supporting industry's production or sales. Trading of financial securities or acquiring the shares of a company in a takeover bid, for example, are activities which do not create new "value added." Hence they do not count toward the gross national product. On the contrary, the income accruing to financial capital is actually a deduction from the economic surplus, which leaves industrial firms with less to reinvest.

Financial capital therefore relates to industrial capital in an inherently ambiguous fashion. On the one hand, it supports industrial investments. On the other hand, it competes with those and reduces their net returns. These two aspects need not clash. Under normal conditions industrial capital will yield more attractive returns than financial capital and will create sufficient surplus to pay for all interest charges without squeezing investment spending. Firms will only borrow funds if they expect investments financed thereby to earn profits in excess of interest costs so that they end up with a net gain. As long as income gains grow faster than debt-servicing charges, taking on debt helps industry to expand. Should financial investments become more attractive than industrial investments and/or should debt-servicing costs outpace profit growth, however, the usually symbiotic relationship between these two forms of capital ruptures and turns into a source of friction. We are facing precisely such a situation today.

Keynes (1936, ch. 24) approached this problem in a very interesting way. He was critical of the standard notion that a moderately high rate of interest was necessary to provide an adequate inducement to save (p. 375). In the *General Theory* he presented saving as a function not of interest rates but of income. Because income depends on investment, saving is ultimately determined by the volume of investment, which in turn benefits from low interest rates. Hence high interest rates are in conflict with full employment.[2] Keynes then went on to argue that capital was likely to become more plentiful over time. Given the downward-sloped schedule of the "marginal efficiency of capital," its greater abundance would result in much lower returns. In this situation the owners of capital could no longer exploit its scarcity-value, and interest rates would also decrease. In this context he spoke of the "euthanasia of the rentier," a class of capitalists he termed "functionless investors" (p. 376).

Keynes was certainly right about the first point. Saving depends more on income than on interest rates. If this were not so, better yields on savings deposits during the 1980s should have reversed America's steadily declining propensity to save (see Table 12.1). He was less on target with his second point, however. The rentier aspect of capitalism has not turned out to be just a transitional phase. Holdings of financial assets relative to gross national product have grown dramatically over the past decade. This was also a period during which interest rates reached historic highs, especially when adjusted for inflation. Obviously capital remains scarce today, at least in relation to unmet needs, giving its owners large returns.

There are several possible reasons why, contrary to Keynes's prediction, capital has not become plentiful enough to lower the rate of interest permanently. Growing affluence in the industrial nations created a seemingly insatiable demand for nonessential consumer goods, a phenomenon Keynes (1930b) himself predicted in his discussion of "relative needs." This conspicuous consumption has often been met with capital-intensive mass-production technologies, as in the case of cars or personal computers. Rapid population growth in the developing world requires massive infrastructure investments which absorb a great deal of capital all at once, as did growth during the postwar "baby boom" in the United States and Europe. Moreover, the nature of government spending has changed since the time of Keynes. Ever since World War II the emphasis of the New Deal on direct employment programs has given way to a growing reliance on government contracts with industry. As already mentioned (in section 8.1), these contracts guarantee extra-high returns and encourage capital-consuming production methods.[3]

While consumerism, demographics, and government subsidies to industry have all contributed to keeping capital relatively scarce, we must also consider what happened when Keynes's prescription of low interest rates was put into practice. The monetary reforms under Roosevelt's New Deal (see chapters 4 and 5) forged a social consensus between creditors and debtors in support of an accommodating "easy money" policy. The Fed used its powers to keep interest rates low, a policy which benefited debtors. At the same time it managed to appease commercial banks, the most important group of creditors in our economy, by favoring private bank money over state-issued currency and thereby encouraging their rapid asset expansion. But with the arrival of stagflation in the 1970s this consensus began to fall apart. Faced with growing losses and risks, creditors revolted against what they perceived to be a prodebtor bias of the

Table 12.1

Declining Savings Versus Growing Financial Capital

Year	Personal saving rate (as percentage of disposable income)	Private financial wealth (as percentage of gross domestic product)
1970–1979	7.8	1.767
1979	7.1	1.714
1980	7.9	1.869
1981	8.8	1.791
1982	8.6	1.865
1983	6.8	1.901
1984	8.1	1.794
1985	6.4	1.867
1986	6.0	1.914
1987	4.3	1.865
1988	4.4	1.868
1989	4.4	1.952
1990	5.1	1.820
1991	5.3	—

Source: Council of Economic Advisers, *Economic Report of the President*, 1992, Washington, DC, Table B-24 (personal saving rate), B-109 (private financial wealth), B-1 (GDP).

Notes: Private national wealth includes credit market instruments, life insurance and pension reserves, security credit, and miscellaneous assets, and is net of liabilities. The 1970–79 period is calculated as yearly average.

postwar monetary regime. Their revolts, whether in the form of regulation-evading innovations, speculation against the dollar, or disintermediation and loan rationing during recurrent credit crunches, eventually forced the Fed to abandon its low-interest policy in October 1979 (see section 7.7). Six months later Congress decided to eliminate the rate ceilings on bank deposits and loans.

The deregulation of interest rates in 1979–80 made it much easier for creditors to charge more for their loans and to transfer the price risk to borrowers (see section 9.3). That shift of market power in favor of creditors contributed to a lasting hike in interest rates, a far cry from the "euthanasia of the rentier" predicted by Keynes. During much of the 1980s financial capital offered very attractive returns. Not only were inflation-adjusted ("real") interest rates high by historic standards, but the gradual decline of nominal rates after 1982 in response to disinflation also boosted security prices and therefore provided additional opportunities for capital gains. This prompted funds to move increasingly from industrial capital where the recovery of profit-rates was only moderate, into financial capital.[4]

That shift in investment preferences during the 1982–90 recovery is evident in the expansion of financial assets relative to gross national product (see Table 12.1). More important, it has contributed to rather remarkable changes in domestic income distribution during the 1980s (see Table 12.2). Reagan's probusiness and anti-union policies (see chapter 8) helped to shift income from wages to profits, while the removal of price controls in credit transactions increased the share that went to interest. This redistribution of income from wages via profits to interest altered the growth pattern of our economy in an ultimately unstable manner. By widening the gap between poor and rich it undermined the social fabric of our society and changed the output mix of our economy from basic needs to luxury products. Middle-class Americans could only maintain their consumption levels by working longer hours, saving less, and borrowing more. Industrial investment has remained stagnant in response to the high cost of capital. With consumers, businesses, and the federal government all having to take on more debt to finance even moderate spending growth, the pattern continuously reproduced the dominant position of financial capital and the conditions for high interest rates. The gradual credit crunch that has unfolded over the last few years has shown that this growth pattern could not be sustained for long.

The debt-dependent growth pattern of the 1980s had its own pitfalls for creditors. Although they benefited from strong credit demand and deregulated interest rates, these very forces also caused large increases in debt-servicing charges. That fixed-cost burden in turn weakened many debtors to the point of default, especially those hit at the same time by deflationary pressures. The 1980s therefore saw growing loan losses on debts to LDCs, farmers, energy producers, real estate developers, and leveraged buyouts. These sectoral debt crises (see section 10.2) have tied up a large portion of interest-bearing capital in debt reschedulings and have made banks wary of extending new loans for fear of causing additional bad-debt losses. Moreover, bank lending also lost market share to more attractive sources of funds (e.g., mortgage brokers, low-cost installment credit offered by retailers and automobile firms). Many of these alternatives involved issue of debt securities, such as commercial paper or junk bonds.

Interest-bearing loan capital was therefore not the primary reason for the revival of finance during the 1980s. Far more important was the rapid growth of fictitious capital (see section 2.6) This form of capital comprises all financial claims whose market value depends on the capitalization of expected future income streams.[5] Since these instruments are marketable, they are more liquid and mobile than is loan capital. Their dissociation from any productive capital also makes them less vulnerable to the vicissitudes of industry. These advantages encourage speculative position-taking in financial markets, with trading profits (realized capital gains) the principal income form of fictitious capital. To the extent that shuffling paper assets absorbs funds which are not spent on industry's

Table 12.2

Shifts in Functional Income Distribution
(as percentage shares of national income)

Year	Wages and salaries	Corporate profits	Net interest
1981	62.3	8.3	9.6
1982	63.2	6.6	10.4
1983	61.9	7.4	9.9
1984	60.5	7.7	10.1
1985	60.8	6.9	10.0
1986	61.2	6.6	10.2
1987	61.2	7.4	9.8
1988	61.0	8.0	9.7
1989	60.9	7.7	10.7

Source: Council of Economic Advisers, *Economic Report of the President*, 1992, Washington, DC, Table B-22.

Notes: Wages and salaries exclude employer contributions for social insurance and to private pension, health, and welfare funds. Corporate profits are measured before tax. They exclude inventory valuation and capital consumption adjustments.

productive capacity, speculation crowds out enterprise—the phenomenon Keynes referred to in the epigraph.

Even though financial speculation has existed throughout the history of capitalism (see Kindleberger, 1978), fictitious capital only became an institutionalized part of our economic system with the monetary reforms of the 1930s. That form of capital is intimately tied to credit-money, a linkage which is rooted in the very process of money creation. By loaning out (excess) reserves gained from deposits, a bank creates new money deposits. As its loan is spent, the process replicates itself with another bank. In the end the banking system as a whole has created a multiple of the original excess reserves in new money (see section 2.4). Such money creation ex nihilo is in itself a source of fictitious capital and the reason why credit-money has no intrinsic value.

The linkage between credit-money and fictitious capital experienced a major extension in the late 1950s, when British banks decided to accept Soviet dollar deposits. This decision gave rise to the so-called Eurocurrency market, which comprises all those deposits denominated in any currency regardless of the country in which the issuing banks are located. Local regulations that affect the cost and nature of domestic deposits do not apply here. That market, which has grown to about $2.3 trillion today, allows banks to operate beyond the reach of central banks and to move funds of truly stateless money around the globe. Much of that movement of funds occurs between banks, with interbank deposits making up slightly more than half of the Euromarket. The absence of any reserve require-ment creates a potentially infinite multiplier effect, since there is no leakage as Eurocurrency deposits flow from bank to bank. In practice, however, there are built-in checks to this process. The multiple expansion stops, for example, when one of the recipients of Eurodeposits prefers to make an interbank loan to a bank in the original country of issue (e.g., a U.S. bank in the case of Eurodollars) instead of a Eurobank or when borrowers decide to convert their Euroloans into local currency.[6]

Money itself became a primary focus of speculation after Bretton Woods broke down and gave way to a system of flexible exchange rates in 1973. Cor-porations and financial institutions have made increasingly large bets on move-ments of currency prices ever since. Their primary vehicle in this endeavor has been futures contracts which give holders the right to buy or sell a currency for a predetermined price at a certain date. These currency futures require investors to put up only between 5 percent and 12 percent of the contract's value in their own money. The rest is borrowed from brokers. Such leveraging creates large gains if the exchange rate moves in the anticipated direction. Since positions can be easily unwound before contracts expire, it is not difficult to limit losses. These features make currency futures an ideal instrument of speculation. Today cur-rency trading across the globe averages $1,000 billion per day (!), most of which is undertaken to hedge risks or to speculate. With deregulation of interest rates in 1979 making securities prices much more volatile, futures contracts also came into widespread use after 1981 for bonds and stocks.[7]

Government securities are another important source of fictitious capital. Is-sued to cover budget deficits, they occupy a key position in our credit system. The Fed trades them to manage bank reserves. Other central banks hold most of their foreign exchange reserves in U.S. Treasuries. Financial institutions like them, because they are free of default risk and very liquid. Global trading of Treasury securities often exceeds $150 billion on any given day. Although that debt instrument is considered safer than any other, its market can be quite risky. Ever since Reaganomics created huge U.S. budget deficits, primary dealers have not been able to absorb greatly increased supplies. This has allowed secondary dealers to enter the market and to build large portfolios with very little capital through repurchase agreements (see section 11.2). Salomon Brothers, one of the key primary dealers, has been found guilty of rigging bids in auctions of Trea-sury securities to corner the market.

Another less obvious form of fictitious capital is the creation of accounting profits to hide or transfer economic losses. These are directly related to credit-money in two ways. Its issue as simultaneous asset and liability, with exactly matching reciprocity for both sides of the transaction (bank and borrowing user), allows all monetary transactions to be recorded by means of double-entry book-keeping in so-called T-accounts—the basic tool of financial accounting. More-over, accounting profits need to be backed by continuous debt financing and therefore depend on endogenous money creation. To the extent that elastic credit-money relaxes the monetary constraint, it frees nominal price movements from underlying value quantities and allows manipulation of balance sheets. In the inflationary 1970s, accounting profits accrued mostly to industrial firms due to the distortions of "historic cost accounting" (see chapter 5). In the 1980s the focus shifted to banks and thrifts, whose use of "regulatory accounting practices" protected impaired loan assets from write-offs and mark-downs (see chapter 10).

The accumulation of fictitious capital is therefore tied to the institution of credit-money in many ways. But why should this form of capital have become so dominant during the past decade? A major reason has been the continuing stagnation of industry, which became more exposed after the disinflation of the early 1980s. Hit by excess capacity and a much higher cost of capital, many firms hesitated to sink a large amount of funds into long-term investment projects with uncertain returns. Much of the income they amassed was reinvested instead in financial assets. Apart from being more liquid, these also promised a chance for higher returns within a shorter period of time than industrial investments. The transition toward a new monetary regime, always a period of competing forms of money, regulatory erosion, and financial innovation, created ample opportunity for new credit instruments and circuits. Many of those facilitated multiple layering of credit and highly leveraged trading strategies to maximize gains. Speculation, which used to be a predominantly cyclical phenomenon before 1979, became a permanent activity and deeply embedded in the structure of our economy during the 1980s.

Financial futures and repurchase agreements were not the only new sources of fictitious capital to emerge in the 1980s and transform securities markets. We also saw a rapidly growing trend of selling and securitizing loans. This transformation of loan capital into fictitious capital made credit more liquid and attracted much new capital into crucial lending areas to compensate for declining household savings (e.g., mortgage-backed securities). Banks pursued money-dealing activities, such as currency trading and payments-processing services, much more aggressively in order to earn fees and to become less dependent on interest income. Also noteworthy in this context was the phenomenal expansion of off-balance-sheet commitments over the past decade (e.g., financial guarantees, swaps, standby letters of credit).

But the principal engine for the rapid growth of fictitious capital after 1982 was the U.S. stock market. Corporations issue stocks to investors as ownership titles. Those stocks are not the same as the actual capital invested by the firm. That capital can exist only once, namely as physical capital in the form of plant and equipment. Stocks are instead mere paper assets which entitle their holders to a share of the future income produced by that capital. As a corollary, the basis of their valuation, which gives us the "market value" of a firm, differs from that of the physical capital they represent, the firm's "book value." Stock prices depend on expectations, may be altered by market manipulation, and tend to move inversely with interest rates. They are thus inherently volatile, always an attractive feature to speculators. The stock market, as had been proved earlier between 1896 and 1907 and in the 1920s, is also a powerful mechanism for industrial restructuring during the downswing phase of a long wave.

12.2. The Cyclical Nature of Corporate Stocks

Common shares traded in the stock market are ownership titles which corporations issue as a source of external funds. They give shareholders a claim on the firm's future profits, either in the form of dividend payouts or capital gains when the stocks appreciate in value. Their valuation, as already indicated earlier (see note 5), is based on the discounted present value of expected yields. Stock prices thus depend primarily on market expectations about the future income potential of corporations and on interest rates.[8]

The special nature of the stock market as a source of fictitious capital leads to pronounced boom-bust cycles. Gradual recovery of stock prices in the wake of spreading optimism typically gives way to speculative euphoria, the so-called bull market. In that situation many investors, expecting price increases to continue, buy up large numbers of shares in the hope of earning capital gains by selling them at higher prices soon thereafter. For a while that process works like a self-fulfilling prophecy, because speculative purchases help to drive up share prices. In those situations market price behavior is likely to be self-reinforcing rather than self-limiting, as assumed in the equilibrium models of standard economic theory. But at some point the values of corporate shares traded in the stock market no longer correspond to the underlying performance capacity of industry. It is in such a situation of overpricing that market sentiments are bound to catch up with the growing divergence between expectations and reality. This adjustment usually comes in the wake of troubling news about industry's mounting difficulties. When it occurs, the shift in expectations tends to be swift and dramatic. As a result, stock prices drop suddenly and then linger on at much lower levels, a so-called bear market.[9]

This boom-bust cycle of the stock market parallels the business cycle of industry in mutually reinforcing fashion. Stock prices are driven by expectations about future corporate profitability. When those improve, as is typical during recoveries, stock prices go up. The opposite is true before and during recessions. Moreover, bull markets facilitate the financing of larger investment volumes in industry. Rising stock prices make it easier for firms to issue new shares and to borrow more. The reverse occurs when stock prices decline and the equity capital base ("net worth") of corporations shrinks. A bear market thus acts as a financial constraint which deepens the recessionary forces in industry. The level of stock prices is also important, because capital gains (or losses) may be significant in determining the level of consumer spending. This so-called wealth effect typically operates in procyclical fashion, as do movements in interest rates, which impact simultaneously on the level of industrial investment and the valuation of stocks.

Financial speculation in the stock market is therefore not entirely detached from the accumulation of industrial capital in the sphere of production. In other words, the autonomy of fictitious capital is only relative. Its capacity for self-expansion is ultimately limited by the performance of corporations. When over-priced shares are becoming increasingly out of line with an underlying deteriora-tion of corporate profitability, then it is only a question of time before the speculative bubble bursts. Furthermore, as Keynes (1936, ch. 12) recognized, speculation is itself detrimental to the health of industry. As it becomes domi-nant, its short-term focus crowds out the long-term planning horizon required in industrial investments. And speculative trading of financial instruments absorbs funds which could have financed investment in productive capital.

Another important aspect of the relation between fictitious and industrial capital is the close association between speculation-driven bull markets and merger waves. We could see those two forces coalesce from 1896 to 1907, when horizontal mergers created many industrial giants; during the 1920s, when hori-zontal mergers established large "number two" firms and vertical mergers gave firms better control over all stages of the production process; during the late 1960s, when many firms diversified into new businesses through conglomerate mergers; and between 1982 and 1987, when takeover mania hit U.S. industry. It is no coincidence that each bull market in U.S. history has been accompanied by a major wave of mergers and acquisitions. After all, one of the principal func-tions of the stock market, as the place in which ownership titles are traded, is to allow firms to acquire the productive assets of other companies. Managers often prefer this (external) method of expansion over (internal) growth based on in-vestment in new plant and equipment. This is especially the case when it is cheaper to buy up existing assets from other firms than to build the same capac-ity from scratch. Such a situation prevails above all during the early stages of recovery, when the market values of corporate shares are still depressed from the preceding downturn and are thus below the much stickier cost-prices of produc-tive capital assets. Later on, mergers themselves tend to become key vehicles for speculative gains, as was the case with the "go-go" conglomerates in the late 1960s or the "raiders" during the 1980s (see below).

A final aspect worth mentioning in the context of the boom-bust cycles of the stock market is the role of financial institutions. Since stock market rallies pro-vide those institutions with large income opportunities, they have a vested inter-est in sustaining such booms by channeling funds into the stock market and expanding trading volumes. The very mobility of shares and the speculative nature of their price formation leave much room for market manipulation. One key method to feed bull markets is the use of common shares as collateral for loans which finance additional stock purchases. As long as share prices are going up, this process is self-expanding. Investors too have a strong incentive to participate in such credit pyramiding, since it allows them to put down less of their own money and thereby to earn relatively larger returns from any given price increase. What we therefore typically find during bull markets are innovations which centralize funds for leveraged purchasing of stocks.[10]

Of course, that practice of leveraging also exacerbates losses during market downturns. For example, when an investor borrows $9 to buy a stock for $10, then a price decline of $1 (10 percent) constitutes a 100 percent loss. It is this credit pyramiding which usually turns market crashes into acute financial crises. Falling stock prices leave outstanding loans partially unsecured, forcing investors to cover the gap by coming up with additional cash in a hurry. Failure to heed these so-called margin calls leads to default. In that situation the lenders will liquidate the stock collateral as soon as possible to limit their losses. Such forced asset sales into a declining market only feed the selling panic. Amid growing losses and spreading defaults, the credit pyramid can collapse like a house of cards. The fictitious nature of speculation-based capital accumulating during bull markets is illustrated most dramatically by its rapid destruction during the early stages of bear markets.[11]

12.3. Stock Market Boom and Merger Wave

The stock market boom of 1982–87 had its roots in underlying changes in the U.S. economy. During the 1970s the stock market had been the victim of intensifying stagflation. That new form of structural crisis involved a gradual deterioration of corporate profitability, with obviously negative consequences for investor confidence and stock prices (see Table 12.3). Even though the financial statements of many U.S. corporations showed record earnings during that period, much of that profit was based on purely fictitious gains created by "historic-cost" accounting of depreciation and inventories (see Figure 5.1). When shareholders realized this accounting manipulation of income, they lost confidence in the accuracy of financial statements and discounted share prices accordingly.

A second reason for the poor stock market performance during the 1970s was the rise in interest rates in the wake of accelerating inflation. Higher interest rates depress stock prices for three reasons. For one, funds get diverted from the stock market into the bond market as yields there become comparatively more attractive. Moreover, greater interest costs take a bigger bite out of corporate gross income and thus tend to lower net income, the bottom-line measure of profit. Finally, higher interest rates reduce the capitalization of anticipated income flows, which forms the basis for the calculation of current share prices.

This stagflation-induced stock market erosion reached its zenith during the Great Recession of 1979–82, when inflation peaked at 14 percent and key interest rates rose above 20 percent. It was precisely the very depth of this crisis which set the stage for a major turnaround in the fortunes of the stock market. To begin with, corporations were forced to cut costs and thereby to improve their

Table 12.3

The Stock Market Malaise of the 1970s

Year	Dow Jones Industrial Average	Standard & Poor's Composite Index (1941–1943 = 10)
1968	906.00	98.70
1969	876.72	97.84
1970	753.19	83.22
1971	884.76	98.29
1972	950.71	109.20
1973	923.88	107.43
1974	759.37	82.85
1975	802.49	86.16
1976	974.92	102.01
1977	894.63	98.20
1978	820.23	96.02
1979	844.40	103.01

Source: Council of Economic Advisers, *Economic Report of the President*, 1992, Washington, DC, Table B-91.

battered balance sheets. Moreover, the collapse of inflation in the aftermath of this downturn (to around 4 percent per year) eliminated much of the accounting bias in financial statements. This helped to restore investor confidence even though reported income was now often lower than it had been in the 1970s. Finally, the disinflation and reduced credit demand during that crisis led to a gradual decline in interest rates after 1982, which boosted stock prices.

A second major factor in the bull market of the 1980s was the shift in U.S. economic policy under President Reagan. The Economic Recovery Tax Act of 1981 (see section 8.1) sharply lowered income taxes for wealthy Americans, reduced the tax rate on capital gains, and increased after-tax profits of corporations through a variety of tax deductions and credits. At the same time, key industries were stimulated by a massive military spending program. Starting in late 1982 the Federal Reserve allowed much more rapid growth in the money supply, which helped to move interest rates gradually lower. With many industries operating at low rates of capacity utilization, spending on new plant and equipment did not pick up much despite improved corporate profits. A major part of the liquidity injections permitted by the Fed was instead absorbed by financial transactions in general and the stock market in particular.

But Reaganomics was more than just a set of economic policy changes. It was above all a conservative counterrevolution against the liberal legacy of Roosevelt's New Deal and Johnson's Great Society. This ideological dimension played a major role in the bull market of the 1980s. Reagan's speeches were filled with boundless optimism about the moral and economic strength of America, a message soon reinforced by a (largely deficit-driven) recovery. His emphasis on the benefits of the "free market" and individualism fed into a deepening "get-rich-quick" mentality of American investors and managers. The race for short-term gains soon became the dominant force in the economy. This bias fostered a climate which favored financial speculation at the expense of industrial investment activities with much longer payoff periods. That shift in investment behavior was reinforced by a variety of social practices, such as the emphasis on current earnings among shareholders and corporate managers, the dominance of finance in business education, and the extremely high salaries for brokers and investment bankers on Wall Street.

The final ingredient of the stock market boom was massive industrial restructuring in the majority of U.S. industries. In key sectors, such as telecommunications, energy, transportation (airlines, railroads, buses, trucks), and finance, this process was triggered by deregulation, which abolished controls on prices and output. Other industries, especially basic manufacturing sectors (e.g., oil, steel, rubber, automobiles, machine tools, chemicals), faced large excess capacities and sharply intensified global competition when the dollar rose by more than 60 percent between 1981 and 1985. Rapid technological change (e.g., electronics, information processing, factory automation, biogenetics) required costly and risky investments on a large scale. All of these forces encouraged greater concentration in affected industries.

This industrial restructuring primarily took the form of mergers and takeovers. Reagan's laissez-faire ideology prevented the government from formulating any coherent industrial policy strategy, even though many industries were given all kinds of subsidies, tax breaks, trade protections, relaxed accounting rules, and regulatory relief. The major impetus for restructuring therefore had to come from the marketplace, especially the stock market. With common shares so undervalued during the 1970s, companies could pay large premiums over market value and still acquire existing assets from other firms more cheaply than expanding internally through reinvestment of profits in new plant and equipment. This preference for external growth was also fed by excess capacity in their traditional lines of business. With many firms selling off disappointing subsidiaries, the stock market soon became a hyperactive trading place for ownership titles to entire production units. The "hands-off" attitude of the Reagan administration with regard to antitrust laws and supervision of financial markets helped to feed this trend.[12]

One characteristic of that merger wave was the huge size of merger transactions, many of which involved several billion dollars (see Table 12.4). The majority of deals in the mid-1980s involved mergers between leading firms in industries undergoing massive restructuring. Often a single deal would set off a whole round of other mergers in the same industry, as firms tried to protect

Table 12.4

The Merger Wave of the 1980s

Year	Mergers and acquisitions	Total value paid (in billions of dollars)	Deals exceeding 100 million dollars	Price/earning ratio paid	Tender offers for publicly traded companies
1979	2,128	43.5	83	14.3	n.a.
1980	1,889	44.3	94	15.2	53
1981	2,395	82.6	113	15.6	75
1982	2,346	53.8	116	13.9	68
1983	2,533	73.1	138	16.7	37
1984	2,543	122.2	200	17.2	79
1985	3,001	179.8	270	18.0	84
1986	3,336	173.1	346	22.2	150
1987	2,302	163.7	301	23.3	116
1988	2,258	246.9	369	21.6	217
1989	2,366	221.1	328	20.9	132

Source: Merrill Lynch, *Mergerstat Review 1989*, pp. 75, 106.

Notes: Mergers and acquisitions are net announcements, excluding cancellations. Average price/earning ratio paid in all transactions. Tender offers are for publicly traded companies and include both uncontested and contested attempts.

themselves against their now much larger competitors. The degree of concentration in those sectors rose rapidly and dramatically.

In 1984 a new type of takeover activity emerged as the leading force in the merger-driven stock market boom, the hostile takeover bids by so-called *corporate raiders*. These raiders were aggressive individuals, such as Carl Icahn, T. Boone Pickens, or Irwin Jacobs, who had the financial backing of the largest investment banks on Wall Street. Speedy access to huge sums of money enabled them to attack even the largest U.S. corporations, such as Goodyear Tire, Trans World Airlines, or U.S. Steel. Many firms were quite vulnerable to such raids, because they had failed to meet the challenges of declining market shares and maturing products. The raiders deftly exploited this weakness by picking under-valued companies as targets and by promising their shareholders rapid capital gains. This made it possible for the raiders to present themselves as populist "champions" of small investors who were taking on entrenched and ineffective management in the interest of disgruntled shareholders.

In reality, of course, the raiders were not quite that altruistic. Their primary motivation was to make a quick profit. Their attacks usually began with secret purchases of shares of the target company. When their position reached 5 percent, the threshold for public disclosure, they would launch a hostile takeover bid for a majority of the shares. These bids offered a high premium over the market price to assure large support from shareholders willing to sell out. Once the bid was launched, several profitable outcomes were possible. In some cases the management under attack bought back the raiders' already accumulated shares at a very high premium ("greenmail") in return for a promise not to launch any future raids. In other instances raiders gained control of the company and shortly thereafter began to sell off its assets. The proceeds from these asset sales were then used to pay off the debt taken on to finance the takeover. Sometimes the raiders held on to acquired assets, especially those with large cash flows. Even failed bids often created gains, because the attack would prompt management into action to raise share prices.

The undervaluation of badly managed companies in the stock market was only one of the conditions that gave rise to the raiders. Another important factor was the growing concentration of stock ownership in the hands of large financial institutions. Although most shares in the United States are still owned by the nearly 40 million individual stockholders, the majority of shares in the larger corporations are held by pension funds, insurance corporations, and mutual funds. Nowadays these institutional investors (see Table 12.5), having come to rely on short-term capital gains as their main source of income, also conduct more than two-thirds of all stock trades. This concentration made it easier for raiders to launch successful bids. They needed the support of only a few shareholders owning large blocks of shares to gain control.[13]

But the most important cause for the predominance of raiders in the 1980s was the financial backing they were given by Wall Street in their attacks on corporate America. This support had its roots in a major reorganization of the securities industry. Following the deregulation of brokerage commissions in 1975, the major firms on Wall Street (e.g., Merrill Lynch, Salomon, Shearson Lehman Hutton, Goldman Sachs, Morgan Stanley Drexel) had faced a steady decline of their traditional activities of stock research and securities trading. After consolidating in the early 1980s (e.g., American Express acquiring Shearson, Prudential buying Bache, Sears taking over Dean Witter), the major securities firms began to look aggressively for new profit opportunities; the takeover game turned out to be the most lucrative. Fee-based investment banking services, such as providing advice and financing for corporate mergers and acquisitions, soon became their key source of income. Thus they had a strong incentive to promote such deals whenever possible (see Table 12.6).

The principal instruments that investment bankers used to finance the takeover bids of raiders were junk-bonds. These are long-term debt instruments which have a low investment rating and are therefore considered quite risky. To compensate investors for this risk, the junk-bonds carry higher yields, ranging 3 to 5 percent above those of Treasury bonds. Before 1980 only very marginal firms had issued junk-bonds, limiting this market to about $5 billion. But then Michael Milken of Drexel launched a successful campaign to convince investors that the default risk of junk-bonds was actually quite low relative to their high

Table 12.5

The Growth of Institutional Investors (in billions of dollars)

Year	Life insurance companies	Other insurance companies	Private pension funds	State and local government employee retirement funds	Mutual funds
1966	162.3	37.3	76.6	38.1	34.8
1973	244.8	69.5	161.7	84.7	46.6
1979	419.3	154.9	386.1	169.7	51.8
1980	464.2	174.3	469.6	198.1	61.8
1981	507.5	185.6	486.7	224.2	59.8
1982	567.5	202.8	575.8	262.5	76.9
1983	632.7	225.3	682.5	311.2	112.1
1984	692.9	241.0	713.9	356.6	136.7
1985	791.1	288.6	848.4	404.7	240.2
1986	900.9	342.2	915.9	469.4	413.5
1987	998.3	391.0	957.5	517.0	460.1
1988	1,125.6	435.0	1,040.6	606.1	478.3
1989	1,268.0	491.3	1,163.5	727.4	555.1

Source: Board of Governors of the Federal Reserve System, *Flow of Funds Accounts, Year-end, 1966–89,* pp. 27–30, September 1990.

Note: Size of different institutional investors measured in terms of total financial assets.

yields. Once large financial institutions, such as mutual funds, pension funds, insurance companies, commercial banks, or thrifts, were willing to invest more of their funds in high-yield junk-bonds, that market was ready for rapid expansion. Soon Drexel began to underwrite new issues of junk-bonds by raiders, and by the end of 1987 that market had grown to $160 billion.

Junk-bonds proved to be a crucial innovation in support of the merger wave by giving raiders rapid access to billions of dollars with which to launch their takeover bids. These high-yield debt instruments were in essence backed by the assets and cash flows of the target company. Consequently, raiders often dismantled their acquisitions by selling off assets or slashing operating costs to generate the cash required for debt servicing. Their enormous financing power made them a threat to even the largest U.S. corporations. To forestall possible raids, a large number of firms took precautionary measures in self-defense. Many tried to boost their stock price by buying up their own shares, spinning off assets, or saving costs through layoffs. Others tried to make themselves less attractive takeover targets by introducing "poison pills," such as huge severance payments to top managers in case of dismissal ("golden parachutes") or two-thirds majorities among shareholders.

Table 12.6

Wall Street's Changing Income Mix (million dollars, unconsolidated)

Year	Commissions	Gains on trading accounts	Gains on investment accounts	Underwriting profits	Margin interest	Mutual fund sales	Other securities-related income
1982	5,972	5,935	597	2,316	1,999	287	3,924
1983	8,326	6,842	728	3,537	2,128	953	4,374
1984	7,095	7,764	714	2,706	2,868	751	6,283
1985	8,238	9,944	1,089	4,250	2,578	1,643	7,176
1986	10,473	12,561	1,143	5,939	2,920	2,801	9,552
1987	12,646	9,973	68	5,157	3,352	2,209	11,680
1988	8,791	11,299	1,394	5,158	3,092	1,413	14,693
1989	10,151	12,343	488	4,120	3,723	1,580	20,338
1990	8,878	13,175	−283	3,243	3,075	1,669	17,389

Source: Securities Industry Association, *Securities Industry Yearbook,* 1985–86, p. 616; 1988–89, p. 762; 1991–92, p. 726.

Note: Revenues of New York Stock Exchange firms doing a public business.

A third response involved so-called leveraged buyouts, in which a company was taken private largely with borrowed money.

The merger mania was a major force in the stock market boom. The takeovers, stock repurchases, and leveraged buyouts shrank the supply of stocks by an estimated $400 billion between 1982 and 1987. With more money chasing fewer shares, stock prices inevitably rose. Restructuring efforts by firms to defend themselves against possible raids also succeeded in pushing up stock prices. Soon the takeover activity itself became a powerful vehicle for massive speculation. Risk arbitrageurs invested in potential takeover targets in the hope of selling their shares at a higher price when the expected bid materialized. By buying up large blocks of shares, they signaled to other traders which firms were likely to be "in play" soon. This speculative frenzy in takeover stocks transformed the way stocks were valued. Many investors no longer based stock prices on such traditional measures as expected earnings, dividend yields, and book value of corporate assets. Instead they increasingly used a different standard of valuation, namely the value a company would have if it were dismembered and its parts sold off. This breakup value justified share prices far in excess of traditional stock market valuations. When one company was taken over, stocks of other firms in that industry would be bid up to reflect the much higher price-earnings multiples just realized by the takeover target.

As is typical for speculation, the euphoria did not last for long. The first setback came in 1986, when a major scandal rocked Wall Street. Investigating suspicious jumps in stock prices of firms just before they became targets of takeover bids, the SEC uncovered massive insider trading. In May 1986 Dennis Levine, a former Drexel employee, pleaded guilty to securities fraud and turned government informant. He led regulators to Ivan Boesky, the largest risk arbitrageur on Wall Street. Boesky, who agreed in November 1986 to pay a $11 million fine and received a three-year prison sentence, revealed that in exchange for advance notification of imminent takeover deals by Drexel he would commit his funds to new issues of junk-bonds financing that takeover attempt. After nearly two years of investigation the SEC concluded that under Milken's leadership Drexel had used its position of dominance as the primary underwriter of junk-bonds to organize the market for its own purposes. The company manipulated stock prices, parked stocks to conceal their ownership, defrauded clients and shareholders, evaded taxes, and violated net capital rules. In order to avoid racketeering charges, Drexel agreed in December 1988 to plead guilty to six criminal charges and to pay a $650 million fine. In April 1990 Milken did the same. Besides having to pay a $200 million fine and $400 million to settle a civil suit by the SEC, he was sentenced in November 1990 to ten years in prison on six fraud and conspiracy charges.[14]

The merger mania of the 1980s certainly enriched raiders, risk arbitrageurs, investment bankers, and a large number of investors, but its overall effect on the U.S. economy has probably been far less positive. It remains to be seen to what

extent the consolidation and corporate restructuring in key sectors has strengthened domestic producers against intensifying international competition. The
massive replacement of equity with costly debt is clearly worrisome, for it has
left many firms highly indebted. This problem is by no means confined to the
raiders using junk-bonds. Between 1982 and 1986 the debt-equity ratio of U.S.
corporations rose from 95 percent to nearly 120 percent. With many firms excessively leveraged, they were clearly vulnerable to adverse economic or financial
developments. The large wave of bankruptcies during the recession of 1990–92
was a direct result of debt-laden financial structures. Moreover, takeovers or
restructurings have often involved layoffs of large numbers of workers and elimination of entire layers of management, undermining employee morale and
sharply increasing stress in the work force. Nor can it be good that many firms
tried to defend themselves against possible raids by taking on more debt, selling
off cash-rich assets, or taking other measures to make themselves less attractive.
In general, the takeover craze has led worried managers to focus even more on
short-term payoffs and less on activities needed for long-term competitiveness,
such as spending on plant and equipment, research and development, or job
training.

12.4. The Computerization of Securities Trading

During the bull market of the 1980s the computer transformed the stock market
in ways unimaginable even a few years before. In many ways, Wall Street was a
perfect target for computerization. Nowhere else is fast and accurate information
so important. And few products in other industries are as intangible. Wall Street's
goods have no physical reality; instead they are nothing but electronic messages
which can be flashed along wires from one computer to another.

The spread of computers in the stock market concentrated on two areas. One
was the trader's desk, where they supplied price information from many different
markets and allowed investors to identify trading opportunities in seconds. The
other was the stock exchanges themselves, enabling those to handle surging
trading volume and linking the trading floor more tightly to brokerage houses.
These uses of computer power accommodated a surge in trading volume at the
New York Stock Exchange (NYSE), the largest U.S. stock market, from a daily
average of 32.2 million shares in 1979 to 165 million in 1989. In addition,
integrated computer networks made it easy to execute huge trades in a matter of
seconds across the globe, thus adding considerably to the global integration of
financial markets.

As in many industries, the use of computers on Wall Street tended to become
a self-feeding process. Traders and investors tried to find ways to use the available computing and software capacity by developing new uses which eventually
required even more powerful computers. The most important boost to this process came from several computer-driven investment techniques which are com-

monly referred to as *program trading*. These techniques linked the stock market to the financial futures market in Chicago, where investors have been able to trade stock-index futures since 1982. Those futures contracts give investors the right to buy or sell a basket of stocks, usually those based on the Standard & Poor 500 index, at a specified future date and at a predetermined price.

Several types of program trading, which together comprise on average about 10 percent of the trading volume at the NYSE today, became popular in the mid-1980s.

• In so-called *stock-index arbitrage* investors exploit price differentials ("spread") between the cash value of the S&P 500 index and the futures contract based on that index. Depending on the spread, traders can lock in a risk-free rate of return by selling or buying futures and at the same time doing the exact opposite with the underlying stocks. Their arbitrage gain is certain no matter in which direction the stock index moves before the futures expire. Between 1984 and 1986 this guaranteed return exceeded the yield on three-month Treasury bills by an average of 4 to 6 percentage points per year. At least $15 billion is currently available for stock-index arbitrage.

• Another technique is *index-funded arbitrage*. Institutional investors have put more than $100 billion into funds that track indexes, most often the S&P 500. One effect of this trend has been that the institutions owning such index funds increasingly trade huge blocks of stocks all at once. In addition, they can boost their returns by exploiting the disparities between the futures and stock markets. For example, if the price of the futures contract drops below the cash value of the index, they can sell their stocks and replace them with cheaper futures.

• A third technique is *portfolio insurance*, which now covers about $60 billion in stocks. This practice allows institutions to hedge against losses by selling futures short during a declining market. Losses in the stock portfolio are then offset by gains in the value of the short positions.

Supporters of these techniques stress their usefulness for traders and institutions. They also point out that program trading has made the stock market much more liquid, allowing investors to conduct huge trades on a continuing basis. Critics complain that program trading has transformed stocks into commodities which are traded randomly in large volumes based on computer signals. The corresponding increase in price volatility undermines the confidence of small investors, since it makes their investments much more uncertain. The concentration of program trading in the hands of a few dozen institutions invites market manipulation, especially in trading strategies to increase the spread between futures contracts and underlying stocks.[15] Finally, the various program trading techniques tend to exacerbate stock market trends. This was brutally illustrated during the crash of October 1987, when computer-driven selling of stocks played a major role in the 508-point decline of the Dow Jones.

12.5. The Stock Market Collapse and Its Effects

During the bull market the Dow Jones index rose from a low of 776.42 in August 1982 to a high of 2722.42 in August 1987. In that five-year period the value of U.S. stocks increased by $1.9 trillion. This spectacular rise is itself one of the reasons for the subsequent crash. At its peak in late August 1987 the stock market was clearly overvalued. Stocks were trading at three times the reported book value, twice the postwar average. And the price-earnings ratio, another traditional valuation measure, had risen to 23, far above the postwar average of 14.5. In that context the crash must be seen as a necessary, though violent, market correction to a more reasonable price level.

The first sign of trouble appeared during 1986, with the SEC investigations of a tight network of key market players who shared secret information on pending deals, used each other to hide their respective stock positions from public disclosure, and provided mutual financial support for their respective deals (see section 12.3). Those insider-trading scandals illustrated both the dramatic erosion of business ethics and the dominance of speculative and market-manipulating practices on Wall Street. Even more worrisome, they pointed to a profound contradiction. On the one hand, the efficient operation of financial markets requires that all interested participants are given easy and speedy access to accurate data. In this sense information is a public good par excellence. On the other hand, information has increasingly become a commodity which is produced, packaged, and sold for profit like any other gigantic "information factory." The scandals showed how a group of powerful players managed to monopolize crucial information for its own gain. Public confidence was shaken, because the rest of the investment community saw itself at a major disadvantage in comparison to these insiders.

The negative impact of the scandals proved to be only temporary however. In January 1987 the stock market staged a major rally in response to bullish forecasts by key analysts. This prompted other forecasters to abandon their more pessimistic predictions, and the stock market exploded in the kind of speculative craze so typical for the last stage of a bull market. In less than nine months the Dow Jones jumped from 1920 to 2720. But during the same period certain important developments began to take shape which ultimately set the stage for the crash in October. These reflected deepening contradictions in the world economy.

The dollar-devaluation strategy agreed to by the leading industrial nations in the Plaza Agreement of September 1985 soon began to create a host of problems. For one, it reawakened inflation fears, as the lower dollar pushed up U.S. import and global commodity prices. In addition, private capital inflows into the United States slowed down when foreign investors began to worry about losses from a devaluing dollar. Finally, the dollar devaluation soon threatened to get out of hand, since the currency speculators dominating the foreign-exchange markets dumped dollars in the expectation of future declines. In February 1987 the Group of Seven therefore decided that the decline of the dollar had gone far enough. In this so-called Louvre Agreement the central banks committed themselves to keeping the key currencies within specified target zones through coordinated intervention (see section 8.4).

The problem with this approach was that the preceding devaluation of the dollar failed to improve the U.S. trade deficit during 1987. Even though U.S. exports began to revive, imports continued to rise as well. Because they were at the same time now more expensive, the trade deficit actually rose month after month. This deterioration put more downward pressure on the dollar, which the Federal Reserve had to counter by letting domestic interest rates move sharply upward. It was precisely this combination of rising interest rates and continuously larger trade deficits that finally killed the bulls on Wall Street.

By early September 1987 the stock market began to react to bad news on trade and interest rates with sharp declines. A week before the crash, investor confidence was hit hard by the announcement of yet another record trade deficit and by talk in Congress of restricting the tax advantages from takeovers. During that week the Dow Jones fell by 90 to 100 points on several days. Then a simmering dispute between Germany and the United States over exchange rates heated up during the weekend of October 17–18. Unusually harsh statements by Treasury Secretary Baker on network television led many to believe that the disunity of the G-7 would hurt the dollar and drive up already sharply higher U.S. interest rates even more. Skittish traders and investors, including a sizable number of those managing Japanese funds, decided on that Sunday to pull more money out of dollar-denominated securities.

When the NYSE opened on Monday, October 19, it was immediately hit with a wave of sell orders. Several factors allowed that early sell-off to rage out of control. Fidelity, the nation's largest mutual fund, unloaded $1 billion in stocks to limit losses from an unusually aggressive investment strategy. An excess in sell orders forced a trading halt in eight of the thirty stocks making up the Dow Jones, creating confusion as to the actual position of that index. This and the growing delays in executing sell orders only fed the panic. Futures fell even more rapidly, so program trading, in particular portfolio insurance, sent "sell" signals for the underlying stocks into computerized execution systems. Block traders, who work for Wall Street's biggest brokerage houses, began to sell positions as quickly as they were forced to buy them from customers. Specialists, charged with assuring orderly market conditions for specific stocks and thus supposed to act as the buyers of last resort, were simply too small to stop the stampede. By the end of the day 600 million shares, about four times the normal daily trading volume, had been sold on the NYSE. The Dow Jones had fallen by 508 points, or 22.6 percent.

This collapse came very close to destroying the intricate techno-structure of the stock market in a mountain of losses, order backlogs, and trade suspensions.

The next day, October 20, the stock market opened with the Dow Jones moving 200 points higher, an extraordinary gain. But soon sell signals from program traders began to drag stock prices down again. Panic resumed, and in less than two hours the Dow Jones plunged by more than 230 points. Trading in key stocks, all options, and most futures contracts had to be halted. Specialists, who had lost two-thirds of their $3 billion in buying power the previous day, withdrew from the market. Many banks, frightened by the steep decline in the value of stocks serving as collateral for loans to securities dealers, simply refused to extend more credit and started calling in major loans. This squeeze threatened many securities firms. But then, during the lunch break, a coordinated crisis-management strategy saved the market from a potentially catastrophic financial "meltdown." The turnaround began with a sharp rebound of the relatively thinly traded Major Market Index (MMI) contract, made up of a basket of twenty blue-chip stocks and the only futures contract still trading at that point. In addition, the Federal Reserve promised troubled institutions unlimited liquidity to cover losses while driving both interest and exchange rates aggressively lower. Bankrupt traders were taken over by other investment banks. Many corporations initiated major buy-back programs to support the prices of their stocks. These measures rallied the market, and at the end of the day the Dow Jones closed 186 points higher.[16]

The immediate aftermath of the crash was filled with predictions of imminent doom. These turned out to be premature. Even though consumers retrenched somewhat, the slowdown in growth proved to be minor and temporary. By early 1988 the U.S. economy was once again accelerating toward an annual growth rate in excess of 3 percent. This strong performance was due mostly to the stimulation from lower interest and exchange rates in response to the crash. Finally, the U.S. trade deficit began to shrink significantly, and the positive effects of booming exports spread across U.S. industry. The economies of Western Europe and East Asia also managed to digest their respective stock market crashes quite well, not least in response to selective stimulation policies. With lower stock prices reducing the costs of takeovers, the merger wave actually accelerated after the crash. Stock prices recovered to a new Dow Jones record of 2999.75 in July 1990, and have since risen to 3600.

Why did the crash seem to have only a limited effect on economic growth? Of crucial importance in this regard was the ability of active crisis management to halt the panic and to contain its ripple effects. Moreover, the very speed of the collapse, even though utterly shocking at the time, may actually have limited its impact. Had the decline been more gradual and taken weeks or even months to unfold, its effects on investor psychology and financial conditions may well have been that much more severe. Also, the dimensions of the crash need to be put into proper perspective. Basically, the stock market returned to a level it had held only nine months earlier. Direct losses from the crash, while certainly heavy for many market participants, did not sink any major financial institutions.

Impressed by its apparent lack of immediate impact on what they like to call the "real" economy, most economists have tended to downplay the significance of the crash of 1987. Yet it is a mistake to reduce that stock market collapse to a one-time event whose only effect was to deflate paper values. The autonomy of fictitious capital vis-à-vis the industrial economy is, after all, only a relative one. When $1 trillion (a million millions) in U.S. equity values is wiped out in a single day, there are bound to be some effects on the rest of the economy.

U.S. regulators understood quite well how close the crash came to causing major damage to the economy. Various reports that analyzed the forces behind the market collapse called for substantial changes in market practices and regulatory constraints to prevent the recurrence of such a collapse. Yet these lofty words have not been followed by decisive action. So far there has only been some tinkering with existing arrangements. The most important regulatory initiative to date has been to impose so-called *circuit breakers*, which automatically stop all stock-related trading when prices or volume reach predetermined limits. There is ongoing debate as to whether computer-driven program trading should be restricted by larger down-payment requirements and price limits for stock-index futures. New rules have been put into place which require specialists to beef up their capital and clarify the behavior of brokers and dealers during a market panic. Another set of proposals aims at the overhaul of reporting requirements and settlement procedures to bring the archaic structure of the stock exchanges in line with the new world of computerized trading.

But this regulatory effort has been hampered by deep ideological splits and turf battles between competing agencies which face different constituencies and conflicting pressures. Until now the Commodity Futures Trading Commission has blocked the SEC's desire to extend its jurisdiction to financial futures. Until that question is resolved, possibly in favor of the SEC, efforts to bring those tightly linked markets under one regulatory umbrella to assure better coordination will not succeed. However, agreement among the heterogeneous constituency of policy-makers is a necessary but not sufficient condition of effective market regulation. The regulators have yet to figure out what kind of regulatory framework we need to deal with the challenges of increasingly linked, globalized, and computerized financial markets. The investigations of the crash by the SEC, Congress, and the Brady Commission have begun to address this question. But their subsequent proposals have barely scratched the surface of this vital issue.

The crash also undermined the financial position of U.S. industry. For one, companies have found it more difficult to tap the stock market for funds, as shattered market confidence caused public offerings and new stock issues to shrink to a trickle after the crash. Moreover, sharply lower stock prices left many firms with a smaller equity cushion against losses. At the same time, high debt levels have increased the likelihood of precisely such losses by saddling many firms with large fixed costs (debt-servicing charges) that consume much of their cash flow.[17] The extent of this problem is best illustrated by the fact that during the past decade U.S. corporations retired nearly $500 billion in equity while piling on almost $1 trillion in new debt. Much of that debt was used to finance takeovers, buyouts, and recapitalizations. Ironically, the crash itself at first exacerbated that imbalance between equity and debt. Lower stock prices made many firms more attractive takeover targets. During 1988 mergers, acquisitions, and leveraged buyouts exploded to a new peak in size and numbers. But soon thereafter, in early 1989, the mountain of debt began to cave in under its own weight.[18]

When the leverage binge of the 1980s started to wind down, its first victims were the junk-bonds. That market, after growing by another $40 billion (to $200 billion) because of the postcrash rush of takeovers in 1988, has suffered serious erosion ever since. First came a series of defaults, including such large borrowers as Integrated Resources (June 1989) and Campeau (September 1989). When nervous investors tried to unload their junk-bonds, the lack of liquidity in that market led to sharp price declines. The correspondingly large increase in yields, with the risk premium for low-rate junk-bonds, over U.S. Treasury bonds rising from 4 percent in mid-1988 to 6 percent a year later, discouraged new issues of junk-bonds. That, in turn, slowed merger activity considerably. The bankruptcy of Drexel in February 1990, marking the end of an era, gave the market another jolt. On top of that, new regulations (e.g., the thrift bailout law of 1989, a directive by the National Association of Insurance Commissioners in April 1990) forced certain financial institutions to rid themselves of junk-bonds. Even though severely shaken, the junk-bond market survived its dramatic price collapse of 1989–91 and may have actually been strengthened by crisis-induced restructuring. Now that Drexel and its price-manipulation strategies have been stopped by government sanction, the market is likely to become more diversified and its trading practices more prudent.

Another early victim of the imploding debt pyramid was leveraged buyouts (LBOs), in which a group of investors put up a little money of its own and borrowed the rest to buy the assets of a company. By 1986 LBOs made up a quarter of all deals on Wall Street, involving such well-known firms as Borg-Warner, Allied Stores, Macy's, Beatrice, and Storer. Besides representing one of the most effective defenses against hostile raiders, LBOs also became popular as big money-makers. Because of the small equity cushion investors could earn a return of up to 50 percent a year and earn large capital gains when they took the firm public again after a few years. Investment banks received hefty fees when the newly private firm sold off pieces of itself and then again later from underwriting its reentry as a public company. In 1988 LBO activity became a frenzy in response to much lower stock prices and gradually declining interest rates, culminating in the $25 billion buyout of RJR Nabisco by Kohlberg Kravis Roberts. But the market, in typical fashion, rewarded the innovators and punished the crowd that followed the pioneers. During 1989 many of the more recent LBOs began to stagger under their heavy debt burdens, adding to the woes of the junk-bond market and hurting banks which had invested heavily in LBOs. The Fed responded by increasing its supervision of banks that were heavily involved in LBO financing, and the SEC required more extensive disclosure by buyout participants. In typical "too little, too late" fashion regulators reacted only when there were clear signs of trouble. At that point of excess their restrictions may have the unintended effect of reinforcing the pullback and thereby making matters worse.

Finally, the entire infrastructure that Wall Street had built between 1982 and 1987 to support the bull market was forced into retrenchment after the crash. Since then, securities firms have found each of their income sources eroding. First, a mass withdrawal of individual investors from the stock market reduced brokerage commissions. Then income from underwriting activity shrank, as public offerings and new stock issues dried up. In early 1989 junk-bonds and LBOs started to experience major difficulties, which put a damper on merger activity. Faced with massive excess capacity in most of their departments, Wall Street firms have laid off thousands of people, sharply lowered bonuses, and cut back operations.

That process of reorganizing and streamlining is bound to change Wall Street in significant ways, probably leading to further consolidation, greater specialization, and eventual deregulation to allow merging of investment banks and commercial banks. Yet these changes are only the beginning of a much broader transformation of our financial system in coming years. The stock market collapse in 1987 illustrated, among other things, that the structure of securities markets has become outdated in the "brave new world" of computerized trading. In that sense, the crash itself must be seen as a crucial moment in an ongoing transition toward a financial system based on "electronic money" (see also section 9.4).

The crash served as a useful reminder that Keynes's words quoted at the beginning of this chapter hold true today. Fictitious capital, more than any other form of capital, has a tendency toward excess. Yet its rapid expansion by euphoric speculators cannot fully escape the reality of industrial stagnation. Its primary driving forces—expectations, interest rates, and the financial maneuvering of market-making institutions—are all vulnerable to shocks and reversals in response to underlying structural imbalances. It is no surprise that the crash was triggered by pressure on the dollar's exchange rates and by rising interest rates. The destabilizing movements in these two prices of money, which directly affected the valuation bases of stocks and other forms of fictitious capital, reflect the limits of an ultimately unsustainable global growth pattern that is based on large U.S. budget and trade deficits. The build-up of fictitious capital during the bull market involved heavy use of debt backed by increasingly overvalued stocks, so the crash left financial institutions and industrial corporations suddenly exposed to the burden of excessive leveraging. Pressed by large debt-servicing charges, both sets of firms now have to trim costs rigorously or face the threat of extinction. By the time this squeeze is over, possibly not for years, restructuring will have run full course. In that sense the crash served as a useful reminder that the intricate, unstable, yet ultimately self-correcting relationship between fictitious capital, interest-bearing capital, and industrial capital is the most important force in the long-wave dynamic of our economic system.

Part V

The International Dimension of Money

13

The Challenges of Global Integration

Until recently the United States had a relatively closed economy which dominated the rest of the world. Under those conditions Americans enjoyed a great deal of independence. Today, however, our economy has become much more open and is no longer dominant. We consume more than we produce, we depend on continuous inflows of foreign capital, and we are now the world's largest debtor nation. All of this has caused a significant loss of autonomy. Our policy options are much more constrained now than they were a generation ago.

We cannot count on the willingness of foreign savers to finance our twin deficits forever. In the meantime, we are running up huge debts to the rest of the world which we have to service. Annual interest payments on our foreign liabilities already approach 1 percent of the United States' GNP. That sum absorbs nearly half of our average growth capacity each year, thus significantly lowering the income gains we can keep for ourselves. As if this were not worrisome enough, we have used a major portion of that foreign debt for activities that do not make our economy more productive in the long run, predominantly excess consumption and a bloated military apparatus. In order to avoid further erosion we need to lower budget and trade deficits substantially.

The "peace and prosperity" days of the Reagan era are long gone. Bush's first term was marked instead by war and recession. At the end of his presidency the budget deficit amounted to $300 billion, while our trade deficit was still a sizable $70 billion. After the bipartisan Budget Accord of October 1990 the Democratic leadership in Congress and President Bush once again became locked into partisan posturing. Neither side was willing to negotiate a shift in spending priorities from the Pentagon, entitlements, and socialization of private losses (e.g., thrift bailout) to productive investments in our infrastructure and labor force. Thus the new Clinton administration has had to start the necessary adjustment toward lower twin deficits from a worse position. How painful that process of change will be depends on other countries, especially their needs for scarce capital competing with ours and their ability to absorb an eventual U.S. trade surplus.

Recessionary conditions in Europe and Japan have already slowed the U.S. recovery and have made further improvements in our trade deficit that much harder to come by.

Today the world economy has become so integrated that no nation, not even the United States, controls its own fate anymore. It is not that our capitalist system has suddenly turned global. The process of its internationalization has been going on for decades now, especially since the end of World War II. What has become different in recent years, however, is the pace and scope of this process. The degree of global integration has taken a leap forward, to the point of creating a qualitatively different kind of economic environment. We are moving toward a *new global economy*.

Capital accumulation has an inherent tendency to expand beyond national borders in all of its aspects—whether exchange, production, or finance (see sections 13.1 and 13.2). But these activities do not expand in a coordinated fashion. Nor does their global extension necessarily result in balanced growth. On the contrary, the dynamic of the world market is anything but stable. In this context it is important to understand that there are certain structural features which are unique to the global economy. These posit a special challenge to economists and policy-makers alike. For example, the international marketplace lacks a fully developed state apparatus. Contract enforcement and stabilization policies depend instead on voluntary agreement between different nation-states. Foreign trade is different from purely domestic exchange in that it involves a second transaction, the conversion of one currency to another, with its own price, the exchange rate. Thirdly, the global economy must have a mechanism for symmetric adjustments and even development if it is to grow properly (see section 13.3).

When we discuss these special features it becomes clear that the prevailing arrangements pertaining to acceptable forms of world money, exchange rates, and capital transfers are central to the global economy. A properly designed international monetary system can be a vehicle for greater integration of different national economies and balanced growth. But such a system can also become a major source of instability, especially when it fails to adjust to underlying structural changes and allows its institutional foundations to become obsolete (see section 13.4).

13.1. The Growing Importance of Foreign Trade

Capitalism tends to expand all of its activities beyond strictly national boundaries. In this section we analyze how this tendency manifests itself with regard to foreign trade, an activity with ancient roots.[1] Economists have long recognized that trade plays a crucial role in the economic development of societies. At first, however, this realization had a decidedly one-sided bias. During the seventeenth century and the first half of the eighteenth century it was widely believed that the national welfare of a country depended on its ability to increase its gold and silver reserves by running continuous trade surpluses. This early theory, known as *mercantilism*, regarded exports as the principal source of wealth. By favoring policies to protect a nation's balance of trade, which included import restrictions as well as the direct use of military force as an instrument of external economic relations, the mercantilists in effect provided an ideological cover for colonialism. Conquest of foreign lands opened up markets in which the manufacturers of the colonial power could undersell local artisans and at the same time secure cheap access to valuable raw materials. Clearly this theory was a far cry from the notion of free and equal exchange among a "community" of nations.

Toward the end of the eighteenth century mercantilism came under attack from the followers of Classical Political Economics, who built a strong case in favor of free trade.

• David Hume (1752) showed that it would be virtually impossible for any country to accumulate precious metals for long. Gold inflows in the wake of persistent trade surpluses would engender inflationary pressures and make that country less competitive. The opposite effects would be felt in the deficit country, where the loss of precious metals would force the least efficient producers out of business and cause wages to decline. Eventually its remaining producers would find their competitiveness improved. That specie-flow adjustment mechanism described by Hume soon became the standard justification for the use of gold as world money.[2]

• Adam Smith (1776) argued that foreign trade benefits all nations doubly by allowing them to rid themselves of a surplus for which there is no demand at home and to receive something in return for which there is demand. Unrestricted exchange among nations would allow the productive powers of each to grow in parallel, thus making their commodities cheaper and their markets larger.

• David Ricardo (1817) made possibly the strongest argument in favor of free trade. His theory of "comparative advantage" powerfully demonstrated the benefits of specialization that result from trade. In his famous example, Portugal is assumed to produce both wine and cloth more cheaply than England. Yet it still benefits Portugal to concentrate most of its resources on wine, where its relative cost advantage is greater, and to import cloth from England despite the higher price it has to pay. This specialization would allow both countries to move resources from inferior to superior uses and to maximize everyone's welfare.[3]

Even though free trade has been the orthodox view among most economists since the days of Smith and Ricardo, in practice very few countries actually followed this prescription. By and large only the strongest industries in the most powerful countries favored such a policy, and in each case they did so to exploit their competitive advantage over others. Between the Congress of Vienna (1814–15) and World War I (1914–18) only Great Britain, then the world's dominant economic power, was firmly committed to free trade; other economies remained strongly protectionist. The United States converted to free trade only after it emerged as the new superpower at the end of World War II, and other industrial countries gradually followed suit.

It was thus more than a century before theoretical dogma actually became widely practiced policy. Protectionism persisted for so long because weaker producers feared loss of market share to more efficient foreign producers and lobbied for help from their respective governments. That fear was certainly justified. To the extent that the leading producers used more modern production technologies, which tended to be more capital-intensive, they enjoyed major unit cost advantages over more backward competitors, provided they operated at high volume. Those economies of scale often outweighed the lower wages typically found among less-advanced competitors in weaker countries. Moreover, the benefits of free trade described by Smith and Ricardo hinged centrally on the assumption of full employment, for only under those conditions would trade-induced specialization be able to redirect labor from less efficient areas to more productive uses. But the downward stickiness of prices and wages, coupled with the fairly immobile and heterogeneous nature of labor resources, made full employment an exception rather than a normal state of affairs. The displacement of domestic output by more efficient foreign producers could then easily add to unemployment, which is why most governments were willing to limit imports.

The postwar conversion of industrial nations to free trade had its roots in the 1930s, when protectionism got out of hand and trade wars erupted, with disastrous results for peace and prosperity. That experience left deep scars. After World War II the United States used its leadership position to build a new international economic order based on open markets. The liberalization of monetary and trading arrangements (e.g., Bretton Woods, 1944; GATT, 1947; the Marshall Plan, 1947) proved to be very successful and convinced many developed countries to abandon protectionism. The creation of the European Economic Community in 1957, followed by the return of its members' currencies to full convertibility a year later, made the economies of Western Europe more integrated while spurring more direct investment by U.S. firms there. That revival of Europe facilitated further reductions in trade barriers under the Kennedy Round (1962–67) and the Tokyo Round (1973–79), each of which lowered tariffs between industrial nations by more than 30 percent. The phenomenal expansion of world trade after World War II was possibly the most important driving force behind the unprecedented global boom of the 1950s and 1960s (see Figure 13.1).

The spread of free trade did not extend to the less-developed countries after most of them had become independent nations between the late 1940s and the early 1960s. Centuries of colonial rule had left those LDCs with a very small industrial base, backward technology, and a few commodities (primary raw materials, agricultural products) as their primary source of export earnings. These

Figure 13.1. **Trade as a Stimulus of Growth in the Postwar Boom**

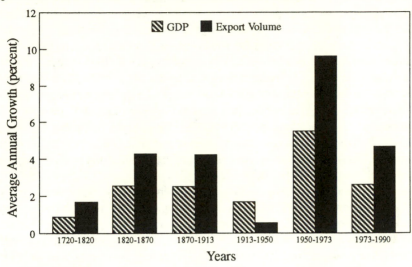

Source: Council of Economic Advisers, *Economic Report of the President*, 1992, Washington, DC, p. 194.

Notes: Bar with rules is GDP growth; black bar indicates export volume growth. The first period GDP is for 1700–1820. Data are for France, Germany, Italy, Japan, the United Kingdom, and the United States. Not all countries are represented in the first two periods.

conditions made them extremely vulnerable. Giving superior foreign producers unrestricted market entry would have made it impossible for those countries to build up their own industrial base. This justified protecting "infant industries" until they could compete with existing foreign producers. The additional investment generated by such protection should more than compensate for the higher costs paid by domestic consumers in the meantime. Moreover, because of massive under- and unemployment commonly found in LDCs, the creation of protected high-cost industries did not draw workers away from more useful occupations or increase the competition for labor but instead put people to work who would otherwise have produced very little at all. A third justification of protectionism by LDCs derived from their adverse terms of trade on the world market. These countries typically had to export cheap raw materials, whose prices often lagged behind those of other products, to pay for imports of the expensive capital equipment they needed for their industrialization efforts. As a result, they suffered more or less inevitable trade deficits and had to ration their scarce foreign-exchange reserves by discouraging imports of consumer goods.[4]

For all of these reasons, many newly independent LDCs ended up adopting a strategy of "import-substituting industrialization," in which the state directly controlled the flow and prices of imports, the allocation of foreign exchange resources, and domestic investment priorities. The combination of free trade among industrial nations and import substitution among LDCs worked quite well for both groups as long as the worldwide boom lasted. But during the late 1960s that long expansion came to an end, and the postwar long wave entered into a downswing phase. At that point the United States had clearly lost its position of absolute dominance (see Figure 13.2). Some of that catching-up by other nations is a natural process. The industries of the leader set very tough competitive standards for their counterparts in other countries, and the absence of any serious challengers tends to make them less aggressive over time. But the ability of Germany and Japan to close the gap with the United States had at least as much to do with conscious policy decisions, combining undervalued exchange rates, generous American aid, active state management of industrial investment, and labor surpluses that kept wages low.

As long as a number of countries are catching up with the technologically dominant nation, the world economy is moving toward a better balance. That process is one of even development and is conducive to rapid growth. This was true in the nineteenth century, when Great Britain dominated, as well as under the Pax Americana of the 1950s and 1960s. But once those countries have caught up with the leader, that very equalization tends to create a much less favorable situation. Tensions between the now roughly equal countries mount, prevailing institutional arrangements in the world economy come under a great deal of pressure, and the long wave moves from expansion to stagnation. We could see this turnaround clearly after 1914, when a century of British hegemony gave way to interimperialist rivalries and worldwide depression.

The loss of America's absolute dominance in the late 1960s also led to deteriorating conditions, albeit of a more moderate kind than those of the interwar period. Bretton Woods broke down in a series of speculative runs against the overvalued dollar between 1968 and 1973 (see section 7.1). That breakdown was a watershed event which had major ripple effects in the world economy. President Nixon's suspension of the dollar-gold convertibility in August 1971 was accompanied by measures that were aimed at improving the competitive position of U.S. industry (e.g., temporary import surcharge, dollar devaluation, wage and price controls). Not only did this "New Economic Policy" signal the end of America's free-trade policy, but it also marked the beginning of trade conflicts among industrial nations which have continued to intensify ever since. The U.S. strategy of dollar devaluation and stimulative macroeconomic policies during much of the 1970s (see section 7.3) backfired by spreading inflationary pressures abroad, a process culminating in the oil-price explosions of 1973 and 1979.

The two oil price hikes had profound effects on the world economy. For one, they forced a large number of deficit countries to adopt restrictive macroeconomic policies at the same time. Previously asynchronous business cycles thus became more synchronized, making subsequent downturns (1973–75, 1979–82) global in nature and much deeper. During the early 1980s the volume of world trade suffered its first postwar decline. Moreover, much higher oil prices made

Figure 13.2. **Catching Up of the Other Industrial Nations**

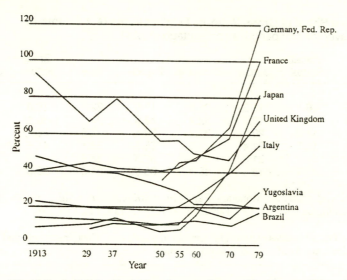

Source: World Bank (1992), *World Development Report*, Washington, DC, p. 21.

Note: Per capita GNP of selected countries as percentatge of U.S. per capita GNP, 1913–79.

most nations a great deal more dependent on trade. The oil producers used a good portion of their sudden wealth to buy high-value imports from the industrial nations for luxury consumption or large industrialization projects. And oil-importing nations had to push exports to pay for suddenly much larger import bills. Table 13.1 illustrates the growing weight of foreign trade during the past three decades in the case of the G-7 nations, with the exception of Great Britain and Canada all heavy buyers of foreign oil supplies.

The trade shares of the major industrial nations seemed to have peaked or at least reached a ceiling in the early 1980s. Much of this apparent stabilization was surely cyclical. In those years, at the bottom of the deepest global downturn since the Great Depression, the GNP figures of the G-7 countries were depressed, even though their trade activity had remained high throughout the recession. But other reasons pointed to a longer-term decline in foreign trade shares, especially when measured in money values rather than in physical volumes. The decade-long global debt crisis (see section 10.1) forced many LDCs to cut imports dramatically and push exports after 1982. This squeeze caused industrial nations to lose valuable export sales, a constraint that hurt the U.S. economy, with its traditional ties to Latin America, in particular. In addition, the export efforts of the LDCs created deflationary pressures in global commodity markets which have kept foreign trade revenues lower than they would have been in a normal price environment. As part of this global commodity deflation, oil prices have

Table 13.1

Trade as a Share of Gross National Product in the G–7 Countries
(annual averages for period; as percentage of total)

Years	United States	Japan	Germany	France	Italy	Great Britain	Canada
1962–66	6.7	16.3	28.9	19.9	22.3	28.0	31.5
1967–71	7.7	16.7	32.7	22.6	24.7	30.1	35.8
1972–76	11.8	20.2	37.7	30.4	32.6	38.1	40.2
1977–81	15.5	21.4	43.8	35.3	38.1	41.5	47.2
1982–86	14.0	21.5	50.4	37.3	35.6	41.7	48.1
1987–91	13.6	15.9	48.6	36.0	31.3	39.8	45.5

Source: International Monetary Fund, *International Financial Statistics Yearbook 1992*, Washington, DC, Country Tables 111, 112, 132, 134, 136, 156, 158.

Notes: Trade includes exports and imports of goods only. Cost, insurance, and freight to point of destination (cif) included in price quoted.

declined during the past decade. They are therefore no longer the factor they were ten years ago, either for consumer nations or for producer nations. The exceptionally steep decline of Japan's foreign trade share between 1987 and 1991 may surprise readers, given that country's worldwide reputation as a first-class trading nation that accumulated consistently large surpluses. We should note here that during the same period Japan's leading firms expanded their direct investments overseas in dramatic fashion, which has made their global trading and production strategies less reliant on exports from the homeland.

The share of exports and imports in the national product of industrial nations may have declined somewhat in recent years, but these activities continue to be of decisive importance for economic growth and development. We could actually argue that in important ways most nations have become even more dependent on trade since the early 1980s. What has changed over the past decade is the underlying pattern of world trade, the result of qualitative shifts which do not show up in aggregate quantitative measures. A much larger portion of trade today involves barter between cash-poor countries or transactions within a globally organized underground economy, neither of which are measured in official trade statistics. Even more rapid has been the growth of product flows between subsidiaries of global production networks. Such intracompany trade is not reported accurately, because much of it involves nonmarket "transfer pricing" for tax evasion purposes as well as "free-enterprise zones" in which multinational corporations benefit from regulatory and cost advantages that keep the value added there artificially low. The strategic importance of this kind of trade is illustrated by the success of newly industrializing countries, especially those in

East Asia, which managed spectacular growth rates during the 1980s by relying on .iigh import levels (as hosts of multinational corporations) and aggressive export-led growth strategies. Probably the most important qualitative shift in trade patterns after 1982, however, was the growing dependence of the world economy on U.S. trade deficits as America assumed the role of the world's "consumer of last resort."

Reagan's macroeconomic policies helped to spur a global recovery. First they increased domestic demand through a combination of tax cuts, large increases in military spending, and a more relaxed monetary policy. That stimulation then spilled over to the rest of the world, as U.S. imports grew rapidly in the wake of a strong dollar appreciation of 74 percent between 1980 and early 1985 (see section 8.2). This allowed other industrial nations and many LDCs to turn their economies around by pushing exports to the United States, still the world's largest single market. The growth pattern emerging during that recovery marked a new stage in the long-run tendency toward global integration. It has tied national economies together as never before and has enabled them to continue the export-led growth strategies they had developed over the previous two decades. In recent years even the U.S. economy has come to rely much more on exports for its own growth. America's need to export will become even more pronounced over the next decade, when it has to service a huge foreign debt. As a result, all industrial countries continue to rely heavily on trade as a source of growth.

But herein also lies the root of a profound contradiction. The more countries come to depend on export-led growth, the greater may be their temptation to abandon the principles of free trade in order to protect their market shares against increasingly intense competitive pressures. We already see signs of movement in this direction. Over the past decade there has been a rather dramatic proliferation of different nontariff barriers, such as import quotas, "voluntary" export restrictions, antidumping charges, application of discriminatory product standards, limited access to domestic distribution networks, export subsidies, or government procurement policies that favor domestic contractors. A growing number of influential economists and policy-makers now speak of "managed" trade based on international market-share agreements or argue in favor of a "strategic trade policy" in which the government assists trade-dependent sectors with great potential for monopoly rents or positive externalities. Whether justified or not, their recommendations concerning trade policy are prescriptions for creeping protectionism.[5]

This trend may have already played its part in the aforementioned decline of foreign trade shares among industrial nations after 1987 (see Table 13.1). If left unchecked, in coming years it could feed trade conflicts among the world's leading economic powers and could cause the eventual disintegration of the global economy into antagonistic trading blocs, a development last witnessed, with disastrous results, during the 1930s.

• In the face of rapidly shrinking market shares the U.S. commitment to free trade has weakened in recent years. Especially vulnerable sectors (e.g., textiles, steel, cars, semiconductors) have been granted protection.[6] The Omnibus Trade and Competitiveness Act of 1988 contained tough provisions to retaliate against countries that engaged in what are deemed to be "unfair" trading practices, especially Japan. Within weeks of his inauguration President Clinton indicated to both Japan and the European Community that he intends to take a much tougher stance that his predecessors on a variety of long-standing trade conflicts. Bilateral treaties with our neighbors (Canada, Mexico) and other close allies (e.g., Israel) have gained in importance. Our commitment to multilateral negotiations has at the same time shown signs of erosion which contributed to a three-year delay in the Uruguay Round and almost prevented its successful conclusion in December 1993. The United States created a free-trade zone with Canada and Mexico, the North American Free Trade Agreement. This trading block may eventually extend to the rest of Latin America and the Caribbean.

• Japan has become an economic superpower by organizing its key industries around exports. This has involved active state intervention to establish investment priorities, the supply of long-term funds to firms at favorable terms, very integrated and concentrated industrial structures, a highly motivated work force that enjoys a great deal of job security and retraining facilities, the famed "just-in-time" inventory management, a strong emphasis on product development, factory automation, and aggressive price policies to undersell foreign competitors. By pushing exports, Japanese firms can obtain a sufficiently large production volume to exploit the economies of scale and learning curves associated with their typically capital- and knowledge-intensive production methods. As a result, they operate at comparatively low unit costs. This in turn facilitates further expansion of their world market shares—a veritable virtuous circle. At the same time major segments of its economy are protected from import penetration. This neomercantilist strategy has made Japan the target of pressure from other industrial nations, especially the United States. Apart from making limited concessions to open its own domestic markets, during the 1980s Japan has invested aggressively abroad in order to bypass protectionist measures against its products. Lately Japan has directed much of its trade, direct investments, and aid to other Pacific Basin countries, a significant step toward greater integration of that region.

• Germany is the world's third major trading power. Most of its trade is with its neighbors, making it the most important trading partner for the other European economies. Reunification in 1990 greatly reinforced its position of dominance in Europe. At the same time, the European Community is now moving toward a greater level of economic and political integration, seeking to create during the 1990s a single-market economy that is comparable in size to the United States. Germany's strong postwar commitment to free trade may prevent a more integrated EC from turning into a "Fortress Europe." At the same time, Germany has always been driven eastward. The collapse of communism in

Eastern Europe has given it the chance to do so as an economic power rather than as a military power. Meanwhile, the combination of high unemployment and political turmoil across Europe has made governments there much more susceptible to protectionist pressures.

Ever since the end of Bretton Woods in the early 1970s the interplay of competition and cooperation between the United States, Japan, and the EC has assumed growing importance. But as long as the cold war persisted, it was overshadowed by the confrontation between East and West. With the disintegration of the Soviet empire this forty-year era of geopolitics has come to an end. Even though the United States once again managed to affirm its leadership role in the Gulf War, helped by a coalescence of interests among industrial nations in favor of preventing Saddam Hussein from controlling OPEC, the projection of military power no longer suffices in the emerging geoeconomic era. When President Bush spoke of a "new world order," he did not spell out how to prevent economic warfare among three roughly equal trading blocs, or what to do about the deepening crisis of economic development in much of the rest of the world. In this context the stalemate of GATT's Uruguay Round in the early 1990s serves as a useful reminder of the dangers ahead.[7]

13.2. The Internationalization of Industrial Capital

So far we have discussed the global economy solely as an amalgam of national economies that have become increasingly linked to each other through the growing volume of trade among them. But there is another aspect to global integration which operates beyond the confines of nations—the multinational corporations (MNCs). These firms run production facilities in a number of countries and increasingly look at the entire world as their "home" market. The trend began when British firms moved abroad in the late nineteenth century, followed by some American firms in the 1920s. But the MNCs are predominantly a postwar phenomenon, taking off during the 1950s with a huge wave of direct investments by U.S. firms. From the mid-1960s onward we can see European and Japanese firms internationalize rapidly in order to catch up with their U.S. and U.K. competitors. In the 1980s they had become large enough to attack the once dominant American competitors on their own home turf (see Table 13.2).

During the past decade MNCs of all industrial nations have greatly expanded their international operations in order to penetrate foreign markets, to bypass potential or actual protectionist barriers, to gain access to natural resources, and to tap cheap labor supplies. Today a few hundred giant corporations straddle the world, controlling a third of all production and an even larger percentage of trade. They exert a pervasive influence in the global economy. This process of internationalization has extended to financial capital, as banks followed their corporate customers abroad. Large money-center banks have set up branches across the globe and in the process have created the so-called Eurocurrency

Table 13.2

Direct Investment Flows

Year	U.S. direct investment abroad	Foreign direct investment in the U.S.
	(in billions of dollars)	
1975	14.2	2.6
1976	11.9	4.3
1977	11.9	3.7
1978	16.1	7.9
1979	25.2	11.9
1980	19.2	16.9
1981	9.6	25.2
1982	2.4	13.8
1983	0.4	11.9
1984	2.8	25.4
1985	17.3	19.0
1986	28.0	25.1
1987	38.6	40.1

Source: U.S. Department of Commerce, International Transactions *Survey of Current Business*, T. 2, p. 78, June 1988.

market. We shall discuss the profound implications of this private banking network further in sections 13.3 and 13.4; here we confine ourselves to the globalization of production.

Orthodox economy theory has little to say about the emergence of MNCs as a dominant factor in the global economy. For neoclassical economists the world is characterized largely by perfect competition between firms subject to nonpolitical market regulation. Assuming free access to markets and resources as well as diminishing returns to scale, small units can always be shown to coexist effectively with large units or even to displace them. In this framework the growth of MNCs can only be attributed to "imperfect markets," which allow stronger firms to use their power at the expense of weaker rivals. The problem with that view is that it presents this process as an exceptional situation rather than as one which is inherent to our economic system.[8]

There are several reasons why the growing concentration and centralization of industrial capital is embodied in the structure of capitalist economies. The marketplace is a battlefield of competition on which weaker firms are eliminated or taken over. Either of these outcomes allows the more efficient survivors to expand their market shares. Moreover, production equipment and methods tend to become more capital-intensive over time. Thus requiring ever more capital in advance as well as increasingly large minimum output levels to spread the overhead, modern production technology eventually moves beyond the reach of small firms. Significant economies of scale also exist in the crucial areas of research and development, labor supply, and access to finance. For all these reasons, most industries will eventually come to be dominated by a few firms ("concentration") which employ ever-larger amounts of capital ("centralization").

The internationalization of industrial capital is a direct by-product of this tendency. With the possible exception of the United States, no domestic market is large enough today for the scale of operations that many industries require. Firms can escape this limitation by selling abroad. This may be done through exports from a national base, but usually it is better to produce directly in those foreign markets. Subsidiaries of MNCs avoid transportation costs, bypass protectionist barriers that confront exporters, use local managers with intimate knowledge of market conditions there, often hire workers who are cheaper and/or more easily disciplined than are those at home, may maintain close relations with government officials of the host country, and usually receive large subsidies from governments that are eager for MNC investment in their countries. All of these advantages allow them to outperform purely national firms that rely on exports. In addition, the support of their parent company in terms of research and development, finance, marketing, and other vital resources usually gives the subsidiaries of MNCs a dominant monopoly position in their local markets.

Multinationals can provide significant benefits to the host countries in which they locate. Their investments bring much-needed capital and foreign exchange which are usually in short supply. They often use more advanced technologies and better-trained managers, thus promoting the diffusion of technical know-how and managerial skills. They also tend to create relatively high-paying jobs and build up a network of local suppliers. Many countries, especially the LDCs, lack indigenous capital to produce on a similar scale to the MNCs. Or they rely too much on state-run production, which usually is less efficient. Their governments therefore tend to welcome foreign firms. The global debt crisis, in particular, has greatly intensified the competition for MNC investment. Countries now bid against each other to offer multinationals the most attractive inducements. This may include a favorable tax status, unlimited repatriation of profits, free access to otherwise rationed foreign exchange for needed imports, direct government subsidies, infrastructure investments (e.g., roads, railroad lines, ports, industrial parks), and prohibition of trade unions or strikes.[9]

Even though the MNCs may well benefit some countries in which they have invested heavily, their overall record is much more ambiguous. They can also have very problematic consequences.

• The corporate giants have concentrated a large portion of their investments in a few countries which already enjoy high incomes (e.g., industrial nations, OPEC countries, newly industrialized countries) while bypassing the majority of LDCs. In that way they have exacerbated the steadily widening gap between poor nations and rich nations.

• Often, especially when investing in LDCs, those firms will obtain a monopoly position in local markets. This enables them to keep prices high and to extract large profits. In sectors in which domestic producers are already active the MNCs have often used their superior technology and financial resources to drive those smaller competitors out of business. The jobs destroyed in that process may outnumber those created by new investments of MNCs.

• With 75 percent of their spending located in industrial nations where labor tends to be scarce and capital plentiful, the MNCs favor capital-intensive technology. Unfortunately, they tend to use the same technology in LDCs, for it is precisely that control over more advanced production techniques which gives them a competitive advantage over local producers. But this kind of technology is not appropriate for developing economies, where labor is abundant and capital is in short supply. The use of capital-intensive technology in LDCs only serves to aggravate the structural imbalances that are commonly found there. Apart from generating little new employment, it will absorb scarce supplies of skilled workers. Most of the costly capital equipment will have to be imported, so there will be large outflows of foreign exchange. Capital-intensive technology typically creates sophisticated and expensive products which are aimed at the world market or local elites and are not accessible to the majority of poorer people. With processes and organizational methods imported from the parent company, the subsidiaries of MNCs are unlikely to build up much local capacity to carry out these functions. For all of these reasons, the actual contributions of MNC investment for LDCs tend to be much less positive than its proponents suggest.

• The MNCs will often move much of their profits out of a country rather than reinvest them in the domestic economy. This is especially true for LDCs where investment opportunities are limited. Such repatriation of profits has a direct impact on a country's balance of payments, money supply, and level of economic activity. The considerable power that MNCs wield as a result can be used to influence government policy.[10]

At a time when many governments and international agencies (e.g., IMF, World Bank) have come to regard MNC investments as the panacea for all kinds of problems in the developing countries, it is worth keeping these negative effects in mind. Most troubling is that the international division of labor created by MNCs tends to promote uneven development across the globe as well as within certain regions. Take, for instance, the internal hierarchy of those firms. Strategic planning occurs at headquarters, often situated in the world's major cities (e.g., New York, London, Tokyo). Regional management tends to concentrate in the capitals of host countries, where political influence is most easily exercised. Production usually takes place in urban areas with special resource advantages (e.g., access to markets, supplies of skilled labor, transportation facilities). This organization benefits the centers of economic development while weakening the peripheries. Once a particular site has been chosen by a few

MNCs, others are likely to follow in order to take advantage of the markets and services created in the process. Certain places, such as São Paulo or Nairobi, have thus developed into major industrial centers out of which MNCs supply large regions. Such geographic concentration of capital promotes stagnation in the rest of the region, where no significant foreign investment takes place and where the market penetration of MNCs forces local producers out of business. Moreover, these industrial centers attract millions of people in search of better employment, most of whom end up in marginal activities and slums. Anyone who has ever experienced the chaos of overgrown Third World cities and the emptiness of the surrounding countryside knows the utter folly of uneven development.

MNCs can even harm the countries in which they originate. The case of Great Britain illustrates this point quite clearly. The world's dominant economic power for more than a century, that country now has a smaller gross national product than Italy. After having built a huge empire that stretched across the globe, its industries took control of resources and markets in the colonies. British firms were not only the first ones to turn global, but they have remained the most multinational to date. No other country, with the possible exception of the Netherlands, has a higher proportion of industrial assets abroad. This presence in overseas markets has helped British firms to maintain their competitive position. At the same time, however, their foreign investments have surely eroded the industrial base of the domestic economy. Great Britain's remarkable deindustrialization in the past few decades has left the country much weakened.

A similar argument, albeit on a smaller scale, can be made for the United States. Over the past twenty-five years American businesses have invested heavily abroad, especially in newly industrializing countries where labor costs much less (e.g., Mexico, Taiwan, South Korea, Singapore). This has enabled them to remain competitive. Whereas the U.S. share of world manufacturing exports declined from 17.1 percent in 1966 to 11.7 percent in 1986, foreign subsidiaries of U.S. firms managed to raise their share from 8.0 percent to 9.8 percent during the same period. But what is good for individual companies may not benefit the economy in the aggregate. The multinationalization of U.S. business has accelerated the deindustrialization of our economy, with manufacturing declining from 30 percent of GNP in 1966 to 21 percent in 1986. Many high-wage jobs in that sector have been lost, replaced by low-wage and low-productivity service-sector jobs. In recent years U.S. multinationals have also begun to shift more of their research and development activities abroad. This worrisome trend is bound to erode our technological capacities and has caused further loss of high-wage jobs. Direct investment abroad by U.S. firms has worsened our trade deficit. It replaces U.S. exports, and MNC subsidiaries ship a considerable portion of their output back to the United States. Those intracompany transactions respond much less to exchange-rate fluctuations, so our large trade deficit has persisted despite a much lower dollar. Finally, the job elimination by U.S. multinationals and generous tax breaks for their foreign income have caused a substantial revenue loss and have thus contributed to our huge budget deficits.[11]

During the past decade we have entered a new phase in the internationalization of industrial capital. It has become increasingly common for goods to be produced in several countries all at once. Companies break down the entire production process into distinct units that require different resource mixes. These can then be located so as to optimize available resource supplies. Labor-intensive assembly, for example, may be moved to low-wage countries (e.g., Mexico, Malaysia), while high-tech design centers may be placed near the top engineering schools (e.g., Silicon Valley, Boston, New Jersey). The interdependent units are coordinated in a way that takes account of their respective size differentials. A component plant, for example, may have a much larger volume capacity than the factories it supplies and can therefore produce for a number of them at the same time. Combining automation, standardization of components, and computer-aided management, these global production networks can easily be retooled to adjust the output mix to changing market conditions.

That trend toward globally integrated production is likely to accelerate. One reason is the growing importance worldwide of intangible services, which lend themselves particularly well to electronic transmission via computer networks and communications satellites (e.g., financial services, business services). Nearly half of today's global trade volume already occurs between subsidiaries of one and the same company. In those intracompany transactions the MNCs may often set nonmarket prices, in order to move their profits from high-tax countries to low-tax countries. Besides minimizing their overall tax burden, firms can use such *transfer pricing* for a variety of other reasons—to reduce the costs of profit-sharing plans with local unions, to bypass selective credit and exchange controls in certain countries, to inflate reimbursements under government contracts, to circumvent domestic price regulations, and so forth. To the extent that those intracompany transactions operate outside direct market constraints, they probably respond much less than normal trade to exchange-rate movements and to other adjustment efforts aimed at correcting external imbalances. All of this implies a growing ability of MNCs to evade, undermine, and manipulate government policy, which poses a major threat to the sovereignty of nation-states.

13.3. Unique Features of the World Economy

Standard theory typically looks at the world economy merely as a quantitative extension of the domestic economy. Keynesian macroeconomic models treat foreign trade as just another component of aggregate demand which is added on to the other spending categories. The neoclassical equilibrium model applies the same optimization rules and free-market principles to trade as it does to all other activities (see note 3). The so-called monetary approach, a version of Monetarism, holds that capital flows between countries automatically equilibrate exchange rates in accordance with purchasing power parity in the goods markets and with uncovered interest parity in the assets markets.[12]

These models ignore the fact that the whole is more than the sum of its parts. The world economy has several unique qualities which are lost when one simply adds up all the national economies into a global aggregate or applies only those behavioral rules that are found in domestic markets. These special features of the global economy are a challenge not only for the economist who tries to theorize about the inner workings of our economic system but also for the government official who is in charge of stabilization policy.

1) Mobility Constraints. Each type of activity—exchange, production, credit financing—tends to expand beyond national boundaries. The form of capital that corresponds to those activities—commodity capital, industrial capital, financing capital—thus has its own global drive. Their respective globalization tendencies are in many ways intertwined and mutually conditioning. For example, trade allows surplus nations to accumulate reserves of gold or foreign currencies with which they can finance asset acquisition abroad—whether as lenders to deficit nations or through direct investments by their producers. Trade also engenders competition over world market shares, which motivates firms to invade the national market turf of their overseas competitors. Multinational companies and transnational banks expand together, facilitating each other's globalization.

This interdependence of activities and forms of capital also exists within any domestic economy (see our discussion of monetary circuits in section 2.3), but its articulation is different in the global economy. There we may encounter specific constraints that do not exist on a national level, and these may impact directly on the international extension of other activities. Take, for example, labor, which is crucial to industry's productive capital. On a national level that resource is highly mobile, because humans can move around freely within their country and do gravitate toward centers of industrial activity in search of jobs. On the international level labor lacks this kind of mobility, because of cultural and language barriers, a natural human attachment to one's homeland, and government restrictions on immigration. Within the global context it is therefore the other component of industrial capital, fixed capital goods, which has to make up for labor's immobility and to move around more freely.[13] Another constraint found only on the international level is the use of government measures to inhibit the free flow of goods and services across borders. The actuality or prospect of such protectionism may induce foreign firms to prefer direct investment over exports as a means of market entry. Finally, money flows between countries may be restricted when currencies are not fully convertible or governments limit profit repatriation by MNCs. Restrictions of that kind hamper the globalization of capital.

2) The Absence of an International State Authority. Orthodox economists generally treat the market economy as if it were entirely divorced from any political regulation. Thus they ignore the fact that the very existence of markets depends on the protection of private property and on the enforcement of contracts by a nonmarket authority. Within national economies that authority is the state, which has the exclusive juridical right to enforce contracts and to maintain social order by physical coercion, if necessary.

Even though direct state control over the actions of individual agents was greatly reduced during the transition from mercantilism to liberalism in the late eighteenth century, the state still plays a major role in regulating national economies. It tries to counteract capitalism's tendency toward economic crisis. It also makes certain that the distribution of resources between classes and regions remains reasonably equitable. The tools used for these objectives, specifically macroeconomic stabilization policies and the redistributive "welfare state," first emerged in the United States during the Great Depression in the form of Roosevelt's New Deal—a reorganization of the U.S. state apparatus which corresponded to the transition from a competitive to a monopolistic accumulation regime. Similar political adjustments occurred in other industrial nations after the end of World War II. In much of Western Europe those reforms went even further than they did in the United States, especially in terms of integrating a more highly organized working class as an active political force.

These different aspects of state intervention reflect the fact that certain political conditions must be established and maintained for any economic system to function properly.[14] If those conditions of stabilization and equity do not exist, then individual entrepreneurship withers away, unrest mounts, the hegemonic system of social organization breaks down, and a growing amount of resources must be devoted to the essentially unproductive provision of coercion to maintain public order. This is as true for Communist economies, as demonstrated by the collapse of the Soviet Union, as it is for capitalist economies. From that perspective Reaganomics can be seen as a dangerous experiment, because it eroded the stabilization capacity of the U.S. government and led to much greater inequity in our society.

The global economy lacks the kind of state power that is capable of enforcing contracts, stabilizing economic activity, and assuring equitable distribution of resources. There is, for example, no fully enforceable system of international law to settle disputes between nations with binding force. If one country decides to appropriate the assets of another country (e.g., Allende's nationalization of Chile's copper mines that were owned by American firms in the early 1970s), it has a legal right to do so that cannot be challenged. Nor do we have policy-making institutions on the international level with the de jure authority to override the sovereignty of nation-states. Hence the way in which the world functions economically, tending toward growing integration, does not correspond to the way in which the world is organized politically, namely as an amalgam of juridically independent nation-states.[15]

As long as economic activities within states far outweighed those between states, the absence of any international political authority endowed with full powers of coercion did not matter much. International economic relations could still be handled by bilateral agreements and treaties between national governments acting on behalf of their respective private-market agents. Yet even at that point states did not interact with each other as autonomous and equal entities, did not form a "community of nations" guided by common interests and mutual respect. Instead, their interactions were based on the projection of power by a few dominant countries and on the subordination of the rest of the world into colonies. The imperialist powers (e.g., Great Britain, France, Germany) managed their relations with each other through a fairly unstructured and frequently shifting system of alliances.

That system proved to be inherently unstable. It invited repeated warfare between the major industrial nations whenever their interimperialist rivalries intensified to the point of destroying the consensus for peaceful coexistence—the Napoleonic Wars of the early nineteenth century, the war between Germany and France in 1870–71, the war between Japan and Russia in 1904–19, World War I, and World War II. The bilateral and ad hoc nature of that international political structure also proved to be increasingly inadequate for global economic management. This structural weakness exploded into the open with full force during the early 1930s, when Great Britain could no longer act as "international lender of last resort," the gold standard collapsed, key countries (e.g., Germany, Argentina) defaulted on their international debt obligations, and trade wars erupted as the various colonial empires turned into protectionist blocs.

That situation changed after the end of World War II, when the United States used its position of absolute dominance to create a new international order. Under its leadership, industrial nations set up a complex set of multilateral institutions to manage economic relations between them.[16] This revolution in the political organization of the world economy included the establishment of a stable international monetary system (Bretton Woods 1944), regulations that governed trade (GATT 1947), mechanisms to transfer capital from surplus to deficit countries (e.g., IMF and World Bank 1945; Marshall Plan 1947), and the creation of supranational federal authorities that promoted economic integration (e.g., the European Economic Community 1957). Together, these institutions for the first time constituted an international state body with the capacity to subordinate national governments. Membership in relevant agencies involves acceptance of its general principles, adherence to its decision-making procedures, and compliance with its agreements. Failure to meet these obligations can lead to sanctions. Those international agencies thus can pressure national governments to adopt certain measures regarded as necessary or to refrain from specific policy options deemed undesirable. A classic case in point is the large number of agreements in the course of the global debt crisis between certain debtor nations and the IMF involving detailed austerity programs (see section 10.1). As those illustrate quite clearly, nowadays the de facto powers of international agencies frequently outweigh the de jure powers of supposedly sovereign nations.

The capacity of subordination does not apply equally to all nations. The make-up of these international agencies has always reflected the global power hierarchy. The IMF and World Bank, for example, function on the basis of voting rights, which are tied to the respective size of member countries. The United States is the one country with veto power in these organizations. The United States, Great Britain, France, Germany, Japan, and Saudi Arabia (in the case of the World Bank also China) are represented in the IMF's governance by their own executive directors. The Security Council, the only body of the United Nations with the power to sanction member countries, has five permanent members (the United States, Russia, China, France, and Great Britain), each of which can veto resolutions it does not like. GATT lacks any enforcement power. It is more a forum of discussion to negotiate rules and codes of behavicr, which then have to be put into effect by agreements between countries based on the principle of reciprocity. A subtle bias in GATT against developing countries manifests itself in the limits on their textile exports under the Multi-Fibre Arrangement or their difficulties in obtaining meaningful concessions from industrial nations during different tariff rounds.

3) The Two-Step Nature of International Transactions. Within a national economy market transactions are relatively simple, involving in each case a transfer of goods, services, or financial assets in return for a monetary payment. This is not the case for market transactions in the global economy, whether they involve trade, direct investments, or credit financing. All of these require an additional step for successful completion, namely the changing of one currency into another at a predetermined rate of exchange. It does not matter whether that exchange of monies occurs before or after the primary transaction, or whether it is done by the buyer or by the seller. What matters is that this second step complicates international economic activities a great deal.

• Some currencies may be subject to exchange restrictions (e.g., the French franc in early 1980s) or may not be convertible at all (e.g., Russian ruble until recently) in which case it will be difficult, if not impossible, for holders of that currency to conduct any kind of transaction with someone from another nation. This problem is still widespread today, for many governments in developing countries or noncapitalist countries impose exchange controls to limit capital flight or nonessential imports.

• Even when currencies are fully convertible, they may be useless to foreign recipients. An Austrian exporter to Brazil, for example, will have no use for cruzados unless he also wants to buy something from Brazil or intends to invest there. Because the cruzado is a soft currency which is frequently subject to sudden devaluations, the exporter will surely prefer to be paid in Austrian schillings. But the Brazilian buyer may not have any schillings available. In order to minimize these difficulties, both sides are better off conducting their transaction in an internationally accepted medium of exchange. Nations have thus come to choose what constitutes world money by multilateral agreement. This choice is fraught with difficulties, for each possible form of international currency has its own distinct shortcomings (see chapter 14 for more).

• Then there is the additional complication of price risk. Companies that do business abroad have to face the possibility that currency prices may fluctuate quite dramatically within a short period of time. If those prices move in the wrong direction, losses can be significant. Firms do have the means to protect themselves against that risk, either in the forward foreign-exchange market or in the currency futures market. But these hedging devices involve their own transaction costs and price risks. Nor do they shield corporate managers from added uncertainty when they decide whether to export their products or to set up production facilities directly in the targeted foreign country. If the currency of that country is expected to fall relative to the domestic currency, a firm might find investing there more attractive than exporting. Should the movement of exchange rates reverse itself, however, this overseas investment will suddenly become less profitable relative to exports. Freely fluctuating exchange rates thus complicate decision-making for multinational firms, which may hamper their investment activity. From that point of view, it is better to maintain relatively stable exchange rates through coordinated market intervention by central banks. But this kind of price manipulation may not allow exchange rates to accurately reflect underlying differences in competitiveness and inflation rates between countries. In the end, such market distortion may exacerbate external imbalances whose subsequent correction will therefore take longer and be more difficult to achieve.

4) External Constraints and Adjustment Policies. Every economic agent faces a monetary constraint—the need to earn income in order to afford spending (see section 2.1). Of course, the supply of loanable funds in the credit system relaxes this monetary constraint temporarily by allowing borrowers to spend beyond their current income. Access to credit supplies differs greatly among different agents. Large corporations, for example, have a much easier time attracting funds from others than do small businesses or middle-class households. The federal government occupies a particularly advantageous position in the credit markets, because it possesses the unique powers of taxation and money creation. But even that privileged agent cannot escape the burdens of excessive indebtedness. Eventually every borrower, including the federal government, will reach a debt limit and will be forced to cut back excess spending.

In the international economy the monetary constraint takes a peculiar form, applying to an entire national economy. If a country runs a trade deficit with the rest of the world, it will use up foreign exchange reserves. Those reserve funds consist of internationally accepted forms of money. They may have accumulated as a result of past surpluses, or they may have been borrowed from sources of funds abroad (e.g., other governments, private banks, international lending agencies). Persistent and large deficits will exhaust a country's reserves and send its foreign debt soaring. Eventually this position becomes untenable, and the country has to reduce its balance-of-payments imbalance.

There are several ways of coping with such an external constraint. The besieged country may try to reduce its trade deficit by protectionist means, creating barriers against imports and/or subsidizing exports. Such direct government intervention is generally opposed by orthodox economists. Protectionism may also violate international trade rules of GATT and is often quite costly. Import barriers invite retaliation by other countries, remove competitive pressures on domestic industry to become more efficient, and hurt consumers by limiting their product choice while forcing them to pay higher prices.

As an alternative to outright protectionism, most governments prefer to shift productive resources from domestic markets to exports. This usually involves a two-pronged policy strategy of reducing consumption and helping to make domestic producers more competitive. Lower consumer spending will reduce imports on its own. Policy-makers typically pursue this goal by cutting public spending.[17] With sales declining at home, many firms will try harder to sell abroad. Should exports fail to increase proportionately at the same time, however, public-spending cuts typically will increase unemployment instead. For this reason governments often combine doses of fiscal restraint with currency devaluation in order to make exports cheaper and imports more expensive. They may also try to lower business costs by restraining wages through legally binding guidelines. Orthodox economists prefer a less direct and interventionist attack on wages, namely, weakening the bargaining power of workers by allowing higher unemployment. It takes less time to cut consumption than to increase output, so some rise in unemployment is usually unavoidable in the wake of fiscal restraint, even with lower exchange rates.

Such adjustment policies run counter to the basic logic of Keynesianism. If countries face large external imbalances as they approach their capacity limits, they may have to abandon full employment as the principal policy objective. Nor can a single country stimulate domestic growth if its main trading partners adopt deflationary policies at the same time. In that situation, doses of policy reflation typically end up triggering rapidly rising trade deficits which eventually force a policy reversal. This external constraint has been the political ruin of many left-leaning governments that try Keynesian policies after election victories, as illustrated by Great Britain's Labour government in 1974–75, by the Carter administration in 1978–79, by Germany's disastrous attempt to act as "locomotive" in 1980, which eventually drove the Social Democrats from power, and by Francois Mitterrand's dramatic switch to austerity in 1983.

An even more problematic situation arises when a large number of countries adopt deflationary adjustment policies at the same time. This was precisely what happened in the aftermath of OPEC's price hikes in 1973 and 1979, which caused trade deficits of oil-importing nations to explode. Their simultaneous austerity policies made subsequent downturns (in 1974–75 and 1981–82) globally synchronized and therefore considerably deeper. Another danger in this context is that currency devaluation, a key ingredient of any adjustment program, may get out of hand if several countries with strong trade ties to each other undertake such a step in short order. In that case the devaluations cancel each other out. Countries may then be tempted to push their currencies even lower. Such "currency wars," a new form of protectionism, plagued Western Europe in the mid-1970s and Latin America during much of the 1980s. Their impact on prices made it more difficult to bring inflation under control. Given these difficulties, it is no surprise that the creditors' strategy for dealing with excessively indebted LDCs has failed to resolve the global debt crisis. The IMF's simultaneous application of stringent adjustment programs in so many countries has made it much more difficult for most of them to overcome their external constraint and has led industrial countries to lose key export markets.

 5) The Problem of (A)symmetry and (Un)even Development. The success of adjustment programs in deficit countries depends on their ability to increase exports. Only then will they find their external constraint relaxed and the deflationary effects of such a restrictive policy on domestic demand offset. But this condition can only be satisfied for the system as a whole if surplus countries are willing to import more and to export less. This they can do by increasing public spending and by allowing higher wages. Rising costs and consumption spending would inevitably reduce their surpluses while facilitating improvements in the trade position of deficit countries. In that way the adjustment process will be symmetrical, with surpluses and deficits being corrected in a balanced fashion. Under these conditions of even development the world economy as a whole will likely enjoy more rapid growth.[18]

In practice, however, international economic relations have been characterized by asymmetrical adjustment and uneven development. Most surplus countries have traditionally refused to play their part in the process. It is not difficult to see why. Symmetrical adjustment would require of them measures, such as higher wages, that are bound to increase business costs and to hurt profits. Domestic industry, which usually has a powerful influence over policy-making in those countries, will therefore often lobby against overly reflationary policies. Moreover, government officials tend to regard trade surpluses as a sign of economic strength and are therefore not inclined to eliminated them voluntarily. Why should they act otherwise? Export-led growth has proved to be the most effective strategy for rapid industrialization, as illustrated in recent years by Japan and other East Asian economies. By accumulating foreign-exchange reserves, surplus countries become net suppliers of funds to other nations. This leaves them in a politically more powerful position than deficit countries. Because international lending agencies (e.g., IMF, World Bank, BIS) depend on contributions of surplus countries for most of their own funding, they have traditionally placed most of the adjustment burden on deficit countries. As long as surplus countries refuse to set aside their short-term national interest, that situation is unlikely to change.

Instead of participating in symmetrical adjustment, surplus countries have preferred to lend their foreign-exchange reserves to deficit countries. These loans earn extra income, which adds to the accumulation of foreign-exchange reserves. They also make it easier for lenders to continue their trade surpluses, since borrowers will often use the credit to buy their products. The international credit system, which transfers funds from surplus countries to deficit countries, consists of different channels. Some of those funds come directly from governments in the form of aid grants, concessionary loans, or export-financing. A more indirect channel is the aforementioned international lending institutions to which surplus countries supply funds and from which deficit countries draw funds. Since the early 1970s the most important transfer mechanism has been the Euromarket, in which transnational banks (TNBs) have acted as financial intermediaries between surplus and deficit countries.

These international credit channels are no substitute for symmetrical adjustment processes that are designed to make the world economy better balanced. On the contrary, they are in effect allowing both surplus and deficit countries to maintain their respective external positions. Moreover, they do not necessarily help chronic deficit countries to close their development gap. A substantial amount of borrowed funds are not targeted toward productive uses.

Each mechanism for capital transfers has its problem. Foreign aid by the industrial nations, which in the past has often proved to be useful in the developing countries, lacks a strong domestic constituency in donor countries and has fallen victim to repeated cuts. Nowadays it has slowed to a trickle in many cases, often replaced by military assistance. Export-financing secures big contracts for the industries of the creditor country, but the large-scale and expensive projects it helps to fund do not necessarily benefit the impoverished masses of the debtor country or create the best kind of infrastructure for economic development there. The same criticism also applies to many of the loans made by the World Bank to the poorest countries. IMF funds to deficit countries are usually short-term, mostly to restore depleted foreign exchange reserves, and tied to rather brutal adjustment policies without much regard for the structural problems of underdevelopment and inequality that caused those deficits to become so onerous in the first place.[19] Because the IMF is controlled by the surplus countries, it has tended to place all of the adjustment burden on the deficit countries. In the current global debt crisis this bias has led the IMF to enforce heavy and multiyear doses of austerity in more than fifty countries, leaving those LDCs in depression conditions and creating a considerable drag on the world economy. That crisis had its origins in a classic case of credit overextension by private banks. For nearly a decade, unregulated Eurobanks had flooded LDCs with loans which they cut off suddenly when Mexico nearly defaulted in August 1982 (see section 10.1).

13.4. International Monetary Arrangements

Limits on activites, the need for an effective international state body, the conversion of payments into an appropriate denomination, the distribution of adjustment burdens, and the problem of uneven development are potential barriers to global integration. They all need to be managed by rules which countries agree to follow. Because international activities are as much monetary circuits as their domestic counterparts are, most of those rules center on regulating money flows between countries—the international monetary system.[20]

1) The Choice of an Internationally Accepted Medium of Exchange. Countries must first agree on what kinds of money to use in transactions between them and on what kinds to keep as reserves for central bank interventions in foreign-exchange markets. Historically we can distinguish several phases in the evolution of world money.

• Until the second half of the nineteenth century the United States and most European countries issued both gold and silver coins. Only Great Britain operated under a gold standard, which it had adopted in 1819. The problem with the bimetallic standard used in most industrial countries was that the legally fixed price ratio of those two precious metals often diverged from the relative market prices. Whenever gold was undervalued at the mint, gold coins would disappear from circulation.[21]

• Between 1855 and 1885 gold output declined slightly, while silver production rose by more than 300 percent. Officially fixed price ratios failed to reflect these output differences, and during the early 1870s the bimetallic standard faced serious difficulties because of the chronic undervaluation of gold. Such imbalance in the supplies of the two principal forms of commodity-money led to a period of tension, which ended with a victory of the "hard money" advocates of gold over the "easy money" protagonists of silver. In 1871 Germany followed political unification with the adoption of a gold standard. This decision added to the demand for gold and destroyed the regional bimetallic standard that had been established by France, Italy, Belgium, and Switzerland in 1865. Finally, the United States ended its seventeen-year suspension of gold payments in 1879 after first limiting the issue of silver coins in 1873 and 1878.

• Between 1879 and 1914 all of the key industrial powers were thus operating on a gold standard. Even though primarily a product of domestic considerations, that standard worked remarkably well on the international level in terms of equilibrating trade balances and capital flows between countries. Orthodox economists (e.g., Frenkel and Johnson, 1976) have argued that this success was due to the automatic and self-adjusting specie-flow mechanism first described by David Hume (see section 13.1). In reality, the international gold standard functioned with a great deal of policy discretion. Crucial in this context were changes in the discount rate by the Bank of England in response to inflows and outflows of

British gold reserves. Because London was the world's dominant financial center, the actions of the Bank of England had an immediate and powerful impact on other countries. When it raised the discount rate, more British surplus capital would be invested at home rather than abroad. When it lowered those rates, capital exports from Great Britain would once again grow faster and increase the world's liquidity.

• Even before its suspension at the very beginning of World War I, the gold standard had increasingly become a sterling standard. Most international transactions were denominated in sterling, and Great Britain was the principal creditor nation at the time.[22] Other countries ended up accumulating large sums of sterling in their reserve accounts, which they could use to settle debts among each other. Gradually, therefore, sterling became an international medium of exchange to supplement gold. Its successor, the gold-exchange standard introduced in the early 1920s, boosted the use of sterling as world money. But that arrangement did not last long. It collapsed in 1931, when Great Britain abandoned its role as international lender of last resort in the face of a global banking crisis and suspended gold payments.

• The Bretton Woods system, set up in 1944, was the first international monetary system based on a multilateral agreement among the leading industrial nations. It was in effect another gold-exchange standard, one which established gold-backed U.S. dollars as the principal form of world money. The system fell apart in August 1971. When foreigners began to lose confidence in the increasingly overvalued dollar, the United States lacked the gold reserves to meet growing reconversion demands from abroad and had to end the gold-dollar link (see section 7.1).

• Since then the international monetary system has evolved into a multicurrency system. The U.S. dollar is still dominant, but German marks and Japanese yen have gradually gained global status as alternative key currencies. This period has also been characterized by new forms of international money. There are the Eurocurrencies issued by private transnational banks in an unregulated network which spans the globe. Although these Eurocurrencies do not, strictly speaking, constitute transaction money, they are a source of "near-money" liquidity and have been able to absorb a growing portion of foreign exchange reserves. In addition, we have seen the first initiatives to create truly international forms of credit-money, most notably the IMF-issued SDRs after 1970 and the European Currency Units (ECUs) introduced by the European Community in 1979. Both are based on a basket of national currencies and are confined to transactions between governments.

2) The Need for Balancing Capital Flows. It is worth noting here that international monetary regimes worked reasonably well whenever strong creditor countries either undertook their own price adjustment or exported part of their surplus abroad. Three examples clearly illustrate this point. In the sixteenth century huge inflows of silver (and, to a lesser degree, gold) from its colonies in the New World caused Spain to experience higher prices first. When that country began to run chronic external deficits, both the inflow of precious metals and inflationary pressures spread to the rest of Europe, where they had strongly stimulative effects. During the gold-exchange standard of the late nineteenth century, the Bank of England maintained a direct relation between gold flows and Great Britain's supply of sterling in international circulation (see above). Bretton Woods worked so well for a while because the United States allowed much of its gold hoard to flow abroad and fed the rest of the world with large supplies of dollars. Within a decade these measures overcame a worldwide liquidity shortage.

This historic record confirms the aforementioned importance of symmetrical adjustment and even development (see section 13.3), which international monetary arrangements have to provide for in order to function well. Unfortunately, the global credit system, as it is currently constituted, does not meet these conditions for stability. On the contrary, once that system came to be dominated by the Euromarket after 1973, it allowed imbalances to build up to dangerous levels. The recycling of petrodollars turned into a classic case of credit overextension, a problem which is endemic to private banking. Easy access to Euroloans allowed deficit countries to delay necessary adjustments until they had taken on too much debt. When Mexico nearly defaulted in August 1982, private banks overreacted once again and cut their LDC loans dramatically. This has made the subsequent global debt crisis more difficult to manage and the adjustment processes of troubled LDCs very painful. Nor have those countries received much help from surplus countries. As long as creditor nations find profitable investment outlets for their foreign-exchange reserves, they are under no pressure to bring down surpluses and to thereby help deficit countries grow out of their problems.

Today's international monetary system therefore suffers from fundamental weaknesses. It prevents timely and orderly adjustments toward better balanced trade patterns. Even worse, given the nature of its capital transfers, the system actually tends to aggravate uneven development. Surplus countries can accumulate more and more financial (paper) assets instead of rewarding their citizens with real goods and services for what they produced. Japan's gap between productivity growth and consumption levels is an especially dramatic case in point here. Private Euroloans and IMF loans to deficit countries are mostly short-term in nature. By and large they do not finance structural investments that may strengthen the productive capacities of chronic deficit countries. Direct MNC investments tend to transfer the kind of technology that is more appropriate for highly industrialized countries than for LDCs. The same is true for export-financing, through which industrial nations secure large foreign contracts for their domestic industries. This bias in favor of excess consumption, capital-intensive technology, and huge construction projects reflects the interests of surplus countries, which use their power as creditors to protect the foreign market shares of their industries. Monopoly licenses for imports and government contracts, which are tied to these international credits, also offer corrupt officials in developing countries ample opportunities for personal enrichment. Crowded out in this collusion of interests are the small-scale and labor-intensive investments that promote local entrepreneurship and allow debtor nations to close their "development gap" from the bottom up.

3) The Determination of Currency Prices. A third feature of any international monetary system concerns the determination of exchange rates. The question is whether currency prices should be allowed to fluctuate freely in response to market forces ("flexible" exchange rates) or be maintained at predetermined levels by central banks ("fixed" exchange rates).

Orthodox economists, especially Monetarists (see Friedman, 1953), generally prefer market determination of currency prices. In theory, at least, such a regime has several important advantages. External imbalances cause counteracting movements in exchange rates, which should restore equilibrium speedily. A balance-of-payment deficit, for example, feeds an excess supply of the country's currency into the foreign-exchange markets. This causes the currency to depreciate. As a result, imports and capital exports decline, while exports and capital imports pick up. The exact opposite sequence occurs with a surplus. Moreover, flexible exchange rates allow for automatic market adjustments in relative prices when the macroeconomic performance standards of different countries change in relation to each other. Fixed-rate regimes typically lack this kind of flexibility. Freed from having to intervene in defense of fixed exchange rates, central banks should also find it much easier to focus on domestic policy objectives.

In reality, however, flexible exchange rates have never worked all that well. During the interwar period some countries pushed their currencies aggressively lower in order to improve the competitiveness of their industries (e.g., France during 1922–26 and again in 1937, Great Britain after 1931, the dollar float in 1933). This practice of "competitive depreciation" reinforced the rising tide of protectionism. Similar currency wars broke out in the 1970s. A second problem has been that the flexible exchange rates have not led to an automatic tendency for the balance of payments to move into equilibrium. Prices adjust more rapidly than do trade volumes, so changes in exchange rates at first have the perverse ("J-curve") effect of exacerbating existing trade imbalances. Moreover, movements in currency prices affect key macroeconomic variables—the level of economic activity, the composition of aggregate demand, inflation rates, interest rates. In light of their powerful impact, central banks have not been able to refrain from manipulating exchange rates as part of their stabilization policy ("managed float"). Finally, currency speculation has been more pronounced whenever exchange rates have been flexible rather than fixed. With the emergence of the Euromarket and currency futures, this activity has come to dominate foreign-exchange markets, often with destabilizing effects. For all of these reasons, flexible exchange rates have only been in force under exceptional circumstances and have never lasted very long.

For most of our history we have operated under fixed exchange rates. Such market regulation has had its own advantages. Most important, it eliminates the aforementioned price risk in international transactions as a source of uncertainty (see section 13.3). As long as gold played a central role in the international monetary system, it made the fixing of exchange rates quite easy by serving as a numeraire on which to base relative prices of different paper monies. The exchange rates of currencies could then be determined by their respective weights in gold. But that price mechanism broke down repeatedly, either due to inflationary shocks in the course of wars (e.g., 1862, 1914) or because of a chronic overvaluation of the key currency that the fixed-rate regime did not correct (e.g., 1931, 1973).

The discussion in this section should make it abundantly clear that stable international monetary arrangements are not easily created and are even more difficult to maintain. When they work, as was the case around the turn of the century or during the postwar boom, they provide the world economy with an institutional framework that is capable of promoting integration and even development. Even then, during periods of relative tranquility, the prevailing features of such a system will often allow structural imbalances to build up which eventually undermine its effectiveness. After the system collapses, it is usually replaced by an amalgam of crisis-management measures which lack sufficient institutional coherence. Such a "nonsystem" of ad hoc and made-do arrangements may not be able to correct existing imbalances or to contain centrifugal forces in the world economy. In that case, pressures will arise for more fundamental reform.

The evolution of international monetary arrangements is rooted in the long waves of capitalist development. Expansion phases have usually depended on major institutional changes which put into place a new order that was capable of stabilizing the world economy. This was surely the case with the introduction of the gold-exchange standard in the 1870s, a process which was completed when the U.S. Congress finally passed the Gold Standard Act of 1900. That same connection was even more evident in the case of Bretton Woods, which laid the foundation for additional reforms (GATT, Marshall Plan, EC). In each instance the new arrangements spurred rapid growth of global trade, pumped large supplies of international liquidity into the world economy, and promoted even development by facilitating the catching-up of other industrial nations. The collapse of prevailing arrangements typically symbolized the end of the expansion phase. Whether we look at the interwar period or at the past two decades, in each case the absence of an effective international monetary system deepened the underlying imbalances that are characteristic of downswing phases—trade conflicts, global debt crises, price instability, and a tendency toward more uneven development.

This pattern suggests that a renewal of worldwide expansion requires major reform initiatives in the area of world money. The creation of a new international monetary system is a vital ingredient in the transition toward a new accumulation regime (see chapter 3). Bretton Woods managed to accomplish this for the monopolistic regime of the postwar period. We now face a similar task for the emerging global accumulation regime. In the next three chapters we shall see why currently prevailing arrangements will not do the job and what kind of alternatives may take their place in the future.

The International Monetary System in Flux

The international monetary system is at the core of the global economy. All other aspects of economic relations between nations derive from prevailing institutional arrangements concerning world money and its circulation. Keynes, during a House of Lords debate in May 1944 on Bretton Woods, put this point succinctly:

> To begin with, there is a logical reason for dealing with the monetary proposals first. It is extraordinarily difficult to frame any proposals about tariffs if countries are free to alter the value of their currencies without agreement and at short notice. . . . In the same way plans for diminishing the fluctuation of international prices have no domestic meaning to the countries concerned until we have some firm ground in the value of money. Therefore, whilst the other schemes are not essential as prior proposals to the monetary scheme, it may well be argued, I think, that a monetary scheme gives a firm foundation on which the others can be built. It is very difficult while you have monetary chaos to have order of any kind in other directions. (Keynes, 1980b, p.5)

Keynes' argument, made on the eve of a new international order for the postwar period, has lost none of its relevance five decades later. The emerging global accumulation regime can only work well with a sound international monetary system.

It is time to heed this lesson. There are many indications that all is not well in this regard. The global distribution of capital flows is clearly out of whack when the richest nation of the world absorbs most of the world's savings and the poorest nations are exporters of capital. Existing institutional arrangements consistently fail to correct balance-of-payments disequilibria between countries and place most of the adjustment burden on the weaker economies. Deregulation of interest and exchange rates has caused those prices of money to fluctuate a great deal. That price volatility in credit and foreign-exchange markets has been a boon for speculators while severely constraining policy-makers.

These signs of trouble are the result of structural weaknesses in the multicurrency system that have evolved since the collapse of Bretton Woods in the early 1970s. Its key features—competing forms of world money, flexible exchange rates subject to intermittent manipulation by central banks ("managed float"), and the mobilization of most capital transfers through a private and largely unregulated banking network—are not conducive to conditions of stability. Nor do they make for a coherent, internally consistent, and well-coordinated system. What we have is actually a "nonsystem," a transitional regime which sooner or later will have to be replaced by a better set of rules.

When we consider what kind of international monetary system may ultimately work best, two sources of knowledge will help—a theoretical understanding of money, and an historic assessment of previous institutional arrangements. Then we can begin to comprehend why each form of world money used so far has had its own unique shortcomings.

We start this chapter by looking at a crucial development of the last few decades, the marginalization of gold, which played such a dominant role for centuries. The last vestiges of commodity-money are thus in the process of disappearing (section 14.1). Yet its replacement, the multicurrency regime we have now, also suffers from fundamental flaws. The currencies of the leading industrial powers—above all, dollars, yen, and marks—may serve as international mediums of exchange. But they do not represent a fully effective form of world money on their own (section 14.2). This structural weakness has been a source of great instability in the global economy (section 14.3). Recent efforts to stabilize this multicurrency system, especially the Louvre Agreement of 1987, are the first steps toward a new regime (section 14.4).

14.1. Gold: True Form of World Money or "Barbarous Relic"?

Control over money has always been crucially important to the exercise of political power. The Pharaohs of ancient Egypt understood this as well as Boris Yeltsin does today. But this source of state rule is fraught with dangers. Many empires have disintegrated as a result of monetary mismanagement, and much of human history has revolved around battles over how to assure stable money as fuel for economic activity and as glue for social agents.

Ever since antiquity, governments have based their legitimacy and power on control over money. In ancient societies this specifically meant preventing private agents from being able to issue their own money, as occurred during the fourth millennium B.C., when the rulers of Egypt, China, and Sumer replaced agrarian money (e.g., wheat, barley, salt, oxen) with money made of metals (e.g., copper, iron, bronze), and again around 700 B.C. with the introduction of the first state-minted coins in Lydia (Eastern Turkey).[1]

Autocratic rulers were able to centralize control over money in the hands of their state apparatus from the very beginnings of human civilization because of the difficulties typically associated with private money creation. Whenever private agents were in a position to issue and use their own money (e.g., farmers growing agrarian products, metalsmiths processing base metals), they gained an essential edge in the marketplace over those who lacked that power. Moreover, the ability to pay for purchases with their own money would often prompt private issuers to generate too much of it. Such excess would frequently feed inflationary pressures, and rising prices tended to undermine social peace. State management of money based its legitimacy primarily on avoiding these difficulties.

All of the major empires of antiquity had leaders who early on set an explicit value for money by specifying exchange rates, metal content of coins, and convertibility guarantees. A classic example was the code of Menes (circa 3250 B.C.), which fixed one part of gold to be equal to 2.5 parts of silver. This bimetallic standard helped to unify Upper and Lower Egypt into one central power and established a long dynasty of Pharaonic rule. Another example was the code of Hammurabi (circa 1745 B.C.), which included a sophisticated monetary stabilization program to finance large reconstruction needs after decades of warfare in Babylon without aggravating already considerable inflationary pressures. The edict of Solon (594 B.C.), an early ruler of Athens, outlawed the debasement of money coins. The next superpower to emerge was Rome, which had switched from agrarian money to metal coins in the fourth century B.C. Debasement of coins a short while later caused an inflationary shock. That disruptive experience led generations of rulers to commit themselves to keeping their coins pure. As a result Rome enjoyed price stability for nearly four centuries, until the death of Tiberius in A.D. 37.

Stable prices and effective management of money played a crucial role in the emergence of hegemonic powers. Yet once an empire was born, the initial discipline waned. Throughout history we see a pattern of powerful nations abusing the privilege of seigniorage by allowing excessive money creation to finance unproductive expenditures associated with the symbols of political rule (e.g., construction of monuments, luxury consumption, military spending). Such mismanagement always produced the same disastrous results—hyperinflation, social unrest, and the eventual collapse of the empire. A good case in point was Sumer, a brilliant civilization emerging along the delta of the Euphrates around 3500 B.C., where centuries of warfare among city-states (Ur, Uruk, Lagash, and others) triggered hyperinflation and the collapse of the kingdom in 2020 B.C. in the wake of a revolution. Another telling example was Alexander the Great, who captured Persia's huge gold hoard in 331 B.C. The eventual transfer of much of that treasure to Macedonia set off violent inflation there and in its wake destroyed the last remnant of the once-mighty Greek empire. Finally, the pattern of abuse found its most dramatic expression in the constant tinkering with the metal content of coins by the emperors of Rome, which began with Nero's desperate debasement in A.D. 64 and ended in the capture of the "eternal city" by invading barbarian tribes in A.D. 476.[2]

The precapitalist societies of antiquity had their own structural limitations and imbalances, which led their political leaders to abandon earlier commitments to responsible money management. Ironically, their very emphasis on the purity of coined money encouraged warfare, because it forced rulers to cope with the chronic scarcity of precious metals by capturing the treasuries and mines of other nations. But large military expenditures and frequent wars proved costly and weakened monetary discipline. Military expansionism among ancient empires was further reinforced by their massive use of slave labor. Since slaves were often literally worked to death, the rate of labor turnover tended to be very high. The state then had to secure a steady supply of replacement workers by invading new territories. The institution of slavery also limited domestic consumption by depressing the wages of "free" citizens. With labor kept artificially cheap, the precapitalist autocracies had a strong bias toward luxury consumption by a tiny class of rich property-owners. Such an unproductive economy provided only limited opportunities to accumulate wealth, prompting widespread hoarding by those with access to money and seizures of private fortunes by the emperors. These confiscatory practices point to a broader problem of monarchic rule in ancient societies where the state apparatus was in the hands of a single person, namely the often-irresistible temptation to abuse state power for the sake of personal enrichment by the leaders. All of these characteristics tended to erode the productive basis of ancient civilizations while increasing the costs of maintaining rule. When monarchs, such as the Roman madman Nero, decided to get out of this squeeze by debasing coins, they ended up eroding public confidence, disrupting the circulation of money, and raising prices.

The fall of Rome in A.D. 476 shifted the center of power to Constantinople, where a new monetary order emerged under Justinian the Great during the sixth century. Byzantine gold coins became a widely accepted international medium of exchange for trade and hoarding purposes. Europe's princes, accepting the gold-based hegemony of Constantinople, struck silver coins, while lesser vassals issued copper and tin coins for local use. Throughout the Middle Ages this monetary pyramid coexisted with barter and agrarian money forms as landlords extracted payments in kind from their serfs. Correspondingly, political rule and economic activity under this feudal mode of production were primarily local in nature (with the exception of Charlemagne's empire during the ninth century). In the last decade of the seventh century, Christian hegemony began to face a direct challenge from a new power which was emerging in the wake of Mohammed's sweeping triumphs. By 690 the Islamic Caliphate had consolidated enough to strike its own gold dinar in competition with Constantinople's bezant and to impose a silver bloc over the territories and trading routes under its control.[3] For the next five centuries the two monetary systems each dominated their own geographic space, while Islamic rulers successfully resisted repeated attacks by Christian armies. During that period the political and military authority of Byzantium declined steadily, challenged by religious competition from the papacy in Rome and by economic competition from Venice. In 1203 the Byzantine order finally collapsed when the crusaders sacked Constantinople.

What followed was a period of great instability. As the Christian princes of Western Europe became kings whose rule extended over entire nation-states, they each struck gold coins to circulate within their domain. Convertibility between the different national coins was limited, and rates of exchange fluctuated. Venice's commercial dominance eventually gave its ducato limited international acceptability during the thirteenth and fourteenth centuries, followed later by the coins of Florence and Genoa.

In the fifteenth century new sources of gold were discovered in Central Europe (e.g., Transylvania, Bohemia). But these supplies soon proved to be inadequate. Moreover, the capture of Constantinople by the Turkish Ottomans in 1453 cut off traditional trade routes from the East. The confluence of these two developments spurred naval expeditions and territorial conquests, as European rulers searched for alternative trade routes and new sources of wealth to plunder—first from the peoples living along the African Gold Coast and then from the Incas, the Aztecs, and the other civilizations of the New World. Those areas provided the bulk of the gold and silver in the sixteenth century. Colombia emerged as a major supplier in the seventeenth century. Large discoveries in Brazil added to gold supplies during the eighteenth century.

This age of "discovery," which culminated in 1492 with Columbus's voyage to America, propelled Spain to a position of global leadership. Its coins dominated international trade for nearly three centuries, even forming the support basis for the U.S. dollar when that currency was first introduced in the 1790s. Although Spain wasted its riches and lost its hegemonic position within a century, this time the abuse of seigniorage had radically different consequences. Whereas the important civilizations of antiquity literally disintegrated in the fires of hyperinflation, the new European nation-states that emerged out of the Middle Ages actually benefited from an influx of precious metals. As global colonial powers they had a substantial amount of foreign labor and raw material reserves to draw from, and cheap access to these resources facilitated an expansion of productive capacity. Moreover, colonialism gave economic activity a new international dimension. The resulting increase in trade provided a much more productive outlet for new money than did the hoards, standing armies, and monumental constructions of ancient rulers. At that point injections of metal money could stimulate more production and trade.

Because of Spain's prodigal spending habits most of the new precious metals brought in from the colonies soon found their way to the rest of Europe, where they helped to create a new commercial bourgeoisie of traders, goldsmiths, and merchant bankers. This infusion of money during the sixteenth and early seventeenth centuries had a powerfully stimulative impact on the continent. It caused a long period of rising prices, which enabled merchants to reap large trading profits and induced artisans to produce more. Once gold began to circulate in large quantities throughout the commercial centers of Europe, much of it ended up with goldsmiths as a store of value. Those then issued certificates against deposits of gold left with them for safe-keeping. The public preferred these paper tokens as a medium of exchange to the rather cumbersome and inefficient gold. As long as the certificates could be turned into a fixed quantity of gold on demand, they also served as a means of payment with which to settle debts.[4]

The goldsmiths soon found that under normal conditions only a fraction of their gold deposits would be withdrawn at any given point in time. This realization led them to issue certificates far in excess of their gold deposits, certificates which they could lend for interest income. Gradually they turned into banks. Their practice of "fractional reserve banking" pumped additional liquidity into the economy. Fed by such a rudimentary credit system, the volume of transactions could expand more rapidly. However, during periods of trouble many goldsmiths/banks faced larger conversion demands, which exceeded their gold reserves. Their inability to meet withdrawals repeatedly touched off financial crises and recessions, during which the level of economic activity was forced back to its metallic core (see section 4.2).

The most important banking centers emerged during the second half of the sixteenth century in the Netherlands, especially Amsterdam and Antwerp, where money issue and banking benefited from free coinage. Dutch maritime and commercial power led to conflicts with Portugal, France, and England throughout the seventeenth century. The Bank of England, it should be noted, was set up in that period to help finance the mounting military expenses of the English monarchs. With the end of the wars of the Spanish succession in 1713 the English pound sterling managed to gain international stature. In 1717 England made gold legal tender, along with silver. In 1774 silver was demonetized. When the rival Bank of Amsterdam closed in 1793, the Bank of England became the dominant financial institution of Europe.

The confluence of merchant capital, artisan production, and gold-based banks laid the foundations for the Industrial Revolution in the eighteenth century. The revolution emerged first in England, where, helped by ample resources (e.g., coal) and rich colonies, conditions for industrialization matured earlier than they did elsewhere. The transformation from mercantilism to industrial capitalism brought with it a greater reliance on international trade, and this in turn required a more stable world monetary system. But that objective was hampered by intense rivalries among European nations. Prolonged warfare fed hyperinflation and social unrest, most notably in France during the 1780s. The end of the Napoleonic Wars in 1815 finally enabled Great Britain to translate economic advantage into political dominance. The British used their hegemonic position to create a new global economic order by putting the pound sterling on a pure gold standard and by abandoning protectionism.[5]

Britain used its dominant global position to impose a "free trade" policy on other nations, both to assure access to cheaper imports and to allow its industries to exploit their competitive edge in the world market. Its success in doing so greatly increased the demand for gold, and by the middle of the nineteenth century the metal was in short supply. That scarcity disrupted economic activity and prompted a search for new supplies. In 1848, just when most of Europe was swept by a major wave of social unrest, California's gold rush began. New sources of gold were also found in Alaska and Australia during the 1850s, followed by the discovery of the largest gold deposits ever in South Africa in 1866. After building up a gold-mining industry in this colony within a few years, Great Britain had assured itself of a steady supply of the money-commodity.

Control over much of the world's gold reserves made it easier for Great Britain to cement its position as the world's principal creditor nation, spending on average about 40 percent (and in some years more than half) of its total investment volume abroad. Because of this incredible propensity for capital exports, unmatched in history, sterling increasingly became used as an international transaction currency. Foreign countries kept both their gold holdings and their sterling reserve balances in London. The Bank of England stood ready to swap currencies and gold on demand within a specified price range and in this way to defend fixed exchange rates. Gold inflows into London enabled the central bank to issue new sterling notes, a significant portion of which British capital exports transferred abroad into international circulation.[6] Gradually, one country after another relegated silver to the status of token money and adopted a gold standard: Germany in 1871; France and the other members of the bimetallic Latin Monetary Union (Belgium, Switzerland, Italy) by 1878; finally the United States in 1879. Even Austria-Hungary and Russia, two heavily indebted and relatively more isolated powers, began to build up large gold reserves.

The international monetary system of the late nineteenth century was hence a gold exchange standard rather than a pure gold standard. At its center was a circuit of gold inflows to London and outflows of sterling. Having been the hegemonic power and key creditor nation for decades, Great Britain had acquired a large stock of assets overseas which earned a steady stream of investment income, equivalent to nearly 8 percent of its GNP each year. It used this income to run a trade deficit which allowed developing countries, such as Argentina or the United States, to earn export income for servicing their foreign debts. With Great Britain's balance of payments the linchpin of a balanced world economy, the Bank of England had a good deal of policy discretion. The central bank regulated Great Britain's capital exports, which supplied the rest of the world with liquidity, by manipulating the discount rate it set on loans to the domestic banking system. After working quite well for thirty-five years, this arrangement collapsed in August 1914, a few weeks after the start of World War I. Shipments of gold to London stopped due to wartime risks, and British banks refused to extend credit, which prevented foreign borrowers from servicing their sterling-denominated debts.

Ironically, Great Britain's earlier triumph in imposing a gold-sterling standard on the rest of the world hastened its downfall as an empire half a century later. The exploitation of its colonies as suppliers of cheap raw materials and as captive markets for its manufacturing products led to revolts against British rule, starting with the United States in the 1770s. Once independent, the former colonies sought to lessen their ties to Great Britain and to diversify their trade relations. Leading British firms were more interested in building a multinational presence than in maintaining a strong industrial base at home. At the same time, after adopting the gold standard in the 1870s, other industrial nations managed to stabilize their domestic economies and to strengthen their productive base. Germany and the United States, especially, accelerated industrialization and improved competitiveness in the last decades of the nineteenth century. By the time Europe went to war in 1914, Great Britain was no longer the undisputed leader of the world economy.

The international gold standard, which had begun to emerge in 1819 and had come into full effect by 1879, functioned well until 1914. Supporters of a gold standard have consistently pointed to this success as proof of the metal's superiority over any other form of world money.[7] Their arguments usually focus on two perceived advantages of gold—its role in the fixing of exchange rates and its enforcement of an automatic adjustment mechanism to equilibrate trade balances between countries.

Since money is essentially national in nature, it is only valid within the country of its issue. Any kind of economic activity that involves agents from two different countries thus requires conversion of foreign money into domestic money. This conversion requirement also applied to gold coins, tokens minted by states solely for home circulation. But the raw material of these coins, gold bullion, did function as an international medium of exchange. It thus represented world money in the truest sense of the word, "the universally recognized embodiment of all wealth," as Marx (1967, p. 142) put it. This global consensus enabled the relative values of different national monies to be expressed in terms of their respective gold weights. Gold thus functioned as the numeraire with which to fix exchange rates.

The international gold standard also contained an automatic adjustment mechanism to correct trade imbalances. Surplus countries experienced net inflows of gold, which allowed both money supply and credit at home to expand more rapidly. This tended to feed inflationary pressures. In turn, rising prices made the industries of the surplus nation less competitive, causing imports to rise and exports to decline. Deficit countries would go through precisely the reverse sequence. Gold outflows forced the money supply and credit activity to shrink.

This reduced economic activity. Once prices (including wages) began to fall, the trade balance would improve in the wake of declining imports and rising exports.

The combination of fixed exchange rates and specie-flow adjustments gave the international monetary system a certain degree of stability, which facilitated the integration of financial markets and the expansion of trade—key factors boosting the world economy around the turn of the century. But these two characteristics of the international gold standard also had their distinct drawbacks. Fixed rates were too rigid and could not adjust properly to reflect underlying changes in the relative competitiveness of different countries. And although the gold standard tended to correct trade imbalances automatically, it did so in a highly destabilizing manner by putting national economies through major inflationary or deflationary shocks.[8] Moreover, the effectiveness of those specie-flow adjustments depended crucially on how rapidly prices responded to changes in the money supply and how sensitively foreign trade reacted to changes in relative money prices. But the monopolization of industry and the spread of forward money contracts (e.g., collective bargaining agreements) increased the downward stickiness of many prices. And the growing integration of national economies made trade patterns gradually less price-elastic. Given those rigidities, deficit countries had to go through increasingly deep and long downturns before their trade balance turned around.

The gold standard also suffered from an inherently limited supply of the money-commodity. Even after all of those discoveries in the middle of the nineteenth century, global gold production actually fell slightly between 1855 and 1885. This relative scarcity prompted the banking system to introduce a variety of new credit tokens (e.g., U.S. greenbacks and national bank notes in 1862–64; checking accounts during the 1880s), which circulated as domestic mediums of exchange. But these money substitutes were still tied to the underlying specie reserves of banks, and that constraint made itself felt in repeated and increasingly violent financial crises (see chapter 4). Concerning international liquidity, the supply of gold eventually proved too limited to finance growing trade and capital flows across the globe. Additional sources of liquidity had to be found. It made sense that these should have come from the leading industrial power. Ever since the Congress of Vienna in 1814–15 Great Britain had dominated the global economy as the world's strongest trading nation, largest exporter of capital, and principal financial center. All of these conditions drew gold to London and injected pounds into international circulation. Other countries accepted that currency as a substitute, because it could be converted into gold on demand.

The international monetary system set up during the 1920s made it even easier to use currency as gold substitute in international transactions. It allowed national currencies to be exchanged with each other directly rather than having to be first converted into gold.[9] Despite this institutional relaxation the gold exchange standard of the interwar period proved to be short-lived. World War I had weakened Great Britain, forcing it to liquidate so many of its assets that its external investment income fell to less than 4 percent of GNP. In 1925 Winston Churchill resumed gold coverage of sterling at the prewar parity. Given Great Britain's short-term debts from World War I and the United States' emergence as the world's leading creditor nation, that ratio clearly overvalued sterling. It could only be put into effect with a massive dose of deflation culminating in the general strike of 1926.[10] Once set, the inherent rigidity of gold-based exchange rates prevented any market correction of that overvaluation.

For a few years the system worked because of large-scale U.S. capital exports which provided European nations with the necessary liquidity to stabilize their currencies and to meet their heavy debt obligations. But although the United States replaced Great Britain as the world's principal creditor, it did not give up its long tradition of protectionism. This limited the stimulative effect of its capital supplies on the global economy. The expansionary monetary policy of the Fed to encourage capital outflows thus came to feed domestic stock market and real estate booms instead. U.S. capital exports dried up in 1928, as Wall Street diverted more and more funds into short-term financing of its bull market. That shift put the British currency under great pressure, especially after France began to convert much of its reserves into gold. The failure of the Kredit-Anstalt Bank of Austria in April 1931 triggered a worldwide panic, which soon led to a massive withdrawal of foreign balances from London. On September 21 Great Britain suspended its gold backing of sterling.

After more than a decade of chaos and disintegration, a unique opportunity presented itself near the end of World War II to create a new global order by multilateral agreement. Previous efforts at international coordination in monetary affairs had always failed (e.g., the 1922 Genoa Conference, the London World Economic Conference of 1933, the 1936 Tripartite Agreement). The Bretton Woods Conference of 1944 marked the first successful effort to regulate the international monetary system through a comprehensive treaty. Its participants, especially Harry Dexter White, of the U.S. Treasury, and John Maynard Keynes, representing Great Britain, had a very clear understanding of the institutional shortcomings that had destroyed previous arrangements. The negotiations, in which the American view prevailed, incorporated many lessons from past failures and led to a new kind of gold exchange standard aimed at avoiding some of the shortcomings of its two predecessors.[11]

• The Bretton Woods agreement set up a powerful central organ, the IMF, to administer a complex system of rules and to provide balance-of-payments assistance to troubled debtor countries. For the first time in history the management of international monetary relations was no longer to be the exclusive domain of governments prone to pursue narrow national interests at each other's expense. Together with the World Bank, the IMF also institutionalized regular capital transfers from surplus countries to deficit countries.

• Bretton Woods introduced a so-called adjustable peg, which allowed otherwise fixed exchange rates to be altered in response to persistent balance-of-payments disequilibria. Such currency price adjustments required consultation with the IMF.

• Finally, Bretton Woods established the U.S. dollar as the new key currency. At the time the United States dominated world trade and production. It also held 70 percent of all gold and foreign-exchange reserves, the result of chronic surpluses during the interwar period. The U.S. government agreed that foreigners could exchange their dollars for its gold reserves on demand at the prewar parity of $35 per ounce, first set in 1934. This convertibility guarantee made the dollar "as good as gold" in international circulation and allowed it to become the unit of account against which other countries could value their own currencies. Once the dollar became universally acceptable world money, America's huge reserve hoard could be turned into a source of global liquidity through orchestrated capital exports. Military commitments abroad, the Marshall Plan, and massive foreign investments all became conduits for transferring dollars overseas in ways that also reinforced U.S. hegemony.[12]

We have already discussed the collapse of Bretton Woods in 1971 (see chapter 7). Suffice it to stress here that the underlying imbalances which led to that breakdown were not only the result of mistaken policies. Their structural roots can be found in the very nature of the gold exchange standard itself: the limited supply of gold; the eventual de facto inconvertibility of the key currency; the inability of a fixed-rate regime based on gold to correct the overvaluation of that currency; the steadily widening balance-of-payments deficits of its issuer. Under these conditions, it was no coincidence that all three gold exchange standards (1879–1914, 1925–1931, 1945–1971) fell apart in a similar fashion. Keynes had called gold a "barbaric relic" in 1933, mostly because of its deflationary impact on domestic economies. With the demise of Bretton Woods forty years later, gold finally stopped being the anchor of the international monetary system. It experienced a short-lived revival in 1979–81, when its traditional role as "safe haven" in times of turmoil resurfaced and supply-siders in the new Reagan administration pushed briefly for a gold standard. But that moment passed without lasting impact, and gold has remained marginal to date.

14.2. National Currencies as International Mediums of Exchange

Ever since 1971 the U.S. dollar has functioned as world money without convertibility into gold. At first sight this inconvertible paper standard seems to avoid many of the shortcomings that characterized the gold exchange standard. Paper currencies are much more practical as mediums of exchange than gold coins or bullion, which are indivisible, difficult to transport, and expensive to store. They are also more attractive as reserve assets, because, unlike gold, they can be reinvested in interest-yielding deposits. Moreover, the issue of key currencies is not subject to the same kind of supply constraint that limited the amount of gold available for monetary transactions. Currency originates within the domestic banking system of the country of issue (see chapter 2) and is then transferred abroad through net outflows of funds from that country. As long as the issuer of key currency runs balance-of-payments deficits, it supplies the rest of the world with additional liquidity. Finally, the removal of gold has allowed for much greater flexibility in currency price adjustments to reflect underlying changes in macroeconomic conditions of the countries concerned.

But appearances are often deceptive. While the advantages of paper currency compared to gold are real, they tell us only part of the story. An international monetary system based on key currencies also has fundamental weaknesses. Those currencies are by their very constitution incapable of effectively fulfilling all of the various functions of money on the global level. They are therefore an incomplete form of world money.

When considering the functions of money, we need to remember a fundamental rule: buyers cannot effectively pay for purchases by issuing their own money to sellers (see section 2.4). Credit-money, a mere token, is nothing but a promise to pay at some future date. Should sellers accept such tokens from buyers, they would in effect give their customers an interest-free loan of indefinite maturity. In the domestic payments system that problem is resolved by indirect means. Credit-money is issued by a third party located outside the marketplace—a bank—which gives the seller an enforceable claim. That claim is satisfied in the "check-clearing" process, whereby the central bank moves an equivalent sum of reserves from the buyer's bank to the seller's bank. Those reserves are debited from the buyer's account and credited to the seller's account.[13]

Let us see how this indirect payments mechanism operates in the world economy for transactions between countries. In the absence of any gold coverage, paper currencies are pure credit-money. They are essentially national in character, with their purchasing power confined to the domestic product. For this reason countries cannot pay for their purchases abroad in their own currency. Instead, they have to convert a sum of domestic credit-money into an internationally accepted form of money, the key currency (e.g., dollars), and to give it to the foreign seller. That sum is consequently lost to domestic circulation. The opposite occurs in the case of exports.

Aggregate purchasing power of the exporting country grows when its exporters convert sums of international money received as payment into domestic money. Exports of capital have the same effect as imports of goods and services, for domestic currency designated for direct or portfolio investments overseas has to be converted first into another form of money that can be spent abroad. Vice versa, capital imports can be treated in the same way as exports of goods and services. All of these transactions presume convertibility of the domestic currency that a country's central bank assures by trading foreign currencies as financial claims.

International transactions thus transfer funds from one country to another. A trade surplus, for example, amounts to an excess sale of goods and services which brings a net inflow of funds from abroad into domestic circulation. It is matched by the central bank's excess purchases of financial claims ("foreign exchange") and consequently shows up as a boost in the reserve position of the surplus country.[14] Conversely, trade deficits result in excess sales of financial claims to finance net imports, as a result of which the foreign-exchange reserves of the deficit country decline. Although import and export activities are obviously initiated by individual market participants, the payments for international trade affect the national economy in its entirety. They have a direct impact on a country's purchasing power ("aggregate demand") and on its foreign-exchange reserves.

Whereas the domestic check-clearing mechanism redistributes funds inside a country, the international payments system changes the total quantity of funds available to a country. This difference reflects the fact that in the world market, countries as a whole are themselves market participants that transfer funds from one to another on behalf of their respective citizens. Since all production takes place within national boundaries (even in the case of MNC investments), the world economy consists only of exchange activities and money transfers in which different national economies confront each other as buyers and sellers. All payment obligations between countries arising from trade and capital movements are thus direct debt from buyer to seller. The same rule, that no domestic buyer or bank can settle its debts effectively by issuing its own money token (see above), also applies to the international payments system. Any country whose currency functions as an international medium of exchange is thus in a uniquely advantageous position. It can finance its imports and capital exports in its own money. This amounts in effect to a continuously revolving line of credit supplied by all foreigners willing to hold that currency as a reserve.

That advantage, the seigniorage benefit, manifests itself in several ways for the beneficiary country that issues world money.

• The producer of world money is the only country able to pay for all overseas transactions in its own currency. It therefore does not have to accumulate and hold foreign-exchange reserves to the degree that other countries do. Although individual buyers and investors of that country must still give up cash to pay for their overseas purchases, its domestic economy does not lose any purchasing power in the process. The money sent abroad flows right back, as foreigners reinvest their reserves in the domestic banking system—be it directly, through Eurocurrency time deposits (which are all backed by domestic demand deposits), or via central banks.

• The national currency that functions as world money originates within the domestic banking system of the issuing country, from which it must subsequently be ejected into international circulation. This can only come about when the issuer runs balance-of-payments deficits that represent a net outflow of funds. Yet that country will typically pile up large trade surpluses due to the dominant world market position of its industries. It will therefore have to expand the volume of capital exports beyond prevailing trade surpluses. Other creditor nations simply recycle previously accumulated surpluses by lending them out, but the issuer of world money can boost its lending activity beyond already earned income. This allows rapid expansion of its foreign assets. Such accumulation of assets abroad creates additional income for investors from the dominant country, which they can use to spend more.

• A country usually gains and sustains world money status for its currency as a powerful creditor nation which turns its large trade surpluses into capital exports (e.g., Great Britain during the nineteenth century; the United States between 1945 and 1971; Japan and Germany during the 1980s). Thus the issuer of the key currency literally serves as the world's banker, and this role can be quite profitable. Its liabilities are the foreign-exchange reserves of other countries, which are usually held in short-term deposits paying money-market rates. On the asset side we find mostly long-term loans and other capital exports. These typically carry higher rates because of their longer maturity. The profits earned from this yield spread are often referred to as "external" seigniorage.[15]

• The balance-of-payments deficits, through which the hegemonic country supplies the world economy with liquidity, can go on indefinitely as long as foreigners are willing to hold new supplies of the key currency in reserve. Those additional reserve holdings absorb the net outflow of funds from the country of issue to the rest of the world, amounting, in effect, to an open-ended line of credit.

• Able to pay for overseas transactions in its own currency and to run continuous balance-of-payments deficits, the issuer of world money faces less of an external constraint than does the rest of the world. It can therefore adopt more stimulative policies than can other countries, whose capacity for deficit spending is limited by their supplies of foreign exchange and their access to credit markets.

But seigniorage also entails certain responsibilities and costs for the issuer of world money. Foreign asset-holders will only accept the key currency as long as they expect it to be a relatively stable store of value. If the value of the world money vis-à-vis other currencies fluctuates a great deal or is likely to depreciate continuously, then this particular medium will become much less attractive as a reserve asset. Its issuer must therefore secure both the internal and the external value of the key currency. The dramatic policy reversal by the Federal Reserve in October 1979 is a classic example of such a stabilization effort and its possibly painful effects on the domestic economy. Most important, the country in question must avoid flooding the world economy with excess supplies of the key currency. If its government violates this rule, as happened with Lyndon

Johnson's "guns and butter" policy in the late 1960s or the reflation-devaluation strategies of Richard Nixon and Jimmy Carter during the 1970s, it will destabilize the international monetary system (see sections 7.1 and 7.3). Should the hegemonic power become a debtor nation, as the United States has been since 1985, it must resist the temptation to depreciate its debts through inflation. That particular "moral hazard" problem will eventually destroy the use of the key currency as a reliable store of value.

Apart from potential difficulties when functioning as international means of payment and store of value, key currencies also pose a unit-of-account problem. They can obviously serve as a reference point for exchange rates of other currencies: One U.S. dollar equals, say, ten Austrian schillings or five French francs; one franc thus exchanges for two schillings. But what determines the relative value of the key currency in the first place? It can only be valued in terms of other currencies, a tautological determination. In any system with x number of currencies we need $(x+1)$ price equations, in which the $(x+1)$th variable acts as numeraire, allowing all x monies to be valued on the same basis. Previously that numeraire had been gold. Whenever countries suspended gold coverage of their currencies, they also removed the objective price standard with which to fix exchange rates. Inconvertibility of currencies and floating exchange rates have therefore always gone hand in hand. Once the dollar became inconvertible in 1971, governments abandoned fixed exchange rates within two years.

Neoclassical economists conveniently sidestep that unit-of-account problem. In their theory (e.g., Friedman, 1953; Johnson, 1972b; Dornbusch, 1976) flexible exchange rates tend toward interest rate and purchasing power parity, a stable level at which current accounts are assumed to be in balance and all capital movements should cease.[16] Unfortunately, this model has very little to do with reality. Over the past two decades we have seen currency prices fluctuate a great deal without necessarily balancing external accounts of individual countries. In section 7.2 we mentioned some of the factors that work against exchange-rate equilibrium—the J-curve effect, overshooting, and competitive devaluations as a form of monetary protectionism ("currency wars"). There are other reasons why the postulated law of uniform prices and interest rates does not operate in reality.

• In the neoclassical theory of flexible exchange rates, capital movements are a marginal phenomenon, of temporary duration, and essentially designed to correct deviations from long-term equilibrium levels. Yet today the vast majority of foreign-exchange transactions are associated with asset transfers rather than with trade in goods and services. These capital flows may be of a long-term nature, may enhance deviations from purchasing power parity, and often trigger cumulative processes toward even greater current account imbalances.

• Many capital movements across the globe are motivated not by the traditional objectives of short-term interest rates or speculative capital gains but by a desire to hold reserves in the key currency. Market participants and asset-holders tend to pick that currency for their transactions and portfolios which best protects them against uncertainty. This protection is a nonpecuniary benefit, akin to the "liquidity premium" of Keynes (1936, ch. 17). Oblivious to the reality of uncertainty, neoclassical economists ignore that special property-protection role of the key currency. Instead, they treat all currencies as equal. If they are truly equal, why do we find capital flight and "black" markets for U.S. dollars in all countries with hyperinflation or official exchange controls?

• Orthodox economists usually look at a single nation in relation to the rest of the world instead of analyzing the global economy as an interdependent system. In that unidimensional perspective the exchange rate appears to be just another price. But it is more than that. Exchange rates constitute nodal points between countries through which business cycles and price movements are transmitted from one national economy to another.

For all of these reasons our current system of flexible exchange rates has proved to be significantly more dysfunctional than originally envisaged by its neoclassical protagonists in the 1970s. Some of its more problematic characteristics—volatile foreign-exchange markets, destabilizing capital flows, and persistent imbalances in current and capital accounts—have introduced a significant element of instability into the world economy. They have clearly contributed to the synchronization of business cycles (see our discussion in chapter 7 of the connection between the U.S. devaluation-reflation strategy under Nixon and Carter, the oil price hikes of 1973 and 1979, and the global recessions shortly thereafter). They have also made world market prices less predictable, thereby complicating long-range planning by private investors and public officials. These problems are neither the result of mistaken policies nor caused by irrational agents refusing to act in accordance with the behavioral prescriptions of neoclassical equilibrium theory. They are structural in nature, direct manifestations of an inadequate form of world money which cannot settle debts properly, may not be a reliable store of value, and has no objective value basis.

14.3. The Instability of Our Multicurrency System

In the absence of any money-commodity (e.g., gold), currency prices lack a proper valuation standard. All currencies can be measured in terms of the key currency, but what determines the value of that currency? For neoclassical economists the lack of numeraire poses no problem. Their models look only at individual exchange rates which are assumed to automatically tend toward equilibrium as defined by interest rate and purchasing power parity. Unfortunately, nobody is certain what those parity levels are, and there is little agreement among economists about equilibrium prices for currencies.[17] It is not enough to argue, in classic free-market fashion, that whatever a currency is presently worth on foreign-exchange markets is by definition the "right" value. Markets do not necessarily reflect rational behavior. They tend toward overreaction and therefore typically exhibit a cyclical pattern. Foreign-exchange markets are no exception. Moreover, currency prices move in response to a variety of forces. Economic fundamentals (e.g., inflation rates, policy mix), speculation, market psychology, technical factors, and central bank interventions all play a major role in determining exchange rates—often with unintended effects.

Even though currency prices have been notoriously unstable since their deregulation in 1973, their movements are not arbitrary.

• Over the long run exchange rates reflect a country's competitiveness in the international hierarchy of nations. When a country manages to strengthen its competitive position in the world market, its external accounts improve and its currency appreciates in response to increased global demand (e.g., Germany, Japan). The reverse occurs when the country in question faces gradual erosion (e.g., Great Britain, United States).[18]

• Woven around this secular trend line we find distinct cycles of four to seven years. This pattern suggests that exchange-rate movements trigger counteracting adjustments in goods and assets markets. But these effects take time to unfold, and in the meantime foreign-exchange markets overshoot. The overshooting sets the stage for the next phase of the cycle, when it has finally begun to turn around such economic fundamentals as inflation and the direction of macroeconomic policy.

• Those multiyear cycles are driven by much shorter-term price fluctuations. At times expectational biases are widely differentiated, and the markets move sideways. But most of the time we can see pronounced price movements in one direction reflecting widely shared market sentiments (see Figure 14.1). These speculative "runs" usually last a few weeks or months before being temporarily interrupted by even shorter countermovements. Because runs outweigh corrections, they reinforce whatever phase of the currency cycle we are in.

Even though there is a certain logic to exchange-rate behavior, the overriding feature of foreign-exchange markets is their price volatility. Before the Louvre Agreement in 1987 key exchange rates (e.g., dollar/mark, dollar/yen) often fluctuated by 1 percent to 2 percent per day. Such instability is quite damaging and costly. Investors must constantly be on guard and must avoid holding their assets in a depreciating currency. Managers find it more difficult to decide whether to export goods or to produce them abroad, for that decision depends to a major extent on the anticipated exchange-rate movements. Multinational firms also find their bottom lines affected by changes in currency prices, because they have to report foreign earnings in their home currency.

It is, of course, possible to protect oneself against those price risks in foreign-exchange markets through forward-market transactions, options, futures, warrants, swaps, or foreign-currency bank accounts.[19] But such protection is not

Figure 14.1 **Exchange Rate Dynamics** ($/DM- rate, 5-day moving average)

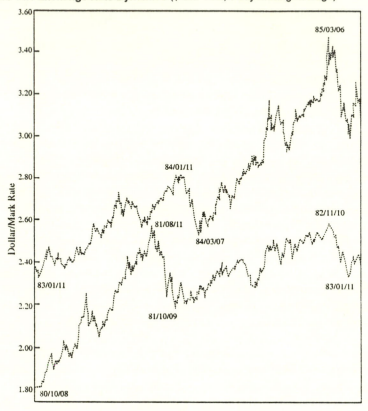

Source: Stephan Schulmeister (1987), "An Essay on Exchange Rate Dynamics," Discussion Paper no. 8(87), Wissenschaftszentrum Berlin—Research Unit Labour Market and Employment, p. 9. Reprinted with permission of the author.

perfect. Each of these hedging techniques carries its own cost, such as the interest-rate differential between the two currencies involved in forward-market transactions or the premiums paid for options and futures. In addition to these transaction costs there are risks. Wrong expectations may cause significant losses.

Investors often try to limit such losses by unwinding their hedges. Such a shift in market positioning tends to have a procyclical effect on currency prices. For example, if the dollar is rising rather than falling as expected, investors will repurchase the dollars they had sold in the forward market. Another practice that reinforces current price movements is the "leading and lagging" of multinational corporations. When those firms expect their home currency to depreciate, they will try to speed up payments to foreigners and to delay getting paid. Such a response makes it more likely that those very expectations come true. Finally, speculators thrive on price volatility and often accelerate ongoing price movements in one direction. They may, for instance, borrow in a currency they think is losing value to buy another that they think will rise. Given all these procyclical market forces, it is not surprising to see a pattern of pronounced price "runs" in foreign-exchange markets.

Currency trading has come to dominate the world economy over the past couple of decades. Fluctuating exchange rates have encouraged a great deal of hedging and speculation. Both activities tend to make prices more volatile and are therefore self-feeding. They may also spin off large numbers of additional trades. When, for instance, futures are bought on the International Monetary Market in Chicago, traders who sell those contracts will typically cover their obligation to deliver the currencies by buying forward contracts from banks. Those banks then usually cover their forward obligations by buying the currency in the spot market. Currency options, warrants, and futures are all highly leveraged instruments which allow investors to move huge sums with very little money of their own. Only a small fraction of today's enormous trading volume represents actual outlays of capital by investors. New telecommunications and computer technologies have also played a major role in the market expansion, linking trading centers across the globe into a single international market.[20]

All of these forces have spurred incredibly rapid growth of the foreign-exchange market since its deregulation in 1973. In the United States alone its daily transaction volume exploded (according to Fed surveys) from an average of $5 billion in 1977 to $23 billion in 1981, $50 billion in 1986, $129 billion in 1989, and $192 billion in 1992. Nowadays global market volume averages (according to triannual surveys by the Bank of England) $1 trillion per day, up from $640 billion in 1989, with most trading centered in London, New York, and Tokyo. Trades are usually in blocks of several million dollars, with no fees charged. Traditional transactions involving trade, tourism, or long-term investments account only for a small fraction of that market. Today about 90 percent of all turnover in the currency markets is day-to-day trading motivated by speculation, hedging against price risk, and short-term portfolio investments in foreign securities markets. Trades are conducted among roughly 10,000 dealers, mostly banks and other financial institutions, for their own accounts or on behalf of their clients (e.g., individuals, investment managers, corporate treasurers). They make money by correctly anticipating short-term movements in currencies and on razor-thin arbitrage profits. Even though the number of currency traders is large, the market is highly concentrated. In 1992 the ten most active institutions handled 41 percent of all currency transactions.

The impact of this massive speculation is mixed at best. There is no question that such a huge volume of day-to-day trading adds liquidity to the market and thus makes it easier for traditional users to reduce their risks from fluctuating exchange rates. In recent years this activity has also become a very important profit center for banks and corporations, albeit an inherently risky one.[21] Extremely leveraged contracts (e.g., a $100,000 investment in options controlling up to $40 million in currencies) can yield very attractive rates of return from only miniscule price movements. But for the same reason losses are often large when currencies move in the wrong direction. Economists who favor flexible exchange rates like to argue that day-to-day traders do not carry large positions for long and therefore affect currency prices only for a few hours at most. The movement of currency prices in the course of weeks or months depends much more on the decisions of longer-term investors (e.g., MNCs, fund managers), government policies, and economic fundamentals. But this argument understates the impact of speculators who like to take advantage of trends or expectations in the market. Most traders use various "oscillator" or "momentum" models to determine buy and sell signals by identifying the behavioral patterns of price series. These models allow speculators to gauge the mood of the market. Their distinctly herd-like behavior in response to widely shared expectations often reinforces existing price trends and makes the currency markets very volatile. Finally, the resources diverted into currency speculation clearly could have been spent more productively elsewhere. In that sense it is fair to say that short-term trading crowds out long-term investments.

That the global economy has become dominated by huge sums of highly mobile capital floating around the globe is no surprise. Such "hot money" merely represents a supply of credit in search of the most profitable short-term investments. Its dramatic expansion since the late 1960s, though surely due to dramatic improvements in communication technology, is directly related to the persistence of huge trade imbalances. Our international monetary system, as currently constituted, lacks an effective mechanism to correct trade imbalances.

Under the gold standard external disequilibria were kept in check by specie flows from deficit countries to surplus countries, which forced both into countervailing adjustments. The convertibility of currency into gold gave ordinary citizens access to the assets of the central bank (i.e., gold). In the face of such a constraint neither money supply nor budget deficits could be allowed to get out of hand. Under Bretton Woods the need to defend fixed exchange rates provided at least a modicum of market discipline. Any country with excessively large trade deficits risked having to devalue its currency. Such a step was regarded as a sign of weakness and was usually accompanied by austerity measures, so it was something to avoid.

The current system does not have any such internal balancing mechanism. Instead it seems to feed imbalances.

• Let us begin with the country whose currency acts as world money. Its economy must run balance-of-payments deficits in order to supply the rest of the world with additional liquidity.

• Surplus countries can avoid their share of the adjustment. Instead of stimulating their own economies, they can continue to run surpluses and relend those to deficit countries.[22]

• As long as debtor nations can tap the global credit markets for more funds, they do not have to bring their external imbalances under control. Under the current system they can also let their currencies slide downward without much ado. Ironically, such currency depreciation tends to make their trade deficits worse at first, because of the J-curve effect (see section 7.2).

• Finally, nowadays most global surplus funds are recycled through the unregulated Euromarket network of private banks and are thus prone to credit overextension. The LDC debt crisis shows how brutal deferred adjustments can be when they finally hit home.

Ever since the early 1960s the Euromarket has dramatically transformed the international monetary system. Once transnational banks accepted deposits in denominations other than that of the country of their location (e.g., dollar deposits held in London), key currencies in international circulation became truly "stateless" money. Surplus countries gained a new investment outlet for their foreign-exchange reserves that offered attractive returns. The movement of funds in the interbank segment of the Euromarket has greatly increased the velocity of the international money supply. That global banking network also operates without reserve requirements, so its deposit multiplier tends to be much larger than in the domestic banking system. For both reasons, the reserve currency country needs to supply less new liquidity. Easy switching of currencies in the Euromarket has complicated central bank management of exchange rates. Eurobanks have also replaced governments and international lending agencies as the primary source of capital transfers from industrial nations to developing countries. This worked during the 1970s. But private credit is much more likely to suffer from overextension than is official aid, and we ended up with a major global debt crisis in 1982. Since then, creditor nations have considered protecting the income and asset values of their banks to be more important than the development needs of poor countries.

The combination of fluctuating exchange rates, inconvertible currencies, and a largely unregulated network of private banks virtually guarantees a great deal of turmoil in the international monetary system. That instability feeds imbalances in trade and capital flows, mostly through discrepancies in national price levels and nominal interest rates. Persistent balance-of-payments deficits and surpluses engender large capital transfers between creditor and debtor nations. Most of that capital is short-term, either used for hedges and speculation in response to volatile exchange rates or diverted into Euromarket deposits and loans to cover balance-of-payments deficits. Our system gives rise to huge amounts of "hot money" racing the globe in search of the highest financial returns while creating a shortage of long-term capital available for economic purposes.

Volatile exchange rates and persistent trade imbalances must be seen in the context of a gradually emerging *multicurrency system*. The dollar is still dominant, though its global position has steadily weakened since the collapse of

Bretton Woods. Germany and Japan, in particular, managed increasingly large trade surpluses once their industries began to dominate world markets. Initially neither country wanted to see its currency become an international medium of exchange. Both feared that world money status might cause their currencies to appreciate and in the process hurt their export industries. During the 1970s they therefore preferred to hoard their surpluses, much like the United States did in the interwar period. But in 1979, with the dollar in sharp decline and oil prices once again exploding, their governments began to realize the benefits of a strong currency in terms of lower import costs. More intense competitive pressures and a cheapening of foreign assets may also prove advantageous for their domestic industries. During the 1980s both countries recycled surpluses more aggressively and became major suppliers of capital to the rest of the world (see Table 14.1). Thus both marks and yen have recently gained in importance as key currencies (see Table 14.2).

Such a multicurrency system is typically a transitional regime. It reflects the reality of a polycentric world economy in which several nations compete for global leadership. The old power has already lost its position of absolute dominance, but no other nation is yet ready to take its place as the new superpower. The transfer of hegemony from one nation to another seems to be a recurrent phenomenon in the world economy. In the seventeenth century Great Britain emerged as the dominant trading nation after Spain had wasted much of the wealth from its colonies on military adventures. During the first half of the twentieth century, especially after World War I, the United States displaced Great Britain as the leading economic power. And now Germany and Japan, the two powers the U.S.-led alliance had defeated in World War II, are in the process of becoming the world's strongest trading nations.

This propensity for leadership changes should not come as a surprise. After all, the industries of the hegemonic power set the standards of competitiveness that others have to meet. They force weaker competitors to improve or fail. Yet they themselves do not face the same kind of challenge. Used to dominating markets, they may be tempted to relax. By the time they finally face serious challenges for market leadership, they may have already lost many of the facilities that once made them winners.[23]

The international monetary system often reinforces this process of shifting power balances. Since the hegemonic power can run continuous balance-of-payment deficits as issuer of world money, it does not face as stringent an external constraint as other nations do. Add to this the fact that the key currency tends to be valued more highly because of the liquidity premium it carries as international medium. Such overvaluation may undermine that country's trade position while benefiting the export industries of its key competitors. It also makes foreign assets cheaper, thus encouraging firms of the leading nation to expand abroad. But excessive multinationalization of its industries can be counterproductive, as so clearly illustrated in the case of Great Britain. The home economy of the

Table 14.1

Balance of Payments of Key Currency Issuers (in millions of US dollars)

Year	Trade balance (+surplus/–deficit)			Capital account (+net imports/-net exports)		
	U.S.A.	Germany	Japan	U.S.A.	Germany	Japan
1975	8,900	16,886	4,935	–22,711	–5,352	89
1976	–9,470	16,007	9,803	–14,683	39	90
1977	–31,940	19,446	17,160	–20,549	–938	–4,427
1978	–33,940	24,106	24,300	–18,079	781	–6,581
1979	–27,540	16,482	1,740	9,755	2,738	–4,398
1980	–25,500	8,694	2,130	–10,260	–1,396	15,776
1981	–27,990	16,074	19,960	–8,502	–29	–1,134
1982	–36,440	24,730	18,080	7,889	–2,064	–11,555
1983	–67,080	21,430	31,460	36,126	–6,613	–19,250
1984	–112,510	22,143	44,260	99,706	–10,704	–32,880
1985	–122,160	28,578	55,990	128,045	–16,068	–49,754
1986	–145,050	55,756	92,820	111,638	–38,331	–70,991
1987	–159,490	70,204	96,420	103,342	–25,688	–49,081
1988	–126,970	79,776	95,000	90,100	–68,755	–63,113
1989	–115,920	77,742	76,890	123,288	–67,455	–69,731
1990	–108,120	71,705	63,580	63,673	–40,925	–44,941
1991	–73,600	23,062	103,090	–16,119	22,784	–81,106

Source: International Monetary Fund, *International Financial Statistics Yearbook 1992*, Washington, DC, pp. 126 and 130.

Note: Capital account includes net errors and omissions but excludes exceptional financing, reserves, and liabilities constituting foreign authorities' reserves.

world money producer may deindustrialize too much as a result. Besides causing extensive job loss, this process could also have detrimental effects on domestic policy. With unions weakened and corporate managers thinking globally, two key constituencies for maintaining a strong industrial infrastructure and investing in human capital at home are less likely to shape public policy.

Investors prefer to have a clearly dominant world money which is capable of protecting their portfolios against uncertainty. The problem with a multicurrency system is that none of the competing forms of world money may perform this function effectively. If there were a stable international store of value, that particular money form would dominate and would crowd out other alternatives. The coexistence of several key currencies therefore indicates by definition the absence of a recognized and secure store of value.

Such a situation is inherently unstable. The competition between different

Table 14.2

Currency Composition of International Reserves

Year	Currency shares of official foreign exchange holdings (percent of total)		
	Dollar	Mark	Yen
1975	78.3	8.8	1.8
1976	77.5	9.3	2.1
1977	77.9	9.0	2.2
1978	76.3	10.7	3.1
1979	72.2	12.5	3.7
1980	68.3	15.3	4.4
1981	70.8	13.2	4.2
1982	70.2	12.4	4.7
1983	71.4	11.7	4.9
1984	69.9	12.2	5.6
1985	65.4	14.6	7.6
1986	68.7	14.2	7.2
1987	66.7	15.6	7.7
1988	64.1	17.2	7.8
1989	60.3	19.1	7.8
1990	56.4	19.7	9.1

Source: International Monetary Fund, *Annual Report 1991*, Washington, DC, pp. 77ff.

national monies for global hegemony may cause frictions between the leading powers. As a worst-case scenario, these tensions may lead the world economy to disintegrate into highly protectionist blocs, as happened during the interwar period. At a minimum the struggle for global dominance may cause policy actions that are contrary to the best interests of these countries (e.g., Great Britain's overvaluation of the pound during the interwar and early postwar period). In a multicurrency system investors are never certain which of the different world monies is going to be the most stable. This uncertainty shortens investment horizons and encourages frequent shifts in currency portfolios. Finally, there is always the possibility of massive and destabilizing capital flows whenever one of these key currencies loses in stature relative to another.

While multicurrency systems are inherently unstable, they do possess a certain resilience. Countries do not suddenly lose or gain hegemony. That process usually takes decades. Newly dominant powers resist seigniorage at first. The United States displayed such an attitude in the interwar period, as did both Germany and Japan during the 1970s. Having finally established a strong world market position, those countries did not want to weaken their export industries by subjecting their currencies to massive appreciation. Only when they finally turn into significant capital exporters, often after years of trade surpluses and reserve hoarding, do these countries begin to supply the rest of the world with enough liquidity for their currencies to become world money. On the demand side, a certain modicum of stability is assured by the propensity of assetholders to congregate around a single monetary standard. Even though the leading currency may face long-term erosion, its depreciation does not necessarily have to trigger a massive sell-off. Sudden flights out of the key currency are mitigated by the fear of realizing capital losses. For all of these reasons, shifts in the composition of world money forms or transitions from one key currency to another tend to be fairly slow processes that stretch over decades.

The present multicurrency standard is no exception. It has already lasted for two decades and may continue for many more years without breaking down. Still, this durability is no reason for complacency. As a matter of fact, in some crucial respects the current situation bears a striking resemblance to the ultimately doomed multicurrency system of the 1920s.

• The dramatic shift of the United States' external investment income, from a surplus averaging 1.5 percent of GNP in the early 1980s to a deficit approaching 2 percent just a decade later, is of the same magnitude as the one experienced by Great Britain during and after World War I. But that deterioration will probably not have quite as damaging an effect on our domestic economy as it did in Great Britain during the interwar period, because not all of America's foreign debt has gone into military spending. Still, servicing this large foreign debt will certainly be quite a burden.

• As was the case with the United States in the 1920s, Japan is now assuming the role of a great creditor nation while still adhering to a neomercantilist policy of running up large trade surpluses. For the global economy to function properly the key creditor nations must eventually open their markets to a large-scale influx of imports. Only then will developing countries earn enough export income to service their overseas loans properly. Both times the absence of a free-trade posture by the new creditor nation limited the effectiveness of its monetary stimulus. Its expansionary monetary policy ended up feeding a real estate and stock market boom which was as spectacular in Japan during the 1980s as it had been in the United States during the 1920s.

• In both transition periods other countries with large growth potential could not pursue expansionary policies because of large external debt burdens or an inability to import capital. During the 1920s that constraint made itself most dramatically felt with regard to Germany's burden of war reparations. In the 1980s it was the debt overhang in Latin America and in other LDCs.

One can easily draw the parallels between the 1920s and the 1980s too far and in the process ignore many crucial differences between the two eras. Today, for example, gold is no longer the anchor of the international monetary system. The absence of such commodity-money has its advantages. Exchange rates can adjust flexibly to changing conditions, and liquidity is no longer scarce. But that very removal of gold also exposes the weaknesses of an inconvertible fiat-money standard. On their own, national currencies are not a proper form of world money. They do not function as an effective unit of account with which to fix stable exchange rates. They allow neither proper settlement of debts nor symmetrical adjustments. And their capacity as an international store of value is seriously hampered by fluctuating exchange rates, especially when several key currencies vie for dominance. This inability of national currencies to carry out essential monetary functions in international circulation manifests itself in many troubling ways, notably volatile exchange rates, persistent external imbalances, global credit overextension, and short-term speculation crowding out more productive long-term investments. If we ever want to have a more stable and better balanced global economy, we need to think of more effective alternatives for world money (see chapters 15 and 16). These, however, will only have a chance if and when the current tinkering with the existing system proves to be insufficient.

14.4. Recent Stabilization Efforts

Growing tensions within the international monetary system during the second half of the 1980s forced policy-makers to respond. In each case their stabilization efforts required multilateral agreement between the leading industrial nations, possibly marking the beginning of a new era characterized by greater international policy coordination to manage an increasingly polycentric world economy. Key initiatives in recent years have focused on the management of the global debt crisis, the harmonization of financial regulations, and coordinated central bank interventions to keep exchange rates within set target zones.

When the LDC debt crisis erupted a decade ago, the industrial nations had to build an international lender-of-last-resort mechanism in a hurry (see section 10.1). Ever since, the United States has been at the forefront in managing this crisis. Its leadership role comes as no surprise. Most LDC loans are in dollars, and U.S. banks are especially exposed to the largest debtors (Mexico, Brazil, Argentina). But the United States could not have dealt with a crisis of such magnitude on its own. Close cooperation with other industrial nations was required to create an effective creditors' cartel. Toward this objective two institutional vehicles in particular have proven highly effective. In the Paris Club, main creditor nations meet on issues pertaining to their official loans to other governments. And the five largest economies have used their control over the IMF to gradually turn this fund from a supplier of short-term emergency loans into a lender making longer-term commitments and enforcing structural reforms.[24]

In recent years the extent of coordination among industrial nations concerning the LDC debt crisis has gradually increased. In 1990 alone there were at least three major initiatives. First the industrial nations agreed to increase the IMF's lending authority by 50 percent to $180 billion while giving the fund new pow-ers to cope with spreading payments arrears. Then the EC and the United States set up a new European Bank of Reconstruction and Development with $12 billion in capital to help meet the urgent needs of former Soviet republics and Eastern European countries for loans and private investment in support of their economic reforms. Finally, the United States, Japan, and the EC used the ongo-ing "Uruguay Round" of world trade negotiations under the auspices of GATT to push LDCs for further removal of trade-related restrictions on private direct-in-vestment flows (e.g., "domestic content" requirements). Such an agreement on capital flows is considered vital to any easing of debt problems in developing countries. In 1991 the industrial nations urged the IMF to provide emergency assistance to those countries hardest hit by the Gulf War (e.g., Egypt, Turkey) and used the Paris Club for debt-forgiveness initiatives (e.g., Poland).

The global debt crisis also convinced bank regulators that some restrictions on the Euromarket subsidiaries of their banks were in order. But unilateral actions, such as the formation of the Interagency Country Exposure Review Committee in the United States during 1983, only could go so far. In an era of intense global competition any country will hurt its financial-services industry if it imposes more burdensome restrictions than elsewhere. In that case capital will simply flow to less heavily regulated areas, one of the key reasons why the Euromarket had grown so rapidly in the first place. The only solution is to impose the same regulatory restraints on all banks no matter where they are located. This requires agreement between the leading financial powers, as occurred in July 1988 when twelve industrial nations decided to impose uniform capital requirements on their respective banks. This treaty was a crucial first step toward building a global regulatory framework for transnational banks capable of bypassing purely na-tional regulations. As financial markets become more integrated, further harmo-nization of rules will follow (see section 11.4).

The most important multilateral stabilization effort in recent years has been with regard to exchange-rate management. Central banks have tried to manipu-late currency prices ever since their deregulation in 1973. In such a "dirty float" a central bank would typically try to slow down depreciation by buying up its own currency. If that central bank ran out of foreign-exchange reserves to sell in the process, it could obtain additional foreign currencies by activating swap agreements with other central banks.[25] But such intervention often proved to be futile. After a $30 billion dollar-rescue package had failed to stem the tide of the key currency in 1979 (see section 7.3), it became clear that no central bank, not even the Federal Reserve, was large enough to fight determined speculation on its own.

At first this realization drove U.S. policy-makers into a laissez-faire posture. The collapse of the dollar in 1979 convinced the Fed that only a drastic reversal of monetary policy toward restraint could avert the demise of the dollar as world money. The subsequent doubling of U.S. interest rates did manage to turn exchange rates around. With the dollar rising in 1980–81, it was easy for the newly elected Reagan administration to apply its "free-market" ideology to the currency markets and to rule out central bank interventions except for emergency situations (e.g., the assassination attempt on Reagan in March 1981). That hands-off policy remained in force for more than four years.

In September 1985 the five leading industrial nations (the United States, Japan, Germany, France, and Great Britain) decided in the so-called Plaza Agreement to intervene actively in the currency markets and to coordinate their actions so as to push the dollar down in an orderly fashion. Why did the Reagan administration, which initiated this historic agreement, abandon its laissez-faire policy? The dramatic appreciation of the dollar between 1981 and 1985 had helped to cause huge U.S. trade deficits, and the Reagan administration faced intense protectionist pressures. It was precisely to avoid a trade war among themselves that the United States and its allies agreed to coordinate exchange rates (see section 8.2). In February 1985 the dollar peaked and began a rather steep decline. Central bankers across the world worried that this speculation-driven slide could get out of hand. They wanted to assure an orderly decline. Because individual interventions had proven futile (e.g., in 1978–79), they were ready to give concerted action a try.

The Plaza Agreement proved to be successful, mostly because market sentiment agreed with the policy objective of the "Group of Five" (G–5) countries to provide for a gradual and orderly depreciation of the dollar. At that point coordination was also made much easier by the fact that for the first time in years growth and inflation rates of the major industrial countries had converged. During 1986 the United States, Japan, and Germany engineered two rounds of simultaneous interest-rate reductions, thereby signaling to the financial markets that central bankers and finance ministers were truly committed to a new era of international economic coordination. Of course, these joint actions of monetary convergence occurred only because all three countries wanted lower interest rates—the United States to counteract a slowdown of its domestic economy, Japan and Germany to slow the appreciation of their currencies in order to protect their manufacturing industries from a further loss of competitiveness.

Emboldened by this success, the G–5 countries soon began to discuss the next step toward a more formalized structure of cooperation. Their debate centered on a proposal made by James Baker at the annual IMF meeting in April 1986. Under this plan, governments would commit themselves to holding exchange rates within secret ranges which had margins of plus and minus 10 percent. In other words, currencies could move 10 percent above or below a set target rate without setting off alarms. But once they breached the margins, action would be taken to ease the pressure. Such a movement of exchange rates beyond their ranges signals governments that their economic policies are at odds and need correction. Participating countries would therefore have to give more weight to the international ramifications of their respective domestic economic policies if they wanted that new regime to work properly.[26]

Initially Baker's plan received only a lukewarm reception. France, with a strong tradition in favor of policy coordination and joint intervention in currency markets, was the only supporter. The U.S. government itself was divided. George Schultz, who had been secretary of treasury during the last days of fixed exchange rates in 1972, and Beryl Sprinkel, the monetarist chairman of the Council of Economic Advisers, both preferred flexible exchange rates. So did Margaret Thatcher, herself a monetarist. The Germans did not want to see their sovereignty over economic policy reduced, and they worried about the inflationary consequences of further interest-rate cuts. Japan feared that the new regime would force the yen to rise so much that its industries would lose valuable export markets.

But then, during the second half of 1986, the dollar decline threatened to get out of hand. After eighteen months of constant depreciation the dollar was 40 percent below its peak, yet its slide was still picking up steam. Growing worries about capital losses led foreign investors to cut back on dollar-denominated assets, prompting central banks to intervene more actively in foreign-exchange markets. By January 1987 private investors overseas had stopped financing the twin U.S. deficits, and a month later the "Group of Seven" (G–5 plus Italy and Canada) formally adopted Baker's proposal in the so-called Louvre Agreement.

The imposition of "target zones" eventually stopped the decline of the dollar—but only through massive intervention by G–7 central banks. In 1987 and 1988 they propped up the dollar five times against market sentiments. Each time they saved the dollar, they made their pledge to stabilize exchange rates more credible. Central bank traders learned how to read and manipulate the markets better. With exchange rates more stable, speculation became less profitable.[27] Still, dollar stabilization proved to be expensive. During 1987 alone the foreign central banks spent $130 billion to support the dollar, pushing the world's foreign-exchange reserves from $559 billion to $790 billion. These dollar acquisitions had the same effect as open-market purchases. As the money supply exploded in Great Britain, Japan and Germany, bond yields there began to rise. That put even more pressure on already rising U.S. interest rates, which eventually punctured the speculative bubble on Wall Street in October 1987.

In the fall of 1988 U.S. interest rates began to rise in response to stronger-than-expected growth and failure to cut the budget deficit just before a presidential election. The tough anti-inflation stance of the Fed caused the dollar to appreciate by about 20 percent between November 1988 and May 1989, breaking through its presumed upper limit against the yen and mark without triggering joint intervention. The Fed tried to slow the movement for fear of jeopardizing the improvements in U.S. trade deficits. Its foreign-currency holdings tripled in the process, from $10.8 billion in June 1988 to $34 billion in July 1989, accompanied by extensive sales of government securities to sterilize its purchases of yen and marks.[28] In the meantime the Bank of Japan and the Bundesbank responded to the renewed inflation threat from weakening currencies and pushed up their interest rates. Domestic considerations had taken over in each country, and rising interest rates strained relations within the G–7. Since then, international economic cooperation has gone adrift.

The erosion of the Louvre Agreement was to be expected. Its features never managed to overcome the intrinsic shortcomings of our multicurrency system. In the end those prevailed.

• To begin with, the officials of the G–7 had a hard time figuring out realistic exchange-rate levels that would allow them to define stable target zones. Economists and policy-makers, within as well as between countries, disagree as to where exchange rates should be. The widely accepted equilibrium level, the so-called purchasing-power parity (PPP), is quite elusive and does not normally correspond to those rates that balance trade.[29]

• Even if we were able to determine PPP with precision, it is unrealistic to believe that market forces or central bank interventions could ever settle exchange rates near PPP levels. The concept of PPP is no longer operational, for two related reasons. To begin with, it only applies to trade. When large cross-border holdings of financial claims exist, as is the case today after an amazing build-up of dollar-denominated financial assets across the globe, the investment demand for that currency swamps its trade-related transaction demand. Moreover, for the PPP principle to work, countries have to restrict the issue of new credit-money to the funding of economic activities (e.g., trade, production). Both of these conditions apply to the European Monetary System (see chapter 15), which is why its experiment with fixed exchange rates had a chance of succeeding.[30] But under Louvre's "managed float" neither condition holds. That arrangement rests on the accumulation of dollar-denominated reserves by foreign central banks. When those institutions buy up excess dollars, they extend permanent credit to the United States. This latest manifestation of dollar seigniorage monetizes U.S. government debt. Having the same effect as an open-market purchase, it is a huge source of global money creation that is not linked to economic transactions.

• The existence of adjustable target zones may actually have encouraged more speculation by inducing private traders to test the margins. Foreign-exchange trading continued to soar after Louvre, and by early 1989 volume had risen enough to overpower central bank interventions once again. Less able to influence exchange rates, the G–7 commitment to the "managed float" waned.

• Central bank trading of foreign currencies to stabilize exchange rates may have counterproductive effects. Take, for example, the efforts to prop up the dollar in 1987 and 1988. Dollar purchases by Great Britain, Germany, and Japan accelerated money creation in those countries, which in turn forced domestic interest rates higher by reviving inflationary expectations. Sterilizing the newly acquired foreign-exchange reserves does not help much. Such a step requires the central bank to sell an equivalent amount of domestic securities, and those open-market sales also raise interest rates.

• Even more disturbing is the fact that joint central bank interventions in defense of target zones reduce market pressure on governments to correct destabilizing policies. Policy-makers can delay necessary adjustments as long as other central banks prop up their currency. The "managed float" thus lacks the one thing most fundamental to maintaining stable exchange rates, namely a mechanism to assure convergence in economic performance among participating member countries.

Under Louvre, the G–7 finance ministers and central bankers have held periodic meetings to review the economic performance of each country. Baker soon understood that this coordination process needed strengthening and that target zones had to be linked to some sort of adjustment mechanism. Toward this goal he proposed in May 1988 that the G–7 countries, besides coordinating their "structural reforms" (e.g., tax reform, financial deregulation), should adopt formal procedures for surveillance of their national economies. First those countries would develop a set of objective indicators to determine performance, including growth, inflation, exchange rates, trade, and payments balances. Then they would use their periodic meetings to establish "monitoring zones" for these economic performance indicators. Though nonbinding, those zones would carry significant weight. If the indicators fell out of the zones, the country concerned would have to consult the others about possible remedial action. Each G–7 country would therefore be under considerable pressure from its allies to make policy corrections deemed necessary to bring its performance back into line. This surveillance proposal was not accepted, mostly because other G–7 countries feared losing their national sovereignty over domestic policy.

At this point, in 1994, we are suspended between two alternatives, neither of which we are willing to endorse wholeheartedly. We do not want to return to freely floating exchange rates, but we hesitate to go down the long road of monetary reform toward a stable exchange-rate regime.

After two decades of turmoil the multicurrency system of flexible exchange rates now seems unacceptable. Volatile currency prices, with their penchant for overshooting, have fed huge "hot money" flows of wandering capital and have subjected the world economy to sharp cycles of inflation and deflation. Those consequences seriously undermined the efficiency of both trade and investment among industrial nations while wreaking havoc on developing countries. The result has been an upsurge in protectionism.

In the face of these dangers, the leading economic powers decided in 1987 to stabilize currency prices. But that new arrangement could not succeed, for there was nothing in the Louvre Agreement to make key currencies any more adequate as world money. Its target zones are adjustable and often left undefended precisely because of their arbitrariness. They do not resolve the unit-of-account problem of defining stable exchange rates which accurately reflect economic fundamentals. Coordinated central bank interventions, especially those in 1987–88 designed to prop up a sagging dollar, are a clear expression of seigniorage. Dollar purchases by foreign central banks finance U.S. budget and trade deficits indefinitely. In the absence of any effective means of payment to settle international debts, there is no way to enforce policy adjustments. Instead, we are left with continuous external account imbalances and unrestrained money creation to monetize corresponding debts.

Torn between laissez-faire and reregulation, the monetary authorities have been unable to act decisively. The "managed" float has been an important move away from the chaos of "free" markets. But further steps are necessary on the long road of reform to give the global economy a stable monetary regime.

15

Supranational Credit-Money

In this chapter we take the question of international monetary reform one step further. Past and current arrangements concerning world money are inadequate to give the emerging global accumulation regime the required degree of cohesion. Our multicurrency system, in which the dollar, the mark, and the yen compete for dominance, ties up huge sums of capital rather unproductively in short-term portfolio management and exacerbates tensions among leading economic powers. The failure of the G–7 nations to follow up on their "managed float" with increased policy coordination shows how difficult it is to reform this system from within.

National currencies are an inadequate form of world money, but at least their use in international transactions avoids the faults of commodity-money. A monetary standard based on strategic commodities, no matter whether gold alone or some combination of raw materials, will always suffer from their relatively inelastic and uncertain supply conditions. Producers of the money commodity will have an outright advantage over others in the marketplace. Even if we reduce the role of the money commodity to that of last-resort reserve and numeraire for exchange rates, as was the case with the gold exchange standard of Bretton Woods, such a hybrid system is prone to break down. Commodity-money and credit-money are essentially incompatible forms of money and do not coexist easily with each other. One or the other will dominate, and each form of dominance will cause its peculiar sources of instability (e.g., inadequate supply of liquidity, loss of convertibility, inequitably distributed adjustment burdens).

Thus we confront the issue of international monetary reform without any of the known options having proved themselves to be workable in the long run. Neither precious metals nor national currencies are effective forms of world money. We must therefore develop a different monetary standard, one based on a truly global currency. Such a supranational credit-money is the next logical step in the historic evolution of money and completes the century-long transition from regimes of commodity-money to credit-money. It is also, as we shall see (especially in chapter 16), the most adequate institutional framework for the kind of global accumulation regime we currently see emerging in the world economy.[1]

Creation of such a new international money form is a very complicated undertaking. To begin with, barring a catastrophic crisis as a catalyst for fundamental reforms, it will not be easy to convince politicians and central bankers to go along with the idea of a universal currency. After all, the ability to issue money is at the core of the nation-state, giving it legitimacy and power vis-à-vis its citizens. Its representatives are not likely to give up this privilege voluntarily. Their resistance does not just reflect a natural unwillingness to break with so fundamental a tradition. Any global money form would surely reduce national sovereignty over economic policy in fairly dramatic fashion. And what politician or central banker would willingly accept such a reduction of power?

Even if we assume sufficient support among participating nation-states for the basic idea, the very notion of supranational credit-money raises difficult questions. What kind of international monetary authority needs to be created to manage elastic issue and unhindered circulation of this supranational credit-money? How will the money-creation process integrate itself with trade and capital flows between nations? Should this money be confined to international transactions, or should it replace domestic currency as well? If it is limited to cross-border exchange and to investments, how should this global currency exchange with the various purely national monies? How should exchange rates be set, and who should have the power to change them? What kind of provisions are necessary to assure a balance in capital access and adjustment burdens between deficit and creditor nations?

Fortunately, we have already some provisional answers to these questions from past and present experimentation. The idea of a truly supranational form of credit-money is not new. Keynes was the first to develop an international payments system based on this money form when he outlined his vision for a postwar order in the early 1940s (section 15.1). In 1968 the IMF began to issue its own liquidity device, SDRs, on a limited basis (section 15.2). And in 1979 the European Community introduced ECUs as the centerpiece of a new monetary regime among its member countries (section 15.3). A crucial debate is now under way in Europe about moving toward a single-currency zone based on an expanded ECU version which, if implemented, would be a major step forward in the historic evolution of world money (sections 15.4–15.6). These various initiatives allow us to analyze (in chapter 16) how a global regime based on supranational credit-money would best operate in practice.

15.1. The Bancor Plan of Keynes

After studying international monetary regimes for nearly thirty years, Keynes had a unique opportunity in the final years of his life to apply his profound theoretical insights on that subject. Working for the British Treasury during World War II, Keynes was put in charge of preparing blueprints for a new international economic order. His radical ideas on world money and trade, even though ultimately pushed aside by the Americans in favor of their own proposals at the Bretton Woods Conference in July 1944, have lost none of their relevance. They still deserve close scrutiny.

In 1941 Keynes proposed the creation of an International Clearing Union, a supranational monetary authority in which national central banks would keep reserve accounts to settle outstanding balances with each other. Those accounts would be denominated in a new kind of world money, which he called *bancor*. All transactions between countries would be routed via those accounts at the clearing union, with bancor thus serving as the official international medium of exchange.[2]

This plan rested on comprehensive exchange controls which would be imposed on both ends of any capital movement to make them more effective. These controls had two purposes. One was to give central banks the monopoly of foreign exchange within their own country. In other words, private agents (e.g., firms buying imports) were not allowed to acquire or reconvert other currencies on their own. Thus deprived of any access to foreign exchange, households and firms could not conduct international transactions other than making remittances through their central bank. The other goal was to distinguish between trade or productive long-term investment, both of which would receive licenses automatically, and unproductive movements of capital for speculation or flight purposes, which would not be approved.

In Keynes' proposal central banks were intermediaries, dealing with their own public through the commercial banking system at home and with each other through the international clearing union. They would buy and sell currencies among themselves only against corresponding debits and credits to their bancor accounts at the clearing union. Let us illustrate how this would work in the case of, say, imports. The firm buying the foreign product would pay by ordering its own bank to send a remittance in the same amount, much like a check, to the central bank, which in turn would present it to the international clearing union for settlement. In the process the importer's checking account at his bank, the commercial bank's reserve account at the central bank, and the central bank's bancor account at the clearing union would all be debited that sum. The clearing union, in turn, would credit the payment to the bancor account of the central bank representing the exporter, who would eventually end up with an equivalent addition in his checking account. Settlements of payments obligations between countries were thus supposed to work very much like the reserve transfers between banks within the domestic check-clearing mechanism (see chapter 2), except that the clearing union would take the place of the central bank as bookkeeper.

Keynes designed this multilateral clearing mechanism as a closed system. Countries would start out with a zero balance. Thereafter, deficit countries would end up with debit balances in their bancor accounts, and surplus countries would accumulate credit balances. Since debits and credits would offset each other in such a closed system, the clearing union as a whole could not be in difficulty. For credits to match debits, the clearing mechanism would have to run like an overdraft system, in which any deficit country could draw additional bancor reserves up to a specified limit. Credit balances of surplus countries would thus automatically support debit balances of deficit countries.

Keynes envisaged that bancors would be measured in terms of a weight of gold and that the various national currencies would be valued in terms of bancor. This regime of fixed exchange rates would then be subject to price adjustments under specific conditions (see below). Bancor would be universally accepted as the equivalent of gold for the purpose of settling international balances. Even though by and large replaced by bancor, gold would still have a limited role as an international medium in Keynes's plan. Central banks could still ship gold to one another as a form of payment, provided they informed the clearing union to make appropriate book entries for clearance in their respective bancor accounts. Any central bank could pay gold into the clearing union and have that amount credited to its account. However, this convertibility did not operate the other way. No central bank could demand gold from the clearing union against its bancor balance, because the latter would only be available for transfer to clearing accounts of other central banks. Yet the clearing union would distribute any surplus gold proportionately among all central banks with credit balances and would deduct those payouts from their accounts.

Another crucial aspect of Keynes's clearing mechanism was its rules for adjustment to prevent excessive imbalances. Each country would be allowed a maximum debit balance. The size of this so-called quota would depend on a country's foreign trade volume and would be subject to regular review. A deficit country would have to take corrective action whenever the annual average debits rose above a certain percentage of its quota. The severity of the adjustment measures required by the clearing union would rise with the deficit threshold being passed: a modest currency devaluation at 25 percent; further devaluation, tighter controls on capital exports, or surrender of its gold reserve at 50 percent; austerity measures or, in case of failure, outright default at 75 percent. Surplus countries whose credit balances exceeded 50 percent of their respective quota, would have to discuss appropriate adjustment measures with the clearing union. Those might include policy reflation (e.g., lower interest rates, higher wages), currency revaluation, removal of trade barriers, or international loans to lesser-developed countries. Finally, as an inducement to maintain equilibrium, both deficit and surplus nations would have to pay charges on their excess debits and credits, which would rise with the imbalance. The two sides could avoid these contributions by arranging for surpluses to be lent out to cover deficits.

Keynes also wanted to use the clearing union in support of additional international stabilization policies by having it collect levies from creditor countries and/or set up clearing accounts for a variety of new multilateral agencies. Those included a Relief and Reconstruction Authority helping war-damaged economies with their rebuilding efforts, a Commodity Control holding stocks of commodities, a Board for International Investment to transfer capital to developing countries, and an International Economic Board to maintain the stability of world prices and to control business cycles. The clearing union could collect debt-servicing charges on behalf of these institutions by automatically debiting the clearing account of the debtor country concerned. It could also easily impose a financial blockage on any country whose belligerent actions the international community (e.g., the United Nations) judged to be a threat to world peace.

The Bancor Plan had major advantages over previous international monetary arrangements. No longer would global liquidity depend on inelastic gold supplies, technological progress in gold mining, and the policies of gold-producing countries. The addition of bancor would guarantee a much more elastic supply of world money, capable of responding automatically to the financing needs that arose out of trade and long-term investments. At the same time, unproductive movements of funds, especially capital flight and speculation, would be severely limited. The new clearing mechanism would also mobilize any surpluses into credits, which would finance debits within a self-balanced overdraft system. In that way it would prevent the shrinking of global liquidity through hoarding of surpluses, as the United States had practiced during the interwar period. Another benefit of the international clearing union would be to force symmetrical adjustments among creditors and debtors, so that the burden of correcting imbalances would not fall entirely on the usually weaker and smaller deficit countries. In addition, a multilateral system could be enforced more easily vis-à-vis individual countries than the multitude of bilateral agreements which had typified international monetary arrangements until then. Finally, Keynes emphasized the benefits of rules over discretion, especially when it came to specifying thresholds, measures, and timetables for adjustments to correct imbalances.

These benefits did not save Keynes's proposal from defeat at the negotiation table. It was the American plan, originally designed by Harry Dexter White of the U.S. Treasury, that carried the day at Bretton Woods. Its position of absolute global dominance enabled the United States to impose its own ideas for a postwar order on the rest of the world. These centered on a stabilization fund, the IMF, as well as on a dollar-based gold exchange standard (see chapter 4).

The U.S. delegation had some serious objections to the Bancor Plan. The concept of an overdraft facility was alien to Americans, even though it was standard banking practice in Great Britain. U.S. attitudes were entirely shaped by expectations of having the strongest currency and being the major supplier of international credit during the postwar period. Because the United States was surely going to be the largest net contributor to the new supranational institution, it wanted to limit its obligation. The U.S. Treasury therefore proposed a fund that was considerably smaller and more conservative in its lending policy than

Keynes's clearing union would have been.[3] The United States also rejected capital controls, which it feared would severely constrain its ability to purchase foreign assets and to set up production facilities abroad. As the largest surplus nation, it did not want to be forced into any corrective adjustments, especially dollar revaluation, which it would have had to make under Keynes's plan. At the same time, the Americans viewed currency depreciation by weaker countries as a threat to U.S. foreign investment and exports. Consequently, the U.S. delegation at Bretton Woods was much more concerned with exchange-rate stability than with liquidity, and that priority is clearly evident in its proposal for what was eventually to become the IMF. Finally, the United States was ready to reap the benefits of seigniorage and in the process turn its huge gold hoard into a source of global liquidity. Thus it wanted a gold-backed dollar, rather than bancor, as world money.

Self-interest also led the United States to squash another idea the British had pushed in the context of Bretton Woods, that of creating an International Trade Organization (ITO) as a close counterpart of the IMF on trade issues.[4] Keynes and Meade understood quite clearly from what had transpired during the inter-war period that a balanced world economy required international coordination on both monetary and commercial fronts. The IMF only had a mandate in the currency and monetary area, not in trade policy. The proposed ITO was supposed to fill that vacuum, regulating trade issues between nations for the first time on a multilateral basis, in the hope of thereby submerging bilateral conflicts and unilateral discretion. The authors of that plan also wanted the reach of the ITO to extend beyond traditional import restrictions (e.g., tariffs, quotas) to domestic policies which give a country unfair trading advantages (e.g., export subsidies, cartels, price discrimination). Finally, the ITO would exert strong pressure on surplus countries to take corrective measures, such as policy reflation or currency revaluation, and in this way would assure a more symmetrical adjustment mechanism in close cooperation with the IMF.

Such an international trade organization never materialized. Having by far the strongest economy at that point, the United States pushed for free trade so that its industries could capture foreign markets more easily. But many other countries, led by Australia and India, resisted this laissez-faire approach. They wanted more room for government intervention to maintain full employment, including protection of domestic industries and use of planning devices to carry out import-substitution strategies that would promote economic development. Between October 1946 and March 1948 three international conferences (London, Washington, Havana) were held to bridge these differences. The Havana Charter, a compromise, was never ratified by the U.S. Congress.

As a by-product of these negotiations, twenty-three countries signed a "Draft Agreement on Tariffs and Trade" in October 1947 at a meeting in Geneva which was called to draw up a preliminary charter for the Havana meeting. After Congress rejected the ITO plan, this draft agreement became the permanent basis for the regulation of trade relations. Known as GATT, this substitute is much closer to the U.S. position than the Havana Charter for an ITO would have been. GATT is a forum for negotiations and a code of rules rather than an organization with enforcement powers. Its effectiveness depends entirely on the willingness of countries to make binding commitments to each other on a reciprocal basis. It adopted the principles of nondiscrimination first established in the "most-favored-nation" clause of the Reciprocal Trade Agreements Act of 1934, the law that reversed more than a century of American protectionism. GATT stressed reduction of protectionism on a multilateral basis, with only limited provisions for the import-substitution strategies of LDCs. Finally, this watered-down version of a trade organization acts separately from the IMF and has no leverage over surplus countries concerning adjustment.

15.2. Special Drawing Rights

By 1960 dollars in international circulation, all supposedly convertible with gold, began to exceed U.S. gold reserves. The emergence of this "dollar overhang" exposed a fundamental contradiction of the Bretton Woods system, which came to be known as the "Triffin dilemma" (see section 7.1). The supply of dollars to the rest of the world required continuous U.S. balance-of-payments deficits, but the long-term stability of the dollar depended on America's ability to return to surplus. The solution to this problem was obvious: cut the U.S. deficit and then make up for the decline in the supply of global liquidity by finding an alternative source of world money. The leading industrial nations, which had met in 1961 as the so-called Group of Ten in the General Agreements to Borrow (GAB), spent the next few years discussing the creation of such a new global liquidity device. Their effort succeeded in 1969 with the introduction of SDRs, which were to be issued by the IMF as a substitute for gold and dollars.[5]

This agreement was a major breakthrough. For the first time in history, nations accepted the idea of a supranational money issued by an international monetary authority. This acceptance came about when a large majority of countries realized that neither static gold supplies nor a weakening dollar could meet the liquidity needs and stability requirements of the world economy any longer. Negotiations pertaining to the details of this new money form proved to be arduous because of clashing interests. The United States refused to cut its own external deficit, prompting surplus countries to reject use of their own reserves to back the new asset. Developing countries pushed hard to get a more than proportional allocation of new SDRs. But the industrial nations rejected such a link of SDRs and aid, insisting that any allocation be in strict proportionality to the respective IMF quotas of participating member countries.[6] Thus only a third of new SDRs went to LDCs with the greatest liquidity needs.

Probably the most important feature of the SDRs is that they are created without backing by any other asset, much like fiat-money created by national governments for domestic transactions. At the time that was a historic first. Never before had there been a legal tender in international circulation that was not convertible into underlying assets such as gold. But the economists who were designing the SDRs realized (finally!) that money did not have to be backed by anything if it had general acceptance as a medium of exchange. Users would be willing to use SDRs or anything else as long as they could count on others accepting it from them. The key question then became what attributes the SDRs had to have to make them globally acceptable as money.

That question of acceptability necessitated rather complex provisions, which I shall summarize briefly.[7]

• To begin with, individual countries have a choice as to whether or not to take part in the SDR scheme. Issues of SDRs by the IMF require approval by an 85 percent majority of the participating countries to assure widespread acceptance. This provision gives both the United States and the European Community a veto right over any allocation of SDRs.

• Only central banks or official lending institutions (e.g., BIS, World Bank) can use SDRs. Hence the number of users has been very limited. So is their use. SDRs are essentially an international reserve asset which deficit countries can convert into gold, dollars, or other key currencies when needed. That need requirement relates primarily to exchange-rate support in the face of large balance-of-payments deficits.

• To make SDRs effective international legal tender, creditors have to accept them in discharge of debts. The problem was that any creditor nation which accepted SDRs from a debtor nation would have to supply an equivalent amount of convertible currency in exchange. Most surplus countries resisted having to give up foreign exchange in return for something they considered less attractive. The acceptance requirement therefore had to be negotiated. First there was a quantitative limit. Any country was committed to hold unneeded SDRs up to three times the size of its total allocation. Any SDR holdings in excess of a nation's total allocation would earn interest (originally set at a low 1.5 percent), thus making them more attractive than gold. In order to assure an equitable distribution of SDR holdings, the IMF could designate which countries must provide the convertible currency.

Although the SDRs are clearly a reserve asset, they also contain certain aspects of a credit instrument. If deficit countries use SDRs excessively, they can be forced to reacquire them—much like a repurchase agreement. A country has to keep at least 30 percent of its average cumulative SDR allocations over a five-year period in reserve at any given point of time. If it uses more than 70 percent of its SDRs, it has to restore its average ratio requirement before the end of that period by repurchasing them from the IMF or from other countries, in exchange for convertible currency. This reconstitution provision aimed to preclude any participating member country from depending solely on SDRs for financing its balance-of-payments deficits and to promote SDR holdings as part of a diversified reserve portfolio.

When first issued in 1970, SDRs were valued in terms of a fixed amount of gold so that one drawing right equaled one dollar. But a year later the United States suspended dollar convertibility into gold, followed by two significant dollar devaluations in late 1971 and early 1973. At that point many countries wanted a different valuation basis, after they realized that the value of their SDR assets would decline whenever the dollar depreciated. In 1974 the IMF complied and began to use a basket of sixteen currencies to value SDRs. Other than the dollar, which was given a proportionately larger role in that basket because of its unique world-money status, the other currencies were weighted on the basis of their respective issuer's proportional share in world exports. Each of those currencies was then converted daily into an equivalent amount of U.S. dollars, and the sixteen amounts were then added up to give the dollar value of one SDR. The procedure could be repeated for each basket currency. This valuation method was much more stable, because currency-price movements would cancel each other out. When one currency depreciated, the other currencies would necessarily appreciate by comparable amounts.[8]

That switch to a basket valuation was not the only IMF measure to make SDRs a more attractive reserve asset. At the same time, still in 1974, it was decided to raise the interest rate on SDRs from the statutory 1.5 percent to a more competitive level. But because the basket-valuation approach gave SDRs an intrinsically more stable value than each of the basket currencies, the IMF proposed keeping the SDR yield below the market average. Such a reverse application of the traditional risk-return trade-off was also strongly favored by certain member nations for different reasons. The United States was eager to protect the reserve-currency status of the dollar and thus wanted to keep the SDRs from becoming too attractive. Chronic deficit countries expected to be net users of SDRs and preferred to pay a lower yield. Apart from this "security discount" the SDR yield was based on only five of the basket's sixteen currencies, a weighted average of American, German, Japanese, British, and French short-term interest rates. Since these countries had relatively strong currencies, interest rates there were typically lower than elsewhere.

The new SDR yield thus ended up being only 5 percent and, under the formula adopted in 1974, would not rise unless the market average exceeded 11 percent. In 1976 the formula was adjusted upward, so that the SDR rate would henceforth be 60 percent of the weighted average of the market rates in those five countries. In 1978 the sixteen-currency basket was changed to make its composition more realistic and to provide for automatic adjustment of currencies and weights in the future. In January 1979 the SDR rate was further increased to 80 percent of the market rate, and in 1981 the IMF proposed raising it to 100 percent. At the same time the basket was reduced from sixteen currencies to the five key currencies, thereby considerably strengthening the capital value of SDRs.

These inducements notwithstanding, SDRs have never managed to fulfill their potential as a substitute for gold or reserve currencies. One reason has been their limited supply. The first allocation of SDRs between 1970 and 1972 amounted to $9.3 billion. An additional 12 billion SDRs, worth about $15 billion at that point, were issued between 1979 and 1981. Today the total amount of SDRs in circulation is less than 3 percent of global reserves.

This marginalization did not have to be. At one point the industrial nations seemed ready to expand the role of SDRs quite significantly. In March 1979, when it had become evident that the dollar-rescue package of November 1978 (see chapter 7) would only halt the slide of that currency temporarily, former IMF Managing Director Johannes Witteveen proposed taking a chunk of the $500 billion in excess dollars out of global circulation. Under his plan foreign central banks, which at that point held about $200 billion in their reserves, could exchange unwanted dollars for new long-term IMF bonds denominated in SDRs. This so-called Substitution Account allowed central banks to diversify their reserve portfolio without dumping dollars on the market. Initially the United States had opposed this plan as an effort to diminish the dollar's international role. But as the dollar resumed its rapid decline, the Carter administration became more sympathetic to the idea. Similarly, European officials gradually warmed to the proposal once they saw the rapidly declining dollar reduce the value of their reserve holdings. Germany, which at first had resisted the substitution account on the grounds that it would enable the United States to run big balance-of-payments deficits with impunity and thereby add to inflationary pressures across the globe, eventually welcomed the plan as a way to prevent the mark from replacing the dollar as a key currency. Still, in April 1980 the industrial nations abandoned the idea, after they failed to agree on the details. Disagreements between the Americans and Europeans centered on the size of the substitution account and on the sharing of risks and costs.[9]

The failure of the Witteveen plan is symptomatic of the inherent shortcomings of SDRs. Any expansion of that liquidity device, either in terms of its quantity or its qualitative role, requires agreement among the leading economic powers—which is very hard to come by. The United States opposes any diminution of the dollar's role as world money; surplus nations with strong currencies (e.g., Germany, Japan) have their own institutional reasons for resisting the growing circulation of SDRs. After all, they must accept newly issued SDRs in exchange for their own currencies, which they have to issue and transfer as part of the government's authorized public expenditure. These SDR deposits cannot be easily disposed of. Unlike other reserve assets (e.g., foreign currency deposits), the central banks of surplus countries cannot use SDRs as a medium of exchange in international transactions. Moreover, even if their compulsory SDR deposits yield rates equivalent to the market average (as has been the case since 1981), those average returns are by definition always less attractive than those which prevail at the same time in at least one of the five countries making up the basket. The same is true for the capital value of their SDR holdings. The law of averages means that the value of at least one of the key currencies in the basket always appreciates more rapidly than does the SDR.

At present, SDRs are not designed to function as world money. Their existence is limited to that of an official reserve asset which deficit countries use to acquire additional liquidity. The irony is that the extraordinarily rapid growth of global liquidity under the system of generalized floating made the original purpose of the SDRs, that of a liquidity device, obsolete. In 1976, therefore, the IMF tried to expand the monetary attributes of SDRs. But these changes under the so-called Second Amendment did not go far enough.

- Since 1976 the SDR has served as the unit of account for all IMF transactions. But the standard basket approach gives one value to the SDR as numeraire and quite another value in its role as reserve asset.[10] This dual valuation has made it difficult to use SDRs as an anchor for computing exchange rates between key currencies, as proposed by the IMF in 1988 for the G–7 target zones.
- The 1976 amendment also increased the use of SDRs in transactions between governments by eliminating several restrictions. SDR transfers could now occur directly between central banks without prior IMF approval, independent of any balance-of-payments need, in exchange for any currency, as a loan (and thus without exchanging an equivalent amount of currency in return), and even in forward or swap operations. These changes turned SDRs into a limited means of payment which governments could use in credit transactions and to settle debts.
- As long as SDRs cannot be held by private parties, their role will be severely limited. In the early 1980s a few transnational banks accepted claims denominated in SDRs and even began to organize a secondary market in which such instruments could be traded. Yet without substitution account or any other method to generate a large supply of SDR claims, any such privatization effort must remain modest.

In conclusion, it is fair to say that after two decades the full potential of the SDRs as a new form of world money is still far from being realized. Although the idea of a truly international form of credit-money is radical, its actual implementation has so far been a first step at best. The SDRs are still a far cry from fully developed money. Any upgrading in that direction will have to conceive of SDRs as a substitute rather than as a supplement to existing forms of world money, as was first recognized in the 1979 proposal for a Substitution Account.

15.3. European Currency Units

Since 1979 the world has witnessed a second experiment with the concept of international credit-money, ECUs, which were defined as "a means of settlement between monetary authorities of the European Community."[11]

ECUs have their origin in the Smithsonian Agreement of December 1971. That arrangement pegged exchange rates of industrial nations at new levels and allowed those rates to fluctuate within wider margins of plus or minus 2.25 percent (compared to the 1 percent margins under Bretton Woods). Three months later the members of the European Community announced that they would maintain their exchange rates vis-à-vis one another within half that margin. From March 1972 onward those EC rates were kept within that narrower "snake." When the collapse of Smithsonian in March 1973 gave rise to generalized floating, the EC member countries announced their intention to keep the snake and to float jointly against the dollar. Great Britain and Italy, which had dropped out of the snake earlier and let their currencies float (in June 1972 and February 1973, respectively), promised to rejoin that fixed-rate arrangement as soon as possible.

The snake failed as a vehicle of economic integration in Europe, however. Key members of the EC decided that they could not adhere to a system of fixed exchange rates, not even one that allowed for occasional adjustments. This was especially true for Great Britain and Italy, both of which remained outside the system. In January 1974 France let its currency float. After rejoining briefly in July 1975, it left the snake for good in March 1976. With France removed, the snake in effect became a mark zone. Germany's smaller neighbors (Belgium, the Netherlands, Luxembourg, Denmark, Norway, Sweden) linked their currencies to the mark because of their extensive economic ties to that hegemonic power in the center of Europe. Great Britain, France, and Italy, on the other hand, preferred to be free of that linkage. By opting for floating, these larger members of the EC thought they could maintain the competitiveness of their industries through currency depreciation.

This strategy of competitive devaluations ultimately backfired. Other trading partners also let their currencies float downward, so devaluations did not help domestic industry much. Instead, they tended to feed inflationary pressures by making imports more expensive and by often being associated with "easy money" policies of the central bank. At the same time, the countries that participated in the snake proved to be much more resistant to inflation. Germany has operated under a strong national consensus in favor of stable prices ever since a devastating encounter with hyperinflation in the early 1920s (see Table 15.1). In this regard, a strong mark helped to keep price increases in check. Linked to the mark, the small economies surrounding Germany reaped these benefits of a strong currency as well. Nor could those countries afford to let their domestic inflation rates rise substantially above that of low-inflation Germany, because prevailing fixed exchange rates might then become impossible to maintain.

Table 15.1

Comparing the "Snake" and Floating

	West Germany		France		Italy		Great Britain	
Year	Inflation	Exchange rate	Inflation	Exchange rate	Inflation	Exchange rate	Inflation	Exchange rate
1972	55.9	91.6	28.3	176.5	15.6	307.7	23.4	193.0
1973	59.9	110.2	30.4	200.6	17.3	326.2	25.1	189.2
1974	64.0	112.9	34.5	185.1	20.5	326.5	29.1	180.4
1975	67.8	119.0	38.6	208.2	24.0	291.9	36.1	171.4
1976	70.9	116.5	42.3	186.7	28.7	229.5	42.7	139.3
1977	73.4	125.9	46.3	181.4	33.2	215.6	48.8	134.7
1978	75.3	145.7	50.5	197.8	37.2	224.3	52.8	148.1
1979	78.4	159.4	55.9	209.6	42.7	229.1	59.9	163.7

Source: International Monetary Fund *International Financial Statistics Yearbook 1992*, Washington, DC, pp. 350–53, 362–65, 428–29, 430–31, 712–13.

Notes: Inflation measured by consumer price index (1985 = 100). Exchange rate by market rate index of domestic currency per U.S. dollar (1985 = 100).

It was precisely this dual outcome of the snake, a failure as an instrument of European integration but a success in its role as a regional currency, that prompted the leaders of the EC to consider a more ambitious version of the snake as its replacement. The departure of Great Britain, Italy, and France— three of the four large EC economies—had stripped the snake of its European dimension. As pounds, lire, and francs moved lower, floating emerged as a new form of monetary protectionism which proved very divisive. It therefore became increasingly clear during the 1970s that further integration within the EC depended not least on bringing these three countries back into a snake-type adjustable-peg system. That issue gained urgency when the precipitous decline of the dollar in 1978 caused much greater divergences among EC currencies.[12] With the need for a common policy vis-à-vis the dollar more clearly felt, the member countries of the EC began to discuss a more broadly based and institutionally improved snake. The result of these negotiations was an agreement in December 1978 to launch the European Monetary System (EMS) at the beginning of 1979.

The principal architects of the EMS were the German Chancellor Helmut Schmidt, French President Valery Giscard d'Estaing, and the president of the EC Commission, Roy Jenkins. Having all been finance ministers, these men understood the intricacies of international monetary arrangements very well. What they designed was a sort of supersnake with three distinct features. To begin with, the remaining EC members (Great Britain, France, Italy, Ireland) were enticed to join the new currency arrangement by allowing their traditionally weaker currencies a larger degree of fluctuations. The second aspect was a partial pooling of member reserves into a multicurrency intervention fund for support operations. Its third and final feature was the creation of a new kind of reserve asset for settlements between central banks within the EC. Let us examine each of these innovative provisions in greater detail.

The new system opted for "fixed, but adjustable" exchange rates, a compromise between genuine floating and the kind of rigidly fixed rates of Bretton Woods. EMS currencies would be linked to each other through an Exchange Rate Mechanism (ERM). If one currency dropped too much against another, the central banks concerned would sell the strong currency in the foreign exchange markets and purchase the weak one in order to maintain prevailing exchange rates. EMS members would set up a fund from which their central banks could borrow to finance their market interventions. If those did not succeed, government officials would meet and adjust the rates within the ERM. Such changes in agreed rates were supposed to be infrequent and to occur only in response to fundamental differences in economic performance. This provision meant that imbalances between member countries should preferably be corrected by shifts in their internal economic policies. If parity changes became unavoidable, any adjustments should involve a degree of symmetry between surplus and deficit countries. In theory, at least, this notion of symmetrical adjustments sounded good (see section 13.4). In practice, however, it once again proved to be a contentious issue between weak- and strong-currency countries, as had been the case at the Bretton Woods Conference (see section 15.1 above).

During the negotiations leading to the EMS it soon became clear that the actual distribution of adjustment burdens depended on how exchange rates were to be fixed within the ERM.

• Germany preferred a system of bilateral rates between all currencies, with a band of permissible fluctuations of plus or minus 2.25 percent. When a weak currency reached the lower edge of this band, a strong currency was automatically at the opposite end. In this so-called "parity grid" approach, both weak- and strong-currency countries would consequently have to intervene at the same time. Under proposed settlement requirements, however, weak-currency countries would have to repurchase their own currencies that had been bought earlier by the strong-currency country.[13] The loss of reserves and the slower growth of the money supply in the wake of such repurchases placed more of the adjustment burden on weak-currency countries. Moreover, under such a grid system of bilateral rates the strength of the mark vis-à-vis all other EMS currencies could force the rest of the EC for extended periods of time into painfully restrictive policies to narrow the inflation differential with Germany.

• For these reasons traditional weak-currency countries favored an alternative that promised to be less burdensome on them. With the backing of Great Britain, the French proposed a so-called basket system based on the ECU as numeraire. This new unit of account was to be valued by a basket of all EMS currencies, akin to the weighted average approach used in the case of SDRs (see section 15.2). Each currency within the EMS would then have a value ("central rate") defined in terms of the ECU, with margins for permissible fluctuations on either side. That approach had two advantages for weak-currency countries. One was to place the duty of market intervention primarily on that country whose currency's market value diverged most from its defined value in ECUs—under normal circumstances, Germany. The other was a much more relaxed provision for buying back one's own currency acquired earlier by another country in the course of intervention. Such repurchases now only became necessary if and when the relative exchange-rate position of the two currencies in question was reversed.

The Germans rejected the French proposal. Having by far the strongest currency in the ECU basket, they did not want to be put in a position of having to bear most of the adjustment burden. They also felt that the settlement and intervention rules of the proposed ECU basket system would prove to be highly inflationary. Germany, forced to intervene in order to keep the mark from rising beyond its permitted level, would have to buy up weak currencies and in the process experience an involuntary increase of its money supply. At the same time, this kind of automatic intervention by the strong-currency country might weaken the pressure on weak-currency countries to keep inflation in check.

The deadlock over that issue was ultimately resolved when the Belgians came up with a compromise formula acceptable to both sides. The solution was to combine the two proposals as much as possible. The bilateral parity grid system favored by the Germans would define the obligations of each EMS member to intervene in the currency markets in support of fixed exchange rates. The ECU basket system proposed by the French would, in turn, signal to any country that the deviation of its currency was such as to warrant policy adjustments. When a currency diverged by more than 75 percent of its permitted maximum deviance, its issuer would have the obligation to respond with adjustment measures, such as changes in the central rate or in monetary policy. The aforementioned repurchase requirement was put into effect as well (see note 13). The central bank, whose currency had to be supported by other EMS central banks, would have to repay all of the credit granted by the latter within six months.

The Belgian compromise put into place a system of great complexity, prompting serious doubts as to whether it was workable.[14] To begin with, the basket approach to valuation prevented the ECU from truly functioning as independent numeraire. Given the way in which the ECU was valued, namely as the weighted average of a currency basket, changes in the relative market values of any currency in that basket automatically affected the value of the ECU. This in turn altered the central rates of all other EMS currencies, because those were, after all, defined in terms of the ECU. Secondly, in practice it proved difficult to combine the parity grid approach and the ECU basket system in a coherent fashion. The EMS members would frequently reach the permissible limits of their bilateral parity grid rates without ever having crossed the 75 percent divergence threshold that triggers adjustment measures. A third problem arose from the fact that the Italian lira had a margin of plus or minus 6 percent, whereas all of the other EMS currencies could only fluctuate within a 2.25 percent margin. Finally, sterling was given a role in determining the ECU value even though Great Britain chose not to participate in the intervention and settlement system of the EMS.

In addition to representing a unit of account for the fixing of exchange rates, the ECU was designed to serve as a reserve asset which EMS members could use to settle official debts among themselves. For that role ECUs had to have a physical presence, be issued by a central institution, and to be held by the monetary authorities of the different participating countries. A new agency, the European Monetary Cooperation Fund (EMCF), was set up to issue ECUs. Each EMS member agreed to put 20 percent of its gold reserves and another 20 percent of its dollar reserves into the fund. Adjustments were made by the EMCF on a quarterly basis to maintain that 20 percent reserve requirement.[15] In exchange for putting this portion of its reserves into a pool, each member country received an equivalent credit denominated in ECUs to draw on. The initial size of the fund was 25 billion ECUs ($33.8 billion), giving participating countries access to a financing facility with at least twice their borrowing capacity from the IMF.

Such an arrangement, swapping gold and dollar reserves for ECUs, made the latter a very different form of supranational credit-money from SDRs.

• Whereas SDRs are allocated on the basis of quotas, ECUs are backed by reserves that determine their distribution. When a deficit country finds its gold and dollar reserves declining, it also loses ECUs each quarter. This is not the case with SDRs.

• Changes in the rate of exchange between dollars and gold leave SDR holdings unaffected. But these relative price changes have a direct impact on ECU holdings, and the precise configuration of that effect depends on the reserve composition of EMS members.

• The EMS revived the use of gold in the settlement of payments imbalances between countries just a few years after the IMF decided to phase out gold as the international reserve asset in favor of SDRs. EMS members could value their gold reserves at the prevailing market price, which rose fourfold in 1979–80 to a peak of more than $800 per ounce. That spectacular price hike right at the beginning of the new system boosted reserves of EMS members with large gold holdings (e.g., France).

• In contrast to the SDRs, which are usually exchanged for basket currencies, the primary use of ECUs is to settle bilateral debts among EMS members. However, creditor central banks were only obliged to accept half of any settlement in ECUs, a more limited acceptance requirement than in the case of SDRs.[16]

The EMS proved to be quite successful. In its first phase, from 1979 to 1983, rates within its ERM were changed about twice a year. These frequent adjustments were in response to still relatively large differences in inflation rates and to divergent economic policies. Even then the exchange-rate changes were kept small, usually less than twice the permissible margin of plus or minus 2.25 percent, and were spread quite evenly among strong-currency and weak-currency countries so that speculators would not gain too much. Starting with the dramatic switch by France's Socialist government toward austerity in March 1983, parity realignments became linked to domestic policy adjustments and thus became a tool for cutting inflation rates.[17] Between 1984 and 1987, at a time of extraordinarily turbulent currency markets, the ERM had already reached such a degree of stability that it required only two relatively minor realignments (in April 1986 and January 1987). All of this meant that ECU currencies have fluctuated much less than other currencies outside the system, as is clear in Figure 15.1. The principal objective of the EMS and its ERM, the stabilization of its members' exchange rates, was thus achieved within a decade.

It is fair to say that the institution of the EMS, contrary to initial predictions of its unworkability, by and large proved to be effective as a new tool of supranational money management among tightly interwoven national economies.

• Inflation declined more rapidly during the last decade within the EMS than in the rest of the EC (Britain, Spain, Portugal), though only at the expense of stubbornly high unemployment. This reflected a deflationary bias in the system, caused primarily by the large weight of the strong German mark within the ECU basket, which pressured other EMS members to keep their monetary and fiscal policies tight for extended periods.

• By reducing exchange-rate risk, the ERM also helped to keep interest rates lower and less variable than they would have been under a system of generalized floating.

• The ERM surely engendered greater monetary policy coordination among its members, forcing countries with comparatively high inflation rates to tighten their money supplies. But during times of stress within the system, such as right after the global stock market crash and sharp dollar decline in late 1987, strong currency countries within the EMS temporarily expanded their money supplies to alleviate the squeeze on the weaker countries.

• The constraint of fixed exchange rates on the domestic money supply also had an indirect effect on fiscal policy by reducing the extent to which excessively large budget deficits could be monetized.

Figure 15.1 **Currency Fluctuations Against ECU, 1979–1987**

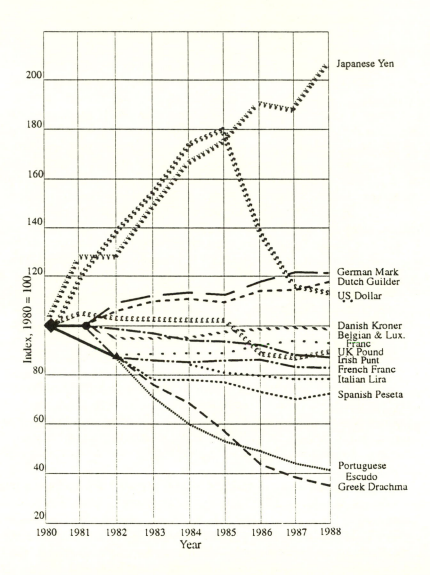

Source: Author's calculation based on data from the Commission of the European Communities, European Economy, no. 48, September 1991, Brussels, p. 126.

Notes: Fluctuations of currencies against the ECU. Black lines, 1980–81 and 1980–82, indicate approximately synchronus exchange-rate movements of several currencies before they diverge.

• Since devaluation was no longer an easy option, balance-of-payments deficits and other real economic divergences gradually came to be regarded as a matter more for domestic policy adjustment than of currency realignment.

• The system's infrequent and small exchange-rate corrections after 1984 raised hopes that earlier imbalances had been finally corrected and had given way to reasonably realistic currency prices.

15.4. Economic and Monetary Union in Europe

The success of the EMS provided the EC with an institutional anchor for further economic integration. The convergence and stabilization brought about during the second phase of the EMS enabled the Europeans to make a bold move in that direction. In December 1985 they decided to introduce a single market over seven years. In the so-called *Single European Act* all twelve member states of the EC committed themselves to remove more than 300 barriers to the movement of goods, people, and capital by the end of 1992.[18]

The prospect of a single market prompted a debate over the future of the EMS, especially in light of the planned capital liberalization by 1992. Policymakers feared that the free movement of capital, with funds invested anywhere within the EC and in any denomination, could trigger massive speculative flows out of weaker countries and thereby undo the EMS. Such fears were not unfounded. The system had shown renewed signs of stress during 1986, as a result of massive capital movements out of dollars and francs into marks. The tensions thereby created were ultimately contained by a series of measures—a currency realignment within the EMS in January 1987, the Louvre Agreement to stabilize the dollar a month later, and the Basel-Nyborg accord of September 1987 to strengthen central bank intervention and policy coordination within the EMS.[19] Even though the crisis passed, it made many EC leaders more aware of what might lie ahead once capital could move freely across the continent.

With the EMS thus restabilized, it was time to consider the long-term role of the system in a fully integrated EC. In February 1988 the fathers of the EMS, Helmut Schmidt and Valery Giscard d'Estaing, called on EC leaders to implement the second stage of their original plan—the creation of a single European central bank and free use of the ECU by companies, banks, and consumers in all twelve member states. The single market, they argued, required such a degree of monetary integration. At their Hanover summit in June of that year, the EC leaders appointed a committee of central bankers and finance experts to study the idea. In April 1989 that committee, headed by the EC Commission President Jacques Delors, published its report proposing an ambitious three-stage plan for "economic and monetary union."[20]

• First Great Britain, Greece, Spain, and Portugal would commit themselves to join the EMS. The twelve EC nations would strengthen coordination of their economic policies, focusing in particular on closer cooperation among central bank governors on such matters as setting interest rates, fighting inflation, and maintaining stable currency prices. This initial phase would end with the liberalization of all capital movements within the EC.

• The Delors Plan then envisaged establishing a framework to set key economic objectives and budget deficit limits. The community would monitor the performance of individual members. If a nation were to run too large a budget deficit, it could be ordered to trim that deficit. During this second stage a European System of Central Banks, similar in structure to the U.S. Federal Reserve, would be introduced. Individual central banks would turn into regional branches of the new EuroFed, thus forming the institutional basis for an EC-wide common monetary policy.

• In the final stage, exchange rates would become irrevocably locked. Members would agree to make the rules for macroeconomic and budgetary policy binding. The EuroFed would assume full responsibility for making the community's monetary policy, intervening in the currency markets, and holding reserves. The process would conclude with the adoption of a single currency for the entire region.

Delors presented his single-currency plan as a central element in the move toward a barrier-free Europe. Once there were a single European capital market in 1992, the current status quo would become untenable. Only with such monetary union, he argued, could there be true economic integration. Adoption of his plan would promote faster growth, would encourage greater efficiency, and would give Europe more clout vis-à-vis the United States and Japan.

These arguments found broad support in the private sector. Surveys clearly indicated that a majority of corporate managers in Europe favored the ECU becoming the main currency for commerce within the EC. This attitude came as no surprise. A single currency promised to yield significant cost savings. Companies could avoid the transaction costs of foreign exchange as well as the costs of hedging against currency fluctuations. They would also have clearer information about prices and costs throughout the EC if those were measured by the same standard of value. Bankers expressed similarly positive sentiments with regard to the Delors Plan, realizing that a single-currency system would greatly facilitate the integration of financial institutions and markets within the EC.[21]

Among governments officials there was broad agreement on the general principle of monetary union as well, and in June 1989 the EC heads of government unanimously decided to move ahead with its implementation. This was followed by a series of preparatory steps. In December 1989 the finance ministers of the EC agreed on uniform minimum capital adequacy standards for banks and for brokerage firms—a key step toward completely unrestricted cross-border operations by financial institutions anywhere within the EC after 1992. In June 1990 the central bankers met in Basel and decided to reorganize the management and policy-making structure of the EC's central banking committee. That powerful committee, headed by Bundesbank President Karl Otto Poehl, gained additional staff and subcommittees to improve the coordination of policies on foreign exchange, monetary issues, and banking supervision. This expansion into what came to be known as the European Monetary Institute was a first step toward creating a EuroFed. In July 1990 the first stage of the Delors Plan officially began. Great Britain and Spain linked their currencies to the ERM, followed shortly thereafter by Portugal, and Greece announced its intention to join a little later.[22]

The objectives of this initial phase—full membership by all twelve EC members in the EMS, liberalization of capital movements within the community, and closer policy coordination among participating countries—were beyond dispute. However, the second and third stages of the Delors Plan proved to be much more controversial. Conflicts soon erupted over the timetable of their implementation and the nature of the new EC-wide monetary authority. Politicians in several countries, most notably France, Belgium, and Italy, were eager to reduce the dominant influence of the German central bank, whose emphasis on fighting inflation had given the EMS a powerfully deflationary bias.[23] They viewed the new EuroFed as the best way to achieve this objective and therefore wanted to see monetary union implemented as soon as possible. This group, sometimes referred to as "institutionalists," argued that only in the face of strict deadlines for each step along the way would countries either shape up or face the consequences of being left behind. A second group within the EC favored a much more cautious approach. These so-called "behaviorists" preferred to make any movement toward a single currency dependent on the proven ability of participating countries to meet stringent conditions (e.g., full EMS membership, fiscal reform) and performance standards (e.g., low inflation).

The strongest opposition to monetary union came from Margaret Thatcher, who insisted that she did not want to cede control over Great Britain's economy to the EC bureaucracy in Brussels.[24] It was difficult to take her argument about "monetary sovereignty" very seriously, considering her country's record in that matter—a stop-and-go pattern of exchange-rate manipulation by the Bank of England and, as a consequence of such unsound money management, surely higher inflation and interest rates than would have been the case had Great Britain been in the EMS. But Thatcher also soon realized that outright rejection of the Delors Plan would leave her isolated within the EC and politically vulnerable at home. She needed to show herself to be more constructive. In October 1989 the British Treasury presented an alternative to Delors's single-currency proposal.

The British plan would let companies and individuals throughout the EC save and spend in whatever currency they chose. In such a competing-currency system governments would have a powerful incentive to lower national inflation rates or risk a loss of confidence in their respective currencies. As a result of such market-based pressure, convergence among member states would increase gradually to a point where further steps toward monetary union might become feasible. The plan also called for turning the ECU from a mere composite into a currency in its own right, with notes and coins, to be used as a thirteenth currency alongside the national currencies. A European Monetary Fund (EMF) would keep its value constant by adjusting interest rates and intervening in currency markets. Such a "hard ECU" would eventually be accepted as a common currency in lieu of national currencies.

Most EC leaders viewed this proposal as a delaying tactic by the British government. Poehl, president of the Bundesbank, rejected its main points as violating what he termed the "indivisibility" of monetary policy. He warned that the inevitable competition between the strongest national currencies and the ECU would lead to damaging "compromises." Market pressure might at one point force the EMF to abandon its "no devaluation" pledge. If that ever happened, confidence in the entire system would collapse. But Germany's powerful central banker also took issue with the Delors Plan and opposed its speedy implementation. If monetary union came about before much greater economic convergence among member states was achieved, the differences in inflation rates and national economic policies would soon, in his opinion, threaten to tear the system apart. In the face of such pressures, Germany might be forced to take measures it did not like, especially excessive stimulation of its economy. Poehl also worried that a European central bank would conduct monetary policy at the level of the lowest common denominator and in this way would accommodate higher inflation across Europe. Why should low-inflation countries like Germany give up their hard currency for something less desirable?

As head of both the Bundesbank and the committee of EC central bank governors, Poehl was in an excellent position to shape the debate over monetary union and to make sure that the behaviorists ultimately prevailed over the institutionalists. By late 1990 his warnings against excessive haste had gained added credibility in the aftermath of German reunification. The spectacular collapse of East German industry, an outcome he had predicted, illustrated clearly what could happen to weaker nations if they linked up with superior economies too soon and at unfavorable exchange rates. In November 1990 Poehl suggested a two-track approach. A core of five or six countries should implement monetary union first; other EC members would join later, after having successfully lowered their domestic inflation.

At a decisive intergovernmental conference in December 1990 the EC heads of state accepted a Dutch "compromise" which went a long way toward Poehl's position. Phase Two would be delayed by a year and would start at the beginning of 1994. During that transitional phase an embryo central bank would be set up to strengthen coordination among EC members, to formulate procedures for an eventual single monetary policy, and to oversee the development of the ECU. The EuroFed that would eventually be created out of this process would be independent of political influence, would possess full control over the management of the single currency it issued, and would have price stability as its primary objective.[25] Countries would have to meet stringent conditions before joining the new institution. These would include full membership in the EMS, an end to the practice of printing more money to finance budget deficits, and substantial progress in economic convergence—particularly in inflation and fiscal policy. By January 1, 1997, the EC members would decide whether or not they were ready to move ahead with the final phase of monetary union. Some countries might require more time and financial assistance to meet monetary union goals.

This compromise formed the basis for the eventual treaty on *economic and monetary union* (EMU), on which the EC leaders agreed at an historic meeting in the Dutch town of Maastricht in December 1991. Under this treaty a single currency was to be introduced as early as 1997, provided that two conditions were met. By 1996 at least seven nations would have to have met tough performance standards on inflation, interest rates, currency stability, and deficit spending.[26] And at that point a majority of the twelve EC member nations would have to vote to proceed with a single currency. Should either of these conditions not be satisfied, then economically robust nations, provided there were at least five of them, could decide to adopt the single currency in 1999 instead. Other countries would join later, whenever their domestic economies were in shape. The Maastricht accord gave Great Britain an opt-out clause to obtain support of Prime Minister John Major. It also provided additional regional aid for the poorer countries (Spain, Portugal, Greece, Ireland) to help them in their efforts to catch up with the rest of the EC. Amendments to the original EC Treaty of Rome, subject to ratification by national legislatures, would incorporate all of these new provisions.

This agreement reflected a growing consensus in the EC that it would have been too dangerous to rush into monetary union. Economically weaker countries (e.g., Greece, Portugal, Great Britain, Spain) worried that moving too fast toward a single currency could cause massive unemployment and slower growth. The richer countries, meanwhile, were reluctant to proceed with the final stage of monetary union unless fiscally troubled governments had taken effective measures to control their huge budget deficits.

Mindful that currency devaluations in the 1970s and early 1980s had inevitably forced interest rates higher to ward off currency crises and looming inflation, the European leaders were committed not to repeat this counterproductive course. Moreover, the positive experience of low-inflation growth in France, Spain, and Italy after these countries had joined the EMS seemed to confirm the advantages of a hard-currency regime over soft-money strategies. These lessons led most EC governments to prefer a tough anti-inflation stance imposed by Germany's central bank to a devalued currency, even if this meant higher interest rates at a time of slow or zero growth. In Maastricht they therefore agreed to model the new EuroFed after the Bundesbank and to impose tough performance criteria on the union members. Those provisions made it much less likely that the EuroFed would be forced to accommodate a high average inflation and support massive deficit spending by member countries. Once implemented, the combination of a solid monetary standard and falling trade barriers should bring about a strong surge in economic growth. European leaders were confident that the new monetary union would spread prosperity throughout the EC, provided it managed to keep inflation low.

15.5. Europe's Currency Crisis of 1992

The Maastricht treaty surely marked a major milestone in the evolution of Western Europe's postwar integration, a new stage in the construction of a confederation among nations that had fought numerous wars with each other for centuries. But at that point it was still only a blueprint, a plan designed and imposed from the top down. Driven by a grandiose vision of Europe's future as a confederation and tightly integrated economy, the politicians who negotiated this historic accord failed to take sufficient account of much messier present realities. Their negligence caught up with them barely nine months later, in the form of the worst monetary crisis since the collapse of Bretton Woods.

One fundamental mistake the political leaders of the EC made in their rush to economic and political union was not to have explained the provisions and implications of their plan to their electorates. In the absence of adequate consultation the European public had a difficult time fully comprehending what was behind Maastricht. Fears, focusing especially on a loss of national identity and meddling by an unaccountable EC bureaucracy in Brussels, soon created a fertile climate for opposition. Public debate also revealed a great deal of latent nervousness about the domination of Europe by a resurgent Germany. Although the heads of state saw in the union treaty a powerful vehicle for peaceful coexistence and a practical way to strengthen European industry, many citizens viewed the proposal as a threat to their national identity and economic interests.

For the union treaty to take effect, it had to be ratified by all twelve members of the EC. Only two, Denmark and Ireland, were constitutionally required to give their citizens a voice in a nationwide referendum. All of the other countries had the choice of ratification through parliamentary approval. In June 1992 the Danes rejected the Maastricht accord by a slim majority. The outcome of that referendum surprised everyone and made it clear that political leaders had not adequately prepared the European people for such a dramatic change in their policy-making structure.

In the immediate aftermath of the Danish vote, President Mitterand announced that he would give French voters a chance to have their say in a nationwide referendum on September 20. Apart from giving the treaty democratic legitimation, Mitterand had several political objectives in mind when he abandoned the safe route of parliamentary ratification in favor of the riskier referendum option. He figured that a sound victory in September would boost his low popularity and would improve the electoral prospects of his party in parliamentary elections shortly thereafter. He also expected the referendum to deepen divisions within the opposition. At the time, polls showed that a large majority of French voters approved of the treaty, making the calculated risk seem small. But France's president, whose shrewdness and political acumen had become legendary, miscalculated badly this time. Politicians opposing the treaty, covering the entire spectrum from Communists to the extreme-right Front National, ran an effective campaign which appealed to nationalist and anti-Mitterand sentiments. Their intense targeting of France's popular vacation spots caught the government off guard, and by the end of the summer the polls showed that the "No" votes had grown into a narrow majority. The prospect of a French rejection, which would have spelled the end for Maastricht, created a climate of uncertainty. This, in turn, set the stage for an unprecedented currency crisis just days before the referendum.

The Danish rejection and France's shifting sentiments raised questions about the future of European integration, and soon those began to preoccupy foreign-exchange traders. This group is especially sensitive to uncertainty and is uniquely positioned to test the intentions of governments. To understand why, we need to keep in mind the special nature of their market—the currency market (see also section 14.3).

• Operating like a computerized auction, highly competitive, free of government regulations, capable of extremely efficient processing of information, and adjusting prices instantaneously, the currency market is the closest real-life approximation of the neoclassical market model we have. It is ironic, yet by no means coincidental, that such a market should thrive on volatility rather than tend toward equilibrium. Its auction-like organization yields widening gaps between bids and offering prices during periods of instability. Some of the largest traders earn much of their currency-trading profits, which in the case of the largest U.S. banks exceed $200 million a year, from such bid-asked spreads. Traders also make money by betting heavily on the market's direction. For both reasons they have a vested interest in price volatility.

• The speculative nature of that market assures such volatility. Currency trading involves the exchange of monies, each of which embodies a relative valuation of the national productive apparatus it represents within a given international hierarchy. This activity is therefore driven largely by market perceptions about strengths and weaknesses of the country issuing the currency in question compared to other countries with which it competes. The trades conducted no longer involve any tangible physical entities, such as coins or paper. Thanks to computerization, they are reduced to electronic bookkeeping entries which modern communications technology transmit across a global network of data-processing units. Instant access to trading information is crucial to this particular market, and activity thrives when expectational biases about trends become widely shared. Finally, market participants use highly leveraged positions which magnify loss and gain. All of those conditions make market-regulated currency prices move a great deal and shift direction suddenly.

• Exchanging monies of different nations, traders basically make bets on the key determinant of a national currency's value—the economic and political performance of the issuer compared to other countries. When two national economies move in opposite directions, the exchange rate of their currencies will change accordingly. Once traders come to believe that prevailing exchange rates are out of line with underlying economic fundamentals or are being undermined by current events, their "animal spirits" will inevitably awaken and may easily grow into a speculative frenzy.

• Able to move huge sums at very short notice, foreign-exchange traders can overwhelm the ability of any government to defend the value of its currency, provided that a widely shared expectational bias moves them massively in one direction.

Because volatile conditions in the foreign-exchange market impact directly on such key macroeconomic variables as a nation's money supply, interest rates, and inflation rates, EC governments had thought it prudent to construct a mechanism for stabilizing their currency prices—the EMS, introduced in 1979. For thirteen years, until those crisis-ridden days of September 1992, it had been widely believed that the EMS system's hitherto successful defense of fixed exchange rates would shield European currency markets from any resurgence of instability. But such optimism turned out to have been premature. In the weeks preceding the French referendum European currency markets were hit by a hurricane of speculation with such force that the very future of the EMS, as the cornerstone of economic and monetary union, hung in the balance.

After the Danish vote, which triggered sudden doubts about the union treaty, currency traders began to question the viability of the proposed transition toward a single-currency regime in less than seven years. Nervousness in the market soon found a concrete focus, as traders began to wonder whether or not exchange rates would have to be realigned before they became irrevocably locked some time in the late 1990s. The more they pondered that question, the likelier such a realignment seemed to them. Significant differences in economic performance and divergent policies among member nations, which had been downplayed during the euphoric days following ratification of the Single European Act in 1987, suddenly took on renewed importance.

Traders had good reason to be nervous. Over the past two years the EC economies had grown apart in terms of performance. By the summer of 1992 their differences had become quite sizable. At the time only three countries—

France, Luxembourg, and Denmark—met Maastricht's stringent performance standards for membership (see note 26). Budget deficits, though still fairly small in France and Denmark, had grown very large in Great Britain, Germany, and Italy. Inflation rates in Greece, Spain and Italy had been consistently higher than, say, in Germany, and they deviated significantly from the EC average. Great Britain remained mired in deep recession, then entering its third year. Other large EC economies (e.g., Germany, France, Italy), though not yet in recession, had seen their growth slow down considerably since 1990.

But successful implementation of economic and monetary union within the prescribed timetable required significant movement in the opposite direction, toward greater convergence. If increasingly disparate conditions within the EC were allowed to persist, economic fundamentals would eventually force a re-alignment of currency prices within the ERM of the EMS. Such a situation could be avoided by coordinated policy initiatives among EC members which held the prospect of moving the different national economies closer together. But this seemed unlikely. In the face of slowing growth the EC governments found that kind of coordination increasingly difficult to sustain. Nervous currency traders had good reason to doubt whether governments, in the face of mounting domestic political pressures amidst rising unemployment, would be willing or able to undertake the painful adjustments such coordination requires. Moreover, any EC-wide move toward greater convergence needed the leadership of Germany, after reunification the undisputed leader of the EC. But at that point the Germans were consumed by internal difficulties—the economic collapse and social disintegration of the former East Germany, a wave of racist violence against foreign asylum-seekers, and deep divisions over policy within the government. In the face of these domestic pressures the German central bank, the most powerful monetary authority within the EMS, had locked itself into a policy course which only exacerbated tensions within the system.

Between July 1988 and July 1992 the Bundesbank had raised interest rates eleven times, pushing the key Lombard rate (which it charges banks for loans) from 4.5 percent to 9.75 percent. These rate hikes had gained momentum in the aftermath of German reunification. Bundesbank officials felt, not without justification, that the federal government had badly mismanaged the process when it allowed East German savers to trade in their old currency at parity (i.e., for an equivalent amount of West German marks) and valued East German industrial assets at an exchange rate of two to one. Those generous terms, while giving East German savers a major boost and thus helping Chancellor Helmut Kohl's reelection chances, had profoundly negative repercussions. On the one hand, they helped to finance a consumer boom in the east. On the other hand, they made East German industry much less competitive and western investments there much less attractive. This difficult situation worsened when the government allowed wage levels in East Germany to rise rapidly to West German pay scales without concomitant improvements in productivity. As a result East German industry collapsed, making the reunification process much more difficult and expensive than originally predicted.

During the election campaign of 1991 Chancellor Kohl had promised that he would not raise taxes, or cut existing federal spending programs, to pay for reunification. These politically motivated decisions, coming on top of major financial commitments to share the costs of the Gulf War and to help Russia, caused the German budget deficit to explode once reunification costs began to mount. The federal government covered the huge transfers (an estimated 180 billion marks in 1992 alone) to its reintegrated eastern provinces by borrowing heavily. Its decision to delay incorporating an additional 370 billion marks ($250 billion) of government debt incurred from the takeover of East German industry's assets and liabilities into the federal budgets of 1994 and 1995 raised the prospect of even larger deficits in the near future. In addition, a strike wave by public-sector employees in early 1992 had forced the Kohl government to accept wage settlements that clearly exceeded the prevailing inflation rate. Even though the German economy slowed down considerably after the initial consumer boom in the east gave way to a depression there, the country's money supply continued to grow at twice the pace targeted by the Bundesbank.

The combination of large-scale government borrowing, generous wage settlements, and rapid money-supply growth caused Germany's inflation rate to double, from 2 percent to 4 percent, within a span of two years. This revived deep-seated fears of higher prices. To assess these fears correctly, we must remember that Germans had been traumatized by hyperinflation during the 1920s. Their fiercely independent central bank, charged in its constitution to make price stability its highest priority, responded in typical fashion by pushing interest rates higher.

Whereas the Bundesbank had gained a reputation as an inflation fighter, its single-minded pursuit of this domestic commitment failed to take into account what ramifications those rate hikes would have for its neighbors and the rest of the world. With exchange rates fixed in the EMS, the international transmission mechanism concerning national monetary policies operates through interest rates. Given the mark's dominating influence in the EMS, other EC countries had to raise their interest rates to keep currency prices within the ranges set by the ERM. Most of those countries already faced high unemployment and slow growth, if not outright recession. Higher interest rates would only aggravate these problems and were therefore counterproductive. Currency traders soon became convinced that this situation was untenable. Their sentiments of skepticism gained force when Bundesbank officials themselves expressed concern over whether currently prevailing exchange rates could be maintained. Capital flows into the mark began to accelerate. By early September this run into the mark had become an avalanche, fed in addition by a weakening dollar and by much lower U.S. interest rates. The more German monetary policy came to be seen as squeezing other countries at a time of global slowdown, the greater was the price that monetary union seemed to exact and the more uncertain became the prospects for Maastricht. Heightened doubts just before the crucial French referendum only gave traders more reason to sell weak currencies and to buy marks. The stage was set for a full-blown currency crisis.

Once it began to feed on itself, that crisis hit the weaker European currencies with devastating ferocity. One currency after another came under attack, forcing central banks to raise interest rates dramatically and to use up most of their reserves in futile efforts to defend prevailing exchange rates. Eventually the prevailing currency-price grid of the ERM, which had remained unchanged since 1987, collapsed. Let us briefly recount the course of this tidal wave of speculation.

1) The Opening Gambit. The crisis began in earnest three weeks before the French referendum, with a massive run against the Italian lira. Italy's enormous budget deficits exceeded 11 percent of its gross national product, which would have to be lowered to 3 percent to comply with Maastricht's membership criteria. Italy's level of national debt clearly exceeded its annual GNP and was almost twice the 60 percent limit set in the union treaty. Long-standing political paralysis and short-lived governments made it unlikely that these targets could be met in less than a decade. With Italy's inflation having risen four times faster than Germany's over the past decade, the lira was the most obvious candidate for future devaluation and the first currency within the EMS to come under attack.

On September 4 the Bank of Italy raised its discount rate by 1.75 percent to a seven-year high of 15 percent—but to no avail. Only heavy central bank intervention during the following week, with the German authorities spending nearly 24 billion marks ($16.2 billion) to prop up the lira, managed to counter that attack. But Bundesbank purchases of lire had the effect of accelerating the domestic money supply in Germany, thereby threatening its efforts at restraint. That side-effect of central bank intervention in the currency markets convinced traders that the Bundesbank was unlikely to relax its tough policy stance anytime soon. They knew that the underlying problem of a strengthening mark had not been resolved, so they began to look for new targets.

2) Scandinavian Jitters. Following the attack on the lira, speculators turned their attention on the Finnish markka and the Swedish krona. The markka in particular made a perfect target. Less than two years earlier the Finns had decided to peg their currency to the ECU in anticipation of applying for EC membership. But they abandoned that link temporarily in December 1991 to devalue the markka by 13 percent. That adjustment proved counterproductive, forcing interest rates there ultimately higher and making Finland's commitment to fixed exchange rates appear shaky. In addition, Finland had seen its foreign-exchange reserves plummet after it lost its major export market in the collapse of the Soviet Union.

Even though not yet officially part of the ERM, the Finnish currency received the support of European central bankers, who bought an estimated 30 billion markkaa ($7.5 billion) to counter the attack. The Bank of Finland first tried to defend its currency by pushing up short-term interest rates, despite the deep recession at home. Ultimately the squeeze was too much to bear, and the government decided to let the markka float on September 8. The currency immediately fell by about 18 percent against the dollar and key EMS currencies.

The Swedes too had pegged their krona to the ECU in May 1991 to prepare for membership in the EC. Currency devaluations in the early 1980s gave traders reason to doubt Sweden's commitment to fixed exchange rates. But that experiment, which contributed to Sweden's comparatively high inflation rates and low growth rates during the 1980s, stiffened the resolve of the new Conservative government to defend the peg whatever the cost. It was only a question of time before traders would test that resolve, and the confrontation unfolded when the turbulence in Finnish markets led to outflows of currency from Sweden. Between July 24 and September 8 Sweden's central bank had raised its key lending rate on loans to commercial banks four times, from 11.5 percent to 24 percent. On September 9, following the Finns' abandonment of their peg, the Riksbank pushed that rate to 75 percent. This drastic step, reinforced by 31 billion ECUs in new loans and credit lines from other central banks to shore up its currency reserves, reversed capital flows. On September 14 the Riksbank lowered the rate to 20 percent, after the government had decided to double the spending cuts proposed in the fiscal 1994 budget. That relaxation proved premature. Soon the krona was under attack again, and two days later the central bank set its lending rate at an incredible 500 percent. The crisis forced the Conservative government to seek an agreement with the Social Democrats for deep cuts in Sweden's legendary "welfare state" benefits and for tax increases to lower the sizable budget deficit. These draconian monetary and fiscal measures came at a time when Sweden was suffering its worst slump since World War II and when Swedish banks were facing severe losses from the collapse of the real estate sector. The government was obviously willing to risk a severe economic crisis in defense of the krona—a very heavy price to pay for maintaining credibility in international financial markets.

3)The First Realignment. Sweden's determined defense of its currency underscored the difficulties of creating an economically united Europe, reinforcing market perceptions that other countries would have to devalue their currencies or raise interest rates sharply. This had the effect of spreading currency speculation to the weaker currencies within the ERM. Selling pressure was especially strong on the lira. On September 10 Italy's new Prime Minister, Giuliano Amato, declared that he would seek special powers for three years to deal with economic emergency situations. If granted, the new powers would allow the government to rescind previously approved spending and borrowing, to change tax rates, and to decide on government debt financing without parliamentary approval. He also announced the first state companies to be privatized, measures to stimulate the stock market, and a crackdown on tax evasion.

This was an impressive step for a new prime minister who had already managed to end the inflationary practice of automatic wage indexation for public officials. But soon doubts arose as to whether Amato had sufficient support within his quarrelsome coalition government to make good on his promises. The attack on the lira resumed, intensifying steadily during and after the battle over the Swedish krona. Amato knew that further interest-rate hikes would doom his plans for spending cuts. With Italy's currency reserves depleted and the lira under intense pressure, devaluation was now the most viable option. But Amato resisted a unilateral decision to that effect. Every realignment within the EMS until then had involved multilateral adjustments. Over the weekend of September 12–13 he negotiated a pact with other EC leaders which tied a 7 percent devaluation of the lira to a cut in German interest rates.

After nearly five years of relentlessly raising interest rates, the Bundesbank finally flinched and reversed course. That move was motivated in part by a desire to influence the outcome of the French referendum. Even though lower interest rates made sense when considering how much the German economy had slowed in 1992, the Bundesbank did as little as it could. It cut its discount rate by 0.5 percent and the more important Lombard rate for supplemental bank borrowings by a paltry 0.25 percent. Moreover, in subsequent interviews German central bank officials made a point of stressing that they did not plan any further rate cuts in the near future. The euphoria in global financial markets following the Bundesbank decision to lower rates therefore fizzled rapidly, once investors realized that they could not expect further cuts. The German-Italian action was not enough to calm the currency markets.

4) The Disintegration of the Exchange Rate Mechanism. Once it became clear that the Bundesbank had not really abandoned its tough policy course, the turmoil in the currency markets grew to unprecedented levels. On September 16 speculation reached hurricane force against several EMS currencies, especially the pound. European central banks spent £10 billion ($17 billion) in defense of the pound. The Bank of England raised its lending rate twice within hours, from 10 percent to 15 percent. Nevertheless, by the end of the day traders had driven the British currency well below its permitted floor in the ERM. At that point Prime Minister Major, who had earlier vowed to defend the pound no matter what the cost, changed his mind. With the British economy going through its worst recession since World War II, a 5 percent increase in interest rates might well trigger depression-like conditions. So Major decided to suspend Great Britain's participation in the ERM and to rescind the second, three-point rate increase. That move paved the way for a devaluation of the pound and enabled the Bank of England to lower its discount rate further, to 9 percent.

The run on the pound also sent other exchange rates into wild gyrations during September 16. The lira in particular faced renewed attack, just three days after its devaluation. By the end of that fateful day, traders had pushed the lira below its floor despite massive intervention by the Bank of Italy. Prime Minister

Amato pledged drastic new budget cuts, but currency traders ignored that vow. The next day the Italians followed the British and announced a temporary withdrawal from the ERM. At the same time, the Spanish government devalued the peseta by 5 percent but decided to leave its currency within the ERM. The near-collapse of the EMS also triggered a spectacular one-day rise of the dollar, to which many investors fled as a haven from the chaos in Europe.

5) The Decisive Battle. Speculators had finally pushed Europe's system of monetary cooperation and economic coordination beyond its capabilities. It was now up to French voters to determine whether the battered system could be salvaged. On September 20 they approved the Maastricht agreement by the slimmest of margins. That ambiguous message from an electorate which up to then had traditionally been among the most fervent supporters of European unity failed to quell growing doubts about the viability of the proposed union treaty.

The inconclusive vote, a bitter quarrel between German and British officials over who was to blame for the turmoil, and Germany's refusal during a G–7 meeting to lower its interest rates convinced traders that the currency crisis was not over yet. With the pound, lira, and peseta already devalued, their attention turned to the French currency. Until then the franc had held up fairly well, reinforced by the strong performance of the French economy, whose budget deficits and inflation rates were smaller than Germany's were. But neither those strong fundamentals nor the improving competitiveness of French industry had prevented unemployment from rising steadily. The narrow outcome of the referendum only reinforced the impression that the government was unpopular and would not have the stomach for a vigorous defense of the franc, with unemployment at 10 percent. The Socialists may inadvertently have contributed to that impression when they promised during the campaign that domestic interest rates would fall, rather than rise, if the voters approved Maastricht.

The attack on the French franc came into full swing on September 23. In a desperate bid to support the franc, the Bank of France raised its key short-term lending rate from 10.5 percent to 13 percent. The currency recovered at first, but that turnaround was brief. When its decline resumed, both the French and German central banks were forced to intervene heavily to shore up the franc. That day the Bank of France bought 50 billion francs ($10 billion), in the process spending about half of its foreign-exchange reserves. And even then the franc closed near the lower edge of its trading band within the ERM. Chancellor Kohl flew to Paris for an emergency meeting with President Mitterand, and both leaders declared their readiness to defend the franc at all cost. The traders took that message seriously and relaxed their selling pressure in subsequent days. The crisis had finally run its course.

The battle over the franc was the decisive one for several reasons. After all, it was the last of the major EMS currencies still fixed to the mark at exchange rates that had been set five years earlier. All others—the pounds, lira, and peseta—had already been devalued. Moreover, the French economy was in much better shape than were those of Great Britain, Italy, or Spain. In terms of key indicators (e.g., growth rate, budget deficit, inflation) it outperformed even the German economy at that point. Had speculators been allowed to force a devaluation of the franc in the face of such strong economic fundamentals, the tough performance and convergence criteria established under Maastricht would have lost all credibility. The French government, of course, might have been tempted to defuse tensions at this critical moment by devaluing its currency, which would have had the added advantage of allowing lower interest rates. But such a step would have reversed a decade of economic policy that had given France lower inflation and smaller budget deficits than Germany. Mitterand did not want to risk losing these tangible benefits of his decade-long pursuit of a hard-money regime and decided to stand firm. Crucial to France's successful defense was strong German support which had been noticeably absent a week earlier during the attack on the pound and lira. Kohl and Helmut Schlesinger, the head of the Bundesbank, knew that any restoration of the EMS as the pillar of future economic and monetary union had to include the franc. After all, the franc-mark peg is the anchor of that system, just as the broader French-German alliance has always been the key to further European integration. They finally drew the line, and the speculators withdrew for the time being.

6) The Aftermath. The currency crisis served as a stark reminder to central bankers and finance ministers of how much their power to control their economies and currencies has eroded. It has left the EMS in tatters. Reserve pools set up under the EMS proved to be inadequate to defend member currencies under attack and were largely exhausted during three weeks of concerted attacks. Massive speculative sell-offs forced both the pound and the lira out of the system. Spain, Portugal, and Ireland had to undertake repeated currency devaluations to stay within the ERM. In addition, both Spain and Ireland imposed capital controls, a step which jeopardized completion of the single-market program in time and contradicted the move toward a common European currency. Subsequent aftershocks prompted Sweden and Norway to follow the example of Finland and break the informal linkage of their currencies to the ERM in favor of devaluation and lower interest rates.

The turbulent events of September 1992 also dealt a serious blow to the prospects for Maastricht. Even though the treaty narrowly survived the French referendum, public sentiment against its provisions has grown strongly across the EC. Ratification has proven especially difficult in Great Britain. Granting Denmark exemption from key aspects of the union treaty in order to gain majority approval in a second referendum, after having made special concessions to Great Britain, has left the EC open to similar demands from other member countries should the treaty ever be reopened for negotiation. This is very likely, since the failure of both Denmark and Great Britain to ratify the treaty during the prescribed period has already invalidated the treaty's timetable. In any process of renegotiation, earlier compromises might easily come undone.

Following the earthquake-like currency crisis, the first priority of European leaders has been to rebuild the EMS into a credible institution that can once again function as the institutional base for the construction of a single-currency zone. Over the past fifteen months there has been some progress in that effort. Spain and Ireland have rescinded their exchange controls. In the face of deepening domestic recession, the Bundesbank has finally undertaken a series of modest interest-rate cuts. This change of course has allowed its partners in the EMS to do the same. The French franc has stabilized, following the electoral triumph of the conservative parties and their adoption of an austerity plan to control France's exploding budget deficits. But the reconstruction of the EMS can only succeed if the pound and lira once again join the system. Even though currency devaluation and lower interest rates have finally produced signs of revival in the British economy, the continuous political erosion of the Major government makes it doubtful that the pound can rejoin the EMS in the near future. Italy, rocked by daily revelations of corruption scandals involving that country's most important politicians and business leaders, faces an even deeper political crisis. The disintegration of its postwar system of coalition government has surely delayed reentry of the lira into the EMS. Apart from getting the pound and the lira back into the ERM grid, the EC might have to realign exchange rates some more and reinforce the intervention capacity of its central banks as part of its rebuilding effort.

At this point (February 1994) several EC members, including Spain, Great Britain, and Italy, lack the political stability and the economic strength to participate fully in the planned transition toward a single-currency zone. It therefore seems increasingly likely that only a core of nations will go ahead with implementation of the original treaty. This group should include Germany, Belgium, the Netherlands, Luxembourg, and France. Austria, Sweden, and Switzerland—all low-inflation countries that have recently applied for EC membership—may also participate in such a single-currency zone. The rest of the EC will form a much looser confederation, with some countries eventually joining the union after having readied their economies for such a step. Such a "two-speed" integration may be the only realistic outcome, but it raises new questions about the nature of European integration. It is quite possible that economic and monetary union confined to the core of Germany and its neighbors might harm the competitive position of countries on the periphery to such an extent that the latter fall behind even more.

15.6. The Uncertain Prospects of the Union Treaty

In the end it may prove impossible to salvage Maastricht. There have been dramatic changes since the treaty was conceived, and these have surely darkened the prospects for political, economic, and monetary union.

• Rapid growth in Western Europe during the late 1980s has given way to a recession which is global in nature. Crisis conditions, most notably very high unemployment and pervasive financial fragility, have fueled social tensions and a sense of vulnerability across the region. Such an unstable environment leaves people more afraid of experiments and governments less able to act decisively.

• A second factor has been the end of the cold war, which over four decades had served as a catalyst for economic integration in Western Europe. With the threat of superpower confrontation on their own soil gone, Europeans feel less pressured to integrate and unify. National and regional interests, long suppressed by the cold war, are now coming to the fore again and create new divisions within the continent. The multiple civil wars in the former Yugoslavia, as the most explosive of the many conflicts arising out of the collapse of communism, have made it abundantly clear how far away the EC nations still are from forging the kind of common foreign and security policies envisaged by the union treaty. Moreover, with Eastern Europe freed of Soviet domination and in the midst of a very difficult transition to a market economy, the question of widening the EC has become as urgent as its deepening. These two challenges may prove to be incompatible, for union among an elite of highly advanced economies may widen the gulf in development levels and living standards between the two halves of Europe.

• Finally, there is the touchy issue of German reunification, which has reinforced the position of that troubled nation in the middle of the continent as the regional superpower. The question is whether Maastricht is a tool of German hegemony or a counterweight to otherwise unfettered expansionism. My feeling is that economic and monetary union among the largest possible number of European nations is the best way to neutralize narrow national interests in Germany and elsewhere. Firmly anchored into an integrated Europe, Germany will have to play by certain "rules of the game" in which its partners have had a say. But we may never have a chance to test this hypothesis. The weight of the past engenders widespread fears of Germany in the rest of Europe which many Germans, especially those born after World War II, resent. Tensions have been fueled by the inflationary shock of German reunification and the Bundesbank's deflationary policy response, which the EMS helped to spread throughout the continent. Unless both sides show a great deal of sensitivity to their shared history of pain and destruction, it is difficult to see how Germany and its neighbors can move forward toward a United States of Europe.

Even though Maastricht may well have been derailed by the confluence of recession, resurgent national interests, and fears of German power, I believe that the vision of an increasingly unified Europe will survive and will foster new initiatives in that direction. Forced to compete with two other powerful blocs, one dominated by the United States and the other by Japan, Europeans will see no alternative to further integration. Hence they have no choice but to maintain a system of fixed exchange rates, even though a reformed ERM may allow for more frequent price adjustments and will require substantially more policy coordination. "Free market" advocates may object to such a conclusion and may point to the currency crisis as one more proof that fixed exchange rates do not work. They have every right to question why there is no crisis when the freely floating dollar declines by 6 percent in a matter of days, while a 1 percent decline of the pegged pound below an artificially set threshold triggers panic. Floating exchange rates obviously provide greater flexibility when adjustments are necessary, and this advantage is a significant one. But in an economically integrated region such as the EC, the benefits of market-determined currency prices become much smaller and the costs of exchange-rate volatility much larger. With the twelve EC member nations inexorably linked by trade and capital flows, unstable currency prices can have potentially very disruptive effects on economic activity.

Even though the currency crisis of 1992 still does not validate arguments in favor of flexible exchange rates, it holds valuable lessons for policy-makers who are trying to rebuild a damaged system of fixed exchange rates within the EC. As European leaders struggle to salvage whatever is left of the union treaty, they will need to understand why the EMS suddenly exploded after working so well for more than a decade. First and foremost, politicians must appreciate their own contribution to the problem. They simply cannot expect to maintain a system of fixed exchange rates if they allow their economies to move too far in opposite directions. Moreover, the only way to counter system-threatening divergence is for member nations to coordinate their macroeconomic stabilization efforts and implement a joint plan of action that brings the different economies closer together. Such coordination can only come about to the extent that each participating government subordinates its national interests to the dictates of the larger community of nations. The currency crisis of 1992 could have been avoided, had national concerns not dominated and blocked any coordinated response to the build-up of centrifugal forces in the region. When traders sense that set exchange rates no longer correspond to underlying performance trends, they will be tempted to test the will of governments by betting against overvalued currencies. Cumulative selling pressure may then soon grow into a full-blown attack. Such a speculative onslaught can engender gigantic trading volumes which overwhelm central bank supplies of foreign-exchange reserves available to defend a particular currency. Even with sufficient reserves, governments find it extremely difficult to maintain prevailing currency prices in the face of massive speculation, because their interventions often have perverse effects (e.g., interest-rate hikes, bulges in the money supply) that may undermine other stabilization objectives. Their best hope is therefore to prevent such an attack in the first place through concerted action.

Even if the policy-makers manage to heed these lessons and to bring Maastricht back on track, they may still face several obstacles which prevent the

EC from ever reaping the benefits of economic and monetary union. Apart from external threats (e.g., the turmoil in Eastern Europe and the former Soviet Union, trade conflicts with the United States and Japan), the EC faces potentially serious complications from implementing the single-currency plan.

1) Turning the ECU into Full-Bodied Money. Lack of public acceptance has so far confined any artificial international money constructs, such as SDRs, to official transactions between central banks. This holds true for the ECU as well. Although the volume of ECU-denominated deposits and bonds has risen steadily in recent years, its commercial use remains marginal.[27] It is doubtful whether the ECU can simply be imposed from one day to the next as the replacement for national currencies without having first come into widespread private circulation. Successful implementation of monetary union may therefore come to depend to a large degree on whether the ECU can gain greater acceptance soon, before the mark has become too dominant. That goal has now become more difficult. Not only did the currency crisis of 1992 reinforce the dominant position of the mark, but in its wake the market for ECU-denominated bonds also suffered major losses.

Despite this setback, it should be possible to build up private use of ECUs over the next decade. Besides reducing price risk, ECU-denominated instruments allow borrowers in weak-currency countries to save interest costs while offering investors from strong-currency countries higher returns. They thus may prove attractive to both sides of the credit transaction, and the ECU market has managed to expand quite rapidly in recent years (see Table 15.2). Moreover, once EC governments and institutions renominate their bonds in ECUs, they will have created a bond market that exceeds the U.S. Treasury market in size. With 60 percent of total EC trade already taking place within the Community, ECU billing would save companies operating in Europe large amounts of money on currency transactions. The problem is one of transition, of how to move from the ECU as an alternative competing with national currencies to a qualitatively quite different stage, in which it replaces them by fiat.

2) The Impossible Triangle of Money Management. The implementation of a single-currency zone has been complicated by the fact that, although capital has been able to move freely within the EC since 1991, monetary union will only come about years later. Deregulating capital movements so early, during the first phase of the transition, may have been a serious mistake. The moment capital and exchange controls were abolished, the EMS changed qualitatively. In the absence of any restrictions on capital flows, the attraction for investors and foreign-exchange traders to shift funds into the strongest currency at the slightest hint of trouble has become that much stronger. Now in a position to move capital even more freely than before, the traders make it more difficult for the monetary authorities to defend weaker currencies against concerted attack. As expensive defense operations absorb most of their foreign-exchange reserves, central bankers inevitably face a painful choice between higher interest rates and currency devaluation.

Table 15.2

Growth of the ECU Market

Year	ECU bond issues (in millions of ECU)	ECU banking assets (in billions of ECU)
1987	9,045	80.8
1988	16,438	100.0
1989	20,317	124.1
1990	25,526	142.7

Source: European Community Commission, "The ECU and Its Role in the Process toward Monetary Union," 1991, Brussels, pp. 131–32.

The liberalization of capital movements within the EC before the end of 1991 has made it impossible for central banks to manage money properly. They can no longer regulate currency prices and at the same time maintain control over interest rates and money supplies. In other words, free capital movements, fixed exchange rates, and autonomy concerning monetary policy are incompatible with each other. Any two of these may be pursued simultaneously, but it is extremely difficult to have all three conditions coexist peacefully. The only EMS member still granted a certain degree of autonomy in the conduct of monetary policy is Germany, the largest country with the strongest currency. Ironically, just when the elimination of capital controls reinforced the dominance of the mark within the system, the mishandling of German reunification triggered an inflationary shock. Given already very high unemployment in Europe and the weakness of the world's other key currencies (dollar, yen) at the time, the Bundesbank could have refrained from pushing interest rates under its control relentlessly higher. In this case the mark would have temporarily weakened, giving Germany's partners in the EMS much-needed breathing space in managing the difficult transition to monetary union. But once the German central bank decided that it needed to contain the threat of higher inflation at home by raising interest rates, all other EMS members had to follow suit or accept market-enforced devaluations of their currencies. In the absence of more effective policy coordination within the EMS, the system may very well experience bouts of instability any time the Bundesbank resumes tightening.

3) Moving Toward Convergence. Unless the macroeconomic performance of still rather heterogeneous economies (the hard-currency bloc around Germany, Great Britain, the Mediterranean countries) converges significantly, capital will surely move from weaker to stronger nations. If those capital movements mainly take the form of currency speculation, then we could see renewed attacks on the EMS before the single-currency plan is completed. Those currency crises will either tear the system apart or force the kind of drastic government actions which convergence requires. The speculative attacks on the krona and the lira during September 1992, for example, forced Swedes and Italians to finally face up to their huge budget deficits and to cut spending programs they had not been able or willing to touch until then.

Rapid financial integration and centralization from 1993 onward will only help to feed the growth of speculative "hot money" flows. With exchange rates essentially fixed, the absorption of large capital movements in foreign-exchange markets can only come about through changing interest rate differentials. Volatile interest rates in turn foster greater uncertainty among investors, thus causing the average rate to be higher because of a larger risk premium.[28] Frequent currency realignments could ameliorate this problem, of course, but only at the expense of undermining confidence in the future viability of monetary union and setting off acute waves of speculation whenever a currency is rumored to be devalued. Credible and effective institutional change promoting convergence within the EC is therefore crucial.

Monetary union only stands a chance if the economies of participating nations become less divergent, but the convergence criteria adopted in Maastricht (see note 26) are simply too stringent. Efforts by individual members to meet those performance standards threaten to keep the entire continent mired in slow growth and unacceptably high unemployment for years to come. After first pushing interest rates to prohibitive levels while growth was already slowing across Europe, most EC governments are now forced to adopt fiscal austerity measures in the mid of a recession. Should restrictive fiscal and monetary policies deepen or prolong the downturn, governments will find it progressively more difficult to meet the budget-deficit and public-debt targets specified in the union treaty. The political crises in Italy, Belgium, Germany, and Spain, which exploded in early 1993 around efforts to control rapidly growing budget deficits, are a harbinger of things to come.

4) The Subordination of Fiscal Policy. When policy-makers discuss the structure of the proposed European System of Central Banks and its conduct of monetary policy for the planned single-currency zone, they often cite the independent German and U.S. central banks as role models. But this comparison, which has even prompted commentators to use EuroFed as a nickname for the new monetary authority, is erroneous in one crucial respect. Both the Bundesbank and the Federal Reserve are operationally tied to the fiscal policies of their respective nations, in that they monetize a portion of the public debt. The EuroFed, by contrast, is supposed to be divorced from that aspect of macroeconomic policy. With taxing powers and spending authority of EC institutions remaining very limited, budgets will continue to be the domain of the individual member states. In the proposed monetary union, however, governments will no longer have the luxury of a domestic central bank which finances deficit spending through additional money creation. Nor will the new European central bank fill the void. The EuroFed will not engage in monetary financing of budget deficits incurred by individual member states.

With debt monetization removed, governments will have to run relatively balanced budgets or tap the capital markets. There they will compete with each other for funds, and the ability to borrow will depend on a state's creditworthiness relative to that of others. Profligate borrowers will find themselves progressively frozen out of the credit markets. Not able to count on the support of the EuroFed, governments that run excessive deficits will therefore at some point come under intense pressure to reduce their red ink. Because it will become much easier for people and capital within the EC to move to lower-tax countries if and when the domestic tax regime has become too oppressive, deficit reduction will focus more on spending cuts than on tax hikes.

Many people, especially those who are inclined to view government spending as wasteful or budget deficits as a primary source of inflation, may welcome such a regime of fiscal discipline. But imposing too much of a constraint on the ability of nation-states to run budget deficits also poses several dangers. For one, governments may not be able to use deficit spending as a means of stimulating their domestic economies out of recession. In the absence of fiscal reflation, future downturns may be deeper and last longer than Europeans have been used to. Furthermore, the generous "welfare state" provisions commonly found in Western Europe (e.g., extensive social insurance coverage, national health service, free public education, housing subsidies) may become untenable under the new system. Existing programs might have to be cut back significantly. At the same time, governments may lack funding to launch new social policy initiatives, no matter how pressing the need. Finally, the already considerable unevenness of regional economic development within the EC is likely to be exacerbated. Forced to keep spending under tighter control, governments may have to eliminate or curtail cross-subsidization channels which move funds from richer to poorer regions.[29]

Deprived of the power to monetize their debts and depending solely on the volatile supply of private investors, governments with excessively large debts may at some point have no choice but to default. Yet any such default risks damaging Europe's financial system in a major way. Because the union treaty does not provide for a bail-out by the EuroFed, profligate countries threatened by default may therefore have to be rescued by the taxpayers in the rest of the EC. We only have to look at the thrift bailout in the United States and remember the centuries of rivalry between European nations to imagine what kind of political passions such a rescue operation would arouse. The only way to avoid this outcome is to make sure that the public finances of member states remain fundamentally sound—through adequate disclosure of information, EC-wide surveillance, and enforcement of minimum public debt maturities. At the same time, financial institutions which buy public debt must be regulated in terms of asset diversification and capital requirements, so that they can survive the default of a public issuer.

5) Monetarist Biases in the Proposed Union Treaty. The abandonment of debt monetization is in line with standard Monetarist thinking. The influence of that theory within the Delors Committee, which drew up the plan for economic and monetary union, can also be seen from its emphasis on price stability as the primary policy objective and its lack of attention to the structural origins of inflation. In this quantitativist notion, price stability is seen to depend on prudent management of the ECU money supply by the EuroFed. The focus of attention thus shifts from the currency to the monetary institution, justifying the notoriously anti-inflationary Bundesbank as the model to copy. This particular bias raises some troubling questions about the future monetary union.

• The primacy of monetary policy over fiscal policy in Delors' single-currency plan gives the proposed EuroFed a great deal of power. Yet the European central bank, run by specialists who enjoy long-term appointments and are subject to only limited supervision by other EC institutions, will largely escape democratic control. One could argue that opposition to monetary policy usually expresses itself in ways other than the electoral process (e.g., capital flight, strikes, a black market for "hard" currencies), but this hardly compensates for giving a few nonelected officials so much discretionary power. This problem exists on a national level as well, but it gains added urgency in the case of supranational organizations which directly reduce national sovereignty.

• Both the Federal Reserve and the Bundesbank were originally designed as decentralized institutions, but they both experienced gradual centralization. A similar evolution can be expected in the case of the EuroFed. This raises the question of the future role of the national central banks. Being turned into regional branches of the EuroFed, they would become primarily supervisors and regulators of domestic financial institutions and markets. Other functions, especially maintaining the payments system and setting discount rates, would in all likelihood be subject to centralization and lost to the governing board of the EuroFed. It is not clear at this point who would ultimately intervene as "lender of last resort" to contain financial crises.

• The EuroFed would have to manage the ECU's exchange rate vis-à-vis all other currencies outside the monetary union, most notably the dollar and the yen. Yet neither the Delors Plan nor the Maastricht treaty specified what constitutes a balanced exchange rate, thus offering no basis for the fixing of currency prices. While the setting of realistic exchange rates is already quite difficult on the national level (see chapter 14), it is made even more complicated on the level of the EC as a whole by the large differences that prevail among its member states. Even if we aggregate their respective current and capital accounts into a European balance of payments, any exchange rates based on such averaging ignore existing variations and may actually worsen them.

These problems—the competition between the mark and the ECU for hegemony, the difficulties of assuring a minimal degree of convergence among vastly different economies when elected officials still define their actions in terms of national interests, the pressure to reduce budget deficits, and the Monetarist biases in favor of "hard money" and low inflation—all contributed to the currency crisis of 1992. That they should have come to the fore so soon and so violently was surely a surprise to the architects of economic and monetary union. But the crisis also served as a useful reminder to European leaders that they need to address those issues before they can hope for successful implementation of the Maastricht treaty. If the politicians manage to do that and in the process create a viable single-currency zone, then the turbulent events of September 1992 may well prove to have been a blessing in disguise.

16

Toward a True Form of World Money

As we move toward a world dominated by trade, global production networks, and huge cross-border movements of capital, the traditional policy apparatus of nation-states no longer suffices. The emerging global accumulation regime requires an additional layer of management and regulation, based on new multilateral arrangements and international policy-making institutions. One of the most pressing issues in this transformation is the replacement of our current multicurrency system with a new kind of universal credit-money that provides the world economy with sufficient liquidity and balanced adjustments. Keynes's Bancor plan, the Special Drawing Rights issued by the IMF, the European Currency Units of the EC are all first steps toward truly stateless money managed by an international monetary authority. Such a money form is, in my opinion, a logical step in the evolution of contemporary capitalism, a distinct possibility as we complete our transition to a global accumulation regime. In this chapter we shall examine how such a uniform money standard might operate in practice.

16.1. Finding a Viable Form of World Money

International monetary reform is necessary, because the system we have now in place is flawed. The use of national credit-money as world money is an inherently unstable arrangement. On their own, dollars, yen, and other key currencies represent fully effective money only at home, within the country of their issue. When they are used in international transactions they fail to perform as means of payment, allowing the issuing country to pay for its overseas obligations in its own money (the so-called seigniorage benefit). Nor do they act as units of account, for they can only be valued in terms of other currencies, whose value they are supposed to define in the first place. Such use of an inadequate money form has fed chronic external account imbalances, volatile exchange rates, massive speculation, and an unstable global (Euro)banking network beyond the reach of government regulators. These problems have tended to become more pronounced over time, as the once all-powerful dollar began to lose ground to other key currencies.

A tripolar arrangement centered on dollars, yen, and marks (eventually replaced by ECUs) might easily become a vehicle for monetary "zones," through which the leading economic powers—the United States, Japan, and Germany—exert their dominant influence over neighboring countries. In other words, the multicurrency system we have today tends to feed dangerous centrifugal tendencies of regional bloc formation and protectionism. Countries that do not belong to any monetary zone could well find themselves on the periphery, without adequate access to capital and markets. Since the three emerging blocs are of approximately equal strength, it is difficult to satisfy the preference of investors for a single dominant currency (see chapter 14). With capital nowadays approaching a state of perfect mobility, huge sums of money constantly flow between the key currencies as investors try to cope with the uncertainty of competing money forms by hedging or speculating. Finally, such a multicurrency system is difficult to manage, because it rests entirely on the discretion of policy-makers of the leading economic powers. And these often have a difficult time setting aside their conflicting national interests. That problem is precisely why the experiments in multilateral coordination under the Louvre Agreement of 1987 or the Maastricht Agreement of 1991 have faltered.[1]

As if these institutional deficiencies were not enough, the multicurrency system also suffers from historic obsolescence. Relying on national currencies to pay for international transactions makes less and less sense in today's integrated world economy, in which most products no longer have a clearly national origin but are produced in several countries at the same time. Half of all world trade, possibly already even more, involves transfers of components, materials, intermediate goods, and highly specialized services within the same global production network rather than traditional trade of finished goods between nations.[2] Firms belonging to such networks engage in a large number of international transactions, and the existence of different currencies greatly complicates their business in terms of transaction costs and exchange risks.

Globally integrated production networks and financial markets are better off with a truly international medium of exchange. Such a stateless money form is the logical next step in the historic evolution of the international monetary system. Over the past two centuries we have gone from a bimetallic standard through a gold standard and two different gold exchange standards to an inconvertible paper standard based on key currencies. This gradual transition from commodity-money to credit-money will ultimately be completed only with the introduction of a new *supranational credit-money*.

How is this new form of world money to function as an alternative to our current multicurrency system? Keynes's Bancor proposal, SDRs, and ECUs provide us with valuable clues. But none of these artifacts functions fully as international money. Bancors never saw the light of day, making it impossible to assess how well they might have worked. But even if Keynes had succeeded in having his plan adopted at Bretton Woods, his new world money would only have acted as an official means of debt settlement through transfer of Bancor-denominated reserve balances from deficit countries to surplus countries. This arrangement would have required extensive controls on private cross-border flows of capital (see section 15.1). SDRs and ECUs have primarily been used as official reserve and debt-settlement devices. Their private use has been extremely limited so far, while they must both compete with other forms of international money. Even governments have often preferred to exchange their SDR or ECU holdings for currencies. This propensity will persist as long as SDRs and ECUs are constructed as baskets of currencies of which at least one performs better than the weighted basket average used to value either SDRs or ECUs. Their valuation as currency baskets also impairs the ability of either to function effectively as an international measure of value and anchor for stable currency prices. Our solution will therefore have to be different from Bancors, SDRs, and ECUs.

One way to deal with the problem of supranational money is to impose a single currency across the globe, much like the Maastricht treaty proposed for the EC. That European nations should want to phase out their own currencies in favor of a supranational substitute is an indication of how much nation-states will see their policy institutions transformed by the force of economic integration. The volume of intra-EC trade, the emergence of a single regional market, and unrestricted cross-border movements of capital all make it much more practical to do business in one money-form than in a dozen different currencies involving considerable transaction costs and exchange risks.

Yet it is highly doubtful whether such a single-currency concept can work for the entire world. The degree of economic integration and interdependence across the world economy is today still much lower than it is within the EC. The same argument applies even more to convergence of economic performance among members, without which monetary union cannot function properly. It is precisely this need for convergence, coupled with the centralization of control, that makes any attempt to introduce a single-currency zone so difficult to implement. The United States' monetary unification (see chapter 4), for example, took more than a century to accomplish. Twice, first in 1811 and then again in 1836, U.S. efforts to set up a central bank failed miserably. The civil war of the 1860s enabled the federal government to introduce national bank notes and impose inconvertible fiat money for the first time, but state banks survived federal efforts to suppress them. During the postwar reconstruction period of the late nineteenth century, which ultimately led to the formation of nationwide markets and industries, the coexistence of different money-forms sparked intense political debates over what kind of monetary regime was best suited to a nationally integrated economy. This issue was only resolved in 1900, when the United States finally completed its return to a gold standard. Not until 1913, when Congress passed the Federal Reserve Act, did the United States have a fully integrated national payments system based on dollars. Significantly, in that same year the U.S. government also began to collect income taxes on a nationwide basis, after decades of political tensions over the issue had finally produced a decisive favorable ruling on the constitutionality of such government power. These tax revenues formed the basis for a new kind of fiscal federalism, through which the U.S. government could organize the kind of resource transfers between states that the convergence requirements of monetary union necessitated. The next year the United States entered World War I as the principal supplier, creditor, and ultimately military force of the anti-German alliance.

The experience of the United States' monetary unification holds valuable lessons for the Europeans as they engage in the creation of a single-currency zone within the EC. Redefining money, the central social institution that guides private initiative and state power, is inevitably difficult. The process is fraught with regional conflict, financial instability, and political crises, as the transition to a new monetary regime transforms the system it is supposed to regulate. Any imposition of a single currency on a system composed until now of several local currencies is a particularly tricky undertaking. Local currencies on their own reflect in their relative values the different levels of labor productivity and industrial competitiveness of their respective areas. Their replacement by a uniform monetary standard subjects the entire system to a new valuation basis and forces corresponding adjustments in its economic structures.

Europe's union treaty got off to a bad start (see sections 15.5 and 15.6), precisely because its architects underestimated the difficulties associated with such a project. The imposition of a single currency on a community of states with different levels of economic development can only work if it is accompanied by new mechanisms of policy coordination and capital transfers that reduce performance differences. In the absence of such regulatory stabilizers, the tension between different national labor standards and a uniform monetary standard cannot be contained and gives rise to destabilizing movements of capital from the weaker periphery to the dominant center. The currency crisis of September 1992, a classic illustration of such a capital-flight process, has destroyed the designs of EC leaders to impose a single-currency zone rapidly, from the top down, and without EC-wide coordination of adjustments. The process, if it is even possible, will surely take much longer than anticipated and will require additional measures. Of special importance in this context will be the expansion of the EC's budgetary and debt-monetization powers to orchestrate capital transfers to less-developed regions, to provide for automatic fiscal stabilizers, and to maintain social programs on a Communitywide basis. Without such fiscal federalism, a single-currency zone in Europe may only be possible for a core of the most prosperous nations whose levels of economic development and labor productivity are fairly similar—Germany, France, Belgium, the Netherlands, Luxembourg, Switzerland, Austria, and possibly also the Scandinavian countries. Such a core zone might make it more difficult for Great Britain, Southern Europe, and Eastern Europe to catch up and join.

If monetary unification in the United States and Europe has proved to be so difficult, it is impossible to imagine a single currency for the entire world economy. Capitalism, its powerful tendencies toward global integration notwithstanding, has not yet evolved to that point. We may never get there, given the propensity for uneven development and the centrifugal forces in our world economy. But that is also precisely why we need to give the emerging global accumulation regime an institutional policy framework which fosters integration and balance. Supranational credit-money, issued and distributed by an international monetary authority according to the needs of a community of nations, has a central role to play in such a system of multilateral regulation. Rather than reaching for the most difficult and utopian version, the introduction of a single currency for the entire world economy, it would be much more realistic to conceive of this new form of world money as used solely in international transactions between countries. This kind of arrangement allows national currencies to exist but confines them to strictly domestic circulation for transactions within their countries of issue. That was precisely the basic idea behind the plan Keynes put forward at the Bretton Woods Conference. But, unlike his Bancor proposal, the supranational credit-money (SNCM) of the future should function fully as money. We therefore need to design an international money form that is based on the institutional characteristics of credit-money (see chapter 2). In practice this means that the following four conditions will have to be satisfied: the creation of SNCM by an agent located outside the marketplace, its issue as a simultaneous asset and liability to both issuer and user, its circulation within a global payments and settlement system, and its proper integration with national currencies as their international extension.

16.2. The Issue of Supranational Credit-Money

A properly constituted SNCM will be able to carry out all of the functions of money and will not just be an international reserve asset with which to settle official debts, as is the case with SDRs or the current ECUs. What we have in mind instead, at least until conditions are ripe for a global single-currency regime (see section 16.7), is a more moderate and flexible proposal of shared sovereignty. Rather than becoming the world's sole money right away, we propose to have the SNCM coexist at least for a while with national currencies in complementary fashion. It will serve as money in all international transactions between countries, while national currencies remain confined to domestic circulation within their respective countries of issue.

There is a certain logic to such a sharing arrangement. Countries trade with each other through individual buyers and sellers. But when it comes to paying for these trades, they relate to each other as entities, as nationally organized ensembles of market participants that are represented internationally by their respective nation-states and central banks. It is precisely because countries conduct monetary transfers in the international economy on behalf of their citizens that cross-border payments by private parties are first routed through their respective central banks. From that perspective, it becomes quite obvious why the SNCM should only be credited or debited to countries as a whole. Were the SNCM allowed to enter a country and fall into the hands of individuals, it would constitute a net asset with immediate purchasing power and would thus violate the principles of credit-money. The only way any stateless form of credit-money can be used by individuals as a simultaneous asset and liability is if purely national payments systems are replaced by an international payments system which individuals can access directly through their banks. This is precisely what happened with the invention of the Eurocurrencies in the 1960s. And this is also what will in all likelihood occur during the third stage of the proposed monetary union in Europe, after 1997, when the ECU becomes the sole currency within the EC. We have rejected such a radical alternative, at least for now (see above), so we need to restrict the use of the SNCM to official transactions between countries. For that purpose, national central banks will keep reserve accounts with an *international monetary authority* (IMA) which issues the SNCM, accompanied by equivalent domestic currency payments to and from individuals.

In every international transaction, be it trade or a flow of capital, the IMA can transfer the requested sum denominated in SNCM from the paying country's reserve account to the recipient country's reserve account by simple double-entry bookkeeping, much like the Fed does when it clears checks between commercial banks. The transaction actually begins earlier, when an individual importer or capital exporter in country A instructs his bank to deliver a money order at the central bank and in the process pays the relevant sum denominated in currency A out of his bank account. When the central bank carries out the money order, the IMA transfers an equivalent amount in SNCM-denominated reserves from country A to country B. Finally, the central bank of country B passes that sum, now denominated in currency B, to the bank of the payee, where it is credited to his account. In sum, international payments are made by and to individual market participants in their own currencies, complemented by transfer of SNCM-denominated funds between countries.

Such a three-step sequence of payments is necessary for the proper integration of global credit-money into the international economy. At first, when issued outside the marketplace, credit-money is a mere token and does not yet possess purchasing power. Any such token—a check, for example—only becomes money subsequently, when it is transferred to a user and as such is integrated into the marketplace as monetary income with the power to purchase output. This poses no particular problem for the domestic economy. But the international economy does not produce anything and consists only of exchange transactions. The issue of new SNCM therefore has no real counterpart in terms of increased output. The only way to avoid feeding inflationary pressures across the globe, then, is to make sure that the creation of SNCM does not increase global purchasing power. In the three-step payments sequence described above, the issue of SNCM does not add to the total amount of money circulating in the world economy. Being linked to equivalent payments by and to individuals in their respective currencies, it only transfers existing purchasing power from one country to another.[3]

Our SNCM proposal differs in important respects from Bancor, SDRs, and ECUs. These predecessors of supranational money were all designed to function only as international means of payment for settlement of official debit balances between countries. In that limited role none of them represents actual credit-money.

- Take Keynes's Bancor, for example. Based on the overdraft principle, it would have given deficit countries a right to draw a certain sum of currencies out of the surplus balances of creditors to cover their debit balances (see section 15.1). As such it was to have been a liability of the issuer, the international clearing union, and an asset for the recipient country. This is not credit-money, which must always be issued as a simultaneous asset and liability to both issuer and user alike. Instead, the Bancor would have functioned solely as a bank guarantee of a deficit country's debt, with the bank in this case being an international clearing union, akin to the issue of bankers' acceptances in foreign trade.

- The SDRs and ECUs, on the other hand, are issued as a simultaneous asset-liability. In both instances the issuer, be it the International Monetary Fund or the European Monetary Cooperation Fund, issues a liability and gains an equivalent sum of the recipient country's currency as a cash asset in return. For the individual member countries the SDRs or ECUs in turn represent reserve assets which they can transfer among each other to settle payment obligations. The problem is that these reserve assets, backed by previously created national currencies, already represent revenue with purchasing power.[4]

Credit-money, on the other hand, is first issued without purchasing power, as mere tokens (like a book of blank checks). These tokens are then transferred through an act of credit extension from the issuer outside the marketplace to users in whose hands they assume the character of money. Only if and when these tokens are integrated among market participants as monetary income revenue through acts of buying goods, services, or financial claims do they actually gain purchasing power (like writing a check to buy something). On the level of the international economy this integration comes about when payments are made for trade, direct overseas investments, or portfolio investments abroad. Consequently, an international credit-money, such as our proposed SNCM, has to be issued to finance all import and capital export transactions rather than just being used as a reserve asset for intergovernmental compensation of external account imbalances. When so confined to the status of merely an international settlement unit, as in the case of Bancor, SDRs, or ECUs, its issue does not meet the criteria for true credit-money. It has only limited monetary attributes as a central bank claim on key currencies which can be cashed in on demand to settle debts.

In sum, the specific issue characteristics of supranational credit-money require that it not function as money in the hands of individual buyers, that it only be issued to a particular country in exchange for an equivalent reduction in domestic purchasing power, and that its issue cover all foreign transactions and not just the net balances.

16.3. The International Payments System

Based on these three issue conditions we can specify how a SNCM-based global payments system might operate (see Figure 16.1).[5] Let us begin with payments for imports and capital exports. Remember that the IMA in charge of issuing SNCM keeps reserve accounts for all participating countries. To pay for imports, for example, a certain sum of revenues will have to be moved from the importing country, *A*, to the exporting country, *B*. The importer in country *A* pays for his purchase in *A*'s money, and the exporter in country *B* receives the payment in domestic currency *B*. The conversion and transfer of the money from *A* to *B* is done through the intermediation of the SNCM. For that purpose the IMA issues the relevant amount in SNCM (as a loan asset) to the importing country, *A*, and simultaneously transfers that sum (as a liability) into the account of the exporting country, *B*. This transfer of SNCM from one country to another is then followed by corresponding changes in the T-accounts of the parties involved in the trade and their respective banks. Such issue of SNCM as simultaneous asset and liability, with its counterbalancing extension in the domestic banking systems of the two countries involved, does not alter the total purchasing power available to the world economy. It only redistributes purchasing power from buyers to sellers.

16.4. Deficit Financing and Adjustment Policy

In the normal course of business, some countries will end up with balance-of-payments surpluses and other countries will run deficits. If these imbalances persist for a while, surplus countries will accumulate excess SNCM in their IMA accounts and deficit countries will end up with SNCM deficiencies in their IMA accounts. How to mobilize the surpluses for financing those deficits is one of the crucial challenges confronting any international monetary regime. Keynes understood, when he proposed overdrafts as the solution (see section 15.1), that such global redistribution of funds from surplus countries to deficit countries is better left to the automatic rules of a global authority than to the profit motive of

Figure 16.1 **International Payments via Issue of SNCM.** Example: U.S. Import of a French Good.

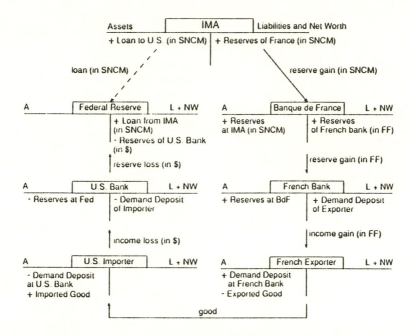

Notes: All transactions between central banks and IMA are denominated in SNCM. All transactions within countries are denominated in their respective currencies and are equivalent to the SNCM amount transferred between countries at currently prevailing exchange rates.

Abbreviations: IMA for International Monetary Authority; SNCM for Supranational Credit-Money; $ for U.S. dollar; FF for French franc; Fed for Federal Reserve; BdeF for Banque de France; A for Assets; L + NW for Liabilitites and Net Worth.

private banks or the politicized foreign assistance of governments. This is one advantage of supranational credit-money.

Going back to Keynes's Bancor proposal fifty years ago, the international monetary authority can organize the global payments system it oversees so that surplus funds are automatically channeled to deficit spending units. For this purpose the IMA should be divided into two separate departments. One is the "monetary department" (M.D.), which issues the SNCM for transfer into the reserve accounts of countries. The other is the "financial department" (F.D.), which borrows and lends SNCM-denominated funds.[6] The two departments are linked with each other through continuous circulation of surplus funds (see Figure 16.2). Surplus countries lend the excess SNCM in their accounts at the M.D. to the F.D. and receive an equivalent quantity of SNCM-denominated claims in return. Deficit countries then borrow these surplus SNCM units from the F.D. in exchange for their own financial claims to cover cash-flow gaps in their M.D. accounts.

Taken together, these four steps form an integrated circuit which transforms monetary revenues into financial claims. In this way any imbalances in the goods markets can be counterbalanced by exactly reciprocal imbalances in financial markets. Excess demand for goods and services ("deficits"), for example, is matched by excess supplies of financial claims ("net debts"). This law of monetary balancing applies both to domestic payments systems and to the global payments system. At the end of that IMA-organized circuit all external account imbalances have been fully covered financially, and all the SNCM units issued during the accounting period are destroyed by returning in full to the original issuer (the IMA) as mere credit tokens. In the process surplus countries have turned creditors of the IMA, while deficit countries have become indebted to the IMA.

The financial intermediation of IMA should provide a fairly stable mechanism for recycling surplus funds. By lending to the IMA rather than directly to deficit countries, surplus countries reduce risk exposure. Debtor nations in turn can expect more reliable supplies of funds from IMA than they currently have from the Euromarket banks or from governments of industrial nations. As we have seen with the global LDC debt crisis, the Euromarket is driven by the profit motive of private banks and, as such, is prone to cycles of overextension and retrenchment. Official foreign-aid programs are skimpy, are heavily politicized, and often come with strings attached.

Loans extended by the IMA to deficit countries will have to be repaid eventually. As long as debtor nations manage to achieve positive trade balances before their debts come due, they generate surpluses which can be used to pay off their loans. Such payments will in turn give IMA's F.D. the funds with which to retire its own debts owed to the surplus countries. The monetary constraint at work here implies that no country can accumulate external deficits forever. Current account deficits will at some point have to be counterbalanced by future surpluses. To make sure this happens, the IMA might have to impose belt-tightening adjustment policies on all countries with chronic deficits and excessive debts. This could be done by linking any credit extension to the adoption of specific policies. The more a country has already borrowed, the more rapidly will it have to bring its deficits under control in order to avoid becoming burdened down by too much debt and risking default.

The experience of the IMF in recent years has clearly shown how politically sensitive the imposition of austerity measures by an international authority on national governments can be. After all, being able to determine one's own domestic policy is at the core of national sovereignty. Of course, critics of the IMF should not forget that the fund tries to do in orderly and coordinated fashion what the market mechanism will otherwise do in more chaotic fashion—creditors forcing

Figure 16.2 **Mobilization of Surplus for Coverage of Deficit.** Example: U.S. Imports from France Equal 1,000 SNCM. U.S. Exports to France Equal 900 SNCM.
Step 1: IMA–M.D. Accounts of U.S. (deficit country) and France (surplus country)

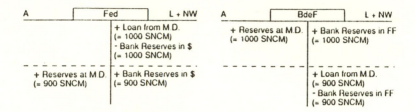

Abbreviation: M.D. for IMA's Monetary Department.

Step 2: The IMA's M.D. as Clearinghouse. The Net Positions of the U.S. and France.

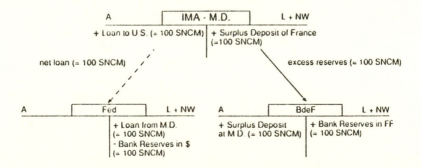

Figure 16.2 *continued*

Step 3: The Recycling of France's Surplus to the U.S. via IMA–F.D.

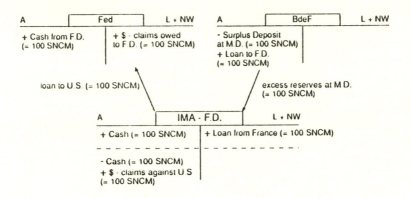

Note: Each transaction in denominated in SNCM, except for dollar-denominated claims of F.D. against the U.S.

Abbreviation: F.D. for IMA's Financial Department.

Step 4: The Coverage("Repayment") of the U.S. Deficit in Its M.D. Account

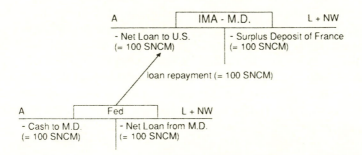

debtors to change behavior in order to protect their income and assets. Moreover, the IMF has often acted as a lightning rod for public discontent, allowing governments to blame a far removed power for unpopular policy shifts which they would not have dared to do on their own. These arguments also hold for our proposed IMA. But in contrast to the IMF, our multilateral institution would enforce adjustments more gradually, before debt levels have gotten out of hand, would coordinate the balancing efforts of different countries, and would have much greater powers as the sole issuer of world money.

Still, because control over a country's domestic policy is always politically touchy, it is best to regulate the issue of adjustment policies as much as possible on the basis of automatic and non-discriminatory rules. Each country would be assigned a borrowing quota in proportion to the size of its national product and its trade volume. Globally those quotas would have to be set so that surpluses exceeded deficits by roughly the amount of money that debtor countries required during any given accounting period in order to repay their maturing loans to the IMA. Whenever a country's debts exceeded a specified percentage of its quota (e.g., 25 percent, 50 percent, or 75 percent), its government would have to undertake certain corrective measures. Those would become tougher and more comprehensive the higher the debt level.

When we look at the global economy as a closed system, it becomes clear that the transactions among nations are a zero-sum game. One country's external deficit is another country's surplus. The ability of debtor nations to reduce or even eliminate their balance-of-payments deficits depends, therefore, not least on the willingness of creditor nations to lower their surpluses. They may even have to endure deficits for a while. If no country can run deficits forever, then it follows that no country can accumulate surpluses ad infinitum. Consequently, there has to be some symmetry in the global adjustment process. Deficit reduction by debtor nations has to go hand in hand with surplus reduction by creditor nations. This is not just a question of fairness. It would be counterproductive for the system as a whole if the entire adjustment burden had to be borne by debtor nations tightening their belts. The reduction of aggregate demand in this case would be felt worldwide. Instead, it would be far better if some of the adjustment came on the surplus side via stimulation of domestic consumption in creditor nations. Not only would that make the deficit-cutting efforts of debtor nations more likely to succeed and less burdensome, but global demand would also remain higher.

The market mechanism, of course, eventually forces adjustments on both sides. But the variables involved in this market correction (e.g., transfer of purchasing power, exchange-rate shifts, credit terms) are such that the imbalances are allowed to build up for a long time. Excessive indebtedness by some and hoarding by others are two sides of the same coin. They coexist in mutually feeding fashion until a crisis erupts and forces often brutal readjustments. At that point power relations in the marketplace tend to create a bias, which places most of the adjustment burden on the weaker debtor nations. Surplus countries, which do not depend on external funding, are in a better position to escape the pressures for change. It is precisely because of these systemic market failures that we need an institutionalized adjustment regime under the supervision of a neutral and nonmarket agency such as our proposed IMA. Under that kind of mechanism, surplus countries will also be subject to policy corrections which are automatically triggered at certain predetermined thresholds. To make sure that those countries cannot escape their responsibilities, they will have to be sanctioned. One possibility is to impose a graduated surtax on excessive surplus reserves.

Although automatic and nondiscriminatory rules help to make IMA prescriptions more acceptable as well as predictable, there must also be some room for policy discretion. The wide range of unique situations and the great heterogeneity in the world economy make it impossible to always apply the same general rules in response. Sometimes the policy-makers at the IMA will have to differentiate and temporarily replace or suspend a rule. What, you may ask, is the point of rules if they are frequently ignored? The important thing is to have an international consensus as to the conditions that warrant such special treatment by the IMA. Most likely are situations in which debtor nations are about to exhaust their borrowing allowances and/or continue to run external deficits despite having put anti-deficit policies into place. At that point some of them could be granted a rescheduling of existing debts or an exceptional one-time increase in their quota. The F.D. may borrow SNCM funds from the M.D. or from surplus countries for this purpose. Freed from the profit motive, an official (extramarket) institution such as the IMA has more flexibility vis-à-vis repayment and adjustment terms than do private banks.

16.5. Global Capital Transfers

Four out of five humans live under conditions of abject poverty in developing countries. In the wake of the global debt crisis these countries have experienced a net outflow of capital over the past decade, while the richest nation, the United States, has become a huge importer of foreign capital. This is not a tenable situation. The strength of the world economy depends on a reversal of this perverse flow of capital. The poorer countries need to import capital on a continuous basis and to use that influx of funds productively for balanced industrialization. Providing them with sufficient funds at reasonable terms also benefits rich nations in terms of larger export markets, greater supplies of cheap labor for industry, and reduced illegal immigration. Even though industrialization in developing countries at times creates massive dislocation in the regions of the industrial nations that formerly depended heavily on labor-intensive manufacturing, it also frees resources there for new types of work. If those are of higher value added than are the jobs lost, rich countries as a whole benefit from the new international division of labor.

The key problem for many developing countries is that they tend to be subject to an especially virulent external constraint. They run chronic and structurally conditioned deficits with the rest of the world. They export only a few commodities with highly volatile world market prices (e.g., metals, foodstuffs). Yet consumption of basic necessities and industrial diversification in those LDCs rely heavily on imports. The resulting trade deficits require continuous imports of capital. The question then is how best to meet this demand for funds and channel it into productive uses that correspond to local needs.

The IMA could play a useful role here, combining the roles of the IMF and the World Bank on a much larger scale (see Figure 16.3). So far we have the F.D. of the IMA receiving excess SNCM deposits from surplus countries and channeling those deposits to the central banks of deficit countries for coverage of their reserve deficiencies and loan repayments (see Figure 16.2). The F.D. could use a portion of these deposits instead—say, up to half—as productive capital which is directly invested in those LDCs. It could simply purchase financial claims issued by private firms and government units within a deficit country.

Such an institutional arrangement, in which the IMA acts as an international investment bank to mobilize up to 50 percent of the world's net surplus for productive expenditures in the developing world, has several advantages over the private Euromarket recycling that brought us the global LDC debt crisis.

• Surplus countries will leave excess funds in the safe hands of the IMA instead of putting them into unsecured Eurocurrency deposits.

• IMA loans will finance infrastructure investments and other capital spending projects that strengthen the industrial base of the recipient country. To the extent that these loans boost the productive capacity of deficit countries, they will more likely be self-liquidating than will private Eurobank loans, which in the past often financed rather unproductive expenditures (e.g., imports of luxury goods, purchases of arms).

• Because the IMA is freed from the private profit constraint of banks, it can adjust its credit terms more flexibly to the needs of the borrower.

• In order to prevent overextension, a common problem in the private Euromarket, IMA's F.D. will limit the net borrowings of each country from its investment fund. Any funds beyond that quota are only forthcoming if combined with simultaneous repayment of old debt. Countries that approach their limit will have sufficient advance warning to reduce deficits or generate additional revenues for debt repayment.

Besides providing for greater financial stability, this investment banking activity of the IMA is bound to stimulate the world economy. It boosts purchasing power in developing countries and thereby increases global markets for capital goods and business services from industrialized countries. These supplies of investment funds from the IMA constitute an import of capital. As such, they

Figure 16.3 **Direct Investment Activity of IMA's Financial Department.** Example: F.D. Loan of 100 SNCM to a Mexican Firm.

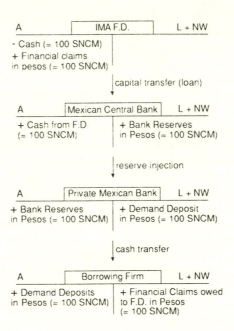

have the same reserve addition and purchasing-power effects as any export of goods and services. Beneficiaries obtain the funds in their own national currency through intermediation of their central bank which receives an equivalent sum of SNCM from IMA's F.D. in the process (see Figure 16.4). This SNCM injection acts as a sort of collateral to insure the privately placed F.D. loans and, because all SNCM eventually returns to IMA's M.D., also partially covers any SNCM shortfall by the recipient country at the M.D. Its balance-of-payments deficit, as defined by the official SNCM shortfall, is thus reduced. Deficit spending automatically becomes monetized on a global scale, just as the institution of national credit-money in the 1930s provided for automatic monetization in the domestic economy (see chapter 5). That leaves developing countries with a less virulent external constraint and with more funds to work their way out of underdevelopment.

16.6. Exchange Rates

In our proposal national currencies circulate only within the domestic economy of their country of issue. Any transaction between countries is carried out in

Figure 16.4 **The IMA as International Investment Bank.** Assumptions: Global Net Surplus of 100 SNCM. F.D. Investment of 50 SNCM.

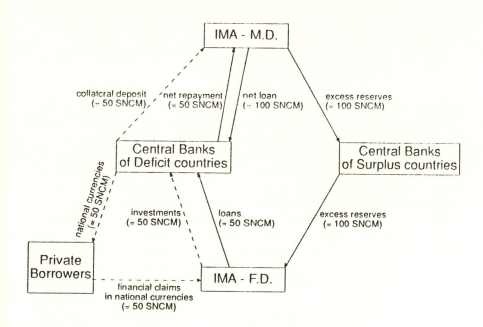

SNCM, which thus functions as the international extension, the universally accepted representative of strictly national monies. In such a global payments system, different currencies are no longer directly exchanged. Instead, they relate to each other indirectly through their respective linkage with the SNCM, which thereby comes to act as numeraire. The relationship between the SNCM and any national currency is that of an absolute price, which establishes the commensurability of different currencies on the same value basis. It is that SNCM price which determines how much one currency is valued relative to another. These relative prices ("exchange rates") of currencies, based on the SNCM as common denominator, properly reflect differentials in purchasing power between the countries involved. The SNCM thus functions as a true international unit of account.

Since the SNCM coexists with national currencies rather than replacing them (as in the case of Europe's proposed economic and monetary union), exchange rates do not have to be irrevocably locked. Instead, they should be subject to adjustments whenever underlying trade imbalances threaten to create unstable conditions. If, for example, a country runs chronic deficits and in the process accumulates SNCM debts beyond a reasonable limit, then the SNCM price of its currency will have to be lowered, in order to restore a better external balance.

Such adjustments should not be confined to deficit countries but should extend (in the opposite direction) to chronic surplus countries as well. The IMA should manage this system of fixed but adjustable exchange rates so that trade among industrial countries is essentially balanced while allowing LDCs to run adequate deficits.

16.7. Moving to a Single-Currency Regime

Our SNCM proposal, even though surely a radical break with existing international monetary arrangements, may itself be only an intermediate stage on the journey toward the ultimate level of monetary integration—the adoption of a single currency for all (domestic and international) transactions worldwide. We still have a long way to go before this idea can become reality. But eventually, perhaps in a generation or two, the globalization of economic activity may have reached such a degree as to make national currencies obsolete.

When multinational firms and transnational banks have become truly global in scope, they will find the price risk and transaction costs of foreign exchange increasingly burdensome. Yet foreign exchange will not be eliminated through a single-currency regime just because the largest corporations and banks want that to happen. Even though both constituencies have a powerful influence over domestic policy, governments follow other interests as well. They do not automatically adopt whatever "big business" proposes. And on the question of money, many governments will be especially attached to the status quo. Controlling the issue of currency is, after all, at the heart of government power and is synonymous with national sovereignty. It has always been a defining issue in the historic evolution of nation-states.

But national sovereignty will have lost much of its meaning once capital moves with ease across borders and foreign transactions absorb a large share of the national product (see Wriston, 1992). At that point even large economies become highly susceptible to international capital flows, yet at the same time less able to control them. Much of what determines how well a national economy performs is decided beyond the boundaries of that nation-state. Strictly national regulation of money no longer suffices when the money functions as capital on a truly global basis. Weaker economies will face capital flight unless they raise interest rates, slash budget deficits, and lower inflation. In the process they will depress domestic activity and end up becoming even more dependent on foreign capital. Stronger economies, which issue key currencies used as an international medium of exchange, must run balance-of-payments deficits to supply the rest of the world with liquidity. At the same time these deficits must not grow too large lest they undermine the market strength of the currency. When several currencies are competing for world money status, as is now the case, huge sums of capital will be tied up rather unproductively in short-term movements between these currencies for hedging and speculative purposes. The countries that issue key currencies will be tempted to protect their interests by building zones of influence which they dominate.

Continued reliance on national money thus becomes a barrier to balanced economic growth. The internationalization of capital requires a supranational form of money, a globally integrated payments system, and multilateral policy coordination. These are the virtues of a single currency for the entire world economy. But such a regime cannot be instituted all at once. It must be preceded by an interim process of adjustments and reforms. Before EC members are in a position to adopt the ECU as a single currency within the community, they will have gone through several distinct phases to prepare the ground for such economic convergence and for monetary union (e.g., the "snake" of the early 1970s, the European Monetary System of 1979–1989, the first two phases of the Economic and Monetary Union in 1990–1996). The same is true for the global economy as a whole.

The SNCM proposal satisfies the basic requirements for such a transition process. It abolishes direct exchange of currencies as a first step toward a single form of universal money. It denationalizes the creation of international liquidity and thereby removes seigniorage from the economic relations of countries. It reins in transnational banks by pushing them from the Euromarket into a settlement and payments system that is run by an international monetary authority. It fosters more gradual correction of disequilibria and more balanced sharing of adjustment burdens. It forces national governments into greater coordination of macroeconomic policy on the basis of clearly defined rules and by limiting their debt-financing capacity. Finally, it favors developing countries by assuring them of greater and easier access to capital. This bias encourages greater economic convergence between nations of different development levels, which the EC experience has shown to be a key prerequisite for the introduction of a single-currency regime.

16.8. The Prospects for Reform

The debates within the EC concerning economic and monetary union illustrate quite clearly how difficult it is to reach agreement on the details of any new international money form and payments system. The questions involved are complex and have a great impact on the policy-making capacity of national governments. What would the precise powers of the new international monetary authority be vis-à-vis the central banks of member countries? How would the borrowing quotas be set and adjusted? Which performance criteria would enter into the determination of exchange rates? Under what conditions would those rates be changed? To what kind of adjustment programs would chronic deficit countries or surplus countries be subjected? Who would make sure that the capital transfers to developing countries are used for productive investment purposes? What would the role of private transnational banks in the new system be?

In theory, of course, these questions can be answered in a logically consistent manner, as my proposal in this chapter has attempted to do. But the translation of these theoretical solutions into practical institutional arrangements cannot be designed by blueprint, nor can it be imposed from above. That process requires detailed multilateral negotiations until a broad consensus among participating member states is reached. Only an extraordinary degree of international cooperation will bring about the introduction of supranational credit-money.

At first glance the conditions for such consensus and cooperation do not seem to be very promising. Even such comparatively modest initiatives as the Louvre Agreement or the Maastricht treaty have seen rapid erosion because of clashing national interests between the key players. As the leading economic powers are busily trying to create their own zones of regional hegemony, their conflicts over trade, access to capital, and the right mix of macroeconomic policies are bound to intensify. In addition, none of the major economic powers currently seems inclined to provide the kind of leadership that is needed to overcome the many divisions. The United States will not want to give up the world-money status of the dollar voluntarily and thereby lose its seigniorage benefit when it already owes the rest of the world so much. Germany is increasingly preoccupied with its own domestic affairs, most notably the consequences of reunification and the resulting clash between fiscal and monetary policy. More generally, the Europeans have their hands full trying to balance a deepening of union ("Europe 1992") with a broadening of integration following the collapse of the Soviet Empire. Japan remains a very insular nation and constrained by an archaic political structure which gives a handful of personalities and a few institutions nearly total control over the nation's resources. Despite its huge surpluses the country is also financially vulnerable, because its banks have relied heavily on land speculation to fuel a bull market and now must face sustained asset deflation.[7]

Yet, whether they want to or not, the industrial nations cannot escape the need to change the international monetary system. One way or another they will have to face the logic of its shortcomings. If they decide to do nothing, they may well end up with the world economy disintegrating into protectionist trading blocs. If they choose to tinker with existing arrangements à la Louvre, they may succeed in temporarily stabilizing one component of the system (e.g., exchange rates) but may cause greater volatility elsewhere (interest rates, capital flows). Ultimately the current system cannot be reformed from within, because the use of national currencies as world money is inherently flawed.

The pressure for reform is evident with regard to all aspects of the international monetary system. For example, after more than a decade of flexible exchange rates most policy-makers have come to realize that currency prices cannot be left to the vicissitudes of market forces. They need some form of regulation which assures stability and discourages speculation. The stabilization of exchange rates through coordinated central bank intervention, begun first under the Plaza Agreement of 1985 and extended in the Louvre Agreement of

1987, has been an important first step toward the resumption of some form of fixed exchange rates. But such market regulation tends to destabilize the other key price of money, interest rates. And here the leading economies have not been able to cooperate effectively. After a few coordinated rate cuts in 1986 and 1987, domestic policy considerations have once again come to dominate. In the late 1980s the Bank of Japan refused to lower its discount rate under pressure, and the Bundesbank raised key rates repeatedly in the early 1990s as a counterweight to exploding budget deficits. This high-interest policy of the world's two leading creditor nations, besides slowing growth across the globe, also eliminated the differential with U.S. rates. As a result capital flows to the United States began to slow considerably in 1990, which aggravated a credit crunch there (see section 10.4).

The long-term stability of exchange rates and interest rates ultimately depends on balanced and steady capital flows between countries. These, in turn, only come about if and when differences in key economic performance criteria (e.g., inflation rates, trade balance, budget deficits) among the countries in question become less pronounced. The introduction of supranational credit-money requires a good deal of convergence beforehand, as the Europeans have discovered in their struggle over economic and monetary union. Consequently, there has to be a transitional period in which participating member states learn how to coordinate their macroeconomic policies and to follow explicit performance targets. The G–7 nations tried this on a purely voluntary basis in the aftermath of Louvre, but they soon allowed domestic policy considerations to dominate once again. More ambitious policy coordination efforts since then have gone nowhere. Unfortunately, such coordination will not happen unless national governments commit themselves to enforcement procedures under multilateral supervision. Once adopted, our SNCM proposal will force national economies to stay within a certain performance range or face corrective sanctions.

Besides trying to manage currency prices among themselves, in recent years the leading industrial nations have also moved toward a somewhat more even-handed management of the global debt crisis. Their money-center banks were finally forced to write down a large chunk of their sovereign loans to a more realistic value level. At the same time, they have gradually expanded the lending capacity of the IMF and the World Bank. Most important, several large debtors have been granted debt relief (e.g., Mexico, Venezuela) and even outright debt cancellations (e.g., Poland), as an incentive to continue ambitious programs of economic restructuring.

The global debt crisis has had a devastating impact on the living standards of developing nations. But the same crisis also destroyed many authoritarian regimes that had squandered billions in corrupt schemes of self-enrichment, capital flight by the rich elites, and commercially unviable projects. The military juntas of Latin America have disappeared, communism has collapsed in Eastern Europe and the Soviet Union, and opposition movements have begun to challenge one-party rule all over Africa. Many of these new democracies have embarked on sweeping deregulation and privatization programs in an effort to control their budget deficits, to expose their hitherto highly protected domestic producers to the rigors of global competition, to rekindle entrepreneurial initiative in their population, and to attract capital from abroad. The postcolonial era of economic nationalism and state-run enterprises has thus come to a rather sudden end, a trend of monumental importance for the long-run evolution of global capitalism.

Just when many LDCs are building new political institutions and economic structures, their private lenders have had to downsize operations in the wake of large losses. Its overextension during the 1970s and panic-like retrenchment in the 1980s left many regulators convinced that sovereign lending needed to be subject to reasonable restraints and close scrutiny. This was only the first step in the creation of a new regulatory framework for international banking operations. The leading industrial nations have also imposed uniform minimum capital requirements for all banks operating within their borders. Reciprocal-access agreements, which the United States recently concluded with the EC as well as with Japan, have standardized regulations pertaining to foreign banks in order to assure equal treatment. The collapse of the Bank of Credit and Commerce International (BCCI) in mid-1991 has revealed how lax the oversight of multinational Eurobanks has been across the world and how easy it is for unscrupulous bankers to exploit the lack of any supervision in offshore banking centers (e.g., Luxembourg, the Cayman Islands, Bahrain) for illicit gain. Bank regulators are using the BCCI scandal to push for more uniform global banking rules.[8]

Stabilization of exchange rates, debt relief for developing economies in exchange for structural reform, the creation of a regulatory framework for the previously unregulated Eurobanks—all of these measures correspond to acute problems in the current international monetary system. They are by and large steps in the direction of our SNCM proposal, which envisages fixed exchange rates, regular capital transfers to LDCs, and the elimination of the private Eurobanking network. They are likely to be followed by even more ambitious initiatives, because the underlying structural deficiencies of the system continuously engender new manifestations of instability.

Still, it would be wrong to view the various multilateral agreements concerning exchange rates, the LDC debt crisis, and transnational banks as the beginning of a comprehensive overhaul of the international monetary system. What we have had so far has been an ad hoc process of adjustments, entirely reactive in nature and looking only at trees without seeing the forest. Policy-makers have responded to specific problems that needed addressing, but their responses have been undertaken in isolation from each other and have lacked overall coordination. Most central bankers and other policy-makers have yet to realize that the system as a whole is flawed. Unless they make that connection, they will not go beyond mere tinkering with existing arrangements, tinkering that leaves current money forms, payments systems, capital transfer mechanisms, and adjustment processes basically intact.

Comprehensive monetary reform has traditionally come about only in the aftermath of cataclysmic events, generally wars or economic crises, which literally destroyed the institutions in place.[9] Only only after a monetary regime has disintegrated and after the consequences of this collapse have made themselves felt in acute crisis conditions have policy-makers usually mustered the will to replace all of the components of the system at once. There is no reason to believe that it will be any different the next time around. Unrealistic ideologies, which distort how markets really work, make it difficult to learn from history.

The most likely trigger for international monetary reform is a crisis of confidence in the dollar. After all, the U.S. currency remains the dominant form of world money, and a refusal by foreigners to hold their reserves or denominate their transactions in dollars would most certainly send shock waves through the world economy. We have already faced such a prospect twice. The first time was in 1971–73, when the fixed-price link between the dollar and gold and other currencies collapsed; the second was in 1979, when only a radical policy shift by the Fed saved the world-money status of the dollar from certain demise. One should keep in mind that in 1931 a similar fate befell the pound, then the world's key currency. At that point the international monetary system simply disintegrated in a global wave of bank failures and country defaults.

It could be argued that the situation today is in no way comparable to the conditions that prevailed in the early 1930s. Ever since President Nixon suspended Bretton Woods in August 1971, we have gradually moved from a dollar-dominated system to a multicurrency system based on three key currencies (dollar, mark, yen) without suffering the kind of cataclysmic crisis of the interwar period. After twenty years of this adjustment, why should we suddenly no longer be able to continue muddling through the transition? The answer to this question depends not least on how we assess the United States' strengths and its ability to maintain the dollar as the principal form of world money. If we are optimistically inclined, we will surely point out that, unlike Great Britain in the early 1930s, the United States is still a dominant superpower. If anything, its global position has become stronger since the collapse of the Soviet Union. Nor do we have to look far to find evidence that the United States is still in a position to project its power globally and in the process to shore up the status of the dollar as the world's leading currency. By taking decisive action against Iraq's bid for control over OPEC and thereby securing global oil supplies at reasonable prices, the Bush administration helped major oil producers (e.g., Saudi Arabia, Kuwait, Iran) as well as industrial nations which depend on imports of Gulf oil (e.g., Germany, Japan). Not only is oil a most strategic commodity traded all over the world, it is also of crucial importance to the dollar. As long as oil transactions across the globe continue to be almost exclusively denominated in dollars, the U.S.

currency will maintain its special key-currency status. Not surprisingly, the dollar rallied in foreign-exchange markets during and after the Gulf crisis.

The euphoria that followed America's military triumph over Iraq did not last long, and the dollar soon began to weaken once again. In mid-1992 its decline accelerated, raising anew questions about its long-term prospects. Since 1985 the dollar has lost more than half of its value vis-à-vis other major currencies, and there is still no end in sight. In light of such sustained depreciation it is doubtful whether the dollar can continue to be the principal form of world money for long. Even though the U.S. share in world trade and output has shrunk to below 20 percent, nearly two-thirds of all trade transactions and reserve holdings are still denominated in dollars. That gap has been bridged by massive international circulation of dollars in the Euromarket, where there is no leakage due to reserve requirements and where the multiplier effect is therefore theoretically infinite. But it is precisely the existence of that private banking network outside the regulatory reach of governments which makes sudden and destabilizing portfolio adjustments that much more likely. It is very easy to switch currencies in the Euromarket.

Ultimately the (in)stability of the dollar depends on U.S. economic policy. Unfortunately, it is very difficult for any financial superpower to manage seigniorage properly over the long run. That benefit allows the issuer of world money to run balance-of-payments deficits without external constraint. The United States ended up abusing that benefit, just as Great Britain did during the interwar period. In the 1980s our nation became a net importer of capital to finance growing trade deficits—a stunning reversal from its original postwar position of power rooted in trade surpluses and large capital exports. The supply of worldwide liquidity via continuous U.S. balance-of-payments deficits is now tied to debt-financed excess consumption of Americans rather than to global investment activities of large U.S. firms.

That kind of global money creation is precarious. The issuer of world money becomes utterly dependent on continuous recycling of dollars circulating abroad back to the point of their origin. These capital imports, besides turning the United States into the largest debtor nation, reduce the supplies of funds for other countries. Moreover, monetary policy becomes subject to conflicting pressures. The United States' ability to attract foreign capital and to maintain the world-money status of its currency requires keeping the dollar strong. At the same time, the competitive world market position of its industries can in the short (and even medium) term be improved only by means of a weaker dollar.

The ensuing conflict between financial capital and industrial capital over the exchange rate has plagued Great Britain since the 1920s, and policy-makers have responded to the contradictory pressures with an endless sequence of "stop-go" policy switches.[10] The same type of conflict, with similarly destabilizing consequences for economic policy, can now be witnessed in the United States. When the dollar comes under too much pressure, the Fed tightens; when growth slows down as a result, the Fed loosens once again. But such an unsteady policy course engenders acute uncertainty and thereby discourages long-term investment activity.

Whereas in recent years U.S. policy-makers have favored a lower dollar to boost exports, most advanced economies will probably fare better with a "hard" currency. Because domestic producers confront more intense competitive pressures from abroad when the currency is valued highly, they will ultimately end up being more efficient. For the same reason inflation will be low, with price increases kept in check by cheap imports. Foreign assets cost less, thus giving the larger firms located in the hard-currency country ample incentives to expand abroad. Finally, investors all across the globe will like the currency, and this in turn will supply the domestic banking system with additional funds. The combination of stable prices and cheap credit, which a "hard" currency thereby encourages, makes for a good investment climate.

It is unlikely that the United States will be able to enjoy the advantages of a strong currency in the years to come, however. After a spectacular rise during the first half of the 1980s, the dollar has steadily drifted downward over the past seven years. In many instances the currency is already priced below the depressed levels of the late 1970s. This decline would have been even more pronounced had the dollar not retained its status as the principal "safe-haven" currency during a period of great turmoil across the globe.[11] If we abstract from relatively short-lived capital flight into the dollar when tensions mount (e.g., the Gulf War, the Soviet coup by communist hard-liners), however, basic market forces point to its continued weakening.

• The U.S. trade deficit may have been cut in half since its peak in 1987 by a combination of cheaper dollar, recession, and some improvements in the competitiveness of U.S. industry, but it is still sizable (currently in excess of $75 billion).

• Although such deficit reduction surely helps to make the United States less dependent on foreign capital, it also reduces the injection of new dollars into the global economy. This reduction of liquidity creation especially hurts those countries with dollar-denominated liabilities. Debt reschedulings and new sovereign loans will therefore become increasingly denominated in currencies other than the dollar (including SDRs and ECUs), a trend which is further reinforced by the global retrenchment of U.S. banks and the rapidly expanding international presence of European and Japanese banks. Such long-term portfolio adjustments in the global debt economy will further weaken the dollar.

• The U.S. trade deficit has fallen by more than half since 1989, but the U.S. budget deficit has more than doubled during the same period. Yet much of that increase lacks the stimulative punch of earlier deficit-spending. U.S. government spending is increasingly channeled into relatively unproductive socialization of losses (e.g., thrift bailout) or maintenance of rather inefficient operations (e.g., military apparatus, health care system). Consequently, the United States is gradually slipping into a dangerous position of continuing to pile up foreign debts while not growing fast enough to service that debt easily out of income gains. In this situation it becomes especially tempting to reduce the effective debt burden through higher inflation and/or a lower dollar.[12]

• Finally, there is the question of how long foreign investors will tolerate the United States' appetite for imported capital. At some point their portfolios will be saturated with dollar-denominated investments. Should the United States then fail to compensate for a relatively high inflation rate through correspondingly higher returns, foreign investors may decide to get out of the dollar altogether. So far we have not witnessed massive dumping of dollars (since 1987), but considering all the forces at work here such a shift in market sentiments remains a distinct possibility.

After twenty years of gradual, albeit occasionally turbulent, adjustment it cannot be claimed that the dollar faces certain collapse. The transition from a dollar-denominated regime to a tripolar regime may proceed without major disruption, and the various issuers of the key currencies—presumably the United States, the EC, and Japan—could ultimately find ways to keep the emerging multicurrency system fairly stable. Such a scenario probably requires a few institutional changes to assure more effective policy coordination and greater convergence among the G–7 nations (e.g., adoption of binding macroeconomic targets). In this case it will be a long time, if ever, before any fundamental reform toward supranational credit-money will materialize.

On the other hand, it is possible that the United States will so mismanage its economy in terms of borrowing requirements or inflation that a major dollar crisis similar to the one in 1979 (see chapter 7) becomes inevitable. Seigniorage is a market failure, because it excludes the issuer of world money from the kind of adjustment pressures which other deficit countries normally face. Thus able to escape the external constraint, the country that issues the key currency will be tempted to run up excessively large deficits and to delay corrective steps until it is too late.

Should a massive flight out of the dollar occur, the international monetary system could be paralyzed. The inability or unwillingness of the United States to act as international lender of last resort during a major financial crisis could have the same result. Fundamental reform of the kind proposed in this chapter is obviously a great deal more likely when the foundations of the current multicurrency system have disintegrated.

Whether we muddle through the current transition or face a major crisis, sooner or later the United States will lose its seigniorage benefit. That loss will either come gradually, as other key currencies gain dominance (e.g., ECUs in the late 1990s), or rather suddenly, through a SNCM-like reform. In either case the United States will have to undergo major policy adjustments and restructuring to adapt its economy to the loss of seigniorage.

Part VI
Restructuring the American Economy

17

The United States at the Crossroads

Ever since the end of World War II the international monetary system has been centered on the dollar as the principal form of world money. The widespread use of its currency as an international medium of exchange has given the United States a special position in the world economy. On the one hand, we Americans have had to supply the rest of the world with adequate supplies of global liquidity. This responsibility has included lender-of-last-resort interventions to help other countries with excessive external deficits and debt-servicing problems, as evidenced by the dominant U.S. role in funding the IMF or in managing the LDC debt crisis. On the other hand, the United States has derived significant advantages as an issuer of world money, being the only country that can pay for its obligations to other countries in its own currency. One consequence of this so-called seigniorage benefit is the ability to run continuous balance-of-payments deficits that are automatically financed by foreigners willing to hold additional dollars (see the last two sections of chapter 5).

Since the breakdown of Bretton Woods in 1971 we have witnessed a gradual erosion of the dollar's international role. This decline has manifested itself in a variety of ways, most notably in a series of devaluations and a long-term loss of market share to other key currencies. The trend is direct result of America's worsening external position over the past twenty-five years. If it continues, then sooner or later the dollar will have ceased to be the primary form of world money.

Such an outcome is virtually certain, should the community of nations ever decide to introduce supranational credit-money (see chapter 16). But even without this kind of reform it is highly probable that the dollar will no longer dominate the international monetary system when the new millennium starts. With regard to trade, production, and capital flows we have already moved away from U.S. hegemony to a much more polycentric world economy. As the international monetary system adjusts to this new reality, other currencies (e.g., mark, yen, and probably after 1999 Europe's ECU) are bound to become as important as the dollar. In other words, the United States is about to lose the seigniorage benefit that it has enjoyed for half a century.

The erosion of the dollar's status as world money is not a smooth process. We have already seen ample evidence of that. Sharp devaluations of the dollar in 1973–74 and 1978–79 destabilized commodity markets, forced interest rates higher, and set off global recessions. Efforts by the leading industrial nations to stabilize the dollar in 1987 under the so-called Louvre Agreement helped to trigger a worldwide collapse of stock prices. Further disruptions of the world economy are likely as the dollar continues to weaken. These may involve a massive flight out of the dollar, global debt crises allowed to deepen in the absence of an effective international lender-of-last-resort mechanism, intensifying trade wars, or a synchronized worldwide downturn.

Even if the world economy as a whole proves to be more resilient to monetary shocks than is assumed here, there can be little doubt that the eventual end of the dollar standard will have profound effects on the U.S. economy. Americans may soon face the same kind of external constraint as anyone else. Specifically, the United States will not be able to borrow as easily as it did in the past. The recycling of international dollars to finance America's twin deficits will inevitably slow down, when global surpluses are increasingly held in denominations other than the dollar and are invested elsewhere. At the same time, the United States will also begin to feel the burden of foreign debt more heavily, once it can no longer freely pay for its obligations overseas in its own currency. The servicing of its debts will then have to come out of real income gains, just as that of other debtor nations does.

Once the dollar no longer predominates as world money, we shall finally feel the full extent of our weakened external position. At that point we may well have to transfer between 1 percent and 2 percent of our GNP abroad each year just to service our foreign debt. That is about half of our current annual growth capacity. Unless we manage to grow faster, we face the prospect of stagnating living standards for years to come. The loss of seigniorage will also make it much harder to finance our twin deficits. We might try to get these deficits under control through austerity measures. But such a traditional response will depress growth rates at a time when a large chunk of our annual income gains must be diverted into servicing our foreign debt.

In the face of these manifestations of external constraint it is imperative to find ways which permit the U.S. economy to expand more rapidly without reigniting inflationary pressures. This can only happen if we overcome certain structural barriers to growth in the U.S. economy. Key among them are slow productivity growth, inadequate investment spending, bias toward the short term, and paralyzed policy-making. That combination of problems calls for full-scale restructuring of our economy.

We begin this final chapter with a discussion of how the United States has abused this seigniorage benefit to the point of having to face its loss in the near future (section 17.1). The consequences of this mismanagement have already become visible in the latest recession, 1990–92, especially the suffocating debt burdens that have fed asset deflation and slowed the growth of our economy (section 17.2).

The challenge we face is considerable. Our economy, as currently structured, may be condemned to stagnation for years to come. It is only by fundamentally restructuring it that we have a realistic chance of growing faster, at least fast enough for national income gains to outpace the increase in total debt-servicing charges. That reorganization has to occur on several fronts. Domestic industry should invest more and better (section 17.3). We must redefine budget priorities to revitalize our government's ability for decisive action in the face of national problems. The nation's fiscal crisis is due as much to political paralysis as to economic stagnation (section 17.4). Our banking system, now under serious stress, needs to be put on a stronger footing. We could also do well with financial institutions and markets that are less prone to speculative activity and more oriented toward improving the long-term growth capacity of our economy (section 17.5). Finally, we must recognize that economic reform is always part of a broader process of social change. More basic reorganization in the direction of community-based and socially beneficial reindustrialization is needed to revive the United States' productive capacities (section 17.6).

17.1. The End of American Hegemony

Given its size and resource base, it was inevitable that the United States would eventually emerge as a superpower. But that status came to our nation more easily because of the destructive tendencies of other powerful nations. During World War I (1914–18) the United States supplied its allies with war materiel and lent them the funds to pay for it. This combination generated boom conditions at home, enabled our firms to capture valuable export markets, and catapulted the United States into prominence as the world's dominant creditor nation. At the same time, the war left most European nations much weakened and indebted. The pattern recurred during World War II (1939–45). Once again we were in a position to profit from warfare elsewhere as supplier of funds and goods, to enter the conflict late and on foreign soil, and to provide the decisive tipping of the scales in favor of our allies.

By the end of World War II the U.S. economy was the only industrial nation that was intact, and it enjoyed a position of absolute dominance. With Europe and Japan in ruins, the new superpower controlled more than 40 percent of global manufacturing capacity and 78 percent of the capitalist world's gold reserves. At that point Americans were finally ready to abandon their traditional isolationism and to use their prominent position to build a new international economic order.

There is no question that this new order played a crucial role in the global boom of the 1950s and 1960s (see chapter 5). The gold-dollar standard introduced at Bretton Woods in 1944 gave the world economy a stable and viable international monetary regime for the first time in three decades, and trade liberalization measures under the auspices of GATT facilitated a very rapid expansion of world trade.

The United States had introduced these institutional arrangements not only to help other countries revive but also to benefit its own industries. This was especially true with regard to Bretton Woods, which established U.S. currency as the primary form of world money. In the aftermath of the war many nations suffered from an acute shortage of dollars needed to pay for essential imports and debt obligations. The problem was overcome when the United States transferred massive amounts of dollars to the rest of the world. Those capital exports gave other countries a highly welcome injection of dollars while reinforcing the United States' status as the world's dominant power.

• Government-assistance programs financed foreign purchases of U.S. goods and in this way secured large export markets for American industry. They also allowed our policy-makers to shape the internal affairs of other nations by making financial support contingent on specific political actions and economic policies to protect U.S. interests in the region.

• In the late 1940s, when the confrontation with the Soviet Union began in earnest, the United States concluded a series of security treaties with allies in Western Europe, Latin America, and Asia. These have involved permanent deployments of American troops in strategic countries (e.g., Germany, Korea), a global network of bases, and large-scale aid to key allies (e.g., Israel, Pakistan)—all channels for dollar transfers abroad.

• Many countries had to borrow dollars to pay for imports, and this international demand for loanable funds gave U.S. banks an edge in global credit markets.

• Countries in need of dollars also tried to attract U.S. firms into their domestic markets by offering them investment incentives (e.g., tax breaks, no-union pledges, easy profit repatriation). During the first postwar decades our largest firms turned multinational, investing aggressively abroad to gain access to cheap resources and to penetrate new markets.

These organized channels of capital exports, which provided the capitalist world with ample injections of liquidity, represented a classic use of seigniorage. The United States, as issuer of world money, was allowed—even required—to run chronic balance-of-payments deficits, which other countries automatically financed by holding dollars as reserve. The dollar transfers were intimately tied to the cold war, especially the United States' military commitments overseas and various official assistance programs, such as the Marshall Plan for Western

Europe or the Alliance for Progress targeted toward Latin America in the early 1960s. In that sense it is fair to argue that the confrontation with the Soviet Union reinforced the superpower status of the United States and gave the international economic order a certain cohesion. The United States projected global power in economic, political, and military terms. As long as these channels of hegemony recycled our surpluses to the rest of the world effectively and brought peace and prosperity to a widening circle of countries, we could legitimately claim to be leader of the "free" world. With the "evil" empire of communism always looming in the background as a threat, American leadership took on a particularly centralizing force. We can justly define the postwar period as a "Pax Americana."

Although Bretton Woods worked remarkably well for more than two decades, the seeds of its eventual destruction in 1971 (see chapter 7) were there from the very beginning. Controlling most of the capitalist world's gold reserves by the end of World War II, the U.S. government was in a position to dictate the price of the precious metal at the Bretton Woods Conference in 1944. Even though commodity prices had tripled on average over the preceding decade, the Americans picked the 1934 gold price of $35 per ounce. This unrealistically low price made it impossible for gold to function effectively as world money, since it could no longer serve as a realistic measure of value. By rendering gold ineffectual, the Americans made sure that the U.S. dollar would take over as world money. In the long run, however, the conscious underpricing of gold hastened the demise of the Bretton Woods system. Not only did it depress the value of U.S. reserves backing the dollar as world money, it also locked in a very high value for the dollar. The two key weaknesses of Bretton Woods, the inadequacy of U.S. gold reserves to back all international dollars in circulation and the chronic overvaluation of the dollar, were therefore enshrined into the system at its very inception.

These contradictions came violently to the fore during the height of the Vietnam War in the late 1960s. This was the first time that the United States exploited its privileged position of monetary hegemony, abandoning its historically cautious fiscal policy and transferring the burden of financing much larger deficits abroad. With the Johnson administration unwilling to pay for the unpopular war through higher taxes, Europeans ended up footing much of the bill. Their central banks were forced to absorb much larger dollar outflows in the wake of rapidly growing U.S. balance-of-payments deficits. Excessive stimulation of domestic demand, always a temptation for the beneficiary of seigniorage whose external constraint is much less stringent than that of any other country, caused U.S. inflation to accelerate rapidly from 1967 onward. This made the relative overvaluation of the dollar even more pronounced. By that point the misalignment of exchange rates had become self-reinforcing, because the artificially cheap mark and yen made it that much easier for the Germans and the Japanese to build up large trade surpluses. When the United States had its first trade deficit in a century, Bretton Woods came undone in a frenzy of dollar selling. In August 1971 European central banks finally decided that they had absorbed enough dollars, prompting Nixon to suspend the gold backing of the dollar.

Seigniorage induced overstimulation of domestic demand, and at the same time it undermined U.S. production capacity on the supply side. Although the leading U.S. firms, especially those that invested heavily overseas, exerted intense competitive pressures on foreign producers because of their size advantage and technological superiority, they lacked the same kind of impetus because of their dominance. The overvaluation of the dollar made the American challenge easier for other industrial nations to stomach. It caused their products to be cheaper than they would have been had Bretton Woods' fixed currency prices more accurately reflected valuation differentials based on average production conditions in different countries. Yet that misalignment of exchange rates did not have a reciprocal effect on American producers, because foreign trade amounted to only about 10 percent of our gross national product during the 1950s and 1960s. At that point the United States was still an essentially closed economy, and in this kind of environment our industrial managers did not take the emerging competitive threat from foreign producers seriously.

Instead, leading U.S. firms experienced the overvaluation of the dollar mostly as an inducement to buy up artificially cheap assets overseas and in the process to expand their market presence in strategic countries. But as they turned increasingly multinational, many became less committed to maintaining a strong industrial base within the United States. The corporate giants lobbied the U.S. government on issues of narrow self-interest (e.g., tax breaks, regulatory relief, protection from foreign competition, sanctions against hostile governments), but they failed to show the same kind of fervor on behalf of broader, potentially costly sources of economic strength (e.g., education, health care, infrastructure). Years of neglect by disengaged business leaders and divided government have now created acute crisis conditions in those crucial areas of public investment.

Our ability to transfer the financing burden of large balance-of-payment deficits onto other nations and to shield ourselves from the full impact of foreign competition reinforced a bias in the U.S. economy in favor of consumption and to the detriment of investment. That distortion has hurt the United States' position in the world economy, making it easier for other industrial nations to catch up. In terms of productivity growth, cost of capital, investment activity, research spending, and other determinants of competitiveness, we have performed worse than others for decades and consequently have lost much of our competitive edge (see Table 17.1).

Those performance differences illustrate negligence on the part of a United States that has become too used to dominance in the global marketplace. An equally important aspect of the data, however, has been the remarkable postwar success of other industrial nations, especially Germany and Japan. It is no surprise that those two nations in particular have emerged as new economic leaders.

Table 17.1

International Comparison of Performance

	United States	Germany	Japan
National saving			
1967–73	16.0	26.9	38.0
1974–79	16.6	22.5	33.0
1980–90	13.6	22.7	31.9
Real business fixed investment			
1967–73	10.9	12.2	15.5
1974–79	11.2	10.9	14.0
1980–90	12.0	12.0	16.5
Real GDP			
1967–73	3.1	4.2	9.2
1974–79	2.5	2.3	3.6
1980–90	2.4	2.1	4.2
Total factor productivity			
1967–73	0.8	3.2	6.2
1974–79	0.0	1.9	1.5
1980–90	0.4	1.0	1.8
GDP deflator			
1967–73	5.0	4.9	6.2
1974–79	7.7	4.7	7.8
1980–90	4.7	3.0	1.6

Source: International Monetary Fund, *World Economic Outlook*, May 1991, Washington, DC, Tables 9 and 10.

Notes: National saving and real business fixed investments measured as percent of GDP (annual average). Real GDP, total factor productivity, and GDP deflator measured as annual changes in percent (average).

Both had been regional powers since the 1870s, and both used their local hegemony for accelerated industrialization. In the process each attempted to dominate its neighbors by force. The disastrous experience of recurrent warfare in the first half of this century, ending in utter defeat, finally led Germans and Japanese to break with their militaristic past and focus instead on socio-economic objectives. After suffering devastating destruction in World War II, both nations had a unique opportunity to rebuild their economies and to reorganize their societies from scratch. With the help of American military protection, financial assistance, and political guidance they succeeded beyond anyone's expectations in creating stability and prosperity. Each developed its own unique model of a mixed economy based on a high degree of coordination between government agencies, union officials, bankers, and corporate managers. Close cooperation among all of these principal actors in the economy has encouraged high investment shares and has facilitated aggressive pursuit of export-led growth strategies.

Even though it was Great Britain and France whose demand for gold conversion of their excess dollars forced President Nixon's hand in August 1971, the successful catching-up by Japan and Germany was the structural cause of the collapse of Bretton Woods. During the 1970s the United States tried hard to maintain the world money status of the dollar by pushing for the complete demonetization of gold and by blocking the issuance of additional SDRs by the IMF. At the same time, the dollar was pushed lower, first in 1971–73 and then in 1977–79, in the hope that thereby cheapened exports and more expensive imports would help to improve the competitive position of U.S. industry. This strategy of monetary protectionism failed doubly. Each time the dollar depreciation triggered speculative flights out of the key currency and global commodity inflation. Moreover, import penetration of key U.S. markets continued to increase despite a lower dollar, which might well indicate accelerating erosion of America's international competitiveness (See Table 17.2).

By late 1979 the erosion of the once-almighty dollar had progressed to the point that its world money status for the first time faced a serious threat. OPEC wanted to be paid in a basket of currencies instead of just dollars, the IMF considered a large "substitution account" to reduce the world's dollar overhang in exchange for new SDRs, and the European Community had just started its own monetary system to shield its currencies from the vicissitudes of the dollar. The time had come for dramatic action to revive the position of the dollar. Starting with Paul Volcker's historic shift to monetary tightening in October 1979 (see section 7.7) and extending to President Reagan's hands-off policy concerning exchange rates during his first term, U.S. policy-makers did their share to strengthen the dollar. The combination of high interest rates and rising exchange rates gave foreign investors very attractive returns on dollar-denominated assets, and the large influx of foreign capital reinforced a dramatic dollar appreciation of 60 percent from its 1979 low. That same combination, of course, pushed many heavily indebted LDCs to the brink of default and triggered a global debt crisis. Unlike Great Britain half a century earlier, at that point the United States was still in a position to act decisively as the international lender of last resort. A central IMF-administered mechanism for emergency loans and debt restructurings was set up to deal with debt-servicing problems on a case-by-case basis (see section 10.1), and a combination of monetary easing and fiscal stimulation in the United States helped to pull the global economy out of a worldwide downturn after 1982.

Ultimately Volcker's monetary policies and Reagan's tax policies broke the inflationary momentum that had built up across the globe during the 1970s. In

Table 17.2

The United States' Declining Competitiveness during the 1970s

(a) U.S. market shares (domestic producers' percentage of total sales)

	1960	1970	1980
Automobiles	95.5	82.8	72.9
Steel	95.8	85.7	83.4
Apparel	98.2	94.8	90.1
Electrical components	99.5	94.4	78.9
Farm machinery	92.8	92.2	80.7
Industrial inorganic chemicals	98.0	91.5	76.2
Consumer electronics	94.4	68.4	53.1
Footwear	97.7	85.4	66.6
Metal-cutting machine tools	96.7	89.4	71.0
Food-processing machinery	97.0	91.9	84.2
Metal-forming machine tools	96.8	93.2	76.2
Textile machinery	93.4	67.1	53.1
Calculating and adding machines	95.0	63.8	57.1

(b) World market shares (U.S. exports as a percentage of world exports)

	1962	1970	1980
Motor vehicles	22.6	17.5	11.4
Aircraft	70.9	66.5	52.2
Organic chemicals	20.5	25.7	15.3
Telecommunications apparatus	28.5	15.2	15.0
Plastic materials	27.8	17.3	12.6
Machinery and appliances (nonelectric)	27.9	24.1	16.6
Medical and pharmaceutical products	27.6	17.5	14.9
Metalworking machinery	32.5	16.8	24.0
Agricultural machinery	40.2	29.6	24.9
Hand or machine tools	20.5	19.1	13.5
Textile and leather machinery	15.5	9.9	7.2
Railway vehicles	34.8	18.4	12.2
Housing fixtures	22.8	12.0	7.8

Source: The *Business Week* Team, *The Deindustrialization of America*, 1982, p. 14. Reprinted from 1982 issue of *Business Week* by special permission, copyright © 1982 by McGraw-Hill, Inc.

the process they also helped to revive the international status of the dollar. But that success did not come without significant cost. The policy reflation during the first half of the 1980s saddled us with huge budget and trade deficits, which turned the United States from the world's dominant creditor nation into its largest debtor nation in less than five years (see Table 17.3). This rapid turnaround represents a rather advanced stage of imperial decay, during which the issuer of world money becomes a net importer of capital and is forced to liquidate foreign assets, much like what happened to Great Britain after World War I.

Table 17.3

Shifting External Positions of the United States, Germany, and Japan
(in billions of U.S. dollars)

	United States		Germany		Japan	
Year	Trade balance	Capital account	Trade balance	Capital account	Trade balance	Capital account
1979	−27.54	9.76	16.48	2.74	1.74	4.40
1980	−25.50	−10.26	8.69	−1.40	2.13	15.78
1981	−27.99	−8.50	16.07	−0.03	19.96	−1.13
1982	−36.44	7.89	24.73	−2.06	18.08	−11.55
1983	−67.08	36.13	21.43	−6.61	31.46	−19.25
1984	−112.51	99.71	22.14	−10.70	44.26	−32.88
1985	−122.16	128.05	28.58	−16.07	55.99	−49.75
1986	−145.05	111.64	55.76	−38.33	92.82	−70.99
1987	−159.49	103.34	70.20	−25.69	96.42	−49.08
1988	−126.97	90.10	79.78	−68.76	95.00	−63.11
1989	−115.92	123.29	77.74	−67.46	76.89	−69.73
1990	−108.12	63.67	71.71	−40.93	63.58	−44.94
1991	−73.60	−16.12	23.06	22.78	103.09	−81.10

Source: International Monetary Fund, *International Financial Statistics Yearbook 1992*, Washington, DC, pp. 126 and 130.

When we look at the legacy of "Reaganomics" (see also chapter 8), we confront a new chapter in the story of our abuse of seigniorage. The twin deficits of the Reagan-Bush era dwarfed earlier instances of fiscal irresponsibility (e.g., Johnson's "guns-and-butter" policy) and far surpassed what used to be considered excessive, say, during the early 1970s. These deficits spurred global recovery after 1982 without reigniting inflation, granted; but the way this came about has certainly undermined our long-term prospects.

• The United States' gradual trend toward a low-investment, low-saving economy only intensified during the Reagan years. In contrast to the predictions of supply-side protagonists, tax cuts geared toward the rich failed to induce more personal savings. Instead, they seem to have been spent mostly on luxury goods. New investment incentives fueled highly speculative shuffling of financial claims ("paper entrepreneurship") but did little to encourage more spending on new plant and equipment. At the same time we reduced our investment in human capital, the most crucial resource in the emerging global accumulation regime. Whatever budgetary savings we as a nation enjoyed from cutting key domestic programs (e.g., low-income housing subsidies, health care, public school education, job training) have long since been outweighed by the social costs of growing poverty and class polarization, which, ironically, these cuts helped to aggravate.

• Throughout the 1980s we Americans consumed more than we produced, with the difference being made up by massive import of foreign capital. The fancies of the richest nation of the world thus diverted scarce capital supplies from poorer countries, where they could have been put to better use for the purposes of industrialization.

• A significant portion of that capital influx financed a huge U.S. rearmament program. Though essential to winning the cold war and certainly a boost to our private sector (especially in terms of employment and corporate profits), the near-doubling of our military budget during Reagan's first term prevented some of our resources from being deployed more productively in the civilian sector.

• Finally, the debt explosion in each sector of the U.S. economy during the 1980s was not least encouraged by our unique ability to pay international obligations in our own currency. As the country issuing the globally accepted means of payment, the United States is able to accumulate more financial liabilities than any other country, because these international claims are still mostly denominated in dollars and therefore do not need to be secured by foreign-exchange reserves or by any other tangible assets. The U.S. government's promise to pay debt-servicing charges is all that backs these debts. In this situation it is difficult to resist the temptation to spend and borrow too much. Americans fell into this trap, especially after Reagan's revival of laissez-faire capitalism had elevated the pursuit of narrow self-interest and instant gratification to the status of ruling dogma.

• When the United States was still a net exporter of capital, our banks enjoyed a competitive edge in the global credit system as they absorbed and channeled excess dollars to ultimate borrowers. But once we became a net importer of capital, the global market share of credit transactions routed through U.S. banks and denominated in dollars began to shrink quite rapidly. The reversal of traditional capital flows has forced our banking sector into a global retrenchment which matches the relative decline in the international circulation of dollars. This aspect of declining monetary hegemony has surely played a major role in our current banking crisis.

Being the issuer of the key currency not only fosters excessive consumption and indebtedness in the domestic economy but also tends to prolong those unhealthy trends beyond prudence. Seigniorage relaxes the external constraint, hence shielding its beneficiary to some extent from the full impact of declining competitiveness. That country can delay adjustments until the cumulative impact of the erosion threatens its very position as world money producer. Given the advanced state of its underlying structural imbalances, the U.S. economy may soon reach that point.

Our ability to finance large deficits and excess spending with reimported dollars has its limits. Key sectors of our economy cannot service old debts with new credit ad infinitum. Sooner or later their liabilities need to be backed by sufficient income gains. Otherwise, debt-servicing charges will absorb too large a portion of cash flow, forcing spending plans to be scaled back. Such a saturation point will also be approached from the supply side of the credit transaction. Eventually foreign investors will have acquired enough assets from the United States and will feel like diversifying. When they do, our domestic "debt economy" will be squeezed.

Sudden withdrawals of foreign funds can send shock waves through our financial system, as evidenced by the silent run out of the Continental Illinois jumbo CDs in early 1984 or the massive profit-taking by Japanese investors that precipitated the stock market collapse in October 1987. Less spectacular but equally significant are gradual portfolio adjustments by saturated foreign investors. The first slowdown of capital flows to the United States came during 1985–86, when Latin American debtors could no longer sustain capital flight and debt-servicing payments, forcing our money-center banks to write down impaired LDC-related assets at a loss of $21 billion in 1987. In early 1990 we saw net liquidations of U.S. securities by foreign investors, especially Japanese institutions. By that point the exchange-rate risk from a falling dollar and rising interest rates elsewhere had made U.S. investments much less attractive. The Fed failed to compensate for the slowing inflow of foreign savings, in the process allowing domestic interest rates to edge higher. This set the stage for a credit crunch and recession which became inevitable when Saddam Hussein's invasion of Kuwait in the summer of 1990 created yet another oil shock.

Since that turning point in early 1990 it has become even more difficult for Americans to attract foreign savings (see Table 17.4). In just two years funding needs exploded across the globe. The moves toward greater integration in Western Europe, the reconstruction needs of Eastern Europe and the former Soviet Union, the rebuilding of Kuwait, and the accelerated industrialization efforts of some developing nations (e.g., Mexico, Thailand) all require massive infusions of capital. Germany is busy with reunification, and Japan has shifted funds to the Pacific Rim while trying to cope with the bursting of its huge speculative bubble in the stock and real estate markets. Moreover, the dollar is now in a mode of sustained decline. This ongoing devaluation cheapens U.S. assets, but it also creates conversion losses for foreign investors. A belated switch to monetary easing by the Fed and the recession-induced weakening of domestic credit demand have also pushed U.S. interest rates down (in some cases to their lowest levels in nearly three decades), which make yields less attractive here than in Europe and Japan. Even the capital flight from Latin America has slowed down as profit opportunities have gradually improved there.

Our economy could not sustain its hectic pace of excess spending and borrowing without massive financing support from abroad. This was the principal

Table 17.4

The United States' Financing Squeeze of the Early 1990s

	1989	1990	1991
Net capital imports	123.3	63.7	−16.1
Budget deficit	−2.8	−4.1	−5.1
Investment	18.3	17.0	15.3
Exchange rate	73.7	69.6	68.4

Source: International Monetary Fund, *International Financial Statistics Yearbook 1992,* Washington, DC, pp.157, 142, 130, 168.

Notes: Net capital imports measured as capital account balance in billions of U.S. dollars. Budget deficit as percentage of GDP. Gross private fixed domestic investment as percentage of GDP. Real effective exchange rate index based on relative consumer prices (1985 = 100)

cause for the recession of 1990–92. Blaming the downturn solely on Saddam Hussein left the Bush administration unprepared for the continuation of bad economic news after victory in the Gulf War. During the election campaign Bush blamed the media for presenting a bleaker picture of the economy than was justified. Occasionally he would urge banks to loosen up and consumers to spend. But exhortations and complaints did not turn our economy around, and the president paid for his inaction with a spectacular defeat by a Democratic candidate who made economic revival the key issue.

17.2. The Return of Debt Deflation

As long as we managed to attract a large chunk of foreign capital, we could mask the underlying long-term weakening of the U.S. economy. Now that those funds have begun to dry up, the debt-financed and consumption-driven growth pattern of the past decade has given way to retrenchment. That squeeze is more than just a cyclical downturn which will be followed in short order by a robust recovery. Underneath a normal recessionary adjustment we find signs of a much deeper malaise, a degree of income erosion, financial fragility, and asset deflation not seen since the Great Depression of the 1930s. These conditions have matured to a point where they constrain every sector of our economy.

1) American Households. Consumers, whose combined spending constitutes two-thirds of total demand, are in dire straits. The boom of the 1980s bypassed most of them, with the bottom 80 percent of families receiving only 6 percent of all after-tax income gains during the Carter-Reagan years.[1] Average real wages have stagnated now for two decades, and inflation-adjusted median household income was lower in 1992 than in 1979. Consumption grew during this period, but only because we saved less, worked longer (including the large-scale entry of married women into the labor force), and took on more debt. These responses could only continue up to a point. Today most American families work as much as they can endure, have run down their savings to a minimum, and have reached dangerously high debt levels. Many households, expecting rising asset prices (e.g., for homes) in future years, took on more debt in the 1980s than they could afford on the basis of their present income. Not surprisingly, personal bankruptcies and foreclosures have reached record postwar levels. The degree of consumer pessimism exhibited during the latest recession (1990–92) expresses a recognition by most Americans that two decades of stagnating income have finally caught up with them and that there is not much prospect for rapid improvement.

2) The Business Sector. A propensity toward much greater leverage, fueled over the past decade by a debt-financed merger boom, has left many enterprises with very high debt-servicing charges and a much weakened financial structure. In that state it is difficult to survive a period of declining revenues, and as a result we have witnessed spectacular bankruptcies during the early 1990s (e.g., Drexel, Campeau, PanAm, Bank of New England, Macy's, Olympia & York). Many of the sectors that experienced rapid growth in the 1980s, such as investment banking and real estate, are facing particularly sharp declines now that the speculative bubbles sustaining their boom have all burst. Small businesses, traditionally a major source of job creation, worker training, and innovation, were hit especially hard by the latest credit crunch.

3) Financial Institutions. The engine of our "debt economy" has fallen on hard times. The disastrous wave of thrift failures has mushroomed into a $300 billion government bailout, as hundreds of savings and loans associations and mutual savings banks have had to be liquidated. Investment banks have only recently begun to recover from a four-year decline following the stock market collapse of October 1987. Many insurance companies face serious cash-flow problems and capital erosion in the wake of heavy losses, while some of their traditional products face growing consumer resistance. Pension funds that are underfunded or used by corporate managers as cash cows give an aging work force much to worry about. Finally, there is a massive shake-out under way among the nation's commercial banks. Technological change (e.g., the spread of "electronic money") and more relaxed structure regulations have caused many of the smaller banks to sell out. Add to this a very large number of bank failures, ranging between 120 and 200 per year over the past decade, due to bad-debt losses on various kinds of loans (e.g., to LDCs, farmers, energy sector, real estate, leveraged buyouts). Our largest banks, which used to dominate the global credit system, are in retreat. Whereas six of the world's ten largest banks were American in 1960, now only two are left among the top fifty. The combination of losses and competitive disadvantages has recently triggered a spectacular merger wave among our largest money-center banks (e.g., Chemical and Manufacturers' Hanover, Bank of America and Security Pacific) in the hope of thereby strengthening their capital base and eliminating wasteful duplication of effort. All of this turmoil among the nation's different financial institutions is manifestation of a credit system that has become fragile in the wake of excessive debt levels and risk taking.

Ironically, the problem of financial fragility first became acute in the early 1980s, when U.S. monetary authorities decided to clamp down on inflation. In the process debtors lost transfer gains which had accrued to them as long as money devalued rapidly (see section 5.3). Strategic sectors, whose heavy reliance on debt had benefited them greatly while inflation accelerated (e.g., commodity-producing LDCs, farmers, energy producers), suddenly found themselves unable to service their debts and facing default. Their desperate efforts to raise cash soon triggered sectoral price wars that were strong enough in 1985–86 to push overall U.S. inflation below 2 percent—a remarkably low level three years into an upswing.

Those first postwar bouts with deflation should have been warning signs. But they were soon drowned out by renewed optimism in the wake of sustained recovery and gradually declining interest rates. Bankers tried to recoup some of their earlier loan losses by lending heavily to booming sectors, especially those enjoying above-average price increases (e.g., housing, financial securities). But such relief proved to be short-lived, built as it was on speculative bubbles that had to burst sooner (stocks in 1987) or later (commercial real estate in 1989). Since then, forced liquidations by defaulting debtors have driven key asset prices down. For example, cooperative apartments in New York City have lost about one-third of their value from their peak in early 1989. We have not witnessed such a debt-deflation adjustment since the 1930s, a key reason why the recession of the early 1990s felt so much worse than GNP and unemployment figures indicated it should.

4) Federal Government. Stimulative fiscal policies pushed the domestic economy out of previous recessions, but we cannot expect such help this time around. Granted, large budget deficits keep the economy from sinking much lower. Automatic fiscal stabilizers, albeit much weakened during the Reagan years, are still at work. Unemployment benefits have already been extended three times since the onset of the current downturn. Late in his term President Bush finally signed a $151 billion transportation bill to create public-sector jobs. Deficit spending by the U.S. government is surely the principal difference between the current situation and the crisis of the 1930s. Its support of income levels prevents the collapse of the economy into outright depression.

Yet federal budget deficits have recently lost much of their stimulative punch. A growing portion of government spending is now directed toward socialization of losses (e.g., bailout of thrifts and banks) and sustaining excess capacity (e.g., the military-industrial complex), activities with very limited positive multiplier effects at best. Moreover, in the face of a $300+ billion deficit for fiscal 1993 there is not much room for additional stimulation. Our budget shortfall has reached a level at which any further widening of deficits at a time of slowing capital inflows from abroad may well clash with private credit demands and in this way abort recovery. Already we can see disturbing signs of this possibility. Although the Fed pushed short-term interest rates to their lowest level in nearly thirty years, long-term rates remained stubbornly high throughout the recession. In early 1992 they even started to rise again, even though inflation rates were still drifting lower.

5) State and Local Governments. That sector tends to be vulnerable in any recession. Most states and municipalities must balance their budgets, yet they face declining tax revenues and increased spending commitments whenever the economy turns down. In the face of recession-induced deficits they often end up having to choose among higher taxes, spending cuts, or a combination of both. Besides being politically unpopular, such doses of fiscal austerity tend to depress the local economy even more. The latest downturn left many governors and mayors in a particularly difficult position. Ever since Reagan's first budget in 1981, the states and cities have had to endure deep cuts in federal grant support while being forced to take over additional spending responsibilities from the U.S. government.[2] Their desperate efforts to balance budgets in recent years have come at a time when the inner cities already face a myriad of deep-seated problems, including crime, homelessness, the spreading AIDS epidemic, a shrinking economic base, and a rapidly aging infrastructure.

This grim picture did not emerge suddenly. Rather, it is the result of two decades of stagnation. For a while American households and businesses tried to counteract that trend and to maintain spending increases by taking on more debt. The dollar's world-money status enabled them to push such leveraging to very high levels by attracting a large chunk of foreign savings. But that process has now reached its natural limit. Slow income gains eventually had to clash with rising debt-servicing burdens, and capital inflows had to slow in the face of declining exchange rates and shrinking interest-rate differentials.

Most Americans are aware that the economic situation has become serious. Feelings of triumph, which swept the country first when the Soviet empire began to disintegrate and then after our victory over Saddam Hussein, dissipated rapidly once the expected recovery failed to materialize in 1991. After three years of zero growth, the mood has turned sour. A majority is clearly dissatisfied with the current status quo, as evidenced by public opinion polls and large protest votes during the 1992 elections. We find a great deal of anxiety about the future and widespread disdain for the "politics-as-usual" attitude of both political parties. But, beyond fear and cynicism, no clear consensus has yet emerged as to what kind of change is best. Instead of providing vision and leadership, our politicians are busy pointing fingers and appealing to the narrow interests of divergent constituencies. In that kind of climate, it is easy for demagoguery to fill the vacuum and give insecure people a variety of easy scapegoats to blame for their troubles. Racism, xenophobia, and insularity are all raising their ugly heads, often fed by the irresponsible utterings of politicians. Such sentiments are not only immoral but also completely counterproductive. They waste energy, limit opportunity, prevent serious debate. Ultimately they steer us away from the kinds of steps we will need to take for economic revival.

17.3. Income Growth, Productivity Gains, and Investment Revival

The squeeze that Americans began to feel a few years ago is unlikely to let up soon. For the next decade, and possibly beyond that, we must transfer at least 1 percent of our GNP abroad each year to service a foreign debt load that already exceeds $600 billion. A resource transfer of that magnitude amounts to more than a third of our country's natural growth rate. Its effect on our living standards may well be lessened if foreign investors reinvest their returns in the United States. But a falling dollar and comparatively low U.S. interest rates may well make that an unattractive option. Of course, as long as the dollar maintains its key currency status we can rely on additional money creation to cover our foreign debt-servicing obligations. But to the extent that the newly created money has no equivalent in actual income gains which are rooted in an expansion of our capital stock at home, such a tactic risks putting too much downward pressure on the dollar. Should this happen, we shall find ourselves in the final phase of abusing seigniorage. Sooner or later we have to pay our foreign debt-servicing charges with true effort.

In order to keep our annual resource transfer overseas from growing much beyond 1 percent of GNP, we should reduce our dependence on foreign capital as soon and as much as possible. Unfortunately, in the short term this can only come about in ways which are likely to depress domestic growth further—by increasing our domestic savings and/or by lowering our aggregate borrowing requirements. In the absence of policy solutions, imbalances will be corrected by market forces; that is, through a recession which reduces trade deficits and private credit demands. We have been going through precisely such an adjustment process since early 1990, but recent improvements in our external position have been jeopardized by a near-doubling of our budget deficit in that same period.

A growing number of Americans, led by a vocal chorus of chief executives, union leaders and politicians, have argued for alleviating the problems of our economy by shielding our industries from imports. But protectionism, whether under the guise of "fair trade," anti-dumping duties, or the aggressive Super 301 provision of the Omnibus Trade and Competitiveness Act of 1988, is no solution. The benefits from unfettered foreign competition outweigh its costs. It forces our firms to be more competitive, encourages lower prices, and gives buyers greater choice. Unfortunately, those benefits tend to be widely dispersed among disorganized consumers whereas the costs are highly concentrated among much better organized producers. This imbalance gives the protectionist lobby an edge in Congress during hard economic times. But their call for import restrictions to save domestic jobs tells only half of the story. Such restraints will cost jobs that depend on imports (e.g., dealers of foreign cars). Furthermore, as other countries are prevented from exporting as much, they will earn fewer dollars and will thus be less able to buy American products. So we may protect relatively uncompetitive jobs and in the process lose inherently more efficient export jobs. This efficiency loss will be even greater if other countries respond in kind against American products. Such retaliatory action must be expected. After all, protectionism is a "beggar-thy-neighbor" policy, an act of aggression which exports unemployment. The net employment effect of import barriers could therefore be negative. Their effect on both allocative and organizational efficiency certainly is.

Ultimately we have no alternative but to improve our international competitiveness and then move the U.S. economy onto a faster growth path. This would help to lower our budget deficit, would improve our ability to save, and would allow us to service our foreign debts properly. It is also the only way in which the average American household can enjoy a rising living standard after having endured two decades of stagnant real income. For the U.S. economy to break out of its long-term stagnation, our productivity gains will have to accelerate. This is more easily said than done. The United States' productivity slowdown over the past quarter of a century has had many different causes. They include redeployment of resources from manufacturing to services, restrictive economic policies depressing actual GNP below the full-employment potential, burdensome regulations of business practices, a large influx of inexperienced workers, oligopolistic practices in support of high prices, the decline of educational standards, heavy-handed management of labor relations undermining workers' morale, a crumbling infrastructure, and rapidly aging plant and equipment.[3]

Whatever its causes, slow productivity growth has been the principal reason why real wages have not risen much since the early 1970s. The two go hand in hand. Business managers worry less about the absolute wage level than about their labor costs per unit of output. This focus makes sense. If a firm offers its workers an average pay increase of 5 percent, which the workers match with a 5 percent increase in productivity, then labor unit costs will have remained constant despite the wage hike. If there is no commensurate productivity gain, then wage increases are either eaten up by higher consumer prices or end up depressing profits and employment.

To be sure, we still enjoy the world's highest productivity level. In manufacturing, Japan's productivity is about 80 percent and Germany's around 75 percent that of the United States. We also have comparatively efficient agriculture and service industries. Consequently, our average output per employee exceeds that of our principal competitors (Canada, Germany, Japan) by a quarter to a third. However, our rivals are closing this gap. And in some key sectors, such as cars, other durable consumer goods, machine tools, or office equipment, they may already be ahead of us. Although our manufacturing sector made great strides during the 1980s through aggressive cost-cutting, productivity gains caused by streamlining tend to be less durable than the ones rooted in genuine improvements in the productive apparatus. Those will only come about if we invest more and spend these additional funds more intelligently.[4]

On the surface the United States' investment levels do not seem to lag much behind those of our key competitors. Japan spends about 28 percent of its gross domestic product on investment, a figure somewhat inflated by exorbitant construction costs in that country. The shares of major Western European economies (Germany, France, Italy) hover somewhere in the low 20+ percent range. Our rate, by comparison, is 19 percent. But that aggregate picture is quite misleading.

• Our investment measures include construction of residential housing and office buildings. In contrast to other industrial nations, the United States has clearly committed too many resources to that sector, especially during the building boom of the 1980s. We are an overbuilt country, thanks to the speculative urges of thrifts or land developers and to a tax code which heavily favors real estate.

• Moreover, we have an older capital stock and correspondingly larger replacement needs than does either Germany or Japan. If we compare investment spending net of depreciation, the United States' share is only half that of the others.

• When it comes to public-sector investment in roads and bridges, mass transit, airports, water and sewer treatment, and communications, our 1.25 percent share places us 55th in the world. Is it any surprise that our infrastructure is literally crumbling?

• Finally, the United States is seriously lagging in research and development spending. At a time when the pace of product development is very rapid and many new industries emerge, we are in danger of losing our technological edge in a growing number of markets. This trend is clearly visible when comparing patents, scientific training, long-term funding of high-risk projects on the frontiers of technology, and corporate rewards for innovation. Not only is our total research and development investment in that field inadequate, but more than half of our capacity in the area is still committed to the Pentagon. Demilitarized Japan and pacifistic Germany divert a much smaller portion to their national defense, perhaps somewhere between 10 percent and 20 percent. Given the increasingly specialized nature of "smart" weapons systems, the spillover effects from military product development have lessened in recent years. Even with regard to the futuristic "Star Wars" technologies, Japanese and Europeans are making a major effort to develop civilian applications.

Productivity improvements will require accelerated capital formation so that American workers have the best tools to work with and so that our product development can keep pace with that of the Japanese. Economists across a broad spectrum, who normally agree on very little, now consider higher investment levels in our domestic economy a matter of great urgency. Less clear cut is how best to achieve that goal.

Industrial investment activity in the private sector is fundamentally shaped by the relationship between expected rates of return, a function of current profitability, and minimum rates of return required, which depend on the cost of capital. American firms prefer shorter payoff periods than do their counterparts in other industrial countries, so they consequently require higher rates of return in their investment decisions. This is not just a question of business culture; it has a great deal to do with financing constraints. German and Japanese firms, for example, have better access to stable long-term funding from financial institutions which often have a direct ownership stake in the firms they support. In other words, they have more patient capital. Assured supplies of external funds permit them to operate with higher leverage, which ceteris paribus translates into higher returns on shareholders' equity. At the same time they also have an advantage concerning their cost of capital. The key differences in that regard are lower long-term interest rates as a result of larger net savings, a better inflation picture, a stronger currency, and smaller risk premiums. Even prices of investment goods, the second determinant of the cost of capital, are more competitive there.

It would be helpful if our firms were to extend their investment horizons and in the process became used to operating with lower required rates of return. Such an adjustment in corporate behavior is not likely unless managerial attitudes change. Too many chief executive officers pay themselves hefty salary increases irrespective of performance and receive "golden parachutes" when their firms are taken over. Much of their pay structure rewards current earnings. That bias inhibits major investment projects whose initial net outlays typically depress profits in the short term. U.S. managers also turn over much more rapidly than do their counterparts in Europe and Japan. Often they do not expect to still be with their present employer when the benefits of their investment decisions materialize. Finally, American producers need shareholders and lenders who commit funds on a long-term basis instead of looking for short-term gains.

Attitudes and incentives among the top echelon of corporate management are only one area in need of reform. Our investment problem has structural aspects as well. For the most part, modern industry is built on capital-intensive technologies and large-scale production processes. High fixed costs ("overhead") must be spread over a large production volume. This may result in lower cost-prices per unit of output, but it also encourages concentrated industrial structures. Market domination by a few large firms invites a variety of inefficiencies which need to be weighed against potential economies of scale. Oligopolies have the power to charge higher prices, tend to restrict output below the optimal level of productive efficiency, emphasize product differentiation and advertising to the point of social wastefulness, prefer to expand by acquiring existing assets in the stock market, and undermine allocative efficiency by erecting barriers to entry. The globalization of markets reinforces competitive pressures, but it tends to produce negative side-effects as well. As they turn multinational, our largest firms become less committed to maintaining a strong industrial base at home. They transfer capital and jobs abroad. Cross-border dealings between their subsidiaries in different countries add to our trade deficit and cost the U.S. government tax revenues.[5] With production facilities abroad they can escape regulatory restrictions (e.g., pollution controls), unions, and policy constraints in this country.

In the face of oligopolistic market power and stateless multinationals, neoclassical economists pretend that our industries still behave as if they operate in the ideal world of perfect competition, where the pursuit of self-interest automatically coincides with socially optimal outcomes. But the private profit motive need not coincide with social welfare, especially in situations in which firms have considerable market power and in which producers' sovereignty reigns. Too many of our managers will invest only if they are convinced of sufficient profit within a certain time period and under acceptable conditions of risk. Projects beyond these limits will not qualify, even those that may have great payoff potential in the long run. Once producers have suffered a period of prolonged stagnation, they will inevitably adjust their expectations and risk tolerance downward. Such caution, coupled with weakening balance sheets, can keep investment levels depressed and the economy mired in a slow-growth posture for quite some time. In addition, enterprises may not pursue the kinds of investments that best contribute to the overall strength of the economy. A good example is the widespread preference among our managers to acquire firms instead of building new capacity from scratch. A large portion of corporate spending is therefore channeled into shuffling existing assets, an activity which adds little to growth. Finally, private firms tend to ignore many socially beneficial investments which contribute only indirectly to their own profitability. Take, for instance, spending on the nation's children, our future work force, or rebuilding our aging infrastructure.

It is in the very nature of our capitalist system that the allocation of our resources, the production process, and the nature of work are guided by the profit motive. This is both its strength and its weakness. The pursuit of self-interest, when properly directed and constrained by market forces, does lend itself to efficient production of goods and services desired by the public. At the same time, such a profit-driven economy encourages concentration of market power and distorts decision-making. Producers will primarily consider their own costs and benefits. But these businesses do not live in a vacuum. They operate within a network of social relations, and their decisions will inevitably have tremendous repercussions for their workers, shareholders, creditors, consumers, competitors, and even governments. Their pursuit of gains, or for that matter cost reductions, often leaves the other parties injured. Plant closures, for example, can have a devastating impact on local communities. The elimination of jobs destroys the livelihood and happiness of people who in turn are prevented from making a useful contribution to the national product. Finally, an economy based on profit will systemically underproduce certain socially beneficial goods and services (e.g., health care, housing, education, mass transit, environmental preservation) while channeling too many resources into creating luxuries of limited social usefulness.

An investment-led strategy for economic revival, which our country urgently needs, can succeed only if it is guided by societal priorities. These ought to be defined in ways that complement the motivational force of private gains. The task cannot be left to the captains of industry and finance alone. As long as the more enlightened and socially responsible among them are put at a cost disadvantage vis-à-vis less scrupulous competitors, they will in the end follow only their own narrow interests. What we face, however, is a national effort that involves all of us.

We as a nation could try to muddle through, hold on to the status quo, believe somehow that things will improve on their own. Such a posture ignores the reality of our decline and denies the need for basic change. Long-term economic stagnation does not necessarily correct itself. Social tensions caused by impoverishment and neglect do not go away. Political paralysis does not suddenly ease. These conditions need to be addressed in pragmatic fashion and with a sense of purpose. Ultimately we have no choice but to start rebuilding our industrial base. If we fail to do this, the malaise will only get worse.

17.4. Restoring Fiscal Sanity

Conservative arguments to the contrary notwithstanding, government has a crucial and constructive role to play in the management of our economic affairs. Operating outside the confines of the marketplace and freed from the profit constraint, it is the only institution that is able to act on behalf of the domestic economy as a whole. To the extent that the pursuit of narrow corporate self-interest contradicts the prerequisites of a strong industrial home base, government must help to bridge that gap.

Our political leaders face a most difficult task in the years ahead. They have to control the huge budget deficit. At the same time they have to lay the foundations for the improved international competitiveness of our economy and guide us into a new geoeconomic era. They must address these issues at a time when the United States is divided, confused, pessimistic, and prone to isolationist sentiments. They have to define a far-reaching agenda for change when they themselves have for the most part lost their sense of direction. Assuming that it is not yet too late for serious change, what should Congress and the president do within their domains? First and foremost, both sides must agree on a program of fiscal restructuring which both contributes to our economic revival and stops the bleeding of red ink. Clinton's first budget proposal, a combination of long-term deficit reduction and modest public-investment measures for short-term stimulation, was a first step in that direction. But a more profound reorientation of our fiscal priorities is needed during his term.

Let us start with taxes. Contrary to widespread sentiments, the United States is not overtaxed. Our tax share is about 30 percent of GNP, compared to a range of 35 percent to 50 percent in other industrial nations. We also have a weak and inefficient system of taxation, especially considering all three levels of government. Many of our taxes are quite regressive, relatively income-inelastic, easy to evade, and prone to encourage counterproductive behavior. We have already made a first step in the right direction with the Tax Reform Act of 1986, which lowered both income tax rates and loopholes. But more needs be done. The question is how to get more tax revenues while encouraging higher levels of investment.

Traditionally, the U.S. government has used tax-based incentives to spur investment spending by private firms. In light of our huge budget deficits, our politicians ought to think twice before further eroding our income tax base in such fashion. New tax breaks would also run counter to the letter and spirit of the 1986 tax reform. It is doubtful to what extent corporate tax breaks actually prompt marginal projects which otherwise would not have been undertaken. Investment tax credits and accelerated depreciation allowances benefit capital-intensive manufacturing sectors most (e.g., steel, chemicals, automobiles), many of which are mature and shrinking. New "growth" sectors, especially those that require highly skilled workers or computer technology, receive proportionately less support from these measures. Sectoral tax breaks, such as oil-depletion allowances or loan-loss reserves for banks, distort the allocation of resources by maintaining excess capacity in declining industries longer than desired. A reduction of the capital gains tax rate, long sought by President Bush, primarily benefits the rich, who gained the most from Reaganomics during the 1980s. It is also biased in favor of real estate and short-term trading of financial securities, two activities of which we already have too much. If any such measure were to be passed, it should apply only to longer-term investments (of at least two years) and to new business formation.

Rather than tinkering on the margins with selective investment incentives, our tax system could use a more radical overhaul. The corporate income tax, which amounts to about 10 percent of federal tax revenues, might as well be abolished. Such a step would give industrial investment activity a powerful boost and would take care of the double taxation problem that afflicts the portion of profit paid out as dividends. At the same time, the United States should introduce a value added tax (VAT), which is easy to collect, hard to evade, and brings in large revenues at relatively low rates. The VAT, already used in all other industrial nations, only taxes consumption and therefore tends to encourage savings.

To compensate for its regressive nature, necessities could be exempted altogether and luxuries could carry higher rates. A new VAT could be coupled with somewhat lower personal income tax rates, but I would make the latter more progressive and raise the marginal tax bracket for the top quintile of households by at least 5 percent. In the absence of effective wealth taxes, rich Americans do not pay their fair share of federal revenues. For the same reason we need to consider removing the cap on Social Security taxes so that better-paid employees contribute the same portion of their salaries as any other wage-earner. I am also in favor of significantly higher gasoline taxes, as currently in place in much of Western Europe. President Clinton's original proposal would have gone even farther than that by taxing all sources of energy. Even though that kind of excise tax would have been regressive, it has the beneficial effects of fighting pollution and making the United States more energy efficient. A higher gas tax could also help to finance needed infrastructure investments, especially an expansion of mass transit capacity.[6] Altogether we need about $200 billion in additional revenues, a tax increase of approximately 13 percent from current levels, for deficit reduction across all levels of government.

Government expenditures need similarly far-reaching restructuring. Our spending priorities are those of a different era and must be altered rather drastically to meet new challenges. Some programs can reasonably be cut, among them military spending and entitlements. Savings in those large budget categories would free much-needed funds for currently underfinanced activities that are vital to our industrial strength. In addition, we need to reform other programs on which we spend too much without adequate returns. If we implement this three-pronged strategy, we can dramatically improve the government's contribution to economic growth without increasing its overall spending levels.

The Pentagon budget is vastly overblown, now that the Soviet Union no longer exists. The end of the cold war warrants a comprehensive overhaul of our national security strategy. Surrounded by friendly neighbors and oceans, we do not need a large force to defend our national territory from invasion. Moreover, several hundred missiles should suffice to deter any nuclear attack. Both objectives could be achieved with an annual budget of $100 billion, one-third of current levels. Anything beyond that would reflect the United States' global engagements as the world's only remaining military superpower. We ought to debate as soon as possible how much we want to be the "global policeman" and impose a unilateral Pax Americana on the rest of the world. If we do, it means foregoing serious efforts at addressing many of our domestic problems. Nor is it at all clear that global projection of our military might makes the world a much safer place. Is it not better to rely on conflict resolution through multilateral negotiations under the auspices of the United Nations? We need to construct a new collective security regime with our old allies and former enemies to replace the obsolete cold war arrangements. The greatest threat to world peace is the proliferation of weapons of mass destruction in sensitive areas where regional powers with a long tradition of hostilities engage in an arms race (the Middle East, the Persian Gulf, South Asia, the Korean peninsula, the former Soviet Union). This problem is best contained through diplomatic means, reinforced by a "carrot-and-stick" approach of sanctions and aid. We could conceivably meet our global commitments by keeping small troop contingents in Europe and by maintaining a rapid deployment force for situations that truly threaten our strategic interests (e.g., disruption of oil supplies). A reduction of our military budget by half or even more over a period of five years will surely have a negative impact on regions that are heavily dependent on bases or weapons procurement, even with a massive conversion effort. But that pain is transitory. And if we miss this opportunity for disarmament, we will lack the public funds for needed social investments and will be worse off in the long run.

Another area which is ripe for major fiscal savings is retiree benefits, our largest entitlement. Senior citizens are well organized and have so far successfully blocked any attack. But thanks to federal income maintenance they are no longer the most vulnerable segment of our population. They have to understand the national interest and make their contribution. Should we continue to protect the income of the elderly while we invest too little in our children? Abstracting from the politics underlying this program, Social Security is an obvious area for economies. Other transfer payments, such as Medicare, disability insurance, federal welfare spending, and unemployment compensation, have already been tightened significantly in recent years. Because Social Security has so many beneficiaries, it only takes fairly minor adjustments to achieve large savings. One widely discussed option is to cancel cost-of-living adjustments for one year. Another is to postpone retirement by a few years, reflecting fairly rapid increases in life expectancy and a coming shortage of skilled labor. In the interest of progressivity we could also tighten benefit caps and/or taxation rules for wealthier retirees. Whatever the cuts, they must be structured so as not to endanger the surplus needed for the retirement of baby boomers after 2010. We might also want to consider further reducing farm-support programs, especially after global deregulation of agriculture following successful completion of the so-called Uruguay Round.

One-third of the budget savings from the military and entitlements should be used for deficit reduction. The rest, perhaps up to $120 billion per year, should be directed into strategic areas of public investment with potentially large future payoffs.

• Having neglected our infrastucture for so long, we now face heavy expenses to fix our transportation systems, telecommunications network, energy grid, public housing stock, water supplies, and sewage treatment facilities. Spending in this area creates jobs, improves the quality of life, and makes our industries more competitive.

• The degradation of our environment has already reached a critical threshold, one at which it begins to impair our resource base. Reversing that trend helps to maintain the production capacity of our economy. Environmental problems are a social cost which the market mechanism cannot address. They therefore become the concern of public policy. At a minimum we need programs that relieve congestion, clean up toxic waste sites, store radioactive materials, improve garbage disposal, and reduce pollution. The U.S. government should also play a much more active role in pursuing multilateral agreements to deal with global ecological dangers, such as acid rain, the greenhouse effect, ozone layer depletion, and the destruction of forests. The United States, the world's largest economy and a major contributor to these problems, should take a global leadership role here. Ultimately none of these issues will ease unless there is a worldwide effort to bring explosive population growth under control.

• We are in the midst of yet another industrial revolution in which radical technological breakthroughs give rise to many new "growth" industries (e.g., fiber optics, consumer electronics, artificial intelligence, robotonics, satellites, biogenetics). Research and development have gained added importance in this age of innovation. Government has a major role to play in this area, especially with regard to basic research, which is by definition far removed from commercial use and thus especially risky. Besides redirecting our considerable defense-based scientific capacity to civilian applications, the U.S. government must also back research activity in universities, laboratories, and industry. Funding of training programs, seed grants for promising projects, and relaxation of antitrust laws concerning joint efforts among competitors are all needed to help our producers to regain technological superiority.

• A large number of Americans, probably a majority, argue that money spent in support of other countries would be better spent at home. Such an "America first" attitude is understandable, in light of our deep-rooted domestic problems and shortage of funds. But it is short-sighted, bordering on the myopic. Foreign aid is certainly not an altruistic giveaway. If targeted well, it will help other countries to prosper, make them politically more stable, and turn them into buyers of our products. Structural adjustments in many developing countries and the transition from command to market economies in what was once the Communist bloc represent major challenges which the rich nations must help to bring to a successful conclusion. Failure on either account will carry a high price tag, including warfare, massive migration, and impoverishment of the entire global economy. Reviving the economies of LDCs and the former Soviet empire, on the other hand, will be the best insurance policy for world peace. These countries, with more than half of the world's population, also represent potentially huge markets for U.S. goods and services. And over the long haul we can afford our imports and foreign liabilities only by capturing new export markets.

Finally, any sensible strategy of reordering our fiscal priorities will have to include reform of our education, health care, and welfare systems. These items are all essential to the productive capacity of our labor force. We spend a great deal of money on each system—without satisfying results. If we restructure government programs in these areas, we might get better results without adding to current spending levels.

• Even though the United States spends more on education than do other nations with similar living standards, Americans lag behind in scholastic achievements. Closing that gap must become a national priority, especially now that we are moving rapidly into a heavily knowledge-based and skill-dependent production regime. Local control over primary and secondary education, coupled with entrenched segregation by race and class, has given us an unequal school system which reproduces social stratification and limits economic opportunities. Only a federal equalizing mechanism can overcome the powerful local coalitions of property owners and political machines that benefit from the status quo. Too much is spent on administrative costs and not enough on direct learning, a wasteful situation which calls for a radical streamlining of the educational bureaucracy. We need to improve teacher training and rewards. The shortage of adequate child care facilities has to be addressed. College students, including adults going back to school, should have access to cheap loans which they can repay as a fixed percentage of future income. Clinton's proposal in that area, especially the federalization of the student-loan program, the possibility of service in community-oriented jobs as a way to earn credits toward college, and repayment schedules as a proportionate function of pay, are right on target, in my opinion. But no amount of reorganization will make much of a difference unless we attract the most qualified people into the teaching profession, demand a great deal more of our students, and involve parents more in the learning process of their children. Better education, including worker (re)training, is essential for lasting productivity gains. At a time when most Americans are already overworked, working smarter is clearly better than working harder.[7]

• The United States has a health care system that costs more than other systems, but still leaves one-third of our population either seriously underinsured or completely unprotected. It is no surprise that sentiment for dramatic change has been growing to the point of making reform possible. The best solution would be a national health insurance system, similar to those in all other industrial nations. Under such an alternative businesses no longer face the cost burden and uncertainties of the current system, and everyone is covered irrespective of employment status. The federal government ends up spending more as the sole insurer or single service provider. But the overall cost of health care to the nation as a whole would be significantly lower than is presently the case. Under such a system we could introduce more effective cost controls, cut red tape, contain adverse selection problems, and end astronomical malpractice insurance premiums. Most countries keep their national health service separate from the general budget and finance it through a payroll tax earmarked for that purpose. Clinton's proposal for "managed competition" stops well short of fully socialized medicine. It will be able to extend insurance to the unprotected, while reducing overall costs, only if it is accompanied by effective government controls of doctors' fees, hospital charges, and drug prices. One way or another, the rationing of health care has become inevitable. Our national debate should be about how such rationing can be handled in the fairest and most cost-effective manner.

• Another area calling for reform is welfare. Although most people rely only temporarily on government assistance during transition periods, a significant number depend on long-term handouts. The latter group ought to have the opportunity of becoming employable again. Recent experiments with "workfare," which make benefit levels contingent on a series of steps by recipients to prepare for eventual reentry into the work force, are a move in that direction. But these efforts can only succeed if they are supplemented with public- and private-sector creation of adequate jobs in poor neighborhoods to improve employment opportunities in the inner cities.

The program of fiscal restructuring outlined here should bring in more revenues, but would do so through better taxes. Cuts in military spending and entitlements are needed to free resources for productivity-enhancing investments in infrastructure, research and development, and human capital. Other than our plan for national health insurance, which should pay for itself, total federal government spending ought to remain at roughly current levels. The goal is to reallocate public funds in order to meet the demands of a new era, one in which industrial competitiveness will play a central role.

Even though the times demand drastic change in the composition of the budget, it is by no means clear that our lawmakers are up to the task. The political culture of the contemporary United States is in real trouble—a poverty of public discourse and debate after five decades of ideological cold war freeze, the partisan finger-pointing and electoral jockeying in an inherently divided government, the corrupting inertia of incumbency, the pervasive influence of highly organized "special interests" on the shape of policy, and a dearth of politicians with the qualities and moral integrity to lead. Yet the revival of our economy will only come about if it goes hand in hand with the restructuring of our budget and the revitalization of our political institutions.

17.5. The Financial Underpinnings of Economic Revival

We will not attain the desired increase in investment levels unless producers have access to long-term funds at affordable terms. But our credit system has become fragile. Its present crisis is a combination of retrenchment and restructuring. In the face of this wrenching adjustment process, it is time to ask ourselves what kind of financial institutions and markets we need in order to support economic revival.

One of the nation's fundamental vulnerabilities is its low level of savings, the raw material of financial intermediation. Such paucity of thrift makes it harder to finance higher investment spending. Nor can we rely on past compensatory mechanisms to close that gap in the future. Foreign capital imports will be harder to come by in the 1990s than they were during the 1980s. And monetary policy loses much of its stimulative punch, as bank lending becomes relatively less important. Lower budget deficits, of course, would free some savings for the private sector. But fiscal austerity may also hurt the recovery, especially if it is not linked to broader restructuring of the budget. Because savings depend much more on income than on interest rates, mindless deficit cutting may end up being counterproductive if it depresses economic activity.[8]

The shortage of savings has certainly had deleterious effects on our financial institutions. It has left banks and thrifts with a correspondingly smaller deposit base and has forced these depository institutions to rely heavily on more volatile and higher-cost borrowed liabilities. Moreover, the scarcity of idle funds must have contributed to the increasingly complex layering of interconnected credit circuits which increased the total borrowing volume by multiple leveraging. Such pyramiding of credit has enhanced the ripple effects from any payment disruption, and this has made our credit system more vulnerable. Finally, savers have aggressively sought higher returns on their capital. This, in turn, has fed a pronounced tendency toward "churning," the constant turnover of securities for short-term trading profits by institutional investors (mutual funds, pension funds, insurance companies). As a result, our capital markets have become more prone to speculative excesses, and stable long-term funding has been even harder to come by. All these practices allowed a huge expansion of financial transactions despite stagnant savings during the 1980s, but they did so at the expense of financial stability.

Now that most speculative bubbles of the past decade have burst, many of the higher-flying institutions and instruments are in full retreat. This is how the market mechanism corrects past excesses. Some of that adjustment, albeit painful, is not at all bad. The elimination of fully one-third of the nation's thrifts puts a serious dent into real estate speculation, in particular slowing land development schemes and office construction, of which we already have too much. With Drexel gone and the riskiest issuers shut out, the junk-bond market has had a chance to reorganize itself. Hard times for corporate raiders and leveraged buyouts have brought some economic sense back to merger and takeover activity. Market manipulation by Salomon and by traders on the Chicago Mercantile Exchange have spurred steps to reorganize both the government securities and the futures markets, especially moves to computerize trading. In general it is safe to predict that the widespread losses and scandals of recent years will make financial institutions more careful for some time to come. Regulators will play their watchdog role more aggressively, and many borrowers will have emerged from the latest recession with stronger balance sheets.

Less clear is how well the credit system will serve the needs of industry over the long haul. When we contemplate the proper structure of the financial system, we need to ask what different institutions and markets contribute to domestic capital formation.

• Large corporations can tap a variety of external funding sources on a global scale, including the Eurobond market and foreign stock markets. Increasingly they rely on the issue of securities rather than on bank loans. Markets provide funds more cheaply and more flexibly than do institutions but are also more volatile and prone to disruption. Investment banks, acting as underwriters, dealers, and brokers of securities, should be able to maintain their crucial role as market-makers. But their importance will continue to decline, as corporations find ways to make themselves less dependent (e.g., private placements, block trading, shelf registration). Nor can the investment banks hope to thrive in the wake of yet another merger wave. They will therefore continue to consolidate and to search for lucrative market niches. Further securitization of loans will surely open more opportunities for market-making. Investment advice and portfolio management for corporate clients may provide a rich source of fees and commissions. Another important avenue of expansion is merchant banking, in which investment bankers put their own capital at risk by investing directly in corporations. Some of them may expand their role as venture capitalists in support of new high-tech firms and of products with promising market potential.

• Smaller firms, which lack access to the securities markets, will continue to rely on bank loans. Their demand for funds should allow many well-run community banks and superregionals to survive the coming shake-out. Our large money-center banks hope for entry into new areas to make up for declining commercial lending and large bad-debt losses. But even if they obtain regulatory approval to do so, their own experience with investment banking in the Euromarket and the problems afflicting insurance products should serve as warning signals. Commercial banks can offer even the largest corporations many specialized services, including credit lines, various payments services, advice, and different "off-balance-sheet" instruments to protect better against volatile interest and exchange rates (e.g., swaps). But these products are surely less attractive than direct ownership of corporate equity. The potential for conflicts of interest, when banks are both creditors and shareholders of industrial firms, and fears of excessive concentration have made policy-makers wary of breaking down the separation between commerce and banking. Yet in the face of intensifying international competition we have to ask ourselves whether we can afford to shut out bank funds from the stock market. After all, we want our firms to expand their capital base and to switch from debt to equity. And we need profitable banks which channel savings into productive investment activities. Moreover, in other countries (e.g., France, Germany) extensive cross-ownership links between banks and industry have surely strengthened the investment capacity and diversi-fication efforts of their leading firms.

• Pension funds and insurance companies have long-term payment commit-ments that can be predicted actuarially with reasonable certainty. That liability structure makes them well suited to carry predominantly long-term assets in their portfolios. Together with mutual funds, they have become America's largest stock market investors. Yet both institutions have increasingly focused on rapid asset turnover ("churning") for short-term capital gains. It might be a good idea to remove their exemption from federal income taxation, if they continue this speculative propensity. Impatient shareholders make it much harder for corporate managers to lengthen their investment horizons.

Over the past decade or two, the U.S. government has played a growing role in the allocation of credit. Its direct loans, loan guarantees, and funding from federally sponsored agencies grew from close to $200 billion in 1970 to about $1.5 trillion in 1990.[9] These programs eliminate gaps in the credit market, pro-vide subsidies for socially desirable activities (e.g., college education), and stim-ulate the economy. A large portion of federally backed funds supports housing and farmers. Even though making mortgages cheaper and easier to obtain contin-ues to be a legitimate public policy objective, both of these sectors suffer from overcapacity. At the same time, federal support for businesses is confined to the notoriously underfunded Small Business Administration and Export-Import Bank. To the extent that the private sector does not generate sufficient funds for long-term investment projects, government enhancement of commercial and in-dustrial loans may be justified.

During the Great Depression the Reconstruction Finance Corporation lent $50 billion over a twelve-year period to banks, insurance companies, railroads, and other enterprises that were threatened with insolvency. The RFC set a precedent for subsequent government bailouts (e.g., Penn Central, Lockheed, Chrysler). But other than such exceptional emergency situations the United States has largely been opposed to the federal government making loans to private firms. For decades such policy was considered too "socialistic" and thus taboo. The standard argument was that market forces pick winners much more effectively than does the government. But now that the cold war is over, we can afford to relax our ideological rigidities a bit and to recognize that conservative govern-ments elsewhere (e.g., Japan's Liberal Democrats, Italy's Christian Democrats, France's Gaullists) used industrial policies to great effect after World War II. We might also want to acknowledge that the United States has long had industrial policies for agriculture and aerospace. But the federal government has tended to develop sectoral assistance programs in haphazard fashion, without overall coor-dination.

Why would virtually all other industrial nations have adopted fairly extensive industrial policy measures, if such intervention is truly as counterproductive as our "free market" advocates claim it is? In reality, the market mechanism may not always allocate resources so well. There exist significant barriers to entry and exit which restrict the mobility of capital. Adjustments in the industrial matrix away from declining sectors and into expanding sectors may take much longer than desired, especially because both federal and state governments often help our older industries slow down their decline. Small businesses, which are responsible for much of the job creation, worker training, and innovation in our economy, often face formidable obstacles. They have less of a safety cushion, fewer economies of scale, and only limited access to external funds. Many firms consider basic research too risky and too far removed from immediate profit opportunities. Their neglect means less of an American presence in the new growth sectors of the future.

Given those conditions, the United States has little to fear of industrial policy. At a minimum we need three initiatives in this area. A new government agency should be set up along the line of Japan's Ministry of International Trade and Industry to coordinate our trade policies, to assess the future of key industries, to monitor their foreign competitors, and to help certain critical sectors (e.g., electronics) stay competitive. A separate agency, possibly an extension of the Pentagon's highly regarded Defense Advanced Research Projects Agency, should bring government and industry together in the development of targeted civilian technologies. Finally, we need a successor to the highly successful RFC. Such an industrial development bank should have a cheap line of credit and adequate capital to support firms of strategic importance.

17.6. Community-Based Economic Development

In the new global economy the United States will have to vie for international leadership with other industrial nations. We will only succeed if our producers become more competitive. The challenge should motivate us to improve education, to expand job training, to rein in soaring health costs, to revamp our tax system, and to select crucial industries for targeted government assistance.

But even if we implement all of these policies, there is no assurance of success. More is needed. Economic revival cannot be left to corporate managers or to national politicians alone. Private industry follows the imperatives of profit, and the federal government is subject to severe budget constraints. Neither represents a vital dimension of societal organization, the communities in which Americans live and work. Governors and mayors, who act on behalf of local communities, have found their capacity for intervention severely curtailed in recent years. Generous concessions to large firms have not prevented them from shutting down operations. And a decade of cuts in federal grant support has left most states and municipalities, which rely on weak taxes and must keep their budgets balanced, in dire fiscal straits.

Yet local communities need leadership and initiative. All across the United States we see towns struggling with street crime, drug abuse, homelessness, chronic unemployment, pervasive corruption, and urban decay. The many social problems found especially in the inner cities are for the most part the result of long-term economic decline. They impose a huge burden on society. A prisoner in New York City, for example, will cost more than $40,000 a year; caring for an AIDS patient, up to $100,000; housing a homeless family in a "welfare hotel," more than $1,500 a month. Were these people able to lead productive lives, they would not only save the government huge expenses but also contribute to the nation's wealth. As living conditions in declining neighborhoods deteriorate, middle-class families and small businesses leave in droves. This vicious circle can literally destroy once thriving communities.

Unless we turn this alarming situation around, we may well end up creating a segregated society in which the rich live in protected enclaves while large segments of our population are condemned to a marginal existence without hope. Poor communities facing the brutal consequences of deindustrialization cannot wait for government initiatives and private-sector investments. Their only salvation lies in self-help, in mobilizing their collective resource of human effort to rebuild the socio-economic base of their run-down neighborhoods. Community-based social-service organizations, not-for-profit institutions, and small-scale cooperatives have a crucial role to play in this reconstruction effort. They know the problems of their communities very well and can build networks of providers and users. Instead of profits, they pursue socially useful objectives. Instead of competing, they cooperate.

These community-oriented producers often provide essential services at low cost. Yet they often lack funding to do as much as they could. It must be a national priority to finance this kind of social investment activity. State and local governments should support innovative pilot projects which, if successful, could lay the foundation for new policy initiatives. Tax-deductible grant support from private foundations is another source of funds that is worth expanding. But more is needed. Governments could complement "free enterprise zones" with community development banks funded by municipal bonds. They could also subsidize commercial bank lending to not-for-profit organizations, either through tax deductions or by amending the Community Reinvestment Act of 1977 accordingly. Pension funds might set aside a certain percentage of their asset base for community reconstruction projects that have good payoff potential. Socially conscious mutual funds could do the same.

Community-sustaining economic development from the bottom up fills a crucial void in a mixed economy that is dominated by global production networks, speculation-prone financial institutions, and big government.[10] Its socially beneficial priorities, which stress health care, housing, education, employment and other expressions of economic democracy, complement the narrow self-interest that reigns in the marketplace. Its emphasis on democratic planning acts as a counterweight to the excessive concentration of economic resources and political power in the hands of a few. As a vehicle for self-empowerment, it allows otherwise disadvantaged groups to help themselves. Our sterile political system needs infusions of citizen participation, economic revival depends on tapping entrepreneurial initiative in the broadest sense, and wealth can be created by a variety of property forms.

The desired opening of our capitalist democracy does not occur only on the ground; it requires rethinking social theory as well. Now that the challenge of communism has passed, American economists can afford a little diversification. Their theorizing need not be confined to mathematical models that are devoid of social content and history. They should recognize that their standard notion of a profit-maximizing "homo oeconomicus" does not cover the full range of human motives. Those who seek an alternative would do well with an interdisciplinary approach which uses political science, cultural anthropology, sociology, and especially social psychology to shed light on group behavior.[11] After all, economics is a social science, not a natural science.

Notes

Chapter 1

1. When that debt comes due, it can under normal conditions simply be rolled over. Old debt is thus replaced by new debt. Provided such refinancing continues, our foreign debt may thus never be repaid. But we do have to service that debt in the form of interest payments to foreign bondholders. These amount to a resource transfer from the United States to the rest of the world, one which already absorbs nearly 1 percent of our annual gross national product. In other words, the U.S. economy has to generate an additional 1 percent per year just to stay even. If we want to avoid squeezing domestic activity (i.e., consumption, investment, government spending), that percentage point is best created by improving our foreign trade balance.

2. The term "megaeconomics" was coined by Walter Russell Mead (1989, p. 429).

3. The origins of neoclassical economics date from the 1870s, most notably William Stanley Jevons (1871), Carl Menger (1871), and Leon Walras (1874). Another early contribution of great importance was that of Alfred Marshall (1890).

4. Modern followers of Walras, such as Gerard Debreu (1959), have recognized how unrealistic this auction process is. Instead, they only specify the conditions necessary to ensure that at least one position of general equilibrium exists.

5. In these neoclassical growth models, such as those of Robert Solow (1956) and Timothy Swan (1956), the burden of adjustment falls entirely on the capital–output ratio.

6. For an excellent discussion of uncertainty and risk in economic theory, see Chapman Findlay and Edward Williams (1985).

7. See in particular William Stanley Jevons (1871), whose proclamation on the very first page of his book that "value depends entirely upon utility" was almost diametrically opposed to the then-dominant classical tradition. It should be noted that utility is a metaphysical concept which cannot be measured objectively and has to be defined in terms of itself. It is the characteristic of commodities that makes individuals want to buy them, and individuals buy commodities to enjoy utility in consuming them.

8. See, for example, Karl Marx (1867), Thorstein Veblen (1942), Joseph Schumpeter (1942), or John Kenneth Galbraith (1967). Despite criticizing capitalism from very different angles, these authors all acknowledged the profound dynamism of this system as a continuous source of broad societal transformations.

9. Some of the more thoughtful neoclassical economists, such as Richard Clower (1967) or Frank Hahn (1973), have recognized that there exists a clear contradiction

between money and equilibrium. Hahn (1983, p. 1), for example, noted that "the most serious challenge that the existence of money poses is this: the best developed model of the economy cannot find room for it."

10. For an excellent survey of these portfolio-choice models, see Lawrence Harris (1981, part III). The author emphasizes the crucial role these models played in the subsequent reformulation of Keynes's *General Theory* back into a standard equilibrium framework, the so-called Neoclassical/Keynesian Synthesis (see John Hicks, 1935, 1937; James Tobin, 1956, 1958).

11. The accounting identity $M \times V = P \times Q$, the so-called Equation of Exchange, was first presented as a cause–effect relationship between money supply M and nominal price level P by Irving Fisher (1911) and was given its modern (Monetarist) reformulation by Milton Friedman (1956).

Chapter 2

1. See Suzanne De Brunhoff (1978, p. 39), Michel Aglietta (1979, p. 328), and Robert Guttmann (1990, pp. 86–89) for more extensive definitions of the "monetary constraint."

2. Robert Frank (1988) has argued that human agents carry a variety of motivations and sentiments into the marketplace. These often induce responses to market signals that are in direct contrast to what neoclassicists consider "rational" behavior. Of particular importance is Frank's argument that humans as social beings may prefer altruism and cooperation over egotism and competition, thus calling into question the neoclassical assumption of self-interest as the overriding motive.

3. These crucial distinctions between expenditures and receipts, between events and observations, and between structural inertia and monetary mobility form the basis for a brilliant sociological analysis of the modern market economy by Dirk Baecker (1988).

4. This "socially necessary labor-time," a concept introduced by Karl Marx (1967, vol. 1), consists of two components. One is the labor activity of workers, which creates new value. We should note that such activity creates different quantities of value per time unit, depending on the skill levels (and reproduction costs) of the work force. The other is that portion of value embodied in the plant, equipment, and inventories which the production process transfers to the output.

5. The founders of neoclassical theory (e.g., Jevons, Menger, Walras, Marshall) did not refer to Marx directly in their works. Not until much later did we see explicit neoclassical attacks, such as the stinging critique of Marx's approach to the transformation problem by Eugen von Böhm-Bawerk (1896).

6. The ensuing analysis of economic activities as monetary circuits was first developed in Karl Marx (1967, vol. 1, chs.1–6). The analysis of John Maynard Keynes (1936) also emphasized the importance of monetary variables on economic activity, especially the downward rigidity of money-wages and liquidity preference. Even though in key respects Keynes's work was much closer to neoclassical analysis (especially its Marshallian variant), Keynes considered Marx's framework of monetary circuits very useful. See, for example, Keynes (1979, pp. 76ff.), where he explicitly approved of the way in which Marx introduced money in terms of forward-moving and interconnected circuits.

7. Don Patinkin (1965) replaced Say's Law with the so-called real balance effect according to which the (excess) demands for goods not only are functions of relative prices but also depend on the real value of money balances. This redefinition restored the logical consistency of the Walrasian general equilibrium model when applied to a monetary economy.

8. According to Karl Marx (1967, vol. 1), money functions as capital to the extent that it mobilizes human labor into value-creating production activities. By paying workers

less than the value they create, employers appropriate a portion of that new value as surplus-value and realize it as profit in output sales. It is worth noting that in his discussion of "capital" Keynes (1936, ch. 16) abandoned neoclassical (utility-based) value theory to express his sympathies for the classical (labor-value) tradition of Smith, Ricardo, and Marx.

9. Neoclassical theory assumes that expectations are either always realized ("rational") or rapidly corrected by error learning ("adaptive"). But, as pointed out by Paul Davidson (1978, ch. 16), neither concept is realistic. The conditions required for rational expectations—uniform access to all relevant information, perfect knowledge, and basic agreement about the future—simply do not exist in reality. Moreover, adaptive learning is difficult. Ongoing changes in the economy often alter hitherto well-established relationships so that past data cannot be reliably projected into the future.

10. In this so-called capital budgeting procedure, corporate managers adjust the expected rate of return for its riskiness on the basis of probability distributions covering a range of possible future scenarios. But this statistical procedure is at best an approximation. Uncertainty is inherently intangible and cannot be measured, precisely because the future is unpredictable. The measurement of risk depends on subjective expectations (of future returns), which are themselves uncertain.

11. For a more extensive discussion of the fundamental difference between logical time in neoclassical equilibrium models and historic time in actual investment decisions, see Stephen Rousseas (1986, ch. 2).

12. This function of money as means of payment is entirely ignored in standard theory, a direct reflection of the latter's very limited notion of credit (see below). But heterodox economists, most notably Karl Marx (1967, vol. 1, ch. 3.3.b) and John Maynard Keynes (1930a, vol. 1, chs. 3 and 15), have identified and analyzed it as a key source of monetary instability.

13. One crucial aspect of this interest-rate structure is the "yield curve," which establishes the relationship between short-term and long-term rates. Since we need to compare securities of similar default risk and liquidity, the yield curve is usually based on comparing government securities of different maturity (i.e., Treasury bills, notes, bonds). Normally that curve is positively sloped, with higher rates for longer maturities.

14. John Maynard Keynes (1913, p. 26), for example, defined a rupee, the Indian currency, as a "note printed on silver." See also Gunnar Heinsohn and Otto Steiger (1983) for a discussion of ancient coins as credit-money.

15. We shall discuss seigniorage and its consequences for the economic and financial relationships between nations in chapters 7, 13, and 14.

16. For some of the primary contributions of this theory of the "dynamic circuit," see Alain Parguez (1975, 1981), and Frederic Poulon (1982), as well as Richard Arena and Augusto Graziani (1985). Many articles by its followers have appeared in *Économie appliquée* and in the series "Monnaie et production" of *Économies et Sociétés*, two leading French economic journals published by the Institut de Sciences Mathématiques et Économiques Appliquées (ISMEA) in Paris. For summaries of that theoretical approach in English see Marc Lavoie (1985) and Augusto Graziani (1989).

17. This model of the "dynamic circuit" can be extended to include a government sector with taxes and public-sector debts. That extension does not alter the basic dynamic of the circuit. Nor do the inclusions of a foreign sector, of bank loans going to consumers, or of a central bank actively manipulating the ability of banks to extend credit.

18. Some circuit theorists, such as Bernard Schmitt (1984) and Alain Parguez (1984), have pushed this point farther and argued that credit-money is actually created by market agents rather than banks. First of all, banks will only extend credit when borrowers make a credible promise of repayment. Moreover, the checks issued in the wake of bank loans are mere tokens and only become money when the borrowers use them for payment.

19. This conclusion rests on a very liberal interpretation of what John Maynard Keynes (1936) and Michal Kalecki (1939, 1971) had to say about the "autonomous" nature of investment behavior in industry.

20. Knut Wicksell (1898), one of the predecessors of modern circuit theory, has himself stressed the importance of interest rates on investment behavior in his discussion of the "indirect mechanism." Similarly, John Maynard Keynes (1936, ch. 11) defined his "marginal efficiency of capital" as an inverse relationship between investment spending and interest rates.

21. The "cost of capital" reflects what both bondholders and shareholders require from the issuing firm in return. It is therefore usually calculated as a weighted and risk-adjusted average of the prevailing market yield on bonds and the rate of return required by shareholders.

22. For example, the daily average volume of (global) trading in U.S. Treasury securities surpassed $100 billion in 1986.

23. Neoclassical theory justifies profit as a reward for abstinence (delayed consumption) and/or risk-taking by the investor. In Marx's "labor theory of value" profit derives from the ability of capitalists to extract surplus-value from the labor-power of their workers (see note 8). Neo-Ricardian theory, such as Piero Sraffa (1960), emphasizes the distributional conflict between capitalists and workers over income shares as key determinant of profit. John Maynard Keynes (1936, ch. 11) related profits to the scarcity of capital. In this context, see also Hyman Minsky (1975, ch. 5). Post-Keynesians view profit as a function either of the firm's market power ("degree of monopoly") to charge prices in excess of unit costs (see Michal Kalecki, 1938, 1939) or of the economy's growth rate and savings propensies of capitalists (see Nicholas Kaldor, 1955; Luigi Pasinetti, 1962).

24. Karl Marx (1967, vol. 3, chs. 21–25) considered the average rate of interest to be primarily determined by the combination of relative competitive pressures and common consent (over the profit-interest distribution) between lenders and borrowers. See also Carlo Panico (1980) on Marx's theory of interest. John Maynard Keynes (1936, ch. 15), while following an approach by and large similar to that of Marx, analyzed interest in addition as a purely monetary phenomenon determined by the interaction between money supply and money demand.

25. This sanguine view of speculation as a stabilizing force dominated especially during the height of the postwar boom, as exemplified by Milton Friedman (1953), Leland Johnson (1960), and John Muth (1961). After nearly two decades of speculation-driven turmoil in the financial markets, it is time to heed the powerful warnings in John Maynard Keynes (1936, ch. 12) and Nicholas Kaldor (1939) of speculation's tremendous potential for destabilization.

26. While careful to stress the interdependence between banks and industry, Hilferding regarded banks as the dominant force in that relation. In contrast, modern variants of this "financial control" hypothesis, such as Robert Fitch and Martin Oppenheimer (1970), Andrew Glyn and Bob Sutcliffe (1972), David Kotz (1978), or John Eatwell (1981), emphasized a conflict of interest between industry and banks. In this context, see also the "mixed monopoly" concept of Paul Sweezy (1972).

27. The concept of "fictitious" capital is also discussed by Friedrich Hayek (1939), one of the founders of the Austrian school of neoclassical economics. There it refers to an increase in bank credit which encourages businesses to invest without a corresponding increase in saving. That situation, according to Hayek, violates the neutrality of money and undermines macroeconomic equilibrium. Of course, we know from our discussion of credit-money in section 2.4 that such increases in bank credit are now the norm. See also Suzanne de Brunhoff (1990).

28. In his brilliant chapter on long-term expectations, John Maynard Keynes (1936, ch. 12) emphasized the dangers of the stock market's predominance, especially in terms of allowing short-term financial considerations to dominate long-term investment plans and speculation to crowd out enterprise (see chapter 12 for more).

Chapter 3

1. The common features of business cycles have led non-orthodox economists, such as Michal Kalecki (1939, 1954) or Richard Goodwin (1967), to formulate models that depict regular fluctuations in economic activity as mechanical, pendulum-like swings.

2. While rising profits and increased investment feed on each other during recovery (see Michal Kalecki, 1942), that process undermines itself. Both Karl Marx (1967, vol. 3, chs. 13 and 15) and John Maynard Keynes (1936, chs. 11 and 16), founders of the most important heterodox traditions in economic theory, recognized a tendency of the profit rate to fall in the wake of increased investment activity as a major barrier to sustained expansion.

3. This "overproduction" tendency is analyzed in Karl Marx (1967, vol. 1, ch. 25; vol. 3, ch. 30; 1968, ch. 17). John Maynard Keynes (1936, ch. 19) viewed the same tendency as a problem of "underconsumption," emphasizing that lower money-wages reduce employment, via lower demand, rather than increase it as claimed by standard theory.

4. For an excellent discussion of the different theoretical approaches to financial crisis, see Martin Wolfson (1986). That book also includes extensive empirical case studies of the major financial crises in the United States since 1966.

5. See Ernest Mandel (1975, ch. 4) and Jan Reijnders (1990) for excellent surveys of the different contributions to long-wave theory, with special emphasis on their respective shortcomings. In addition, the recurrent phenomenon of prolonged stagnation has been the subject of interesting analyses, most notably by Alvin Hansen (1941), Josef Steindl (1952), and Paul Sweezy (1982).

6. Starting with Karl Marx (1967, vol. 2, chs. 20–21), extensive discussions of such two-sector reproduction schemes can also be found in Michal Kalecki (1971), Rosa Luxemburg (1951), Ernest Mandel (1968), Joan Robinson (1956), and Paul Sweezy (1942).

7. One of the great insights by John Maynard Keynes (1936) was to have recognized the strategic importance of the wage-productivity balance. See especially his chapters on "The Theory of Prices" (pp. 299–303) and "Notes on the Trade Cycle" (pp. 324–326).

8. This two-directional interdependence between profits and investment has been analyzed in Michal Kalecki (1942).

9. Contributions of "Regulation Theory" in English include Michel Aglietta (1979, 1982), Robert Boyer (1979, 1987), Alain Lipietz (1985, 1987), and Pascal Petit (1986). A brief introduction to the principal arguments and concepts of this approach can be found in Michel De Vroey (1984) and Robert Boyer (1990).

10. "Regulation" is defined here much more broadly than its traditional use in the United States to denote government interference in the marketplace by use of its coercive powers. Regulation Theory employs the term in its French meaning, describing the ways in which a multitude of decentralized decisions and activities are made compatible in support of the system's expanded reproduction.

Chapter 4

1. The concept of "monetary regime" is not my own. It has occasionally been used by neoclassical economists, such as in Karl Brunner and Alan Meltzer (1982, 1985). But

there it refers strictly to standard concerns regarding money, in particular monetary policy targets and money-demand estimates.

2. The Coinage Act of 1792 established the United States Mint to issue a new basic monetary unit, the dollar, in the form of full-bodied coins whose metallic commodity value and face value were supposed to be equivalent. The dollar was defined as being equal to 371.25 grains of silver and/or 24.75 grains of gold, for a mint ratio of 15:1 between silver and gold.

3. Sir Thomas Gresham, a British finance minister during the reign of Queen Elizabeth I (1533–1603), observed that lighter-weight or worn coins circulated freely as medium of exchange while full-weight coins were removed from circulation and instead held as a store of value.

4. The central bank's control mechanism over state banks is described in David Kidwell and Richard Peterson (1984, ch. 5). If the central bank wanted to limit the volume of a particular bank's loans and notes, it would accumulate a large quantity of those notes and then present them for redemption. This drained the issuing bank's specie reserves, forcing the latter to reduce its notes or face bankruptcy. The central bank rewarded satisfactory operating policies by holding on to the notes or paying them out into circulation rather than redeeming them, thus allowing that state bank to retain its reserves.

5. Charles Kindleberger (1978, p. 124) points out that the demise of the Second Bank was due not least to its greedy and corrupt directors. These had tried to enrich themselves through a variety of unscrupulous practices, which added to then-rampant credit-financed speculation. The end of the bank contributed to the collapse of speculative bubbles, followed by a major financial panic in 1837 and depression in the wake of widespread debt repudiation during the early 1840s.

6. The problems with "free banking" became so bad in the early 1840s that the federal government was forced to set up an independent treasury payment system that completely bypassed the banks. Only twenty years later, after the outbreak of the Civil War, did the Treasury once again come to rely on commercial banks.

7. This large variety of circulating bank notes led to rampant counterfeiting. According to David Kidwell and Richard Petersen (1984, p. 99), the "Bank Note Reporter and Counterfeit Detector," a monthly register, listed more than 1,000 counterfeit bank notes in 1860.

8. For analyses of money-supply variations under the gold standard and of early banking in the United States, see Richard Cooper (1982), David Dewey (1903), or John Gurley and Edward Shaw (1957).

9. This $300 million borrowing program included the issue of $50 million worth of so-called demand notes. Those were in essence money, since they were immediately redeemable by the government (in gold or silver) and acceptable as payment for public dues. At first distrustful, the public (e.g., soldiers, government suppliers, banks) accepted this form of money only after Treasury officials and commanding army officers publicly declared their willingness to be paid in demand notes.

10. With the Greenbacks backed by government bonds, the Treasury's capacity to print new money depended on its ability to issue these securities. For this purpose it empowered the banker Jay Cooke to become the sole marketing agent of these securities. In return for this monopoly and generous commissions, Cooke hired 2,500 subagents to distribute newly issued bonds all across the Union. For a discussion of this first security-underwriting operation in U.S. history see Max Shapiro (1980, pp. 140–151).

11. The circuit discussed here shows that the Civil War inflation cannot be blamed simply on the excessive issue of paper money. The causality obviously ran from speculative hoarding and price hiking via the budget deficit to money creation, and not the other way around. Inflation was thus a device, rather than the consequence of a flawed set of policies.

12. Of course, government contracts, which assured a high level of aggregate demand, were not the only reason driving the industrial boom. Profits benefited from a decline of real wages (by an average of 35 percent for male workers) and a massive switch to cheaper female labor. Pro-business policies, such as refusing to tax companies, high tariffs as a source of tax revenues and for protection of domestic industry, and large subsidies (e.g., free land and construction grants for railroad companies) helped too.

13. See Robert Boyer and Benjamin Coriat (1984, pp. 8–11). The authors of this excellent paper also discuss (pp. 18–36) the profound influence of the Greenback Era on the evolution of specifically American economic theories. Its analysis by Wesley Mitchell (1903, 1908), for example, gave rise to the so-called Institutionalists, a paradigm which stressed quantitative analyses of business-cycle fluctuations and the role of policy institutions. And Irving Fisher (1911) applied his findings of the Greenback Era to redefine the Quantity Theory of Money for inconvertible paper money.

14. As already illustrated above (in Figure 4.1), this 50 percent reduction in the bank-created money-supply was compensated for by the return to a bimetallic standard in 1878–79, which helped to increase the circulation of precious metal coins and certificates as alternative money-forms.

15. O. M. W. Sprague (1968) has pointed out that during this crisis-prone period no single institution in the United States was capable of effectively acting as lender of last resort. Without capacity to issue money, the Treasury could only intervene after having accumulated budget surpluses, a rare situation. And the dominating New York banks, which still tended to follow the real-bills doctrine of a self-regulating money-supply (on the basis of trade bills), failed to keep sufficient reserves for any extraordinary cash requirements.

16. It should be noted that 1913 was a major turning point in U.S. economic policy-making. Apart from establishing a central bank, the United States also introduced the personal income tax that year. And in response to the rapid increase in industrial concentration following the merger boom of the late 1890s and 1900s, the U.S. government drastically expanded its antitrust powers in the Clayton and Federal Trade Commission acts of 1914.

17. With checks clearing at par and at no cost, they became even more popular with the public, to the point of establishing demand deposits as the principal form of modern money. The Fed ran its check-clearing system on a national basis, linking its regional Banks by wire transfer and air courier service. State banks, which were not part of the Federal Reserve System, participated through the correspondent network with member banks.

18. See Jeffry Frieden (1987, pp. 25–41) for more details on this clash between the "internationalism" of Wall Street and the "isolationism" of Washington during the 1920s.

19. Under this arrangement the world's currencies were defined by their respective gold content to fix their rates of exchange. But different currencies (in the form of government-issued paper money) could now be directly exchanged with each other, without gold as an intermediary.

20. Keynes made his early mark criticizing the structural deficiencies of the international monetary system that emerged after World War I. The negative economic and political repercussions of high reparation payments imposed on the losers was the subject of John Maynard Keynes (1919). And warning policy-makers of the deflationary pressures from a return to a gold standard, John Maynard Keynes (1923) proposed a system of managed money as an alternative to gold, which he termed a "cruel and barbarous relic."

21. In effect, one out of every six banks in the United States failed between 1921 and 1929. But most of those failures occurred among small local and regional banks, with only one-fifth of them being members of the Federal Reserve System.

22. There were two reasons for this prohibition of stock ownership by banks. One was that stocks, with their typically large price fluctuations, were considered too risky an investment for banks. The other was the well-founded fear that such ownership would result in excessively large concentrations of resources and power in the hands of bank-industry conglomerates.

23. With a 10 percent margin, a 10 percent price increase translated into a 100 percent return on capital. The increased value of the securities could then be used as collateral for additional margin credit. In 1929 more than 40 percent of all investors were margin buyers.

24. See, in particular, John Kenneth Galbraith (1954) and Charles Kindleberger (1973) for interesting analyses of this crisis.

25. Despite these serious mistakes by the Fed, Milton Friedman and Anne Schwartz (1963a) are wrong to blame the Great Depression solely on the central bank's erroneous policy. Their Monetarist interpretation abstracts entirely from other contributing factors, most notably industry's overproduction, structural changes in the financial system, the destabilizing role of speculation, and the fragility of the international monetary system.

26. The FOMC consists of twelve members, the seven governors and five presidents of the regional Federal Reserve banks. The latter are selected on a rotating basis among the twelve banks, with the exception of a permanent seat for the president of the Federal Reserve Bank of New York, where the Fed's open-market operations are conducted. Now the principal policy-making body of the central bank, the FOMC meets regularly (at least eight times per year) to set monetary policy goals.

27. These margin requirements (Fed Regulations T, U, and G) were part of a broader regulatory framework for the securities markets that eventually succeeded in restoring investor confidence. The Securities Act of 1933 and the Securities and Exchange Act of 1934 required regular and accurate disclosure of information to investors, imposed registration procedures for issue and trading of securities, and outlawed previously widespread market manipulation techniques (e.g., insider trading, misrepresentation, pooling of funds, price pegging). The Securities and Exchange Commission (SEC) was set up to administer the regulations.

28. Keynes, representing Great Britain at Bretton Woods, argued vehemently against the gold-dollar standard. Opposed to any system based on a national currency, he wanted the IMF to be run as a Clearing Union which could issue a new form of world-money, the Bancor, for settlement of international payment obligations. But this idea was opposed by the United States and thus never adopted. For a discussion of Keynes's highly innovative proposal, see Robert Guttmann (1985), as well as section 15.1 below.

Chapter 5

1. Excess reserves arise when banks hold more reserves than the amount required by the central bank, which is usually defined as a set percentage of their deposit liabilities. Banks can create new money up to the amount of their individual excess reserves. But the banking system as a whole can create a multiple of the original excess reserves in new money, because the circulation of checks transfers reserves from one bank to another. The size of that multiplier depends (inversely) on various leakages in the reserve-transfer process (e.g., reserve requirements, cash withdrawals).

2. Public demand for new currency (instead of demand deposits) is met by cash withdrawals from banks. The Fed replenishes depleted cash balances by transferring newly issued notes and coins to the banks affected.

3. Even the state as the other issuer of credit-money cannot immediately use its own currency (e.g., Federal Reserve notes) for purchases of goods and services. First any new

currency has to be transferred (by double-entry bookkeeping) from the central bank as the issuing agency to other government units entitled to spend on behalf of the public sector.

4. The Quantity Theory of Money, the standard paradigm in monetary theory (see chapters 1 and 2), avoids this problem by assuming stability of both the credit multiplier (linking the monetary base and money supply) and the velocity of money (linking the money supply and the gross national product). These constancy assumptions imply that banks tend to loan out all their excess reserves and that money demand (the reciprocal of velocity) is a constant portion of income.

5. For more on this procyclical trade-off in bank strategy see also Robert Guttmann (1987, pp. 4–5).

6. The prime rate is the interest rate banks charge their best (corporate) customers. As such it sets a floor for all other bank loans. Any change in the prime rate sets off corresponding rate adjustments for the other types of loans, such as mortgages, consumer loans, or broker loans. For a discussion of the government's use of "moral suasion" in the early 1970s to keep the prime rate from rising, see Charles Henning, William Pigott, and Robert Haney Scott (1978, pp. 265–268).

7. This theory of financial crises as a result of the Fed's policy mistakes has been most developed by Milton Friedman, the leading exponent of postwar Monetarism in the United States. See, above all, his discussion of the Great Depression in Milton Friedman and Anne Schwartz (1963a, 1963b), as well as Milton Friedman (1970). For an excellent critique of this position see Martin Wolfson (1986, pp. 27–39, 182–187).

8. Not surprisingly, this trend toward oligopolization and administered pricing was first recognized and analyzed by economists during the 1930s. In this context, see the path-breaking works of Adolf Berle and Gardiner Means (1932), Edward Chamberlin (1933), or Joan Robinson (1933).

9. Henry Ford (1926) understood the far-reaching implications of switching from batch production to the assembly line extremely well. The same is true for Frederick Taylor (1912), who developed the practice of "scientific management."

10. In his criticism of standard classical price theory, John Maynard Keynes (1936, ch. 21) formulated the wage–productivity balance by concluding that the price level was proportional to the wage rate divided by the "efficiency of labor." In other words, the ratio (balance) between money wages and labor productivity is the proximate determinant of the price level. Keynes stressed the downward rigidity of money wages, the result of organized labor's growing ability to resist wage cuts.

11. Having repressed the classical notion of "value," defined as the quantity of labor-time necessary to produce a commodity under average production conditions, neoclassical economists view this external value of money simply as an inverse function of the general price level. This is misleading. If, for example, prices rise in line with an increase in the underlying value of commodities, money still represents the same quantity of value and thus retains its purchasing power. When instead defined as a decline in the value of money, inflation can be properly rooted in specific accumulation conditions, which determine both the quantity of value embodied in output and the formation of prices. For more detail on the devaluation of (credit-)money as an inherent tendency of "monopolistic regulation," see Robert Guttmann (1984).

12. Long-term capital gains, when "realized" through sale of assets above the purchasing price, were given preferential tax treatment. Until the 1986 tax reform 60 percent of these gains were exempted from income tax. This encouraged shareholders to favor capital gains over dividends, thus allowing firms to keep their pay-out ratios relatively lower and retain a larger portion of profits for reinvestment.

13. The growing dominance of fixed costs from mechanization and debt has led companies to attempt such stabilization in a variety of ways. These have included regula-

tion of payment obligations by forward-money contracts (including trade credit from suppliers, prearranged lines of credit from banks, collective bargaining agreements, deferred tax payments and other accruals), mergers for better control purposes, administered prices instead of self-destructive price wars, diversification of the firm's asset portfolio, and planned obsolescence to assure larger replacement demand for maturing products.

14. U.S. corporations began to adopt depreciation accounting on a widespread scale after the dramatic industrial expansion during World War I and the brutal postwar depression. Before 1920 the absence of depreciation in cost-pricing tended to exacerbate the procyclical fluctuations of profit. During recovery periods, when investment outlays increased rapidly, corporate income was overstated. Sooner or later, especially during deflationary downturns, the inevitable loss in usefulness and value of machinery or buildings would translate into a sudden reduction of profits.

15. Both depreciation charges and accounting profits are sources of fictitious capital (see section 2.6), which result from the relaxation of monetary constraint in a regime of elastic credit-money. Accounting profits in particular are directly tied to that institutional money form. Since credit-money is issued as a simultaneous asset and liability for both issuer and user in exactly matching reciprocity, it allows all monetary transactions to be recorded by double-entry bookkeeping between the two sides—the basis of financial accounting. It is then up to (often quite arbitrary) accounting rules to determine the valuation of assets and liabilities or the measurement of cash flows.

16. Originating in precapitalist societies of antiquity and the Middle Ages, seigniorage denoted the profit that princes or kings made from the coinage of money (see chapter 14). With the emergence of monetary regimes based on credit-money, government came to benefit from its privilege of money creation in more indirect ways. Internal seigniorage refers to inflation-induced additions of tax revenues derived from the monetization of public debts. External seigniorage accrues to the country issuing the key currency functioning as world money. That country typically builds up long-term assets while owing short-term liabilities, thus earning net income from a positive yield spread.

Chapter 6

1. The most original theoretical explanation of this mutually feeding profit-investment link can be found in Michal Kalecki (1942; 1971, ch. 7). Standard theory recognizes that investment is a direct function of profit. What Kalecki did was to illustrate how the share of income going toward profit depends in turn on the volume of investment.

2. Measured in constant dollars, U.S. military spending grew by 43 percent between 1965 and 1968, while government transfer payments to individuals rose by 39 percent. The fiscal restraint of 1968 (a 10 percent income-tax surcharge, a $6 billion cut in spending) was in part offset by an easing of monetary policy. Central bank tightening in December 1965 slowed money supply growth to 2.8 percent, resulting in a growth recession that year. But the money supply grew 6.4 percent in 1967 and 7.3 percent in 1968.

3. There a distinction was made between "profit inflation" of the demand-pull variety and "income inflation." In his analysis of the latter, Keynes discussed the relationship of changes in wages, prices, and productivity to stress the importance of a balance between wage growth and productivity gains for price stability.

4. For an early version of this argument, see Milton Friedman (1968). Harry Johnson (1972a) contains a relentless Monetarist attack on Keynesian cost-push theories.

5. Estimates by the U.S. Commerce Department in 1979, a year of very high inflation, suggested that corporate profits may have been overstated by an astounding $50 billion—a gap of 30 percent to 40 percent between reported and "real" earnings. At a corporate tax rate of 48 percent, this amounted to an "excess tax liability" of more than

$20 billion. Steel companies paid out more in dividends than their inflation-adjusted earnings, thereby in effect liquidating themselves. While steel was the worst example of the hidden ravages of inflation, the problem was also acute for other capital-intensive industries, such as automobiles, paper, or chemicals.

6. Hyman Minsky (1975, 1982) has analyzed this situation of overextension ("Ponzi financing") as a gradual yet inevitable outcome of continuous debt financing.

7. During inflationary periods interest rates will gradually rise. Older financial assets, originally issued at lower coupon rates, will then have to be discounted at the (now higher) market rate. This causes their present value (market price) to decline, thereby allowing them to stay competitive with newer financial assets of the same type offering those higher yields. In this devaluation process holders of these older instruments experience a capital loss, however.

8. Economists define "core" inflation as the underlying rate at which prices would rise even in the absence of any excessive demand pressure or such "shocks" as sudden, sharp increases in oil or food prices. Cost-of-capital calculations, which confirm the rapid rise of the measure in the United States during the 1970s and early 1980s, can be found in George Hatsopoulos and Stephen Brooks (1986), Albert Ando and Alan Auerbach (1988), as well as in George Hatsopoulos, Paul Krugman, and Lawrence Summers (1990).

9. Each of the recent credit crunches created and was in turn fed by bursting speculative bubbles. See, for example, the collapse of Real Estate Investment Trusts and banks involved in currency speculation (e.g., Herstatt, Franklin National) in 1974–75, the heavy losses for the Hunt Brothers and their bankers in the silver market in 1980, and the spectacular failures of Penn Square and Drysdale in 1982.

10. According to 1980 estimates by the *American Machinist*, a trade publication, nearly 70 percent of metal-cutting machinery in U.S. industry was then at least ten years old, compared to only 41 percent in Japan. That 70 percent figure was about 10 percent higher than in 1960 and some 30 percent above the level during the early postwar years. A McGraw-Hill survey in 1981 showed staggering percentages of plant and equipment considered outdated in some U.S. industries—42 percent for railroads, 34 percent for rubber, and 24 percent for auto manufacturers.

Chapter 7

1. All data are from International Monetary Fund (1981, pp. 29–42).

2. Even though the United States' trade surplus grew considerably during the Kennedy years, its balance-of-payments deficits continued to accelerate due to direct investments by U.S. corporations in the Common Market and short-term portfolio investments in foreign instruments carrying higher interest rates. The capital controls of 1964 consisted of an "interest equalization" tax (of 15 percent, later raised to 30 percent) on foreign currencies and a voluntary program of "credit restraint" on bank loans to foreign companies and residents.

3. The Bancor Plan was spelled out in John Maynard Keynes (1943). A more detailed presentation of the "Triffin Dilemma" can be found in Robert Triffin (1960).

4. The status of the dollar as the principal form of world money since 1945 has thus been especially beneficial to the United States. While individual U.S. consumers and producers still have to pay for their imports out of their own pocket, their dollars flow back into the United States as an increased supply of funds to the domestic financial markets. Foreigners reinvest their excess dollars in the U.S. banking system either directly, through Eurodollar (time) deposits that are backed by U.S. demand deposits, or via their central banks.

5. From 1965 to 1972 the United States is estimated to have spent $141 billion on the military adventure in Vietnam. Its inflationary financing of those expenditures during 1965–68 caused much larger external U.S. deficits. To the extent that other (surplus) countries agreed to hold the excess supplies of dollars thereby engendered, they in effect ended up providing financial support for the war.

6. Other than acting as means of debt settlement, the SDRs did not carry out any of money's other functions. The surplus nations accepting SDRs had to issue and transfer their own currencies to the IMF in exchange as part of their budgetary appropriations. Their compulsory SDR deposits paid below-market rates set by the IMF and could not be disposed of as a medium of exchange in international transactions. Moreover, new issues of SDRs depended on U.S. permission. Viewing the SDRs as a possible threat to the dominance of the dollar as world money, the United States used its veto power after 1972 to block creation of additional SDRs.

7. For example, the Euromarket allowed U.S. banks to evade U.S. controls on capital exports in 1964 and 1968. By setting up branches abroad, U.S. banks bypassed the restriction on foreign lending. Their best customers, multinational corporations, could now simply go to their Euromarket subsidiaries for loans. The U.S. government welcomed this innovation, since it helped to maintain foreign investment activity by U.S. firms without further adding to the net dollar drain.

8. Between the end of 1969 and the end of 1971 private overseas investors reduced their dollar holdings from $28.2 billion to $15.1 billion in a series of speculative "runs" out of the dollar. During the same period, foreign central banks increased their official dollar holdings from $16 billion to $50.6 billion.

9. Reflecting the rapid internationalization of banks and corporations during the preceding decade, by the early 1970s currency fluctuations had come to play a much larger role in determining their balance sheet performance. This forced both banks and corporations to pay much more attention to the foreign exchange markets. Soon they developed sophisticated international money-management techniques, such as manipulating the timing of payment flows and foreign exchange transactions in line with exchange-rate expectations (e.g., corporate "leads and lags").

10. See, for example, Milton Friedman (1953) and Harry Johnson (1972b). Even some Keynesians, such as James Meade (1966), favored flexible exchange rates.

11. It usually takes between 12 and 24 months for volume adjustments to begin to outweigh initial price changes in response to exchange-rate movements and to move the trade balance in the desired direction. The J-curve was first discussed in Stephen Magee (1973).

12. According to official estimates (see Michael Andrews, 1984; Bank of England, 1986; Michael Sesit, 1989; Allen Myerson, 1992), the daily volume of foreign exchange transactions exploded across the globe during the 1980s, growing at an annual compound rate of 30 percent and approaching $1 trillion per day in 1992. This figure is somewhat inflated, since it involves double counting of cross-border exchange trades among banks. The U.S. share (of $192 billion) compares to daily averages of $150 billion for domestic trades of U.S. government securities and $6.2 billion on the New York Stock Exchange. Trade and direct investment in long-term assets absorb only around 15 percent of these currency trades. The rest goes into outright speculation, risk hedging, and short-term portfolio investments.

13. For more details on the depreciation-reflation strategy of the United States during the 1970s see Robert Guttmann (1989a).

14. Both the "boom-bust" cycles and propensity for speculation in commodity markets derive from the strategic role of these raw materials as basic inputs in industry. When the economy grows rapidly, many sectors increase their inventories of commodities at the same time. The opposite, simultaneous cutbacks, occurs during recessions. The

demand for oil grew at especially high rates during the 1970s, boosted both by a low-price policy in the United States and cheaper oil imports in other industrial nations due to a lower dollar.

15. That concordat, an agreement between central banks of the leading industrial powers ("Group of Ten") under the auspices of the Bank for International Settlements (BIS), consisted of two parts. The first, a deliberately vague statement in late 1974, dealt with central bank responsibilities as lender of last resort when Eurobanks encountered liquidity problems. It also authorized the BIS to create a Standing Committee on Banking Regulations and Supervisory Practices (Cooke Committee), which issued a set of principles on international bank supervision in August 1975.

16. This speculative run out of the dollar in 1977–78 generated hefty gains for U.S. banks betting against their own currency. For example, Citibank reported a 700 percent increase in profits from foreign exchange trading (from $13 million in 1977 to $105 million in 1978). The losers in this process were the central banks of Europe and Japan, which were forced to hold more depreciating dollars than they wanted.

17. After 1974 the U.S. government undertook a special effort to lure OPEC money into Treasury securities, which helped to finance its budget deficits and also took some pressure off the Eurobanks. But in mid-1979 this circuit broke down when OPEC countries stopped buying U.S. securities. Instead, their surplus went into the Euromarkets, where much of it could be shifted out of dollars.

18. For an excellent discussion of this accommodating Federal Reserve policy in the 1950s and early 1960s, with money-market conditions as its primary operating target, see Jack Guttentag (1966).

19. See the discussion of Monetarism's rising influence at the Fed in Andrew Brimmer (1971) and Andrew Bartels (1985).

20. The first time the Fed actually had made a monetary aggregate, in this case bank credit, a policy objective was under the so-called proviso clause in May 1966. The Fed's FOMC instructed the manager of its Trading Desk at the Federal Reserve Bank of New York to conduct open-market operations with a view toward maintaining specified conditions in the money market, provided that the behavior of bank credit was deemed appropriate under the circumstances. But the Fed did not adopt explicit goals for bank credit or any other measure of the money supply until early 1970, another period of tightening.

21. BHCs also had a lower tax burden than banks. Multibank holding companies, regulated under the 1956 act, were formed largely as a means of circumventing state branching restrictions under the McFadden Act of 1927. Many large banks formed one-bank holding companies to engage in nonbanking activities, from which they otherwise were precluded under the Glass-Steagall Act of 1933. Even after their regulation in 1970 the Federal Reserve defined the scope of banking-related activities for BHCs much more broadly than those of banks.

22. For a discussion of liability-management strategies and their detrimental effects on the Fed's ability to control the money creation process by private banks, see James Earley and Gary Evans (1982), as well as the articles in Thomas Havrilevsky and John Boorman (1980, part II).

23. State-chartered banks generally not only had lower reserve requirements than national banks, but also more relaxed supervision and examination by their state regulators. In addition, many states allowed them to count Treasury bills toward their reserves, whereas the reserves of national banks (vault cash, deposits with the Federal Reserve) yielded no interest.

24. The Fed also helped thrifts by extending Regulation Q ceilings to their deposits and setting those 0.25 percent above comparable ceilings for banks. This made it easier for thrifts to compete with banks for deposits and to counter disintermediation.

25. By channeling funds into the booming real estate industry, REITs had managed to expand very rapidly during the early 1970s. Between 1970 and 1974 their assets grew from \$4.8 billion to \$21.8 billion. Since REITs financed projects deemed too risky by banks, they were especially vulnerable to a cyclical turnaround in the housing market.

26. The Fed's program of credit restriction included an increase and broadening of the reserve requirements on borrowed liabilities of banks, a 3 percent surcharge to the discount rate on frequent borrowings by large banks, a special 15 percent deposit requirement on consumer credit and money-market funds, and a voluntary credit restraint program for banks, which included a request to stop lending for purely speculative and financial purposes.

Chapter 8

1. The policy reforms of the New Deal in the 1930s found their theoretical justification in John Maynard Keynes (1936). This influential classic, which started a revolution in economic thinking, called for active state intervention in the economy to assure full employment. Specifically, the government should stimulate total demand in the economy through deficit spending and a low-interest policy of its central bank. Those prescriptions became standard liberal policy after World War II.

2. The new Accelerated Cost Recovery System allowed vehicles to be written off in three years, machines in five years, and industrial plant and other real estate structures in fifteen years (soon thereafter extended to nineteen years). This speed-up in depreciation added to cash flow, reduced taxable income, gave firms larger tax deductions, and made capital goods de facto cheaper.

3. This last provision returned the poorest one-third to their effective tax burden of a decade earlier. From 1975 onward that income group had suffered a particularly steep increase in its tax burden. Pushed by Democrats, that relief also found support among conservative Republicans. They saw it as preferable to antipoverty programs and liked its profamily bias.

4. In recent years the Pentagon has tried to increase competition. But its efforts in this direction have so far failed. Contractors supposedly bidding against each other have operated like an informal cartel, coordinating their bids and sharing contracts through subcontracting agreements.

5. Recently the Pentagon has experimented with different pricing formulas to encourage efficiency, such as fixed-price contracts in which producers may keep any cost savings below the set limit as extra profit and must pay any overruns out of their own pockets. But given the inherently uncertain nature of product development using sophisticated and often untested technologies, it is extremely difficult to predict costs. Firms have used this argument effectively to resist these types of contracts.

6. The key findings of these studies are discussed in Edward Pound (1986) and Tim Carrington (1986).

7. Under this accounting method, contractors can count all contract-related reimbursements as current income and delay booking already incurred costs until completion of the contract.

8. On Keynesian monetary theory, see Paul Davidson (1978). Milton Friedman (1968) spells out most clearly how Monetarists view money and monetary policy. Good summaries of the debate between Monetarists and Keynesians can be found in Thomas Humphrey (1979) and Lawrence Harris (1981).

9. For the supply-side theory's view of money and monetary theory, see Victor Canto and others (1983) or Marc Miles (1984).

10. The number of corporate acquisitions rose from 1,526 valued at \$34.2 billion in 1979 to a peak of 4,022 valued at \$190 billion in 1986. During the same period, the number of takeovers rose from 3 in 1979 with a combined value of \$6.2 billion to 34 in 1986 valued at \$68.6 billion.

11. For a discussion of this U.S. saving shortfall and its far-reaching implications for our economy, see Robert Guttmann (1989b).

12. That Plaza Agreement comprised the United States, Great Britain, France, West Germany, and Japan as signatories. Later, in the Louvre Agreement of February 1987, Canada and Italy were also included, giving rise to the so-called Group of Seven (G–7).

13. Supply-siders, such as Paul Craig Roberts (1989), have argued that the comparatively low inflation rate for capital goods and the change in the asset mix toward short-lived equipment generating more depreciation during the 1980s exaggerate the decline of the (net) investment share. But their argument ignores the growing replacement needs due to aging capital stock and the comparatively small capacity-enhancing effects of short-lived equipment, such as computers. Heavy machinery and plant together still account for 82 percent of industrial capacity. And during 1988 these big-ticket items grew by only 0.3 percent in U.S. manufacturing, after suffering slight declines in the previous two years.

14. The bailout of the thrifts may ultimately cost \$500 billion, including interest. Cleaning up nuclear weapons plants could amount to \$100 billion over a ten-year period. Doing the same for the 1,200 toxic waste sites designated a priority by the Environmental Protection Agency's Superfund is now estimated at a staggering \$750 billion. The much-needed modernization of our air traffic control system is estimated at \$25 billion. Repairing bridges and road surfaces of our interstate highway system also requires huge expenditures over the next two decades, with some estimates as high as \$500 billion. If the federal government is really serious about dealing with the drug crisis, it will have to spend billions more on treatment and preventive education than is currently budgeted. Furthermore, the demands for federal help to young families for child-care expenses and to the elderly for long-term health care are mounting.

15. These accounting gimmicks included government sales of public assets (e.g., loans, land) that raise cash now at the expense of future income, overly optimistic economic forecasts by the Office of Management and Budget underestimating the size of future deficits, moving expenses from one fiscal year into another, and "off-budget" expenditures.

16. A dollar decline of, say, 10 percent raises import prices by that amount unless foreign firms accept lower profit margins to maintain market shares. It then takes a 10 percent reduction in import volumes to reduce the United States' total import bill. The same occurs in reverse for exports, whose volume would have to grow by 10 percent in order to make up for the decline in export prices.

17. A dramatic illustration of this trend has been the growing importance of trading in currency futures as an independent profit center for banks and corporations in the 1980s. A highly original analysis of the relationship between growing exchange-rate volatility after 1973 and the transformation of foreign exchange markets into speculative circuits is the one by Stephan Schulmeister (1987).

18. This long-term trend toward higher levels of indebtedness in the private sector of the U.S. economy has been analyzed most thoroughly by Hyman Minsky (1982).

19. During the Reagan recovery we Americans consumed on average about 4 percent per year more than we produced. This means that between 1982 and 1990 we consumed nearly \$1 trillion in products we have not yet paid for and did not produce.

20. The remaining portion of the world money supply includes other key currencies, most notably the yen and the mark. But their issuers, Germany and Japan, are creditor

nations—in contrast to the United States. And then there are supranational forms of world money, such as the Special Drawing Rights (SDRs) of the IMF and the European Currency Units (ECUs) within the Common Market. They are primarily used as reserve assets of central banks and in official transactions between them. Gold still plays an important role as reserve asset for certain countries, but is otherwise a declining force in the international monetary system.

Chapter 9

1. The extent of this override differed, depending on the type of lending institution and the loan category. State usury laws, which subjected state-chartered institutions to more restrictive maximum ceilings than nationally chartered institutions, were eliminated. Ceilings on certain agricultural and business loans were suspended for three years. The act nullified rate ceilings on mortgages unless the states passed new ones within three years. DIDMCA also raised the statutory rate ceiling for federally chartered credit unions from 12 percent to 15 percent.

2. The new reserve requirements applied equally to each depository institution: 3 percent of its first $25 million of demand deposits (including NOW and ATS accounts); 12 percent of its demand deposits in excess of that amount (with the Fed allowed to alter that requirement within a range of 8 to 14 percent and raising it to 18 percent in emergencies); 3 percent of corporate time and savings deposits with maturities of less than four years (set within a possible range of 0 to 9 percent). The act eliminated reserve requirements on personal time and savings deposits.

3. Selective credit controls have been an important ingredient of monetary policy in other industrial nations, especially France and, in less explicit fashion, Japan. In the United States they are only favored by post-Keynesian economists (e.g., Stephen Rousseas, 1986, ch. 6), with John Maynard Keynes (1930a) himself approving this measure under certain conditions.

4. Money-market mutual funds, which in 1978 had only amounted to $10.9 billion, grew from $74.4 billion in 1980 to a peak of $232.3 billion in December 1982. MMMFs reinvest most of their funds in instruments of money-center banks and large firms. Cash management accounts, introduced by Merrill Lynch in 1977, combine a high-yielding money-market fund, access to brokerage services, check-writing privileges, a credit card (or debit card) for cash withdrawals, and a line of credit. Checks, cash, and credit line are all backed by the value of securities held in the account. See Tim Carrington (1982) for details on the rapid spread of CMAs in the early 1980s.

5. Details of the evolution toward class-tiered banking and its emergence as a political issue are discussed in Daniel Hertzberg (1984), Bianca Riemer (1985), and Phillip Zweig (1985a).

6. For an interesting discussion of how banking innovation and financial deregulation have made central bank targeting of monetary aggregates more difficult, see Anthony Solomon (1982), then president of the Federal Reserve Bank of New York.

7. The endogeneity of credit-money is also discussed in Marc Lavoie (1984), Stephen Rousseas (1986, ch. 5), and Robert Guttmann (1989c, chs. 1 and 4).

8. One such measure, the so-called Divisia aggregates, looks at the interest rates of different deposits, under the theory that there exists an inverse relation between yield and liquidity. All deposits with monetary attributes are then given different weights depending on their degree of liquidity. A second measure, the so-called debit-weighted money index, assigns different weights to various categories of money according to how often they turn over. Traditional no-interest demand deposits, for example, turn over 350 times per year, compared to only 16 times for NOW accounts and 3 times for MMMFs.

9. Depository institutions had to set up new computer and reporting procedures. They also have had to keep a larger cushion of excess reserves in order to avoid being caught short. Short-term interest rates became somewhat more volatile as reserve-deficient institutions rush into the money market at the end of each two-week reporting period. For more on the difference between "lagged" and "contemporaneous" reserve accounting, see *Business Week* (1980) and Michael Quint (1981).

10. We shall examine many examples of such excessive risk-taking by banks and thrifts in chapters 10 and 12. It is worth recalling here that the Glass-Steagall Act of 1933 introduced deposit-rate ceilings precisely to limit the destabilizing effects of price competition on the investment behavior of banks.

11. For an interesting discussion of what caused the high real interest rates during the 1980s, see Paul Davidson (1986).

12. ATM networks and other plans in the direction of "electronic" banking are discussed in *Business Week* (1982b).

13. The Fed's check-processing practice of crediting and debiting reserve accounts of banks at different times has encouraged a whole host of manipulations by financial institutions. Most notorious is the elaborate check-overdraft scheme run by E. F. Hutton against as many as 400 banks during the early 1980s, which gave that brokerage house as much as $250 million in interest-free loans on some days. After years of investigation and legal wrangling, Hutton finally pleaded guilty to 2,000 counts of mail and wire fraud in May 1985, for which it paid a fine of $2 million. For more details on this case, see *Business Week* (1985a).

14. In 1986 the Fed simplified the format of electronic fund transfer messages to reduce the amount of manual processing required of banks. At the same time, it also changed the fee structure charged on the float that results from overnight processing of electronic fund transfers. As a result, most banks ended up paying less per transaction.

15. Before 1980 correspondent banks typically cleared checks for their respondent customers, managed their reserves and spare cash, and lent them money when necessary.

16. The Fed's price list set off immediate controversy. Banks complained that the "private sector adjustment factor," required by Congress to compensate for the central bank's exemption from taxation and interest payments on investments in plant and equipment, was too low. The Fed was forced to raise this surcharge from 12 percent to 16 percent.

17. For example, a computer malfunction at the Bank of New York paralyzed the Treasury bond market in November 1985 for 28 hours. The bank required a one-day discount loan of $20 billion (at an interest expense of $4 million) from the Federal Reserve Bank of New York so it could pay for securities received.

18. Henry Watson (1985, 1986) has given very interesting reasons why the Fed should move out of the wire-transfer business and leave it entirely in private hands.

Chapter 10

1. As a result of that first oil shock and the global recession that followed in its wake (1973–75), Britain, France, and Mexico required financial bailouts.

2. In 1973 commercial banks held only 45 percent of total LDC and Eastern Europe debt. But following cutbacks by governments and international lending agencies, such as the International Monetary Fund or the World Bank, that share rose to 65 percent by 1982.

3. Smuggling, corruption, underinvoicing of imports, or overinvoicing of exports all make it quite easy to move funds surreptitiously out of any country. It should also be noted that banks, especially U.S. and Swiss banks, actively court wealthy citizens of

debtor nations to deposit funds with them. Much of the capital flight out of LDCs in the early 1980s was prompted by political uncertainties, overvalued local currencies, and domestic interest rates lagging behind inflation. For more empirical data on the scope of this problem, see *Business Week* (1983), Gary Hector (1985), George Ayittey (1986), and John Williamson (1987a).

4. See Art Pine (1982) and Peter Norman (1983) for details of this lending cutback. The U.S. banks, for example, reduced their lending to developing countries from $43 billion in 1981 to only $25 billion in 1982.

5. Art Pine (1983) provides fascinating details of the pivotal leadership role played by Volcker in this crisis, especially his battle against reluctant Treasury officials whose inexperience with international financial affairs and rigid adherence to a "free market" ideology made it difficult for them to appreciate fully the seriousness of the LDC debt problem.

6. For more details on these "regulatory accounting practices" pertaining to nonperforming and rescheduled bank loans, see Robert Guttmann (1989d, pp. 90–95).

7. A 1992 study by the I.M.F. Assessment Project, a nonpartisan group of economists, concluded that countries following IMF adjustment programs ultimately managed to increase their growth more and reduce their trade deficits faster than countries that did not follow the fund's prescriptions. But those countries paid a heavy price for this success, having to slash spending on housing, health care, or economic aid programs (e.g., food subsidies) and to raise prices of imported goods in the wake of often massive currency devaluations. See Steven Greenhouse (1992) for more details on that study.

8. Toward these objectives lawmakers set up the Interagency Country Exposure Review Committee, comprising the Fed, the FDIC, and the Comptroller of Currency. These regulators meet three times a year to evaluate LDC debtors and to give commercial banks guidelines as to their treatment of doubtful foreign loans. The committee has since then gradually tightened loan-loss accounting rules, forcing banks to recognize troubled loans earlier and to set aside reserves for them more readily.

9. The settlement provided for $6 billion in new loans with a twelve-year maturity and a comparatively low interest rate (i.e., 13/16 percent above the LIBOR rate banks charge one another for funds in London), rescheduling of $44 billion in outstanding loans over twenty years at the same rate, and additional contingency funds should Mexico's growth slump.

10. Even though European and Japanese banks had already taken steps to cushion themselves against Third World debt loss, they too set aside additional reserves in 1987.

11. In a debt–equity swap a debt note is sold in the secondary market at a discount. The purchaser then takes that note to the central bank of the debtor country and cashes it in for an amount of local currency equivalent to its face value. That money can be used to purchase equities in that country, a potentially profitable way for multinationals to gain control over a country's resources. In a debt-for-bond swap foreign-currency debt is converted at the prevailing discount price into local-currency obligations, mostly government bonds, which can be traded or converted into equity. These bonds carry low yields, such as the 6 percent over 25 years in the case of Brazil's exit bonds, which also had a ten-year grace period on principal.

12. In this deal Mexico exchanged about 41 percent of its $48.5 billion in commercial bank debt for new exit bonds at a discount of 35 percent. This conversion reduced its total liability by about $7 billion. But Mexico had to borrow an additional $5.7 billion from Japan, the World Bank, and the IMF to finance a $7 billion collateral fund that guarantees interest and principal payments on the discounted debt. Mexico agreed to use $3.3 billion of these funds to buy U.S. Treasury zero-coupon bonds, which back and ultimately pay

off its exit bonds. Finally, banks also offered Mexico $1.5 billion in new loans over four years.

13. In 1986–87 the IMF set up a "structural adjustment facility" of $11.4 billion in soft loans (ten-year maturity, five-year grace period, 0.5 percent interest rate) for very poor nations committed to longer-term economic restructuring programs. Of these funds, 80 percent have been allocated to the countries of sub-Saharan Africa. In 1988 the fund also introduced a special contingency fund to aid countries whose economic-adjustment programs are threatened by events beyond their control (e.g., sharp rises in world interest rates, natural disasters, import price hikes).

14. Income from farm assets measures the contribution of capital and thus differs greatly from the familiar farm income measure. Specifically, it excludes the farm operator's contribution to profit (his labor and management) and makes no deduction for interest expenses.

15. Federal assistance during the early 1980s included price-support programs in which the government bought up excess output at a set price, "payment-in-kind" programs in which farmers received some of the government-stored surplus in return for idling some of their land, and export subsidies. In 1985 Congress passed a five-year farm bill that slashed price-support levels of most major crops to spur farm exports and shrink surpluses. In order to cushion the blow of lower prices, the government increased cash payments to farmers and provided additional export subsidies.

16. For a discussion of the crisis among farm banks, see Charles McCoy and Marj Charlier (1985) and Charles McCoy (1987). The broader effects of the farm debt crisis on the U.S. economy are analyzed well in Marj Charlier (1985).

17. The FCS consists of three independent banking networks that together comprise 37 regional banks and more than 700 local lending units. The Federal Land Banks offer long-term mortgages on farm land. The Production Credit Associations provide short-term funds to cover the costs of growing and harvesting crops. And the Banks for Cooperatives lend to agricultural, aquatic, and public utility cooperatives. The entire three-tier system is regulated by the Farm Credit Administration, a federal agency.

18. See Aloysius Ehrbar (1985), Charles McCoy (1985), and Art Pine (1987) on the crisis of the FCS, various initiatives to rescue the system, and the far-reaching repercussions of its potential failure on the U.S. economy.

19. Participations are loan syndications in which participating banks receive the income from the loan payments. The originating bank continues to service the loan and keeps the borrower's deposits. Interesting accounts of Penn Square's spectacular failure are Mark Singer (1985) and Phillip Zweig (1985b).

20. Between 1973 and 1979 thrifts were allowed to offer various deposit certificates carrying market rates, make more consumer loans, increase their borrowing capacity, issue commercial paper and Eurodollar securities, and introduce variable-rate mortgages.

21. Those promissory notes were issued only to institutions whose net worth had fallen below 3 percent of liabilities. About 100 thrifts with net worths below 0.5 percent were considered too sick and thus ineligible. The regulators paid interest on the notes. But they did not incur any other expenses in this swap unless an institution holding notes actually failed, an outcome the FDIC and FSLIC could influence to some degree. By the end of 1985 about 700 thrifts had received such capital assistance, at an estimated cost of $1.8 billion to the FSLIC.

22. "Good will" is normally defined as the amount paid to acquire a company in excess of its tangible book value. Purchase accounting turned this concept on its head, applying it to the excess of book value over market value. For more on purchase accounting and its extensive use in thrift bailouts, see Christian Hill and John Andrew (1982).

23. Besides gaining most of the powers of commercial banks under DIDMCA 1980 and DIA 1982, thrifts were in many respects even more attractive than banks. They enjoyed special tax benefits as well as more lenient accounting and capital rules. Thrift holding companies could also engage in real estate development, insurance, and securities underwriting—activities denied to bank holding companies.

24. A recent study, widely reported in the press (see Paulette Thomas, 1990), estimated that outright fraud only accounted for $5 billion, or 3 percent, of total federal government losses on S&Ls. It should be noted that the author of this study (Bert Ely) is a thrift consultant and may therefore not have used objective judgment. In reality, fraud may have played a much more significant role in thrift failures, even though it is at times hard to separate from mismanagement. A study by the House Government Operations Committee in 1987, for example, showed fraud to have been the leading cause of failure among 30 S&Ls in California. In July 1990 the Justice Department targeted 100 S&Ls as high-priority cases for investigation of alleged improprieties.

25. For details of FIRREA of 1989 see Christian Hill and Paulette Thomas (1989) or Nathaniel Nash (1989).

26. The "too big to fail" doctrine has come under a great deal of criticism since then. But it is doubtful whether the FDIC had any alternative at the time. Without such protection it probably would have had to discount the LDC loans held by Continental Illinois to their true market value. This in turn would have forced other money-center banks to do the same, something that both regulators and banks wanted to avoid at the time.

27. What makes such manipulation of financial statements possible in the first place is the very institution of credit-money. Constituting simultaneously an asset and a liability for both issuer and user, that form of money rests entirely on double-entry bookkeeping. In our cash-flow economy all monetary transactions are thus recorded via so-called T-accounts. Within that framework both timing of cash flows and valuation of assets, itself just a procedure of discounting future cash flows to present value, can be altered quite easily (see chapter 5).

28. In this context, a House Banking Committee report (see Kenneth Bacon, 1991a) highlighted the disproportional impact of supervisory failures by the Comptroller of Currency. Even though that agency regulates only about one-third of the nation's banks, failures under its jurisdiction have accounted for 73 percent of the net losses to the deposit insurance fund since 1986. That year the Comptroller decided to scale back annual on-site examinations of small banks in favor of more limited examinations targeted at specific problem areas.

29. Jeffrey Bardos (1988) presents an interesting analysis of how this Basel Agreement came about.

30. The Treasury wanted banks to pay insurance premiums based on risk and to transfer riskier activities to uninsured affiliates. Its plan would also have limited the number of insured accounts per depositor and the insurance coverage for pension funds and other big depositors. Congress wanted the FDIC to abandon its "too big to fail" policy and subject undercapitalized banks to restrictions on growth and dividend payouts.

Chapter 11

1. The valuation of bank loans depends on bankers assessing the creditworthiness of their corporate customers on the basis of a long-standing personal relationship. This stability of loan values is reinforced by special regulatory accounting rules that allow banks to ride out cyclical fluctuations by having them keep assets on their balance sheets at book value rather than having to mark them down "to market." Since 1992, the FASB has required banks and other companies to disclose the fair market value of all financial assets in footnotes to their financial statements.

2. Commercial paper, an unsecured promissory note, has a maximum maturity of 270 days to avoid time-consuming registration and prospectus requirements imposed by the

SEC. Most of it is issued by industrial firms, consumer finance companies, and bank holding companies—either directly or through dealers. The secondary market for such paper is small, since it is so heterogeneous and mostly held until maturity. Its key buyers are insurance companies, nonfinancial businesses, bank trust departments, and state and local government pension funds. Most paper is backed by a credit line from a bank which collects a fee for that service.

3. Other financial intermediaries have suffered a similar fate. The market share of life insurance companies, for example, fell from 13 percent in 1975 to 11.4 percent in 1987. Investment banks have also suffered market erosion, starting with the deregulation of brokerage commissions in 1975. Public utilities now routinely auction off their new issues rather than using underwriters. Shelf-registration of new securities months before their issue has intensified competition among investment bankers for the underwriting business. New practices, such as private placement and block trading, have also cut into the traditional market-making business of investment bankers.

4. Already by 1984, for example, one-third of the banks on the FDIC's problem list made heavy use of brokered deposits. The same was true for half of the banks which failed that year. The abuse was even more pronounced in the case of insolvent thrifts that the FSLIC had permitted to stay open (see section 10.3).

5. Millions of Americans have a stake in that huge market, either because of their own direct investments or through pension and money-market funds. In addition, foreigners now hold more than $400 billion in U.S. Treasuries, and many of these holdings constitute a basic foreign-currency reserve of foreign nations. Finally, the government securities market is also crucial for the execution of U.S. monetary policy, since the Fed conducts its open-market operation there to manage bank reserves.

6. In the reverse repos Drysdale tended to borrow bonds that were almost due for semiannual coupon payments by the government and therefore included a relatively large amount of accrued interest for which it did not have to pay. The firm then sold the same issues for a price which included the accrued interest.

7. Most of these securities pool residential mortgages, which are fairly standard and often backed by a government agency. Commercial mortgages are far more difficult to pool, because they tend to be much less homogeneous and lack federal guarantees. Fewer than 10 percent of these are therefore securitized.

8. Certain variants of mortgage-backed securities, such as collateralized mortgage obligations (CMOs), introduced in 1983, or Real Estate Mortgage Investment Conduits (REMICs), created by the Tax Reform Act of 1986, were explicitly designed to reduce prepayment risk. They let underwriters channel interest and principal payments from a mortgage pool more efficiently into various maturities with different yields or maturities. See Ann Monroe (1986a, 1986b) for more details on risk-containment innovation in the mortgage-backed securities market.

9. Lee Berton (1985) reports that a major portion of Community S&L's revenues and assets derived from questionable accounting methods used in connection with EPIC's limited partnerships. See also Steven Swartz (1985) for an excellent account of EPIC's complex web of transactions.

10. Financial institutions are not the only ones using off-balance-sheet liabilities. Under "defeasance," for example, an industrial company buys government securities at a discount and places them in a trust, pledging future income from those to pay off interest and principal due on its own bonds as they mature. In this way the firm can scratch the debt from its balance sheet. At the same time it records a paper profit on its income statement, because the discounted government securities cost less than the potential cost of retiring its own debt at face value. For more details on this and other so-called asset-liability management techniques, see Lee Berton (1983) and Ann Monroe (1985).

11. In July 1984 First National Bank of Chicago sold off nonperforming loans to a limited partnership set up by Bear, Stearns & Co. In September 1984 Citicorp created its own buyer of bad loans. That firm, Chatsworth, would sell commercial paper guaranteed by Travelers. In May 1988 First Republic, facing imminent failure, decided to package nonperforming loans into bonds and sell those at a deep discount. The proceeds from that sale would be used to recapitalize the bank. Mellon launched a similar bad-loan bond issue in July 1988. Both recapitalizations were arranged by Drexel as an extension of its junk-bond business.

12. For example, a corporation might become nervous about paying higher variable rates and thus wish to lock in a fixed rate. The other party in that swap, expecting interest rates to decline, likes to receive a fixed rate and to pay out a variable rate.

13. For more details on the evolving market structure for loan securitization, see Christine Cumming (1987). Beverly Hirtle (1987) provides an interesting analysis of the market in financial guarantees.

14. The Independent Bankers Association, which represents about 7000 small banks, has less than 10 percent of the staff and budget of the American Bankers Association. But it tends to speak with a unified voice, while the ABA, trying to represent all bankers, is vulnerable to the competing interests of a highly diverse membership. For more on the power of the IBA compared to the much larger ABA, see Christopher Conte (1983).

15. For a discussion of efforts by money-center banks to set up nationwide networks of bank-related activities following the BHC Act of 1970, see Daniel Hertzberg (1983) and *Business Week* (1984). Both articles emphasize the particularly aggressive expansion strategy of Citibank, which helped it to become the nation's largest bank.

16. Apart from the McFadden Act of 1927 and the Bank Holding Company Act of 1956, merger-based expansion strategies of banks are also subject to the Bank Merger Act of 1960, which was passed in response to a decade-long merger wave involving more than 1,500 banks. That act stipulated, among other things, several criteria for evaluating bank mergers and subjected all acquisitions involving FDIC-insured banks to prior approval by a federal bank supervisory agency. It was amended in 1966 to incorporate pertinent sections of the Sherman and Clayton antitrust acts.

17. Thrifts also tend to have lower operating costs than commercial banks, because they often generate more deposits per branch and provide fewer services.

18. Superregionals and their strategies are discussed in Felix Kessler (1984), *Business Week* (1986a), and Gary Hector (1988).

19. This difference disappeared at the end of 1992, when the Basel Agreement required all banks in the United States, Europe, and Japan to have the same risk-weighted capital-asset ratios of 8 percent (see section 10.4).

20. See Tim Carrington (1980), and *Business Week* (1984b) for analyses of how Merrill Lynch, the nation's largest broker, expanded aggressively into real estate, insurance, and commercial bank services.

21. See Richard Davis (1986) for more details.

22. The reorganization and dramatic expansion of Citibank's investment banking operation is detailed in *Business Week* (1986b). George Anders (1987) discusses how Wells Fargo Investment Advisors managed to become the biggest single investor in the stock market. *Business Week* (1988) analyzes the remarkable transformation of Bankers Trust into a merchant bank which today derives more than half of its income from selling loans, trading securities (e.g., corporate bonds, commodities, currency options, and futures), and financing leveraged buyouts.

23. See Gary Hector (1983) for more details.

24. Victor Saulsberg (1987) lists the different nonbanking activities that are allowed in each state.

25. During the stock market boom of the 1920s, commercial banks had participated in nearly two-thirds of all new stock and bond issues. Many banks were found to have lent money on favorable terms to their investment affiliates. They also gave preferential treatment to loan requests by firms whose securities they were allowed to underwrite. They stuffed their trust departments with securities issued through their investment affiliates. Finally, those affiliates often supported stock prices of parent banks.

26. Proposals by the Fed and the FDIC on how to integrate commercial and investment banking while maintaining an effective "fire wall" around money creation are spelled out in Robert Litan (1986) and Gerald Corrigan (1987a).

27. For detailed case studies of these internal frictions within commercial banks trying to take on Wall Street on its own turf, see Linda Sandler (1984) and Philip Zweig (1986).

28. Low profit margins in an intensely competitive environment and the costs of government regulation make it questionable how attractive banks would be for industrial corporations in the first place.

29. Schumer's core banking proposal, which differed in significant respects from Litan's "narrow" banking idea, was first put forward by Lowell Bryan (1991).

30. For empirical evidence concerning the adverse effects of increased concentration in local bank markets, see Mark Green and Glenn von Nostitz (1992)

31. There is a great deal of public opposition to bank mergers. Postmerger rationalization imposes heavy social costs in terms of branch closings, unemployment, and service cuts. Local community groups often organize against mergers on the grounds that those would sever existing ties between banks and community. In their battles they make use of the Community Reinvestment Act (CRA) of 1977, which requires regulatory agencies to rate U.S. financial institutions under their jurisdiction as to how well they serve their local communities. These CRA ratings are important, because they must be taken into consideration by the regulators when ruling on proposed bank mergers.

32. Several post-Keynesian economists working on Wall Street have clearly recognized the dangers of banking deregulation. Albert Wojnilower (1980) and Henry Kaufman (1986) in particular have stressed the destabilizing consequences of new bank products on monetary policy and financial market risks.

33. For more on the secretive Cooke Committee, see Michael Moffitt (1983, pp. 232–35) and Stephen Fay (1984).

34. Gerald Corrigan (1987b) presents an interesting summary of these equal-access and rule-harmonization issues in the construction of an international regulatory framework for globally integrated banking and securities markets.

Chapter 12

1. John Gurley and Edward Shaw (1960), a classic on that subject, provides an excellent example of that orthodox view.

2. Keynes (1936, p. 375) concluded: "Thus it is to our best advantage to reduce the rate of interest to that point relatively to the schedule of the marginal efficiency of capital at which there is full employment."

3. All these reasons for continued capital scarcity figure prominently in Hyman Minsky (1975, pp. 151–155).

4. This trend manifested itself in a variety of ways, including purchases of financial institutions by industrial firms, the growing importance of corporate pension funds, and the priority given to takeovers over expanding existing lines of business.

5. The capitalization of income (for claims perpetually yielding the same fixed amount at regular intervals) involves dividing the amount expected annually by the prevailing average rate of interest adjusted for risk. For example, if a stock is expected to

yield an annual income of $100 and the relevant rate of interest is 5 percent, then that stock would be valued at $2,000. More generally, the fair market value of any investment is determined by discounting all its expected future payments to present value at an appropriate rate of capitalization, usually the prevailing rate of interest for instruments of similar risk.

6. Strictly speaking, a Eurocurrency deposit is not money, because it is a time deposit rather than a transaction deposit with check-writing privileges. Its only monetary attribute is its backing by a demand deposit in the original country of issue. As the Eurodeposit moves from bank to bank and multiplies, the underlying domestic demand deposit remains the same, with only the name of its holder changing. For more details on the Euromarket, see Paul Einzig and Brian Quinn (1977) and Edward Frydl (1982), as well as Ivor Pearce and William Hogan (1982).

7. An excellent discussion of the causes behind growing financial market volatility can be found in Robert Shiller (1988).

8. Standard theory holds that stock market prices move randomly and cannot be predicted accurately. The basis for this "random walk" hypothesis (see Burton Malkiel, 1973) is that stock prices are based on evaluations of all available information and that the market responds quickly to any new information, especially surprises. This "efficient market" theory was first formulated by Eugene Fama (1970), a classic in the field of finance.

9. George Soros (1987) described the boom-bust behavior of the stock market quite powerfully. The analysis of speculative bubbles in the stock market led Eugene Fama and Kenneth French (1988), as well as Gikas Hardouvelis (1988), to conclude that, contrary to the traditional random walk hypothesis, stock prices are indeed predictable over a longer time horizon.

10. During the 1920s, for example, U.S. banks used a combination of trust departments, broker loans, and underwriting of securities to manipulate both the demand-side and the supply-side of the stock market (see section 4.7).

11. Ever since 1934 the Federal Reserve has imposed so-called margin requirements on broker loans to limit such leveraging. Currently individuals can only borrow up to 50 percent against the value of the stocks they buy on credit. Despite this restriction, credit pyramiding continues, mostly by large institutional investors, which nowadays are a much bigger force in the stock market than are individual investors. Nor do margin requirements apply to derivative instruments, such as stock-index futures or options.

12. Between late 1982, when the stock market rally began, and the beginning of 1987, some 12,200 companies and corporate divisions, worth at least $490 billion, changed hands. That figure represented nearly one-fifth of the current market value of all traded stocks.

13. Pension funds, the largest institutional investors, occupy a special role in our society. Financed by equal contributions from employers and employees as a fixed percentage of nominal wages, they constitute a form of "forced savings" to protect the living standards of workers after their retirement. At the same time, pension funds possess ideal attributes for long-term financial investments, such as tax exemption, constant inflows, and predictable timing of outflows. By turning workers into shareholders, these funds symbolize a move toward a more "populistic" capitalism. The problem, of course, is that retirement benefits depend on the returns pension funds earn from their investments. A portion of the social wage is thus based on fictitious capital.

14. Drexel's market abuses extended beyond strictly illegal activities. In the absence of any publicly quoted price information on junk bonds, it actively manipulated the pricing of those instruments. For example, it would offer discounts to its own employees and to investors who were willing to hold large positions in certain junk bonds, while selling the same bonds to others at a premium for its own profit. In addition, Drexel set up

a complex cross-financing network in which issuers used some of their borrowed funds to buy each other's junk bonds. For more details on Milken's junk-bond empire and strategies, see James Stewart and Daniel Hertzberg (1988) or Connie Bruck (1988).

15. In January 1989 an FBI sting operation turned up allegations of widespread cheating of customers, market manipulation, fraud, and tax evasion by futures traders at the Chicago Mercantile Exchange and the Chicago Board of Trade. See *Business Week* (1989) or Jeff Bailey and Scott McMurray (1989).

16. Among the most fascinating accounts of the stock market crash and the ultimately successful management of this crisis are James Stewart and Daniel Hertzberg (1987), who won the Pulitzer Price for this article, and Tim Metz (1988). Both analyses argued that the crucial rebound of the MMI index during the lunch hour of October 20 may very well have been the result of a market-rigging effort by key investment banks.

17. At that point interest payments already absorbed an alarming 30 percent of U.S. industry's cash flow. This was several percentage points above the records reached during the worst postwar recessions of 1973–75 and 1979–82.

18. A basic proposition of corporate finance, formulated first in a path-breaking article by Franco Modigliani and Merton Miller (1958), has been that a company's market value depends on its earnings power and not on its financial structure. This only holds true when leverage is moderate. But high levels of debt relative to assets or equity depress a firm's market value, because financial markets become increasingly reluctant to provide additional financing. Therefore, the process of adding debt and removing equity is inherently self-limited.

Chapter 13

1. The earliest evidence of organized, deliberate, long-distance trading dates back to about 11000 B.C., in Western Asia. See the excellent discussion of early signs of trading and its profound repercussions on the social organization of human society in Leon Festinger (1983, ch. 9).

2. It is in this analysis of the monetary effects of the trade balance under a gold standard by David Hume (1752) that we find the first formulation of the Quantity Theory of Money, still the dominant view of money's effects on the economy.

3. Bertil Ohlin (1933), with the help of Eli Heckscher, extended those classical arguments into a general equilibrium framework. In their neoclassical trade theory, countries with different resource endowments are shown to focus on products that use more of those inputs they have in rich supply. Such specialization has the effect of equalizing prices throughout the world. It also maximizes producer efficiency and consumer choice, while breaking down the barriers between nations. For a complete treatment of comparative advantage, see also Charles Kindleberger and Peter Lindert (1978, ch. 2).

4. This "terms of trade" justification for LDC protectionism was first put forward by Raul Prebisch (1959). In this context, see also the hypothesis of "unequal exchange" between less-developed and industrialized economies by Arghiri Emmanuel (1972) and Samir Amin (1974).

5. The concept of "managed" or "fair" trade is particularly popular among the Cambridge Economic Policy Group (e.g., Francis Cripps and Wynne Godley, 1978) advising the British Labour Party, as well as certain post-Keynesian economists (Robert Reich, 1990) and leaders of the Democratic Party (e.g., Richard Gebhardt) in the United States. Such selective protectionism is usually justified as part of a broader industrial policy strategy to help mature industries modernize their outdated structures. The proponents of "strategic trade policy" (e.g., Paul Krugman, 1986), on the other hand, want industrial

policy to be directed toward new high-tech industries in which economies of scale, the learning curve, and entry barriers all play a major role.

6. According to World Bank data, the share of America's nonoil imports subject to such nontariff barriers grew from 17 percent in 1981 to 25 percent in 1986.

7. This latest round of multilateral negotiations among the 106 member countries of GATT was supposed to liberalize trade in services, protect patents and copyrights in technology transfers, and deregulate trade in agricultural products. It broke down when the EC refused U.S. proposals to eliminate subsidies to farmers.

8. John Dunning (1981) presents an excellent review of this "market imperfections" approach. Steven Hymer (1979), on the other hand, explains the MNCs as part of a structural tendency in our economic system toward increasingly concentrated and centralized capital, the view shared by most radical and neo-Marxist economists.

9. These concessions to MNCs have reached their most developed form in the so-called free trade zones (e.g., along the Mexican–U.S. border, or in the coastal provinces of Southeast China), where foreign firms enjoy complete freedom regarding imports, exports, and labor.

10. That power of MNCs may extend to their country of origin. American multinationals have repeatedly shaped foreign policy objectives of the U.S. government. CIA-backed coups against Mossadegh in 1953 in response to his threatened nationalization of Iran's oil industry, against Guatemala's Arbenz in 1954 on behalf of the United Fruit Company, and against Allende in Chile during 1973 after U.S. firms with large holdings there (e.g., ITT, Anaconda, Kennecott) had participated directly in a campaign of destabilization are only a few examples in a long chain of U.S. interventions to protect the interests of its MNCs abroad.

11. See *Business Week* (1986c) and Gerald Epstein (1990) for more details on the negative effects of direct foreign investment by American firms on the U.S. economy. A recent Commerce Department study (see Silvia Nasar, 1991) reported that the streamlining of U.S. manufacturing in the early 1980s revived productivity growth and allowed that sector to regain some of its lost ground in recent years. Its shares of domestic GNP and of world exports are now the same as they were in 1979–80.

12. For these different Monetarist "flow" and "asset market" models of exchange-rate adjustments, see Rudiger Dornbusch (1976), Jacob Frenkel (1976), or Jacob Frenkel and Harry Johnson (1976).

13. In recent years labor has become much more mobile across the globe. Many multinational firms now prefer to hire people with some work experience in other countries or to send managers to overseas subsidiaries as part of their career track. Education, especially on the university level, is increasingly open to foreign students, who often use study abroad as a way to leave their own countries for good. Demographic imbalances in the world, with stagnant and rapidly aging populations in the industrialized world and very rapid population growth in most developing countries, induce huge movements of people from the overpopulated regions into richer areas where labor is scarce.

14. There is a long and rich theoretical tradition, from Thomas Hobbes (1651) to Ralph Miliband (1969) and Nikos Poulantzas (1980), of attempts to specify the political conditions that are necessary for capitalism to function both as a hegemonic system of social organization and as a stable system of economic structures.

15. Robin Murray (1975), in his very interesting analysis of the world economy, has termed this difference between its economic functioning and its political organization "the problem of territorial non-coincidence."

16. Apart from these institutions for international economic management, after the war the United States entered into various security arrangements and military alliances with other industrial nations (e.g., NATO with Western Europe, ANZUS in the Southern

Pacific, Japan) and developing countries (e.g., SEATO in Southeast Asia, OAS in Latin America). Those two structures are complementary, with the U.S. projection of military might itself a means of transferring capital to its compliant allies and influencing the behavior of other governments.

17. In exceptional situations, depending on political conditions at the time, they may also tax luxury consumption by the wealthy. In this context, see the progressively higher value-added taxes on luxury products adopted in many EC countries during the 1980s or the new U.S. tax imposed on certain items of conspicuous consumption (e.g., expensive cars, yachts) under the budget agreement between President Bush and Congress in October 1990.

18. John Maynard Keynes (1943, 1980a), when formulating Britain's bargaining position at the Bretton Woods Conference, argued forcefully that even burden-sharing between deficit and surplus countries was a necessary condition for achieving and maintaining full employment in the world economy.

19. Cheryl Payer (1974, 1982) has given us an important account of how both the IMF and the World Bank operate in the "Third World." Her detailed case studies make it quite clear that the interventions of these institutional agencies often coincide with the interests of the elites in developing countries but by and large fail to promote more even development.

20. Kenneth Dam (1982) provides an interesting account of how rules and other institutional features of the international monetary system have evolved historically.

21. In that situation a holder of gold would sell it in the market, buy silver, and then exchange the silver coins at the mint for a gain. In addition, holders would melt gold coins for their bullion content or export them to a country in which gold was not undervalued. This crowding out of one metal by the other is the famous Gresham's law (see section 4.2).

22. Between 1879 and 1914 Great Britain spent 40 percent of its total investment abroad. Foreign investments absorbed about half of its total current savings, a proportion matched by no nation since then.

Chapter 14

1. From about 5000 B.C. onward, farming gradually turned from a communal activity into a private activity, as land became individual property. By imposing metals as medium of exchange, rulers regained control over the money supply because they owned most of the mines. With technological advances in metal processing during the second millennium it became increasingly easy for skilled craftsmen to produce the rings, arrowheads, or axes which functioned then as the medium of exchange. This led rulers (first the Minoans, then in China, finally in Asia Minor) to introduce state-issued money symbols, from which evolved the metal coin.

2. More details of how the kings of Sumer, Alexander the Great, and the emperors of Rome mismanaged the coinage of metal money can be found in the excellent account of hyperinflations by Max Shapiro (1980, chs. 1, 2).

3. As Robert Mundell (1972) noted, the Islamic silver bloc encircled the Byzantine gold bloc for centuries. Traces of the dinar were found in a great arc stretching from the Pyrenees (on today's Spanish-French border) via Scotland through Scandinavia and the Baltics to Samarkand and along East–West trading routes all the way into northern Africa.

4. See Duncan Innes (1981, p. 12) for more on these certificates as a substitute for gold.

5. Gold had come to play a dominant role in Great Britain much earlier, and by 1792 the country was de facto on a gold standard. The Peel Act of 1819 made that evolution

official. In 1846 Great Britain abandoned its protectionist stance when Parliament repealed the Corn Laws, which had imposed prohibitive tariffs on imported grains thirty years earlier.

6. That management of the international monetary system was based on a complex set of interactions between two separate departments of the Bank of England. Its Issue Department held the central bank's gold; the Bank Department was responsible for the issue of sterling notes. The connection between gold reserves and currency supply was regulated by the coverage provisions of the Bank Charter Act of 1844.

7. The most recent push for a return to a gold standard came shortly after Reagan's election victory from supply-siders, such as Robert Mundell (1981), Arthur Laffer and Charles Kadlec (1981), Lewis Lehrman (1981), and Jude Wanniski (1981).

8. Supply-siders (e.g., Roy Jastram, 1977) have stressed the price "stability" during the nineteenth century as one of the great advantages of the gold standard. In reality prices were anything but stable. They moved up and down. While these movements may have canceled each other out over time, they still represented a great deal of instability.

9. Paper currencies had begun to replace gold coins and bullions a long time ago. Even before 1913 many nations held much of their reserves in currency form (see Peter Lindert, 1969). After 1917, when the Bank of England stopped minting gold sovereigns, currencies came to be widely used as the international medium of exchange in lieu of gold coins. As a result, the share of currencies held by European central banks rose from 12 percent of total reserves in 1913 to 42 percent in 1928 (see Ragnar Nurkse, 1944).

10. For a summary of the debates surrounding this fateful decision, see Donald Winch (1972, ch. 5). The numerous warnings by John Maynard Keynes (1981) against such a step subsequently proved to be valid.

11. See Kenneth Dam (1982, ch. 4) for a detailed account of the Bretton Woods Conference and agreement.

12. Both Harry Magdoff (1969) and Walter Russell Mead (1988) have analyzed this mutually reinforcing connection between orchestrated capital exports and U.S. hegemony under Bretton Woods from a variety of interesting angles.

13. See Robert Guttmann (1985, pp. 3–4) for a more detailed explanation of why payment obligations from buyer to seller need a third party for proper settlement.

14. It should be noted that this net inflow of funds also shows up as a direct increase in the domestic money supply of the surplus country. The key link here is the central bank purchases of foreign exchange in the process. Having the same effect as any open market purchase, these transactions expand bank reserves and thus the money supply. At times the central bank might neutralize ("sterilize") the effect of the inflow on the domestic money supply by counteracting its foreign exchange purchases with simultaneous open-market sales.

15. It was Charles Kindleberger (1985) who coined the phrase "external seigniorage" for windfall gains accruing to the government from the yield spread between short-term liabilities and long-term assets. He chose that term carefully to set it apart from the standard (and purely domestic) definition of seigniorage, which refers to revenue gains for the government from an acceleration of inflation made possible by more rapid money creation.

16. The neoclassical theory of flexible exchange rates has two equilibrium positions. The condition of interest-rate parity applies to asset markets and is short-term, whereas long-run equilibrium applies to purchasing-power parity in the markets for goods and services. The latter condition is assumed to be the dominant one, implying a primacy of commodity markets over asset markets.

17. The degree of confusion among economists about the "correct" (equilibrium) level of exchange rates at any time is beautifully documented in *Business Week* (1988b).

18. The definition of exchange rates as a measure of a country's relative competitiveness corresponds to our notion of money's value developed first in section 5.4. There we argued that the "purchasing power" of money depends on the relationship between productivity and wages prevailing in domestic industry. That ratio, which John Maynard Keynes (1980b, vol. 26, pp. 32–37) termed the "efficiency wage," is both a crucial indicator of economic strength and a principal determinant of the price level.

19. In the forward market anyone can buy or sell currencies for future delivery at a specific price and certain date to lock in a set exchange rate. Options give their holders the right, without obligation, to buy or sell a currency at a predetermined price for a set period of time. Futures are like options, except that the transaction is set for a certain date rather than stretched over an entire period. Warrants allow investors to sell a foreign currency at a set rate to the company that issues the warrant. In swaps, two parties trade obligations in different currencies.

20. Trading rooms of banks and brokers are linked by satellites, transoceanic cables, microwave stations, and fiber optics. Traders watch news and prices on video screens. Computers provide backup accounting, help analyze data to predict market behavior, and run programs that dictate buying and selling. Tape recorders on phone lines record deals. Backup confirmation comes electronically or by telex. The synergy of these various technologies has allowed currency markets to become as large as they are today. See Walter Wriston (1992) for a fascinating study of how technology has transformed foreign-exchange trading in recent years.

21. See Charles Stevens (1987a) or Robert Guenther and Charles Stevens (1988) for some of the problems BankAmerica and Bankers Trust encountered in their foreign-exchange operations.

22. A surplus country is at some point likely to face both external and internal adjustment pressures. Other countries may challenge its neomercantilist obsession with accumulating continuous surpluses. And its workers, wanting to be rewarded for producing these surpluses, will push for more consumption. But such pressure is qualitatively quite different from being subjected to an automatic adjustment mechanism, as was the case under the gold standard.

23. In a fascinating study of what makes nations and industries succeed in the world market, Michael Porter (1990) identified intense competitive pressure as the most important microlevel attribute. Other factors include resource supplies, having a sizable home base of buyers demanding high-quality products, and the development of industry "clusters," in which a free flow of ideas with supplier and related industries promotes innovation.

24. The five leading industrial nations, which together control 42 percent of the IMF's capital (the United States, 19 percent; Germany and Japan, 6 percent each; France and Great Britain, 5.5 percent each), have repeatedly increased its lending capacity as the debt-servicing problems of many LDCs deepened. They have also allowed the IMF to set up new funds for borrowers with special needs and to make longer-term loans coupled with structural adjustment programs.

25. It should be noted that the monetary results of such foreign currency trades are similar to that of open-market operations. Foreign currency sales thus have ceteris paribus a restraining effect on the domestic money supply, which central banks can counteract ("sterilize") by buying government securities.

26. For a theoretical justification of the ideas underlying Baker's proposal, such as the notion of "crawling target zones," see John Williamson (1987b).

27. See Thomas O'Boyle (1987) for a description of currency trading strategies by the German central bank to maximize the impact of its market interventions. Charles Stevens (1987b) documents the steep decline in foreign-exchange profits by large U.S. banks in the aftermath of Louvre.

28. These transactions involved significant losses for the Fed. Its purchases of depreciating currencies caused $511 million in capital losses during 1988; its sales of government securities reduced its net interest income.

29. Purchasing power parity defines an exchange rate at which a currency buys approximately the same amount of goods and services in the domestic market and abroad after having been exchanged for the local money. One reason why it is difficult to determine PPP levels is that relative prices of goods and services differ from country to country, making baskets incomparable.

30. EMS rules require every member country to repay credits granted by other central banks in support of its currency within six months. This keeps cross-border holdings of financial claims small relative to the huge volume of intra-EC trade. For more details about why these conditions do not hold in the international monetary system, see Paul Fabra (1990).

Chapter 15

1. Even such normally pragmatic central bankers as Alan Greenspan (1986) and Paul Volcker (1990) have argued that ideally the world economy would and should have a single currency.

2. There are several versions of Keynes's "Bancor" plan. Earlier drafts of 1941–42 appeared in Keynes (1980a, vol. 25, ch. 1). His official version, published as a White Paper by the British government (see Keynes, 1943; also reprinted in J. Keith Horsefield, 1969, vol. 3), was already watered down to make it more acceptable to the Americans.

3. The stabilization fund was only a sixth of Keynes's clearing union. Moreover, the fund's concept of subscriptions implied a more conservative lending policy than the clearing union's concept of quotas. For more on that difference, see John Maynard Keynes (1980a, ch. 3), as well as Kenneth Dam (1982, pp. 81–84). Marcello de Cecco (1979) analyzes the differences between the Keynes Plan, the White Plan, and the final IMF Articles of Agreement pertaining to capital controls.

4. The "father" of the ITO was James Meade, then economic adviser to the British government, whose proposal for a Commercial Union was adopted by the U.K. Board of Trade in 1942. Keynes played a major role in shaping that proposal and subsequent refinements of the British position on commercial policy. His key contributions on that subject from December 1941 to December 1945 can be found in John Maynard Keynes (1980b, ch. 2).

5. Detailed accounts of the debates and proposals concerning the introduction of SDRs can be found in Group of Ten (1965) and Margaret De Vries (1976).

6. Each country joining the IMF has a quota (or subscription) of monetary assets it must contribute. This quota is a function of its size relative to other countries in terms of trade volume, GNP, and international reserve holdings. Quotas also determine how much countries can borrow from that pool, as well as their voting strength in the IMF's collective decision-making process.

7. For more details on these provisions, see Kenneth Dam (1982, pp. 151–167).

8. The basket-valuation approach is discussed more thoroughly in Jacques Polak (1974, 1979).

9. The United States wanted to keep the new fund small, at about $12 billion, whereas the IMF staff argued that a larger fund of at least $40 billion was needed to make any difference. The parties also failed to agree on who would pay the SDR interest. The EC rejected the U.S. position that the exchange-rate losses suffered by the IMF from any dollar decline should be borne "jointly."

10. On the one hand, SDRs function as numeraire when expressing exchange rates, such as 1 SDR equals 1.35 dollars. On the other hand, when the United States holds, say, 1 billion SDRs, the actual value of these reserve holdings may be quite different from $1.35 billion, irrespective of whether or not the U.S. government kept its currency prices pegged through market intervention. That so-called transaction value depends how the dollar moves in relation to all the other currencies in the basket.

11. See European Communities Monetary Committee (1979, p. 40)

12. When investors abandoned the dollar, they did not move funds equally into all the European currencies. During 1978 they bought especially large amounts of German marks and Swiss francs, causing both currencies to appreciate against French francs or sterling far in excess of what would have been justified by inflation-rate differentials between those countries.

13. This repurchase requirement precludes any seigniorage benefit for deficit countries and allows the adjustment process to work in classical fashion. The problem with the rule is that it applies even in instances which have little to do with the weak-currency countries themselves, such as central bank interventions necessitated by a flight of capital out of dollars and into the strong-currency country.

14. See, for example, Samuel Brittan (1978), who predicted that the compromise proposal would prove too complicated to be managed properly and for this reason would fail to perform well.

15. These adjustments were designed to take account of changes in reserve quantities, gold prices, and dollar exchange rates.

16. For more detail on these original provisions concerning the EMS, see Philip Trezise (1979).

17. That particular currency realignment in March 1983 marked a critical test for the EMS. Central banks and finance ministers wrangled for two days in Brussels over a new set of exchange rates, and at one point France even threatened to withdraw from the system. Finally, a compromise was reached when Germany agreed to revalue the mark by 5.5 percent, while the franc was devalued only by 2.5 percent. In return, the French committed themselves to a policy of sustained austerity.

18. This decision was an effort to revive the EC, which at that point had become bogged down on several fronts (e.g., Great Britain's revolt against its disproportionately large budget contributions, the fiscally burdensome Common Agricultural Policy, prolonged entry negotiations with Portugal and Spain, and a growing inability to make effective decisions).

19. The agreements of Basel and Nyborg provided for more active central bank defense of currencies within existing fluctuation margins and for additional short-term credits to finance this increase in market intervention. Policy coordination among EMS members was improved, using economic indicators as a guide. Finally, reserve holdings of the central banks in the system were to become more diversified, a step designed not least to promote greater use of the ECU.

20. Philip Revzin (1988) discusses the Schmidt-Giscard proposal. The original Delors Plan appeared in European Community Commission (1989). An updated version, which designated the ECU as the single EC-wide currency and proposed setting up a EuroFed at the beginning of 1993, appeared in August 1990 (see European Community Commission, 1990). The Maastricht Treaty proposed a much slower timetable introducing the first stage of the Euro Fed in 1994 and the single currency by 1999.

21. For extensive analyses of the Delors Plan and the supposed advantages of a single-currency zone in Europe, see Alain Jean (1990) and Philippe Jurgensen (1991), as well as Michael Emerson (1991). A survey by Ernst & Young and the National Institute of Economic and Social Research (see Association for the Monetary Union of Europe,

1990) documents in great detail the broad support of EC managers and bankers for the plan.

22. In addition to economic and monetary union, European leaders decided in June 1990 to make the EC a more unified and efficient organization by simplifying its institutional structure, creating greater democratic checks and balances, and facilitating joint decision-making. This so-called political union would eventually include a collective foreign policy and common defense structure for the EC as well.

23. After three catastrophic bouts with hyperinflation in half a century, Germans have become highly sensitive to even minor upticks in domestic inflation. Unlike most other central banks, the Bundesbank is explicitly required by law to maintain the mark's purchasing power.

24. For an interesting discussion of national sovereignty in the context of European monetary integration, see Bernard Schmitt (1988).

25. These specifications for the EuroFed are clearly modeled after the German Bundesbank, especially in terms of political autonomy and the priority given to fighting inflation.

26. These performance criteria include an inflation rate within 1.5 percent of the EC's best national rate, a budget deficit below 3 percent of GDP, a public debt ceiling of 60 percent of GDP, a currency that has not been devalued within the EMS for two years, and long-term interest rates no more than two points above the EC's lowest levels.

27. ECU deposits now exceed $100 billion, and the volume of ECU-denominated bonds has risen above $75 billion (see Candace Cumberbatch, 1989; *Business Week*, 1990). Still, ECUs currently account for less than 2 percent of all EC bank lending. Only 2 percent of EC trade and 5 percent of all Eurobonds are denominated in ECUs.

28. In a monetary union, interest rates are supposed to converge. Once expectations of exchange-rate changes diminish, borrowers will want to borrow in low-interest currencies, while savers seek lending opportunities in high-interest currencies. These market forces will reduce existing interest-rate differentials. "Hot money" flows have the opposite effect and thus threaten to undo one of the key benefits of monetary union.

29. Poorer regions will also lose their ability to become more competitive through currency devaluations and might be more vulnerable to a flight of increasingly mobile capital. The Delors Plan envisaged to compensate underdeveloped regions through grants, but that subsidy plan may end up as messy as the Common Agricultural Policy without fostering more balanced development.

Chapter 16

1. The "target zones" for exchange rates under this experiment have actually reinforced the movement toward distinct monetary blocs. Early efforts to coordinate interest-rate movements have stopped since German reunification and Japan's financial turbulence have put monetary authorities in both countries under a good deal of stress. Initial plans for broader coordination of macroeconomic policy, of the kind envisaged for the second phase of economic and monetary union within the EC, have led nowhere.

2. See Robert Reich (1991) for an excellent discussion of these global production networks and the multinational character of their products.

3. In one of the more interesting analyses of international (credit-)money, Bernard Schmitt (1977, pp. 111–123) has identified this redistributive function as the key characteristic of effective world money.

4. As mentioned earlier, SDRs are issued against a basket of five key currencies from which SDR-holders can draw. These currencies are provided by the leading industrial powers as a budget allocation, much like any official foreign assistance (see section 15.2).

ECUs, on the other hand, are backed by gold and dollar reserves that participating countries managed to accumulate as net gains from previous foreign transactions.

5 For additional details involving the issue of SNCM as simultaneous asset and liability, see Robert Guttmann (1988, pp. 270–82).

6. The creation of new money and the financial intermediation of existing money are two functions that all banks combine. Their institutional separation into two different departments among central banks originated with the reorganization of the Bank of England in 1844.

7. When the speculative bubble burst and stock prices began to decline rapidly during 1990–91, Tokyo's leading brokerage houses shielded their largest domestic clients from losses. That scandal revealed clearly the highly centralized, collusive, and market-manipulating nature of Japan's managerial class.

8. For details of proposals by the Fed, the EC Commission, and the BIS for more effective policing of transnational banks in the wake of the BCCI scandal, see Kenneth Bacon (1991b).

9. During the Civil War, for example, the United States introduced inconvertible fiat money (Greenbacks), national banks with their own standardized notes, and a deficit-financing mechanism. A series of financial panics around the turn of the century led to the creation of the Fed in 1913. World War I gave rise to a modified and less restrictive gold standard. The Great Depression led to the institution of credit-money and comprehensive banking reform. World War II ended with Bretton Woods, which in turn lasted until the Vietnam War.

10. See Andrew Glyn and Bob Sutcliffe (1972), as well as John Eatwell (1981), for more details.

11. Gold used to be the other principal "safe haven" in times of crisis and turbulence. But low inflation and high "real" interest rates have made the precious metal a much less attractive reserve asset in recent years. Moreover, its key producers—South Africa, Russia, and Brazil—have great economic and political difficulties at home, which prompt them to sell off larger quantities of gold. The market is therefore glutted. This situation is likely to continue for some time, not least because new technology has made gold mining much more efficient.

12. Inflation benefits the borrower, because it reduces the effective debt burden by devaluing the principal. A lower dollar (relative to other currencies, especially those of the creditor nations) has the same effect, because America's foreign debt is denominated in its own currency.

Chapter 17

1. A recent study by the Congressional Budget Office, discussed at length by Silvia Nasar (1992), found, on the basis of tax returns, that the richest 1 percent of American families gained 60 percent of the growth in the average after-tax income between 1977 and 1989. They gained an even more amazing 77 percent of the pretax income growth. At the same time, the bottom fifth lost 9 percent, an indication of a dramatic shift in income distribution.

2. A surprisingly large number of governors also treated a one-time revenue gain from asset sales before the phase-out of the tax break on capital gains as if it were a long-term source of additional income. This overestimation of future tax inflows prompted many states to launch long-term capital projects just before the onset of the recession.

3. Lester Thurow (1985), in a very thorough analysis of America's productivity slowdown, likened its many causes to "a thousand small cuts."

4. It should be noted that these international productivity comparisons are based on purchasing-power parity exchange rates to take account of cross-country differences in relative prices. If we use market exchange rates, then our productivity advantage vis-à-vis other industrial nations shrinks considerably.

5. American multinationals often undertake labor-intensive operations, such as assembly, abroad and then reimport the product of these processes at a higher value added. This practice explains much of our trade deficit with Canada, Mexico, and Taiwan. Moreover, the MNCs often set prices in those intra-company transactions so that recorded profits are moved to subsidiaries in low-tax countries (i.e., "transfer pricing").

6. Tax reform should extend to state and local governments, which traditionally have been left with weaker revenue sources. State sales taxes and local property taxes could be replaced by a portion of the federal VAT. If our VAT rate averaged 10 percent, between one-third and one-half of its revenues could be apportioned to the states and municipalities, based on relative needs.

7. Juliet Schor (1992) convincingly documented how much more American families have had to increase their average work time during the last decade.

8. For a more detailed discussion of America's savings shortfall, see Robert Guttmann (1989b).

9. Government institutions making direct loans to private individuals and institutions include the Farmers Home Administration, the Commodity Credit Corporation, the Export-Import Bank, and the Small Business Administration. Loan guarantees are granted by the Federal Housing Administration and the Government National Mortgage Association, among other institutions. The most important government-sponsored agencies empowered to issue their own securities are the Federal National Mortgage Association, the Farm Credit Administration, and the Student Loan Marketing Association. For more details on these credit programs, see Howard Schuman (1988, pp. 178–182).

10. Gar Alperovitz and Jeff Faux (1984) have offered a detailed blueprint for rebuilding America on the basis of community-sustaining economics.

11. For more on "socio-economics," a new alternative to mainstream neoclassical economics which takes account of humans as socially defined and interdependent agents, see Amitai Etzioni and Paul Lawrence (1991).

Acronyms and Abbreviations

ABA	American Bankers Association
ACH	automated clearinghouse
ARM	adjustable-rate mortgage
ASEAN	Association of South East Asian Nations
ATM	automated teller machine
ATS	automatic transfer of savings
BBS	Bevill, Bressler & Schulman
BCCI	Bank of Commerce and Credit International
BHC	bank holding company
BIS	Bank for International Settlements
CD	certificate of deposit
CEBA	Competitive Equality Banking Act
CHIPS	Clearing House Interbank Payments System
CMA	cash management account
CMO	collateralized mortgage obligation
CRA	Community Reinvestment Act
DIA	Depository Institutions Act
DIDC	Depository Institutions Deregulation Committee
DIDMCA	Depository Institutions Deregulation and Monetary Control Act
EC	European Community
ECU	European Currency Unit
EEOC	Equal Employment Opportunity Commission
EFT	electronic funds transfer
EMCF	European Monetary Cooperation Fund
EMF	European Monetary Fund
EMS	European Monetary System
EMU	economic and monetary union
EPA	Environmental Protection Agency
EPIC	Equity Programs Investment Corporation

ERM	Exchange Rate Mechanism
ERTA	Economic Recovery Tax Act
Fannie Mae	Federal National Mortgage Association
FASB	Federal Accounting Standards Board
FCA	Financial Corporation of America
FCS	Farm Credit System
F.D.	financial department of the IMA
FDIC	Federal Deposit Insurance Corporation
FDICIA	Federal Deposit Insurance Corporation Improvement Act
Fed	Federal Reserve System
FHLBB	Federal Home Loan Bank Board
FIRREA	Financial Institutions Reform, Recovery and Enforcement Act
FOMC	Federal Open Market Committee
Freddie Mac	Federal Home Loan Mortgage Corporation
FSLIC	Federal Savings and Loans Insurance Corporation
G–5	Group of Five (France, Germany, Great Britain, Japan, the United States)
G–7	Group of Seven (Canada, France, Germany, Great Britain, Italy, Japan, the United States)
GAB	General Agreements to Borrow
GATT	General Agreement on Tariffs and Trade
GDP	gross domestic product
Ginnie Mae	Government National Mortgage Association
GM	General Motors
GNP	gross national product
IBA	Independent Bankers Association
IBRD	International Bank for Reconstruction and Development (World Bank)
IMA	international monetary authority
IMF	International Monetary Fund
IO	interest only
IRA	Individual Retirement Account
ITO	International Trade Organization
LBO	leveraged buyout
LDCs	less-developed countries
LIBOR	Louston Inter-Bank Offering Rate
LSB	limited-services bank
MCP	management consignment program
M.D.	monetary department of the IMA
MMDA	money-market deposit account
MMI	Major Market Index
MMMF	money-market mutual fund
MNC	multinational corporation

MSB	mutual savings bank
NAFTA	North American Free Trade Agreement
NATO	North Atlantic Treaty Organization
NIF	note issuance facility
NLRB	National Labor Relations Board
NOW	negotiable order of withdrawal
NYSE	New York Stock Exchange
OAS	Organization of American States
OBS	off-balance-sheet
OPEC	Organization of Petroleum Exporting Countries
OSHA	Occupational Safety and Health Administration
PO	principal only
PPP	purchasing-power parity
RAP	regulatory accounting principles
REIT	Real Estate Investment Trust
REMIC	Real Estate Mortgage Investment Conduit
repo	repurchase agreement
RFC	Reconstruction Finance Corporation
RP	repurchase agreement
RPDs	reserves available for private nonbank deposits
RTC	Resolution Trust Corporation
S&L	savings and loan association
SDI	Strategic Defense Initiative
SDRs	Special Drawing Rights
SEATO	Southeast Asia Treaty Organization
SEC	Securities and Exchange Commission
SNCM	supranational credit-money
TNB	transnational bank
UAW	United Auto Workers
VAT	value added tax

Bibliography

Aglietta, Michel (1979), *A Theory of Capitalist Regulation:* The US Experience (New Left Books: London).
―――. (1982), *Regulation and Crisis of Capitalism* (Monthly Review Press: New York).
Alperovitz, Gar, and Jeff Faux (1984), *Rebuilding America: A Blueprint for the New Economy* (Pantheon Books: New York).
Amin, Samir (1974), *Accumulation on a World Scale* (Monthly Review Press: New York).
Anders, George (1987), "Using Rote and Math Wells Fargo Succeeds as a Money Manager," *Wall Street Journal* (3/23).
Ando, Albert, and Alan Auerbach (1988), "The Cost of Capital in the U.S. and Japan: A Comparison," *Journal of the Japanese and International Economies,* 2, pp.134–158.
Andrews, Michael (1984), "Recent Trends in the U.S. Foreign Exchange Market," *Federal Reserve Bank of New York Quarterly Review,* 9(2), pp. 39–47.
Arena, Richard and Augusto Graziani (eds.) (1985), *Production, Circulation, et Monnaie* (Presses Universitaires de France: Paris).
Association for the Monetary Union of Europe (1990), *A Strategy for the Ecu* (Kogan Page: London).
Ayittey, George (1986), "The Real Foreign Debt Problem," *Wall Street Journal* (4/8).
Bacon, Kenneth (1991a), "Panel Criticizes Comptroller in Bank Failures," *Wall Street Journal* (9/9).
―――. (1991b), "Multinational Banks Are Likely to Face Stricter Oversight in U.S. and Europe," *Wall Street Journal* (8/23).
Baecker, Dirk (1988), *Information und Risiko in der Marktwirtschaft* (Information and Risk in the Market Economy) (Suhrkamp: Frankfurt).
Bailey, Jeff, and Scott McMurray (1989), "Futures Shock: Traders Are Indicted for Running the Pits by Their Own Rules," *Wall Street Journal* (8/3).
Bank of England (1986), "The Market in Foreign Exchange in London," *Quarterly Review,* September, pp. 379–382.
Bardos, Jeffrey (1988), "The Risk-based Capital Agreement: A Further Step Towards Policy Convergence," *Federal Reserve Bank of New York Quarterly Review,* 12(4), pp. 26–34.
Bartels, Andrew (1985), "Volcker's Revolution at the Fed," *Challenge,* September-October, pp. 35–42.
Batra, Ravi (1987), *The Great Depression of 1990* (Simon and Schuster: New York).
Berle, Adolf, and Gardiner Means (1932), *The Modern Corporation and Private Property* (Macmillan: New York).

Berton, Lee (1983), "Loose Ledgers: Many Firms Hide Debt to Give Them an Aura of Financial Strength," *Wall Street Journal* (12/13).

————. (1985), "Community S&L's Accounting for 1984 Stirs Wide Debate," *Wall Street Journal* (9/5).

Böhm-Bawerk, Eugen v. (1896), *Zum Abschluss des Marxschen Systems*, translated into English in 1949 by Paul Sweezy as *Karl Marx and the Close of His System* (Augustus Kelley: New York).

Bowen, William (1960), *The Wage-Price Issue: A Theoretical Analysis* (Princeton University Press: Princeton, NJ).

Boyer, Robert (1979), "Wage Formation in Historic Perspective: The French Experience," *Cambridge Journal of Economics*, 3(3), pp. 98–118.

————. (1987), *Labour Flexibility in Europe* (Oxford University Press: Oxford).

————. (1990), "Regulation," in J. Eatwell, M. Milgate, and P. Newman (eds.), *The New Palgrave: Marxian Economics* (Macmillan: London), pp. 331–335.

Boyer, Robert, and Benjamin Coriat (1984), "Les Greenbacks 'Revisités': Innovations dans les Institutions et l'Analyse Monetaires Americaines (1862–1913)," CEPREMAP mimeo no. 8420, Paris.

Brimmer, Andrew (1971), "The Political Economy of Money: Evolution and Impact of Monetarism in the Federal Reserve System," *American Economic Review*, 61, pp. 344–352.

Brittan, Samuel (1978), "EMS: A Compromise That Could Be Worse than Either Extreme," *The World Economy*, 2, pp. 1–30.

Bruck, Connie (1988), *The Predators' Ball* (Simon and Schuster: New York).

Brunner, Karl, and Alan Meltzer (eds.) (1982), *Monetary Regimes and Protectionism* (North-Holland: Amsterdam).

————. (1985), *Understanding Monetary Regimes* (North-Holland: Amsterdam).

Bryan, Lowell (1991), *Bankrupt: Restoring the Health and Profitability of Our Banking System* (HarperCollins: New York).

Business Week (1980), "A Sensitive Plan to Stabilize Rates" (9/8).

————. (1982a), *The Reindustrialization of America* (McGraw-Hill: New York).

————. (1982b), "Electronic Banking" (1/18).

————. (1983), "An Exodus of Capital Is Sapping the LDC Economies" (10/3).

————. (1984), "The First Nationwide Bank Is Already Here" (1/9).

————. (1985a), "What Did Hutton's Managers Know—And When Did They Know It?" (5/20).

————. (1985b), "Playing With Fire" (9/16).

————. (1986a), "Banking's Balance of Power Is Tilting Towards the Regionals" (4/7).

————. (1986b), "Is This Any Way to Run an Investment Bank? Citibank Thinks So" (7/28).

————. (1986c), "The Hollow Corporation" (3/3).

————. (1988a), "Bankers Trust Could Beat the Street at Its Own Game" (4/4).

————. (1988b), "Oh, Dear, Where Should the Dollar Be?" (7/4).

————. (1989), "Life In the Pits Will Never Be the Same" (2/6).

————. (1990), "Will the Franc, the Lira, and the Pound Become Collectors' Items?" (10/1).

Canto, Victor, David Joines, and Arthur Laffer (eds.) (1983), *Foundations of Supply-Side Economics: Theory and Evidence* (Academic Press: New York).

Carrington, Tim (1980), "Diversified Offering: Merrill Lynch Expands from Stocks to Gamut of Financial Services," *Wall Street Journal* (9/10).

————. (1982), "Cash Management Accounts Proliferating As Banks, Brokers Vie for People's Money," *Wall Street Journal* (11/15).

————. (1986), "Pentagon Contracts Offer High Profits, GAO Study Finds," *Wall Street Journal* (12/24).

Chamberlin, Edward (1933), *The Theory of Monopolistic Competition* (Harvard University Press: Cambridge, MA).

Charlier, Marj (1985), "Farm Fallout: Rural Crisis May Hurt Rest of the Economy, Many Experts Believe," *Wall Street Journal* (12/24).

Clower, Richard (1967), "A Reconsideration of the Microfoundations of Monetary Theory," *Western Economic Journal*, 6(1), pp. 1–9.

Conte, Christopher (1983), "Country Cousins: Small-Town Bankers Fight to Keep Curbs on Big Rivals' Growth," *Wall Street Journal* (6/3).

Cooper, Richard (1982), "The Gold Standard: Historical Facts and Future Prospects," *Brookings Papers on Economic Activity*, no.1, pp. 1–56.

Corrigan, Gerald (1987a), *Financial Market Structure: A Longer View* (Federal Reserve Bank of New York: New York).

————. (1987b), "A Perspective on the Globalization of Financial Markets and Institutions," *Federal Reserve Bank of New York Quarterly Review*, 12(1), pp. 1–9.

Cripps, Francis, and Wynne Godley (1978), "Control of Imports as a Means to Full Employment and the Expansion of World Trade: the UK Case," *Cambridge Journal of Economics*, 2(3), pp. 327–334.

Cumberbatch, Candace (1989), "European Currency Unit Finds Favor as EC Nations Topple Trade Barriers," *Wall Street Journal* (8/28).

Cumming, Christine (1987), "The Economics of Securitization," *Federal Reserve Bank of New York Quarterly Review*, 12(3), pp. 11–23.

Dam, Kenneth (1982), *The Rules of the Game: Reform and Evolution in the International Monetary System* (University of Chicago Press: Chicago).

D'Arista, Jane (1991), "No More Bank Bailouts: A Proposal for Deposit Insurance Reform," Briefing Paper, Economic Policy Institute, Washington, DC.

Davidson, Paul (1978), *Money in the Real World*, 2d ed. (Macmillan: London).

————. (1986), "A Post Keynesian View of Theories and Causes for High Real Interest Rates," *Thames Papers in Political Economy*, London (UK).

Davis, Richard (1986), "The Recent Performance of the Commercial Banking Industry," *Federal Reserve Bank of New York Quarterly Review*, 11(2), pp. 1–11.

Debreu, Gerard (1959), *Theory of Value: An Axiomatic Analysis of Economic Equilibrium* (Wiley: New York).

De Brunhoff, Suzanne (1978), *The State, Capital and Economic Policy* (Pluto Press: London).

————. (1990), "Fictitious Capital," in J. Eatwell, M. Milgate, and P. Newman (eds.) *The New Palgrave: Marxian Economics* (Macmillan: London), pp. 186–187.

De Cecco, Marcello (1979), "Origins of the Post-War Payments System," *Cambridge Journal of Economics*, 3(1), pp. 49–61.

De Vries, Margaret (1976), *The International Monetary Fund, 1966–1971* (International Monetary Fund: Washington, DC).

De Vroey, Michel (1984), "A Regulation Approach Interpretation of the Contemporary Crisis," *Capital and Class*, no. 23, pp. 45–66.

Dewey, David (1903), *Financial History of the United States* (New York).

Dornbusch, Rudiger (1976), "Expectations and Exchange Rate Dynamics," *Journal of Political Economy*, 84(6), pp. 1161–1176.

Dunning, John (1981), *International Production and the Multinational Enterprise* (Allen and Unwin: London).

Earley, James, and Gary Evans (1982), "The Problem Is Bank Liability Management," *Challenge*, January-February, pp. 54–56.

Eatwell, John (1981), *Whatever Happened to Britain?* (Duckworth: London).

Ehrbar, Aloysius (1985), "Facts vs. the Furor over Farm Policy," *Fortune* (11/11).

Einzig, Paul, and Brian Quinn (1977), *The Eurodollar System* (St. Martin's Press: New York).

Emerson, Michael (1991), *The ECU Report* (Pan Books: London).

Emmanuel, Arghiri (1972), *Unequal Exchange* (New Left Books: London).

Epstein, Gerald (1990), "Mortgaging America: Debt, Lies and Multinationals," *World Policy Journal*, 8(1), pp. 27–59.

Etzioni, Amitai, and Paul Lawrence (1991), *Socio-Economics: Toward a New Synthesis* (M. E. Sharpe: Armonk, NY).

European Communities Monetary Committee (1979), *Compendium of Community Monetary Texts* (European Economic Community: Brussels).

European Community Commission (1989), *Report on Economic and Monetary Union in the European Community* (Brussels).

————. (1990), *Economic and Monetary Union: The Economic Rationale and Design of the System* (Brussels).

Fabra, Paul (1990), "Stop Fine-Tuning the Global Economy," *Wall Street Journal* (5/2).

Fama, Eugene (1970), "Efficient Capital Markets: A Review of Theory and Empirical Work," *Journal of Finance*, 25(2), pp. 383–417.

Fama, Eugene, and Kenneth French (1988), "Permanent and Temporary Components of Stock Prices," *Journal of Political Economy*, 96(1), pp. 246–73.

Fay, Steven (1984), "Central Bankers Have a Hot Line Too," *Fortune* (10/1).

Festinger, Leon (1983), *The Human Legacy* (Columbia University Press: New York).

Findlay, Chapman, and Edward Williams (1985), "A Post Keynesian View of Modern Financial Economics: In Search of Alternative Paradigms," *Journal of Business Finance and Accounting*, 12(1), pp. 1–18.

Fisher, Irving (1911), *The Purchasing Power of Money: Its Determination and Relation to Credit, Interest, and Crises* (Macmillan: New York).

Fitch, Robert, and Martin Oppenheimer (1970), "Who Rules the Corporations?" *Socialist Revolution*, 1 (4–6).

Ford, Henry (1926), *My Life and Work* (Garden City Publishing Co.: Garden City, NY).

Frank, Robert (1988), *Passions Within Reason: The Strategic Role of the Emotions* (Norton: New York).

Frenkel, Jacob (1976), "A Monetary Approach to the Exchange Rate: Doctrinal Aspects and Empirical Evidence," *Scandinavian Journal of Economics*, 78(2), pp. 200–224.

Frenkel, Jacob, and Harry Johnson (eds.) (1976), *The Monetary Approach to the Balance of Payments* (Allen and Unwin: London).

Frieden, Jeffry (1987), *Banking on the World: The Politics of American International Finance* (Harper and Row: New York).

Friedman, Milton (1953), "The Case for Flexible Exchange Rates," in M. Friedman, *Essays in Positive Economics* (University of Chicago Press: Chicago). pp. 157–203.

————. (1956), *Studies in the Quantity Theory of Money* (University of Chicago Press: Chicago).

————. (1968), "The Role of Monetary Policy," *American Economic Review*, 58(1), pp. 1–17.

————. (1970), "A Theoretical Framework for Monetary Analysis," *Journal of Political Economy*, 78(1), pp. 193–238.

Friedman, Milton, and Anne Schwartz (1963a), *A Monetary History of the United States 1867–1960* (Princeton University Press: Princeton, NJ).

————. (1963b), "Money and Business Cycles," *Review of Economics and Statistics*, 45(1), pp. 32–64.

Frydl, Edward (1982), "The Eurodollar Conundrum," *Federal Reserve Bank of New York Quarterly Review*, 7(1), pp. 11–19.

Galbraith, John Kenneth (1954), *The Great Crash: 1929* (Houghton Mifflin: Boston).

————. (1967), *The New Industrial State* (Houghton Mifflin: Boston).

Garvy, George (1943), "Kondratieff's Theory of Long Cycles," *Review of Economic Statistics*, 25(4), pp. 203–220.

Giddy, Ian (1979), "Measuring the World Foreign Exchange Market," *Columbia Journal of World Business*, 14(4), pp. 36–48.

Glyn, Andrew, and Bob Sutcliffe (1972), *British Capitalism, Workers, and the Profits Squeeze* (Penguin: Harmondsworth, UK).

Goodwin, Richard (1967), "A Growth Cycle," in C. H. Feinstein (ed.), *Capitalism and Economic Growth* (Cambridge University Press: Cambridge, UK), pp. 54–58.

Graziani, Augusto (1989), "The Theory of the Monetary Circuit," *Thames Papers in Political Economy*, London.

Green, Mark, and Glenn von Nostitz (1992), "Survival of the Fattest? Bank Mergers Are Taxing Consumers," *Nation* (1/27).

Greenhouse, Steven (1992), "I.M.F. Is Found to Spur Growth, at Social Cost," *New York Times* (3/10).

Greenspan, Alan (1986), "Coordination Could Be Washed Out," *Wall Street Journal* (7/10).

Greider, William (1988), *Secrets of the Temple: How the Federal Reserve Runs the Country* (Simon and Schuster: New York).

Group of Ten (1965), *Report of the Study Group on the Creation of Reserve Assets* (Ossola Report), Washington, DC.

Guenther, Robert, and Charles Stevens (1988), "Bankers Trust Foreign Exchange Woes Are Tied to Intricate Trading Strategy," *Wall Street Journal* (7/22).

Gurley, John, and Edward Shaw (1957), "The Growth of Debt and Money in the United States, 1800–1950: A Suggested Interpretation," *Review of Economics and Statistics*, 39, pp. 250–263.

————(1960), *Money in a Theory of Finance* (Brookings Institution: Washington, DC).

Guttentag, Jack (1966), "The Strategy of Open Market Operations," *Quarterly Journal of Economics*, 80(1), pp. 1–30.

Guttmann, Robert (1984), "Stagflation and Credit-Money in the USA," *British Review of Economic Issues*, 6(15), pp. 79–119.

————. (1985), "Crisis and Reform of the International Monetary System," *Thames Papers in Political Economy*, London.

————. (1987), "Changing of the Guard at the Fed," *Challenge*, November-December, pp. 4–9.

————. (1988), "Crisis and Reform of the International Monetary System," in P. Arestis (ed.), *Post-Keynesian Monetary Economics: New Approaches to Financial Modelling* (E. Elgar: London), pp. 251–299.

————. (1989a), "World Money and International Economic Relations," in W. Vaeth (ed.), *Political Regulation in the 'Great Crisis'* (Ed. Sigma: Berlin), pp. 71–89.

————. (1989b), "The Saving Shortfall Reconsidered," *Challenge*, September-October, pp. 47–51.

————. (1989c), *Reforming Money and Finance: Institutions and Markets in Flux* (M. E. Sharpe: Armonk, NY).

————. (1989d), "The Socio-Economic Foundations of Financial Accounting," *British Review of Economic Issues*, 11(24), pp. 75–102.

————. (1990), "The Regime of Credit-Money and Its Current Transition," *Économies et Societes*, 24(6), pp. 81–105.

Hahn, Frank (1973), "On the Foundations of Monetary Theory," in M. Parkin and A. Nobay (eds.), *Essays in Modern Economics* (Longmans: London), pp. 230–242.

————. (1983), *Money and Inflation* (MIT Press: Cambridge, MA).

Hansen, Alvin (1941), *Fiscal Policy and Business Cycles* (Norton: New York).

Hardouvelis, Gikas (1988), "Evidence on Stock Market Speculative Bubbles: Japan, the United States, and Great Britain," *Federal Bank of New York Quarterly Review*, 13(2), pp. 4–16.

Harris, Lawrence (1981), *Monetary Theory* (McGraw-Hill: New York).

Hatsopoulos, George, and Stephen Brooks (1986), "The Gap in the Cost of Capital: Causes, Effects, and Remedies," in R. Landau and Dale Jorgensen (eds.), *Technology and Economic Policy* (Ballinger: Cambridge, MA), pp. 221–280.

Hatsopoulos, George, Paul Krugman, and Lawrence Summers (1990), "U.S. Competitiveness: Beyond the Trade Deficit," in Philip King (ed.), *International Economics and International Economic Policy: A Reader* (McGraw-Hill: New York), pp. 108–137.

Havrilevsky, Thomas, and John Boorman (eds.) (1980), *Current Perspectives in Banking: Operations, Management, and Regulation* (AHM Publishing: Arlington Heights, IL).

Hayek, Friedrich (1939), *Profits, Interest, and Investment* (Routledge: London).

Hector, Gary (1983), "The Banks Invade Wall Street," *Fortune* (2/7).

————. (1985), "Nervous Money Keeps On Flowing," *Fortune* (12/23).

————. (1988), "How Banking Will Shake Out," *Fortune* (4/25).

Heinsohn, Gunnar, and Otto Steiger (1983), "Private Property, Debts, and Interest, or: The Origins of Money and the Rise and Fall of Monetary Economies," *Studi Economici*, (38)3.

Henning, Charles, William Pigott, and Robert Scott (1978), *Financial Markets and the Economy* (Prentice-Hall: Englewood Cliffs, NJ).

Hertzberg, Daniel (1983), "Interstate Banking Spreads Rapidly Despite Laws Restricting Practice," *Wall Street Journal* (12/19).

————. (1984), "Lack of Balance: Smaller Customers Get Less Service at Banks and Pay More Charges," *Wall Street Journal* (10/18).

Hicks, John (1935), "A Suggestion for Simplifying the Theory of Money," *Economica*, 2(1), pp. 1–19.

————. (1937), "Mr. Keynes and the 'Classics': A Suggested Interpretation," *Econometrica*, 5(1), pp. 147–159.

Hilferding, Rudolf (1985), *Finance Capital* (Routledge and Kegan Paul: London), first published in German in 1910.

Hill, Christian, and John Andrew (1982), "U.S. Expected to Cut Costly Efforts to Force Mergers of Troubled S and Ls," *Wall Street Journal* (2/17).

Hill, Christian, and Paulette Thomas (1989), "New Fiscal Game: Big Thrift-Rescue Bill Is Likely to Realign the Financial System," *Wall Street Journal* (8/7).

Hirtle, Beverly (1987), "The Growth of the Financial Guarantee Market," *Federal Reserve Bank of New York Quarterly Review*, 12(1), pp. 10–28.

Hobbes, Thomas (1651), *Leviathan*, ed. C. B. MacPherson (Penguin: Harmondsworth, UK, 1968).

Horsefield, J. Keith (1969), *The International Monetary Fund, 1945–1965* (International Monetary Fund: Washington, DC).

Hume, David (1752), "Of Money" and "Of the Balance of Trade" in D. Hume, *Essays, Moral, Political and Literary*, reprinted in 1875, (Longmans, Green: London).

Humphrey, Thomas (1979), "Some Current Controversies in the Theory of Inflation," in Federal Reserve Bank of New York, *Federal Reserve Readings on Inflation*, pp. 114–125.

Hymer, Steven (1979), *The Multinational Corporation* (Cambridge University Press: Cambridge, UK).

Innes, Duncan (1981), "Capitalism and Gold," *Capital and Class*, 14, pp. 8–35.

International Monetary Fund (1981), *International Financial Statistics—Yearbook* (Washington, DC).

Jastram, Roy (1977), *The Golden Constant: The English and American Experience, 1560–1976* (John Wiley and Sons: New York).

Jean, Alain (1990), *L'Ecu, le SME et les Marches Financiers* (The Ecu, the EMS and Financial Markets) (Les Editions d'Organisation: Paris).

Jevons, William Stanley (1871), *Theory of Political Economy* (Macmillan: London).

Johnson, Harry (1972a), *Inflation and the Monetarist Controversy* (North-Holland: Amsterdam).

———. (1972b), "The Case for Flexible Exchange Rates, 1969," in H. Johnson, *Further Essays in Monetary Economics* (Harvard University Press: Cambridge, MA).

Johnson, Leland (1960), "The Theory of Hedging and Speculation in Commodity Futures," *Review of Economic Studies*, 27, pp. 139–151.

Jurgensen, Philippe (1991), *ECU, Naissance d'Une Monnaie* (ECU, Birth of a Currency (J. C. Lattes: Paris).

Kaldor, Nicholas (1939), "Speculation and Economic Stability," *Review of Economic Studies*, 7, pp.1–27.

———. (1955), "Alternative Theories of Distribution," *Review of Economic Studies*, 23, pp. 83–100.

Kalecki, Michal (1938), "The Determinants of Distribution," *Econometrica*, 6, pp. 97–112.

———. (1939), *Essays in the Theory of Economic Fluctuations* (Allen and Unwin: London).

———. (1942), "A Theory of Profits," *Economic Journal*, 52, pp. 258–267.

———. (1954), *Theory of Economic Dynamics*, (Allen and Unwin: London).

———. (1971), *Selected Essays on the Dynamics of the Capitalist Economy, 1933–1970* (Cambridge University Press: Cambridge, UK).

Kane, Edward (1981), "Impact of Regulation on Economic Behavior: Accelerating Inflation, Technological Innovation, and the Decreasing Effectiveness of Banking Regulation," *Journal of Finance*, 36(2), pp. 355–367.

Kaufman, Henry (1986), *Interest Rates, the Markets, and the New Financial World* (Times Books: New York).

Kennedy, Paul (1987), *The Rise and Fall of the Great Powers: Economic Change and Military Conflict from 1500 to 2000* (Random House: New York).

Kessler, Felix (1984), "Here Come the Regional Superbanks," *Fortune* (12/10).

Keynes, John Maynard (1913), *Indian Currency and Finance* (Macmillan: London).

———. (1919), *The Economic Consequences of the Peace* (Macmillan: London).

———. (1923), *Tract on Monetary Reform* (Macmillan: London).

———. (1930a), *A Treatise on Money* (Macmillan: London).

———. (1930b), "Economic Possibilities for Our Grandchildren," reprinted in J. M. Keynes, *The Collected Writings of John Maynard Keynes* (Macmillan: London), vol. XI, 1973, pp. 321–332.

———. (1936), *The General Theory of Employment, Interest, and Money* (Macmillan: London).

———. (1937), "Alternative Theories of the Rate of Interest," *Economic Journal*, 47(186), pp. 241–252.

———. (1943), *Proposals for an International Clearing Union*, Cmnd. 6437, London.

———. (1979), *The Collected Writings of John Maynard Keynes, vol. 29: The General Theory and After: A Supplement*, ed. by D. Moggridge (Macmillan: London).

———. (1980a), *The Collected Writings of John Maynard Keynes, vol. 25: Activities 1940–1944: Shaping the Post-War World, The Clearing Union*, ed. by D. Moggridge, (Macmillan: London).

———. (1980b), *The Collected Writings of John Maynard Keynes, vol. 26: Activities*

1941–1946: Shaping the Post-War, Bretton Woods and Reparations, ed. by D. Moggridge, (Macmillan: London).

————. (1981), *The Collected Writings of John Maynard Keynes, vol. 19, Activities 1922–29: The Return to Gold and Industrial Policy*, ed. by D. Moggridge, (Macmillan: London).

Kidwell, David, and Richard Peterson (1984), *Financial Institutions, Markets, and Money*, 2d ed. (Dryden Press: New York).

Kindleberger, Charles (1973), *The World in Depression, 1929–39* (University of California Press: Berkeley, CA).

————. (1978), *Manias, Panics, and Crashes* (Basic Books: New York).

————. (1985), "The Dollar Yesterday, Today, and Tomorrow," *Banca Nazionale del Lavoro Quarterly Review*, no. 155, pp. 295–308.

Kindleberger, Charles, and Peter Lindert (1978), *International Economics*, 6th ed. (Irwin: Homewood, IL).

Knox, John J. (1903), *A History of Banking in the United States* (Bradford Rhodes and Co.: New York).

Kondratieff, Nikolai (1926), "Die Langen Wellen der Konjunktur" *Archiv für Sozialwissenschaft und Sozialpolitik*, 56(3), pp. 573–610.

Kotz, David (1978), *Bank Control of Large Corporations in the United States* (University of California Press: Berkeley).

Krugman, Paul (1986), *Strategic Trade Policy and the New International Economics* (MIT Press: Cambridge, MA).

Laffer, Arthur, and Charles Kadlec (1981), "The Point of Linking Dollar to Gold," *Wall Street Journal* (10/13).

Laidler, David (1976), "Expectations and the Phillips Trade Off: A Commentary," *Scottish Journal of Political Economy*, 23(1), pp. 55–72.

Lavoie, Marc (1984), "The Endogenous Flow of Money and the Post Keynesian Theory of Money," *Journal of Economic Issues*, 18(4), pp. 771–797.

————. (1985), "Credit and Money: The Dynamic Circuit, Overdraft Economics, and Post-Keynesian Economics," in Mark Jarsulic (ed.), *Money and Macro-Policy* (Kluwer-Nijhoff: Dordrecht, Netherlands).

Lehrman, Lewis (1981), "The Case of the Gold Standard," *Wall Street Journal* (7/30).

Lindert, Peter (1969), *Key Currencies and Gold, 1900–1913*, Princeton Studies in International Finance, no. 24 (Princeton, NJ).

Lipietz, Alain (1985), *The Enchanted World: Inflation, Credit, and The World Crisis* (Verso: London).

————. (1987), *Mirages and Miracles: The Crises of Global Fordism* (Verso: London).

Lipin, Steven and Marj Charlier (1992), "Gathering Stream: As National Banking Nears, Mergers Sweep Across State Borders," *Wall Street Journal* (6/22).

Litan, Robert (1987), *What Should Banks Do?* (Brookings Institution: Washington, DC).

Luxemburg, Rosa (1951), *The Accumulation of Capital* (Routledge and Kegan Paul: London).

Magdoff, Harry (1969), *The Age of Imperialism* (Monthly Review Press: New York).

Magee, Stephen (1973), "Currency Contracts, Pass-Throughs and Devaluation," *Brookings Papers in Economic Activity*, 1, pp. 303–325.

Malkiel, Burton (1973), *A Random Walk Down Wall Street* (Norton: New York)

Mandel, Ernest (1968), *Marxist Economic Theory* (Merlin: London).

————. (1975), *Late Capitalism* (New Left Books: London).

Marshall, Alfred (1890), *Principles of Economics* (Macmillan: London).

Marx, Karl (1867), *Das Kapital*, vol. 1 (Meissner: Hamburg).

————. (1967), *Capital*, vols. 1–3 (International Publishers: New York), first published in German in 1867, 1885, and 1894 respectively.

―――. (1968), *Theories of Surplus-Value*, vol. 2 (Progress Publishers: Moscow), first published in German in 1905–10.

McCoy, Charles, (1985), "Out of Options: Farm Credit System, Buried in Bad Loans, Seeks Big U.S. Bailout," *Wall Street Journal* (9/4).

―――. (1987), "Deterioration of Nation's Farm Banks Continues Apace, Latest Fed Data Show," *Wall Street Journal* (2/11).

McCoy, Charles, and Marj Charlier (1985), "Banks Give Farmers Loans and Pray for Bailout," *Wall Street Journal* (6/6).

McKinnon, Ronald (1984), *An International Standard for Monetary Stabilization* (Institute for International Economics: Washington, DC).

Mead, Walter Russell (1988), "The United States and the World Economy: From Bretton Woods to the Bush Team," *World Policy Journal*, 6(1), pp. 1–45.

―――. (1989), "The United States and the World Economy, Part II," *World Policy Journal*, 6(3), pp. 385–468.

Meade, James (1966), "Exchange-Rate Flexibility," *Three Banks Review*, no. 70, pp. 3–27.

Menger, Carl (1871), *Grundsaetze der Volkswirtschaftslehre* (Foundations of Macroeconomic Theory) (Braumueller: Vienna).

Metz, Tim (1988), *Black Monday: The Catastrophe of October 19, 1987 . . . And Beyond* (William Morrow: New York).

Miles, Marc (1984), *Beyond Monetarism: Finding the Road to Stable Money* (Basic Books: New York).

Miliband, Ralph (1969), *The State in Capitalist Society* (Weidenfeld & Nicholson: London).

Minsky, Hyman (1964), "Longer Waves in Financial Relations: Financial Factors in the More Severe Depressions," *American Economic Review*, 54(3), pp. 324–355.

―――. (1975), *John Maynard Keynes* (Columbia University Press: New York).

―――. (1982), *Can 'It' Happen Again?* (M. E. Sharpe: Armonk, NY).

Mitchell, Wesley (1903), *A History of Greenbacks* (University of Chicago Press: Chicago).

―――. (1908), *Gold, Prices, and Wages under the Greenbacks Standard* (University of California Press: Berkeley).

Modigliani, Franco, and Merton Miller (1958), "The Cost of Capital, Corporation Finance, and the Theory of Investment," *American Economic Review*, 48(2), pp. 261–297.

Moffit, Michael (1983), *The World's Money: International Banking from Bretton Woods to the Brink of Insolvency* (Simon and Schuster: New York).

Monroe, Ann (1985), "Financial Ploys: Companies Now Get Funds Through Array of Arcane Maneuvers," *Wall Street Journal* (1/16).

―――. (1986a), "Mortgage-Backed Bond Innovations Are Proliferating," *Wall Street Journal* (10/29).

―――. (1986b), "New Era Dawns for Market in Mortgage-Backed Issues," *Wall Street Journal* (11/10).

Mundell, Robert (1972), "The International Financial System," in A. Acheson and others (eds.), *Bretton Woods Revisited* (University of Toronto Press: Torontc), pp. 91–104.

―――. (1981), "Gold Would Serve into the 21st Century," *Wall Street Journal* (9/30).

Murray, Robin (1975), "The Internationalisation of Capital and the Nation State," in H. Radice (cd.), *International Firms and Modern Imperialism* (Penguin: Harmondsworth, UK), pp. 107–134.

Muth, John (1961), "Rational Expectations and the Theory of Price Movements," *Econometrica*, 29, pp. 315–335.

Myerson, Allen (1992), "Currency Markets Resisting Powers of Central Banks," *New York Times* (9/25).

Nasar, Silvia (1991), "American Revival in Manufacturing Seen in U.S. Report," *New York Times* (2/5).

————. (1992), "The 1980s: A Very Good Time for the Very Rich," *New York Times* (3/5).

Nash, Nathaniel (1989), "Totaling Up the Thrift Bailout Plan," *New York Times* (8/27).

Norman, Peter (1983), "Banks Reduce Lending to the Third World amid Rising Concern over Debt Problems," *Wall Street Journal* (1/19).

Nurkse, Ragnar (1944), *International Currency Experience: Lessons of the Interwar Period* (League of Nations: Geneva).

O'Boyle, Thomas (1987), "Bundesbank Trader Still Has Currency-Market Clout," *Wall Street Journal* (3/26).

Ohlin, Bertil (1933), *Interregional and International Trade* (Harvard University Press: Cambridge, MA).

Okun, Arthur (1975), "Inflation: Its Mechanics and Welfare Costs," *Brookings Papers on Economic Activity*, 6(2), pp. 351–390.

Panico, Carlo (1980), "Marx's Analysis of the Relationship Between the Rate of Interest and the Rate of Profits," *Cambridge Journal of Economics*, 4, pp. 363–378.

Parguez, Alain (1975), *Monnaie et Macroeconomie* (Economica: Paris).

————. (1981), "Ordre social, Monnaie, et Regulation," *Économie Appliquée*, 34(2–3), pp. 383–448.

————. (1984), "La Dynamique de la Monnaie," *Économies et Sociétés*, 18(4), pp. 83–118.

Pasinetti, Luigi (1962), "Rate of Profit and Income Distribution in Relation to the Rate of Economic Growth," *Review of Economic Studies*, 29, pp. 267–279.

Patinkin, Don (1965), *Money, Interest, and Prices*, 2d ed. (Harper and Row: New York).

Payer, Cheryl (1974), *The Debt Trap: The International Monetary Fund and the Third World* (Monthly Review Press: New York).

————. (1982), *The World Bank: A Critical Analysis* (Monthly Review Press: New York).

Pearce, Ivor, and William Hogan (1982), *The Incredible Eurodollar* (Allen and Unwin: London).

Petit, Pascal (1986), *Slow Growth and the Service Economy* (Frances Pinter: London).

Phelps, Edmund (1967), "Phillips Curves, Expectations of Inflation, and Optimal Unemployment over Time," *Economica*, 34(3), pp. 254- 281.

Phillips, A. W. (1958), "The Relation Between Unemployment and the Rate of Change in Money Wage Rates in the United Kingdom, 1861–1957," *Economica*, 25(4), pp. 283–299.

Pine, Art (1982), "Leery Lenders: Uneasy Western Banks Pulling Back on Loans to the Poorer Nations," *Wall Street Journal* (7/1).

————. (1983), "Extra Duty: Fed's Chief Took on Big Role in Attacking World's Financial Ills," *Wall Street Journal* (3/14).

————. (1987), "Rescue Operation: Farm Credit System Seems Certain to Win Huge Federal Bailout," *Wall Street Journal* (7/3).

Polak, Jacques (1974), *Valuation and Rate of Interest of the SDR*, IMF Pamphlet Series no. 18 (International Monetary Fund: Washington, DC).

————. (1979), "The SDR as a Basket of Currencies," *IMF Staff Papers*, 26(4), pp. 627–653.

Poole, William (1976), "Rational Expectations in the Micro Model," *Brookings Papers on Economic Activity*, 2, pp. 436–505.

Porter, Michael (1990), *The Competitive Advantage of Nations* (Free Press: New York).

Poulantzas, Nikos (1980), *State, Power, Socialism* (New Left Books: London).

Poulon, Frederic (1982), *Macroeconomie Approfondie* (Advanced Macroeconomics) (Cujas: Paris).

Pound, Edward (1986), "Defense Contractors Repeatedly Deceive U.S., Reap Windfall Profits, Panel Says," *Wall Street Journal* (5/7).

Prebisch, Raúl (1959), "Commercial Policy in the Underdeveloped Countries," *American Economic Review*, 49(2), pp. 251–273.

Quint, Michael (1981), "Taming the Renegade Money Supply," *New York Times* (12/20).

Reich, Robert (1990), "We Need a Strategic Trade Policy," *Challenge*, July-August, pp. 38–42.

———. (1991), *The Work of Nations: Preparing Ourselves for 21st Century Capitalism* (Knopf: New York).

Reijnders, Jan (1990), *Long Waves in Economic Development* (Edward Elgar: Aldershot, UK).

Revzin, Paul (1988), "Fathers of Europe's Monetary System Push Creation of a Joint Central Bank," *Wall Street Journal* (2/23).

Ricardo, David (1817), *Principles of Political Economy and Taxation* (J. Murray: London).

Riemer, Bianca (1985), "Liberty, Justice, and Bank Accounts for All?" *Business Week* (7/1).

Roberts, Paul Craig (1989), "Investment Is Fine—It's the Critics Who Are Wrong," *Business Week* (8/21).

Robinson, Joan (1933), *The Economics of Imperfect Competition* (Macmillan: London).

———. (1956), *The Accumulation of Capital* (Macmillan: London).

Rosenberg, Sam, and Tom Weisskopf (1981), "A Conflict Theory Approach to Inflation in the Postwar U.S. Economy," *American Economic Review*, 71(2), pp. 42–47.

Rousseas, Stephen (1986), *Post Keynesian Monetary Economics* (M. E. Sharpe: Armonk, NY).

Rowthorn, Robert (1977), "Conflict, Inflation, and Money," *Cambridge Journal of Economics*, 1(3), pp. 215–239.

Sandler, Linda (1984), "Entry Problems: Investment Banking Proves a Tough Field for Commercial Banks," *Wall Street Journal* (9/19).

Sargent, Tom, and Neill Wallace (1976), "Rational Expectations and the Theory of Economic Policy," *Journal of Monetary Economics*, 2(2), pp. 169–184.

Saulsberg, Victor (1987), "State Banking Powers: Where Are We Now?" *FDIC Regulatory Review*, April, pp. 1–16.

Schmitt, Bernard (1977), *L'Or, le Dollar et le Monnaie Supranationale* (Gold, the Dollar, and Supranational Money) (Calmann-Levy: Paris).

———. (1984), *Inflation, Chomage, et Malformations de Capital* (Inflation, Unemployment, and the Disfigurements of Capital) (Economica: Paris).

———. (1988), *L'Ecu et les Souverainétés Nationales en Europe* (The Ecu and National Sovereignty in Europe) (Dunod: Paris).

Schor, Juliet (1992), *The Overworked American: The Unexpected Decline of Leisure*, (Basic Books: New York)

Schulmeister, Stephan (1987), "An Essay on Exchange Rate Dynamics," Discussion Papers (IIM/LMP 87 - 8), Wissenschaftszentrum Berlin für Sozialforschung, Berlin (West).

Schuman, Howard (1988), *Politics and the Budget: The Struggle Between the President and the Congress* (Prentice-Hall: Englewood Cliffs, NJ).

Schumpeter, Joseph (1912), *Theorie der Wirtschaftlichen Entwicklung* (Duncker und Humbolt: Berlin). Published in English in 1934 as *The Theory of Economic Development* (Harvard University Press: Cambridge, MA).

———. (1939), *Business Cycles*, vols. 1–2 (McGraw-Hill: New York).

———. (1942), *Capitalism, Socialism, and Democracy* (Allen and Unwin: London).

Sesit, Michael (1989), "Japanese Influence Grows in Global Currency Market," *Wall Street Journal* (9/14).

Shapiro, Max (1980), *The Penniless Billionaires* (Times Books: New York).

Shiller, Robert (1988), "Causes of Changing Financial Market Volatility," in Federal Reserve Bank of Kansas City, *Financial Market Volatility*, pp. 1–22.

Singer, Mark (1985), *Funny Money* (Knopf: New York).

Smith, Adam (1776), *An Inquiry into the Nature and Causes of the Wealth of Nations* (London).

Solomon, Anthony (1982), "New Strategies for the Federal Reserve?" *Challenge*, April, pp. 19–24.

Solow, Robert (1956), "A Contribution to the Theory of Economic Growth," *Quarterly Journal of Economics*, 70(1), pp. 65–94.

Soros, George (1987), *The Alchemy of Finance: Reading the Mind of the Market* (Simon and Schuster: New York).

Sprague, O. M. W. (1968), *The History of Crises Under the National Banking System* (A. M. Kelley: New York), first published in 1910.

Sraffa, Piero (1960), *Production of Commodities by Means of Commodities* (Cambridge University Press: Cambridge, UK).

Steindl, Josef (1952), *Maturity and Stagnation in American Capitalism* (Oxford University Press: Oxford).

Stevens, Charles (1987a), "BankAmerica Finds Accounting Errors of $26 Million in Foreign Exchange Line," *Wall Street Journal* (10/8).

———. (1987b), "Rate Stability Hurts Currency Traders," *Wall Street Journal* (10/26).

Stewart, James, and Daniel Hertzberg (1987), "Terrible Tuesday: How the Stock Market Almost Disintegrated a Day After the Crash," *Wall Street Journal* (11/20).

———. (1988), "Street Fight: SEC Accuses Drexel of a Sweeping Array of Securities Violations," *Wall Street Journal* (9/8).

Stockman, David (1986), *The Triumph of Politics* (Harper and Row: New York).

Swan, Timothy (1956), "Economic Growth and Capital Accumulation," *Economic Record*, 32(63), pp. 334–361.

Swartz, Steven (1985), "Epic Was a Complex but a Lucrative Venture," *Wall Street Journal* (10/21).

Sweezy, Paul (1942), *Theories of Capitalist Development* (Monthly Review Press: New York).

———. (1972), "The Resurgence of Financial Control: Fact or Fancy?" in P. Sweezy and H. Magdoff, *The Dynamics of U.S. Capitalism* (Monthly Review Press: New York), pp. 113–145.

———. (1982), "Why Stagnation?" *Monthly Review*, 34(2), pp. 1–10.

Taylor, Frederick (1912), *Shop Management* (Harper & Brothers: New York).

Thomas, Paulette (1990), "Fraud Was Only a Small Factor in S and L Losses, Consultant Asserts," *Wall Street Journal* (7/20).

Thurow, Lester (1985), *The Zero Sum Solution: Building a World-Class American Economy* (Simon and Schuster: New York).

Tobin, James (1956), "The Interest-Elasticity of Transactions Demand for Cash," *Review of Economics and Statistics*, 38(3), pp. 241-247.

———. (1958), "Liquidity Preference as Behavior Towards Risk," *Review of Economic Studies*, 25(1), pp. 65–86.

Todd, Walker (1991), "Time to Stop Bailing Out the Banks," *Nation* (9/16).

Trezise, Philip (ed.) (1979), *The European Monetary System: Its Promise and Prospects* (Brookings Institution: Washington, DC).

Triffin, Robert (1960), *Gold and the Dollar Crisis* (Yale University Press: New Haven, CT).

Veblen, Thorstein (1899), *The Theory of the Leisure Class: An Economic Study of Institutions* (Macmillan: London).

Volcker, Paul (1983), "How Serious Is U.S. Bank Exposure?" *Challenge*, May-June, pp. 11–19.

———. (1990), "Reflections of a Central Banker," *Wall Street Journal* (10/16).

Walras, Leon (1874), *Éléments d'Économie Politique Pure* (Lausanne; definitive ed. Pichon: Paris, 1926). Published in English as *Elements of Pure Economics* (Irwin: Homewood, IL).

Wanniski, Jude (1981), "A Supply-Side Case for a Gold Standard," *Business Week* (12/7).

Watson, Henry (1985), "End the Check-Churning Frenzy," *Wall Street Journal* (5/24).

———. (1986), "Fed Drives Out Competitors in Bank Fund Transfers," *Wall Street Journal* (3/13).

Wicksell, Knut (1898), *Geldzins und Gueterpreise* (G. Fischer Verlag: Jena). Published in English in 1934 as *Interest and Prices* (Macmillan: London).

Williamson, John (1987a), *Capital Flight and Third World Debt* (Institute for International Economics: Washington, DC).

———. (1987b), *Targets and Indicators: Blueprint for the International Coordination of Economic Policy* (Institute for International Economics: Washington, DC).

Winch, Donald (1972), *Economics and Policy* (Fontana: London).

Wojnilower, Albert (1980), "The Central Role of Credit Crunches in Recent Financial History," *Brookings Papers on Economic Activity*, no.2, pp. 277–326.

Wolfson, Martin (1986), *Financial Crises: Understanding the Postwar U.S. Experience*, (M. E. Sharpe: Armonk, NY).

Wriston, Walter (1992), *The Twilight of Sovereignty: How the Information Revolution Is Transforming Our World* (Scribner: New York).

Zweig, Philip (1985a), "Small Depositors May Pay More Fees Under Next Year's Bank Deregulation," *Wall Street Journal* (12/24).

———. (1985b), *Belly Up* (Crown: New York).

———. (1986), "Growing Pains: Some Big Banks Find Entering New Fields a Tough Transition," *Wall Street Journal* (8/1).

Index

Bank of the United States (1791), 66
Bank reform, 279–86
  commerce and banking fusion, 283–84
  commercial and investment integration,
    282–83
  core banks, 284–85
  and market discipline, 285–86
  nationwide banking, 281–82
Banks
  borrowing by, 114
  commodity-to-credit transition, 63–86
  credit between, 112–14
  and credit-money, 29–37, 87–115
  crises, 77–78, 88, 92, 95
  and deposit insurance reform, 249–57
  deregulation of, 199–207
  failures, 88, 95, 161, 162, 163, 241–42,
    254, 429, 495n.21
  first in United States, 65–67
  global collapse (1931), 88
  liabilities, 159–60
  mergers, 511n.31
  money-center, 271, 277–78
  national system established, 74
  reform of, 279–86
  restructuring of, 258–92
  safety of, 94
  size distribution, 96
  and stock market, 496n.22
  types of, 85
See also Central banking; Commercial
    banking; Interstate banking;
    Investment banking; National
    banking; Regional banking; Reserve
    banking system; State banking;
    specific banks
Barter economy, 24–25, 87
Basel Agreement (1988), 252, 274,
    510n.19
Basel Concordat (1975), 148, 289,
    501n.15
Basel-Nyborg accord (1987), 403
Basket valuation, 393, 399
BCCI. See Bank of Commerce and Credit
    International
Bear market, 302
Behaviorists, 405
Belgium, 347, 405
Bevill, Bressler & Schulman, 268, 269
BHCs. See Bank holding companies
Bills of exchange, 65

Bimetallic monetary standard, 64–69, 72,
    347, 355
BIS. See Bank for International Settlements
Block traders, 315
Blumenthal, W. Michael, 149
Board for International Investment, 389
Boesky, Ivan, 311
Bonds, 80, 81, 263–64, 268, 318
See also Junk bonds
Boom-bust cycles, 40, 302, 500–501n.14
Brady Commission, 317
Brady Plan, 237
Brazil, 225, 229, 230, 235, 236, 238
Bretton Woods system, 114–15, 206, 348, 351
  collapse of, 137–43, 151, 163, 328, 333,
    373–74, 449, 460, 462
  conference (1944), 86, 89, 102–3, 341,
    353, 362–63, 387, 398, 458,
    515n.18
  problems with, 459
  prospects of, 429, 431
  and U.S. delegation, 390
See also Bancor Plan
Britain. See Great Britain
Brokerage commissions, 308
Broker loans, 82
Bryan, William Jennings, 72
Budget, U.S., 112, 170, 176–79
See also Deficits; Deficit spending
Budget Accord (1990), 323
Bull market, 174, 302, 303, 305, 306, 312,
    314
Bundesbank, 382, 406, 408, 411, 415,
    418, 422, 423, 447, 520n.23
Bush, George
  and bank regulation, 254, 255, 259
  and budget deficit, 323
  and capital gains tax, 477
  and global economy, 333
  and Gulf War, 467
  and oil transactions, 449–50
  and public-sector jobs, 469
  Reaganomics legacy, 166–67
  and savings and loan crisis, 242, 247, 248
See also Reagan-Bush era
Bush, Neil, 242
Bush administration. See Bush, George
Business cycles, 8, 54
  dynamics of, 45–49
  and global economy, 328–29, 368
  long waves compared with, 49, 223

About the Author

Robert Guttmann is a professor of economics at Hofstra University and has in recent years also taught as a visiting professor at the Université Paris-Nord. He studied at the University of Vienna and the Free University of Berlin before receiving advanced degrees in economics at the University of Wisconsin and in London. Professor Guttmann has written widely on industrial policy and on issues in money and banking in a global setting, with publications in Austria, Germany, Italy, France, Britain, and the United States.